9000929249

BIG RED
BOOK OF
SPANISH IDIOMS

Also available:

Gordon & Stillman/*The Big Red Book of Spanish Verbs*

Gordon & Stillman/*The Red Pocket Book of Spanish Verbs*

THE
BIG RED
BOOK OF
SPANISH IDIOMS

12,000
SPANISH AND ENGLISH EXPRESSIONS

Peter Weibel

McGraw·Hill

New York   Chicago   San Francisco   Lisbon   London   Madrid   Mexico City
Milan   New Delhi   San Juan   Seoul   Singapore   Sydney   Toronto

Library of Congress Cataloging-in-Publication Data

Weibel, Peter, 1947–
    The big red book of Spanish idioms / Peter Weibel.
       p.   cm.
    Includes index.
    ISBN 0-07-143302-3
    1. Spanish language—Idioms.   I. Title.

  PC4460.W45   2004
  463'.13—dc22   2004050405

1 2 3 4 5 6 7 8 9 0 AGM/AGM 3 2 1 0 9 8 7 6 5 4

ISBN 0-07-143302-3

Interior design by Terry Stone

Contents

Acknowledgments

I wish to convey my special thanks to Kim, my wife, and Ron Nagel. Their help and support made it possible to finish this project.

My appreciation also goes to Christopher Brown, the editor of this book, for his advice and suggestions. Last but not least, I would like to thank Susan R. Moore for her meticulous review of the book.

Introduction

In the early 1970s I went on vacation to Galicia, Spain. On the thirty-four-hour train journey from Bern, Switzerland, to La Coruña I got into conversation with a Spaniard. He was very knowledgeable about Spanish literature and recommended to me the writings of Cela; this was the first time that I had heard of this author.

Many years later, in late 1989, a headline in the arts pages of a newspaper caught my attention: "The Nobel Prize for Literature goes to Camilo José Cela." This prompted me, finally, to acquaint myself with his works. Typical of his style is *La Colmena*, a novel peppered with colloquial and slang expressions. As I read it, I felt the need for a reference for English speakers that dealt comprehensively with such Spanish terms, so I began to jot down words. From these beginnings I developed this dictionary of commonly used Spanish expressions that are often difficult to find in standard dictionaries. My sources have been as diverse as the expressions themselves: Nobel Prize–winning authors and Juan Pérez (the man in the street), professors and students, contemporary and classical literature, dictionaries, movies, and newspapers from across the Spanish-speaking world.

The Big Red Book of Spanish Idioms is a comprehensive reference designed to open up the world of idiomatic Spanish to English-speaking learners, including students, travelers, and language-lovers, who have an intermediate or advanced level of understanding of Spanish. The dictionary contains a broad collection of over 4,000 commonly used idiomatic and colloquial expressions in Spanish and almost 8,000 English translations. Particular care has been taken to match like with like, so that Spanish idioms are matched with idiomatic English expressions of a similar tone or register. This feature also makes the dictionary a particularly helpful reference for Spanish-speaking learners of English.

Using the Dictionary

1. LOCATION OF A SPANISH EXPRESSION

To look up a particular Spanish phrase or expression in order to find its English equivalent, turn to the main Spanish-English dictionary. Each expression is listed under one particular Spanish headword, and the headwords appear in alphabetical order, though initial articles (*el, la, el/la, las, los*) are not alphabetized. The idiomatic expressions (preceded by ▶) are listed below the headword:

la nueva piece of news
▶ coger a alg. de nuevas (fig.) to take s.o. by
surprise
▶ hacerse de nuevas (fig.) to act surprised,
to pretend to be surprised, to pretend not to
have heard/known anything [about it]

To allow for useful groupings by sense, the idiomatic expressions are not necessarily listed in alphabetical order.

In some instances, your selection of a key word within an expression may not match the chosen headword in this dictionary. To allow for this, numerous cross-references are included, indicated by ▷. The correct location of the expression in the dictionary is indicated by the boldfacing of the headword:

▷ aburrido (ser algo ~ a más no **poder**)
▷ adornar (quedarse para ~ **altar**es)
▷ confianza (**ganar**se la ~ de alg.)

These cross-references are integrated alphabetically within the dictionary. Whenever a Spanish word is both a headword and a cross-reference, its cross-references are listed below the idiomatic expressions in alphabetical order.

Some entries and English equivalents are also followed by cross-references (indicated by ▷) to idiomatic expressions where a more extensive list of English equivalents is provided. These further expressions are equally appropriate but for the purposes of saving space were not duplicated for every appropriate idiomatic expression.

palmarla (pop.) to cash/hand in one's chips
(fam., hum.) ▷ **cascar[la]**
la nana grandma/granny (fam.)
▶ del año de/en el año de la nana (fam.)
donkey's years ago ▷ año de **Maricastaña**

2. ENGLISH MEANINGS

The English meaning of every headword is provided, except where no equivalent exists and the word is only comprehensible within an idiomatic expression.

Every Spanish idiomatic expression is followed by at least one English equivalent. As far as is possible, the English expression has been selected to match the tone or register of the Spanish phrase. Note that in many instances the literal meaning of the headword will not match the English equivalent of following idiomatic expressions.

Some Spanish entry phrases have more than one sense in English. These senses are numbered (a), (b), etc.

el cerro hill
▶ irse por los cerros de Úbeda (fig.) (a) to talk
[a lot of] nonsense or rubbish (fam.) or rot
(fam., Br.E.), to give silly or ridiculous or
absurd answers (b) to wander from the sub-
ject/point, to go off at a tangent (fig.)

For clarity, some English entries are prefaced by explanatory tags that may indicate the context or provide the neutral term in English:

▶ la lana (fam., Méjico) (money): dough (sl.,
Am.E.), bread (sl.), sugar (sl.), brass/dosh/
lolly (sl., Br.E.), wampum (sl., Am.E.)

3. EXAMPLE SENTENCES

Example sentences and phrases that incorporate the idiomatic expression are indicated by ◆ and are followed by their English translation. Over 1,800 examples are included in instances where it is judged particularly helpful to see the context in which an expression is used:

la sarta series
▶ una sarta de (fig., fam.) [whole] series of,
[whole] string or catalogue of (fig.) ◆ *una
sarta de mentiras a string/pack of lies* ◆ *una
sarta de disparates a load/pack of nonsense
or rubbish (Br.E.) (fam.)* ◆ *Nos soltaron una
sarta de insultos. They hurled a string of
insults at us.*

4. ENGLISH-SPANISH DICTIONARY AND INDEX

If you are looking for a Spanish equivalent of an English expression, consult the English-Spanish Dictionary and Index. The English expressions are listed alphabetically by key word. The words *to* (as part of the infinitive) and *to be* (before an adjectival expression) are not alphabetized. Wherever the key word is not the first term in the expression, the full expression usually appears in parentheses with the key word represented by a tilde ~.

The English expression is followed by one or more equivalent Spanish idiomatic expressions. This may serve your immediate requirements, but for a more complete treatment of these Spanish expressions, locate them in the Spanish-English dictionary under their respective headwords. The headword is always indicated in bold text:

buttocks las **cacha**s
canard el **cuento** chino
come what may salga lo que salga/saliere
    (▷ **salir**)
to be **dead tired** estar **muerto** [de cansancio]
luck (trusting to ~) a la buena de Dios
    (▷ **bueno**)
to see (oh, I ~!) ¡acabáramos! (▷ **acabar**)
to talk turkey [with s.o.] **cantar**las claras [a alg.]
to vamoose **largar**se

Exceptions
Bold type is not used when the headword is the first word in the expression:

to be **dead on one's feet** caerse de
    cansancio/sueño

Or when the Spanish entry is an article + noun in the singular:

chatterbox la cotorra
crowd una nube

Abbreviations

▷	see	*véase*
adj.	adjective	*adjectivo*
adv.	adverb	*adverbio*
alg.		*alguien* (someone)
Am.E.	American English	*inglés norteamericano*
Br.E.	British English	*inglés británico*
Esp.	Spain	*España*
euph.	euphemism	*eufemismo*
fam.	familiar/colloquial	*familiar/coloquial*
fig.	figurative	*[en sentido] figurado*
hum.	humorous	*humorístico*
iron.	ironical	*irónico*
o.s.	oneself	
pej.	pejorative	*peyorativo*
pop.	popular	*lenguaje popular*
prov.	proverb	*proverbio*
sl.	slang	*argot/jerga*
s.o.	someone (*alguien*)	
s.th.	something (*algo*)	
vulg.	vulgar	*vulgar*

Spanish-English Idiomatic Dictionary

Over 4,000 Spanish idiomatic phrases and expressions (indicated by ▶) are presented under Spanish headwords that appear in alphabetical order. Many expressions are followed by example sentences (marked ◆). Also included are numerous cross-references (preceded by ▷) that indicate in bold the appropriate headword under which that expression can be found. For a more complete explanation of conventions and abbreviations used in this dictionary, consult the Introduction.

abarcar to include
▶ Quien mucho abarca, poco aprieta. (prov.) You can bite off more than you can chew. (prov.) Don't bite off more than you can chew. (prov.)

la abeja bee
▶ estar como abeja en flor (fig.) to feel really great, to feel on top of the world (fam.), to feel completely at home (fam.), to be in one's element ◆ *Los niños salieron corriendo a retozar en la piscina. Allí están como abeja en flor.* The children dashed off for a romp in the swimming pool. There they are in their element[s].

el/la ablandabrevas (fam.) good-for-nothing, washout (sl.), dead loss (fig., fam.)

abocar a (fig.)
▶ estar abocado al fracaso to be doomed to fail/failure (plan/etc.)
▶ estar abocado a un desastre to be heading for a disaster
▶ verse abocado a un peligro to be facing danger, to see danger looming ahead (fig.)

el aborto miscarriage
▶ ser un aborto del diablo (fig.) to be as ugly as sin/hell (fam.), to be incredibly ugly

abrasarse to burn [up], to burn to the ground
▶ abrasarse de sed (fig.) to have a raging thirst, to be dying of thirst (fig.), to be parched (fam.)
▶ abrasarse de calor (fig.) to nearly die in the heat (fig.), to be dying of the heat (fig.)
▶ abrasarse de amores (fig.) to be burning with love (fig.), to be madly in love
▶ abrasarse en deseo (fig.) to be ablaze/aflame with desire (fig.)

el abrigo coat, shelter
▶ Este niño es de abrigo. (fig., fam., Esp.) This child is a real handful. (fig., fam.)
▶ Ese tío es de abrigo. (fig., fam., Esp.) You've got to watch [out for] that guy.

la abuela grandmother
▶ ¡... mi abuela! (fam.) ... my foot! (fam.) ◆ *¡Cansado, mi abuela!* Tired, my foot! ◆ *¡Tarea difícil, mi abuela!* Difficult task, my foot!
▶ ¡Cuénteselo a su o cuéntaselo a tu abuela! (fam.) Tell that to the marines! (fam., Am.E.) Pull the other one! (fam., Br.E.)
▶ no necesitar abuela (pop., hum., Esp.) to blow one's own horn (Am.E.) or trumpet (fig., fam.), to be full of o.s. (fig.) ◆ *No necesita abuela.* He doesn't need anyone else to blow his trumpet for him. He's always blowing his own horn. He is modest! (iron.)
▶ ... éramos pocos y parió la abuela (fam., hum.) ... and that was all we needed! ... and that was the last straw! (fam.) ... as if we didn't have enough problems! (fam.) ◆ *Perdió todo el dinero en el juego–éramos pocos y parió la abuela* He gambled all the money away, and that was all we needed! ◆ *... y encima dejó el coche hecho chatarra–éramos pocos y parió la abuela. ...* and on top of everything he totaled the car. That was the last straw!
▷ abuela (estar más **muerto** que mi ~)

la abundancia abundance, wealth
▶ De la abundancia del corazón habla la boca. (prov.) When the heart is full, it's the mouth that overflows.
▶ nadar en la abundancia (fig.) to be rolling in money (fig., fam.)

Abundio (fam.)
▶ ser más tonto que Abundio (fam.) to be as daft as a brush (fam., Br.E.) ▷ ser más tonto que **Carracuca**

▷ aburrido (ser algo ~ a más no **poder**)

▷ aburrimiento (**pudrirse** de ~)

aburrirse to be bored
▶ aburrirse como una ostra o una almeja o un mono (fam.) to be bored to death or to tears (fam.)

acabar to end, to finish, to conclude, to complete
▶ ¡Se acabó! (fam.) That's the end of that!

▶ ¡Acabáramos! (fam.) Oh, I see! Now I get it! Now I understand! You could have said that right away! ◆ *Vivieron diez años en España. ¡Acabáramos! Por eso hablan tan bien español. They lived in Spain for ten years. Oh, I see!/Now I understand! That's why they speak Spanish so well.*

▶ i[Esto] es el acabóse! (fam.) This is the absolute limit! (fam.) This is the last straw! (fam.) This beats the Dutch! (fam.)

▶ Como presidente/etc. es el acabóse. (fam.) As a president/etc. he's a complete disaster. (fig.)

▶ ser el acabóse de feo (fam.) to be as ugly as sin/hell (fam.), to be incredibly ugly

acaparar to hoard

▶ acaparar la palabra (fig.) not to let anybody get a word in edgewise (Am.E.) or edgeways (fig.)

▶ acaparar la atención [de todos] (fig.) to occupy everybody's attention, to hog the limelight (fig., fam.)

▶ acaparar todas las miradas (fig.) all eyes are on s.o. ◆ *Ella acaparó todas las miradas. All eyes were on her.*

▷ acaso (más vale un "**por si** ~" que un "¿quién pensara?")

▷ aceite (apagar el **fuego** con ~)

▷ aceite (**balsa** de ~)

▷ aceite (extenderse/etc. como una **mancha** de ~)

▷ aceituna (cambiar el **agua**/**caldo** a las ~s)

▷ aceituno (**olivo** y ~, todo es uno)

la acera sidewalk

▶ ser de la otra acera (fig., fam.) (a) to be a member of the other party, to be a competitor (b) to be gay (fam.), to be homosexual

▷ acero (tener **nervio**s de ~)

aclarar to clarify

▶ aclarar las cosas (fig.) to clear the air/atmosphere (fig.) ◆ *Al principio hubo muchas tensiones entre ellos, pero finalmente aclararon las cosas. At first there were a lot of tensions between them, but finally they cleared the air.*

▷ acostarse con las **gallina**s

Adán Adam

▶ en traje de Adán o como Adán en el paraíso (fig., hum.) in one's birthday suit

(hum.), in the raw (fam.), in the nude, in the buff (fam., hum., Br.E.), starkers (fam., hum., Br.E.), stark naked (fam.), naked ◆ *Cuando era joven iba a nadar en traje de Adán. When he was young, he [often] went swimming in his birthday suit.*

▷ adornar (quedarse para ~ **altar**es)

▷ adornar la **frente** a alg.

▷ adornarse con **pluma**s ajenas

▷ aflojar la **cuerda**/las **rienda**s

▷ afuera (de **boca**/**dientes** [para] ~)

▷ agarrarse a los faldones de alg. (▷ **faldón**)

▷ agarrarse a un **clavo** ardiendo/a un **pelo**

▷ agente de la **porra**

▷ agigantado (a **paso**s ~s)

el agosto August

▶ hacer su agosto (fig., fam.) to make a killing (fam.), to make a packet (fam.), to make a haul (fam.), to make a bomb (fam.), to hit the jackpot (fig., fam.), to make one's pile (fam.), to feather one's nest (fam.) ◆ *Con ese contrato hizo su agosto. He made his pile with that contract. He made a packet with that contract.*

▷ agrio (tener el **vino** ~)

el agua water

▶ Agua pasada no mueve molino. (prov.) It's no use crying over spilt milk. (prov.)

▶ Del agua mansa líbreme Dios que de la brava me libro yo. Still waters run deep. (prov.)

▶ estar más claro que el agua (fig., fam.) to be as clear as vodka (fig.), to be as clear as crystal (fig.), to be crystal-clear (fig.), to be as plain as the nose on your face, to be as plain as a pikestaff (Br.E.) ◆ *Lo que dice está más claro que el agua. What he says is as clear as vodka or is crystal-clear.*

▶ echar agua en el mar (fig.) to carry coals to Newcastle (fig.) ◆ *Llevarle hielo a un esquimal es como echar agua en el mar. Taking ice to an Eskimo is like carrying coals to Newcastle.*

▶ coger agua en cesto (fig.) to waste one's time, to labor in vain

▶ estar con el agua al cuello (fig.) to be up to one's neck in debt or in problems (fam.), to be over a barrel (fig., fam.)

▶ tener a alg. con el agua al cuello (fig.) to have s.o. over a barrel (fig., fam.)

▶ hacérsele a alg. la boca agua to make s.o.'s mouth water ◆ *Se me hacía la boca agua mirando los dulces. Looking at the sweets made my mouth water.*

▶ venir como agua de mayo (fam., Esp.) to come at just the right time, to be a [real] godsend (fig.), to be just what s.o. needs/needed, to be just what the doctor ordered (fig., fam.), s.th. couldn't have come at a better time ◆ *El dinero me vino como agua de mayo. The money was just what I needed or was a real godsend.*

▶ cambiar el agua a las aceitunas (fam., hum.) (men): to have a slash (sl., Br.E.), to take or have (Br.E.) a leak (sl., hum.), to have a pee/piddle (fam., Br.E.), to spend a penny (euph., fam., Br.E.)

▶ bailar el agua a alg. (fig.) to dance attendance on s.o. (fig.)

▶ llevar el agua a su molino (fig.) to carry grist to one's own mill (fig.), to turn things to one's advantage

▶ sacar agua de las piedras o de un palo seco (fig.) ◆ *Sacarle la información a él es como sacar agua de las piedras. Trying to get information from him is like trying to get blood out of a stone. (fig.)*

▶ ser agua pasada to be water under the bridge (fam.), to be a thing of the past ◆ *El lío con ella es agua pasada. The affair with her is a thing of the past.*

▶ ha corrido/pasado mucha agua bajo el puente a lot of water has flowed under the bridge ◆ *Ha corrido mucha agua bajo el puente desde entonces. A lot of water has flowed under the bridge since then.*

▶ Nunca digas de esta agua no beberé. Never say never. Never be or don't be too sure.

▶ sin decir agua va (fam.) without so much as a by-your-leave or as a word of goodby[e] or as an explanation/etc., without [any] warning ◆ *Se fue sin decir agua va. He left without so much as a by-your-leave.*

▶ las aguas vuelven a su cauce (fig.) things are settling down, things return to normal ◆ *Una vez que las aguas vuelvan a su cauce te hablaré del asunto. I'll talk to you about the matter once things settle down. ◆ Las aguas han vuelto a su cauce después de los disturbios. Things have returned to normal after the disturbances.*

▶ estar entre dos aguas (fig.) to sit on the fence (fig.), to be undecided

▷ agua (cambiar el ~ al **canario**)

▷ agua (de **perdidos**, al ~)

▷ agua (**nadar** entre dos ~s)

▷ agua dulce (el **marinero** de ~)

▷ agua fría (caer/sentar como un **jarro** de ~)

▷ agua fría (echar un **jarro** de ~ a alg.)

▷ agua fría (el **gato** escaldado del ~ huye)

▷ agua turbia (**pescar** en ~s ~s)

▷ aguantar (el **papel** todo lo aguanta)

▷ aguantar **carro**s y carretas

▷ aguantar el **chaparrón**/[la] **mecha**/lo **suyo**

▷ aguar la **fiesta**

▷ aguijón (▷ **coz**: dar coces contra el ~)

▷ águila (tener **ojo**s de ~)

la aguja needle

▶ buscar una aguja en un pajar (fig.) to look for a needle in a haystack (fig.)

▶ meter aguja para sacar reja (fig.) to set/throw a sprat to catch a mackerel or a whale (fig., Br.E.)

▶ entender/conocer la aguja de marear (fig., fam.) to have got the hang of it (fam.), to know one's way around

▷ aguja (meterse por el **ojo** de una ~)

ahogarse to drown

▶ ahogarse en un vaso de agua (fig.) to cause/start a tempest in a teapot (Am.E.) or a storm in a teacup (Br.E.) (fig.), to get worked up about nothing [at all], to get all upset over nothing

▷ ahuecar el **ala**

el aire air

▶ ser libre como el aire (fig.) to be [as] free as [the] air (fam.), to be footloose and fancy-free (fam.) ◆ *No creo que mi hermano se case. Le gusta ser libre como el aire. I don't think that my brother will get married. He likes being footloose and fancy-free.*

▶ estar en el aire (fig.) to be up in the air (fig.) ◆ *Todo está todavía en el aire. It's still all up in the air.*

▶ azotar el aire (fig.) to waste one's time, to labor in vain, to flog a dead horse (fig., fam.), to be a waste of time, to be a wasted effort ◆ *Hablarle de aumentar los sueldos es como azotar el aire. Talking to him about increasing the salaries is like flogging a dead horse or is a complete waste of time.*

▶ darse aires de valiente to [try to] act tough

▶ darse aires de grandeza to play lord of the manor (Br.E.), to give o.s. grand airs, to act high and mighty (fam.), to act big (fam.), to act the big shot (fam.)

▶ beber los aires (poético) to run like the wind (fig.)

▶ beber los aires por algo/alg. to long/yearn for s.th., to be crazy about s.th./s.o. (fam.). to be madly in love with s.o. (fam.)

▷ aire (**sustentarse** del ~)

el ajo garlic

▶ echar ajos [y cebollas] (fam.) to swear [horribly], to rant and rave (fam.), to eff and blind (fam., Br.E.), to let fly (fig.), to let rip (fam.)

▶ andar/estar en el ajo (fam.) (a) to be mixed up in it (fig.), to be involved (b) to be in the know, to be in on the secret, to be in on it (fam.)

▶ Quien o el que se pica, ajos come. (fam., Esp.) If the cap/shoe fits, wear it. (fig.)

▷ ajo (**tieso** como un ~)

el ala wing

▶ ahuecar el ala (fam.) to beat it (sl.), to do a bunk (sl., Br.E.), to make off

▶ caérsele a alg. las alas [del corazón] s.o.'s heart falls/sinks, to lose heart ◆ *Se me cayeron las alas del corazón. My heart fell. I lost heart.*

▶ cortar las alas a alg. to clip s.o.'s wings ◆ *José se tomaba muchas libertades. Su jefe tuvo que cortarle las alas. José was taking a lot of liberties. His boss had to clip his wings.*

▶ arrastrar el ala (fig.) to be down in the dumps/mouth (fam.), to be depressed

▶ arrastrar el ala a alg. (fam.) to court/woo s.o. ◆ *Hace mucho que le arrastra el ala a ella. He's been courting her for a long time.*

▶ dar alas a alg. to encourage or embolden s.o. ◆ *Basta darle alas y lo conseguirá. Just encourage him and he'll make it.* ◆ *¡Qué apuesta más estúpida! ¡Y tú le diste alas! What a stupid bet! And you even encouraged him to make it.*

▷ ala (esconder/meter la **cabeza** bajo el ~)

el alacrán scorpion

▶ ser un alacrán (fig.) to have a vicious/wicked tongue

la alafia verbosity, wordiness

▶ pedir alafia (fam.) to eat humble pie (fig.), to eat crow (fam., Am.E.), to beg for mercy

la albarda packsaddle

▶ poner dos albardas a un burro (fig.) to repeat o.s. unnecessarily, to use pleonasm

la albondiguilla little meatball

▶ la albondiguilla (pop.) (dry nasal mucus): bogey (sl., Br.E.), booger (fam., Am.E.)

▶ hacer albondiguillas (pop.) to pick one's nose

▷ alcachofa (tener **corazón** de ~)

▷ alcohol (**quita**rse del ~)

el alcornoque cork oak

▶ un [pedazo de] alcornoque (fig., fam.) idiot, nincompoop (fam.), blockhead (fam.), dope (fam.), clod (fam.), numskull/dumbo (fam., Am.E.), twit (fam., Br.E.), dolt

la aldaba doorknocker

▶ tener buenas aldabas (fig., fam.) to have [powerful/influential] friends in the right places, to have [a lot of] influence/pull

▶ las aldabas (fam.) (breasts): knockers (sl.), tits (fam.), boobs (fam.), hooters (sl., Am.E.)

▷ alegre (estar ~ como unas **castañuela**s)

▷ alegre (ser ~ de **cascos**)

▷ alegre (tener el **vino** ~)

la alegría joy, cheerfulness

▶ las alegrías (pop., Esp.) male genitals, naughty bits (fam., Br.E.)

▷ alegría (no caber en el **pellejo** de ~)

▷ alegría (no **caber** en sí de ~)

▷ alegría (**rebosar** de ~)

▷ alegría (**vestir** el rostro de ~)

el aleluya hallelujah

▶ el aleluya (fam.) (person): beanpole (fig., fam., hum.)

el alfiler pin

▶ estar prendido con alfileres (fig.) to be unreliable, to be insufficient, to be shaky (fig.) ◆ *Esta teoría está prendida con alfileres. This theory is shaky. This is a shaky theory.*

▶ estar de veinticinco alfileres (fig.) to be dressed up to the nines (fam.), to be dressed to kill (fam.), to be all spruced up, to be all dolled up (fam.), to be all decked out (fam.), to be in one's glad rags (fam., Br.E.), to be in one's Sunday best (fam.)

▶ ponerse de veinticinco alfileres (fig.) to get dressed up to the nines (fam.), to get all spruced up, to get all dolled up (fam.), to spruce or doll (fam.) o.s. up, to put on one's glad rags (fam., Br.E.), to put on one's finery

▶ no caber ni un alfiler (fig.) (hall/train/cinema/etc.): to be absolutely packed, to be packed out, to be jam-packed (fam.), to be jam-full (fam.), to be crowded out, to be chock-a-block (fam.), there's no room to swing a cat (fam.) ◆ *No cabía ni un alfiler en el tren. The train was packed out. You couldn't have squeezed anyone else into the train. There was no room to swing a cat in the train.* ◆ *No cabe ni un alfiler en esta caja. You can't squeeze/get another thing into this box.*

▷ alforja (sacar los **pies** de las ~s)

el algodón cotton

▶ guardar/tener a alg. entre algodones (fig.) to wrap s.o. [up] in cotton wool (fig.), to pamper/coddle s.o., to mollycoddle s.o. (fam., pej.), to spoil s.o. (pej.), to handle/treat s.o. with kid gloves (fig.), to bring s.o. up as mommy's (Am.E.)/mummy's (Br.E.) boy or darling (fam.)

▶ criar a alg. entre algodones (fig.) to wrap s.o. [up] in cotton wool (fig.), to bring s.o. up as mommy's (Am.E.)/mummy's (Br.E.) boy or darling, to pamper/coddle s.o. [in his childhood], to mollycoddle s.o. [in his childhood] (fam., pej.) ◆ *Juan fue criado entre algodones. Juan was brought up as mummy's boy. Juan had a pampered childhood.*

el alguacil bailiff

▶ comer más que un alguacil (pop.) to eat like a horse (fig., fam.), to feed/stuff one's face (fam.), to stuff o.s. (fam.), to make a [real] pig of o.s. (fam.)

la alhaja jewel, gem

▶ ¡Menuda/buena alhaja! (fam., iron.) He's/she's a real gem! (iron.) He's/she's a fine one! (iron.)

la alharaca fuss

▶ hacer [muchas] alharacas to make a [lot of] fuss [about/over s.th.], to make a [great] song and dance [about s.th.] (fig., fam.) ◆ *¡No hagas tantas alharacas! Don't make such a fuss!* ◆ *Los padres hicieron muchas alharacas cuando su chiquillo empezó a caminar. The parents made a great song and dance when their child started walking.*

▶ sin alharacas ni bambollas (fam.) without any fuss, without much ado, quietly

el alma soul

▶ arrancarle a alg. el alma (fig.) to deeply hurt/wound s.o. (fig.), to shock s.o. (fig.) ◆ *Lo que dijo nos arrancó el alma. We were deeply wounded by what he said.*

▶ partírsele a alg. el alma (fig.) to break s.o.'s heart, to be heartbroken ◆ *Se le partió el alma a ella. It broke her heart.*

▶ llegarle algo a alg. al alma (fig.) to be deeply affected or shaken by s.th., to be shocked by s.th. (fig.), to be deeply touched or moved by s.th. (fig.) ◆ *Su muerte nos llegó al alma. We were deeply affected by her death.* ◆ *Sus palabras me llegaron al alma. I was deeply moved by his words.*

▶ caérsele a alg. el alma a los pies (fig.) s.o.'s heart sinks into his boots, to become [very] disheartened ◆ *Se me cayó el alma a los pies. My heart sank into my boots.*

▶ no poder con su alma (Esp.) s.o. can't stand/take it any more or any longer ◆ *No puedo con mi alma. I can't stand it any longer.*

▶ tener el alma en un hilo (fig.) (a) to be on tenterhooks (fig.), to be/sit on pins and needles (fig., Am.E.) (b) to be scared stiff (fam.), to be scared to death (fam.), to have one's heart in one's mouth (fam.), to be worried to death (fam.) ◆ *Mientras esperábamos las noticias teníamos el alma en un hilo. We were sitting on pins and needles while [we were] waiting for the news.* ◆ *En aquel momento tuvo el alma en un hilo. He was scared to death at that moment.*

▶ írsele a alg. el alma tras algo (fig.) to long/yearn for s.th., to fall for s.th.

▶ vender el alma al diablo (fig.) to sell one's soul [to the devil] (fig.) ◆ *Hubiera vendido su alma al diablo para obtener ese abrigo de pieles. She would have sold her soul to the devil for that fur coat. She would have done anything to get that fur coat.*

▶ mojarse hasta el alma (fam.) to get soaked to the skin, to get wet through, to get soaking/dripping wet, to get drenched

▶ ir como alma que se lleva el diablo (fam.) to run like mad/hell (fam.), to run like a bat out of hell (fam.), to run hell for leather (fam.), to go like the clappers (fam., Br.E.) ◆ *Fueron como alma que se lleva el diablo. They ran like mad.*

▷ alma (▷ **negro**: tener el ~ negra)
▷ alma (estar con el ~ en un **puño**)

▷ alma (**pedazo** del ~)
▷ alma de **cántaro**

la almeja shellfish, clam. (Am.E.)
► la almeja (vulg., Esp.) (vagina) ▷ el conejo
▷ almeja (**aburrirse** como una ~)

la almendra almond
► almendras (fam.) bullets ◆ *Cosieron al traidor a almendras.* They riddled the traitor with bullets.

la almohada pillow
► consultar algo con la almohada (fig.) to sleep on s.th. (fig.) ◆ *No puedo tomar una decisión así, de buenas a primeras. Primero tengo que consultarlo con la almohada.* I can't make a decision just like that. First, I have to sleep on it.
► dar vueltas a la almohada (fig.) s.o. can't sleep, s.o. can't fall asleep, to toss and turn (in bed)
► La mejor almohada es una conciencia tranquila. (prov.) With a clear conscience you sleep well.

la alpargata canvas sandal
► no tener ni para unas alpargatas (fig.) not to have a penny or a red cent to one's name, not to have two [brass] farthings to rub together (fam., Br.E.), to be as poor as a church mouse (fig.)
► ir/venir a golpe de alpargata to go/come on Shank's pony (Br.E.) or on Shank's mare (Am.E.) (hum.), to walk, to hoof it (fam.)
▷ alpargata (vivir/estar donde **Cristo** perdió la ~)

el altar altar
► quedarse para adornar altares (fig.) to be/become an old maid (fam.), to be left on the shelf (fig.)
► tener a alg. en los altares (fig.) to have the greatest respect for s.o.
► llevar a una al altar (fig.) to lead a girl or a woman to the altar ◆ *Finalmente la llevó al altar.* Finally he led her to the altar.

alucine (fam.)
► ser un/de alucine to be great/super (fam.), to be far out (sl.), to be fantastic (fam.), to be terrific (fam.), to be brilliant/brill (fam., Br.E.), to be wonderful, to be amazing (fam.), to be incredible (fam.), to be glorious, to be divine (fig., fam.), to be heavenly (fam.) ◆ *Es un alucine. It's great/fantastic.*

◆ *¡Qué alucine! It's brill! It's far out!* ◆ *Las vacaciones en España fueron de alucine. The vacation in Spain was super or absolutely wonderful.* ◆ *La vista es de alucine. The view is splendid/glorious.* ◆ *Este vino es de alucine. This is a heavenly wine.*

▷ alzar **cabeza**
▷ alzar **cabeza** (no ~)
▷ alzar el **codo/vuelo**

la amapola poppy
► ponerse como una o más rojo que una amapola to turn as red as a poppy (fam.), to turn as red as a beet (fam., Am.E.), to blush like a or go as red as a beetroot (fam., Br.E.), to go bright red ◆ *Se puso más rojo que una amapola. He went bright red.*

▷ amargura (apurar el **cáliz** de [la] ~ hasta las heces)
▷ amargura (llevar/traer a alg. por la **calle** de la ~)
▷ amarillo (el **periódico** ~)
▷ amarillo (la **prensa** amarilla)

el amén amen
► en un decir amén (fig.) in next to no time, in a flash, in a trice, in a jiffy (fam.), in a tick (fam., Br.E.), before you can say Jack Robinson (fam.) ◆ *Estoy allí en un decir amén. I'll be there before you can say Jack Robinson.* ◆ *Todo pasó en un decir amén. It was all over in a flash.* ◆ *Lo hizo en un decir amén. He did it in a jiffy.*
► decir amén a todo (fig.) to say yes to everything, to agree to everything
► llegar a los amenes (fig.) to show up at the end (of an event/etc.) (fam.)

▷ amigo (tener **cara** de pocos ~s)
▷ amo (ser el ~ del **cotarro**)

el amor love
► hacer algo por amor de/a alg. to do s.th. for s.o.'s sake or for s.o. ◆ *Lo hizo por amor a ella. He did it for her.*
► hacer el amor a/con alg. (fam.) to make love to/with s.o., to sleep with s.o. (euph.)
► ¿Qué tal andas/etc. de amores? (fam.) How's your/etc. love life?
► estar al amor de la lumbre (fig.) to be/sit by the fireside/fireplace
▷ amor (**abrasarse** de ~es)
▷ amor (de malas en el **juego**, de buenas en ~es)

▷ amor (desgraciado en el **juego**, afortunado en ~es)
▷ amor (¡**Salud**, ~ y pesetas!)

la andanada broadside
▶ soltar la/una andanada a alg. (fig., fam.) to give s.o. a [good] telling-off (fam.) ▷ zurrar la **badana** a alg. (b)
▶ soltar una andanada de insultos a alg. (fig., fam.) to unleash a volley/stream of abuse at s.o. (fig.)
▷ andar por las **nubes**

la andorga (fam.) paunch
▶ llenarse la andorga to stuff o.s. (fam.), to feed/stuff one's face (fam.), to make a [real] pig of o.s. (fam.), to eat like a horse (fig., fam.)

el anillo ring
▶ [no] caérsele a alg. los anillos (fig., fam.) s.th. isn't going to or won't kill s.o., [not] to be beneath s.o., [not] to be beneath s.o.'s dignity. ◆ *No se te caerán los anillos por fregar los platos. Washing the dishes isn't going to kill you or won't kill you.* ◆ *No creo que se me caigan los anillos por disculparme ante ella. I don't feel it's in any way beneath my dignity to apologize to her.* ◆ *No se me cayeron los anillos por eso. It didn't kill me.* ◆ *¿Se lo pido a ella? ¡No lo dices en serio! Se le caerán los anillos. Shall I ask her to do it? You must be joking! That sort of thing is beneath her [dignity].*
▶ venir/sentar [a alg.] como anillo al dedo (fam.) (a) to come at just the right time, to be a [real] godsend (fig.), to be just what the doctor ordered (fig., fam.), to be just what s.o. needs/needed, s.th. couldn't have come at a better time (b) to fit/suit [s.o.] to a T, to fit [s.o.] like a glove ◆ *El dinero me vino como anillo al dedo. The money was just what I needed. The money was a real godsend.* ◆ *Este vestido te sienta como anillo al dedo. This dress fits you like a glove or fits you perfectly.* ◆ *Esa fecha nos viene como anillo al dedo. That date suits us to a T. That date's perfect for us.*
▷ anís (no ser **grano** de ~)

las anteojeras blinkers (Br.E.)/blinders (Am.E.)
▶ llevar las anteojeras puestas (fig., fam.) to be blinkered (fig., Br.E.), to have blinders on

(fig., Am.E.) ◆ *Simplemente no vee que este plan dará [buen] resultado. Debe de llevar o parece llevar las anteojeras puestas. He just doesn't see that this plan will prove a success. He must have blinders on.*
▶ ver las cosas con anteojeras (fig., fam.) to be narrow-minded, to suffer from tunnel vision (fig.)

la antigualla (pej.) old thing, [piece of] old junk (pej.) ◆ *Quiero deshacerme de esas antiguallas. I want to get rid of that old junk.* ◆ *¿A esa antigualla le llamas coche? (fig.) Do you call that old heap of metal (fam.) or that old banger (fam.) or that old crock (fam., Br.E.) or that old relic (fam.) or that old wreck (fig., fam.) a car?* ◆ *una antigualla (libro) (fig.) out-of-date [and worthless] book, old tome* ◆ *una antigualla (costumbre o cuento/chiste/etc.) (fig.) (custom/story/joke/etc.): old chestnuts (fam.), old hat (fam.), it's out of the Ark (fig.), it went out with the Ark (fig.)* ◆ *una antigualla (persona) (fig.) (person): has-been (fam., pej.), back number (fam., pej.), old crock (fam., Br.E.), old relic (fam.), walking antique (fig., hum.)*

el año year
▶ ¡Tal día hará un año! (fig., fam.) A fat lot I care! (fam., iron.) I don't care/give a damn! (fam.)
▶ quitarse/restarse años (fig.) to lie about one's age, to be older than one says/admits ◆ *Las mujeres siempre se quitan años. Women always lie about their ages. Women are always older than they admit.*
▶ Dentro de cien años todos calvos. (prov.) Eat, drink and be merry, for tomorrow we die. (fig.) It will all be the same in a hundred years.
▷ año (**llevar** a alg. un/etc. ~)
▷ año (no hay **bien** ni mal que cien ~s dure)
▷ año (una **tostada** de ~s)
▷ año de la **nana/pera/polca** (del ~/en el ~)
▷ año de **Maricastaña**

el apagabroncas (pop.) bouncer (fam.)

la apaña (pop.) lover

el apaño (pop.) (a) fiddle (fam., Br.E.), put-up job (fam.), piece of juggling (with figures/etc.) (fig.) (b) [love] affair (c) lover
▷ aparecer por [el] **escotillón**

apiparse (fam.) (a) to stuff o.s. (fam.), to feed/stuff one's face (fam.), to guzzle (b) to get tanked up (sl.), to guzzle

▷ apostar[se] la **cabeza**/el **cuello** a que ...

▷ apretar la **cuerda**

▷ apretar las **calzadera**s

▷ apretar las **clavija**s/los **tornillo**s/las **tuerca**s a alg.

▷ apuro (**sacar** a alg. de un ~)

la araña spider
▶ matar la araña (fig.) to waste one's time

arder to burn
▶ estar alg. que arde (fig.) to be fuming/seething (fig., fam.) ♦ *Tu amigo está que arde. Your friend's fuming.*
▶ arder de entusiasmo [con/por algo] (fig.) to be as keen as mustard [on s.th.] (fam.)

el ardite (histórico) coin of little value
▶ no valer un ardite (fig.) not to be worth a bean (fam.), not to be worth a [brass] farthing (Br.E.) or a red cent (Am.E.) (fig.), not to be worth a [tinker's] damn/cuss (fam.), not to be worth anything ♦ *Este coche no vale un ardite. This car isn't worth anything.*
▶ no importar a alg. un ardite (fig.) s.o. couldn't care less (fam., Br.E.), not to give/care a [tinker's] damn/cuss (fam.), not to give/care a monkey's (sl., Br.E.), not to give/care a rap (fig., fam.) ♦ *No me importa un ardite lo que digan/piensen. I don't give a damn what they say/think.* ♦ *No me importa un ardite lo que hagas. I couldn't care less what you do.* ♦ *No le importan un ardite tus problemas. He doesn't care a rap for your problems.*

▷ arena (aportar/poner su **grano**/granito de ~)

▷ arena (**sembrar** en la ~)

el arma weapon
▶ el arma (vulg.) (penis) ▷ el calvo
▶ pasar a una por las armas (fig., pop.) to screw a woman (vulg.) ▷ **calzar**[se] a alg.
▶ ser de armas tomar (fam.) to be a tough customer (fam.), you've got to watch [out for] s.o. ♦ *Es de armas tomar. He's a tough customer.* ♦ *Esos tíos son de armas tomar. You've got to watch out for those guys.*
▶ una mujer de armas tomar (fam.) battle-ax[e] (fam.), shrew, butch (sl.), virago, termagant, Xanthippe (fig.)

▷ arma (ser un ~ de dos **filos**)

▷ armar **camorra**/[un] **cisco**/[un] **jaleo**

▷ armar la de **Dios** es Cristo/la de **San Quintín**

▷ armar la gorda (▷ **gordo**)

▷ arrancar algo de **raíz**

▷ arrancarle a alg. el **alma**

▷ arrancarle a alg. **lágrima**s

▷ arrastrar algo/a alg. por el **fango**/por los **suelos**

▷ arrastrar el **ala**

▷ arrastrar el **ala** a alg.

▷ arrastrar los **pies**

el arrastre dragging
▶ estar alg./algo para el arrastre (fam.) (a) (s.o.): to have had one's day, to be over the hill (fam.), to be [a bit] long in the tooth (b) (s.th.): to have had it (fam.), to be ready for the breaker's yard or scrapyard or scrapheap ♦ *Mi coche está para el arrastre. My car has had it. My car's ready for the scrapheap.*

arrear to hurry along
▶ ¡Arrea! Get moving! Make it snappy! (fam.) Sharp's the word! (fam.)
▶ ¡El que venga detrás, que arree! (fig.) Devil take the hindmost. (prov.) Every man for himself [and the devil take the hindmost].

arreglar to arrange
▶ arreglárselas (fam.) to manage, to get along/by, not to be at a loss as to what to do, to find a way (fig.) ♦ *¿Cómo te las arreglas? How do you manage?* ♦ *Se las arregla siempre. He's never at a loss as to what to do.* ♦ *Sabe arreglárselas. He can take care of himself. He can look after himself.* ♦ *¡Allá se las arregle [él]! He has to sort that out himself! (fig.) That's his problem! That's his funeral! (sl.) That's his look-out! (fam.) On his [own] head be it!*
▶ arreglárselas para + infinitivo to manage/contrive to + infinitive ♦ *No sé cómo se las arregló para convencer a su jefe. I don't know how she managed to convince her boss.*

arriba above, up
▶ codearse con los de arriba (fam.) to belong to the upper crust (fam., hum.), to belong to the upper class[es], to move in high circles (fig.), to rub shoulders (fig.) or hobnob with upper-crust people (fam., hum.)

▷ arrojar hasta los **huesos**

▷ arroyo (huir del **toro** y caer en el ~)

el arroz rice
▶ haber arroz y gallo muerto (fig., fam.) to be a real feast/a slap-up (sl.) meal, to be a slap-up do (sl., Br.E.) ◆ *Hubo arroz y gallo muerto. It was a real feast. It was a slap-up do.*

arrugarse to get wrinkled
▶ arrugarse (fig., fam.) to get scared, to get the wind up (sl.)

el arte art, skill
▶ no tener arte ni parte en algo (fam.) to have nothing whatsoever to do with a matter ◆ *No tuvimos arte ni parte en el asunto. We had nothing whatsoever to do with it.*
▷ arte de **birlibirloque**

el asa handle, grip
▶ el asa (fig., fam.) (nose): beak/hooter (fam., hum.), conk (sl., Br.E.), snout (fam.), schnozzle (fam., Am.E.)
▶ tener a alg. por el asa (fig., fam.) to have s.o. in one's grip (fig.)
▷ asador (poner toda la **carne** en el ~)

asar to roast
▶ asar a alg. a preguntas (fig., fam.) to pester or plague (fam.) s.o. with questions
▶ asarse vivo (fam.) to be roasting (fig.), be dying of the heat (fig.)

el ascua ember, live coal
▶ arrimar el ascua a su sardina (fig., fam.) to work things to one's own advantage, to put one's own interests first, to look after Number One (fam.) ◆ *Siempre arrima el ascua a su sardina. He always puts his own interests first.*
▶ estar en/sobre ascuas (fig., fam.) to be on tenterhooks (fig.), to be/sit on pins and needles (fig., Am.E.), to be like a cat on hot bricks or on a hot tin roof (fig.), to cool/kick one's heels (fam.) ◆ *Mientras esperábamos las noticias estábamos sobre ascuas. We were sitting on pins and needles while [we were] waiting for the news.*
▶ tener a alg. en/sobre ascuas (fig.) to keep s.o. on tenterhooks (fig.), to have s.o. on the hook (fam.), to keep s.o. in suspense ◆ *¡Dímelo ahora! ¡No me tengas en ascuas más tiempo! Tell me now. Don't keep me on tenterhooks any longer!*

el asidero handle, grip
▶ tener buenos asideros (fam.) to have [powerful/influential] friends in the right places, to have [a lot of] influence/pull (fig.)

el asiento seat
▶ calentar el asiento o pegársele a alg. el asiento (fig., fam.) to stay [too] long (on a visit), to overstay one's welcome ◆ *Anoche se le pegó el asiento. He stayed too long last night.*
▷ asiento (ser [un] **culo** de mal ~)

el asno donkey
▶ asno muerto, la cebada al rabo (fig.) to lock the barn door after the horse is stolen (fig., Am.E.), to lock/shut the stable door after the horse has bolted/gone (fig., Br.E.)

el asperges sprinkling with holy water
▶ quedarse asperges (fam.) to come away or be left empty-handed, to end up with nothing

el asta horn, antler
▶ dejar a alg. en las astas del toro (fig.) to leave s.o. in the lurch (fig.), to leave s.o. high and dry (fig.), to leave s.o. in a jam/fix (fam.), to leave s.o. in a tight spot (fam.)
▶ poner a alg. en las astas del toro (fig.) to get s.o. into a [hell of a (sl.) or into a real or into a right] mess (fig.), to get s.o. into a [real] jam/fix (fam.), to get s.o. into a [very] tight spot (fam.)
▷ astilla (de tal **costilla/palo**, tal ~)

el asunto business, matter, affair
▶ el asunto (pop.) (penis) ▷ el calvo

el atajo shortcut
▶ echar/tirar por el atajo (fig.) to take the easiest way out, to seek a quick solution
▶ No hay atajo sin trabajo. (prov.) No pains, no gains. (prov.)

atar to tie [up]
▶ atar corto a alg. (fig.) to keep s.o. on a tight rein (fig.), to keep s.o. on a short leash (fig., Am.E.)
▷ atar (estar/ser **loco** de ~)
▷ atención (**acaparar** la ~ [de todos])
▷ atención (**prestar** ~ a alg./algo)
▷ atender a alg. a **cuerpo** de rey

el atolladero puddle, mire
▶ meterse en un atolladero (fig.) to get o.s. into a [fine/nice] mess (fig.), to get o.s. into a fix/jam (fam.)
▶ sacar a alg. del atolladero (fig.) to get s.o. out of a jam/fix (fam.), to get s.o. off the hook (fam.)
▶ haber salido del atolladero (fig.) to be off the hook (fam.), to be out of the wood (Br.E.) or woods (Am.E.)

el atranco (fig.) jam (fam.), fix (fam.), tight spot (fam.), awkward situation
▶ no saber como salir del atranco to be at a loss as to what to do [next], to be at one's wits' end, to be at the end of one's rope or one's tether (Br.E.) (fig.)
▶ No hay barranco sin atranco. (prov.) No pains, no gains. (prov.)

atravesado crossed, oblique
▶ tener algo o a alg. atravesado (fig., fam.) s.o. can't stand s.th./s.o. (fam.), s.o. can't stomach s.th./s.o. (fam.), s.th./s.o. sticks in s.o.'s gullet (fig.) ◆ *Tengo atravesado tu comportamiento. I can't stomach your behavior.* ◆ *Lo tengo atravesado. I can't stand him. He sticks in my gullet.*

el atún tuna
▶ un [pedazo de] atún (fig.) idiot ▷ un [pedazo de] **alcornoque**
▶ querer ir por atún y a ver al duque (fam.) to want to have it both ways, to want to have one's cake and eat it [too] (fig.), to want to kill two birds with one stone (fig.)
▷ aurora (acabar como el **rosario** de la ~)

la ausencia absence
▶ brillar alg./algo por su ausencia (fam.) (a) (person): to be conspicuous by one's absence (b) s.th.: there's a distinct lack of ◆ *Brilla por su ausencia. He's conspicuous by his absence.* ◆ *El orden brilló por su ausencia. There was a distinct lack of order.*

ausente absent
▶ Ausente sin culpa, ni presente sin disculpa. (prov.) The absentee is always [in the] wrong.

el avispero wasp's nest
▶ meterse en un avispero (fig.) to stir up a hornet's nest (fig.), to get o.s. into trouble
▷ ayer (▷ **nacer**: no nació alg. ~)
▷ ayer (ser **periódico** de ~)
▷ ayuda (costar **Dios** y ~ a alg.)
▷ ayuda (necesitar **Dios** y [su] ~)
▷ azotar el **aire**

el azote whip
▶ azotes y galeras (fam.) monotonous fare, same old muck or same old rotten food (fig., fam., pej.)

la azotea flat roof, terrace roof
▶ estar mal de la azotea (fam.) to be crazy ▷ no estar bueno de la **cabeza**

B

la baba slobber, dribble
- ▶ caérsele a alg. la baba con/por alg./algo (fig., fam.) to be drooling over s.o./s.th. (fig.), to be/go soft on s.o. (fam.), to dote on a child, to be crazy/wild about s.o./s.th. (fam.), to be besotted or infatuated with s.o./s.th., to be thrilled to bits or delighted with s.th. (plan/idea/etc.) ◆ *Se les cae la baba con sus nietas. They dote on their granddaughters.* ◆ *Se le cae la baba por ella. He's soft on her. He's crazy about her.* ◆ *Se nos cae la baba por ese coche. We're drooling over that car. We're wild about that car.* ◆ *Se me cae la baba por esta idea. I'm thrilled to bits or infatuated with this idea.*
- ▶ cambiar babas (pop.) to have a good old snog (sl., Br.E.), to kiss
- ▷ baba (llorar a **moco** y ~)

Babia
- ▶ estar en Babia to have one's head in the clouds, to be away with the fairies (fam.), to be remote from it all (fig.), to be miles away (fig.), to have one's mind on other things, to be out to lunch (fam., Am.E.), to be daydreaming, to be woolgathering (fam.)

el bacalao codfish
- ▶ el bacalao (pop., Esp.) (vagina) ▷ el conejo
- ▶ cortar el bacalao (fig., fam., Esp.) to call the tune/shots ▷ llevar la **batuta**
- ▷ bachiller Trapazas (▷ el **trapaza**)

la badana tanned sheepskin
- ▶ zurrar la badana a alg. (fig., fam.) (a) to tan s.o.'s hide (fig., fam.), to beat s.o. up (fam.), to give s.o. a [good] tanning or hiding or thrashing or clobbering (fam.), to let s.o. have it (fam.) (b) to give s.o. a [good] dressing-down or wigging (Br.E.) or telling-off or ticking-off (Br.E.) or tongue-lashing or roasting (fam.), to give s.o. a piece of one's mind, to read the riot act to s.o. (fig., hum.), to haul s.o. over the coals (fig.), to give s.o. a rocket (fig., fam., Br.E.), to come down on s.o. like a ton of bricks (fam.)

bailar to dance
- ▶ ¡Que me/nos quiten lo bailado! (fam.) Nobody can take away the good times I've/we've had.
- ▷ bailar (▷ **feo**: tocarle a alg. ~ con la más fea)
- ▷ bailar (▷ **pelar**: bailan que se las pelan)
- ▷ bailar al compás de la **música** de alg.
- ▷ bailar al **son** que le tocan a alg.
- ▷ bailar el **agua** a alg.
- ▷ bailar en la **cuerda** floja
- ▷ balazo (**coser/freír** a alg. a ~s)

la balsa pool, pond
- ▶ balsa de aceite (fig.) ◆ *El mar/lago está como una balsa de aceite. The sea/lake is as smooth as a millpond/as smooth as glass.* ◆ *Este pueblo es una balsa de aceite. This village is [as] quiet as the grave or is [as] quiet as a Sunday-school party. This is a very sleepy village.* (fig.) ◆ *Todo iba como una balsa de aceite. Everything was going swimmingly (fig.) or very smoothly.* ◆ *La asamblea fue una balsa de aceite. The meeting went off very smoothly.*
- ▷ bambolla (sin **alharaca**s ni ~s)

bañar to bathe
- ▶ ¡Anda a bañarte! (pop.) Go jump in a lake! (fam.) Go take a running jump! (fam.) Go fly a kite! (fam., Am.E.) Go fry an egg! (fam.) Go climb a tree! (fam.) Take a hike! (fam., Am.E.) Go to hell! (fam.) Get lost! (fam.) Piss off! (sl., Br.E.)

el baquetazo lash (with a switch)
- ▶ echar a alg. a baquetazo limpio (fig., fam.) to throw s.o. out, to kick s.o. out (sl.), to boot s.o. out (fam.)
- ▶ tratar a alg. a baquetazo limpio (fig., fam.) to be tough with s.o. (fam.), to give s.o. a hard time (fam.), to treat s.o. harshly

el bar (americano) bar
- ▶ el bar de ligue o de alterne (fam.) singles bar, a joint (sl.) where people go to pick s.o. up (fam.)

la baraja deck, pack of cards (Br.E.)
- ▶ jugar con/a dos barajas (fig.) to play a double game
- ▶ O jugamos todos o se rompe la baraja. Either we all do it/we all go/etc. or nobody does.

la barba beard, chin
- ▶ barba a barba (fam.) face to face ◆ *Ayer nos encontramos barba a barba por primera vez. We met face to face for the first time yesterday.*
- ▶ hacer la barba a alg. (fig.) (a) to get on s.o.'s nerves (fam.), to get on s.o.'s wick (fam., Br.E.) (b) to flatter s.o., to butter s.o. up (fam.), to suck up to s.o. (fam.), to fawn on s.o. (fig.), to soft-soap s.o. (sl.)
- ▶ con toda la barba (fam.) ◆ *ser un hombre con toda la barba to be a real man* ◆ *ser un líder con toda la barba to be a real/true leader* ◆ *mentir con toda la barba to tell a barefaced lie, to lie through one's teeth (fam.)* ◆ *un coche/etc. con toda la barba a car/etc. with all the trimmings*
- ▶ en mis/etc. propias o mismísimas barbas (fam.) from right under my/etc. nose, from under my/etc. very nose, from right in front of me/etc. ◆ *Le robaron el coche en sus mismísimas barbas. They stole his car from under his very nose.* ◆ *Nos robaron el coche en nuestras propias barbas. They stole our car from right in front of us or from right under our noses.*
- ▶ subirse a las barbas de alg. (fam.) to take liberties with s.o., to be disrespectful to s.o., to get cheeky (Br.E.) or fresh (Am.E.) with s.o. (fam.), to get too familiar with s.o. (fam.)
- ▶ decir algo en las barbas de alg. (fam.) to say s.th. to s.o.'s face
- ▶ Cuando las barbas de tu vecino veas arder, pon las tuyas a remojar. You should learn from other people's mistakes.
- ▷ barbaridad (gastar una ~ en **trapos**)

el barbas (fam.) bloke/guy with the beard (fam.), [old] hairy face (fam.) ◆ *¿Quién te lo dijo? Ese barbas allí. Who told you that? That guy with the beard over there.*

- ▷ barquero (decirle a alg. las **verdad**es del ~)

la barra bar (legal system)
- ▶ no pararse en barras (fig.) to stop at nothing

- ▶ sin pararse en barras (fig.) inconsiderately, unscrupulously, regardless ◆ *El gobierno actuó sin pararse en barras. The government took drastic action or measures.*

el barranco ravine
- ▶ No hay barranco sin atranco. (prov.) No pains, no gains. (prov.)

barrer to sweep
- ▶ barrer hacia/para dentro (fig., fam.) to look after Number One (fam.), to put o.s. first
- ▶ barrer en su propia casa (fig.) to put one's own house in order [first] (fig.) ◆ *Siempre se queja de otra gente. Dile que barra en su propia casa. He's always complaining about other people. Tell him to put his own house in order first.*
- ▶ barrer con algo (fig.) to make a clean sweep of s.th. (fig.)
- ▶ barrer con todo (fig.) to wipe the slate clean (fig.)

la barrera barrier
- ▶ El pensamiento no tiene/conoce barreras. (prov.) You can think what you like.
- ▶ ver los toros desde la barrera (fig.) to watch from the sidelines, to sit on the fence, not [to want] to have anything to do with it or with the matter

el barrido sweeping
- ▶ servir lo mismo para un barrido que para un fregado (fam.) to be a/the [general] dogsbody (sl.), to be a jack-of-all trades, to be a/the handyman, s.o. who can turn his hand to anything ◆ *Aquí sirve lo mismo para un barrido que para un fregado. He's the general dogsbody [around] here.* ◆ *Sirve lo mismo para un barrido que para un fregado. He can turn his hand to anything.*

la barriga belly
- ▶ llenarse la barriga (fam.) to stuff o.s. (fam.), to make a [real] pig of o.s. (fam.)
- ▶ Barriga llena, corazón contento. (prov.) A full stomach makes for a happy heart. (prov.)

barrigón (fam.) potbellied
- ▶ Al que nace barrigón es al ñudo que lo fajen. (prov., Cono Sur). A leopard never changes or cannot change its spots. (prov.)

el barrio area or part of a town, district
- ▶ irse al otro barrio (fam., hum.) to kick the bucket (fam.) ▷ **cascar**[la]

▶ mandar a alg. al otro barrio (fam.) to send s.o. to glory (fam.), to do s.o. in (fam.)

el barro clay, mud
▶ el barro (fam.) (money): dough (sl., Am.E.), bread (sl.), sugar (sl.), brass/dosh/lolly (sl., Br.E.), wampum (sl., Am.E.)
▶ tener barro a mano (fam.) to have money to burn (fig.)

la bartola (fam.)
▶ echarse/tenderse/tumbarse a la bartola to take it easy, to have an easy/a lazy time of it, to do nothing

los bártulos (fam.) belongings, things, stuff (fam.), gear (fam.), goods and chattels (fam., Br.E.)
▶ liar los bártulos (a) to pack one's bags/things (b) to die, to peg out (fam.), to kick the bucket (fam.)

el basilisco (mitología) basilisk (mythology)
▶ estar hecho un basilisco (fig., fam.) to be hopping mad (fam.), to be terribly angry, to be [really] fuming (fig., fam.), to be livid (fam., Br.E.), to be seething [with rage] (fig., fam.), to be wild with rage (fam.)
▶ ponerse como un basilisco (fig., fam.) to get terribly angry, to blow/flare up (fig.), to blow/pop one's cork (sl.), to go ape (fam., Am.E.) ▷ salirse de sus **casillas** ◆ *Cuando se entere se pondrá como un basilisco. When he finds out he'll get terribly angry.*

el bastón baton, stick
▶ empuñar el bastón (fig.) to take command, to take charge
▶ meter el bastón (fig.) to intervene, to intercede
▶ meter un bastón en la rueda o bastones en las ruedas [de alg.] (fig.) to put a spoke in s.o.'s wheel (fig., fam., Br.E.), to throw a spanner (Br.E.) or a monkey wrench (Am.E.) in[to] the works (fam.) ◆ *Me metió un bastón en la rueda. He put a spoke in my wheel.* ◆ *Casi echó nuestros planes por el suelo cuando de repente se rajó. Él sí que metió bastones en las ruedas. He almost ruined our plans when he suddenly backed out. He really threw a monkey wrench into the works.*
▷ batalla (**ganar** la ~)
▷ batalla (**ganar**le la ~ a alg.)

las Batuecas backward region of Extremadura
▶ estar en las Batuecas (fig., fam.) to have one's head in the clouds, to be away with the fairies (fam.), to be remote from it all (fig.), to be miles away (fig.), to have one's mind on other things, to be daydreaming

la batuta baton
▶ llevar la batuta (fig.) to call the tune/shots (fig.), to play first fiddle (fig.), to wear the pants (Am.E.)/the trousers (Br.E.) (fig.), to carry the ball (fig., Am.E.), to rule the roost (fig.), to be the boss (fig.), to run the show (sl.), to be firmly in command ◆ *Su esposa lleva la batuta. His wife calls the tune/plays first fiddle.*

el baúl trunk (travel), chest
▶ cargar el baúl a alg. (pop.) to pass the buck to s.o. (fig., fam.), to pin the blame on s.o., to leave s.o. holding the baby (Br.E.) or the bag (Am.E.) (fam.)
▶ el baúl (fig., fam.) belly, paunch
▶ henchir el baúl (pop.) to stuff o.s. (fam.), to feed/stuff one's face (fam.), to make a [real] pig of o.s. (fam.), to eat like a horse (fig., fam.)

el bautismo baptism
▶ romper el bautismo a alg. (fam.) to smash s.o.'s head/face in (fam.), to knock s.o.'s block off (fam.), to brain s.o. (fam.)

la baza (playing cards): trick
▶ la baza maestra (fig.) masterstroke
▶ meter baza [en] (fig., fam.) to interfere (in the conversation/etc.), to butt in [on] (fam.), to shove/put/stick one's oar in (fam.), to put in one's [own] two bits (fam.), to put in one's [two] pennyworth (fam., Br.E.), to put in one's two cents[' worth] (fam., Am.E.) ◆ *Siempre quiere meter baza. He always wants to put in his own two bits or his two cents' worth.*
▶ no dejar meter baza a nadie (fig., fam.) not to let anybody get a word in edgewise (Am.E.) or edgeways (fig.)
▶ no dejar meter baza a alg. (fig., fam.) not to let s.o. get a word in edgewise (Am.E.) or edgeways (fig.) ◆ *No nos dejó meter baza. He didn't let us get a word in edgeways.*

la beata lay sister
▶ la beata (pop.) peseta

▶ la beata (fam., pej.) sanctimonious woman, churchy type (pej.), pious Annie (iron.), excessively pious woman, goody-goody (fam., pej.)

▶ De día beata, de noche gata. (pop.) During the day pious Annie, during the night a bit of all right (sl., Br.E.) or hot stuff (fig.) or mistress.

▷ beber (a ~ y a tragar, que el **mundo** se va a acabar)

▷ beber (sin **comer**lo ni ~lo)

▷ beber a **morro**/a **palo** seco/a **pote**/a todo **pasto**

▷ beber como un **descosido**/una **esponja**

▷ beber hasta **tumbar** a alg.

▷ beber los **aires**

▷ beber los **aires** por algo/alg.

▷ beber los **vientos**

▷ beber los **vientos** por algo/alg.

▷ beber más que **siete**

▷ beberle a alg. las **palabras**

▷ beberse las **lágrimas**

el becerro bull calf

▶ adorar el becerro de oro (fig.) to worship the golden calf (fig.) ◆ *Me parece que le interesa sólo el dinero. Diste en el clavo. Siempre ha adorado el becerro de oro.* It seems to me that he's only interested in money. You hit the nail on the head. He's always worshipped the golden calf.

el Belén Bethlehem

▶ estar en Belén (fig., fam.) to have one's head in the clouds, to be away with the fairies (fam.), to be remote from it all (fig.), to be miles away (fig.), to have one's mind on other things, to be daydreaming

la bellota acorn, bud (carnation)

▶ si le/etc. menean, da bellotas (fig.) he's/etc. as thick as they come (fam.) ▷ ser más tonto que **Carracuca** ◆ *Si les menean, dan bellotas.* They're as thick as they come.

la bendición blessing, benediction

▶ echar la bendición a algo/alg. (fig.) to say goodby[e] to s.th. (fig.), to give s.th./s.o. up for lost, to not want to have anything more to do with s.th./s.o. ◆ *Puedes echar la bendición a tu cartera.* You can say goodbye to your wallet. ◆ *Será mejor echar la bendición a él.* It will be best to have nothing more to do with him.

el bendito (fig.) good/simple soul (fam.)

▶ dormir como un bendito to sleep like a baby (fig.), to sleep like a log (fam.)

▷ benedictino (tener una **paciencia** de ~)

▷ beneficio (sin **oficio** ni ~)

el beo (pop., Esp.) (vagina) ▷ el conejo

el berenjenal aubergine field (Br.E.), eggplant field (Am.E.)

▶ meterse en un berenjenal (fig., fam.) to get o.s. into a pickle (fam.), to get o.s. into a jam/fix (fam.), to get o.s. into a tight spot (fam.), to get o.s. into a mess (fig.) ◆ *¡En buen berenjenal nos hemos metido!* We've got ourselves into a real pickle! This is a pretty kettle of fish! (fam., iron.) We've got ourselves into a fine mess! (fig.)

▷ berenjenal (huir del **perejil** y dar en el ~)

la berza cabbage

▶ el/la berzas (fam.) washout (sl.), dead loss (fig., fam.), idiot, imbecile, dummy (fam.), moron (fam.) (all pej.)

▶ mezclar berzas con capachos (fig.) to jumble things up, to get things in a complete mess (fig.), s.o.'s place/etc. is in a complete mess (fig.) or is a[n absolute] shambles (fig.), everything's topsy-turvy (fam.) in s.o.'s place/etc. ◆ *No le digas a ese berzas que vaya por el documento. Mezclará berzas con capachos en el archivador.* Don't tell that idiot to get the document. He'll jumble things up or things will be all jumbled up in the filing cabinet. ◆ *Mezcló berzas con capachos en el/su cajón.* He jumbled things up in the drawer. Things were all jumbled up in his drawer. ◆ *Mezclaron berzas con capachos en su casa.* They got things in a complete mess in their house. Everything was topsy-turvy in their house. Their house was a shambles.

▷ besar la **cruz/tierra**

bestial bestial, brutal

▶ bestial (fig., fam.) great (fam.), fantastic (fam.), (to be) the business (sl., Br.E.), huge ▷ cojonudo (a), (b) ◆ *Es bestial.* It's fantastic. It's the business. ◆ *Tenemos un hambre bestial.* We're famished. (fam.) We're incredibly hungry.

▷ besugo (tener **ojos** de ~)

la Biblia Bible
▶ ser la biblia (fig., fam.) to be the tops (fam.), to be [really] super/great/magic (fam.)
▶ saber la biblia en verso (fam.) to know everything, to know about [absolutely] everything
▶ contar la biblia en verso (fam.) to tell in minute or in great detail, to tell down to the last detail, to give a blow-by-blow account ◆ *Nos contó la biblia en verso. He told us about it in minute detail.*
▷ biblioteca (la **rata**/el **ratón** de ~)

el bicho [wild] animal
▶ No hay/había bicho viviente. (fig., fam.) There isn't/wasn't a living soul here/there. There isn't/wasn't a sod here/there. (sl., Br.E.) ◆ *No hay bicho viviente en la calle. There isn't a living soul in/on the street.*
▶ todo bicho viviente (fig., fam.) everyone, everybody, each and every one of them; every Tom, Dick and Harry (fam.); every man jack [of them] (fam.), every living soul, [all] the world and his wife (fam., Br.E.), every mother's son [of them], everyone and his brother (fam., Am.E.), all the odds and sods (sl., Br.E.) ◆ *Vino todo bicho viviente. Everyone came. The world and his wife came.*
▶ ser un mal bicho (fig., fam.) to be a nasty piece of work (fig., fam.), to be a nasty (fig.) character, to be a mean son of a bitch (sl., Am.E.), to be a rotter (sl., Br.E.)

el bien good
▶ hacer [el] bien sin mirar a quién to do good to all alike, to cast one's bread [up]on the waters
▶ Haz bien y no mires a quién. (prov.) Do good to all alike.
▶ No hay bien ni mal que cien años dure. (prov.) Nothing lasts forever. Nothing goes on forever. There's an end to everything.
▷ bien (no hay **mal** que por ~ no venga)

el bigote mustache (Am.E.), moustache (Br.E.)
▶ menear el bigote (fam.) to scoff (fam., Br.E.), to feed/stuff one's face (fam.)
▶ tener bigote o tres pares de bigotes (fam.) (a) to stick to one's guns (fig.), to stick to one's decision (b) to be [very] difficult or complicated or tricky ◆ *Este problema tiene tres pares de bigotes. This is a very difficult problem.*

▶ de bigote (pop., Esp.) ◆ *una cochinada de bigote* s.th. that's incredibly disgusting/rotten ◆ *Cometieron una falta de bigote. They made a huge mistake.* ◆ *hacer un calor de bigote* to be sweltering, to be sizzling/scorching hot ◆ *Esta idea está de bigote. This is a fantastic/great idea.*

la bilis bile
▶ exaltársele a alg. la bilis (fig., fam.) to get very cross (fam.) ▷ ponerse como un **basilisco** ◆ *Se le exaltó la bilis. He got very cross.*
▶ descargar la bilis contra/en alg. (fig., fam.) to vent one's anger/spleen on s.o. (fig.), to take it out on s.o. (fam.)
▶ [tener que] tragar bilis (fig.) to suppress/stifle one's anger, to force o.s. not to get angry, [to have] to put up with it, [to have] to take it, [to have] to lump it (fam.) ◆ *Me insultaron y tuve que tragar bilis. They insulted me and I had to take it.*

birlibirloque (fam.)
▶ [como] por arte de birlibirloque by magic, as if by magic ◆ *hacer desaparecer algo como por arte de birlibirloque to magic s.th. away*

bizantino Byzantine
▶ discusiones bizantinas (fig.) protracted and pointless/unresolvable/idle discussions or arguments, hair-splitting ◆ *Fue una discusión bizantina. It was a protracted and idle discussion.* ◆ *Siempre se meten en discusiones bizantinas. They always get involved in protracted and pointless/etc. discussions. They're always splitting hairs.*

bizco cross-eyed
▶ quedarse bizco (fig., fam.) to be very impressed, to be amazed, to be dumbfounded, to be astounded, to be stunned (fig.), to be flabbergasted, to be lost for words ◆ *Cuando abrió el regalo se quedó bizco. When he opened the present he was lost for words.*
▶ dejar bizco a alg. (fig., fam.) to impress s.o. strongly, to amaze s.o., to stun s.o. (fig.), to leave s.o. open-mouthed (with wonder or amazement)

la blanca (pop.) (cocaine/heroin): snow (sl.); (cocaine): coke (sl.)

la blanca old Spanish copper coin
▶ la blanca (fig., Esp.) money

► estar sin blanca o no tener blanca (fam.) to be broke (fam.) ▷ estar sin un **cuarto** o no tener [ni] un cuarto

blanco white

► no distinguir lo blanco de lo negro (fam.) not to have the foggiest [idea] (fam.), not to have the faintest idea (fam.), not to have a clue (fam.), not to know left from right (fam.)

► estar tan lejos como lo blanco de lo negro (fam.), no parecerse ni en el blanco de los ojos (fam.) (persons; views/etc.): to be totally different personalities, to be poles apart (fig.), to be as different as night and day (Am.E.)/as chalk and cheese (Br.E.) (fam.), not to look in the least bit alike ♦ *Aunque son gemelos, están tan lejos como lo blanco de lo negro. Although they are twins, they are as different as chalk and cheese.* ♦ *Sus hermanos no se parecen ni en el blanco de los ojos. Her brothers don't look in the least bit alike.*

► hacer de lo blanco negro (fam.), volver en blanco lo negro (fam.) to make out that white is black, to distort/twist things (truth/facts) (fig.)

► quedarse en blanco s.o.'s mind goes blank or is a blank (fig.), to fail to see the point

► blanco y en botella, leche truism, triviality, triteness, platitude (fig.)

▷ blanco (la **noche** blanca)

▷ blanco (ponerse más ~ que la **pared**/que una **sábana**)

el blanco target

► dar en el blanco (fig.) to hit the mark (fig.), to score a bull's-eye (fig.), to be right on (fam., Am.E.), to be spot-on (fam., Br.E.), to strike/hit home (fig.) ♦ *Dio en el blanco con ese regalo. He was spot-on or right on with that gift/present.* ♦ *Tu observación dio en el blanco. Your remark struck home.*

► cargar el blanco a alg. (fig.) to pass the buck to s.o. (fig., fam.), to pin the blame on s.o., to leave s.o. holding the baby (Br.E.) or the bag (Am.E.) (fam.)

▷ blanco (**tirar** más allá del ~)

blandengue weak, soft

► ser un blandengue (fam.) to be a weakling (fig.), to be a softy (fam.), to be a wimp (fam.) (pej.)

▷ blasfemar como un carretero

el bledo

► [no] importar a alg. un bledo (fig.) not to give/care two hoots (fam.) ▷ no importar a alg. un **ardite**

▷ bobo (la **caja** boba)

la boca mouth

► andar algo/alg. de boca en boca (fig.) to be going/doing the rounds, to be the subject of gossip, to set [a lot of] tongues wagging ♦ *El rumor anda de boca en boca. The rumor is going the rounds.* ♦ *En aquel momento la noticia ya anduvo de boca en boca. The news was already common knowledge at that [point in] time.* ♦ *Ella anda de boca en boca. She's the subject of gossip.* ♦ *Desde ese incidente anda de boca en boca. Since that incident he's set a lot of tongues wagging.*

► andar algo en boca de todos (fig.) everybody is talking about s.th., to be on everybody's lips, to be the talk of the town ♦ *Su nombre anda en boca de todos. His/her name is on everybody's lips.* ♦ *El escándalo anda en boca de todos. Everybody is talking about the scandal. The scandal is the talk of the town.*

► traer en bocas a alg. (fam.) to gossip about s.o., to run s.o. down (fam.)

► mentir con toda la boca to tell a barefaced lie

► Pide por esa boca. (fam.) Just ask. All you have to do is ask.

► írsele la boca a alg. to blurt out s.th., to talk thoughtlessly ♦ *Se le fue la boca. He blurted it out.*

► coserse la boca (fig.) to keep one's mouth shut, to keep mum (fam.), to keep quiet, not to say/breathe a word, s.o.'s lips are sealed (fig.), to keep s.th. under one's hat (fam.) or to o.s.

► no descoser la boca (fam.) not to open one's mouth, not to say/breathe a word

► no decir esta boca es mía (fam.) not to open one's mouth, not to say/breathe a word ♦ *No dijo esta boca es mía. He didn't say a word.*

► sin decir esta boca es mía (fam.) without saying a word ♦ *Se fue sin decir esta boca es mía. She left without saying a word.*

► decir algo con la boca chica to say s.th. just to be polite, to say s.th. without really meaning it, to say s.th. insincerely

▶ decir lo que se le viene a la boca a alg. not to mince one's words (fig.), to speak one's mind ◆ *Digo lo que se me viene a la boca. ¡Ahora sí que la has cagado! I won't mince my words. You've really screwed things up now!*

▶ hablar con boca de ganso to repeat s.th. (other people's opinions/ideas/etc.) parrot fashion

▶ de boca [para] afuera lip service, (to support s.th./s.o.) in name only, not to be sincere [in what one says] ◆ *Apoyaron nuestra idea de boca para afuera. They were [only] paying lip service to our idea.* ◆ *Habló o lo dijo de boca afuera. He said one thing and meant another. He didn't mean what he said. He wasn't sincere in what he said.*

▶ a pedir de boca to one's heart's content, for the asking, (to come up) roses, as much as one wishes, just the way you want it to, just fine, perfectly ◆ *Ayer cenamos a pedir de boca. We dined to our heart's content yesterday.* ◆ *Todo salió a pedir de boca. Everything or it all turned out perfectly or just fine or just the way we/etc. wanted it to. Everything came up roses.*

▶ estar en la boca del lobo (fig.) to be in great danger

▶ meterse en la boca del lobo (fig.) to put one's head in the lion's mouth (fig.), to go/venture into the lion's den (fig.)

▶ quitarse algo de la boca (fig.) to go/do without, to scrimp and save ◆ *El padre se lo quita todo de la boca para que su hijo estudie. The father does without in order to pay for his son's [higher] education.*

▶ no tener qué llevarse a la boca to be on the breadline (fig., fam.), not to have a penny or a red cent to one's name, not to have two [brass] farthings to rub together (Br.E.), to be as poor as a church mouse (fig.)

▶ Quien o el que tiene boca, se equivoca. (prov.) To err is human. (prov.)

▶ En boca cerrada no entran moscas. (prov.) If you keep your mouth shut, you won't put your foot in it. (fam.) Mum's the word. (fam.) Silence is golden. (prov.)

▶ Por la boca muere el pez. (prov.) Talking too much can be dangerous. Silence is golden. (prov.)

▷ boca (de la **abundancia** del corazón habla la ~)

▷ boca (dejar a alg. [con] mal **sabor** de ~)

▷ boca (del **plato** a la ~ se pierde la sopa)
▷ boca (echar **candado** a la ~)
▷ boca (hacérsele a alg. la ~ **agua**)
▷ boca (írsele a alg. la **fuerza** por la ~)
▷ boca (sacar el **hígado** por la ~)
▷ boca (**tapar** la ~ a alg.)

el bocado morsel, bite, mouthful

▶ un buen bocado (fam.) (woman/girl): [real] smasher (Br.E.), [real] looker (fam.), real beauty

▶ el bocado sin hueso sinecure, cushy job (sl., Br.E.), soft job

el/la bocazas (fig., fam.) gasbag (fam.), windbag (fam.), blabbermouth (fam.), bigmouth (fam.)

la boda wedding

▶ No hay boda sin tornaboda. (prov.) There's no rose without a thorn. (prov.)

▷ boda (ser la **vaca** de la ~)

el bofia (fam.) cop (fam.), copper (fam.), pig (sl.)

la bofia (fam.) cops (fam.), fuzz (sl.), pigs (sl.), filth (sl., Br.E.), heat (sl., Am.E.)

la bola ball

▶ dejar que ruede la bola to let things take their course

▶ estar como [una] bola de billar (fig.) to be as bald as a coot (fam., Br.E.), to be as bald as a cue ball (Am.E.) or as a billiard ball (Br.E.)

▶ dorar la bola a alg. (fig., fam.) to sweet-talk s.o. (fam.), to soft-soap s.o. (fam.)

▶ no rascar bola (fam./vulg.) not to do a stroke of work

▶ las bolas (pop.) (testicles) ▷ las **canicas**

▶ estar/ir en bolas (fam./vulg.) to be starkers (fam., hum., Br.E.), to be stark naked (fam.) ◆ *Fue a bañarse en bolas. He went skinny-dipping. (fam.)*

▶ estar hasta las bolas (fam./vulg.) to be pissed off (sl.)

▶ darle por o romper las bolas a alg. (fig., fam./vulg.) to piss s.o. off (sl.), to get on s.o.'s tits (vulg.) or wick (fam.) (Br.E.), to get on s.o.'s nerves (fam.)

▶ pillar a alg. en bolas (fam./vulg.) to catch s.o. with his pants (Am.E.) or with his trousers (Br.E.) down (fam.), to catch s.o. on the hop (fam.), to catch s.o. red-handed ◆ *Estaba robando el contenido de la hucha de*

su hermano cuando la madre entró en el cuarto. Lo pilló en bolas. He was plundering his brother's piggy bank when the mother entered the room. She caught him red-handed.
▷ bola (no dar **pie** con ~)

la bolichada casting of the net
▶ la bolichada (fig., fam.) stroke of luck, lucky break

la bolina lead, bowline
▶ echar de bolina (fig., fam.) to talk/act big (fam.), to puff o.s. up (fig.), to act the big shot (fam.)

la bollera (pop.) lesbian, dyke (sl.), dike (sl.)

el bollo bread roll
▶ el bollo (pop., Esp.) (vagina) ▷ el conejo
▷ bollo (¡no está el **horno** para ~s!)

el bolo skittle
▶ el bolo (pop., Esp.) (penis) ▷ el calvo
▶ echar a rodar los bolos (fig., fam.) to kick up a row (fam.), to create a disturbance

el bolsillo pocket, purse
▶ meterse a alg. en el bolsillo (fig.) to twist s.o. [a]round one's little finger
▶ consultar con el bolsillo (fam.) to count one's cash, to do one's sums (fam.), to consider one's financial circumstances
▶ rascar[se] el bolsillo (fig., fam.) to cough up (fam.), to fork out (fam.), to stump up (fam., Br.E.)

el bombero fireman, firefighter
▶ un bombero (fam., Esp.) idiot, blockhead (fam.)
▶ el golpe de bombero (fam., Esp.) real booboo (sl., Am.E.), nonsense, crazy idea

el bombo big drum
▶ darse bombo (fig., fam.) to blow one's own horn (Am.E.) or trumpet (fig.), to shoot a line (fam.), to puff o.s. up (fig.), to swank (fam.), to brag
▶ dar bombo a alg. (fig., fam.) to give s.o. exaggerated praise, to praise s.o. to the skies (fam.), to write s.o. up in a big way
▶ dar bombo a algo (fig., fam.) to [heavily] beat the drum for s.th. (fig.), to hype s.th. up (sl.), to crack s.th. up (fam.), to give s.th. a lot of hype (sl.), to ballyhoo s.th. (fam.)
▶ a bombo y platillo (fig., fam.) with great/much fanfare (fig.), with a lot of hype (sl.), (to make) a great song and dance [about s.th.] (fig., fam.) ◆ *El pacto se firmó a bombo y platillo.* A great song and dance was made about the signing of the treaty. ◆ *Lo anunciaron a bombo y platillo.* It was announced with great fanfare. It was ballyhooed. *(fam.)*

el bonete cap, biretta
▶ un gran bonete (fam.) bigwig (fam.), big shot (fam.), big noise (sl.), big cheese (sl.), big wheel (fam.), top nob (sl., Br.E.)

la boquilla mouthpiece
▶ de boquilla (fig., fam.) (to [only] pay) lip service ▷ de **boca** para afuera ◆ *Lo prometieron de boquilla.* They made a promise they didn't intend to keep.

el borbollón ▷ borbotón

el borbotón welling up, bubbling
▶ hablar a borbotones o a borbollones (fam.) the words come tumbling or spluttering or gushing out, to talk in a torrent (fig.)

▷ borracho (ser un ~ **perdido**)

el borrego lamb, yearling ram
▶ No hay tales borregos. (fig., fam.) There isn't any such thing. There's no such thing. It's nothing of the sort. It's enough to make a cat laugh. (fam.)

el borrón blot, smudge
▶ Borrón y cuenta nueva. (fig.) [Let's] forget it. Let's make a fresh start. Let bygones be bygones.
▶ hacer borrón y cuenta nueva (fig.) to make a clean break with s.th. [and start again] (fig.), to wipe the slate clean [and start again] (fig.), to let bygones be bygones

la bota boot
▶ morir con las botas puestas (fig.) to die with one's boots on (fig.), to die in harness (fig.) ◆ *Dice que prefiere morir con las botas puestas a morir en la cama.* He says he prefers dying with his boots on to dying in bed.
▶ ponerse las botas (fig., fam.) (a) to line one's pockets, to feather one's nest (fig.), to make one's pile (fam.), to make a haul or a killing (fam.), to hit the jackpot (fig., fam.), to strike it rich (fig.), to rake it in (fig., fam.) (b) to enjoy o.s. immensely, to enjoy s.th. to the full (c) to make a pig of o.s. (fam.), to stuff o.s. (fam.), to have a blow-out (sl.) (d) to shamelessly take advantage of s.th. ◆ *Con*

ese contrato se puso las botas. He made a killing with that contract. ◆ *Cuando estábamos de vacaciones, nos poníamos las botas. We always enjoyed the vacation (Am.E.) or the holidays (Br.E.) to the full.* ◆ *Como pagaba otra persona se pusieron las botas. Somebody else was paying so they really stuffed themselves.*

▷ bota (**gota** a gota se llena la ~)

el bote thrust, jump, can, boat

▶ dar el bote a alg. (fig., pop.) (to dismiss): to chuck/boot s.o. out (fam.), to fire s.o. (fam.), to sack s.o. (fam.), to give s.o. the chuck/boot/sack (fam.), to give s.o. the kiss-off (sl., Am.E.), to send s.o. packing (fig.), to give s.o. the pink slip (Am.E.), to give s.o. his marching orders (fam.)

▶ darse el bote (pop.) to beat it (sl.), to split (sl.)

▶ tener a alg. en el bote (fam.) to carry/have s.o. in one's pocket (fig.) ◆ *Don Corleone tiene muchos jueces y políticos en el bote. Don Corleone carries/has many judges and politicians in his pocket.*

▶ tener algo en el bote (fam.) s.th. (contract/etc.) is in the bag (fig., fam.), s.th. is buttoned up (fig., fam.), to have s.th. all sewn up (fam.)

▶ chupar del bote (fig., fam.) (a) to scrounge (fam.), to sponge (fam.) (b) to line one's pockets, to feather one's nest (fig.), to look after Number One (fam.) (c) to curry favor [with s.o.], to creep [into s.o.'s favor] (fig.)

▶ estar de bote en bote (sala/tren/cine/etc.) (hall/train/cinema/etc.): to be absolutely packed, to be packed out, to be jam-packed (fam.), to be jam-full (fam.), to be crowded out, to be chock-a-block (fam.), there's no room to swing a cat (fam.) ◆ *El restaurante estaba de bote en bote. The restaurant was chock-a-block.*

▷ bote (ser **tonto** del ~)

la botella bottle

▶ la media botella (fig., fam., hum.) nipper (fam., Br.E.), little lad

▶ darle a la botella (fam.) to drink, to hit the bottle (fam.)

▷ botella (▷ **temblar**: dejar una ~ temblando)

▷ botella (▷ **temblar**: una ~ está temblando)

▷ botella (gafas de **culo** de ~)

▷ Botero (las **caldera**s de Pe[d]ro ~)

la botica (fam.) pharmacy, fly/flies (on pants/trousers)

▶ tener la botica abierta (fam., hum.) to have one's fly/flies undone

▷ boticario (encajar/caer como **pedrada** en ojo de ~)

▷ boticario (venir como **pedrada** en ojo de ~)

la botija bulbous, earthenware jug

▶ estar hecho una botija (fam.) to be as fat as a pig/sow (fam., pej.), to be as round as a barrel (fam.), to be a tub of lard (fam.), to be a fatso (sl., pej.)

las bragas panties (Am.E.), knickers (Br.E.)

▶ pillar a alg. en bragas (fam.) to catch s.o. with his pants (Am.E.) or with his trousers (Br.E.) down (fam.), to catch s.o. on the hop (fam.) ◆ *¡Será posible! Trató de mangar un collar de perlas. El joyero la pilló en bragas. Would you believe it! She tried to walk off with a pearl necklace. The jewel[l]er caught her with her pants down.*

▶ estar hecho una braga (fam.) to be completely exhausted, to be knackered (sl., Br.E.)

▷ estar hecho **cisco**

▷ bragas (no se pescan **trucha**s a ~ enjutas)

la bragueta fly/flies (on pants/trousers)

▶ tener braguetas (vulg.) to be a real man

el braguetazo (pop.) marriage for money

▶ dar un/el braguetazo to marry for money, to marry a rich woman

la brasa live coal, ember

▶ estar [como] en brasas (fig.) to be on tenterhooks (fig.), to be/sit on pins and needles (fig., Am.E.), to cool/kick one's heels (fam.) ◆ *Mientras esperábamos las noticias estábamos como en brasas. We were sitting on pins and needles while [we were] waiting for the news.*

▷ brasa (huir de la[s] **ceniza**[s] y caer/dar en la[s] ~[s])

▷ brasa (huir del **fuego** y caer en las ~s)

▷ brasa (salir de las **llama**s y caer en las ~s)

el brazo arm

▶ no dar su brazo a torcer (fig.) not to let s.o. twist one's arm (fig.), to stand fast (fig.), to hold/stand one's ground (fig.), not to give in

▶ estar/quedarse con los brazos cruzados (fig.) to sit back and do nothing, to sit on one's hands (fig., fam., Am.E.), to twiddle one's thumbs (fig.), to watch with one's arms crossed, to stand/sit around doing nothing

► **luchar a brazo partido (fig.)** to fight bitterly (fig.), to fight tooth and nail (fig.), to go at it hammer and tongs (fam.)

► **estar hecho un brazo de mar (fam.)** to be immaculately dressed, to be dressed up to the nines (fam.), to be dressed to kill (fam.)

▷ **brazo (darle a alg. la/una mano y se toma el ~)**

la breva early fig

► **la breva (fig., fam.)** (a) luck, stroke of luck, lucky break, chance piece of good luck (b) plum job (fig., fam.)

► **No caerá esa breva.** There's no such luck. That's an illusion. A fat chance you've/etc. got. (sl., iron.)

► **Está madura la breva. (fig.)** The time is ripe. ◆ *Estuvo madura la breva para un cambio. The time was ripe for change.* ◆ *Actuaré cuando esté madura la breva. I will act when the time is ripe.*

► **ser una breva (fam.)** to be child's play (fig.), to be a cinch (sl.), to be a pushover (sl.), to be a piece of cake (fam.), to be a snap or a breeze (fam., Am.E.), to be a doddle (fam., Br.E.), to be as easy as pie (sl.) ◆ *El examen fue una breva. The exam/test was child's play.*

► **chuparse [una] buena breva (fam.)** to cream off the best (fig., fam., Br.E.), to skim the cream off (fig.)

► **pescar una buena breva (fam.)** to do [very] well, to come off [very] well

▷ **breva (de higos a ~s)**

▷ **breve (lo bueno, si ~, dos veces bueno)**

Briján

► **saber más que Briján (fam.)** to be very smart, to know every trick in the book (fam.), to know the lot (fam.)

▷ **brillar alg./algo por su ausencia**

brincar to jump up and down, to hop

► **estar alg. que brinca (fig., fam.)** to be hopping mad (fam.) ▷ **estar hecho un basilisco** ◆ *Tu amigo está que brinca. Your friend's hopping mad.*

la broma joke, fun

► **no estar para bromas** to be in no mood for jokes/laughter

► **estar de bromas** to be in a joking mood

► **entre bromas y veras** half-joking[ly], half-serious[ly] ◆ *Lo dijeron entre bromas y veras. They said it kind of half-jokingly, half-seriously.*

► **mezclar bromas con veras (fig.)** to apply a carrot-and-stick policy or a policy of the carrot and the stick (fig.) ◆ *El gobierno mezcló bromas con veras para cambiar la opinión del pueblo. The government applied a policy of the carrot and the stick in order to change the people's opinion.*

la bronca (fam.) (a) row (fam.), set-to (fam.), racket (fam.), scrap (sl.) (b) ticking-off/telling-off (fam., Br.E.), scolding ◆ *Anoche se armó una bronca bestial. There was an almighty row last night.* ◆ **buscar bronca** to look for trouble, to look for a fight ◆ **echar la gran bronca a alg.** to give s.o. a terrific telling-off/ticking-off or bollocking (sl., Br.E.), to come down on s.o. like a ton of bricks (fam.), to really bite s.o.'s head off (fam.)

bruto brute

► **estar bruto (pop.)** to be randy (fam.), to be horny (sl., vulg.)

► **ponerse bruto (pop.)** to get randy (fam.), to get horny (sl., vulg.)

▷ **bruto (ser más ~ que la pila de un pozo)**

el buche crop (bird), maw (cow/etc.)

► **llenarse el buche (fam.)** to stuff o.s. (fam.), to make a [real] pig of o.s. (fam.)

► **sacar el buche a alg. (fig.)** to get s.th. out of s.o., to make s.o. talk

► **no caberle algo a alg. en el buche (fig.)** s.o. can't keep s.th. to himself, s.o. can't keep his mouth shut (fam.) ◆ *No le cabe nada en el buche a él. He can't keep anything to himself. He can never keep his mouth shut.*

bueno good

► **Lo bueno, si breve, dos veces bueno. (prov.)** Brevity is the soul of wit. (prov.)

► **Bueno está lo bueno [pero no lo demasiado]. (fam.)** Leave well enough alone. You can have too much of a good thing. You can take things too far.

► **Lo que es bueno para uno es bueno para el otro.** What's sauce for the goose is sauce for the gander.

► **ser bueno como el oro (negocio o método o éxito/etc.)** to be a sure-fire . . . (fam.) (business or method or success/etc.)

▶ **a la buena de Dios** (fam.) trusting to luck, on the off-chance, on a wing and a prayer, at random ◆ *Fuimos a Sevilla a la buena de Dios. We went to Seville on the off-chance [of finding good weather/a hotel room/etc.].*

▶ **por las buenas o por las malas** willy-nilly, by hook or by crook, like it or not, whether one likes it or not, by fair means or foul ◆ *Tienes que hacerlo por las buenas o por las malas. You have to do it willy-nilly. You have to do it whether you like it or not.*

▶ **de buenas a primeras** just like that, suddenly, all of a sudden, without [any] warning, right off the bat (Am.E.), out of the blue ◆ *No puedo tomar una decisión así, de buenas a primeras. I can't make/take (Br.E.) a decision just like that.*

▶ **de los buenos** (fam.) tremendous, terrific, good, real, decent, sound, severe (all: fam.) ◆ *Nos echó un sermón de los buenos. He gave us a terrific/severe wigging or lecture.* ◆ *Es una mentira de las buenas. It's a great big lie. (fam.) It's a whopping great lie. (fam.)*

▷ bueno (no estar ~ de la **cabeza**)

el buey ox

▶ **trabajar como un buey** (fig.) to work very hard, to work like an ox or like a bull (fig.) ▷ echar/sudar la **hiel**

▶ **Habló el buey y dijo mu.** (un dicho; hum.) What did you/etc. expect of him/etc.? (iron.) ◆ *Disparataron de lo lindo. Habló el buey y dijó mu. They talked utter nonsense. What did you expect of them?*

▶ **a paso de buey** (fig.) at a snail's pace (fig.), [as] slow as or slower than molasses [in January] (fig., Am.E.) ◆ *Allí hay una cola de coches que se extiende hasta 10 millas. Se puede ir sólo a paso de buey. There's a 10-mile traffic jam. You can only drive at a snail's pace. The traffic is as slow as molasses in January.* ◆ *Estoy impaciente esperando las noticias. El tiempo parece pasar a paso de buey. I'm anxiously awaiting the news. Time seems to be moving at a snail's pace.*

el bulto vague/indistinct shape

▶ **buscar el bulto a alg.** (fig., fam.) (a) to crowd s.o. (fam., Am.E.), to push s.o. (fig.) (b) to have it in for s.o. (fam.), to be out for s.o.'s blood (fig.)

▶ **coger/pescar el bulto a alg.** (fam.) to collar s.o., to nab s.o. (fam.)

▶ **menear/sacudir el bulto a alg.** (fam.) to thrash s.o. (fig.), to give s.o. a thrashing ▷ arrimar **candela** a alg.

▶ **escurrir/escapar/huir el bulto** (fam.) to dodge (fig.), to duck out [of it] (fam.), to cop out [of it] (sl.), to skive off (fam., Br.E.), to make o.s. scarce (fam.), to sneak away ◆ *De nuevo escurrió el bulto. He skived off again.* ◆ *Cada vez que teníamos mucho que hacer, ese tío escurría el bulto. Whenever we had a lot to do, that guy ducked out.*

▶ **sacar el bulto** (pop.) to beat it (sl.), to clear off (fam.), to skin out (sl., Am.E.)

el buñuelo (Spain): fritter, doughnut

▶ **el buñuelo** (fig., fam.) bad or botched (fam.) job, botch (fam.), botch-up (fam.)

▶ **mandar a alg. a freír buñuelos** (fam.) to tell s.o. to go fry an egg (fam.) ▷ mandar a alg. a freír **espárragos**

▶ **¡Vete a freír buñuelos!** (fam.) Go fry an egg! (fam.) ▷ ¡Véte a freír **espárragos**!

la burra she-donkey

▶ **la burra** (fam., Esp.) bicycle, bike, pushbike (Br.E.)

▶ **írsele a alg. la burra** (fam.) to tell tales [out of school] (fig.), to blab [it out] (fam.), not to keep it to o.s., not to keep one's mouth shut (fam.) ◆ *Se le fue la burra a ella. She didn't keep her mouth shut.*

▷ burra (la **panza** de ~)

la burrada drove of donkeys

▶ **la burrada** (fig.) silly/stupid thing [to do], stupid act/saying/etc.

▶ **costar una burrada** (fig., fam.) to cost a tidy sum, to cost a pretty penny (fam.), to cost a packet (sl.), to cost a bomb (fam., Br.E.), to cost an arm and a leg (fam.), to cost a fortune, to be shockingly expensive (fam.)

▷ burral (la **edad** ~)

el burro donkey

▶ **apearse de su burro** (fig., fam.) to climb down (fig., fam.), to back down (fam.), to recognize one's error/mistake, to think better of it

▶ **no apearse de su burro** (fig., fam.) to persist in one's error, to remain stubborn ◆ *Aunque le aconsejaron que no lo hiciese, no se apeó de su burro. Even though they advised him not to do it, he persisted in his error.*

▶ no ver tres en un burro (fam.) (a) to be [as] blind as a bat (fam.) (b) (due to darkness/fog/etc.): s.o. can't see his hand in front of his face, s.o. can't see a thing ◆ *Su abuelo no ve tres en un burro. His grandfather is blind as a bat.* ◆ *Está tan oscuro que no veo tres en un burro. It's so dark that I can't see my hand in front of my face.* ◆ *La niebla estuvo tan densa que no vimos tres en un burro. The fog was so thick that we couldn't see a thing.*

▶ como un burro en una cacharrería (fig., fam.) like a bull in a china-shop (fig.) ◆ *Se comportó como un burro en una cacharrería. He was like a bull in a china-shop.*

▶ [Una vez] puesto en el burro. (fam.) In for a penny, in for a pound. (Br.E.) In for a dime, in for a dollar. (Am.E.)

▶ Quien nace [para] burro muere rebuznando. (prov.) A leopard never changes or cannot change its spots. (prov.)

▷ burro (la **panza** de ~)

▷ burro (no morir de **cornada** de ~)

▷ burro (poner dos **albarda**s a un ~)

▷ buscar **bronca/camorra**

▷ buscar el **bulto** a alg.

el busilis (fam., Esp.)

▶ Ahí está el busilis. There's or that's the rub/snag. (fig.) That's where the problem is/lies. That's why [it doesn't work/etc.].

▶ dar en el busilis to hit the mark (fig.), to hit the nail on the head (fig.) ◆ *Diste en el busilis con esa observación. You hit the mark with that remark.*

C

caballero riding
▶ estar caballero en su opinión (fig.) to stick firmly to one's opinion

el caballero rider, knight, gentleman
▶ Poderoso caballero es don Dinero. (prov.) Money talks. Money makes the world go round.

el caballo horse
▶ ir/venir en el caballo de San Francisco (fam., hum.) to go/come on Shank's pony (Br.E.) or on Shank's mare (Am.E.) (hum.), to walk, to hoof it (fam.)
▶ como un caballo en una cacharrería (fig., fam.) like a bull in a china-shop (fig.) ◆ *Se comportó como un caballo en una cacharrería. He was like a bull in a china-shop.*
▶ A caballo regalado no hay que mirarle o no le mires el diente. (prov.) Don't look a gift horse in the mouth. (prov.)
▷ caballo (dar un **gallo** para recibir un ~)
▷ caballo (**sota**, ~ y rey)

el cabe stroke (refers to argolla, a game like croquet)
▶ el cabe de pala (fig., fam.) unexpected opportunity/chance, lucky break, stroke of luck, chance piece of good luck

el cabello hair
▶ partir/hender un cabello en el aire (fig.) to split hairs
▶ no faltar un cabello a algo (fig.) to be [as good as] finished/complete/done
▶ traer algo por los cabellos (fig.) to be farfetched (fig.) ◆ *Me parece traído por los cabellos. I think it's far-fetched.* ◆ *Lo has traído por los cabellos. It (what you've said) is farfetched.*
▶ llevar a alg. de un cabello (fig.) to twist s.o. [a]round one's little finger
▶ colgar/pender o estar colgado/pendiente de un cabello (fig.) to hang or be hanging by a hair/thread (fig.) ◆ *El futuro de la firma cuelga de un cabello. The firm's future hangs by a hair.* ◆ *Su vida pendía o estaba pen-*

diente de un cabello. His/her life was hanging by a thread.
▷ cabello (coger/asir la **ocasión** por los ~s)

caber to go or fit in/into
▶ no caber en sí de alegría (fig.) to be beside o.s. with joy, to be overwhelmed or wild (fam.) with joy
▷ caber (no ~ en el **pellejo**)
▷ caber (no ~ en el **pellejo** de alegría/orgullo)
▷ caber (no ~ ni un **alfiler**)
▷ caber (no ~le a alg. en la **cabeza**)

el cabestro halter
▶ llevar a alg. del cabestro (fig.) to lead s.o. by the nose (fam.)

la cabeza head
▶ un[a] cabeza de corcho (fam.) numskull (fam.), blockhead (fam.) ▷ un [pedazo de] **alcornoque**
▶ un[a] cabeza torcida (fam.) hypocrite
▶ un[a] cabeza de turco (fig., fam.) scapegoat, fall guy (fam., Am.E.), whipping boy (fig.)
▶ un[a] cabeza de chorlito (fig., fam.) scatterbrain
▶ tener la cabeza a pájaros to be a scatterbrain, to be scatty (fam., Br.E.), to be scatterbrained or featherbrained
▶ tener la cabeza llena de pájaros (fig., fam.) to be living in cloud-cuckoo-land, to be living in never-never land, to be living in a dream/fantasy world
▶ La cabeza blanca y el seso por venir. There's no fool like an old fool. (prov.)
▶ no estar bueno de la cabeza (fam.), estar ido/mal/tocado de la cabeza (fam.), tener pájaros en la cabeza (fig., fam.) to be crazy (fam.), to be nuts (fam.), to be off one's nut (fam., Br.E.), to be off one's rocker (fam.), to be as nutty as a fruitcake (fam., hum.), to be off one's head (fam.), to be soft in the head (fam.), to be round the bend (fam., Br.E.), to have lost one's marbles (fam., hum., Br.E.), to have bats in one's/the belfry

▶ apostar[se] la cabeza a que ... (fam.) to bet s.o. anything he likes [that] . . . , you can bet your life (fam.) or your bottom dollar (fam., Am.E.) [that] . . . , it's dollars to doughnuts [that] . . . (fam., Am.E.) ◆ *Me apuesto la cabeza a que no lo hacen. I bet you anything you like they don't do it. You can bet your life they won't do it.*

▶ Apostaría la cabeza. (fam.) You can bet your life on that. (fam.) You can bet your bottom dollar on that. (fam.)

▶ afirmar con la cabeza to nod [yes]

▶ negar con la cabeza to shake one's head

▶ dar con la cabeza en las paredes (fig.) (a) to get furious, to get mad (fam.), to tear one's hair [out] (fig.), to go spare (fam., Br.E.), (s.th. is enough) to drive s.o. spare or up the wall (fam.), s.o. could kick himself or feels like kicking himself (fam.) (b) to be pig-headed, to be as stubborn as a mule (fig.) ◆ *... y encima he perdido el tren. ¡Podría dar con la cabeza en las paredes!* . . . *and on top of everything I've missed the train. It's enough to drive me spare! I feel like kicking myself! I could tear my hair out!*

▶ calentar la cabeza a alg. (fig., fam.) to fill s.o.'s head (with s.th.), (s.th.) makes s.o.'s head spin (fig.) ◆ *Esas fórmulas matemáticas nos calentaron la cabeza. These mathematical formulas made our heads spin.* ◆ *El profesor nos calentó la cabeza con esas fórmulas matemáticas. The teacher filled our heads with these mathematical formulas.*

▶ calentarse la cabeza (fig., fam.) s.o.'s head is/starts spinning (fig.), to get tired out, to get fagged out (fam., Br.E.) ◆ *Me calenté la cabeza con tanto estudiar. I studied so hard that my head started spinning or that I got fagged out.*

▶ quebrarse/romperse la cabeza (fig., fam.) to rack one's brains (fig.)

▶ esconder/meter la cabeza bajo el ala (fig.) to bury one's head in the sand (fig.) ◆ *Acepta la realidad. No metas la cabeza bajo el ala. Face [up to] the facts. Don't bury your head in the sand.*

▶ meterse de cabeza en algo (fig., fam.) to throw o.s. or plunge into s.th. (work/etc.) (fig.)

▶ no saber dónde volver la cabeza not to know any more whether one is coming or going, to have an awful lot on one's plate (fam.) or on one's mind ◆ *Estoy hasta aquí de trabajo. ¡Ya no sé dónde volver la cabeza! I'm up to my neck/eyeballs in work. I don't know any more whether I'm coming or going.*

▶ andar/ir de cabeza con algo (fam.) to be up to one's eyeballs or eyes or ears or neck in s.th. (work/debt/etc.), to be snowed under with s.th. (fig.) ◆ *Ando de cabeza con tanto trabajo. I'm up to my eyes in work. I'm snowed under with work.*

▶ levantar/alzar cabeza (fig., fam.) to get on one's feet again (after a business failure/etc.) (fig.), to recover (from s.th.), to pick o.s. up (fig.), to get back on one's feet (after an illness) (fig.), to recover one's health ◆ *Ha sufrido varios fracasos profesionales. Pasará algún tiempo antes de que levante cabeza. He's had several failures in his work. It will take him some time to recover from them or to get on his feet again.*

▶ no levantar/alzar cabeza (fig., fam.) (a) not to get on one's feet again (after a business failure/a setback/etc.) (fig.), not to recover (from a business failure/a setback/etc.) (b) to be totally depressed or dejected, to be down in the dumps/mouth (fam.) (c) to be very ill/sick (d) to keep one's head down, to have one's head buried in one's work, to be totally engrossed in or wrapped up in (fam.) one's work

▶ no caberle a alg. en la cabeza (fig., fam.) s.o. [just] doesn't/can't understand ◆ *No me cabe en la cabeza que no le guste ir a España. I just can't understand that he doesn't feel like going to Spain.*

▶ subírsele algo a alg. a la cabeza (fig.) s.th. (wine/success/etc.) goes to s.o.'s head ◆ *El éxito se le ha subido a la cabeza. His/her success has gone to his/her head.*

▶ vestirse por la cabeza (fam., hum.) to be a female, to be a cleric, to be a clergyman ◆ *¿Quién es? Se viste por la cabeza. Who is it? It's a woman.*

▶ tener la cabeza en su sitio o bien puesta (fam.) to have one's head screwed on (Br.E.) or screwed on tight (Am.E.) (fam.), to be no fool

▶ llevarse las manos a la cabeza to throw one's hands in the air, to throw up one's hands (in dismay/shock/etc.)

▶ llevar de cabeza a alg. (fig., fam.) to drive s.o. crazy/mad (fam.), to drive s.o. round the bend (fam., Br.E.) ◆ *Lleva de cabeza a todo el mundo. He drives everybody crazy.*

▶ bailarle algo a alg. por la cabeza (fig.) s.th. goes round and round in s.o.'s head ◆ *La idea me baila todavía por la cabeza. The idea is still going round and round in my head.*

▶ Más vale ser cabeza de ratón que cola de león. (prov.) It's better to be a big fish/frog in a small pond than a small fish/frog in a big pond. (prov.) It's better to be the head of a dog than the tail of a lion. (prov.)

▷ cabeza (▷ **nacer**: nació alg. de ~)

▷ cabeza (**llevar** a alg. la ~)

▷ cabeza (no tener **pies** ni ~)

▷ cabeza (tener la ~ como una **olla** de grillos)

▷ cabeza (tener la ~ llena de **serrín**)

▷ cabeza (tener la ~ más dura que un **picador**)

▷ cabeza (tirarse los **trastos** a la ~)

▷ cabeza ajena (▷ **escarmentar**: nadie escarmienta en ~)

▷ cabeza ajena (**escarmentar** en ~)

la cabezada butt (with the head), nod[ding], nodding off

▶ darse de cabezadas (fam.) to rack one's brains (fig.)

▶ echar una cabezada o cabezadita (fam.) to have/take a nap, to have a snooze (fam.), to get a bit of or some shut-eye (fam.), to have/get forty winks (fam.), to catch some Zs (sl., Am.E.)

▷ cabezadita (echar una **cabezada** o ~)

el/la cabezota (fam.) pig-headed person, mule (fig.)

el cable cable, hawser

▶ echar un cable a alg. (fam.) to give s.o. a helping hand, to help s.o. out of a jam/fix (fam.), to help s.o. out of a tight spot (fam.), to get s.o. off the hook (fam.), to bail s.o. out (fig.)

el cabo end, point

▶ estar al cabo de algo o de la calle (fig., fam.) to know all about s.th., to know what the score is (fam.), to know what's going on, to have got/gotten (Am.E.) to the bottom of s.th. ◆ *Estoy al cabo de lo que están tra-*

mando. I know exactly what they're up to. ◆ *Estamos al cabo de la calle. We know what the score is. We've got to the bottom of it.*

▶ no tener cabo ni cuerda to make no sense whatsoever, there's no rhyme or reason [to s.th.], s.o. can't make head[s] or tail[s] of s.th. (fam.), to be absurd, to be ridiculous ◆ *Para mi/nosotros esto no tiene cabo ni cuerda. I/we can't make head or tail of it.* ◆ *Este plan no tiene cabo ni cuerda. This plan makes no sense whatsoever. This is an absurd plan.*

▶ atar/unir cabos (fam.) to put two and two together (fig.), to tie up loose ends (fig.), to draw conclusions, to make sense, to make head[s] or tail[s] of it (fam.) ◆ *¿Puedes atar cabos? Can you make head or tail of it?*

▶ al fin y al cabo (fam.) at long last, in the end, after all, when all is said and done, at the end of the day (fig.) ◆ *Al fin y al cabo no se divorciaron. They didn't get divorced after all.* ◆ *Es inútil darles consejos. Al fin y al cabo hacen siempre lo que quieren. It is pointless/useless to give them advice. In the end they always do as they please.*

▶ de cabo a cabo, de cabo a rabo (fam.), de punta a cabo from A to Z, from beginning to end, from start to finish, from cover to cover, inside out (to know), like the back of one's hand (to know) ◆ *Leí ese libro de cabo a cabo. I read that book from cover to cover.* ◆ *Conoce la ciudad de cabo a rabo. He knows the city like the back of his hand.*

la cabra goat

▶ la cabra (fam.) motorbike, motorcycle

▶ estar como una cabra (fam.) to be crazy

▷ no estar bueno de la **cabeza**

▶ estar más loco que una cabra (fam.) to be completely crazy/nuts (fam.), to be as mad as a hatter (Br.E.), to be as mad as a March hare (fam.)

▶ meter las cabras en el corral a alg. (fam.) to intimidate s.o., to cow s.o.

▶ La cabra siempre tira al monte. (prov.) A leopard never changes or cannot change its spots. (prov.)

cabrillas (a) fleecy or cotton-wool clouds, cirrocumuli (b) (waves): white horses

▷ cabrillas (pedir **leche** a las ~)

▷ cabrito (apartar las **ovejas** de los ~s)

el cabrón billy goat
▶ el cabrón (vulg.) (abuse): swine (fam.), bastard (sl.), son of a bitch (vulg., Am.E.) ◆ *El muy cabrón me robó el coche. The bastard stole my car.*

la caca (fam., en lengua infantil) poop (Am.E.) or pooh (Br.E.) (used to or by children), excrement
▶ la caca (fig.) filth (fig.)
▶ ocultar/tapar la caca (fig., fam.) to cover s.th. up (fig.), to hush s.th. up

cacarear to cackle, to crow
▶ cacarear algo (fig., fam.) to [boastfully] broadcast s.th. (fig., fam.), to crow about s.th., to boast about s.th., to brag about s.th. ◆ *La estrella de la pantalla cacareó su propia fama. The movie star (Am.E.)/film star broadcasted her own fame or crowed about her own fame.* ◆ *Fue un triunfo muy cacareado. It was a much-vaunted or much-trumpeted triumph. There was a lot of boasting or crowing about the triumph.* ◆ *La tan cacareada hospitalidad dejó mucho que desear. The much-praised or much-ballyhooed (fam.) hospitality left much to be desired.* ◆ *Siempre cacareaban. They were always bragging.*
▶ cacarear y no poner huevos (fig., fam.) to be nothing but or just empty boasting, to be nothing but or just braggadocio, to be all mouth and no trousers (fam., Br.E.), to be all talk and no action ◆ *Su hermano siempre cacarea y no pone huevos. Everything that comes out of his brother's mouth is just empty boasting. His brother is all mouth and no trousers.*

la cacha haunch (small game), hilt, handle
▶ las cachas (pop.) buttocks
▶ meter el cuchillo hasta las cachas en algo to stab the knife up to the hilt into s.th.
▶ estar metido hasta las cachas en algo (fig., fam.) to be up to one's eyeballs/eyes/ears in s.th. (work/debt/etc.)
▶ meterse hasta las cachas en algo (fig., fam.) to be totally wrapped up in s.th. (work/etc.) (fam.)

▷ cacharrería (como un **burro/caballo/ele-fante** en una ~)

el cadáver corpse
▶ tener un cadáver en el armario (fig.) to have a skeleton in the cupboard (Br.E.) or in the closet (Am.E.) (fig.)
▷ caer (llegar como caído del **cielo**)

caerse to fall [over]
▶ caerse redondo (fam.) to collapse/fall in a heap, to keel over (fig.)
▶ caerse de cansancio/sueño (fam.) to be ready to drop (fam.), to be dead on one's feet (fig., fam.), to be dog-tired (fam.)
▶ caerse de tonto/etc. (fam.) to be very stupid/etc.
▶ caerse [muerto] de miedo (fam.) to be scared to death (fam.), to be terrified
▶ no tener donde caerse muerto not to have a penny or a red cent to one's name, not to have two [brass] farthings to rub together (Br.E.), to be as poor as a church mouse (fig.)
▶ caerse de/por su propio peso to be obvious, to be self-evident, to go without saying
▶ caerse [a/en pedazos] de viejo (fam.) ◆ *Se cae de viejo. He's very old and frail. He's so old he can hardly walk.* ◆ *Su bicicleta se cae a pedazos de vieja. His bicycle is so old it is falling to pieces or it is falling apart.*
▷ caérsele a alg. el **alma** a los pies
▷ caérsele a alg. la **baba** con/por alg./algo
▷ caérsele a alg. la cara de **vergüenza**
▷ caérsele a alg. la **casa** encima/a cuestas
▷ caérsele a alg. la **venda** de los ojos
▷ caérsele a alg. las **alas** [del corazón]
▷ caérsele a alg. los **anillos** ([no] ~)

el café coffee
▶ estar de mal café (fig., fam.) to be in a bad mood
▶ tener mal café (fig., fam.) to have bad/evil intentions, to have a nasty temper, to have a spiteful/nasty nature or disposition, to be a nasty piece of work (fam.), to be a bastard (fam.)

la cafetera coffee pot
▶ la cafetera [rusa] (fam.) (car): jalop[p]y, old heap of metal (fam.), old crock (fam., Br.E.), old banger (fam.) ◆ *¿A esa cafetera rusa le llamas coche? Do you call that old heap of metal a car?*
▶ estar como una cafetera (fam.) to be crazy, to be nuts (fam.) ▷ no estar bueno de la **cabeza**

27

el cagachín (**fig., pop.**) swine (fam.), bastard (fam.), son of a bitch (vulg., Am.E.)

la cagalera (**pop., vulg.**) (diarrhea): trots (fam.), runs (fam., Br.E.), shits (sl., vulg.), Montezuma's revenge (hum.)

cagar (**pop., vulg.**) to shit (vulg.), to take or have (Br.E.) a shit/crap (vulg.)
▶ cagar algo (**pop., vulg.**) to make a botch of s.th. (fig.), to mess s.th. up (fig., fam.), to cock s.th. up (sl., Br.E.), to ball or balls (Br.E.) s.th. up (sl.)
▶ cagarla (**pop., vulg.**) to drop a clanger (sl.), to screw or cock (Br.E.) it/things up (sl.), to ball or balls (Br.E.) it/things up (sl.), to mess it/things up (fig., fam.), to blow it (sl.) ◆ *¡Ahora sí que la hemos cagado! Now we've really cocked things up!*
▶ cagarse (**pop., vulg.**) to shit o.s. (vulg.)
▶ cagarse de miedo (**fig., pop., vulg.**) to shit o.s. [for fear] (fig., vulg.) ◆ *Nos cagamos de miedo. We shit/shat ourselves. We were scared shitless. (vulg.) We were in a blue funk. (fam., Br.E.)*
▶ cagarse en algo/alg. (**fig., pop., vulg.**) not to give a shit (vulg.) or a damn (fam.) about s.th./s.o. ◆ *¡Me cago en el gobierno! To hell with the government! (fam.) Screw the government! (vulg.)*
▶ ¡Me cago en diez o en la mar! (**pop., vulg.**) Shit! (vulg.) Damn [it]! (fam.)

el cagatintas (**pej.**) ink-shitter (pej.), hack writer (pej.), penpusher (fam., pej.), petty clerk (pej.)

Caín Cain
▶ pasar las de Caín (**fam.**) to have a ghastly time, to go through hell (fam.), to die a thousand deaths (fam.)
▶ venir con las de Caín (**fam.**) to have evil intentions

la caja box
▶ la caja boba/idiota/tonta (**fam.**) (TV): box (fam.), goggle box (fam., Br.E.), [boob] tube (fam., Am.E.)
▶ echar/despedir a alg. con cajas destempladas (**fig., fam.**) to kick s.o. out (fam.), to send s.o. packing (fig.) ▷ dar el **bote** a alg.

el cajón big box
▶ el cajón de sastre (**fig., fam.**) motley collection, hotchpotch (fig., Br.E.) or hodge-podge (fam., Am.E.), jumble, mess (fig.) ◆ *El informe anual es un cajón de sastre. The annual report is a hotchpotch or is a jumble of different things. ◆ Su oficina está como [un] cajón de sastre. His office is in utter disorder or is in a terrible mess or is an absolute shambles. (fig.)*

la cal lime
▶ cerrar algo a cal y canto (**fig.**) to shut or close s.th. firmly/tight/securely
▶ de cal y canto (**fig.**) durable/lasting/solid (peace or building or basis/etc.), unshakable (conviction/etc.), firm, as solid as a rock (fig.)
▶ dar una de cal y otra de arena (**fam.**) (a) to be a weathercock (fig.), to blow hot and cold (fig.), to chop and change (fam., Br.E.) (b) to apply a policy of the carrot and the stick or a carrot-and-stick policy (fig.) ◆ *El gobierno dio una de cal y otra de arena para cambiar la opinión del pueblo. The government applied a policy of the carrot and the stick in order to change the people's opinion.*

la calabaza pumpkin
▶ la calabaza (**fig.**) nut (sl.) ▷ la cebolla
▶ una calabaza (**fig., fam.**) dope (fam.), idiot ▷ un [pedazo de] **alcornoque**
▶ dar calabazas a alg. (**fam.**) (a) (student/candidate): to fail, to flunk (fam., Am.E.), to plough (sl., Br.E.) (b) (suitor): to give the brush-off (fam.); (lover): to jilt ◆ *Le dieron calabazas en español. They ploughed him or he was ploughed or he was flunked in Spanish. ◆ Ella le dio calabazas. She gave him the brush-off. ◆ Ella le dio calabazas a su amante. She jilted her lover.*

la calada soaking
▶ dar una calada a alg. (**fig., fam.**) to give s.o. a [good] dressing-down or ticking-off (Br.E.) (fam.), to haul s.o. over the coals (fig.) ▷ zurrar la **badana** a alg. (b)
▷ calado (estar ~ hasta los **huesos**)

la calamidad disaster, calamity
▶ ser alg. una calamidad (**fam.**) s.o.: to be utterly useless, to be a dead loss (fig., fam.), to be a washout (sl.), to be a [complete] disaster (fig., fam.) ◆ *Como presidente es una calamidad. As a president he's a disaster.*

el calcetín sock

▶ el calcetín (pop.) (condom): rubber (fam., Am.E.), johnny (fam., Br.E.), French letter (fam., Br.E.)
▶ ir/venir a golpe de calcetín to go/come on Shank's pony (Br.E.) or on Shank's mare (Am.E.) (hum.), to hoof it (fam.), to walk

la caldera ca[u]ldron, kettle

▶ las calderas de Pe[d]ro Botero (fig., fam.) hell

el caldo broth

▶ revolver el caldo (fig.) to stir it/s.th. up again (fig.)
▶ amargar el caldo a alg. (fig.) to spoil s.o.'s fun, to spoil all the fun, to spoil s.th./things for s.o., to cause s.o. trouble
▶ hacer el caldo gordo a alg. (fig.) to play into s.o.'s hands, to make it/things easy for s.o.
▶ cambiar el caldo a las aceitunas (fam., hum.) (men): to have a slash (sl., Br.E.), to take or have (Br.E.) a leak (sl., hum.), to have a pee/piddle (fam., Br.E.), to spend a penny (euph., fam., Br.E.)
▶ poner a alg. a caldo (fam.) to give s.o. a dressing-down (fam.), to tell s.o. what you think of him

el calé o calés (pop.) (money): dough (sl., Am.E.), bread (sl.), sugar (sl.), brass/dosh/lolly (sl., Br.E.), wampum (sl., Am.E.)

las calendas calends

▶ en las Calendas griegas (fam., hum.) on the Greek calends (hum.), in a month of Sundays (fam.), in a coon's age (sl., Am.E.), never ◆ Pagarán en las Calendas griegas. They'll pay on the Greek calends. They'll never pay. ◆ Siguiendo así, terminarán el trabajo en las Calendas griegas. Continuing like that, they won't finish the job in a month of Sundays.
▷ calentar el asiento
▷ calentar la cabeza/los cascos a alg.
▷ calentarse la cabeza
▷ calentura de pollo

la calientapollas (vulg., Esp.) sexually provocative woman, prick-teaser (vulg.), cockteaser (vulg.)

caliente warm, hot

▶ Ande yo caliente y ríase la gente. I don't give a damn what other people say/think (fam.) I couldn't care less what other people say/think. I dress for comfort, not for other people.
▷ caliente de cascos

el cáliz chalice

▶ apurar el cáliz de cicuta o de [la] amargura o de dolor hasta las heces (fig.) to drain/drink the cup of sorrow or the cup of bitterness [down] to the last drop (fig.)

callar to be quiet

▶ callar[se] como un muerto o como una piedra (fam.) to shut up like a clam (fam.), s.o.'s lips are sealed (fig.), to keep absolutely quiet, not to breathe a word
▶ Quien calla otorga. Silence gives/implies consent.
▷ callar (▷ el sabio: es de sabios el ~)

la calle street

▶ echarse a la calle (fig.) to take to the streets, to demonstrate, to riot, to express one's outrage
▶ hacer la calle (fam.) (prostitute): to walk/work the streets (fam.), to be on the game (fam.)
▶ llevar/traer a alg. por la calle de la amargura (fam.) to give s.o. a [very] difficult time, to make s.o.'s life a misery (fam.), to make life hell for s.o. (fam.)
▶ desempedrar la calle (fig., fam.) to dash along/through the street, to shoot off
▶ echar a alg. a la calle (fam.), poner a alg. de patitas en la calle (fam.) to kick s.o. out (fam.), to boot s.o. out (fam.), to fire s.o. (fam.) ▷ dar el bote a alg.
▶ plantar a alg. en la calle (fig., fam.) to pitch s.o. into the street (fig.) ▷ dar el bote a alg.
▷ calle (estar al cabo de la ~)

el callo callus

▶ dar el callo (fig., fam., Esp.) to keep one's nose to the grindstone (fig.) ▷ echar/sudar la hiel
▶ criar callos (fig.) to develop a thick skin (fig.), to become inured, to become hardened (fig.), to toughen [o.s.] up (make physically or emotionally resilient) ◆ Tiene la sensibilidad a flor de piel. Debería criar ca-

llos. She's very easily hurt. She should develop a thick skin.

▷ calor (▷ **cojón**: hacer un ~ de cojones)
▷ calor (▷ **traer/traérselas**: hace un ~ que se las trae)
▷ calor (**abrasarse** de ~)

el Calvario Calvary, Stations of the Cross
► ser un calvario (fig.) to be an ordeal (fig.), to be a misery (fam.), to be torture (fig.), to be hell (fam.) ◆ *Vivir allí fue un calvario. Life was hell there.* ◆ *La oveja negra de la familia hizo de la vida de sus padres un verdadero calvario. The black sheep of the family made his parents' life a real misery.*

calvo bald, baldheaded
► el calvo (pop.) (penis): prick (vulg.), cock (vulg.), dick (vulg.), pecker (vulg., Am.E.), dong (vulg., Am.E.)
► Ni tanto ni tan calvo. (fig.) Don't exaggerate. It's not that bad. ◆ *Casi morimos. ¡Ni tanto ni tan calvo! We almost died. Don't exaggerate! It was not that bad.*
▷ calvo (dentro de cien **años** todos ~s)

la calzadera lace for abarcas (sandals)
► apretar las calzaderas (fig., fam.) to take to one's heels, to beat it (sl.)

calzar (shoes/etc.): to put on, to wear
► calzar algo (fig., fam.) to get s.th. (fam.), to twig s.th. (fam., Br.E.), to catch on to s.th. (fam.), to grasp s.th. (fig.), to understand s.th.
► calzar poco (fig., fam.) to be slow on the uptake, to be pretty dim (fam.), to be a bit dense (fig.)
► calzar[se] a alg. (pop., Esp.) to screw s.o. (vulg.), to fuck s.o. (vulg.), to bang s.o. (vulg.), to bonk s.o. (vulg.), to have it off/away with s.o. (sl., Br.E.), to lay s.o. (sl.), to ball s.o. (sl., Am.E.), to shag s.o. (vulg., Br.E.)
► calzarse a alg. (fig., fam.) to have/keep s.o. under one's thumb (fig., fam.) ◆ *Hace un año que esa mujer de armas tomar se calza a él. That Xanthippe has been keeping him under her thumb for a year.*
► calzarse algo (fig., fam.) to get s.th., to manage to get s.th., to succeed in getting s.th. ◆ *Me calcé el empleo. I got the job.*
► calzárselos (fam.) (punishment/ticking-off/etc.): to deserve it, to serve s.o. right ◆ *El jefe les echó una bronca fenomenal. Se*

los calzaron. The boss gave them a terrific ticking-off. They deserved it. It served them right.

el calzón trousers (Br.E.), pants (Am.E.)
► meterse en sus calzones (fig.) to mind one's own business ◆ *¡Métete en tus calzones! Mind your own business!*
► llevar o ponerse los calzones (mujer) (fig.) (woman): to wear the pants (Am.E.)/trousers (Br.E.) (fig.) ▷ llevar la **batuta** ◆ *Su esposa lleva los calzones. His wife wears the pants.*

los calzoncillos underpants (Am.E.), pants (Br.E.)
► dejar a alg. en calzoncillos (fig., fam.) to fleece s.o. [of everything] (fig.), to milk s.o. [dry] (fig.), to bleed s.o. [white/dry] (fam.)

la camada litter (animals)
► la camada (fig., pej.) band/gang [of thieves], bunch of no-gooders (fam., pej.)
► ser lobos de una misma camada (fig., pej.) to be tarred with the same brush (fam., pej.), to be birds of a feather ◆ *Son lobos de una misma camada. They're tarred with the same brush.*

la camándula (fig., fam.) smartness, shrewdness, cunning
► tener muchas camándulas to be very shrewd/crafty, to be as sly as they come (fam.), to know every trick in the book (fam.)

el camarón shrimp, prawn
► Camarón que se duerme, se lo lleva la corriente. (prov.) Time and tide wait for no man. (prov.) Don't miss the boat. (fig.) Board the boat before it sails or before it has set sail. (fig.)

el cambiazo (fam.) dishonest switch (fig.)
► dar el cambiazo a alg. to dishonestly switch s.th. ◆ *No es el diamante auténtico. Me han dado el cambiazo. It isn't the real diamond. They have switched it for a fake one.*

▷ camello (hacer de una **pulga** un ~)

el camelo (fam.) blarney (fam.), leg-pulling (fam.), joke, hoax, lie, bull (sl., Am.E.), con (sl.), swindle ◆ *Esto es un camelo. It's all a swindle.* ◆ *Lo que dijo fue puro camelo. What he said was a pack of lies or a load of bull.*

▶ dar [el] camelo a alg. (a) to make fun of s.o., to pull s.o.'s leg (fam.), to kid s.o. (fam.), to have s.o. on (fam.) (b) to take s.o. for a ride (fam.), to fool s.o., to put one/it over on s.o. (fam.), to con s.o. (sl.)

▶ oler a camelo there's s.th. fishy about it (fam.), to smell/sound fishy (fam.) ◆ *Aquí huele a camelo. There's s.th. fishy here.* ◆ *Eso me huele a camelo. That smells fishy to me. There's s.th. fishy about that.* ◆ *Esta noticia me huele a camelo. This piece of news sounds fishy to me.*

▷ camino (con **pan** y vino se anda el ~)
▷ camino (**tirar** por un ~)

el camión truck (Am.E.), lorry (Br.E.)

▶ estar como un camión (fam., Esp.) (woman): to have a great/fantastic figure or build, to look smashing (fam.), to be a real knock-out (sl.) ◆ *Su novia está como un camión. His girlfriend has a great figure.*

la camisa shirt

▶ no llegarle a uno la camisa al cuerpo (fig.) to jump out of one's skin, to be scared stiff (fam.), to be scared to death (fam.), to be terrified, to be frightened or scared out of one's wits, to get the fright of one's life ◆ *En aquel momento no me llegó la camisa al cuerpo. I was scared stiff at that moment. I was frightened out of my wits at that moment.*

▶ casarse con una mujer en camisa (fig.) to marry a woman without a dowry

▶ jugar hasta la camisa to lose one's shirt (fig.), to gamble away everything [one owns]

▶ dar hasta la camisa (fig., fam.) to give the shirt off one's back (fig.) ◆ *Ella te daría hasta la camisa. She'd give you the shirt off her back.*

▶ meterse en camisa de once varas (fam.) (a) to bite off more than one can chew (fam.) (b) to interfere in or poke one's nose into (fam.) other people's affairs (c) to get o.s. into a pickle (fam.), to get o.s. into a jam/fix (fam.), to get o.s. into a tight spot (fam.), to get o.s. into a mess (fig.)

la camorra (fam.) row (fam.), fight, set-to (fam.), scrap (sl.) ◆ *armar camorra* to kick up a row (fam.), to start/pick a fight ◆ *buscar camorra to look for trouble or for a fight*

la campana bell

▶ echar las campanas al vuelo to set the bells ringing, to peal the bells

▶ echar las campanas al vuelo (fig.) to rejoice, to be all excited, to jump for joy, to celebrate [prematurely], to shout about s.th., to proclaim or shout s.th. from the rooftops (fig.) ◆ *No eches las campanas al vuelo antes de tiempo. Don't rejoice too soon. Don't celebrate prematurely.* ◆ *No queremos echar las campanas al vuelo hasta no estar seguro. We don't want to start shouting about it or shouting from the rooftops until we know for sure.*

▶ oír campanas y no saber dónde (fam.) (a) to have heard s.th. or noises to that effect, not to know exactly (b) to grope in the dark (fig.), to be [totally] in the dark (fig.), not to have a clue (c) to get hold of the wrong end of the stick (fig.) ◆ *¿Sabes qué ocurrió? He oído campanas y no sé dónde. Do you know what happened? I've heard s.th. about it, but I don't know exactly. I only have a vague idea.* ◆ *Oigo campanas y no sé dónde. I'm totally in the dark. I'm groping in the dark.*

▶ querer tocar las campanas y asistir a la procesión to want to be in two places at once

▶ tocar la campana (pop., Esp.) (to masturbate): to jerk off (vulg.), to jack off (vulg.), to toss off (vulg., Br.E.), to wank or have a wank (vulg., Br.E.)

el campanario belfry, bell tower

▶ subirse al campanario (fig., fam.) to go up the wall (fig.), to go spare (fam., Br.E.), to go off at the deep end (fam.) ▷ salirse de sus **casillas**

el campaneo pealing, bell ringing

▶ el campaneo (fam.) (esp. women): swinging/swaying of the hips, hip-swinging

la campanilla small bell

▶ tener muchas campanillas (fam.) to be a bigwig (fam.), to be a big noise (sl.), to be a big shot (fam.), to be a big cheese (sl.), to be a big wheel (fam.), to be a fat cat (fam., Am.E.), to be a top nob (sl., Br.E.)

▶ de muchas campanillas (fam.) important, distinguished, high-class, big (fam.), grand ◆ *Es una dama de muchas campanillas. She's a grand lady.*

campante (fam.) self-satisfied, smug

▶ quedarse/estar tan campante (fam.) to act as if nothing had happened, not to bat an eyelid (Br.E.) or eyelash (Am.E.) (fig.), not to turn a hair (fig.), . . . as cool as a cucumber (fig.) ◆ *Fue declarado culpable por los jurados y allí estaba tan campante. He was found guilty by the jury and he acted as if nothing had happened/and he didn't bat an eyelid/and there he sat as cool as a cucumber.*

campar to camp
▶ campar con su estrella (fig.) to be lucky, to be in luck, to be successful
▶ campar por sus respetos (fig.) to act independently, to act on one's own hook (fam.), to do as one pleases, to strike out on one's own (fig.)

la cana white hair
▶ peinar canas (fig.) to be old
▶ echar una cana al aire (fam.) (a) to have an easy day of it, to cut loose (sl.), to go on a fling (fam.), to have a fling (fam.), to whoop it up (fam.), to let one's hair down (fig.) (b) to be unfaithful (to one's husband/wife/etc.), to two-time (one's husband/wife) (fam., Am.E.), to have an affair or a fling (fam.) (with another man/woman) ◆ *Ayer echamos una cana al aire. We cut loose yesterday.* ◆ *Cada vez que su marido estaba en viaje de negocios echaba una cana al aire. Every time her husband was away on business she was unfaithful to him. She always two-timed her husband when he was away on business.*

el canario canary
▶ el canario (pop., Esp.) (penis) ▷ el calvo
▶ cambiar el agua al canario (pop., hum., Esp.) (men): to have a slash (sl., Br.E.), to take or have (Br.E.) a leak (sl., hum.), to have a pee/piddle (fam., Br.E.), to spend a penny (euph., fam., Br.E.)

la canción song
▶ ¡[Siempre] la misma canción! (fig., fam.) The same old story [every time]! Here he/etc. goes again! Can't he/etc. change the record!? (fig., fam.)
▶ Ha vuelto a la misma canción. (fig., fam.) He's/she's riding his/her hobby-horse again. (fig.) He's/she's on his/her hobby-horse again. (fig.) He's/she's onto his/her favorite or pet subject/topic again.

el canco (pop., Esp.) (gay): queer/fairy/faggot (sl., pej.), pansy (fam., pej.), queen (sl.), poof[ter] (sl., pej., Br.E.), fag (sl., pej., Am.E.), arse bandit (vulg., Br.E.)

el candado padlock
▶ echar candado a la boca/a los labios (fig.) to keep a secret to o.s., not to breathe/say a word, to keep mum (fam.), to keep one's mouth shut (fam.)

la candela candle
▶ estar con la candela en la mano (fig., fam.) to be dying, to be at death's door
▶ acabársele a alg. la candela (fam.) to snuff it (fam., Br.E.) ◆ *Se le acabó la candela. He snuffed it.*
▶ arrimar candela a alg. (fam.) to give s.o. a [good] clobbering or hiding or tanning or thrashing (fam.), to beat s.o. up (fam.), to tan s.o.'s hide (fig., fam.), to let s.o. have it (fam.)

el candelero candlestick
▶ estar algo/alg. en [el] candelero (fig.) (s.th.): to be of keen current interest, (s.th./s.o.): to be rated highly, to be in the limelight (fig.), to be the center or focus of attention; (s.o.): to be high up (fig.), to be in a position of authority
▶ poner algo/a alg. en [el] candelero (fig.) to bring s.th./s.o. into the limelight (fig.) or into the center of attention, to give/get s.o. a high post, to build s.o. up (fam.)

la candelilla small candle, glowlight
▶ hacérsele a alg. candelillas los ojos (fig.) to be tipsy, to be tiddly (fam.), to have had one too many (fam.) ◆ *Se te hacen candelillas los ojos. You're tipsy.*

el candil oil lamp
▶ pescar al candil (fig.) to fish in troubled waters (fig.)
▶ arder en un candil (fig., fam.) (a) (wine): to be very strong (b) to be pretty strong stuff (fig., fam.) ◆ *Este vino arde en un candil. This wine is very strong.* ◆ *Lo que dijo ardió en un candil. What he said was pretty strong stuff.*
▶ buscar con un candil (fam.) to search high and low
▶ Ni buscando con [un] candil. (fam.) There aren't many of that sort around. You won't see the likes of that again in a hurry. (fam.)

la canela cinnamon
▶ ser canela fina (fig.) to be wonderful, to be splendid, to be exquisite, to be fantastic (fam.), to be heavenly (fam.), to be divine

(fig., fam.), to be pure nectar (fig.), to be very special, to be exceptional ◆ *Esa mujer es canela fina. That woman is wonderful. She is an exceptional woman.* ◆ *Este jarrón de porcelana es canela fina. This is a very exquisite porcelain vase.* ◆ *Este vino es canela fina. This wine is divine or is pure nectar.*
▶ ser la flor de la canela (fig.) to be the very best, to be the crème de la crème (fig.), to be the best that money can buy (pop.)

el canelo cinnamon tree
▶ hacer el canelo (pop., Esp.) to be exploited (fig.), to be taken for a ride (fam.), to be taken in (fam.)

el cangrejo crab
▶ ponerse rojo como un cangrejo, ponerse como un cangrejo asado to blush like a lobster (fig.), to blush like a or go as red as a beetroot (fam., Br.E.), to turn as red as a beet (fam., Am.E.), to go bright red

el canguro kangaroo
▶ el/la canguro/cangura (fig., Esp.) baby-sitter ◆ *Hace de cangura dos veces por semana. She baby-sits twice a week.*

la canica marble (little ball)
▶ las canicas (pop., Esp.) (testicles): balls (pop., vulg.), nuts (vulg., Am.E.), marbles (vulg., Br.E.), bollocks (vulg. Br.E.), goolies (sl.)

el canónigo canon
▶ vivir como un canónigo (fig., fam.) to live an easy life

▷ cansado (▷ **nacer**: nació alg. ~)
▷ cansado (estar ~ del **plantón**)

▷ cansancio (**caerse** de ~)
▷ cansancio (estar **muerto** [de ~])

el/la cantamañanas (fam., pej.) unreliable person, person who is all talk and no action (fam.) ◆ *Es un cantamañanas. He's all talk and no action. He's an unreliable bloke. You can't believe a word he says.*

cantar to sing
▶ cantar (fam.) to sing (sl.), to squeal (sl.), to talk (fam.), to blab (fam.), to spill the beans (sl.)
▶ cantar de plano (fam.) to make a full confession, to tell all one knows, to come clean (fam.)

▶ cantar algo a alg. (fam.) to rave to s.o. about s.th. ◆ *Siempre me cantan ese restaurante. They're always raving to me about that restaurant.*
▶ cantar las cuarenta a alg. (fam.) to give s.o. a piece of one's mind, to tell s.o. a few home truths
▶ cantarlas claras [a alg.] (fam.) not to mince one's words (fig.), to speak frankly/out, to talk turkey [with s.o.] (sl., Am.E.), to tell s.o. straight, to give it to s.o. straight ◆ *Las canté claras. I didn't mince my words.* ◆ *Se las canté claras a ellos. I told them straight. I gave it to them straight. I talked turkey with them.*
▶ cantar victoria (fig.) ◆ *Gracias a Dios se han ido. No cantes victoria. Thank God they're gone. Don't speak too soon.* ◆ *No cantes victoria antes de tiempo. Don't count your chickens before they are hatched. (fig.)* ◆ *Es pronto para cantar victoria. I'm/we're not out of the wood (Br.E.) or woods (Am.E.) yet. (fam.)*
▷ cantar (canta la **chicharra**)
▷ cantar (**carta**[s] canta[n])
▷ cantar (otro **gallo** cantaría si ...)
▷ cantar (quien nacè **chicharra** muere cantando)
▷ cantar (ser **coser** y ~)
▷ cantar el **kirie**
▷ cantar la **cartilla** a alg.
▷ cantar la **gallina/palinodia**

el cantar song
▶ Eso es otro cantar. (fig., fam.) That's [quite] another story or matter or kettle of fish. That's [quite] a different story or matter or kettle of fish. That's a different ball game. (fig., fam.)

el cántaro pitcher, jug
▶ los cántaros (fam.) (breasts): knockers (sl.), tits (fam.), boobs (fam.), hooters (sl., Am.E.)
▶ un alma de cántaro (fig., fam.) nincompoop (fam.), numskull (fam.) ▷ un [pedazo de] **alcornoque**
▶ Tanto va el cántaro a la fuente, que al fin se rompe. (prov.) There's a limit to everything. You/etc. shouldn't push your/etc. luck. (fam.) You/etc. won't get away with it/that forever.
▶ a cántaros (fig.) in plenty, plenty of, pots/ piles/heaps of (fam.) ◆ *llover a cántaros to rain in torrents, to come down in buckets/*

sheets, to rain cats and dogs, to be pouring [down or with rain], to be bucketing down (Br.E.), the floodgates of heaven open (fig.) ◆ *Gana dinero a cántaros. He makes pots of money. He's raking it in.*

la cantilena chant, song, ballad
▶ ¡[Siempre] la misma cantilena! (fig., fam.) The same old story [every time]! Here he/etc. goes again! Can't he/etc. change the record!? (fig., fam.)
▶ Ha vuelto a la misma cantilena. (fig., fam.) He's/she's riding his/her hobby-horse again. (fig.) He's/she's on his/her hobby-horse again. (fig.) He's/she's onto his/her favorite or pet subject/topic again.

el canto song, singing
▶ al canto del gallo (literal/fig.) at daybreak, at the crack of dawn (fam.), at cockcrow (literal/fig.) ◆ *Ayer nos levantamos al canto del gallo. We got up at the crack of dawn yesterday.*

el canto stone, pebble, edge, border
▶ darse con un canto en los dientes o en los pechos (fam.) to be well pleased, to count o.s. lucky ◆ *Puedes darte con un canto en los dientes. You can count yourself lucky.*
▶ [por] el canto de un duro (fig.) almost, [very] nearly, (to come) very close to, (to come) within a whisker of (fam.), (to be/come) teeth within an ace of (fig.), by the skin of one's teeth (fam.), (to be/have) a close/narrow shave (fig., fam.) or a close call (fam.) ◆ *Me faltó el canto de un duro para ganar. I came within an ace of winning. I came within a whisker of winning.* ◆ *Le faltó el canto de un duro para perder el tren. He very nearly missed the train.* ◆ *Me salvé por el canto de un duro. I had a narrow shave/escape. It was a close shave/call.* ◆ *Por el canto de un duro nos atropellan. We just missed being run over by the skin of our teeth.*
▷ canto (cerrar algo a **cal** y ~)
▷ canto (de **cal** y ~)

la caña reed
▶ la caña (fig., fam.) (person): beanpole (fig., fam., hum.)
▶ dar caña a alg./algo (fam.) (a) to give s.o. a beating ▷ arrimar **candela** a alg. (b) to attack s.th. (fig.), to slam s.th. (fam.), to slag s.th. off (sl., Br.E.), to pan s.th. (fam.) ◆ *Le*

dieron caña a la prensa. They [really] attacked the press. ◆ *Los críticos le dieron caña a la novela. The critics panned the novel.*
▶ dar/meter caña (fam.) to step on it (fam.), to step on the gas (fam.) ◆ *¡Dale caña! Step on it!*
▶ Las cañas se vuelven lanzas. A joke can easily turn into s.th. unpleasant. A joke can easily turn serious.
▷ caña (hay **toros** y ~s)

cañón (adj. inv., adv., fam., Esp.) fabulous[ly] (fig., fam.), marvellous[ly] (fam.), great (fam.), wonderful[ly], fantastic[ally] (fam.), gorgeous (fam.), stunning[ly], staggering[ly] (fig.), brillant[ly] (fam., Br.E.) ◆ *Ella está cañón. She's gorgeous.* ◆ *una idea cañón a fantastic idea* ◆ *Lo has hecho cañón. You've done it brillantly. You've done a great job.* ◆ *Me lo pasé cañón. I had a wonderful or a great time.*
▷ cañón (estar/morir al **pie** del ~)
▷ cañonazo (matar **moscas** a ~s)

la capa cape, cloak
▶ la capa [de ladrones] (fig.) receiver [of stolen goods], fence (fam.), uncle (sl.)
▶ dar la capa (fam.) to give the shirt off one's back (fig.) ◆ *Ella te daría la capa. She'd give you the shirt off her back.*
▶ hacer de su capa un sayo (fig.) to do what one likes with one's own things, to do as one pleases, to make one's own decisions, to act freely
▶ tirar a alg. de la capa (fig.) to drop a hint to s.o.
▶ defender algo a capa y espada (fig.) to fight tooth and nail to defend s.th. (fig.), to put everything one has into the defense of s.th., to defend s.th. to the last ditch (fig.), to take up the cudgels for s.th. (fig.)
▶ una película/etc. de capa y espada cloak-and-dagger film/etc.
▷ capa (si **Dios** de ésta me escapa, nunca me cubrirá de tal ~)
▷ capacho (mezclar **berzas** con ~s)
▷ capar **moscas** (mandar a alg. a ~)
▷ capirote (hacer **mangas** y ~s de algo/alg.)
▷ capirote (ser **tonto** de ~)
▷ capítulo (tener **voz** en ~)
▷ capricho (ser **juguete** de los ~s de alg.)

el capuchón (clothing): big hood
▶ ponerse el capuchón (pop.) to be put behind bars (fig.), to be put in clink (sl.), to be put in the can (sl., Am.E.), to be put in the jug (sl.), to be put in the slammer (sl.), to be locked up

la cara face
▶ tener cara de nalgas (fig., pop.) to have chubby cheeks, to be chubby-cheeked
▶ tener cara de pan (fam.) to have a round face, to be moon-faced
▶ tener cara de pocos amigos to look black (fig.), to look like or as black as thunder, to look grumpy, to look surly, to have a sour (fig.) or cross (fam.) look on one's face
▶ tener más cara que espalda (pop.) to be very impertinent/impudent, to be a cheeky devil (fam., Br.E.), to be as bold as brass (fam.), to have such a nerve (fam.)
▶ dar/sacar la cara por alg. to stand up for s.o., to stick up for s.o.
▶ plantar cara a alg. to confront s.o., to defy s.o., to stand up to s.o.
▶ saltar a la cara a alg. (fig., fam.) to jump down s.o.'s throat (fam.), to snap at s.o.
▶ lavar la cara a alg. (fig.) to suck up to s.o. (fam.), to toady to s.o., to lick s.o.'s boots (fig.), to adulate s.o.
▶ se le ve/nota/conoce a alg. en la cara one can tell just by looking at s.o., one can tell just by the look on s.o.'s face ♦ *Se te ve en la cara que no dices la verdad. One can tell just by looking at you or just by the look on your face that you don't tell the truth.*
▷ cara (▷ **escribir**: tener algo escrito en la ~)
▷ cara (▷ **nuevo**: ponerle a alg. la ~ nueva)
▷ cara (caérsele a alg. la ~ de **vergüenza**)
▷ cara (dar a alg. con la **puerta** en la ~)
▷ cara (tener la ~ como el **cemento**)
▷ cara (tener **monos** en la ~)
▷ cara de **pascuas** (tener ~)
▷ cara de **rallo**
▷ cara de **vinagre** (poner ~)

la carabina carbine
▶ ser [como o lo mismo que] la carabina de Ambrosio (fam.) to be utterly useless, to be a dead loss (fig., fam.)
▶ la carabina (fam.) chaperon[e] ♦ *hacer/ir de carabina to go [along] as or play chaperon, to play gooseberry (fam., Br.E.)* ♦ *sentirse de carabina to feel like a fifth wheel (fig., fam.)*

el caracol snail, spiral (form)
▶ ¡Caracoles! (fam., euph.). (amazement/surprise): Good heavens! (fam.) Blow me! (fam., Br.E.) (anger): Damn it! (fam.)
▶ hacer caracoles (fig., fam.) (drunk): to reel, to stagger, to weave about

el carajillo (Esp.) black coffee with a dash of brandy

la carantoña (fam.) (a) grotesque mask (b) grotesque or ugly face, ugly mug (sl.) (c) painted hag (pej.), mutton dressed up as lamb (fam., Br.E.)
▶ hacer carantoñas a alg. (a) to make sheep's eyes at s.o. (b) to flatter s.o., to butter s.o. up (fam.), to soft-soap s.o. (fam.)

la carcajada guffaw, peal of laughter
▶ soltar la carcajada to burst out laughing
▶ reír[se] a carcajadas to roar with laughter, to guffaw

el carcamal (fam., pej.) (person): old crock (fam., Br.E.), [old] wreck (fig., pej.)
▷ cárcel (dar con los/sus **huesos** en la ~)
▷ cárcel (**pudrirse** en la ~)
▷ cárcel (**zambullir** a alg. en la ~)

la careta mask
▶ quitarse la careta (fig.) to drop the mask (fig.), to show [o.s. in] one's true colors ♦ *Nunca se sabe qué piensa ese tío. No se quita la careta. You can never tell what that guy is thinking. He doesn't show his true colors.*
▶ quitarle la careta a alg. (fig.) to unmask s.o. (fig.), to expose s.o.

la carga load, burden
▶ dar con la carga en tierra o en el suelo (fig.), echarse con la carga (fig.) to chuck it all in/up (fam., Br.E.), to chuck the whole thing (fam.), to throw in the sponge/towel (fig.), to give up ♦ *Probemos al menos una vez más. Es demasiado prematuro echarse con la carga. Let's try at least one more time. It's too early/soon to throw in the towel.*

cargar to load
▶ cargarse a alg. (fam.) (a) to kill s.o., to bump s.o. off (sl.), to finish s.o. off (fam.), to do s.o. in (fam.), to croak s.o. (sl.), to deep-six s.o. (sl., Am.E.) (b) to have it off

with s.o. (sl., Br.E.) ▷ **calzar[se] a alg.** ◆ *¡Me lo cargaré! I'll bump him off!*

el cariz weather situation
▶ **ir tomando algo mal cariz** (fig.) s.th. (situation/etc.): to be beginning to look bad, to be getting serious, not to like the look of s.th. ◆ *Esto o esta cosa va tomando mal cariz. I don't like the look of this. This business is beginning to look bad.* ◆ *La situación política va tomando mal cariz. The political situation is beginning to look bad.*

la carlanca (fig., fam.) shrewdness, cunning
▶ **tener muchas carlancas** to be very shrewd/crafty, to be as sly as they come (fam.), to know every trick in the book (fam.)

la carne flesh, meat
▶ **herir a alg. en carne viva** (fig.) to hurt/wound s.o. deeply (fig.), to cut s.o. to the quick (fig.)
▶ **poner toda la carne en el asador** (fig.) (a) to put all one's eggs in one basket (fig., pop.), to go the whole hog (fam.), to stake one's all (fig.), to shoot the works (fam.) (b) to do everything in one's power, to move heaven and earth, to leave no stone unturned (fig.)
▶ **ponerle o ponérsele a alg. [la] carne de gallina** (fig.) to give s.o. or get gooseflesh/goose pimples/goose bumps (Am.E.) (fig.), to give s.o. or get the creeps (fam.), to give s.o. or get the heebie-jeebies (fam.), to send shivers down s.o.'s spine (fig.) ◆ *Nos pone la carne de gallina. It gives us gooseflesh.* ◆ *Esa escena me puso la carne de gallina. That scene gave me goose pimples. That scene sent shivers down my spine.* ◆ *Se me puso carne de gallina. I got the creeps/heebie-jeebies.*
▶ **tener carne de perro** (fig., fam.) to have an iron (fig.) constitution
▶ **ser de carne y hueso** to be only human, to have feelings too, to have the same feelings as other people ◆ *¿Él cree que no sufrimos? Nosotros también somos de carne y hueso. He thinks we don't suffer? We're only human. We have feelings too.*
▶ **no ser carne ni pescado** (fig.) to be neither fish nor fowl (fig.), to be neither one thing nor the other.
▶ **temblarle a alg. las carnes** (fig.) to tremble from head to foot, to tremble all over
▶ **perder carnes** (fam.) to go thin, to lose weight

▶ **en carnes [vivas]** (fig.) naked, stark naked (fam.), starkers (fam., hum., Br.E.), in the buff (fam., hum., Br.E.) ◆ *Fuimos a bañarnos en carnes. We went skinny-dipping. (fam.)*
▷ **carne (ser uña y ~)**

el carnero wether, ram
▶ **No hay tales carneros.** (fig., fam.) There isn't any such thing. There's no such thing. It's nothing of the sort. It's enough to make a cat laugh. (fam.)

▷ **caro (salirle algo a alg. ~)**

carpetazo (fam.)
▶ **dar carpetazo a algo** (plan/proyecto/etc.) s.th. (plan/project/etc.): to shelve (fig.), to leave on the shelf (fig.), to put on ice (fig.), to put on one side, to do nothing about

Carracuca (fam.)
▶ **estar más perdido que Carracuca** to be really in the soup (fam.), to be in a fine/real mess (fig.), to be in a real jam/fix (fam.), to be in a very awkward or difficult situation
▶ **ser más viejo que Carracuca** to be as old as the hills (fig., fam.), to be as old as Methuselah (fig.)
▶ **ser más feo que Carracuca** to be as ugly as sin/hell (fam.), to be incredibly ugly
▶ **ser más tonto que Carracuca** to be as thick as they come (fam.), to be as thick as two short planks (fam.), to be as thick as a brick (fam.), to be a real thicko (sl., Br.E.), not to be exactly an Einstein (fam.), s.o. must have been at the back of the queue when they were handing brains out (fam., hum.)

▷ **carrera (plantar la ~)**
▷ **carreta (aguantar carros y ~s)**

el carretero cart driver
▶ **blasfemar/jurar como un carretero** (fam.) to swear like a trooper (fam.), to swear horribly
▶ **fumar como un carretero** (fam.) to smoke like a chimney (fig.)

el carrillo cheek
▶ **comer o mascar a dos carrillos** (fam.) to gobble (fam.), to scoff (fam., Br.E.) (fam.), to tuck in (fam.), to tuck it away (fam.), to eat greedily, to stuff o.s. (fam.), to feed/stuff one's face (fam.), to make a [real] pig of o.s. (fam.), to eat like a horse (fig.)

▶ **comer a dos carrillos** (fig.) (a) to have more than one iron in the fire or string to one's bow (fig., fam.), to have more than one [well-paid] job, to moonlight (sl.), to have the best of both worlds (b) to run with the hare and hunt with the hounds (fig., Br.E.) ◆ *Ten cuidado al negociar con él. Come a dos carrillos. Be careful negotiating with him. He runs with the hare and hunts with the hounds.*

el carro cart, wagon
▶ **untar el carro a alg.** (fig., fam.) to grease s.o.'s palm (fig., fam.), to bribe s.o.
▶ **aguantar carros y carretas** (fig.) to put up with anything
▶ **¡Para el carro!** (fig., fam.) Hold your horses! (fam.) Cool it! (fam.) Keep your shirt on! (fam.) Keep your hair on! (fam., Br.E.)

el carroza (fam., Esp.) (a) old fogey (fam., pej.), old geezer (fam.), a man who has antiquated ideas, square (sl.) (b) old gay lecher, old queen (sl.)

la carta card, playing card
▶ **jugar la última carta** (fig.) to play one's last [trump] card (fig.)
▶ **jugárselo todo a una [sola] carta** (fig.) to put all one's eggs in one basket (fig.), to risk everything on one throw
▶ **jugar a cartas vistas** (fig.) to put one's cards on the table (fig.)
▶ **poner las cartas boca arriba** (fig.) to put/lay one's cards on the table (fig.) ◆ *Pon las cartas boca arriba y dime qué verdaderamente piensas. Put your cards on the table and tell me what you really think.*
▶ **no saber a qué carta quedarse** (fig.) not to know what to think/believe, to be in a dilemma, to be undecided
▶ **tomar cartas en un asunto** (fig.) to take a hand in a matter, to come in on an affair, to intervene in a matter, to step in (fig.) ◆ *Tenemos que tomar cartas en el asunto. We have to intervene [in the matter]. We have to step in.*
▶ **Carta[s] canta[n].** (prov.) To have it in black and white. To have it in cold print. (fig.) ◆ *¿Y no hay la menor duda? Cartas cantan. And there's no doubt whatsoever? I/we have it in black and white. Here it is in cold print.*

la carta letter
▶ **echar una carta al correo** (fig., fam.) to do one's business (fig., fam.), to relieve o.s. ◆ *Está echando una carta al correo. He's doing his business. ◆ Tengo que echar una carta al correo. I must just pay a visit. (euph., Br.E.) I have to go to the loo (Br.E.) or to the john (Am.E.). (fam.) Nature calls. (fam.)*

la cartilla primer, elementary treatise
▶ **cantar/leer la cartilla a alg.** (fam.) to give s.o. a [severe] ticking-off (fam., Br.E.), to read the riot act to s.o. (fig., hum.), to take s.o. to task (fig.), to give s.o. a good talking-to (fam.)
▶ **no saber [ni] la cartilla** (fam.) not to know a single thing, not to have the foggiest [idea] (fam.), not to have the faintest idea (fam.), not to have a clue (fam.)

el cartucho cartridge
▶ **quemar el último cartucho** (fig.) to play one's last card (fig.)
▶ **haber quemado su último cartucho** (fig.) to have shot one's bolt (fig.) ◆ *No sabe a qué santo encomendarse. Ha quemado su último cartucho. He's at the end of his tether. He's shot his bolt.*
▶ **luchar hasta quemar el último cartucho** (literal/fig.) to fight on to the last ditch (literal/fig.), to die in the last ditch (literal/fig.) ◆ *En la batalla de Álamo lucharon hasta quemar el último cartucho. At the Álamo they died in the last ditch. ◆ El sindicato [obrero] luchó hasta quemar el último cartucho. The [labor/trade] union fought on to the last ditch.*

la casa house
▶ **caérsele a alg. la casa encima o a cuestas** (fig.) the bottom falls out of s.o.'s world ◆ *Cuando se entere de eso se le caerá la casa encima. The bottom will fall out of her world when she finds out about that.*
▶ **echar/tirar la casa por la ventana** to go to enormous expense, to spare no expense, to push the boat out (fig.), to roll out the red carpet (for s.o.) (fig.), to give s.o. the red-carpet treatment (fig.) ◆ *Para la boda de su hija echó la casa por la ventana. He spared no expense or he [really] pushed the boat out for his daughter's wedding.*
▷ casa (**barrer** en su propia ~)
▷ casa (en ~ de **herrero**, cuchillo de palo)

▷ casa (en ~ del **gaitero/tamborilero** todos son danzantes)

casar[se] to marry, to get married
▶ casarse por detrás de la iglesia (fam.) to move in with each other, to set up house together, to shack up together (sl.), to live together, to cohabit ◆ *Se casaron por detrás de la iglesia. They moved in with each other. They set up house together.* ◆ *Viven casados [por] detrás de la iglesia. They're shacked up together. They live together.*
▷ casarse con una mujer en **camisa**
▷ casarse de **penalty**

el cascabel little bell
▶ poner el cascabel al gato (fig.) to bell the cat (fig.), to stick one's neck out (fam.), to take on a risky or dangerous assignment/job

cascar to crack, to break
▶ cascar (fam.) to chat, to shoot the breeze/ bull (fam., Am.E.), to chatter, to talk a lot
▶ cascar[la] (pop.) (to die): to snuff it (fam., Br.E.), to kick the bucket (fam.), to peg out (fam.), to pop off (fam.), to pop one's clogs (fam.), to croak (sl.)
▶ cascar a alg. (pop.) (a) to bump s.o. off (sl.) ▷ **cargar**se a alg. (a). (b) (sport/etc.): to beat s.o. hollow (fam.), to slaughter s.o. (fig., fam.)
▶ cascársela (vulg.) (to masturbate) ▷ tocar la **campana** ◆ *Ese viejo verde se la casca cada día. That dirty old man or randy old goat jerks off every day.*

la cáscara shell (egg/nut/etc.)
▶ No hay más cáscaras. (fig.) There's no choice. There's no alternative. There's no other way.
▶ ¡Cáscara[s]! (fam.) (amazement/surprise): Blow me! (fam., Br.E.) Well I'm blowed! (fam., Br.E.)

el cascarón [broken] eggshell
▶ llevar todavía el cascarón pegado al culo (pop.) to be still wet behind the ears (fig., fam.)

el/la cascarrabias (fam.) cantankerous or quick-tempered man/woman or person, irritable sort; (woman): battle-ax[e] (fam.), shrew, virago, termagant, Xanthippe (fig.)

el casco helmet
▶ el casco (fig.) head, nut (sl.)
▶ caliente de cascos (fig.) hot-headed
▶ romper los cascos a alg. to smash/bash s.o.'s head in (fam.)
▶ romperse los cascos (fig.) (a) to rack one's brains (fig.) (b) to kill o.s. with brainwork (fam.)
▶ romper/calentar los cascos a alg. (fig.) to get on s.o.'s nerves (fam.), to get on s.o.'s wick (fam., Br.E.), to get s.o. worked up ◆ *Me rompe los cascos con sus lamentaciones. Sus lamentaciones me calientan los cascos. He gets on my nerves with his whining. His whining gets me worked up.*
▶ ser ligero/alegre de cascos (fam.) to be frivolous, to be flighty

casi almost
▶ De casi no se muere nadie. (prov.) A miss is as good as a mile. (prov.)

la casilla small house, hut
▶ salirse de sus casillas (fig., fam.) to go through the roof (fig., fam.), to hit the roof (fig., fam.), to get one's monkey up (hum.), to fly off the handle (fam.), to blow/lose one's cool (sl.), to blow one's top (sl.), to blow one's stack (sl.), to blow/pop one's cork (sl.), to get [very] cross (fam.)
▶ sacar a alg. de sus casillas (fig., fam.) to get s.o.'s goat (sl.), to get s.o.'s monkey up (hum.), to make s.o. cross (fam.), to get s.o. worked up, to get up s.o.'s nose (fam.), to drive s.o. crazy (fam.), to drive s.o. round the bend (sl.), to drive s.o. spare (fam., Br.E.)

el casquete skullcap
▶ echar un casquete (pop., Esp.) to have a screw (vulg.), to screw (vulg.), to fuck (vulg.), to bang (vulg.), to bonk (vulg.), to shag (vulg., Br.E.), to ball (sl., Am.E.), to have it off/away (sl., Br.E.), to get a/one's leg over (sl., Br.E.), to have a shag (vulg., Br.E.), to get one's rocks off (sl., Am.E.)

▷ casta (de ~ le viene al **galgo** ser rabilargo)

la castaña chestnut
▶ sacar las castañas del fuego a alg. (fig.) to pull s.o.'s chestnuts out of the fire for him (fig.), to do s.o.'s dirty work for him
▶ ser algo/alg. una castaña (fam.) (s.th./s.o.): to be a drag (fam.)

▶ dar la castaña a alg. (fam.) to cheat s.o., to swindle s.o., to con s.o. (fam.), to make a fool out of s.o.

▶ dar a alg. para castañas (fam.) to punish s.o. ◆ *Hay que darle para castañas. He has to be punished.*

▶ cogerse una castaña (fam.) to get drunk, to get canned/pissed (sl., Br.E.) ◆ *Ayer nos cogimos una castaña. We got drunk/canned yesterday.*

▶ conducir a toda castaña (fam.) to drive flat out (fam.)

▷ castaña (parecerse como un **huevo** a una ~)

el castaño chestnut tree

▶ pasar de castaño oscuro (fam.) to be really too much, to be really out of line (fam.), to be really the limit, to be pretty strong stuff (fam.), to be a bit thick (sl.), to be beyond a joke, to be close to the bone (fam.), to take the biscuit (fam., Br.E.), to be the height of cheek (fam., Br.E.) ◆ *Esto pasa de castaño oscuro. This is beyond a joke.* ◆ *Lo que dijeron pasó de castaño oscuro. What they said was really too much or was really out of line.*

la castañuela castanet

▶ estar [alegre] como unas castañuelas (fig.) to be very merry, to be very chipper (Am.E.) or chirpy (Br.E.) (fam.), to be as happy as a clam/lark (fam., Am.E.), to be as happy as a sandboy/as Larry (fam., Br.E.), to be in high spirits

el castellano Castilian, Spanish

▶ hablar en castellano [puro y llano] (fig.) to speak openly/freely or straightforwardly, to say s.th. in plain English (fig.) ◆ *Hablaron en castellano. They spoke openly.* ◆ *Lo dijo en castellano puro y llano. He said it in plain English.*

Castellón de la Plana

▶ ser de Castellón de la Plana (hum.) (woman): to be flat-chested, to be [as] flat as a board (fam.), to be as flat as a pancake (fam.), not to be exactly well stacked (sl., iron.)

castigador punitive

▶ el/[la] castigador[a] (fam.) (man): woman-izer, philanderer, lady-killer (fam.), wolf

(fig., fam.); (woman): sexually provocative woman, seductress, Circe (fig.)

el castillo castle

▶ hacer castillos en el aire (fig.) to build castles in the air or in Spain (fig.)

▶ hacer castillos de arena (fig.) to build on sand (fig.) ◆ *Esta inversión es demasiado insegura. No hago castillas de arena. This investment is too insecure. I don't build on sand.*

▶ hacer un castillo de un grano de arena (fig.) to make a mountain out of a molehill (fig.)

▶ derrumbarse como un castillo de naipes (fig.) to fold up or collapse like a house of cards (fig.) ◆ *Su ambicioso proyecto se derrumbó como un castillo de naipes. His ambitious project collapsed like a house of cards.*

los cataplines (pop.) (testicles) ▷ las **canicas**

el catarro catarrh, cold

▶ Al catarro, con el jarro. (fam.) When you have a cold, drink some booze or have a toddy.

▷ cauce (las **aguas** vuelven a su ~)

el caucho rubber

▶ quemar el caucho (fam.) to tear [along] (fam.), to race/speed [along], to drive/go flat out or [at] full lick (fam.)

caudino (histórico)

▶ pasar por las horcas caudinas (fig.) to suffer a humiliating defeat, to be humiliatingly defeated

▶ ser pasar por las horcas caudinas (fig.) to be a terrible experience, to be a terrible ordeal (fig.), to be torture (fig.) ◆ *Fue pasar por las horcas caudinas tener que disculparme ante él. It was a terrible ordeal having to apologize to him.*

▷ cazar (~las al **vuelo**)

▷ cebada (**asno** muerto, la ~ al rabo)

cebar to feed, to fatten

▶ cebarse en algo (fig.) (a) to become absorbed or engrossed or immersed in s.th. (b) to revel in s.th. (fig.), to gloat over s.th. ◆ *Se cebó en un estudio. He became absorbed in a study.* ◆ *cebarse en la matanza o en la sangre* to revel in or gloat over the bloodshed, to be bloodthirsty

▶ **cebarse en alg.** (fig.) to take one's anger/fury out on s.o. (sl.), to vent one's anger/fury on s.o. (fig.)

▶ **Se ceba la peste/el fuego.** (fig.) The plague/fire is raging.

el cebo feed, bait

▶ **morder el cebo** (fig.) to swallow/take the bait (fig.)

la cebolla onion

▶ **la cebolla** (pop.) (head): onion (sl.), nut (sl.), bean/conk (sl., Am.), bonce/noddle (sl., Br.E.)

▷ cebolla (echar **ajo**s y ~s)

Ceca

▶ **andar de la Ceca a la Meca** to run/chase from pillar to post (fig.) ◆ *Había tantas formalidades burocráticas. Tuve que andar de la Ceca a la Meca para obtener los papeles.* It was red tape all the way. I had to run from pillar to post to get the [identity] papers.

la ceja eyebrow

▶ **tener a alg. entre ceja y ceja** (fam.) to have a grudge against s.o. ▷ tener a alg. **atravesado**

▶ **tener algo metido entre ceja y ceja** (fam.) to have a bee in one's bonnet [about s.th.] (fam.), to be set on s.th.

▶ **quemarse las cejas** (fig., fam.) to study/work far into the night, to burn the midnight oil, to cram (fam.), to swot (fam., Br.E.), to bone up (fam.)

▶ **estar hasta las cejas de algo/alg.** (fig.) to be fed up to the back teeth with s.th./s.o. (fam.), to be utterly fed up with s.th./s.o. (fam.), to be sick and tired of s.th./s.o. (fam.), to be cheesed off with s.th./s.o. (fam., Br.E.) ▷ estar hasta [más allá de] la **coronilla** de algo

cejijunto having eyebrows that meet

▶ **cejijunto** (adj., fig.) frowning, scowling

▷ celemín (meter/poner la **luz** bajo el ~)

el cemento cement

▶ **tener la cara como el cemento** (fig., fam.) to stick it on (fam.), to be quite shameless [about making outrageous demands or asking an outrageous price], to feel no shame [about . . .] ◆ *Cuando pidió ese precio tuvo la cara como el cemento.* He was quite

shameless about asking that price. He had the nerve to ask that price.

el cencerro cowbell

▶ **estar [loco] como un cencerro** (fig.) to be [completely] crazy (fam.) or crackers (sl., Br.E.) ▷ no estar bueno de la **cabeza**

la ceniza ash[es]

▶ **escribir algo en la ceniza** (fig.) to write s.th. off

▶ **huir de la[s] ceniza[s] y caer/dar en la[s] brasa[s]** (fig.) to jump out of the frying pan into the fire. ◆ *Atracó un banco para pagar sus deudas. Huyó de las cenizas y dio en las brasas.* He held up a bank to pay [off] his debts. He jumped out of the frying pan into the fire.

▷ centella (echar **rayo**s y ~s)

▷ céntimo (**pellizcar** los ~s)

cepillar to brush

▶ **cepillar[se] a una** (pop.) to screw a woman (vulg) ▷ **calzar**[se] a alg.

▶ **cepillar[se] a alg.** (pop.) to kill s.o. ▷ **cargar**se a alg. (a)

el ceporro old vine stock

▶ **un ceporro** (fig.) idiot, oaf ▷ un [pedazo de] **alcornoque**

▶ **dormir como un ceporro** (fam.) to sleep like a log (fam.)

▶ **dormirse o quedarse dormido como un ceporro** (fam.) to go out like a light (fig., fam.) ◆ *Estuve tan cansado que me dormí como un ceporro.* I was so tired [that] I went out like a light.

la cera wax

▶ **No hay más cera que la que arde.** (fam.) That's all there is. What you see is what you get. That's the best I/we can do.

▷ cera (alzarse/salirse con el **santo** y la ~)

▷ cerdo (a cada ~ le llega su **San Martín**)

el cero zero

▶ **ser un cero a la izquierda** (fam.) to be a walking/real zero (fam., Am.E.), to be a real zilch (sl., Am.E.), to be a nobody (pej.), to be a dead loss (fig., fam.), to be a [complete] washout (fam.), to be utterly useless

cerrado closed, shut

▶ **ser más cerrado que un cerrojo** (fam.) to be as thick as two short planks (fam.), to be as thick as a brick (fam.) ▷ ser más tonto que **Carracuca**

▷ cerrar algo a **cal** y canto/a **piedra** y lodo
▷ cerrar todas las **puerta**s a alg.

el cerro hill
▶ irse por los cerros de Úbeda (fig.) (a) to talk [a lot of] nonsense or rubbish (fam.) or rot (fam., Br.E.), to give silly or ridiculous or absurd answers (b) to wander from the subject/point, to go off at a tangent (fig.)

▷ cerrojo (ser más **cerrado** que un ~)

la cerviz neck, nape of the neck
▶ doblar/bajar la cerviz (fig.) to submit, to bow down, to humble o.s.
▶ ser de dura cerviz to be stubborn, to be headstrong

César Caesar
▶ O césar o nada. (fig.) All or nothing.

el cesto [large] basket
▶ estar hecho un cesto (fam.) to be [blind] drunk (fam.), to be [totally] plastered or sloshed (fam.), to be [totally] smashed or stoned (sl.), to be [totally] canned or pissed (sl., Br.E), to be legless (fam., Br.E.), to be tight (fam.), to be as pissed as a newt (sl., Br.E.), to be as drunk as a lord (fam., Br.E.), to be [as] drunk as a skunk (fam., hum., Am.E.), to be drunk to the gills (fam.), to have had one over the eight (fam.), to have had one too many, to be out of one's head (sl.), to be three sheets to or have three sheets in the wind (sl.)

chachi (adj. inv., adv., pop.) great (fam.), brilliant[ly] (fam., Br.E.) ▷ cojonudo (a) ◆ *Lo pasamos chachi. We had a great or fantastic or smashing time.*

chalado (pop.)
▶ estar chalado to be nuts (fam.), to be bonkers (sl., Br.E.) ▷ no estar bueno de la **cabeza**
▶ estar chalado por alg. to have a crush on s.o. (fam.), to be crazy/nuts about s.o. (fam.)

la chamusquina scorching, smell of burning
▶ oler a chamusquina (fig., fam.) things are getting hot (fam.), there's trouble brewing, there's s.th. nasty (fig.) coming ◆ *Aquí huele a chamusquina. Things are getting hot here. There's trouble brewing [here].*

el chaparrón cloudburst, downpour
▶ aguantar el chaparrón (fig., fam.) to [patiently] endure the lecture or wigging (fam., Br.E.)
▶ soltar un chaparrón de insultos a alg. (fig.) to hurl a barrage (fig.) or stream of insults at s.o.

el chapero (fam., Esp.) rent boy (fam., Br.E.), ass peddler (fam., Am.E.), male [gay] prostitute

la chaqueta jacket
▶ ser más vago que la chaqueta de un guardia (fam.) to be bone idle (fam., Br.E.), to be very lazy
▶ cambiar de/la chaqueta (fig., pej.) (a) to change sides, to be a turncoat, to turn traitor (b) to trim one's sails to the wind (fig.) ◆ *Es un oportunista. Siempre cambia de chaqueta. He's an opportunist. He always trims his sails to the wind.*

el Charly (pop.) (cocaine): coke (sl.), snow (sl.)

el charol varnish
▶ darse charol (fig., fam.) to swank (fam., Br.E.), to brag, to boast, to show off, to act the big shot (fam.), to act big (fam.)

el chasis chassis
▶ quedarse en el chasis (fig., fam.) to be a bag of bones (fam.), to be all skin and bone (fam.), to be nothing but skin and bone (fam.), to be terribly thin, to be as thin as a rake (fam.)

la chata bedpan
▶ la chata (fam.) (a) stocky woman (b) sawn-off shotgun

chateo (fam.)
▶ andar/ir de chateo to go on a drinking expedition, to go on a bat (sl., Am.E.), to go on a pub-crawl (fam., Br.E.), to do the bars/pubs (fam.), to go from one bar/pub to another

la chaveta cotter pin, cotter
▶ la chaveta (fig., fam.) nut (sl.) ▷ la cebolla
▶ estar mal de la chaveta (fam.) to be nuts (fam.) ▷ no estar bueno de la **cabeza**
▶ perder la chaveta (fam.) to go mad/crazy (fam.), to go nuts (fam.), to go ape (fam., Am.E.), to go bonkers (sl., Br.E.), to go off one's rocker (fam.), to flip one's lid (fam.)

▶ perder la chaveta por alg. (fam.) to lose one's head over s.o. (fig.), to go crazy/nuts about s.o. (fam.), to have a crush on s.o. (fam.) ◆ *Perdió la chaveta por ella. He lost his head over her. He had a crush on her.*

la chicha chicha (corn/maize brandy or wine)
▶ no ser ni chicha ni limonada (fam.) to be neither one thing nor the other, to be neither fish nor fowl (fig.)

la chicharra cicada
▶ la chicharra (jerga del hampa) wallet, billfold (Am.E.), purse
▶ Canta la chicharra. (fam.) It's very/terribly hot.
▶ hablar como una chicharra (fig., fam.) s.o. wouldn't stop talking, to talk a mile a minute (fam., Am.E.), to talk nineteen to the dozen (fam., Br.E.), s.o. could talk the hind legs off a donkey (fam.)
▶ Quien nace chicharra muere cantando. (prov., Chile). A leopard never changes or cannot change its spots. (prov.)
▷ chico (ponerse como el ~ del **esquilador**)

chiflado (fam.)
▶ estar chiflado to be nuts (fam.), to be cracked (fam.), to be bonkers (sl., Br.E.)
▷ no estar bueno de la **cabeza** ◆ *Ella y su hermana están completamente chifladas. She and her sister are completely cracked.*
▶ estar chiflado por alg. to have a crush on s.o. (fam.), to be crazy/nuts about s.o. (fam.)

la chimenea chimney
▶ fumar como una chimenea (fig., fam.) to smoke like a chimney (fig., fam.)

la China China
▶ acá y en la China (fam.) everywhere ◆ *Las cosas son así acá y en la China. That's the way things are everywhere.*
▶ ni aquí/acá ni en la China (fam.) neither here nor anywhere ◆ *Las cosas no funcionan así, ni aquí ni en la China. That's not the way things work, neither here nor anywhere.*
▷ China (¡Naranjas de la ~!)

la china small stone, pebble
▶ la china (fam.) (money): dough (sl., Am.E.), bread (sl.), sugar (sl.), brass/dosh/lolly (sl., Br.E.), wampum (sl., Am.E.)
▶ aflojar/soltar la china to cough up (fam.), to fork out, to stump up (fam., Br.E.)

▶ poner chinas a alg. (fig.) to put or place obstacles in s.o.'s path/way (fig.), to make things difficult for s.o.
▶ tocarle a alg. la china (fig., fam.) to have bad luck, to have to carry the can (fam., Br.E.) ◆ *Nos tocó la china. We had to carry the can.*

la chinche bedbug
▶ el/la chinche (fig., fam.) pest (fig.), bore, nuisance, pain in the neck (fam.), pain in the ass (Am.E.) or in the arse (Br.E.) (vulg.), annoying individual/person
▶ caer/morir como chinches (fam.) to drop/die like flies (fam.), to go down like ninepins (fig., fam.)
▷ chinche (tener **sangre** de ~s)

chino; el chino Chinese; Chinese
▶ ser chino algo para alg. (fam.) (a) to be Chinese to s.o. (fig., fam.), to be all Greek to s.o. (fig., fam.), to be above s.o.'s head (b) to be double Dutch to s.o. (fam., Br.E.) ◆ *Lo que dijeron fue chino para mí. What they said was all Greek to me or was above my head.* ◆ *Tu discurso fue chino para ellos. You were talking over their heads.*
▶ engañar a alg. como a un chino (fam.) to play s.o. for a sucker (fam.), to take s.o. for a ride (fam.)
▶ tener la paciencia de un chino (fig.) to have the patience of Job (fig.) or of a saint (fam.)
▷ chino (el **cuento** ~)
▷ chino (¡Naranjas chinas!)

la chiquita little girl
▶ no andarse con/en chiquitas (fam.) not to fuss about details, to come/get [straight] to the point, to get [straight] down to business or brass tacks (fam.), to come straight out [with s.th.], not to beat about/around the bush (fig., fam.), not to pull [one's] punches (fig., sl.), to lay it on the line (fam.) ◆ *No me anduve en chiquitas para decírselo a ellos. I came straight out with it. I didn't beat about the bush or pull my punches when it came to telling them.*

la chiribita spark
▶ echar chiribitas (fig., fam.) to be [really] fuming (fig., fam.), to be livid (fam., Br.E.)
▷ estar hecho un **basilisco**

la chirigota (fam.) joke
▶ tomarse algo a chirigota not to take s.th. seriously, to take s.th. very lightly, to take s.th.

as a joke ◆ *Todo se lo toman a chirigota. They don't take anything seriously. They take everything very lightly.*

la chispa spark
- ▶ echar chispas (fig., fam.) to be hopping mad (fam.) ▷ estar hecho un **basilisco**
- ▶ tener mucha chispa (fig.) to sparkle with wit (fig.)
- ▶ ni chispa de (fig.) not the least bit of, not an ounce/iota/atom of (fig.), not a scrap of, not a spark of (fig.), (not to know) beans (about s.th.) (sl., Am.E.) ◆ *No tiene ni chispa de inteligencia. He doesn't have a spark of intelligence.* ◆ *No entienden ni chispa de eso. They don't know beans about that. They don't know the least bit or the first thing about that.*

chistar
- ▶ sin chistar [ni mistar] (fam.) without a word, without so much as a word ◆ *Lo aceptaron sin chistar ni mistar. They took it without a word.*
- ▶ no chistar not to say/utter a word

la chita anklebone
- ▶ a la chita callando (fam.) on the quiet (fam.), on the sly, stealthily ◆ *Salió a la chita callando. He left on the quiet.*

chivarse (fam.) to grass/sneak (sl., Br.E.), to rat/squeal (sl.), to snitch (fam.)
- ▶ chivarse contra/de alg. [con/a alg.] to inform on s.o. [to s.o.], to grass/rat/sneak on s.o. [to s.o.], to squeal/snitch on s.o. [to s.o.], to blow the whistle on s.o. (fam.) ◆ *Se chivaron. They grassed. They squealed.* ◆ *Ella se chivó contra él. She ratted/sneaked on him. She blew the whistle on him.* ◆ *Ella se chivó contra él al profesor. She sneaked on him to the teacher.* ◆ *El traficante de drogas fue detenido por la policía porque alg. se chivó contra él. The drug dealer was arrested by the police because somebody ratted/grassed on him.*

el chivatazo (fam.) tip-off (fam.)
- ▶ dar el chivatazo to give a tip-off

el chivato, la chivata (fam.) grass/sneak (sl., Br.E.), stool pigeon (fam.), telltale (fam., Br.E.), snitch (fam.), canary (sl., Am.E.), informer
- ▷ chocar (¡choca esos **cinco**!)

el chocho (pop.) (vagina) ▷ el conejo

el chocolate (fig., pop.) (marijuana): hash/pot (fam.), grass/shit/weed (sl.), tea (sl., Am.E.)

la cholla (fam.) (a) nut (sl.) ▷ la cebolla (b) brains (fam.), nous (fam.), gumption (fam.)

el chorizo chorizo (typical Spanish paprika sausage)
- ▶ el chorizo (pop.) (penis) ▷ el calvo
- ▷ chorlito (**cabeza** de ~)
- ▷ chorrera (¡Y un **jamón** [con ~s]!)

el chorro jet of water
- ▶ hablar a chorros (fig.) to talk in a torrent (fig.), to talk a mile a minute (fam., Am.E.), to talk nineteen to the dozen (fam., Br.E.), s.o. wouldn't stop talking
- ▶ sudar a chorros (fig.) to sweat buckets/streams (fam.), to be dripping with sweat
- ▶ llover a chorros to rain in torrents, to come down in buckets/sheets, to rain cats and dogs, to be pouring [down or with rain], to be bucketing down (Br.E.), the floodgates of heaven open (fig.) ◆ *Ayer llovió a chorros. It rained in torrents yesterday. It was pouring yesterday. The floodgates of heaven opened yesterday.*
- ▶ soltar el chorro [de la risa] (fig.) to burst out laughing (fig.), to roar with laughter

la chuleta chop, cutlet
- ▶ la chuleta (fig., fam.) box or clip (fam.) round the ears
- ▶ la chuleta (argot) (school): crib (fam.), trot/pony (sl., Am.E.)

la chupa (histórico) doublet (historical)
- ▶ la chupa (pop., Esp.) jacket
- ▶ poner a alg. como chupa de dómine (fig., fam.) to give s.o. a tremendous ticking-off or wigging (fam., Br.E.); (criticism/etc.): to attack s.o. violently (fig.), to give s.o. a sound pasting (sl.), to slam s.o. (fam.), to slag s.o. off (sl., Br.E.), to have a real go at s.o. (fam.), to tear s.o. to pieces or to shreds (fig., fam.) ◆ *En la prensa le pusieron como chupa de dómine. They gave him a sound pasting in the press.* ◆ *Los críticos pusieron al escritor como chupa de dómine. The critics tore/pulled the writer to pieces.*

chupar to suck
▶ ¡Chúpate ésa! (fam.) Put that in your pipe and smoke it! (fam.)
▷ chuparle a alg. la **sangre**
▷ chuparse el **dedo**
▷ chuparse el **dedo** (no ~)
▷ chuparse los **dedos** [por algo]

el chupatintas (fam., pej.) penpusher (fam., pej.), ink-shitter (pej.), petty clerk (pej.), minor bureaucrat (pej.), hack writer (pej.)

¡Chus! Come here! (dog)
▶ no decir [ni] chus ni mus (fam.) to keep one's mouth shut (fam.), not to say a word, to keep mum (fam.)

chutar to shoot (at goal)
▶ ir que chuta (fam.) to go swimmingly (fig.) or very well, to go fine ◆ *Todo va que chuta. Everything's going fine.*
▶ chutarse (fam.) (drug): to shoot/jack up (sl.), to give o.s. a shot/fix (sl.), to give o.s. a jab (sl., Br.E.)

el chute (fam.) (drug injection): shot (sl.), fix (sl.)

el cicatero, la cicatera (a): (fam.); (b): (jerga del hampa) (a) miser, penny-pincher (fam.), skinflint (fam.), tightwad (fam., Am.E.), scrooge (fig., fam.) (b) pickpocket
▷ cicuta (apurar el **cáliz** de ~ hasta las heces)

el ciego blind man
▶ Lo ve un ciego. (fig.) You can see that with half an eye. (fam.) Anyone can see that.
▶ En tierra de ciegos o en el país/reino de los ciegos el tuerto es [el] rey. In the country of the blind the one-eyed man is king.
▷ ciego (dar **palos** de ~)
▷ ciego (ser más ~ que un **topo**)

el cielo sky
▶ estar en el séptimo o quinto cielo (fig.) to be in seventh heaven (fam.), to be over the moon (fam.), to be on cloud nine (fam.) ◆ *Está en el séptimo cielo. Ganó un millón de dólares. She's in seventh heaven. She won a million dollars.*
▶ venir como llovido o llegar como caído del cielo (fig.) to come like manna from heaven (fig.), to be a [real] godsend (fig.), to come at just the right time, s.th. couldn't have come at a better time, to be just what s.o.

needs/needed, to be just what the doctor ordered (fig., fam.) ◆ *El dinero me vino como llovido del cielo. The money was a real godsend. The money was just what I needed.*
▶ caerle a alg. como llovido del cielo (fig.) to fall/drop into s.o.'s lap (fig.) ◆ *Si crees que todo te va a caer como llovido del cielo, estás muy equivocado. If you think everything will fall into your lap, you've got another think coming.* ◆ *No le va a caer como llovido del cielo. It won't drop into his lap.*
▶ [re]mover cielo y tierra [para + infinitivo] to move heaven and earth [to + infinitive]
▶ aunque se junten el cielo y la tierra not for anything in the world, not for love [n]or money, not for all the tea in China, not for all the whiskey in Ireland ◆ *No me lo perderé aunque se junten el cielo y la tierra. I won't miss it for anything in the world.*
▷ cielo (**clamar/escupir** al ~)
▷ ciencia (ser un **pozo** de ~)
▷ ciento y la **madre**

el cierne [time of] pollination
▶ estar en ciernes (fig.) to be in its infancy (fig.) ◆ *La empresa está aún en ciernes. The enterprise is still in its infancy.*
▶ ser un escritor/etc. en ciernes (fig.) to be a budding writer/etc., to be a writer/etc. in the making

el cierre locking device
▶ echar el cierre (pop.) to shut one's trap (sl.), to pipe down (fam.), to belt up (fam., Br.E.) ◆ *¡Echa el cierre! Shut your trap! Pipe down! Belt up!*

la cigüeña stork
▶ pintar la cigüeña (fig., fam.) to play lord of the manor, to act the big shot (fig.), to act high and mighty (fam.)

el cimbel decoy
▶ el cimbel (pop.) (penis) ▷ el calvo

cinco five
▶ saber cuántas son cinco (fam.) to be no fool, to know a thing or two (fam.), to know what's what (fam.)
▶ decir a alg. cuántas son cinco (fam.) to tell s.o. what's what (fam.), to tell s.o. a thing or two (fam.), to give s.o. a piece of one's mind
▶ ¡Choca esos cinco! (fam.) Give me five! (fam.) Put it there! (fam.)

la cintura waist

▶ meter a alg. en cintura (fig.) to make s.o. listen to or see reason, to bring s.o. under control ◆ *Tenemos que meterle en cintura. We have to make him listen to reason.*

el cinturón belt

▶ apretarse el cinturón (fig.) to tighten one's belt (fig.), to draw in one's horns (fig.) ◆ *Durante la recesión tuvimos que apretarnos el cinturón. We had to tighten our belts during the recession.*

ciscar (pop.) to soil, to dirty

▶ ciscarse de miedo (fig., pop.) to shit o.s. [for fear] (fig., vulg.) ◆ *Nos ciscamos de miedo. We shit/shat ourselves. We were scared shitless. (vulg.) We were in a blue funk. (fam., Br.E.)*

▶ ciscarse en algo (fig., vulg.) not to give a shit/fuck about s.th. (vulg) ◆ *¡Me cisco en el gobierno! I don't give a shit about the government! Screw the government! (vulg.) To hell with the government! (fam.)*

el cisco coaldust

▶ armar [un] cisco (fig., fam.) to kick up a stink/row (fam.), to make trouble ◆ *Se armó un tremendo cisco. There was an almighty stink/row.*

▶ estar/quedar hecho cisco (fam.) to be completely exhausted, to be completely shattered or whacked (fam., Br.E.), to be completely washed out (fam.), to be totally worn out (fig.), to be completely bushed (fam.), to be completely pooped (sl., Am.E.), to be completely knackered (sl., Br.E.), to be completely drained (fig.), to be completely done in/up (fam.), to be completely beat (fam., Am.E.), to be dead-beat (fam.), to be all in (fam.), to be shagged out (sl., Br.E.), to be dog-tired (fam.)

▶ hacer algo cisco to shatter s.th., to smash s.th. to pieces, to tear s.th. to bits

clamar to clamor

▶ clamar en el desierto (fig.) to be a voice crying in the wilderness (fig.), to preach in the wilderness (fig.), to talk at deaf ears (fig.), to talk to the winds (fig.) ◆ *Nadie estaba escuchando. Clamaste en el desierto. Nobody was listening. You were a voice crying in the wilderness. You were talking at deaf ears.*

▶ clamar al cielo to cry out to heaven, to stink to high heaven (fig., fam.), to be a scandal, to be outrageous ◆ *Esto clama al cielo. This cries out to heaven.*

▷ clandestinamente (mudarse ~)

▷ claro (estar más ~ que el **agua**)

▷ claro (ser más ~ que el **sol**)

clavado nailed

▶ dejar clavado a alg. (fig.) to leave s.o. speechless (fig.), to floor s.o. (fam.), to dumbfound s.o. ◆ *Su pregunta me dejó clavado. His question left me speechless. I was completely floored by his question.*

▶ ser clavado a alg. o ser alg. clavado (fam.) to be the spitting image or the spit and image of s.o. (fam.), to be a dead ringer for s.o. (fig., fam.) ◆ *Es su madre clavada. She's the spit and image of her mother. ◆ Eres clavado a mi hermano. You're a dead ringer for my brother.*

▶ a las seis clavadas (fam.) at 6 [o'clock] sharp, at 6 on the dot (fam.), on the dot of 6 (fam.), at 6 [o'clock] on the nose (fam.)

la clavija dowel, pin

▶ apretar las clavijas a alg. (fig., fam.) to put the pressure on s.o. (fig.), to tighten up on s.o. (fig.), to put the screws on s.o. (fig.)

el clavo nail

▶ dar en el clavo (fig.) to hit the nail on the head (fig.), to be right on (fam., Am.E.), to be spot-on (fam., Br.E.) ◆ *Tu observación dio en el clavo. Your remark hit the nail on the head. ◆ Dio en el clavo con ese regalo. He was right on with that gift/present. ◆ Damos en el clavo con nuestra predicción. Our prediction was spot-on.*

▶ dar una en el clavo y ciento en la herradura (fig., fam.) to be wrong nine times out of ten

▶ agarrarse a un clavo ardiendo to clutch at straws (fig.), to do anything ◆ *Están tan necesitados que se agarrarían a un clavo ardiendo. They're so needy they would do anything [to help themselves].*

▶ remachar el clavo (fig.) to make matters worse

▶ poner un clavo a una (pop.) to bang a woman (vulg.) ▷ **calzar**[se] a alg.

▶ ¡Por los clavos de Cristo! Por los clavos de una puerta vieja! (hum.). For heaven's sake! For goodness' sake!

la clueca broody hen
▶ **ponerse como una gallina clueca** (fig., fam.) to puff o.s. up (fig.), to act big (fam.), to act the big shot (fam.)

la coba (fam.) flattery, cajolery
▶ **dar coba a alg.** to play up to s.o., to butter s.o. up (fam.), to soap s.o. up (fam.), to soft-soap s.o. (fam.), to sweet-talk s.o. (fam., Am.E.), to suck up to s.o. (fam.), to toady to s.o.
▷ cobarde de siete **suelas**
▷ cobrar una **miseria**

el cobre copper
▶ **batir[se] el cobre** (fig.) to work very hard, to work with a will, to exert o.s., to make a tremendous effort, to bust a gut (fam., Am.E.), to put one's back into it
▶ **batirse el cobre por + infinitivo** (fig.) to work/go all out to + infinitive ◆ *Me batí el cobre por terminar el trabajo. I worked all out to finish the job.*
▶ **batirse el cobre** (fig.) (debate/etc.): to be a tough/pitched battle (fig.), things get a bit rough/tough, both/all sides are driving a hard bargain ◆ *En la última reunión se batieron el cobre. Things got a bit rough at the last meeting.* ◆ *Durante la negociación se batieron el cobre. During the negotiation[s] both sides were driving a hard bargain.* ◆ *Nos batimos el cobre en el debate. The debate took it out of us.*
▶ **enseñar el cobre** (América Latina) to show [o.s. in] one's true colors ◆ *Nunca se sabe qué piensa ese tío. No enseña el cobre. You can never tell what that guy is thinking. He doesn't show his true colors.*

la coca (fam.) (a) (cocaine): coke (sl.), snow (sl.) (b) nut (sl.) ▷ la cebolla (c) biff/rap on the nut (fam.) or on the head

cocer to cook
▶ **cocerse** (fig., fam.) (a) to get drunk, to get sloshed or plastered (fam.), to get tight (fam.), to get canned or pissed (sl., Br.E.), to get tanked up (sl.), to get smashed or stoned (sl.), to get legless (fam., Br.E.), to get as pissed as a newt (sl., Br.E.) (b) to be cooked up (fig.), to be hatched [out] (fig.) ◆ *Este complot se coció ayer. This plot was hatched yesterday.*

▶ **estar cocido** (fig., fam.) to be drunk, to be plastered or sloshed (fam.), to be tight (fam.), to be canned or pissed (sl., Br.E.), to be pie-eyed (fam.), to be in one's cups ◆ *estar completamente cocido to be blind drunk (fam.), to be smashed out of one's mind (sl.)*
▶ **cocérsele a alg. los sesos** (fig.) s.o.'s head is/starts spinning (fig.) ◆ *Estudiaba hasta que se me cocían los sesos. I was studying until my head started spinning.*
▷ cocer (dejar a alg. ~ en su propia **salsa**)
▷ cocerse en su propia **salsa**

el cochazo (fam., Esp.) big flashy car (fam.), luxury flash car (fam.), whacking great car (fam.), flashy cruisemobile (sl.)

el coche car
▶ **ir/venir en el coche de San Francisco o de San Fernando** (hum.) to go/come on Shank's pony (Br.E.) or on Shank's mare (Am.E.) (hum.), to walk, to hoof it (fam.)

el cocinero cook
▶ **haber sido cocinero antes que fraile** (fig., fam.) to know what one is doing, to be no beginner, to be no novice

el coco coconut
▶ **el coco** (fig., fam.) (a) nut (sl.) ▷ la cebolla (b) brains (fam.), nous (fam.), gumption (fam.)
▶ **comer el coco a alg.** (pop.) to brainwash s.o., to befuddle s.o.'s brain (with words, in order to manipulate), to soft-soap or sweet-talk (Am.E.) s.o. (into doing s.th.) (fam.) ◆ *Durante la dictadura comían el coco a todo el pueblo. During the dictatorship all the people were brainwashed.* ◆ *La hija le comió el coco a su madre para que le diese dinero. The daughter sweet-talked her mother into giving her money.*
▶ **comerse el coco** (pop.) to rack one's brains (fig.), to think hard, to worry a lot
▶ **estar hasta el coco de algo** (fam.) *to be utterly fed up with s.th. (fam.)* ▷ estar hasta [más allá de] la **coronilla** de algo
▷ cocodrilo (llorar/derramar **lágrimas** de ~)

el cocotazo (fam.) biff/rap on the nut (fam.) or on the head
▷ codearse con los de **arriba**

el codo elbow

▶ alzar/empinar el codo (fam.) to bend/lift one's elbow (fam.), to hoist one or a few (sl., Am.E.), to belt one or a few down (fam., Am.E.), to have a drink or a few drinks

▶ comerse/roerse los codos de hambre to be on the breadline (fig.), not to have a bite to eat, to be utterly destitute

▶ romperse los codos (fam.) to cram (fam.), to swot (fam., Br.E.), to bone up (fam.)

▶ hablar por los codos (fam.) to talk too much, to talk nineteen to the dozen (fam.), to talk one's head off (fam.)

▶ mentir por los codos (fam.) to lie through one's teeth (fam.), to tell huge lies

▶ llevar a alg. codo con codo (fig., fam.) to arrest s.o.

▷ coger (~las al **vuelo**)

el cogote back of the head/neck

▶ estar hasta el cogote de algo (fam.) to have had it up to here with s.th. (fam.), to be fed up to the back teeth with s.th. (fam.)

el cojón (pop., vulg.) (testicle): ball (pop., vulg.)

▶ no valer un cojón not to be worth a shit (vulg.), not to be worth a damn (fam.)

▶ los cojones (testicles) ▷ las **canicas**

▶ tocarse los cojones (fig.) to do bugger all (vulg.) or damn all (fam.) or sod all (sl.) (Br.E.), to do sweet f.a. (fam.), to sit on one's butt (Am.E.) or on one's backside (Br.E.) (fam.)

▶ tener cojones to have balls (vulg.), to have guts (fam.), to have gumption (fam.), to have bottle (fam., Br.E.), to have pluck (fig.)

▶ tocar/hinchar los cojones a alg. (fig.) to piss s.o. off (sl., Br.E.), to get up s.o.'s nose (fam., Br.E.)

▶ estar con los cojones de corbata to be in a flat panic, to be scared stiff (fam.), to be frightened or scared out of one's wits (fam.)

▶ salirle a alg. de los cojones to say what one damn well (fam.) or bloody well (sl., Br.E.) likes ◆ Decimos lo que nos sale de los cojones. We say what we damn/bloody well like.

▶ hacer un frío de cojones to be cold enough to freeze the balls off a brass monkey (fam., Br.E.), to be bloody (sl.) or damn[ed] (fam.) cold

▶ hacer un calor de cojones to be bloody (sl., Br.E.) or damn[ed] (fam.) hot

cojonudo (adj., pop.) (a) great (fam.), super (fam.), magic (fam.), splendid, magnificent, wonderful, fantastic (fam.), amazing (fam.), incredible (fam.), awesome (sl., Am.E.), brilliant (fam., Br.E.), outstanding (fig.), terrific (fam.), marvelous (fam.), smashing (fam.) (b) huge, enormous, colossal, gigantic, monumental ◆ un tío cojonudo a great guy/bloke ◆ una chavala cojonuda a smashing chick/bird ◆ un día cojonudo a glorious/wonderful day ◆ un apetito cojonudo a huge appetite

la col cabbage

▶ Entre col y col, lechuga. (prov.) A change is a good thing. Variety is the spice of life. (prov.)

la cola tail, glue

▶ hacer/guardar cola to queue [up] (Br.E.), to line up, to stand in line (Am.E.)

▶ tener/traer cola (fig.) to have [grave] repercussions (fig.) or consequences ◆ Ese asunto va a tener cola. That is going to have consequences.

▶ Aún falta/queda la cola por desollar. (fig.) The main difficulty or the most difficult part is yet/still to come. The worst is yet/still to come.

▶ no pegar ni con cola (fam.) ◆ Eso no pega ni con cola. (fam.) That has nothing whatsoever to do with it. That's utter rubbish (fam.) or nonsense. ◆ Esa corbata y esa chaqueta no pegan ni con cola. That tie and that jacket just don't go together. That tie just doesn't go with that jacket. ◆ Lo que dijiste no pegó ni con cola. What you said was utter nonsense.

el colador sieve

▶ dejar algo/a alg. como un colador (fig., fam.) to riddle s.th./s.o. with bullets, to make a lot of holes in s.th. ◆ Dejaron al traidor como un colador. They riddled the traitor with bullets. ◆ Las polillas dejaron mi chaqueta de lana como un colador. The moths made/ate a lot of holes in my cardigan.

▶ tener la cabeza como un colador (fig., fam.) to have a memory like a sieve (fig.)

colar to strain [off], to filter

▶ colar (fam.) to pass muster (fig.), to wash (fam.) ◆ Esta excusa no va a colar. This excuse will not pass muster. *This excuse will not wash [with me/etc.].*

▶ colar algo (por un sitio o por la aduana) (fam.) to smuggle/slip s.th. through (a place/the customs)

▶ colar algo a alg. (fam.) to foist/palm s.th. off on s.o. ◆ *Trataron de colarnos una imitación. They tried to foist a fake off on us.*

▶ ¡A mí no me la cuelas! I'm not going to swallow that! You must think I'm stupid! Don't [even] try to fool me!

el coleto (histórico) doublet (historical), jerkin (historical)

▶ decir algo para su coleto (fig., fam.) to say s.th. to o.s.

▶ echarse algo al coleto (fam.) (a) (beverage/drink): to down (fam.), to knock back (fam.), to drink down (b) (food): to put away (fam.), to polish off (fam.), to eat right up (c) (book/etc.): to devour (fig.), to read right through ◆ *Me eché un sándwich al coleto. I put a sandwich away.* ◆ *Me eché el libro al coleto. I read the book right through.*

colgado hanging

▶ dejar a alg. colgado (fig.) to let s.o. down, to fail s.o., to stand s.o. up, to leave s.o. in the lurch (fig.), to leave s.o. high and dry (fig.), to leave s.o. out in the cold (fig.) ◆ *Como me dejaron colgado, tuve que hacerlo todo yo. Since they left me in the lurch, I had to do it all myself.*

▶ estar colgado de las palabras de alg. (fig.) to hang on s.o.'s every word, to hang on s.o.'s lips (fig.)

▶ quedar colgado (fig., fam.) to get hooked [on drugs] (fam.), to have a monkey on one's back (fam., Am.E.)

▷ colgar de un **cabello/hilo**

colmar to fill [to the brim]

▶ colmar a alg. de algo (honores o alabanzas o favores/etc.) (fig.) s.th. (honors/praise/favors/etc.): to heap on s.o. (fig.), to lavish on s.o., to shower upon s.o., to shower s.o. with ◆ *Los padres colmaron a sus hijos de regalos. The parents showered presents/gifts upon their children.*

▶ colmar la medida (fig.) to be the last straw, to take the biscuit (fam., Br.E.), to have had just about all one can take ◆ *¡Esto colma la medida! This is the last straw! This takes the biscuit! I've had just about all I can take!*

el colmillo eyetooth

▶ enseñar los colmillos (fig.) to show one's teeth (fig.)

▶ escupir por el colmillo (fig.) to talk big (fam.), to brag

el color color

▶ ponerse de mil colores to blush to the roots of one's hair, to go bright red

▶ salírsele/subírsele a alg. los colores to blush [with shame], to go red [with shame], to flush [with anger/excitement/pride/strain/etc.] ◆ *Se le subieron los colores por vergüenza. He/she blushed with shame.*

▷ color (para cada **gusto** se pintó un ~)

la coma comma

▶ contar algo con puntos y comas to tell s.th. in minute or in great detail, to tell s.th. down to the last detail, to give a blow-by-blow account of s.th. ◆ *Nos lo contó todo con puntos y comas. He told us all about it down to the last detail.*

comer to eat

▶ El comer es como el rascar, todo es cuestión de empezar. (hum.). Eating is like scratching: Once you start, you don't want to stop or you can't stop.

▶ comer[se] a alg. vivo (fig., fam.) (threat): to skin s.o. alive (fig., fam.), to make mincemeat of s.o. (fig., fam.), to have s.o.'s guts for garters (fam., Br.E.) ◆ *Cuando se entere de eso, te comerá vivo. When he finds out about that, he'll make mincemeat of you.*

▶ comerse a alg. crudo (fig., fam.) to be head and shoulders above s.o. (fam.), to be more than a match for s.o., to be streets ahead of s.o. (fam.), to knock spots off s.o. (fam.), to outshine s.o. (fig.), to beat s.o. hollow (contest/sports/etc.) (fam.) ◆ *Uno de los jugadores de ajedrez se los comió crudos a todos los otros. One of the chess players was more than a match for all the others.*

▶ comerse los santos to be a sanctimonious or an excessively pious man/woman or person, to be a holy Joe (sl., Br.E.), to be a churchy type (pej.), to be a pious Annie (pej.) ◆ *Juan se come los santos. Juan is a holy Joe.*

▶ Está para comérsela. (fig., fam.) She looks a treat. (fam.) She's a real dish. (fam.) She's a feast for the eyes. (fam.)

▶ ¿Con qué se come eso? (fig., fam.) What on earth's that? (fam.)

▶ con su/etc. pan se/etc. lo coma/etc. (fam.) that's his/etc. look-out (fam.), that's his/etc. funeral (sl.), that's his/etc. problem ◆ *¡Con tu pan te lo comas! That's/it's your problem!*

▶ estar algo diciendo cómeme (fam.) to be looking very appetizing or delightful or tempting ◆ *Los pasteles están diciendo cómeme. The pastry is looking very appetizing.*

▶ comer a alg. la envidia (fig.) to be eaten up or consumed with envy ◆ *Le come la envidia. He's eaten up with envy.*

▶ sin comerlo ni beberlo (fig.) through no fault of one's own, without having [had] anything to do with it or any part in it ◆ *Tuve que indemnizarlo por los daños ocasionados sin comerlo ni beberlo. I had to compensate him for the damage even though I didn't have anything to do with it.*

▷ comer (se juntaron el **hambre** y las ganas de ~)

▷ comer a dos **carrillo**s/a todo **pasto**/a más no **poder**

▷ comer a lo gran señor (▷ el **señor**)

▷ comer como un **decosido**/un **gorrión**/una **lima**/un **pajarito**/un **sabañón**

▷ comer con los **ojos**

▷ comer el **coco** a alg.

▷ comer más que un **alguacil**/que un **sabañón**/que **siete**

▷ comerse a alg. con los **ojos**

▷ comerse el **coco**

▷ comida (dar un buen **golpe** a la ~)

▷ comida (**regar** una ~ con vino)

▷ comida (una ~ de **rechupete**)

la comidilla (fam.)

▶ ser la comidilla de la ciudad o de la gente o del público to be the talk of the town ◆ *Sus romances son la comidilla de la ciudad. His love-affairs are the talk of the town.*

comido full (to have eaten)

▶ [lo] comido por [lo] servido (fam.) it's not worth it, it's not worthwhile, it doesn't pay (fig.), it's just enough to live from hand to mouth (wage[s]/salary) ◆ *¿Cómo es? Es comido por servido. How is it? It doesn't pay. It's not worthwhile.* ◆ *¿Cuánto pagan? Lo comido por lo servido. How much do they pay? It's just enough to live from hand to mouth.*

la comilona (fam.) blow-out (fam.), binge (fam.), great nosh-up (sl.), spread (fam.), feast, slap-up meal (fam., Br.E.) ◆ *¡Qué comilona! What a blow-out!* ◆ *Sirvieron una comilona suntuosa. They laid on a magnificent spread.*

el comino cumin

▶ el comino (fig., fam.) little squirt (fam.)

▶ no valer un comino (fam.) not to be worth a bean (fam.) ▷ no valer un **ardite**

▶ [no] importar a alg. un comino (fam.) s.o. couldn't care less (fam., Br.E.) ▷ no importar a alg. un **ardite**

el comistrajo (fam., pej.) awful food, muck/ swill (fig., fam., pej.)

▷ compás (bailar al ~ de la **música** de alg.)

la componenda (fam.) (a) compromise, [provisional/temporary] settlement or arrangement (b) wheeler dealing or wheeling and dealing or horse trading (esp. in politics) (fam.), shady deal (fam.) ◆ *El senador estuvo hasta la coronilla de las componendas [políticas] y dimitió. The senator was fed up with the wheeler dealing or with the wheelings and dealings and resigned.*

componer to put together, to compose

▶ componérselas (fam.) to manage, to get along/by, not to be at a loss as to what to do, to find a way (fig.) ◆ *¿Cómo te las compones? How do you manage?* ◆ *Se las compone siempre. He's never at a loss as to what to do.* ◆ *Sabe componérselas. He can take care of himself. He can look after himself.* ◆ *¡Allá se las componga [él]! He has to sort that out himself! (fig.) That's his problem! That's his funeral! (sl.) That's his look-out! (fam.) On his [own] head be it!*

▶ componérselas para + infinitivo to manage/ contrive to + infinitive ◆ *No sé cómo se las compuso para convencer a su jefe. I don't know how she managed to convince her boss.*

la composición composition

▶ hacer[se] su o una composición de lugar (fig.) to weigh up the pros and cons (of one's/ the situation), to take stock (of one's/the situation) (fig.) ◆ *Hice mi/una composición de lugar y decidí irme. I took stock of my situation and decided to leave.*

▷ comprar algo a **huevo**

▷ comprar algo por un **pedazo** de pan

comulgar to receive/take communion
▶ no comulgar en la misma iglesia (fig.) not to suit each other or one another
▶ comulgar con ruedas de molino (fig., fam.) to swallow anything (fig.), to be easily taken for a ride (fam.), to fall for anything (fam.), to be pretty thick (fam.)
▶ no comulgar con ruedas de molino (fam.) to be no fool, to be nobody's fool, s.o. wasn't born yesterday

la concha shellfish, scallop shell, tortoiseshell, snail shell
▶ tener muchas conchas (fam.), tener más conchas que un galápago (fam.) to be very crafty, to be a sly one (fam.)
▶ meterse en su concha (fig.) to retreat/retire/withdraw into one's shell (fig.)
▷ conciencia (la mejor **almohada** es una ~ tranquila)

la coneja doe rabbit
▶ la coneja (fig., pop.) babymachine (fig., fam., hum.)

el conejo rabbit
▶ el conejo (vulg.) (vagina): pussy (pop., sl.), fanny (vulg., Br.E.), beaver (sl., Am.E.), cunt (vulg.), twat (vulg.)
▶ los conejos (vulg.) (testicles) ▷ las **canicas**
▷ confiado (**pecar** de ~)
▷ confianza (**ganar**se la ~ de alg.)
▷ conocer (más vale **malo** conocido que bueno por ~)
▷ conocer (ser más conocido que el **tebeo**)
▷ conocer a su **gente**
▷ conocer algo al **dedillo**
▷ conocer algo como la **palma** de la mano
▷ conocer el **paño**
▷ consultar algo con la **almohada**
▷ consultar con el **bolsillo**
▷ contar las **estrellas** (tratar de ~)
▷ contar los **garbanzos**
▷ contento (estar más ~ que unas **pascuas**)

contonearse (women): to swing/sway one's hips

el contoneo (women): swinging/swaying of the hips, hip-swinging

contrapelo: a contrapelo (adv.) (to brush/comb): the wrong way

▶ venirle algo a alg. [muy] a contrapelo (fig., fam.) to go [totally] against the grain with s.o. (fig.) ◆ *Nos vino muy a contrapelo. It went totally against the grain with us.* ◆ *Apoyarlo me viene a contrapelo. It goes against the grain with me to support him.* ◆ *Por mucho que me venga a contrapelo tengo que hacerlo. However much it goes against the grain [with me] I have to do it.*
▷ conversación (cortar el **hilo** de la ~)

la coña annoyance
▶ dar la coña a alg. (pop.) to get on s.o.'s nerves or wick (Br.E.) (fam.), to pester s.o.

el coño (vulg.) (vagina) ▷ el conejo
▶ ¡Vete al coño! (vulg.) Piss off! (vulg.) Fuck off! (vulg.) Go to hell! (fam.)
▶ ¿Qué coño te importa? (vulg.) That's none of your bloody business! (fam., Br.E.) That's none of your goddam[n] business! (sl., Am.E.) Why the hell does it matter to you? (fam.)

el copete tuft of hair
▶ gente de alto copete (fam.) important or socially prominent people, bigwigs (fam.), big shots (fam.), top nobs (fam., Br.E.), big names, top brass (fam.), VIPs (sl.)
▶ tener mucho copete (fig.) to be stuck-up (fam.), to be haughty ◆ *Ese tío sí que tiene mucho copete. That guy isn't half stuck-up. (fam., Br.E.)*

la copla verse, folksong
▶ andar en coplas (fam.) to be the talk of the town, to be common knowledge ◆ *La noticia ya anda en coplas. The news is already common knowledge.*
▶ ¡Ni en coplas! (fam.) No way! Not on your life! Certainly not!

el corazón heart
▶ tener corazón de alcachofa (fig.) to be quite a philanderer or womanizer, to be a ladykiller (fam.)
▶ no caberle a alg. el corazón en el pecho (a) to be beside o.s. with joy, to be bursting with joy (fig.), to be overjoyed (b) to be very generous/kind, to be the very soul of kindness
▶ tener el corazón en su sitio o bien puesto (fig.) s.o.'s heart is in the right place (fig.) ◆ *No siempre hace lo que es justo, pero tiene el corazón en su sitio. He doesn't always do what is right, but his heart is in the right place.*

▷ corazón (**barriga** llena, ~ contento)
▷ corazón (de la **abundancia** del ~ habla la boca)
▷ corazón (hacer de **tripa**s ~)
▷ corazón (la **prensa** del ~)
▷ corazón (llegarle a alg. a las **tela**s del ~)
▷ corazón (**ojos** que no ven, ~ que no siente)
▷ corazón (**pedazo** del ~)
▷ corazón (tener **pelo**s en el ~)

el corbatín bow tie
► salirse por el corbatín (fam.) to be very thin, to be skinny (fam.), to be as thin as a rake (fam.)

▷ corcho (**cabeza** de ~)

el cordero lamb
► No hay tales corderos. (fig., fam.) There isn't any such thing. There's no such thing. It's nothing of the sort. It's enough to make a cat laugh. (fam.)
► Ahí está la madre del cordero. (fam.) There's or that's the rub/snag. (fig.) That's where the problem is/lies. That's why [it doesn't work/etc.].

▷ cordero (un **lobo** con piel de ~)

la cornada thrust with the horns
► Más cornadas da el hambre. (fig.) It could be worse. It could have been worse. Starving would be worse. Starving would have been worse. Worse things happen at sea. (fam., Br.E.) ◆ ¿Estuviste muy mal? Más cornadas da el hambre. Were you in a very bad way? It could've been worse. Worse things happen at sea.
► no morir de cornada de burro (fam., hum.) to be a coward, to be chicken (sl.), not to risk anything at all ◆ ¡Nadie muere de cornada de burro! Don't be chicken! Don't be [such] a coward! Risk s.th.[for a change]! Be more adventurous! ◆ Ese tío no morirá de cornada de burro. That guy is a coward. That guy doesn't risk anything at all.

cornudo horned, antlered
► el cornudo (fig.) cuckold

el coro chorus, choir
► hacer coro a/con alg. to chime in with s.o. (fig.), to agree with s.o., to go along with s.o.

la coronilla crown/top of the head
► estar hasta [más allá de] la coronilla de algo (fam.) to be [utterly] fed up with s.th. (fam.), to be fed up to the back teeth with

s.th. (fam.), to be sick to the teeth of s.th. (fam.), to be sick and tired of s.th. (fam.), to have had it up to here with s.th. (fam.), to be cheesed off with s.th. (fam., Br.E.), to blow/stuff s.th. for a lark (sl.) ◆ Estoy hasta más allá de la coronilla del asunto. I am fed up to the back teeth with the whole thing. I'm utterly fed up with the whole ball of wax. (fam., Am.E.)
► andar/bailar de coronilla to lean/bend over backwards (to do s.th. or please s.o.) (fam.), to do one's utmost (to please s.o.), to pursue s.th. very diligently

▷ corral (estar/sentirse como **gallina** en ~ ajeno)
▷ corral (meter las **cabra**s en el ~ a alg.)
▷ corral (vivir/sentirse como **pava** en ~)
▷ correo (echar una **carta** al ~)

correr to run
► correrse (fam.) (to have an orgasm): to come (fam.); (man): to shoot off (vulg., Br.E.)
► correrla (fam.), correr sus mocedades (fam.) (youth): to sow one's wild oats ◆ Cuando éramos jóvenes la corríamos. When we were young or in our young days we were sowing our wild oats.
▷ correr (▷ **pelar**: corre que se las pela)
▷ correr a más no **poder**
▷ correr como el **diablo**
▷ correr como **gato** por ascuas

el/la correve[i]dile (fam.) (a) [old] gossip (fam.), tattletale (b) telltale, tattletale, informer, sneak (fam., Br.E.), grass (fam., Br.E.), snitch (fam.)

corrido worldly-wise
► ser más corrido que un zorro viejo (fam.) to be as sly as they come (fam.), to know every trick in the book (fam.)
► ser [un] toro corrido (fig.) to be an old hand, to be an old fox (fig.), to be a cunning old devil (fam.)
► ser [una] liebre corrida (fig.) to be an old hand, to be an old fox (fig.), to be a cunning old devil (fam.)

corriente normal
► corriente y moliente (fam.) ordinary, run-of-the-mill ◆ Fue una comida corriente y moliente. It was just an ordinary meal.

▶ salir algo corriente y moliente (fam.) to go off smoothly, to go off without a hitch, to turn out well ◆ *Todo salió corriente y moliente. Everything went off smoothly.*

la corriente stream, current

▶ tomar la corriente desde la fuente (fig.) to get to the bottom of it/s.th. (fig.)

▶ llevar/seguir la corriente a alg. (a) to dance to s.o.'s tune (fig.) (b) to humor s.o., to play along with s.o., to give s.o. his head (fam.) ◆ *Me seguía la corriente para que me callase o para que no protestase. He was humoring me to try to keep me quiet.*

▶ dejarse llevar de/por la corriente (fig.) to swim/go with the tide (fig.), to howl/run with the pack (fig.), to go along with the crowd, to follow the crowd

▶ ir/navegar contra la corriente (fig.) to swim/go against the tide (fig.)

▷ corriente (**camarón** que se duerme, se lo lleva la ~)

el corro (of people): circle, ring

▶ escupir en corro (fig., fam.) to put in one's [own] two bits (fam.), to put in one's two cents[' worth] (fam., Am.E.), to chime in (fig.), to butt into the or in on the conversation (fam.), to join in the conversation ◆ *Siempre tiene que escupir en corro. He always has to put in his own two bits or his two cents' worth.*

▷ cortar (ni **pinchar** ni ~)
▷ cortar algo de **raíz**
▷ cortar las **ala**s/los **vuelo**s a alg.
▷ cortar por lo **sano**
▷ cortar **traje**s
▷ cortar un **traje** a alg.

cortés polite

▶ Lo cortés no quita lo valiente. Politeness and firmness aren't mutually exclusive. Politeness doesn't have to be a sign of weakness.

corto short

▶ ser más corto que las mangas de un chaleco to be as thick as two short planks (fam., Br.E.) ▷ ser más tonto que **Carracuca**
▷ corto (▷ **largo**: a la corta o a la larga)
▷ corto (**atar** ~ a alg.)

cosechar to harvest

▶ cosechar lo que uno ha sembrado (fig.) to reap what one has sown (fig.)

▶ Se cosecha lo que se siembra. (prov.) As you sow, so you reap. (prov.) As ye sow, so shall ye reap. (fig.)

coser to sew

▶ coser a alg. a tiros/balazos (fig.) to riddle s.o. with bullets (fig.) ◆ *Cosieron al traidor a tiros. They riddled the traitor with bullets.*

▶ ser coser y cantar (fam.) to be child's play (fig.), to be a cinch (sl.), to be a pushover (sl.), to be a doddle (fam., Br.E.), to be a breeze (fam., Am.E.), to be a piece of cake (fam.), to be as easy as falling off a log, to be as easy as pie (sl.), to be like shooting fish in a barrel (fig., Am.E.) ◆ *El examen fue coser y cantar. The exam/test was child's play.*

▷ coserse la **boca**

las cosquillas tickling

▶ tener malas cosquillas, no sufrir cosquillas s.o. can't take a joke

▶ buscar las cosquillas a alg. to annoy s.o., to rile s.o. (fam.)

▶ hacer cosquillas a alg. (fig.) to arouse/tickle s.o.'s curiosity (fig.)

los costados line of ancestors, ancestry

▶ por los cuatro costados (fig.) thoroughly, wholly, through and through, to the core (fig.), true-blue, red-hot (fam.), dyed-in-the-wool (fig.), whole-hog (sl.), one hundred percent or per cent (Br.E.), out-and-out, confirmed, absolute, inveterate, hopeless ◆ *Pepe es español por los cuatro costados. Pepe is Spanish through and through. Pepe is wholly or thoroughly Spanish. Pepe is Spanish to the core.* ◆ *un partidario por los cuatro costados a red-hot or dyed-in-the-wool supporter, a whole-hogger (sl.)* ◆ *una patriota por los cuatro costados a whole-hog patriot, a hundred-percenter (Am.E.)* ◆ *Es un solterón por los cuatro costados. He's a confirmed bachelor.* ◆ *Es un malvado por los cuatro costados. He's an out-and-out villain.* ◆ *Es una holgazana por los cuatro costados. She's an absolute idler.*

el costal sack, bag

▶ ser un costal de mentiras (fig.) to be an out-and-out liar, to be a chronic liar

▶ ser un o estar hecho un costal de huesos (fig.) to be a bag of bones (fam.), to be all skin and bone (fam.), to be nothing but skin and bone (fam.)

▶ vaciar el costal (fig., fam.) to spill the beans (sl.), to talk (fam.), to blab (fam.)

▷ costal (ser **harina** de otro ~)

▷ costar la de **San Quintín**

▷ costar los cinco **sentido**s

▷ costar un **dineral/huevo/pico/riñón/sen-tido**

▷ costar un **huevo** [+ infinitivo]

▷ costar un **ojo** de la cara

▷ costar una **burrada/riñonada**

la costilla rib

▶ De tal costilla, tal astilla. (prov.) The apple doesn't fall far from the tree. (prov.) Like father like son. (prov.) A chip off the old block.

▶ mi [cara] costilla (fig., fam., hum.) my better half (fam.)

▶ medir las costillas a alg. (fam.) to give s.o. a thrashing (fam.) ▷ arrimar **candela** a alg.

▶ tener a alg. sobre sus costillas (fam.) to be lumbered with s.o. (fam.)

▷ costumbre (la ~ es otra/segunda **naturaleza**)

la costura seam

▶ sentar las costuras a alg. (fig., fam.) to give s.o. a hiding (fam.) ▷ arrimar **candela** a alg.

▶ meter a alg. en costura (fig.) to make s.o. listen to or see reason, to bring s.o. under control ◆ *Tenemos que meterle en costura. We have to make him listen to reason.*

el cotarro night shelter (for tramps/etc.)

▶ el cotarro (pop.) clique

▶ alborotar el cotarro (fig., fam.) to stir up trouble (fig.), to make trouble

▶ ser el amo del cotarro (fam.), dirigir el cotarro (fam.) to rule the roost (fig.) ▷ llevar la **batuta**

la cotorra budgerigar, magpie

▶ la cotorra (fig., fam.) gasbag (fam.), windbag (fam.), chatterbox (fam.)

▶ hablar más que una cotorra (fig., fam.) s.o. wouldn't stop talking, to just go on and on, to be a real chatterbox (fam.), to have a motormouth (fam.), to talk nineteen to the dozen (fam., Br.E.), to talk a mile a minute (fam., Am.E.), s.o. could talk the hind legs off a donkey (fam.)

la coyunda halter

▶ la coyunda (fig., hum.) yoke of marriage (hum.)

la coz kick

▶ soltar la/una coz a alg. (fam.) to be rude to s.o., to snap at s.o.

▶ tratar a alg. a coces (fig.) to treat s.o. very badly/rudely, to treat s.o. like dirt (fam.), to be very rude to s.o.

▶ dar coces contra el aguijón (fig.) to kick against the pricks (fig.), to rebel ◆ *Los empleados dieron coces contra el aguijón cuando no recibieron el aumento salarial [que les habían] prometido. The employees kicked against the pricks when they didn't get the wage increase promised them.*

▷ crecer como la **espuma**

▷ creces (▷ **pagar**: ¡[Ya] me las pagarás con ~!)

el credo credo

▶ en un credo (fig.) in next to no time, in a flash, in a jiffy (fam.), in a trice, in a tick (fam., Br.E.), before you can say Jack Robinson (fam.) ◆ *Todo pasó en un credo. It was all over in a flash.* ◆ *Terminó el trabajo en un credo. He finished the work in next to no time.*

creederas (fam.)

▶ tener buenas creederas to swallow anything (fig.), to be terribly gullible

▷ creer algo a **puño** cerrado

▷ creer que todo el monte es **orégano**

▷ criar a alg. en **estufa**

▷ criar a alg. entre algodones (▷ **algodón**)

▷ criar **callo**s

▷ criar la **víbora** en el seno

▷ criar **moho** (no ~)

▷ criar **moho** (no dejar ~ a alg./algo)

la criba sieve

▶ pasar algo por la criba (fig., fam.) to sift through s.th. (fig.), to go through/over s.th. with a fine-tooth comb (fig.), to scrutinize s.th. ◆ *Pasaron las solicitudes por la criba. They sifted through the applications carefully.*

▶ estar hecho una criba (fig.) to be riddled with holes (fig.), to be full of holes

la crisma chrism, holy oil

▶ la crisma (fam.) head

▶ romper la crisma a alg. (fig., fam.) to knock s.o.'s block off (fam., Br.E.), to bash s.o.'s head in, to smash s.o.'s face in

▶ romperse la crisma (fig., fam.) to break one's neck, to crack one's head open (fam.), to brain o.s. (fam.)

el cristal crystal, glass
▶ verlo todo con cristal ahumado (fig.) to take a gloomy view of everything

cristiano Christian
▶ en cristiano (fam.) in Spanish (lit.), in plain English or Spanish or German/etc. (fig.)
▶ hablar en cristiano to speak Spanish (lit.), to say/tell s.th. in plain English or Spanish or German/etc. (fig.), to express o.s. clearly, to make sense with what one says ◆ *Ahora estamos en España. ¡Habla en cristiano! We're in Spain now. Speak Spanish!* ◆ *¡Habla o dímelo en cristiano! Tell me or say it in plain English!*

Cristo; el cristo Christ, crucifix
▶ vivir/estar donde Cristo dio las tres voces o donde Cristo perdió la alpargata/la gorra (fam.) to live/be: at the back of beyond (fam.), in the middle of nowhere (fam.), [way] out in the sticks (fam.), [way] out in the boonies (sl., hum., Am.E.) or boondocks (fam., hum., Am.E.), at a godforsaken place (fam.) ◆ *Ya hace mucho tiempo que viven donde Cristo dio las tres voces. They've been living at the back of beyond for a long time now.*
▶ ¡Hasta verte, Cristo mío! (fam.) Cheers! (fam.) Down the hatch! (fam.) Bottoms up! (fam.)
▶ Cristo y la madre (fam.), todo cristo (pop.) everyone, everybody ▷ todo **bicho** viviente
▶ poner a alg. como un Cristo (fam.) to call s.o. all the names under the sun, to heap abuse on s.o.
▶ sentarle algo a alg. como a un santo cristo un par de pistolas (fam., hum.) s.th. doesn't suit s.o. at all, s.th. looks awful on s.o. ◆ *Esta camisa te sienta como a un santo cristo un par de pistolas. This shirt doesn't suit you at all. This shirt looks awful on you.*
▷ Cristo (armar la de **Dios** es ~)
▷ Cristo (¡Por los **clavos** de ~!)
▷ crudo (**comer**se a alg. ~)

la cruz cross
▶ besar la cruz (fig.) to bow to the inevitable (fig.)
▶ ser una cruz para alg. (fig.) to be a millstone [a]round s.o.'s neck (fig.)

▶ Cada uno lleva su cruz. (fig.) Each of us has his cross to bear. (fig.)
▶ meter la espada/etc. hasta la cruz en algo to drive the sword/etc. up to its handle into s.th.
▶ desde la cruz hasta la fecha from A to Z, from beginning to end
▶ ¡Cruz y raya! (fam.) Stop it! Enough of that! That's quite enough!

cuajado curdled, coagulated
▶ cuajado de (fig.) full of, covered with, studded (fig.) or dotted with (stars or flowers or animals/etc.), bristling with (mistakes/etc.), swarming or crawling with (insects/people), teeming with (mistakes or animals or people), thick or caked with (dirt/etc.), interlarded with (quotations/etc.) ◆ *El cielo está cuajado de estrellas. The sky is studded with stars.* ◆ *La playa está cuajada de turistas. The beach is teeming or crawling or swarming with tourists.* ◆ *La Pradera estaba cuajada de bisontes. The prairie was dotted with bison.* ◆ *El suelo está cuajado de hormigas. The ground is crawling with ants.* ◆ *Sus pantalones están cuajados de suciedad. His pants (Am.E.)/trousers (Br.E.) are thick with dirt or filth.* ◆ *Una corona cuajada de joyas. A crown covered with jewels.* ◆ *Tiene la frente cuajada de gotas de sudor. His forehead is dotted with beads of sweat.* ◆ *El texto está cuajado de faltas. The text is bristling with mistakes.*
▷ cuarenta (**cantar** las ~ a alg.)

la cuaresma Lent
▶ ser más largo que una cuaresma (fig.) to just go on and on, to take forever (fam.), not to half take a long time (fam., Br.E.) ◆ *La reunión fue más larga que una cuaresma. The meeting just went on and on.* ◆ *Esto sí que es más largo que una cuaresma. This is really taking forever. It doesn't half take a long time.*

el cuarto quarter, fourth part
▶ el cuarto (histórico) ancient coin
▶ [los] cuartos (fam.) (money): dough (sl., Am.E.), bread (sl.), sugar (sl.), brass/dosh/lolly (sl., Br.E.), wampum (sl., Am.E.)
▶ tener muchos cuartos to be rolling in money (fam.), to have pots of money (fam.), to be loaded (fam.), to be stinking rich (fam.)

► administrar/manejar los cuartos to hold the purse strings

► ¡estar sin un cuarto o no tener [ni] un cuarto (fam.) to be [absolutely/flat] broke (fam.), not to have a penny or a red cent to one's name, not to have two [brass] farthings to rub together (Br.E.), not to have a bean (sl., Br.E.), to be on the rocks (fam.)

► echar su cuarto a espadas to put in one's [own] two bits (fam.), to put in one's two cents[' worth] (fam., Am.E.), to put/stick/ shove one's oar in (fam.) ◆ *Siempre tiene que echar su cuarto a espadas. He's always got to stick his oar in. He always has to put in his own two bits or his two cents' worth.*

► dar un cuarto al pregonero (fig.) to tell the world [about it/s.th.], to tell all and sundry [about it/s.th.], to tell everyone one's private business ◆ *Yo que tú no daría un cuarto al pregonero. I would keep quiet about it if I were you.*

Cuba Cuba

► Más se perdió en Cuba. (hum., Esp.) It's not the end of the world. (fam.) It could be worse. It could have been worse. Worse things happen at sea. (fam., Br.E.) ◆ *Ayer me dieron el bote. Más se perdió en Cuba. I was fired yesterday. That's not the end of the world.*

la cuba wine cask

► estar hecho una cuba (fam.) to be [completely] sloshed (fam.), to be three sheets to or have three sheets in the wind (sl.) ▷ estar hecho un **cesto**

▷ cubero (a **ojo** de buen ~)

el cubo bucket

► llover a cubos (fig.) to rain in torrents, to come down in buckets/sheets, to rain cats and dogs, to be pouring [down or with rain], to be bucketing down (Br.E.), the floodgates of heaven open (fig.) ◆ *Ayer llovió a cubos. The rain or it came down in buckets yesterday. It was bucketing down yesterday. The floodgates of heaven opened yesterday.*

la cuchara spoon

► meter su cuchara (fam.) to chime in (fig.), to put in one's [own] two bits (fam.), to put in one's [two] pennyworth (fam., Br.E.), to put in one's two cents[' worth] (fam., Am.E.), to butt into or in on (a conversation/etc.) (fam.), to put/stick/shove one's oar in (a conversation/an affair/etc.) (fam.), to

get in on the act (fam.) ◆ *Siempre tiene que meter su cuchara. He's always got to stick his oar in. He always has to put in his own two bits or his two cents' worth.*

► meter algo a alg. con cuchara (fam.) to spoon-feed s.o. with s.th. (fig.), to have a hard job getting s.o. to understand s.th. ◆ *Se lo metimos con cuchara. We spoon-fed him with it. We had a hard job getting him to understand it.*

► un oficial de cuchara (fig., fam.) (in the military): an officer who has risen from the ranks, a ranker

el cucharón ladle

► servirse/despacharse con el cucharón (fig.) to make sure one gets the lion's share, to look after Number One (fam.)

el cuchillo knife

► remover el cuchillo en la llaga (fig.) to turn the knife in the wound (fig.), to rub salt in[to] the wound (fig.) ◆ *Juan se siente muy abatido porque ha perdido mucho dinero al póquer. Paco está removiendo el cuchillo en la llaga diciendo cuánto ganaron los otros jugadores. Juan is feeling miserable about losing a lot of money at poker, and Paco is rubbing salt into the wound by saying how much the other gamblers won.*

▷ cuchillo (en casa de **herrero**, ~ de palo)

el cuello neck

► apostar[se] el cuello a que ... (fam.) to bet s.o. anything he likes [that] . . . , you can bet your life (fam.) or your bottom dollar (fam., Am.E.) [that] . . . , it's dollars to doughnuts [that] . . . (fam., Am.E.) ◆ *Me apuesto el cuello a que no lo hacen. I bet you anything you like they don't do it. You can bet your life they won't do it.*

▷ cuello (estar con el **agua**/el **dogal**/la **soga** al ~)

▷ cuello (tener a alg. con el **agua** al ~)

la cuenta count[ing], bill

► La cuenta es cuenta. (prov.) Business is business. (prov.)

► la cuenta de la vieja (fig.) counting on one's fingers

► pasar la cuenta a alg. (fig.) to make s.o. pay for it (fig.)

► ajustar cuentas con alg. (fig.) to get even with s.o. (fig.), to settle a score with s.o. (fig.)

◆ *¡Ya ajustaré cuentas con él!* I'll get even with him!
▶ tener cuentas pendientes con alg. (fig.) to have accounts or an account to settle with s.o. (fig.), to have a bone to pick with s.o., to have a crow to pluck with s.o.
▶ dar cuenta de alg. (pop.) to bump s.o. off (sl.)
▶ dar en la cuenta de algo to get wise to s.th. (fam.)
▶ Ahora caigo en la cuenta o me doy cuenta. [Now] the penny has dropped. (hum., Br.E.)
▶ Por fin cayó en la cuenta o se dio cuenta. The penny finally dropped. (hum., Br.E.)
▶ Está con la cuenta. (fam.) She has the curse [of Eve]. (fam.) She has the rag on. (sl.) She's on the rag. (sl., Br.E.)
▷ cuenta (echar la ~ sin la **huéspeda**)
▷ cuenta ([hacer] **borrón** y ~ nueva)
▷ cuenta (hacer las ~s de la **lechera**)
▷ cuenta (la ~ de la **lechera**)

el cuentagarbanzos (hum.) miser, penny-pincher (fam.), skinflint (fam.), tightwad (fam., Am.E.), scrooge (fig., fam.)

el cuento story, tale
▶ el cuento chino (fam.) lie, hoax, canard, load of baloney (sl.), load of bull (sl., Am.E.), load of rubbish (fam., Br.E.), cock-and-bull story (fam.), tall story (fam.)
▶ el cuento de viejas (fam.) old wives' tale

la cuerda rope, cord, string, spring (in a watch)
▶ apretar la cuerda (fig.) to take a tougher line, to tighten up (fig.)
▶ aflojar la cuerda (fig.) to ease up
▶ estirar la cuerda (fig.) to go too far, to overdo it (fig.)
▶ bailar en la cuerda floja (fig.) to perform a skillful balancing act (fig.), to keep it with both sides/parties ◆ *El negociador bailó en la cuerda floja.* The negotiator performed a skillful balancing act.
▶ dar cuerda a alg. (fig., fam.) to encourage s.o. to talk, to let s.o. ride his hobby-horse (fig.) ◆ *Parece que le han dado cuerda a ella.* She just goes on and on. She wouldn't stop talking.
▶ tirar de la cuerda a alg. (fig.) (a) to get/keep s.o. under control, to hold s.o. back (b) to winkle everything out of s.o. (fig., Br.E.), to drag everything/it out of s.o. (fig., fam.) ◆

Siempre hay que tirarle de la cuerda. You always have to drag/winkle everything out of him. ◆ *No lograron tirarle de la cuerda.* They were unable to or couldn't drag it out of him.
▶ bajo cuerda (fig.), por debajo de cuerda (fig.) under the counter (fig.), by stealth, in an underhand way, on the side, behind the scenes ◆ *Lo pusieron a la sombra por haber vendido alcohol bajo cuerda.* He was clapped in jail for selling liquor under the counter.
▶ la cuerda no da más (fig.) to be on one's last legs (fam.)
▶ estar contra/en las cuerdas (fig.) to be on the ropes (fig.), to be up against it (fam.)
▶ aún quedar cuerda a alg. (fig.), aún tener cuerda (fig.) to have still some steam left (fig.) ◆ *Aún le queda cuerda.* He has still some steam left in him.
▶ La cuerda se rompe siempre por lo más delgado. (fig.) The weakest goes to the wall. (fig.)
▷ cuerda (no tener **cabo** ni ~)

cuerdo sane, wise
▶ De cuerdo y loco todos tenemos un poco. (prov.) We're all a little crazy in one way or another.

el cuerno horn (animal)
▶ irse al cuerno (fam.) to fall through/flat, to come to nothing, to break up, to be spoiled/ruined (party/etc.), to be/go on the rocks (marriage) (fam.) ◆ *Todos nuestros planes se fueron al cuerno.* All our plans fell through. ◆ *Su matrimonio se fue al cuerno.* Their marriage broke up. Their marriage went on the rocks. (fam.)
▶ mandar a alg. al cuerno (fam.) to tell s.o. to go to hell (fam.) ▷ mandar a alg. a freír **espárrago**s
▶ mandar algo al cuerno (fam.) to chuck s.th. (job/etc.) in/up (fam., Br.E.) ◆ *Voy a mandar mi trabajo al cuerno y a buscarme otro.* I'm going to chuck my job in and look for another one. ◆ *Lo mandé todo al cuerno. I chucked it all in. I chucked the whole thing.*
▶ oler a cuerno quemado (fam.) to be suspicious, to smell/sound fishy (fam.), to be a fishy business (fam.) ◆ *Esto me huele a cuerno quemado. I'm suspicious about/of this. This seems suspicious to me.* ◆ *Esta cosa huele a cuerno quemado. There's something fishy about this.* ◆ *Esta noticia me huele a*

cuerno quemado. This piece of news sounds fishy to me.

▶ romperse los cuernos (fam.) to work one's butt (Am.E.) or one's tail off (fam.)

▶ andar/verse en los cuernos del toro (fig.) to be in great danger, to be sitting on top of a volcano (fig.)

▶ meter/poner [los] cuernos a alg. (fig., fam.) to cuckold s.o., to cheat on s.o. (fam., Am.E.), to be unfaithful to s.o.

▶ poner a alg. en/por o levantar a alg. a/hasta los cuernos de la luna (fig.) to praise s.o. to the skies, to heap praise on s.o. (fig.), to sing s.o.'s praises ◆ *La puso en los cuernos de la luna. He praised her to the skies.*

▷ cuerno (coger el **toro** por los ~s)

el cuero wineskin, leather, skin

▶ el cuero (fam.) (a) drunkard (pej.), boozer (fam.), dipso (fam.), toper, lush (sl.), old soak (fam.) (b) football, soccer ball (Am.E.) (c) wallet

▶ estar hecho un cuero (fam.) to be [completely] sloshed (fam.), to be three sheets to or have three sheets in the wind (sl.) ▷ estar hecho un **cesto**

▶ en cueros [vivos] (fam.) stark naked (fam.), in the buff (fam., hum., Br.E.) ◆ *Fue a bañarse en cueros. He went skinny-dipping. (fam.)*

▶ dejar a alg. en cueros [vivos] (fig., fam.) to fleece (fig.) or relieve (hum.) or rob s.o. of everything, to bleed s.o. dry/white (fam.), to clean s.o. out (sl.)

el cuerpo body

▶ echarse algo al cuerpo (fam.) to have s.th. to eat/drink

▶ vivir a cuerpo de rey (fam.) to live like a king (fig.), to live the life of Riley (fig.), to live on the fat of the land

▶ tratar/atender a alg. a cuerpo de rey (fam.) to wine and dine s.o., to entertain s.o. lavishly, to lay on the works for s.o. (fam.), to treat s.o. like royalty, to lavish attentions on s.o.

▶ a cuerpo gentil (fig.) without [any] outside help, by o.s., single-handedly ◆ *Lo hice a cuerpo gentil. I did it without outside help.* ◆ *Salió adelante o hizo carrera a cuerpo gentil. He pulled himself up by his [own] bootstraps.*

▷ cuerpo (**hurtar**le el ~ a algo)

el cuesco stone (fruit)

▶ el cuesco (vulg.) loud fart (vulg.)

la cuesta slope

▶ hacérsele algo a alg. [muy] cuesta arriba [+ infinitivo] (fam.) to be an/[a real] uphill struggle [+ gerund] (fig.), to have a [very] hard time [+ gerund], to find s.th. [very] difficult/hard [to + infinitive], to go [totally] against the grain with s.o. [to + infinitive] ◆ *Se nos hace cuesta arriba trabajar con este frío. We find it difficult to work in this cold.* ◆ *Se me hace muy cuesta arriba colaborar con él. It goes totally against the grain with me to collaborate with him.*

▷ cuestión de **gabinete**

▷ cuidado (▷ **pecar**: nunca se peca por demasiado ~)

▷ culata (salirle a alg. el **tiro** por la ~)

▷ culebra (echar **sapos** y ~s)

el culo (pop.) arse (Br.E.) or ass (Am.E.) (vulg.), butt (fam., Am.E.), bum (fam., Br.E.), backside (fam.), bottom (fam.)

▶ un culo de vaso (fig., fam.) fake jewel or gem[stone]

▶ gafas de culo de vaso o de culo de botella (fig.) pebble [lens] glasses (fig., fam.)

▶ andar/ir con el culo a rastras (fig., fam.) to be on one's last legs (fam.), to be on one's beam-ends (fam., Br.E.), to be [flat] broke (fam.)

▶ romperse el culo (fam.) to work one's tail off (fam.) ▷ echar/sudar la **hiel**

▶ ser [un] culo de mal asiento (fam.) s.o. can't sit still for a minute, to be a restless soul, to never stay in one place for long, to keep changing one's job or one's flat or one's apartment (Am.E.)/etc.

▶ tomar/confundir el culo por las témporas (fig., pop.) to mix up everything (fig.), s.o. can't tell his arse (Br.E.) or ass (Am.E.) from his elbow (fam.)

▶ pasarse algo por el culo (vulg.) to piss on s.th. (fig., vulg.), not to give a shit about s.th. (vulg.) ◆ *Estos reglamentos me los paso por el culo. I don't give a shit about these regulations.*

▶ ¡Vete a tomar por culo! (vulg., Esp.) Piss off! (vulg.) Fuck off! (vulg.) Screw you! (vulg.) Get stuffed! (vulg.)

▶ mandar a alg. a tomar por culo (vulg., Esp.) to tell s.o. to piss/fuck off (vulg.), to tell s.o.

to get stuffed (vulg.) ◆ *La mandó a tomar por culo. He told her to piss off.*

▶ mandar algo a tomar por culo (vulg.) to chuck s.th. (job/etc.) in/up (fam., Br.E.) ◆ *Lo mandé todo a tomar por culo. I chucked it all in. I chucked the whole thing.*

▶ traer de culo a alg. (fam., Esp.) to drive s.o. nuts (fam.), to drive s.o. bananas (sl.), to drive s.o. round the bend (fam., Br.E.) ◆ *Trae de culo a todo el mundo. He drives everybody crazy.*

▶ a culo pajarero (adv., fam.) naked ◆ *La fulana fue arrestada porque hizo la calle a culo pajarero. The hooker was put under arrest because she walked the streets naked.*

▷ culo (dar una **patada** en el ~ a alg.)

▷ culo (llevar todavía el **cascarón** pegado al ~)

▷ culo (poner a alg. el ~ como un **tomate**)

▷ culpa (**ausente** sin ~, ni presente sin disculpa)

la cumbre top (of a mountain)

▶ sentirse en la cumbre (fig.) to feel one's oats (fam., Am.E.)

▷ curar (estar curado de **espanto**)

▷ curar (más vale **prevenir** que ~)

▷ curiosidad (**reventar** de ~)

CH

Las palabras que empiezan por "ch" aparecen bajo la letra C en su correspondiente orden alfabético.

Words beginning with "ch" are listed at the appropriate alphabetical position under letter C.

D

dabute[n], dabuti (adj. inv., adv., fam.)
great (fam.), super (fam.), fantastic[ally]
(fam.) ▷ cojonudo (a) ◆ *Lo pasamos*
dabuti. We had a great/fantastic or smashing
time.

daca (fam.)
▶ andar al daca y toma to argue back and
forth, to bicker

el dado die, dice
▶ estar como un dado to look very promising,
to go extremely well
▶ correr el dado (fig.) to be lucky

la danza dance
▶ meterse en o estar/andar metido en [la]
danza (fam.) to get/be caught up or mixed
up (fam.) or involved in it/in a business/in
a shady affair, to be in on it (fam.) ◆ *¿Quién*
está/anda metido en la danza? Who's mixed
up or involved in this [business]?
▷ danza (meter los **perros** en ~)

dar to give
▶ Donde las dan, las toman. (prov.) An eye
for an eye [and a tooth for a tooth]. (prov.)
Tit for tat.
▶ A quien dan no escoge. (prov.) Beggars
cannot or must not be choosers. (prov.)

dares y tomares
▶ andar en dares y tomares [con alg.] to
bicker/squabble [with s.o.], to argue back
and forth

deber to owe
▶ no quedar a deber nada (fig.) to give s.o.
tit for tat

decir to say
▶ Dime con quién andas y te diré quién eres.
You can judge a person by the company he
keeps.
▶ el qué dirán what people may/might/will
say ◆ *Me cago en el qué dirán. I don't give*
a shit what people might/will say.

la dedada thimbleful
▶ la dedada de miel (fig., fam.) crumb of
comfort

el dedillo little finger
▶ conocer algo al dedillo (fig.) to know s.th.
like the back of one's hand (fig.), to know
s.th. inside out (fam.) ◆ *Conozco la ciudad*
al dedillo. I know the city like the back of my
hand.
▶ saber algo al dedillo (fig.) to know s.th.
backwards and forwards, to have/know s.th.
off pat (Br.E.) or down pat, to have s.th. at
one's fingertips ◆ *Supo la lección al dedillo.*
He had the lesson off pat.

el dedo finger, toe
▶ el dedo veintiuno (pop.) penis, eleventh finger (fam.)
▶ darle a alg. un dedo y se toma hasta el
codo (fig.) give s.o. an inch and he'll take a
yard/mile
▶ poner el dedo en la llaga (fig.) to put one's
finger on the spot (fig.), to touch on a sore
spot/point (fig.), to hit a raw nerve (fig.) ◆
Perdóname, no fue mi intención ofenderte.
No me daba cuenta de que ponía el dedo
en la llaga. Sorry, I didn't mean to offend you.
I didn't realize that I was touching on a sore
spot.
▶ chuparse el dedo (fig., fam.) to come away
empty-handed, to end up with nothing
▶ no chuparse el dedo (fig., fam.) to be no
fool, to be nobody's fool, s.o. wasn't born
yesterday (fig.) ◆ *¡Pero yo no me chupo el*
dedo! Do you think I was born yesterday?!
▶ chuparse los dedos [por algo] (fig.) to drool
[over s.th.] (fig.), to smack one's lips [over
s.th.] (fig.), to rub one's hands (fig.)
▶ pillarse los dedos (fig.) to burn one's fingers
(fig.), to singe one's wings (fig.)
▶ meter a alg. los dedos en la boca to [skill-
fully] sound s.o. out (fig.), to try to get s.o.
to talk
▶ meter a alg. los dedos por los ojos (fig.) to
throw dust in s.o.'s eyes (fig.) ◆ *Me metió los*
dedos por los ojos y acabó vendiéndome el
reloj más caro. He threw dust in my eyes and
I ended up buying the most expensive watch.
▶ no tener dos dedos de frente (fig.) not to
be exactly a shining or leading light (fig.),
to be pretty dim (fam.)

▶ ir[se] a dedo (fam.), hacer dedo (fam.) to hitch/thumb a lift (Br.E.) or a ride (Am.E.) (fam.), to thumb it (fam.) ◆ *Nos fuimos a casa a dedo. We hitched/thumbed a lift home.*

▷ dedo (venir/sentar [a alg.] como **anillo** al ~)

▷ defecto (más vale pecar por **exceso** que por ~)

defender to defend

▶ defenderse bien (fam.) to keep one's end up, to hold one's own

▷ defender algo a **capa** y espada

defraudar defraud

▶ defraudar el sueño (fig.) to work through the night, not to get a wink of sleep all night

▷ dehesa (tener el **pelaje/pelo** de la ~)

▷ dejar (no dejes para **mañana** lo que puedes hacer hoy)

delante in front [of]

▶ no ponérsele a alg. nada por delante (fig.) to pursue one's goal (fig.) ruthlessly, not to let anything get in one's way ◆ *A ese tío no se le pone nada por delante. That fellow doesn't let anything get in his way.*

▷ delgado (**hilar** ~)

▷ delgado (la **cuerda** se rompe siempre por lo más ~)

▷ demasiado (**bueno** está lo bueno, pero no lo ~)

el demonio devil, demon

▶ estudiar con el demonio (fig.) to be a very shrewd operator (fam.)

▶ darse a todos los demonios (fam.) to swear horribly, to rant and rave (fam.), to eff and blind (fam., Br.E.), to let fly (fig.), to let rip (fam.)

▶ ponerse hecho un demonio (fam.) to go berserk (fam.) ▷ ponerse como un **basilisco**

▶ mandar a alg. al demonio (fam.) to tell s.o. to go to hell (fam.) ◆ *La mandó al demonio. He told her to go to hell.*

▶ saber a demonios (fam.) to taste awful/foul

▶ oler a demonios (fam.) to smell awful/foul

▶ ¿Qué demonios estás/etc. haciendo aquí? (fam.) What the devil/hell are you/etc. doing here? (fam.)

la depre (fam.) depression (dejection)

▶ tener la depre, estar con la depre to be down in the dumps (fam.), to be feeling down/low, to have the blues (fam.)

▷ derecho (**hecho** y ~)

▷ derecho como una **vela**

▷ desaparecer por [el] **escotillón**/por el **foro**

▷ desastre (▷ **abocar a**: estar abocado a un ~)

descabezar to behead

▶ descabezar un sueñecito (fam.) to have/take a nap, to have a snooze (fam.), to get a bit of or some shut-eye (fam.), to have/get forty winks (fam.), to catch some Zs (sl., Am.E.)

descacharrante (fam.) a [real] scream (fam.), hilariously funny, [as] funny as a barrel of monkeys (fam.) ◆ *Estuvo descacharrante. It was a scream. It was hilariously funny.* ◆ *Es descacharrante. He's/she's a real scream. He's/she's as funny as a barrel of monkeys.*

descojonarse (pop., Esp.) to piss (vulg.) or wet o.s. laughing, to kill o.s. laughing (fam.)

descolgarse to let o.s. down

▶ descolgarse con algo (fig., fam.) to blurt out s.th., to come out with s.th., to suddenly [and unexpectedly] say/announce s.th. ◆ *Se descolgó con esa estupidez. He blurted out that silly remark.* ◆ *A último momento se descolgaron con que no podían venir. At the last minute they said/announced that they couldn't come.*

▷ desconfiar hasta de su **sombra**

▷ descoser (no ~ la **boca**)

descosido unstitched

▶ como un descosido/una descosida (fam.) like a madman/madwoman (fig.), like a maniac (fig.), like mad, immoderately, wildly ◆ *reír[se] como un descosido to laugh one's head off (fam.), to split one's sides laughing (fam.)* ◆ *gritar como un descosido to shriek/shout one's head off (fam.), to scream/shout at the top of one's voice or lungs* ◆ *hablar como un descosido to talk a mile a minute (fam., Am.E.), to talk nineteen to the dozen (fam., Br.E.)* ◆ *estudiar/trabajar como un descosido to study/work like mad* ◆ *comer como un descosido to eat to excess, to stuff o.s.*

(fam.), *to feed/stuff one's face (fam.)*, *to pig out (fam., Am.E.)* ◆ *beber como un descosido to drink an awful lot, to drink like a fish* ◆ *gastar como un descosido to spend [one's] money wildly, to spend [one's] money like it's going out of style or like there was no tomorrow (fam.)* ◆ *repartir golpes como un descosido to lash out wildly, to lash out like a maniac*

descoyuntarse de risa (fam.) to kill o.s. laughing (fam.), to die laughing (fam.), to crack up (fam., Am.E.), to crease up (fam., Br.E.), to be in stitches (fam.)

▷ descubrir el **pastel**

▷ desdicha (ser el **rigor** de las ~s)

desembuchar (bird): to regurgitate

▶ desembuchar [algo] (fig., fam.) to spill the beans (sl.), to come clean [about s.th.] (fam.), to reveal or divulge s.th. (secret/etc.) ◆ *Es un secreto. No [lo] desembuches. It's a secret. Don't reveal it.*

▷ desempedrar la **calle**

▷ deseo (**abrasarse** en ~)

▷ desesperar (▷ **esperar**: quien espera, desespera)

▷ desfachatez (¡Qué **solemne** ~!)

desgañifarse (fam.) to shout one's head off (fam.)

desgañitarse (fam.) to shout one's head off (fam.)

desgargantarse (fam.) to shout/scream o.s. hoarse, to shout until one is [as] hoarse as a crow (fam.)

▷ desierto (**clamar/predicar** en el ~)

el desliz slip, slide

▶ el desliz (fig.) faux pas, slip (fig.), slip-up (fig.), gaffe, lapse, indiscretion ◆ *Tuvo un desliz. He made a faux pas.*

deslizar to slip, to slide

▶ deslizar algo a alg. (fig.) to slip s.o. s.th.

▶ deslizarse (fig.) to slip or sneak away/off

▶ deslizarse por [entre] las mallas (fig.) to find a loophole (fig.)

▷ desmañado (ser ~ a más no **poder**)

▷ desollar (aún falta/queda la **cola**/el **rabo** por ~)

▷ despedir a alg. con **caja**s destempladas

▷ despedirse a la francesa (▷ **francés**)

despotricar [contra] (fam.) to rant and rave (fam.), to rant/rave [about], to complain [about], to rail [against] ◆ *Despotricaron contra él. They railed against him.*

desternillarse de risa (fam.) to kill o.s. laughing (fam.), to die laughing (fam.), to crack up (fam., Am.E.), to crease up (fam., Br.E.), to be in stitches (fam.)

desvertebrar algo (red de espionaje/de narcotraficantes; grupo terrorista; pandilla/etc.) (fig.) (spy/drugtrafficking ring; terrorist group; gang/etc.): to break up, to smash ◆ *Ayer desvertebraron una red de espionaje. They smashed a spy ring yesterday.*

▷ devoción (no es **santo** de mi ~)

▷ día (▷ **pensar**: el ~ menos pensado)

▷ día (~s de **Maricastaña**)

▷ día (ser el **hombre** del ~)

▷ día (ser más **largo** que un ~ sin pan)

▷ día (ital ~ hará un **año**!)

▷ día (todo el **santo** ~)

▷ día (un ~ **puente**)

▷ día (un ~ **sí** y otro no)

▷ día (un ~ **sí** y otro también)

el diablo devil

▶ ¡El diablo sea sordo! (fam.) Touch wood! (Br.E.) Knock on wood! (Am.E.)

▶ el diablo predicador (fig., fam.) devil as a moralizer, wolf in sheep's clothing (fig.) ◆ *Ten cuidado con el director. Parece que no le cabe el corazón en el pecho, pero es un diablo predicador. Beware of the manager. He seems to be the very soul of kindness, but he's a wolf in sheep's clothing.*

▶ vivir/estar donde el diablo perdió el poncho (fam., América del Sur) to live/be at the back of beyond (fam.) ▷ vivir/estar donde **Cristo** dio las tres voces

▶ ¡Que el diablo cargue con él/etc.! (fam.) He/etc. can go to hell! (fam.)

▶ mandar a alg. al diablo (fam.) to tell s.o. to go to hell (fam.) or to go to blazes (sl.), to send s.o. packing (fig.) ◆ *Yo que tú la mandaría al diablo. If I were you, I'd send her packing.*

▶ mandar algo al diablo (fam.) to chuck s.th. (job/etc.) in/up (fam., Br.E.) ◆ *Voy a man-*

dar mi trabajo al diablo y a buscarme otro. *I'm going to chuck my job in and look for another one.* ◆ *Lo mandé todo al diablo.* I chucked it all in. I chucked the whole thing.

▶ como el/un diablo (fam.) ◆ *correr como el diablo to run like the devil (fam.), to run like crazy (fam.), to run like hell (sl.)* ◆ *Me dolió como un diablo. It hurt like the devil. (fam.) It hurt like hell. (sl.) It hurt like mad/crazy. (fam.)* ◆ *Esto pesa como el diablo. This is damn[ed] heavy. (fam.)*

▷ diablo (▷ **pintar**: no es tan feo el ~ como le pintan)
▷ diablo (▷ **pintar**: ¿Qué ~ te pintas tú/etc. por aquí?)
▷ diablo (encender una **vela** a Dios y otra al ~)
▷ diablo (ir como **alma** que se lleva el ~)
▷ diablo (no se puede servir a **Dios** y al ~)
▷ diablo (no servir a **Dios** ni al ~)
▷ diablo (ser capaz de contar los **pelo**s al ~)
▷ diablo (ser de la **piel** del ~)
▷ diablo (ser un **aborto** del ~)
▷ diablo (**tentar** al ~)
▷ diablo (vender el **alma** al ~)

el diamante diamond
▶ ser un diamante en bruto (fig.) to be a rough diamond (Br.E.) or a diamond in the rough (Am.E.) (fig.)

la diana bull's-eye
▶ dar en la diana, hacer diana (literal/fig.) to score a bull's-eye (literal/fig.), to hit the mark (fig.), to hit/strike home (fig.) ◆ *Diste en la diana con esa observación. You hit home with that remark.*

la dicha [good] luck
▶ Nunca es tarde si la dicha es buena. (prov.) Better late than never. (prov.)

el dicho saying, proverb
▶ Del dicho al hecho hay mucho trecho. (prov.) It's one thing to say s.th. and another to actually do it. There's many a slip 'twixt cup and lip. (prov.) Actions speak louder than words. (prov.)
▶ Dicho sin hecho no trae provecho. (prov.) It's one thing to say s.th. and another to actually do it. There's many a slip 'twixt cup and lip. (prov.) Actions speak louder than words. (prov.)

el diente tooth
▶ poner los dientes largos a alg. (fig., fam.) (a) to make s.o. jealous, to make s.o. green with envy (fig.) (b) to make s.o.'s mouth water (fam.)
▶ de dientes [para] afuera (fig., fam.) hypocritically, insincerely, lip service, (to support s.th./s.o.) in name only, not to be sincere [in what one says] ◆ *Habló o lo dijo de dientes para afuera. He said one thing and meant another. He didn't mean what he said. He wasn't sincere in what he said.* ◆ *Apoyaron nuestra idea de dientes afuera. They were [only] paying lip service to our idea.* ◆ *Lo prometieron de dientes para afuera. They made a promise they didn't intend to keep.* ◆ *No creemos que lo hayan sentido. Lo dijeron de dientes para afuera. We don't think they were sorry. They just said they were.*

▷ diente (a **caballo** regalado no hay que mirarle/no le mires el ~)
▷ diente (darse con un **canto** en los ~s)
▷ diente (**Dios** da pan a quien no tiene ~s)
▷ diente (**hincar** el ~ [a/en algo])
▷ diente (**ojo** por ojo, ~ por ~)

diestro right
▶ a diestro y siniestro, a diestra y siniestra at random, wildly; left, right and centre (Br.E.); left and right (Am.E.) ◆ *Repartió golpes a diestro y siniestro. He threw out punches left, right and centre. He lashed out wildly.* ◆ *Las bombas caían a diestra y siniestra. The bombs were falling left and right.*

▷ diez (▷ **cagar**: ¡Me cago en ~!)
▷ diez (▷ **último**: estar en las ~ de últimas)

la digestión digestion
▶ cortarse la digestión (fam.) to get an upset stomach
▶ ser de mala digestión (fig., fam.) to be unbearable, to be detestable

dimes y diretes (fam.) verbal exchange, bickering, squabbling
▶ andar en dimes y diretes [con alg.] to bicker/squabble [with s.o.], to argue back and forth

el dineral huge amount of money
▶ costar un dineral (fam.) to cost a tidy sum
▷ costar una **burrada**

el dinero money
- ▶ alzarse con el dinero (fig., fam.) to take the money and run, to make off with the money (fam.)
- ▶ cambiar el dinero (fig.) to sell at no profit
- ▶ Los dineros del sacristán cantando se vienen y cantando se van. (prov.) Easy come, easy go. (prov.)
- ▷ dinero (estar **mal/podrido** de ~)
- ▷ dinero (ganar ~ a **cántaros**/a **pote**)
- ▷ dinero (**hinchar**se de ~)
- ▷ Dinero (poderoso **caballero** es don ~)
- ▷ dinero (**rebosar** en ~)
- ▷ dinero (tener ~ a **punta** pala)
- ▷ dinero (tener ~ hasta la **pared** de enfrente)
- ▷ dinero (tener la **mar** de ~)

diñarla (pop.) to kick the bucket (fam.)
- ▷ **cascar**[la]

Dios God
- ▶ vivir como Dios en Francia to live the life of Riley (fig.), to live/be in clover (fig.)
- ▶ necesitar Dios y [su] ayuda (fam.) to face a very difficult task/job, to need a lot of help
- ▶ costar Dios y ayuda a alg. [+ infinitivo] (fig., fam.) to take s.o. a supreme effort [to + infinitive], to have a terrible job [to + infinitive] ◆ *Nos costó Dios y ayuda. It took us a supreme effort.* ◆ *Me costó Dios y ayuda hacerlo. I had a terrible job to do it.*
- ▶ para alg. no hay más Dios [ni Santa María] que ... (fam.) . . . means the world to s.o. ◆ *Para él no hay más Dios ni Santa María que el juego. Gambling means the world to him.* ◆ *Para ellos no hay más Dios que sus coches. Their cars mean the world to them.*
- ▶ armar la de Dios es Cristo (fam.) to raise hell (fam.), to raise Cain (fam.), to cause a tremendous fuss (fam.), to cause an almighty row (fam.)
- ▶ como Dios manda (fig.) properly, as is proper, well ◆ *[Com]pórtate como Dios manda. Behave properly/well.*
- ▶ Si Dios de esta me escapa, nunca me cubrirá de tal capa. (fam.) If God helps me out this time, I'll never get involved in such an affair or in this kind of thing again.
- ▶ Rogar a Dios por santos mas no por tantos. Enough is as good as a feast. (prov.)
- ▶ servir a Dios y al diablo (fam.) to run with the hare and hunt with the hounds (fig., Br.E.) ◆ *Ten cuidado al negociar con él.*

Sirve a Dios y al diablo. Be careful negotiating with him. He runs with the hare and hunts with the hounds.
- ▶ no servir a Dios ni al diablo (fam.) to be utterly useless, to be a dead loss (fig., fam.)
- ▶ No se puede servir a Dios y al diablo. (prov.) No man can serve two masters. (prov.)
- ▶ Dios los cría y ellos se juntan. (prov.) Birds of a feather flock together. (prov.)
- ▶ Dios da pan a quien no tiene dientes. (prov.) It's an unfair world. (prov.)
- ▶ A Dios rogando y con el mazo dando. (prov.) God helps those who help themselves. Put your trust in God and keep your powder dry. (prov.)
- ▷ Dios (▷ **bueno**: a la buena de ~)
- ▷ Dios (▷ **estornudar**: cada uno estornuda como ~ le ayuda)
- ▷ Dios (▷ **madrugar**: a quien madruga, ~ le ayuda)
- ▷ Dios (a la **gracia** de ~)
- ▷ Dios (del **agua** mansa líbreme ~ que de la brava me libro yo)
- ▷ Dios (el **hombre** propone y ~ dispone)
- ▷ Dios (encender una **vela** a ~ y otra al diablo)
- ▷ Dios (mi madre/etc., que ~ tenga en la **gloria**)
- ▷ Dios (ser más **feo** que pegar a ~)
- ▷ Dios (**tentar** a ~)

diquelar algo (pop.) to get s.th. (fam.), to twig s.th. (fam., Br.E.), to catch on to s.th. (fam.) ◆ *¿Lo has diquelado? Did you twig it? Have you caught on to it?*
- ▷ discordia (la **manzana** de la ~)
- ▷ disculpa (**ausente** sin culpa, ni presente sin ~)
- ▷ discusión (▷ **bizantino**: discusiones bizantinas)
- ▷ divertirse **horrores**
- ▷ divertirse la **mar**

la docena dozen
- ▶ la docena del fraile (fam.) baker's dozen, long dozen

el dogal hangman's noose
- ▶ estar con el dogal al cuello (fig.) to be in an awful or in a real jam/fix (fam.), to be in a very tight spot (fam.)
- ▷ dolor (apurar el **cáliz** de ~ hasta las heces)

▷ dómine (poner a alg. como **chupa** de ~)

▷ dorar la **bola** a alg.

▷ dorar la **píldora**

▷ dormir a **pierna** suelta

▷ dormir como un **bendito/ceporro/leño/lirón/tronco**

▷ dormir como una **peña**

▷ dormir con los **ojos** abiertos

▷ dormir de narices (▷ **nariz**)

▷ dormir la **mona**/el **vino**

▷ dormir sobre un lecho de **rosa**s ([no] ~)

▷ dormirse como un **ceporro/santo/tronco**

▷ dormirse sobre los/sus **laurel**es

dos two

▶ en un dos por tres (fam.) in next to no time, in a flash, in a jiffy (fam.), in a trice, in a tick (fam., Br.E.), before you can say Jack Robinson (fam.) ◆ *Todo pasó en un dos por tres. It was all over in a flash.* ◆ *Terminó el trabajo en un dos por tres. He finished the work in next to no time.*

el dragón dragon

▶ el dragón de seguridad (fig., fam.) chaperon[e]

▷ duda (sin **sombra** de ~)

el duende ghost, goblin

▶ tener duende (Andalucía) to have that certain s.th., to have charm/magic, to have a special appeal

el dueño owner, proprietor

▶ Cual el dueño, tal el perro. (prov.) Like master, like man. (prov.)

dulce; el dulce sweet; sweet, candy

▶ entre dulce y amargo (fig.) bittersweet (fig.)

▶ A nadie le amarga un dulce. (fig.) Something pleasant is always welcome. Nobody says no to a bit of luck.

▶ El mucho dulce empalaga. (prov.) Enough is as good as a feast. (prov.)

▷ duque (querer ir por **atún** y a ver al ~)

duro hard

▶ tomar las duras con las maduras (fam.) to take the rough with the smooth (fig.), to take the bitter with the sweet (fig.) ◆ *Mi vida ha tenido sus altibajos. Tenía que aprender a tomar las duras con las maduras. My life has had its ups and downs. I had to learn to take the bitter with the sweet.*

▷ duro (a quien cuida la **peseta** nunca le falta un ~)

▷ duro ([por] el **canto** de un ~)

E

el ecuador equator
▶ pasar el ecuador (fig.) (work/studies/etc.): to be halfway through [it], to have got half out of the way, to have got half over [and done] with

la edad age
▶ la edad ingrata (fam.)/burral (pop.)/del pavo (fam.) awkward age, green years (fig.)

el eje axis
▶ partir algo/a alg. por el eje (fig.) (a) to mess up s.th. (fig.), to muck up s.th. (fig.), to ruin s.th., to wreck s.th. (fig.), to cause s.o. a lot of trouble (b) to floor/stump s.o. (fam.), to knock s.o. for a loop (Am.E.) or for six (Br.E.) (fam.), to knock s.o. sideways (fam.) ◆ *Me partió por el eje. He caused a lot of trouble for me.* ◆ *Partieron nuestros planes por el eje. They mucked up or ruined our plans.* ◆ *Nos partió por el eje con su pregunta. We were completely floored by his question.*

el elefante elephant
▶ como un elefante en una cacharrería (fig., fam.) like a bull in a china-shop (fig.) ◆ *Se comportó como un elefante en una cacharrería. He was like a bull in a china-shop.*
▷ elefante (hacer de una **pulga** un ~)

el elemento element
▶ estar en su elemento (fig.) to be in one's element
▶ encontrarse en seguida en su elemento (fig.) to take to s.th. like a duck to water (fam.)

el embozo turndown (bedsheet)
▶ quitarse el embozo (fig.) to drop the mask (fig.), to show [o.s. in] one's true colors (fig.) ◆ *Nunca se sabe qué piensa ese tío. No se quita el embozo. You can never tell what that guy is thinking. He doesn't show his true colors.*

el embustero liar, cheat
▶ Antes se coge al embustero que al cojo. (prov.) Your lies will always catch up with you in the end.

empalmarse (pop.) to get a hard-on (vulg.), to get randy (fam.), to get horny (sl.)

empantanado swampy
▶ dejar empantanado a alg. (fig.) to leave s.o. in the lurch (fig.), to leave s.o. high and dry (fig.) ◆ *Me dejaron empantanado y tuve que hacerlo todo yo. They left me high and dry and I had to do it all myself.*

emperejilar[se] (fam.); **emperifollar[se]** (fam.) to titivate [o.s.] (fam., hum.), to spruce/doll (fam.) [o.s.] up, to get [all] dolled up (fam.) ◆ *Emperejilaron a sus hijos. They titivated their children.* ◆ *Nos emperifollamos. We spruced ourselves up. We got dolled up.*

empollar (fam.) to cram (fam.), to swot (fam., Br.E.), to bone up (fam.)
▶ empollar algo to cram s.th., to swot up [on] s.th., to mug up [on] s.th. (fam., Br.E.), to bone up on s.th.

emporrado (fam.) high (on drugs) (fam.), stoned (sl.), out of one's head (sl.) ◆ *Estaban todos emporrados cuando llegó la bofia. They were all high when the cops arrived.*

emporrarse (fam.) to smoke pot (sl.), to get high on grass (sl.)

▷ enamorado (estar ~ hasta los **tuétanos**)

el enchufado, la enchufada (fam.) person who has a cushy job (fam.)

enchufar a alg. (fig., fam.) to get s.o. a cushy job (fam., Br.E.), to get s.o. a post/etc. ◆ *Enchufó a su amigo en la empresa. He fixed/set his friend up with a cushy job in the firm. He pulled some strings (fig.) or used his influence to get his friend a post/job in the firm.*

enchufarse (fam.) to wangle o.s. a job/etc. (sl.), to get a post or a position or a cushy job (fam., Br.E.) (through contacts), to get advantages (through contacts)

el enchufe (fig., fam.) good connection, useful contact, drag (sl., Am.E.) ◆ *Hay que* *tener enchufes. You've got to have connections or contacts. You've got to have friends in high or in the right places.* ◆ *Tienen un enchufe en el ministerio. They've got a useful contact or a drag in the ministry. They can pull strings/wires at the ministry.*

▷ enchufe (**huérfano** de ~s)

el enchufillo (fam.) cushy job (fam., Br.E.)

el enchufismo (fam.) cronyism (fam.), string-pulling (fam.), wire-pulling (fam.), favoritism, old-boy network (Br.E.), the use of contacts to obtain advantages or favors

la encrucijada intersection, junction
▶ estar en la/una encrucijada (fig.) to be at the/a crossroads (fig.)

endiñar (pop.)
▶ endiñar algo a alg. to lumber s.o. with s.th. (fam., Br.E.), to land s.o. with s.th. (fam.), to saddle s.o. with s.th. (fam.), to unload s.th. on [to] s.o. (fam.) ◆ *Me endiñaron todo el trabajo y se fueron a la playa. They lumbered me with all the work and went off to the beach.* ◆ *Creo que nos va a endiñar la culpa de todo. I think he'll pin the blame for everything on us.*

endosar (fam.) ▷ endiñar

la ene name of the letter N/n
▶ la ene de palo (fam.) gallows ◆ *llevar a alg. a la ene de palo to send s.o. to the gallows*

▷ enfermedad (ser peor el **remedio** que la ~)

enfrascar to bottle
▶ enfrascarse en algo (fig.) to become absorbed or immersed in s.th. (fig.), to become wrapped up in s.th. (fam.), to become engrossed in s.th. (fig.), to immerse/bury o.s. in s.th. (fig.) ◆ *Se enfrascaron en su trabajo. They buried themselves in their work. They became wrapped up in their work.* ◆ *enfrascarse en un libro to become absorbed or engrossed in a book, to bury o.s. in a book*

▷ engañar a alg. como a un **chino**

▷ engreído (ser ~ como **gallo** de cortijo)

▷ enojo (tener **pronto**s de ~)

el ensalmo incantation
▶ [como] por ensalmo as if by magic ◆ *Desaparecieron como por ensalmo. As if by magic they disappeared.*

▷ ensayo (lanzar un **globo** de ~)

▷ enseñar (querer ~ el **padrenuestro** al cura)

entendederas (fam.) brains (fig.)
▶ ser corto de entendederas, tener malas entendederas to be slow on the uptake, to be pretty dim (fam.), to be a bit dense (fig.)

▷ entender (no ~ ni **papa/patata**)

el entendedor understanding person, expert
▶ Al buen entendedor, pocas palabras [le bastan]. (prov.) A word to the wise is sufficient/enough. (prov.) A nod is as good as a wink.

enterrar to bury
▶ enterrar a alg. (fig.) to outlive s.o.
▶ enterrarse en vida (fig.) to break off contact with people, to cut o.s. off from the world, to become a hermit/recluse (fig.)

▷ entierro (... **vela** en este ~)

▷ entierro (ser/sonar como **guitarra** en un ~)

las entrañas entrails
▶ echar las entrañas (fam.) to spew one's guts out (sl.), to throw up violently

▷ entrañas (**pedazo** de las ~)

el entresijo mesentery
▶ tener algo/alg. muchos entresijos (fig.) (a) s.th.: to have its snags (fig.), to have its ins and outs (fam.), to be very complicated (b) s.o.: to be a deep one (sl.)

▷ entusiasmo (**rebosar** de ~)

▷ envidia (estar **muerto** de ~)

▷ envidia (**morir**se/**perecer**se/**reventar** de ~)

▷ equivocarse (quien tiene **boca**, se equivoca)

erizado bristly
▶ erizado de problemas o de faltas o de citas/etc. (fig.) bristling with problems/mistakes/etc., interlarded with quotations/etc. (fig.) ◆ *El texto está erizado de faltas. The text is bristling with mistakes.*

▷ errar (▷ **hablar**: quien mucho habla, mucho yerra)

la erre name of the letter R/r
▶ erre que erre (adv., fig.) stubbornly, pigheadedly, doggedly ◆ *Insistió, erre que erre, en su opinión. He insisted stubbornly on his opinion.*

el erudito, la erudita scholar, learned person

▶ el erudito/la erudita a la violeta (fam.) pseudo-intellectual, soi-disant scholar/expert

▷ escándalo (un ~ **padre**)

escandaloso scandalous, shocking

▶ escandalosamente (fam.) extremely, dreadfully (fam.), scandalously, shockingly (fam.), terribly (fam.), incredibly (fig.), outrageously ◆ *Tiene ojos escandalosamente azules. His eyes are incredibly blue.* ◆ *Es escandalosamente guapa. She's outrageously good-looking.* ◆ *Precios escandalosamente altos. Scandalously or shockingly or outrageously high prices.* ◆ *Su discurso fue escandalosamente aburrido. His speech was terribly boring.*

▷ escapar el **bulto**
▷ escapar[se] por un **pelo**

escarmentar to learn one's lesson (fig.), to learn the hard way ◆ *Salió escarmentado de la experiencia. He learned his lesson.*

▶ escarmentar a alg. to punish s.o. severely (in order to deter), to teach s.o. a lesson (fig.)
▶ escarmentar en cabeza ajena to learn by someone else's mistakes
▶ Nadie escarmienta en cabeza ajena. One only learns from one's own mistakes.
▶ De los escarmentados nacen los avisados. (prov.) Once bitten twice shy. (prov.)

escoñar algo (pop.) to screw s.th. up (sl.), to cock s.th. up (sl., Br.E.), to ball or balls (Br.E.) s.th. up (sl.), to mess s.th. up (fig., fam.), to botch s.th. [up] (fig.), to bugger s.th. up (sl.)

▶ escoñarse (pop.) to fail, to fall through/flat, to come to nothing, to break up (marriage/etc.), to be spoiled/ruined (party/etc.) ◆ *El plan se escoñó. The plan fell through.*

▷ escorpión (tener una **lengua** de ~)

la escotilla hatch

▶ atrancar las escotillas (fig.) to batten down the hatches (fig.)

el escotillón trapdoor

▶ aparecer por [el] escotillón (fig., fam.) to suddenly turn up (fig.)
▶ desaparecer por [el] escotillón (fig., fam.) to disappear without trace, to vanish into thin air

escribir to write

▶ estar escrito (fig.) to be meant to be, to be [written] in the stars, to be fated to + infinitive, to be destined [by fate] to + infinitive ◆ *Estaba escrito que no iba a verla nunca más. He was destined never to meet her again.*
▶ tener algo escrito en la frente/cara (fig.) to have s.th. written all over one's face (fig.) ◆ *Tiene la envidia escrita en la frente. Envy is written all over his face.*
▶ Sobre esto no hay nada escrito. (fig.) This is open to argument. One can argue about this.

▷ escribir [algo] a vuela **pluma**

escupir to spit

▶ ser escupido el padre/etc. (fam.) to be the spitting image or the spit and image of one's father/etc. (fam.) ◆ *Es escupida la madre. She's the spitting image of her mother.*
▶ escupir al cielo (fig.) to cut off one's nose to spite one's face

espachurrarse (fam.) to go wrong ◆ *Todo se espachurró. Everything went wrong.*

la espada sword

▶ estar entre la espada y la pared (fig.) to be [caught] between the devil and the deep blue sea (fam.), to be [caught] between a rock and a hard place (fam.), to be on the horns of a dilemma, to be in a difficult situation
▶ poner a alg. entre la espada y la pared (fig.) to drive s.o. into a corner (fig.)

▷ espada (más fuerte es la **pluma** que la ~)
▷ espada (una película/etc. de **capa** y ~)

la espalda back

▶ donde la espalda pierde su honesto nombre (fam.) posterior (euph.), behind (fam., euph.), backside (fam.), bottom (fam.), butt (fam., Am.E.), bum (fam., Br.E.)
▶ tener anchas/buenas espaldas (fig.) to have a thick skin (fig.), to be thick-skinned (fig.) ◆ *Lo que dijeron los críticos le dejó completamente frío. Tiene muy anchas espaldas. What the critics said ran off him like water off a duck's back. He has a very thick skin.*

▷ espalda (echarse algo entre **pecho** y ~)
▷ espalda (quedarse con algo entre **pecho** y ~)
▷ espalda (tener el **santo** de ~s)
▷ espalda (tener más **cara** que ~)

el espanto fright, amazement, astonishment
▶ estar curado de espanto (fig., fam.) not to get scared easily, to have seen plenty worse, nothing surprises s.o. any more, to be hardened or callous (fig.) ◆ *A nosotros no nos parece tan malo, será que ya estamos curados de espanto. It doesn't seem so bad to us. We're [probably] pretty hardened. We've seen plenty worse.*

el espárrago asparagus
▶ el espárrago (fig., fam.) (person): beanpole (fig., fam., hum.)
▶ mandar a alg. a freír espárragos (fam.) to tell s.o. to go fry an egg or to go [and] jump in a lake or to go fly a kite (Am.E.) or to go climb a tree or to go [and] take a running jump (fam.), to tell s.o. where to go (fam.), to tell s.o. to go to hell (fam.), to tell s.o. to get lost (fam.) ◆ *La mandó a freír espárragos. He told her to get lost.*
▶ ¡Vete a freír espárragos! (fam.) Go fry an egg! (fam.) Go fly a kite! (fam., Am.E.) Go climb a tree! (fam.) Go jump in a lake! (fam.) Go take a running jump! (fam.) Take a hike! (fam., Am.E.) Go to hell! (fam.) Get lost! (fam.)

la espátula spatula
▶ estar como una o hecho una espátula (fig., fam.) to be as thin as a rail (fam., Am.E.), to be as thin as a rake (fam., Br.E.)

el espejo mirror
▶ mirarse en alg. como en un espejo (fig.) to look up to s.o. as a model, to idolize s.o., to adore s.o.

▷ esperanza (**huérfano** de ~)
▷ esperanza (**rayo** de ~)

esperar to wait, to hope, to expect
▶ Quien espera, desespera. (prov.) A watched kettle/pot never boils. (prov.) The waiting gets you down.
▶ esperar sentado (fam.) to be waiting in vain, to wait till the cows come home (fam.), to whistle for s.th. (fam.) ◆ *¡Ya puedes esperar sentado! You've got a long wait coming! You're in for a long wait! You can/may whistle for it! (fam.)* ◆ *Si quiere más dinero, va a tener que esperar sentado. If he wants more money, he can wait till the cows come home or he can whistle for it.*

el espinazo backbone
▶ doblar el espinazo (fig., fam.) to have no backbone (fig.), to knuckle under, to eat crow (fam., Am.E.), to eat humble pie (fig.) ◆ *Defendió sus derechos. No dobló el espinazo He stood up for his rights. He didn't knuckle under. He didn't eat humble pie.*

la espita spigot (Am.E.), tap (Br.E.)
▶ la espita (fig., fam.) drunkard (pej.), boozer (fam.), dipso (fam.), toper, lush (sl.), old soak (fam.)

la esponja sponge
▶ arrojar/tirar la esponja (fig.) to throw in the sponge/towel (fig.), to pick up one's marbles (fig., fam., Am.E.), to give up ◆ *Probemos al menos una vez más. Es demasiado prematuro tirar la esponja. Let's try at least one more time. It's too early/soon to throw in the sponge.*
▶ pasar la esponja sobre algo (fig.) to forget all about s.th.
▶ la esponja (fig.) sponger (fam.), scrounger (fam.)
▶ la esponja (fig., fam., hum.) drunkard (pej.), boozer (fam.), dipso (fam.), toper, lush (sl.), old soak (fam.)
▶ beber como una esponja (fig.) to be a heavy drinker, to drink like a fish

la espuela spur
▶ calzar la[s] espuela[s] a alg. (fig.) to knight s.o.

la espuma foam
▶ crecer como la espuma (fig.) (a) (plant): to shoot up (fig., fam.) (b) (business/etc.): to flourish (fig.) or prosper greatly/fast/rapidly, to flourish like the green bay tree (fig.) ◆ *La empresa está creciendo como la espuma. The company is prospering greatly/rapidly.*

el espumarajo foam, froth
▶ echar espumarajos (fig.) to foam at the mouth (fig.), to foam/splutter with rage (fig.)

el esqueleto skeleton
▶ menear/mover el esqueleto (fig., fam., hum.) to shake one's stuff (fig., fam.), to shake a leg/hoof (fam., hum.), to dance
▷ esquilar (ir por **lana** y volver esquilado)

el esquilador sheepshearer
▶ ponerse como el chico del esquilador (fig., fam.) to feed/stuff one's face (fam.) ▷ comer o mascar a dos **carrillos**

esquilmar to harvest
▶ dejar esquilmado a alg. (fig., fam.) to suck s.o. dry (fig.), to bleed s.o. dry/white (fam.), to clean s.o. out (sl.), to fleece (fig.) or relieve (hum.) or rob s.o. of everything

la esquina corner
▶ estar de/en esquina con alg. (fig.) to have fallen out with s.o. (fam.)

esquinar to form a corner with
▶ esquinarse con alg. (fig.) to fall out with s.o. (fam.)
▶ estar esquinado con alg. (fig.) to have fallen out with s.o. (fam.)

el esquinazo (fam.) sharp corner
▶ dar [el] esquinazo (fig.) to disappear around the corner
▶ dar [el] esquinazo a alg. (fig.) (a) to shake s.o. (pursuer) off (fig.), to give s.o. (pursuer) the slip (fig.) (b) to stand s.o. up (fam.)

la estaca stake, post
▶ plantar la estaca (fam.) to take or have (Br.E.) a shit/crap (vulg.), to shit (vulg.)

la estacada fence
▶ dejar a alg. en la estacada (fig.) to leave s.o. in the lurch (fig.), to leave s.o. high and dry (fig.) ◆ Como me dejaron en la estacada, tuve que hacerlo todo yo. Since they left me high and dry or in the lurch, I had to do it all myself.
▶ quedarse en la estacada (fig.) to be left in the lurch (fig.), to be left high and dry (fig.)

el estallido bang, explosion
▶ Está para dar un estallido. (fig., fam.) The situation is extremely tense. The situation is about to explode. (fig.)

estar to be [located]
▶ Ni están todos los que son, ni son todos los que están. (prov.) Appearances can be or are deceptive. (prov.) You can't always go by appearances. Things aren't always what they seem.

la estatua statue
▶ merecer una estatua (fig.) to have rendered outstanding services

▶ quedarse hecho una estatua (fig.) to be/stand rooted to the spot (fig.) ◆ Se quedaba hecho una estatua cuando oía la serpiente de cascabel. She stood rooted to the spot when she heard the rattlesnake.

el estirón (fam.) jerk
▶ dar un estirón (fig., fam.) to grow fast/quickly, to shoot up (fig., fam.) ◆ Su hijo dio un estirón. His son shot up.

el estómago stomach
▶ el sello del estómago (fam.) canapé, small [but robust] hors d'oeuvre or starter
▶ tener buen estómago (fig.) to have a strong stomach (fig.), to have a thick skin (fig.), to be thick-skinned (fig.) ◆ Lo que dijeron los críticos le dejó completamente frío. Tiene muy buen estómago. What the critics said ran off him like water off a duck's back. He has a very strong stomach.
▶ echarse algo al estómago (fam.) to put s.th. away (fam.), to polish s.th. off (fam.), to eat s.th. right up ◆ Me eché un sándwich al estómago. I put a sandwich away.
▶ tener a alg. sentado en el estómago (fig., fam.) s.o. can't stomach s.o. (fam.) ▷ tener a alg. **atravesado** ◆ Tengo a ese tío sentado en el estómago. I can't stomach that guy.
▶ revolver el estómago a alg. (fig.) to turn s.o.'s stomach (fig.), to make s.o.'s stomach turn (fig), to make s.o. sick to his stomach (fig.) ◆ La campaña electoral me revuelve el estómago. The election campaign turns my stomach. ◆ Al verlo, se me revolvió el estómago. My stomach turned at that sight. ◆ Se me revolvió el estómago. It made my stomach turn. It made me or I was sick to my stomach.

estornudar to sneeze
▶ Cada uno estornuda como Dios le ayuda. (fig.) (sense): Everybody does their best.

la estrella star
▶ tratar de contar las estrellas (fig.) to attempt the impossible
▶ Unos nacen con estrella y otros nacen estrellados. (prov., hum.) Some are born under a lucky star and some are born seeing stars. (hum.) Fortune smiles on some but not on others.
▶ ver las estrellas (fig.) (pain): to see stars (fig.) ◆ Vi las estrellas cuando di con mi

cabeza contra la puerta. I saw stars when I bumped my head against the door.

▷ estrella (**campar** con su ~)

▷ estrella (no hay nada **nuevo** bajo las ~s)

el estrellato stardom

▶ lanzar a alg. al estrellato to help s.o. to rise to stardom, to make s.o. a star

el estribo stirrup

▶ estar con un pie en el estribo (fig.) (a) to have one foot in the grave (fig.), to be at death's door (b) to be on the point of leaving, to be about to leave ◆ *Mi abuelo tiene 92 años. Está con un pie en el estribo. My grandfather is 92 years old. He has one foot in the grave.* ◆ *No pudimos hablar con él. Estuvo con un pie en el estribo cuando nos encontramos con él. We couldn't talk to him. He was about to leave when we met him.*

▶ estar/andar sobre los estribos (fig.) to watch/look out, to be on one's guard

▶ perder los estribos (fig.) to lose one's temper/head, to lose/blow one's cool (fam.)., to lose one's rag (fam., Br.E.), to fly off the handle (fam.), to get hot under the collar (fam.)

▶ tomar[se] la del estribo (fam.) to have one for the road (fam.) ◆ *Vamos a tomar la del estribo. ¡Barman! Let's have one for the road. Bartender!*

el estropajo dishcloth

▶ poner a alg. como un estropajo (fig.) to shower insults on s.o., to lambast[e] s.o. (fig.)

▷ estudiar como un **descosido**

▷ estudiar con el **demonio**

la estufa stove

▶ criar a alg. en estufa (fig.) to pamper/coddle s.o. [in his childhood], to mollycoddle s.o. [in his childhood] (fam., pej.) ◆ *Juan fue criado en estufa. Juan had a pampered childhood.*

▷ etapa (**quemar** ~s)

Eva Eve

▶ las hijas de Eva (fig., fam.) daughters of Eve (fig.), women

▶ en traje de Eva (fig., hum.) in one's birthday suit (hum.), in the raw (fam.), in the nude, in the buff (fam., hum., Br.E.), starkers (fam., hum., Br.E.), stark naked (fam.), naked ◆ *Cuando era joven iba a nadar en traje de Eva. When she was young, she [often] went swimming in her birthday suit.*

el evangelio gospel

▶ lo que dice alg. es el evangelio (fig., fam.) (a) to speak the gospel truth (fig.) (b) what s.o. says is accepted or taken as gospel truth (fig.) ◆ *Lo que dice es el evangelio. He speaks the gospel truth.* ◆ *Para ella todo lo que digan es el evangelio. She takes/accepts everything they say as gospel truth.*

▶ hacer evangelio de algo (fig.) to make s.th. into a dogma

▶ ser tan seguro como el evangelio (fig., fam.) to be absolutely certain, to be dead certain (fam.), to be a dead cert (fam., Br.E.), to be a sure-fire . . . (fam.) ◆ *Es cosa tan segura como el evangelio. It's a dead cert.*

el exceso excess

▶ pecar por exceso (fig.) to overdo it (fig.) ◆ *Al hacer la estimación pecaron por exceso. They were overambitious in their estimate.* ◆ *Peca por exceso de confianza [en sí mismo]. She's overconfident. She errs on the side of overconfidence.* ◆ *Más vale pecar por exceso que por defecto. It's better to have/bring/etc. too much/many than too little/few. It's better to do too much rather than too little.*

▷ éxito **padre**

el expediente expedient

▶ cubrir el expediente (fig.) to do just enough to get by

explicaderas (fam.)

▶ tener buenas explicaderas to be good at explaining things [away], to have the gift of [the] gab (fam.)

F

la faena piece of work
▶ hacer una faena a alg. (fam.) to play a dirty/nasty trick on s.o. (fig.)

▷ falda (el **gobierno** de ~s)

el faldón coattail
▶ agarrarse a los faldones de alg. (fig.) to cling to s.o. (fig.), to put o.s. under s.o.'s protection, to take refuge with s.o. (fig.)

▷ falta (dar **quince** y ~ a alg.)
▷ falta (hacer tanta ~ como los **perro**s en misa)

faltar to be lacking
▶ ¡No faltaba/faltaría más! (a) Don't mention it! You're welcome! (b) [But] of course! Naturally! Certainly! (c) That's all I/we need[ed]! That'd be really great! (iron.). Certainly not! No way! (fam.)

▷ faltar (no ~ un **cabello** a algo)

la fama fame
▶ Unos cardan la lana y otros tienen/llevan/cobran la fama. (prov.) Some do [all] the work and others get [all] the credit. One does [all] the work and the other [one] gets [all] the credit.

el fango mud, mire
▶ arrastrar algo/a alg. por el fango (fig.) to run s.th./s.o. down (fam.), to drag s.o.'s name through the mud/mire (fig.)

el farol lantern
▶ echarse/marcarse un farol (fam.) to swank (fam.), to brag, to shoot a line (fam.)

el farolero lamplighter
▶ el farolero, la farolera (fig., fam.) braggart, hot-air artist (fam.), bigmouth (fam.), loudmouth (fam.)

el farolillo Chinese lantern
▶ ser el farolillo rojo (fig.) to be the back marker (Br.E.); (sports): to be the tailender (fam.), to be the bottom-of-the-table team, to be the team in last place

fas (fam.)
▶ por fas o por nefas rightly or wrongly, by hook or by crook, at any cost, at all costs ◆ *Por fas o por nefas tenemos que terminarlo hoy. We must finish it today at all costs.*

fastidiar to annoy, to bore
▶ ¡La hemos fastidiado! (fam., Esp.) Now we're in a right/fine mess! (fig.) Now we've blown it! (fam.)

▷ fecha (desde la **cruz** hasta la ~)

el felpudo coconut mat[ting], doormat
▶ el felpudo (pop., Esp.) bush (woman's pubic hair) (sl.)

feo ugly
▶ tocarle a alg. bailar con la más fea (fig.) to get the dirty/short end of the stick (fam.), to draw/get the short straw (fam.) ◆ *Siempre nos toca bailar con la más fea. We always draw the short straw.*
▶ ponerse algo feo to begin to look bad, to get ugly/nasty (fig.), to get unpleasant, not to like the look of s.th. ◆ *Las cosas se están poniendo feas. Things are beginning to look bad or are getting nasty.* ◆ *Esto se está poniendo feo. This is getting ugly. I don't like the look of this.*
▶ ser más feo que Picio o que el pecado o que un susto a medianoche o que pegar a Dios o que pegar a la madre (fam.) to be as ugly as sin/hell (fam.), to be incredibly ugly

▷ feo (▷ **acabar**: ser el acabóse de ~)
▷ feo (ser ~ a más no **poder**)
▷ feo (ser más ~ que **Carracuca**)

la férula cane, rod
▶ estar bajo la férula de alg. (fig.) to be under s.o.'s thumb (fig.), to be under s.o.'s rule or domination, to be tied to s.o.'s apron strings (fig.)

la fiera wild animal
▶ entrar en el cubil de la fiera (fig.) to beard the lion in his den (fig.)

▶ ser una fiera para/en algo (fig., fam.) to be a demon/fiend for s.th. (fig.) ◆ *Es una fiera para el trabajo. He's a demon for work.*

la fiesta party, celebration

▶ aguar la fiesta to spoil the fun/party, to be a wet blanket (fig., fam.), to be a spoilsport, to be a killjoy ◆ *Se aguó la fiesta. All the fun was spoiled.* ◆ *Él es muy divertido, pero su hermano siempre nos agua la fiesta. He's great fun, but his brother always spoils our party.* ◆ *La noticia del accidente aéreo nos aguó la fiesta a todos. The news of the plane crash put a damper on us all. (fig.)*

▶ no estar para fiestas (fig.) to be in no mood for fun/jokes, to be in a bad/foul mood

▶ hacer fiestas a alg./a un animal to caress s.o., to fondle s.o., to play up to s.o., to butter s.o. up (fam.), to soft-soap s.o. (fam.), to fawn on s.o. (fig.), to rub up against s.o.'s legs (dog/cat), to ruffle a dog's/cat's fur/neck ◆ *Hizo fiestas a ella. He played up to her.* ◆ *Mientras él leía, ella hacía fiestas al gato. While he was reading, she was ruffling the cat's neck.* ◆ *Su perro nos hizo fiestas. His dog fawned on us or rubbed up against our legs.*

▶ hacer fiestas a alg. (fig.) (guest/etc.): to make a great fuss of/over ◆ *Siempre hacen fiestas a sus huéspedes. They always make a great fuss of their guests.*

▶ dejar la fiesta en paz (s.th. negative): not to bring up any more, not to talk about any more

▷ figura (**genio** y ~ hasta la sepultura)

el filo edge

▶ ser un arma de dos filos (fig.) to be a double-edged sword (fig.)

▶ estar en el filo de la navaja (fig.) to be on a razor's edge (fig.), to be balanced on a knife-edge (fig.) ◆ *El futuro de la firma está en el filo de la navaja. The firm's future is balanced on a knife-edge.* ◆ *Su vida estaba en el filo de la navaja. His/her life was on a razor's edge.*

▷ fin (al ~ y al **cabo**)

▷ fino (**hilar** muy ~)

finolis (fam.)

▶ meterse a finolis to act/play the elegant/refined man or woman

la firma signature

▶ echar una firma (pop.) to relieve o.s.

▷ flaco (las **vacas** flacas)

flamenco Flemish

▶ ponerse flamenco (fig., fam., Esp.) to get cheeky (fam., Br.E.), to get fresh/sassy (fam., Am.E.), to get impertinent or impudent, to get importunate or pushy (fam.)

▷ flan (**temblar** como un ~)

▷ Flandes (poder pasar por las **pica**s de ~)

▷ Flandes (poner una **pica** en ~)

▷ flaqueza (sacar **fuerza**s de ~)

la flauta flute

▶ sonar la flauta [por casualidad] to be a fluke, to be sheer luck, to be a lucky coincidence or guess ◆ *Sonó la flauta por casualidad. It was sheer luck. It was a lucky coincidence.* ◆ *¡Y sonó la flauta por casualidad! It's nice to be lucky!* ◆ *Si me suena la flauta, ... If I get a bit of luck, . . .* ◆ *¿Sabías de verdad la contestación o es que sonó la flauta por casualidad? Did you really know the answer or was it a lucky guess?*

▷ flauta (hoy le da a alg. por **pito**s y mañana por ~s)

▷ flauta (cuando no es por **pito**s, es por ~s)

▷ flauta (cuando **pito**s ~s, cuando ~s pitos)

el flechazo arrow shot

▶ ser un flechazo (fig., fam.) to be love at first sight ◆ *Con ellos fue un flechazo. With them it was love at first sight.*

la flor flower, blossom, surface

▶ ir de flor en flor (fig.) to play the field (fam.), to flit from one man/woman to another

▶ estar en la flor de la vida (fig.) to be in the prime of life

▶ caer en flor (fig.) to die [too] early

▶ segar en flor (fig.) to nip s.th. in the bud (fig.), to scotch a rumor (fig.) ◆ *Había problemas en el vestuario, pero el entrenador segó en flor. There was trouble in the locker room, but the coach nipped it in the bud.* ◆ *Es un rumor malicioso. Tenemos que segar en flor. It's a vicious rumor. We have to scotch it.*

▶ la flor y nata (fig.) cream (fig.), pick, crème de la crème (fam.), best ◆ *La flor y nata de la sociedad. The cream/pick of society.* ◆ *Separaron o se llevaron a la flor y nata de*

los alumnos. They creamed/skimmed off the best or brightest (fig.) pupils.
▶ echar flores a alg. to pay s.o. [pretty] compliments
▶ echarse/tirarse flores to blow one's own horn (Am.E.) or trumpet (fig.)
▶ pasársela en flores (fig.) s.o.'s life is a bed of roses (fig.), not to have any problems or worries ◆ *Se la pasaba siempre en flores. His life was always a bed of roses.*
▶ a flor de on a level with, close to ◆ *a flor de tierra at ground level, close to the ground* ◆ *a flor de agua at water level, close to the surface of the water*
▶ a flor de piel ◆ *tener la sensibilidad a flor de piel to be very easily hurt (fig.) or offended* ◆ *tener los nervios a flor de piel to be all on edge, s.o.'s nerves are all on edge, to be ready to explode (fig.)* ◆ *tener el mal genio a flor de piel to be quick to lose one's temper, to tend to flare up very quickly (fig.), to tend to fly into a temper or off the handle (fam.)*
▶ dar en la flor de + infinitivo to fall into the [bad] habit of + gerund ◆ *Han dado en la flor de llegar tarde. They've got into the habit of being late.*
▷ flor (estar como **abeja** en ~)
▷ flor (ser la ~ de la **canela**)

el floreo compliments, meaningless or insubstantial phrases/talk
▶ andar en o andarse con floreos (fam.) (a) to turn on the old charm (fam.) (b) to beat about/around the bush (fig.), to make excuses, to prevaricate ◆ *Le gusta andar en floreos. He likes to turn on the old charm.* ◆ *No se anduvo con floreos. He didn't beat about the bush.*

flote
▶ ponerse/salir a flote (fig.) to get out of a jam/fix (fam.), to get on one's feet again (fig.), to get back on one's feet (fig.)
▶ poner/sacar algo/a alg. a flote (fig.) to get or put s.th./s.o. back on its/his feet (fig.), to get s.th./s.o. going [again] (fig.) ◆ *Tratan de poner la empresa a flote. They're trying to get the company back on its feet.* ◆ *Sacaron el país/la economía a flote. They got the country back on its feet. They got the economy going again.* ◆ *Puso a ella a flote. He put her back on her feet.*
▶ mantenerse a flote (fig.) to keep/stay afloat (fig.), to keep going (fig.), to keep the wolf

from the door (fig.), to keep one's head above water (fig.) ◆ *Puede mantenerse a flote. He can stay afloat.* ◆ *La empresa se mantiene a flote. The firm is managing to stay afloat or to keep going.*

la foca seal
▶ la foca (fam.) fatty (fam.), fatso (fam.), rolypoly (fam.), fat woman

follar to blow [on] with bellows
▶ follar [a alg.] (pop., vulg.) to have a screw (vulg.), to have a shag (vulg., Br.E.), to get one's rocks off (sl., Am.E.), to get a/one's leg over (sl., Br.E.), to have it off/away [with s.o.] (sl., Br.E.), to screw/fuck [s.o.] (vulg.), to shag [s.o.] (vulg., Br.E.) ▷ **calzar[se]** a alg.
▶ follarse (pop.) to fart silently (vulg.), to let one off silently (fam.)

el follón noiseless firework (rocket)
▶ el follón (pop.) silent fart (vulg.)

el fondo bottom, depth
▶ emplearse a fondo to do one's utmost, to do one's level best, to do everything in one's power, to leave no stone unturned (fig.), to do a very thorough job

el foro back of the stage
▶ desaparecer por el foro (fam.) to sneak/slip away [unnoticed]

el forofo (fam.) fan (fam.), enthusiast, buff (fam.)
▶ ser forofo de algo/alg. to be a real fan of s.th./s.o., to be crazy or mad (Br.E.) or wild about s.th./s.o. (fam.) ◆ *Es forofo de fútbol. He's a football or soccer (Am.E.) fan.*

forrado lined
▶ estar forrado (fig., fam.) to be loaded (fam.), to be well heeled (fam.), to be rolling in it (fam.)
▷ fortuna (**sonreír**le a alg. la ~)
▷ foto (**tirar** una ~)
▷ fracaso (▷ **abocar a**: estar abocado al ~)
▷ fraile (haber sido **cocinero** antes que ~)
▷ fraile (la **docena** del ~)

francés French
▶ despedirse a la francesa (fam.) to take French leave (Br.E.), to sneak away
▷ Francia (vivir como **Dios** en ~)

▷ frazada (no estirar los **pies** más de lo que da la ~)

el fregado scrubbing, washing-up
► meterse en un fregado (fig., fam.) to get involved in a nasty (fig.) affair/business
► dar un fregado a alg. (fig., fam.) to give s.o. a dressing-down (fam.), to give s.o. a wigging (fam., Br.E.)
▷ fregado (servir lo mismo para un **barrido** que para un ~)

freír to fry
► freír a alg. (fig., pop.) to blow s.o. away (sl.), to waste s.o. (sl.) ▷ **cargar**se a alg. (a)
► freír a alg. a tiros/balazos (fig.) to riddle s.o. with bullets (fig.) ◆ *Frieron al traidor a tiros. They riddled the traitor with bullets.*
► freír a alg. a preguntas (fam.) to bombard s.o. with questions (fig.)
► Al freír será el reír. (prov.) He who laughs last laughs longest/loudest. (prov.) The proof of the pudding is in the eating. (prov.)
▷ freír **buñuelos** (mandar a alg. a ~)
▷ freír **buñuelos** (¡Vete a ~!)
▷ freír **espárragos** (mandar a alg. a ~)
▷ freír **espárragos** (¡Vete a ~!)

el frenillo frenulum
► no tener frenillo en la lengua (fig., fam.) not to mince one's words (fig.), to speak one's mind ◆ *Habla en plata. No tiene frenillo en la lengua. He speaks bluntly. He doesn't mince his words.*

el freno bit, bridle, break
► morder/tascar el freno (fig.) to suppress/stifle one's anger, to restrain o.s., to hold back (fig.)
► correr sin freno (fig.) to live/lead a dissolute life
► ¡Echa el freno, Ma[g]daleno! (fam., Esp.) Put a sock in it! (sl., Br.E.) Cool it! (fam.) Keep your hair on! (fam., Br.E.) Keep your shirt on! (fam.) Hold your horses! (fam.)

la frente forehead, front
► adornar la frente a alg. (fam.) to cuckold s.o.
► acometer algo de frente (fig.) to take the bull by the horns (fig.), to grapple boldly with s.th. (fig.) ◆ *Nos vimos enfrentados a un grave problema. Lo acometimos de frente y lo solucionamos. We were faced with a serious problem. We took the bull by the horns and solved it.*
► con el sudor de su/etc. frente (fig., fam.) by the sweat of his/etc. brow ◆ *Me ganaba los garbanzos con el sudor de mi frente. I earned my bread and butter (fam.) by the sweat of my brow.*
▷ frente (▷ **escribir**: tener algo escrito en la ~)

la fresca cool part of the day, fresh/cool air
► soltar/decir cuatro frescas a alg. (fig.) to give s.o. a piece of one's mind (fam.), to come down on s.o. like a ton of bricks (fam.)

fresco fresh, cool
► ¡Estamos frescos! (fig., fam.) That's all we need[ed]! Now we're in a right/fine mess! (fig.) Now we've blown it! (fam.)
► dejar fresco a alg. (fig.) to take s.o. for a ride (fam.), to disappoint s.o.
► quedarse fresco (fig., fam.) to be disappointed, to be taken for a ride (fam.), to be taken in (fam.)
► decir algo tan fresco to say s.th. as cool as you please, to say s.th. quite boldly/brazenly ◆ *Me lo dijo tan fresco. She said it to me as cool as you please or quite brazenly.*
► quedarse/estar tan fresco to remain/be totally unperturbed ▷ quedarse/estar tan **campante** ◆ *Se quedó tan fresco ante su hostilidad. He was totally unperturbed by her hostility.* ◆ *Ella estaba muerta de miedo pero él estaba tan fresco. She was scared to death but he was as cool as a cucumber or he was totally unperturbed.*
▷ fresco (ser más ~ que una **lechuga**)

el fríjol bean
► ganarse los fríjoles (fam.) to earn/make a living, to earn one's daily bread (fam.), to earn one's bread and butter (fam.), to earn one's crust (fam.)

frío cold
► quedarse frío (fig.) (a) to be completely shocked or taken aback (fig.), to have a very unpleasant or nasty (fig.) surprise (b) to get cold feet (fig.) (c) to kick the bucket (fam.) ▷ **cascar**[la] ◆ *Cuando lo oí me quedé frío. I was completely taken aback when I heard it.*
▷ frío (▷ **cojón**: hacer un ~ de cojones)
▷ frío (▷ **pelar**: hacer un ~ que pela)
▷ frío (hacer un ~ de **perros**)

la friolera (fam.) trifle, mere nothing ◆ *Nos cobró la friolera de 5,000 francos. (iron.) He only charged us 5,000 francs. (iron.)*

frito fried

▶ estar frito de algo/alg. (fig., fam.) to be fed up to the back teeth with s.th./s.o. (fam.), to be cheesed off with s.th./s.o. (fam., Br.E.) ▷ estar hasta [más allá de] la **coronilla** de algo

▶ tener/traer frito a alg. (fam.) to drive s.o. spare (fam., Br.E.), to get on s.o.'s nerves or wick (Br.E.) (fam.) ◆ *Ese tío me tiene/trae frito. That guy drives me spare.*

▶ dejar frito a alg. (fig.) to waste s.o. (sl.) ▷ **freír** a alg.

▶ quedarse frito (fig.) to kick the bucket (fam.) ▷ **cascar**[la]

el fu hiss (cat)

▶ no ser ni fu ni fa (fam.) (a) to be neither one thing nor the other, to be neither fish nor fowl (fig.) (b) to be fair to middling (fam.), to be so-so (fam.) ◆ *Uno de los tres hermanos es listo, otro tonto y el otro [no es] ni fu ni fa. One of the three brothers is bright, one's stupid and the third's neither one thing nor the other.* ◆ *El espectáculo no fue ni fu ni fa. The show was so-so.*

el fuego fire

▶ Donde fuego se hace, humo sale. (prov.) Where there's smoke, there's fire. (prov.) There's no smoke without fire. (prov.)

▶ huir del fuego y caer en las brasas to jump out of the frying pan into the fire ◆ *Atracó un banco para pagar sus deudas. Huyó del fuego y cayó en las brasas. He held up a bank to pay [off] his debts. He jumped out of the frying pan into the fire.*

▶ estar entre dos fuegos (fig.) to be [caught] between the devil and the deep blue sea (fam.), to be [caught] between a rock and a hard place (fam.), to be on the horns of a dilemma, to be in a difficult situation

▶ jugar con el fuego (fig.) to play with fire (fig.) ◆ *Corrió un gran riesgo. Parece que le gusta jugar con el fuego. He took a big risk. He seems to like playing with fire.*

▶ echar leña al fuego (fig.), apagar el fuego con aceite (fig.) to add fuel to the fire/flames (fig.) ◆ *Estaba hecho un basilisco. Su hermano echó leña al fuego cuando empezó a reírse de él. He was seething with rage. His*

brother added fuel to the fire when he started to laugh at him.

▶ matar a alg. a fuego lento (fig.) to make life hell for s.o. (fam.)

▶ echar fuego por los ojos (fam.) s.o.'s eyes blaze or are ablaze with anger/indignation

▶ a fuego y hierro/sangre with fire and sword, with great violence

▶ poner algo a fuego y sangre to lay s.th. (a place/etc.) waste ◆ *Los invasores pusieron la cuidad a fuego y sangre. The invaders laid the town waste.*

▷ fuego (▷ **cebar**: se ceba el ~)

▷ fuego (sacar las **castañas** del ~ a alg.)

la fuente spring

▶ beber en buena fuente o en fuente fidedigna (fig.) to have s.th. from a good/reliable source (fig.) ◆ *La información no es falsa. Bebimos en fuente fidedigna. The information is not false. We have it from a reliable source.*

▷ fuente (tanto va el **cántaro** a la ~, que al fin se rompe)

▷ fuente (tomar la **corriente** desde la ~)

▷ fuerte (la **ley** del más ~)

la fuerza strength, vigor, power

▶ írsele a alg. la fuerza por la boca to be all talk [and no action] (fam.), to be all mouth [and no trousers] (fam., Br.E.) ◆ *Siempre se le va la fuerza por la boca. He's always all talk and no action.*

▶ sacar fuerzas de flaqueza (a) to make a virtue of necessity (b) to take heart, to pluck up (fig.) or screw up or summon up [one's] courage, to bring o.s. to do s.th., to screw o.s. up to do s.th. ◆ *Saqué fuerzas de flaqueza y se lo dije. I plucked up my courage and told [it to] her.*

el ful (pop.) (marijuana): hash/pot (fam.), grass/shit/weed (sl.), tea (sl., Am.E.)

la fulana (fam.) prostitute, whore, tart (sl.), hooker (sl., Am.E.), floozie (fam.), slut (fam.), slag (fam., pej., Br.E.)

fumar to smoke

▶ fumarse algo (fam.) (a) not to go/come to s.th., to stay away or be absent from s.th., not to show up at s.th. (fam.), to skip s.th. (fam.), to skive off s.th. (fam., Br.E.), to play truant, to play hooky (fam., Am.E.) (b) (money/etc.): to dissipate, to blow (sl.), to squander ◆ *Se fumó la clase. He skived off class/school. He didn't go to class/school. He played truant/hooky.* ◆ *Se fumó sus ahorros. He squandered/blew all [of] his savings.*

▷ fumar (no ~ más que **papel**)
▷ fumar como un **carretero**/una **chimenea**

la función show, spectacle

▶ habrá función (fig., fam.) there will be trouble, there will be a row (fam.) ◆ *¡Vamos! Si no, habrá función en casa. Come on, let's go!,* otherwise there will be trouble at home or otherwise we'll get a [good] scolding at home.

▷ funerala (tener un **ojo** a la ~)

fusilar to shoot, to execute by firing squad

▶ fusilar algo (fig., fam.) to plagiarize s.th., to lift s.th. (fig.), to crib s.th. (fig.), to pirate s.th., to copy s.th. illegally ◆ *El profesor le echó la gran bronca a él porque fusiló la redacción. He was hauled over the coals by the professor because he cribbed the essay.*

G

el gabinete cabinet
▶ plantear la cuestión de gabinete (fig.) to propose a vote of confidence

▷ Gaceta (**mentir** más que la ~)

▷ gafas de **culo** de botella/vaso

▷ gaita (**tamboril** por ~)

el gaitero bagpiper
▶ En casa del gaitero todos son danzantes. (prov.) The apple doesn't fall far from the tree. (prov.) Like father like son. (prov.) Like mother like daughter. (prov.)

la gala full/best dress
▶ llevarse la gala to carry off the palm (fig.), to take the cake (fig.), to triumph, to win
▶ ser la gala de (fig.) to be the best of, to be the pride [and joy] of ◆ *La prestigiosa universidad es la gala de la ciudad.* The prestigious university is the pride of the city.
▶ vestir sus primeras galas de mujer (fig.) (society): to make one's début/debut

▷ galápago (tener más **conchas** que un ~)

▷ galera (**azote**s y ~s)

el galgo greyhound
▶ De casta le viene al galgo ser rabilargo. (prov.) Like father like son. (prov.) Like mother like daughter. (prov.) A chip off the old block. The apple doesn't fall far from the tree. (prov.)
▶ ¡Échale un galgo! (fig., fam.) You can kiss it/that goodby[e]! (fam.) You can write that off! (fig.) You won't see that/him/her again! ◆ *Aún no me ha devuelto el dinero. ¡Échale un galgo!* He hasn't paid me back the money yet. You can kiss it goodbye!
▶ ¡Vete a espulgar un galgo! (fam.) Go to hell! (fam.) Go to blazes! (sl.)

▷ galgo (hacer la **rosca** [de ~])

la gallina hen
▶ el/la gallina (fam.) chicken (fam.), coward, sissy (fam.), s.o. who couldn't fight his way out of a paper bag (fam.) ◆ *Es un gallina. He's a chicken. He couldn't fight his way out of a paper bag. (fam.)*

▶ matar la gallina de los huevos de oro (fig.) to kill the goose that lays the golden eggs (fig.), to saw off one's own branch (fig.)
▶ acostarse con las gallinas to go to bed early
▶ levantarse con las gallinas to get up at the crack of dawn, to rise with the lark
▶ cantar la gallina (pop.) to climb down (fig., fam.), to come down a peg or two (fam.)
▶ estar/sentirse como gallina en corral ajeno to be/feel like a fish out of water, to feel very uneasy, to feel very/wholly out of place, to feel like a square peg in a round hole ◆ *Aquí estoy como gallina en corral ajeno. I'm like a fish out of water here.* ◆ *En la universidad nos sentíamos como gallina en corral ajeno. At the university we felt like a square peg in a round hole.*
▶ ¡Hasta que/cuando meen las gallinas! (pop.) Pigs might fly! (iron.) Till hell freezes over! (fam.) If I never see you again it will be too soon! (hum.)
▶ cuando meen las gallinas (fig., fam.) when pigs learn to fly (iron.), in a month of Sundays (fam.), in a coon's age (sl., Am.E.), never ◆ *Pagarán cuando meen las gallinas. They'll pay when pigs learn to fly. They'll never pay.* ◆ *A este paso terminarán el trabajo cuando meen las gallinas. At this rate they'll never finish the job or they won't finish the job in a month of Sundays.*

▷ gallina (ponerle o ponérsele a alg. [la] **carne** de ~)

▷ gallina (ponerse como una ~ **clueca**)

el gallito (fig., iron.) cock of the roost/walk (often pej.), tough guy (iron.)

el gallo rooster, cock
▶ dar un gallo para recibir un caballo (fig.) to set/throw a sprat to catch a mackerel or a whale (fig., Br.E.)
▶ ser engreído como gallo de cortijo to be as proud as a peacock
▶ alzar/levantar el gallo (fig., fam.) to act the big shot (fam.), to put on airs, to brag
▶ andar de gallo (fig.) to make a night of it, to be a night owl (fam.)
▶ bajar el gallo a alg. (fig.) to take s.o. down a peg or two (fig.)

▶ pelar gallo (fam., Méjico) (a) to make tracks (sl.) (b) to kick the bucket (fam.) ▷ **cascar[la]**

▶ matarle a alg. el gallo [en la mano] (fam., Méjico/etc.) to shut s.o. up (fam.)

▶ en menos que canta un gallo in next to no time, in a flash, in a jiffy (fam.), in a trice, in a tick (fam., Br.E.), in the twinkling of an eye (fig.), before you can say Jack Robinson (fam.) ◆ *Lo hizo en menos que canta un gallo. He did it in a jiffy.* ◆ *Solucionó el problema en menos que canta un gallo. He solved the problem in the twinkling of an eye.*

▶ otro gallo cantaría o otro gallo me/etc. cantara si ... it would be quite a different matter if . . . , things would be very different if . . . ◆ *Otro gallo cantaría si hubiesen elegido presidente al otro candidato. Things would be very different if the other candidate had been elected president.*

▶ [Aquí] hay gallo tapado. (fam., América Latina) There's s.th. fishy [here]. (fam.) There's s.th. fishy going on [here]. (fam.) I/we [can] smell a rat [here]. (fam.) ◆ *Aquí hay gallo tapado. There is s.th. fishy going on here. I smell a rat here.*

▶ entre gallos y medianoche (fam.) in the middle of the night, in the or at (Br.E.) dead of night ◆ *Me telefonearon entre gallos y medianoche. They called/phoned me in the middle of the night or in the dead of night.*

▷ gallo (al **canto** del ~)
▷ gallo (haber **arroz** y ~ muerto)
▷ gallo (**pata**s/**rabo**s de ~)

la gana desire, wish

▶ Me entraban unas ganas locas de llorar. (fam.) I felt a terrible urge to cry.

▶ Donde hay gana, hay maña. (prov.) Where there's a will, there's a way. (prov.)

el ganado [live]stock

▶ el ganado (fig., pop.) entire herd (fig., pej.), all those present, all the people, a whole lot/bunch [of them] (fam.)

la ganancia gain, profit

▶ andar de ganancia (fig.) to be lucky, to be in luck, to be on a lucky streak, to have a streak/run of [good] luck

▶ no arrendarle la ganancia a alg. (fig.) s.o. wouldn't like to be in s.o.'s shoes (fig.), s.o. wouldn't like to swap places with s.o., not to envy s.o. ◆ *No te arriendo la ganancia. I* wouldn't like to be in your shoes. I don't envy you.

ganar to gain, to earn

▶ ganar a alg. para algo to win s.o. over to s.th.

▶ ganar a alg. en algo to excel/beat/outdo s.o. at/in s.th. ◆ *No hay quien le gane en ajedrez. There's nobody who can beat him at chess.*

▶ ganar la batalla (fig.) to win the battle (fig.)

▶ ganarle la batalla a alg. (fig.) to get the better of s.o.

▶ llevar/tener [todas] las de ganar (a) to hold all the aces or trumps (fig.) (b) to have a streak/run of [good] luck

▶ ganarse la confianza de alg. to win s.o.'s trust

▶ ganarse la voluntad de alg. (a) to win s.o.'s favor (b) to win s.o. over

▶ ganársela (pop.) to get a hiding/thrashing (fam.), to get it (fam.), to cop it (Br.E.) ◆ *Como se enteren, te la vas a ganar. If they find out, you're going to get/cop it.*

▶ Lo ganado por lo gastado. (prov.) Easy come, easy go. (prov.)

▷ ganar algo a **pulso**
▷ ganar **terreno**
▷ ganar una **miseria**
▷ ganarse los **fríjol**es/los **garbanzo**s/el **pan**/ el **puchero**/la **vida**

la gandaya (fam.)

▶ ir por o correr la gandaya to laze around, to bum around (fam.), to loaf around

el gansarón young goose

▶ el gansarón (fig., fam.) (person): beanpole (fig., fam., hum.)

▷ ganso (hablar con **boca** de ~)

▷ garabato (muchas **mano**s en un plato hacen mucho ~)

el garañón stud jackass

▶ el garañón (fig., pop.) [randy] goat (fig., fam.), lecher

el garbanzo chickpea

▶ ser el garbanzo negro [de la familia] to be the black sheep [of the family] (fig.) ◆ *Su hijo es el garbanzo negro de la familia. Siempre se mete en problemas con la policía. Her son is the black sheep of the family. He always runs into trouble with the police.*

▶ contar los garbanzos (fig.) to be very stingy/miserly

▶ ganarse los garbanzos (fam.) to earn/make a living, to earn one's daily bread (fam.), to earn one's bread and butter (fam.), to earn one's crust (fam.)

▷ garbanzo (en toda/cualquier **tierra** de ~s)

la garganta throat, gullet

▶ tener una garganta de oro (fig.) to have a voice of gold (fig.), to have an excellent singing voice

▶ tener un nudo en la garganta (fig.), hacérsele a alg. un nudo en la garganta (fig.) to have/get/feel a lump in one's throat (fig.), to choke up (fam.), to choke [with] (fig.), to be choked [with] (fig.) ◆ *Teníamos un nudo en la garganta [de la emoción]. We choked with emotion. We choked up.* ◆ *Tenía un nudo en la garganta [de temor]. I was choked with fear.* ◆ *Se le hizo un nudo en la garganta. He got/felt a lump in his throat. He choked up.*

la gárgara gargle, gargling

▶ mandar a alg. a hacer gárgaras (fig., fam.) to tell s.o. where to get off (fam., Br.E.)

▷ mandar a alg. a freír **espárrago**s

el garguero; el gargüero (pop.) throat, gullet

▶ mojarse el garguero to wet one's whistle (hum.), to hoist one (sl., Am.E.), to belt one down (fam., Am.E.), to have a drink

el garlito fish trap

▶ caer en el garlito (fig.) to fall/walk into the trap (fig.)

▶ coger a alg. en el garlito (fig.) to catch s.o. (at it or doing s.th.), to catch s.o. red-handed, to catch s.o. in the act ◆ *Anoche nos entraron ladrones. Afortunadamente pasó la policía y los cogió en el garlito. Our house was broken into last night. Fortunately the police drove by and caught the burglars in the act.*

la garra claw

▶ gente de la garra (fam.) good-for-nothings who live from/by or who make their living from/by stealing/robbing

▶ tener garra (fig., fam.) to have zip (fam.), to have bite (fig.) ◆ *La obra no tiene garra. The play lacks bite or has no bite to it.* ◆ *Esta música tiene garra. This music has zip.* ◆ *El partido no tenía garra. There was no fight-*

ing spirit in the game/match. (Br.E.) ◆ *No tiene garra. It's boring.*

▶ echar la garra a algo (fig., fam.) to grab s.th., to seize s.th.

▶ echar la garra a alg. (fig., fam.) to seize s.o., to arrest s.o. ◆ *La policía echó la garra a los ladrones. The police arrested the thieves.*

▶ caer en las garras de alg. (fig., fam.) to fall into s.o.'s clutches (fig.)

▶ sacar a alg. de las garras de alg. (fig., fam.) to free s.o. from s.o.'s clutches (fig.) ◆ *La sacó de las garras de su suegra. He freed her from the clutches of her mother-in-law.*

garrafal (adj., fig., fam.) huge, enormous, colossal (fam.), gigantic, monumental ◆ *Incurrieron en una falta garrafal. They made a huge mistake.*

gastar to spend

▶ gastarlas (fam.) ◆ *ya saber cómo las gasta alg.* to know exactly what kind of [a] person s.o. is or how s.o. carries on (fam.) or how nasty (fig.) s.o. can be/get ◆ *Ya sé cómo las gasta él. I know exactly what kind of a person he is.* ◆ *Todos sabemos cómo las gastan. We all know how they carry on. We all know how nasty they can get.* ◆ *Así las gasto yo. That's the way I am.*

el gasto expense, expenditure

▶ Es lo que hace el gasto. (fig., fam.) That's the point. That's the important thing.

▷ gata (de día **beata**, de noche ~)

el gato cat, tomcat

▶ llevar[se] el gato al agua (fam.) to take the cake (fig.), to pull off s.th. difficult ◆ *A ver quién se lleva el gato al agua. Let's see who takes the cake.*

▶ ser para el o pal gato (fig., fam.) to be for the birds (fam.), not to know why one bothered ◆ *No valía la pena. Fue para el gato. It wasn't worthwhile. I don't know why I bothered.* ◆ *¿Qué sacaste tú de eso? Fue pal gato. What was in it for you? It was for the birds.*

▶ jugar al gato y al ratón con alg. (fig.) to play cat and mouse with s.o. (fig.), to play a cat-and-mouse game with s.o.

▶ dar a alg. gato por liebre (fam.) to con s.o. (sl.), to swindle s.o., to take s.o. in (fam.), to sell s.o. a bill of goods (fam., Am.E.), to sell s.o. a goldbrick (fam., Am.E.), to pull the wool over s.o.'s eyes (fam.)

▶ lavarse a lo gato (fam.) to make do with a lick and a promise (fam.), to give o.s. a cat-lick (fam.)

▶ correr como gato por ascuas (fam.) to run [away] like crazy/mad (Br.E.) (to escape from danger) (fam.)

▶ [Aquí] hay gato encerrado. (fam.) There's s.th. fishy [here]. (fam.) There's s.th. fishy going on [here]. (fam.) I/we [can] smell a rat [here]. (fam.) ◆ *Aquí hay gato encerrado.* There's s.th. fishy going on here. I smell a rat here.

▶ No hay/había ni un gato. (fam.) There isn't/wasn't a living or blessed soul here/there. There isn't/wasn't a sod here/there. (sl., Br.E.)

▶ cuatro gatos (fig., fam.) ◆ *Ayer asistieron/ vinieron cuatro gatos.* Only a few people par-ticipated/came yesterday. ◆ *[Allí] hay cuatro gatos.* There's only a handful of people [there]. ◆ *En aquel pueblo no quedan más que cuatro gatos.* There's hardly a soul left in that village.

▶ Hasta los gatos quieren zapatos. Even the most ordinary people aim high or are am-bitious.

▶ De noche todos los gatos son pardos. (prov.) At night all cats are gray/grey. (prov.) No one will notice [in the dark].

▶ El gato escaldado del agua fría huye. (prov.) Once bitten twice shy. (prov.)

▶ Cuando el gato duerme, bailan los ratones. (prov.) When the cat's away, the mice will play. (prov.)

▶ Cuando el gato va a sus devociones, bailan los ratones. (prov.) When the cat's away, the mice will play. (prov.)

▷ gato (buscar cinco/tres **pies** al ~)
▷ gato (poner el **cascabel** al ~)
▷ gato (tener siete **vidas** [como los ~s])

el gaznate throat, gullet
▶ mojar/refrescar el gaznate (pop.) to wet one's whistle (hum.), to hoist one (sl., Am.E.), to belt one down (fam., Am.E.), to have a drink

la gazuza (fam.) ravenous hunger

▷ generoso (**pecar** de ~)

el genio disposition, nature, genius
▶ no poder con el genio (fam.) to [tend to] fly off the handle (fam.)

▶ tener el genio vivo to be quick-tempered, to be hot-tempered, to be short-tempered

▶ tener mal/mucho genio to have a bad/vio-lent temper, to have a or be on a very short fuse (fam.)

▶ llevar el genio a alg. (fam.) to give s.o. his head (fam.), to humor s.o., to give in to s.o., not to dare to contradict s.o. ◆ *Nos seguía la corriente para que nos callásemos o para que no protestásemos.* He was humoring us to try to keep us quiet.

▶ Genio y figura hasta la sepultura. (prov.) A leopard never changes or cannot change its spots. (prov.)

▷ genio (tener el mal ~ a **flor** de piel)

la gente people
▶ gente de pelo/pelusa (fam.) well-to-do people, well-heeled people (fam.)

▶ gente gorda (fam.) upper-class people, up-per crust (fam.), bigwigs (fam.), big cheeses (sl.), big shots (fam.), fat cats (fam.), big wheels (fam.)

▶ conocer a su gente (fig.) to know who one is dealing with

▶ hacer gente (fig., fam.) to attract or draw (fig.) a crowd ◆ *El orador hizo gente.* The speaker attracted/drew a crowd.

▷ gente (ande yo **caliente** y ríase la ~)
▷ gente (ser la **comidilla** de la ~)
▷ gente de alto **copete**/de la **garra**

el gesto gesture, expression on one's face
▶ afirmar con el gesto to nod one's agreement, to nod in agreement, to agree with a nod

▶ hacer gestos to make or pull (Br.E.) faces

gil, gilí (adj., fam., Esp.) dumb (fam., Am.E.), daft (fam., Br.E.), stupid, silly

el/la gilipollas (pop., Esp.) prat (sl., pej.), git (sl., pej., Br.E.), wanker (vulg., Br.E.), jerk (sl., pej., Am.E.), dickhead (vulg.), twat (vulg.), twerp (sl.), dummy (fam.)

gilipollear (pop., Esp.) to do s.th. stupid, to be stupid

el globo globe, sphere, balloon
▶ el globo (fam.) (condom): rubber (fam., Am.E.), johnny (fam., Br.E.), French letter (fam., Br.E.)

▶ los globos (fam.) (breasts): knockers (sl.), tits (fam.), boobs (fam.), hooters (sl., Am.E.)

▶ lanzar un globo de ensayo (fig.) to fly a kite (fig.)

▶ tener un globo [impresionante] (fam.)
(drunk or on drugs): to be high [as a kite/as
the sky] (fam.), to be [really] out of one's
head (sl.), to be [totally] stoned (sl.) ◆ *Tiene
un globo. He's high/stoned.* ◆ *Anoche tuviste
un globo impresionante. You were high as a
kite or as the sky last night.*

la gloria glory
▶ un pedazo de gloria (fig., fam.) [little] darling ◆ *Su hija es un pedazo de gloria. His
daughter is a little darling.*
▶ estar en su[s] gloria[s] (fig.) to be in seventh
heaven, to be on cloud nine (fam.), to be in
one's element, to be as snug as a bug in a rug
(fam.) ◆ *Está en su gloria. Ganó un million
de dólares. She's in seventh heaven. She won
a million dollars.* ◆ *Le gusta muchísimo escribir. Está en sus glorias cuando está tra-
bajando en una novela. He loves to write.
He's in his element when he's working on a
novel.* ◆ *Los niños salieron corriendo a retozar en la piscina. Allí están en sus glorias.
The children dashed off for a romp in the
swimming pool. There they are in their element[s].*
▶ saber a gloria to taste delicious/glorious, to
taste divine (fig., fam.) or heavenly (fam.),
to taste absolutely wonderful ◆ *Sabe a gloria. Sabe a más. It tastes delicious. I hope
there's more where that came from.*
▶ oler a gloria to smell divine (fig., fam.) or
heavenly (fam.), to smell glorious, to smell
absolutely wonderful
▶ mi madre/etc., que en gloria esté o que
Dios tenga en la gloria my mother/etc., God
rest her/etc. soul
▷ gloria (sin **pena** ni ~)

el gobernante ruler
▶ la gobernante (fam.) madam[e]

el gobierno government
▶ el gobierno de faldas (fam.) petticoat government

la golondrina swallow
▶ Una golondrina no hace verano. (prov.)
One swallow does not make a summer.
(prov.)

el golpe blow
▶ no dar golpe (fam.) not to do a hand's turn
(fam.), not to lift a finger (fam.), to sit on
one's hands (fig., fam., Am.E.)

▶ dar un buen golpe a la comida (fam.) to dig
in (fam.), to feed/stuff one's face (fam.)
▶ dar el último golpe a algo (fig.) to add/put
the finishing touch[es] to s.th. ◆ *Dio el último golpe a su obra. He put the finishing
touches to his work.*
▶ dar un golpe de timón (fig.) to alter course
[radically], to make a [radical] change of direction (fig.), to do a flip-flop (fig., fam.,
Am.E.)
▶ de golpe y porrazo (fam.) all of a sudden,
suddenly, on the spot, without thinking, just
like that ◆ *De golpe y porrazo tomaron una
decisión. They made a decision just like that.*
▷ golpe (ir/venir a ~ de **alpargata/calcetín**)
▷ golpe (repartir ~s como un **descosido**)

la goma gum, rubber
▶ la goma (fig., fam.) (condom): rubber (fam.,
Am.E.), johnny (fam., Br.E.), French letter
(fam., Br.E.)
▶ la goma (fam., América Central) (after
drinking): hangover (fam.) ◆ *Ayer estuve de
goma. I had a hangover yesterday.*

▷ gordiano (cortar el **nudo** ~)

gordo thick, fat
▶ caerle gordo a alg. (fam.) not to like s.o., s.o.
can't bear/stand s.o., to get on s.o.'s wick
(Br.E.) or on s.o.'s nerves (fam.) ◆ *Ese tío me
cae gordo. I can't stand that guy. I can't bear
that fellow. That guy gets on my wick.*
▶ hacer la vista gorda [a algo] (fig.) to turn a
blind eye [to s.th.] (fig.), to close/shut one's
eyes [to s.th.] (fig.), to pretend not to see/no-
tice [s.th.], to wink at s.th. (fig.), to look the
other way (fig.), to turn one's head the other
way (fig.) ◆ *Hizo la vista gorda. He pre-
tended not to have seen [it]. He looked the
other way.* ◆ *Hicieron la vista gorda a/ante
ese asunto. They turned a blind eye to that
affair. They winked at that affair.*
▶ hacer de lo gordo (vulg.) to take or have
(Br.E.) a crap/shit (vulg.), to shit (vulg.)
▶ armar la gorda (fam.) to cause a huge scandal, to kick up a tremendous fuss (fam.), to
kick up an almighty row (fam.), to raise Cain
(fam.), to cause/make a terrible scene (fam.)
◆ *Armaron la gorda. They caused a huge
scandal.* ◆ *Se armó la gorda. There was an
almighty row.* ◆ *Aquí se va a armar la gorda.
Now the fat is in the fire.* ◆ *Cuando se enteren, se va a armar la gorda. When they
find out there's going to be a terrible scene.*

▷ gordo (▷ **ver**: no haberlas visto nunca más gordas)

▷ gordo (**gente** gorda)

▷ gordo (las **vacas** gordas)

▷ gordo (ser un **pájaro** ~)

▷ gordo (sudar la **gota** gorda)

▷ gordo (tener la **lengua** gorda)

▷ gordo (un **pez** ~)

el gorgojo grub, weevil

► el gorgojo (fig., fam.) dwarf, midget, runt (fig.)

la gorra cap

► andar/vivir de gorra (fig.) to cadge, to scrounge (fam.), to sponge (fam.), to sponge a living (fam.), to live at s.o. else's expense

▷ gorra (vivir/estar donde **Cristo** perdió la ~)

el gorrazo (fam.)

► dar el gorrazo a alg. to scrounge/sponge on s.o. (fam.)

el gorrión sparrow

► comer como un gorrión (fam.) to eat like a bird (fig.), to pick at one's food

el gorro [round] cap

► estar hasta el gorro de algo (fam.) to have had it up to here with s.th. (fam.) ▷ estar hasta [más allá de] la **coronilla** de algo

la gota drop

► ser una gota de agua en el mar (fig.) to be [just] a drop in the ocean (fig.) ◆ *Esta suma es una gota de agua en el mar. This sum is a drop in the ocean.*

► la gota que desborda/colma el vaso (fig.) the straw that/which breaks the camel's back (fig.) ◆ *Hizo novillos otra vez. Fue la gota que desbordó el vaso. He played truant again. That was the straw which broke the camel's back.*

► hasta la última gota (fig.) to the full/last ◆ *Lo saboreamos hasta la última gota. We savored it to the full.*

► no quedarle a alg. gota de sangre en las venas (fig.) to freeze [with fear/horror] (fig.), to be petrified or paralyzed with fear/horror (fig.)

► parecerse como dos gotas de agua to be as like as two peas [in a pod]

► sudar la gota gorda (fig.) (a) (anxiety/strain): to sweat blood. (b) to sweat buckets (fig.), to sweat like a pig/bull (fig.)

► Gota a gota se llena la bota. (prov.) Constant dripping wears away a stone. (prov.) Little strokes fell great/big oaks. (prov.)

la gotera leak (in the roof)

► ser una gotera (fig.) to be one thing after another, just not to come to an end ◆ *Es una gotera. It's one thing after another. It just doesn't come to an end.*

► goteras (fig., fam.) aches and pains ◆ *Está lleno de goteras. He's full of aches and pains.*

el gozo enjoyment, pleasure

► [todo] mi/etc. o el gozo en el/un pozo (fam.) my/etc. hopes are dashed, I'm/etc. sunk (sl.), it's all ruined, it's all off (fam.), that's/it's torn it (fam.) ◆ *Su gozo en el pozo. His hopes are dashed.* ◆ *¡Todo nuestro gozo en un pozo! We're sunk! It's all ruined!* ◆ *¡Todo el gozo en un pozo! It's all ruined! It's all off!*

la gracia grace, joke, humor

► ser una triste gracia (fam.) to be horrible, to be enough to make you weep ◆ *¡Es una triste gracia! Horrible! It's enough to make you weep!*

► hacerle a alg. gracia de algo to spare s.o. s.th., to excuse s.o. s.th. ◆ *¡Hazme gracia de los detalles! Spare me the details!* ◆ *Nos hizo gracia de una humillación. He spared us a humiliation.*

► a la gracia de Dios (fam.) trusting to luck, on the off-chance, on a wing and a prayer, at random ◆ *Fuimos a Sevilla a la gracia de Dios. We went to Seville on the off-chance [of finding good weather/a hotel room/etc.].*

► reírle a alg. la[s] gracia[s] (fam.) to humor s.o., to applaud s.o. ironically

gracioso graceful, witty, funny

► hacer el gracioso (fig.) to act or play the fool/buffoon

granar to seed

► ir que grana (fig., fam.) to go/run like clockwork (fig.) ◆ *Todo va que grana. Everything goes like clockwork.*

▷ grandeza (darse **aires** de ~)

granel

► a granel (fig.) ◆ *Hay comida y bebida a granel. There's food and drink in abundance. There's stacks/loads of food and drink. (fam.)* ◆ *Hubo palos a granel. The blows came thick and fast. He/etc. was dealt an endless stream* of blows. ◆ *Me hicieron preguntas a granel.* They asked me hundreds or a barrage of questions. (fig.) They bombarded me with questions. (fig.)

▷ granero (un **grano** no hace ~ pero ayuda al compañero)

▷ granito (aportar/poner su **grano**/~ de arena)

el grano grain

▶ aportar/poner su grano o granito de arena (fig.) to do one's bit (fam.) ◆ *Ha servido fielmente a la patria. Ha aportado su grano de arena.* She has served her country faithfully. She has done her bit. ◆ *Durante la guerra puso su granito de arena.* He did his bit in the war.

▶ tomar algo con un grano de sal (fig.) to take s.th. with a grain/pinch of salt (fig.) ◆ *Tienes que tomar todo lo que dice con un grano de sal. Él no siempre dice la verdad.* You've got to take anything he says with a pinch of salt. He doesn't always tell the truth.

▶ apartar/separar el grano de la paja (fig.) to separate the wheat/grain from the chaff (fig.)

▶ no ser grano de anís (fig.) not to be peanuts (fam.), to be no chickenfeed (sl.), to be no small matter, to be important ◆ *Gana cien mil dólares al año, que no es grano de anís.* He earns one hundred thousand dollars a year, which is no chickenfeed.

▶ ir al grano (fam.) to get [straight] down to business or to brass tacks (fam.), to come/get [straight] to the point, to get down to the nitty-gritty (fam.) ◆ *¡Vamos al grano!* Let's get down to brass tacks!

▶ Un grano no hace granero pero ayuda al compañero. (prov.) Every little helps.

el granuja (fig., fam.) guttersnipe, ragamuffin, rascal, urchin, scalawag (fam., Br.E.), rogue

▷ gravedad (**vestir** el rostro de ~)

el/la grifota (fam.) pot-smoker (fam.), dopehead (sl.)

la grilla female cricket

▶ ¡Ésa es grilla [y no canta]! (fig., fam.) That's a likely story! (iron.) Tell that to the marines! (fam., Am.E.)

▷ grillo (la **olla** de ~s)

el gris (fig., fam.) cold wind

▶ hace un gris there's a cold wind [blowing]

▶ corre un gris que pela a piercing wind is blowing, the wind is [as] cold as a witch's caress

▷ gritar a más no **poder**

▷ gritar como un **descosido**

el guante glove

▶ echar el guante a alg. (fig., fam.) to arrest s.o., to nab s.o. (fam.)

▶ arrojar el guante a alg. (fig.) to throw down the gauntlet to s.o. (fig.)

▶ recoger el guante (fig.) to take up the gauntlet (fig.), to take up the challenge

▶ echar un guante (fam.) to take a collection ◆ *Echó un guante a beneficio de las víctimas.* He took a collection on behalf of the victims.

▶ tratar a alg. con guante de seda to handle/treat s.o. with kid gloves (fig.) ◆ *Tiene la sensibilidad a flor de piel. Hay que tratarla con guante de seda.* She's very easily offended. You have to handle her with kid gloves.

▶ quedarse más suave que un guante (fig.) to become/be as meek as a lamb (fig.)

▷ guapo (▷ **nariz**: ser ~ de narices)

▷ guapo (ser la **mar** de ~)

la guardia guard[ing]

▶ estar en guardia [contra] (fig.) to be on one's guard [against], to watch out [for]

▶ ponerse en guardia [contra] to take precautions [against]

▷ guardia (ser más vago que la **chaqueta** de un ~)

Guatemala Guatemala

▶ salir de Guatemala y entrar en Guatepeor (fam.) to jump out of the frying pan into the fire ◆ *Atracó un banco para pagar sus deudas. Salió de Guatemala y entró en Guatepeor.* He held up a bank to pay [off] his debts. He jumped out of the frying pan into the fire.

▷ Guatepeor (salir de **Guatemala** y entrar en ~)

el guiñapo rag, tatter

▶ poner a alg. como un guiñapo (fam.) to run s.o. down (fam.), to pull s.o. to pieces (fam.), to tear s.o. to pieces/bits/shreds (fig., fam.) ◆ *Los críticos pusieron al escritor como un guiñapo.* The critics pulled the writer to pieces.

guiñar to blink
▶ guiñarla (pop.) to kick the bucket (fam.)
▷ **cascar**[la]

guipar algo (fam.) to cotton/catch on to s.th.
(fam.) ◆ *Lo he guipado. I've cottoned on
to it.*

el güiro (pop.) nut (sl.) ▷ la cebolla

guisar to cook
▶ guisárselo y comérselo (fig., fam.) you've/
etc. made your/etc. bed, now you/etc. must
lie in/on it (fig.) ◆ *Ella se lo guisa, [y] ella
se lo come. She has made her bed, now she
must lie in it.* ◆ *Como uno se lo guisa, así
se lo come. As you make your bed, so you
must lie in it.*

▷ guiso (muchas **manos** en la olla echan el
~ a perder)

la guita (fam.) (money): dough (sl., Am.E.),
bread (sl.), sugar (sl.), brass/dosh/lolly (sl.,
Br.E.), wampum (sl., Am.E.)

la guitarra guitar
▶ ser/sonar como guitarra en un entierro
(fig.) to be quite/wholly inappropriate, to be
quite/wholly out of place ◆ *Lo que dijiste
sonó como guitarra en un entierro. What
you said was quite out of place.*
▷ guitarra (**rascar** la ~)

el güito (pop.) nut (sl.) ▷ la cebolla

la gurrina (pop., Esp.) (penis) ▷ el calvo

el gustazo great pleasure
▶ el gustazo (fam.) malicious or fiendish (fig.)
delight/glee ◆ *Les dio un gustazo verla fra-
casar. They took a fiendish delight in seeing
her fail.*

el gusto taste, pleasure
▶ dar gusto verlo to be a sight for sore eyes,
to be a treat to see it (fig.) ◆ *Dio gusto verlo.
It was a sight for sore eyes. It was a treat to
see it.* ◆ *¡Mira qué sal tiene para moverse!
Da gusto verlo. Look how gracefully she
moves! It's a treat to see it.* ◆ *Estoy muerto de
hambre. Da gusto ver esta comida. I'm simply starving. This meal is a sight for sore eyes.*
▶ Sobre gustos no hay nada escrito. Para
cada gusto se pintó un color. There's no accounting for taste[s].
▶ Hay gustos que merecen palos. (fam.)
There's no accounting for taste[s]! (iron.) ◆
*Llevaba zapatos naranjados, pantalones
purpúreos, una blusa gris y el pelo fue
teñido de verde claro. Hay gustos que merecen palos. She was wearing orange shoes, pur-
ple pants, a gray blouse and her hair was dyed
bright green. There's no accounting for taste!*
▶ Quien por su gusto padece, vaya al infierno
a quejarse. Everyone must bear/face the
consequences of his actions.
▶ En la variedad está el gusto. (prov.) Variety is the spice of life. (prov.)
▷ gusto (▷ **llover**: nunca llueve a ~ de todos)
▷ gusto (no ser **plato** de su ~)

H

la haba bean
- ▶ Son habas contadas. (fig., fam.) There's no doubt about it. It's a sure thing. It's a a certainty. There are no two ways about it. You can bet your bottom dollar on that. (fam., Am.E.)
- ▶ En todas partes cuecen habas. It's the same the whole world over.
- ▷ haba (ser más tonto que una **mata** de ~s)

haber to have
- ▶ ser de lo que no hay (fam.) ◆ *Esto es de lo que no hay. Would you believe it! (fam.)* ◆ *Eres de lo que no hay. You're impossible! (fam.) You're the limit! (fam.)*
- ▶ habido y por haber ◆ *todos los presidentes habidos y por haber all presidents past and future* ◆ *Pertenecen a la firma todos los inventos habidos y por haber. All inventions present and future belong to the firm.* ◆ *todas las diversiones habidas y por haber all the fun of the fair* ◆ *Pregúntale a mi padre. Ha leído todo lo habido y por haber sobre este tema. Ask my father. He's read absolutely everything there is to read on this subject.*
- ▶ habérselas con alg. to have to do/deal with s.o., to be up against s.o. (fam.), to cross swords with s.o. (fig.) ◆ *¡Se las habrán conmigo! They'll have me to deal with!*

el hábito habit
- ▶ ahorcar/colgar los hábitos (fig.) to leave the priesthood, to give up the cloth (monk), to give up one's profession
- ▶ El hábito no hace al monje. (prov.) Clothes do not make the man. (prov.) Appearances can be or are deceptive. (prov.)
- ▶ El hábito hace al monje. (prov.) Clothes make the man. (prov.) Fine feathers make fine birds. (prov.)

hablar to speak, to talk
- ▶ ¡Ni hablar! (fam.) No dice! (sl., Am.E.) [That's] out of the question! Nothing doing! (fam.) No way! (fam.)
- ▶ i... ni hablar! (fam.) . . . my foot! (fam.) ◆ *¡Dama, ni hablar! Lady, my foot!* ◆ *¡Tarea difícil, ni hablar! Difficult task, my foot!*

- ▶ Quien mucho habla, mucho yerra. (prov.) The more you talk, the more mistakes you'll make.
- ▷ hablar (▷ **tonto**: ~ a tontas y a locas)
- ▷ hablar a **chorro**s
- ▷ hablar a la **pared**
- ▷ hablar como una **chicharra**/un **descosido**
- ▷ hablar de **trapo**s
- ▷ hablar en **castellano/cristiano/plata**
- ▷ hablar más que una **cotorra**/que un **sacamuelas**/que **siete**/que una **urraca**
- ▷ hablar sin **ton** ni son

hacer to make, to do
- ▶ hacer lo que otro no puede hacer por uno (fam.) to go to the restroom
- ▶ hacerla buena (fam., iron.) to make a fine mess of it (fig.) ◆ *¡Ahora sí que la has hecho buena! Now you've [really] done it! A fine mess you've made of it!*

el hacha ax[e]
- ▶ desenterrar el hacha de guerra (fig.) to take up the hatchet (fig.)
- ▶ enterrar el hacha de guerra (fig.) to bury the hatchet (fig.)
- ▶ ser un hacha [en/para algo] (fig., fam.) to be a genius [at s.th.], to be a crackerjack [at s.th.] (fam., Am.E.), to be a whiz[z] [at s.th.] (fam.), to be an ace . . . ◆ *Es un hacha en las matemáticas. He's a genius at mathematics. He's a brilliant mathematician.* ◆ *Es un hacha para el deporte. He's an ace sportsman or a sports ace.*
- ▷ hacha (tener una **lengua** de ~)

la hache name of the letter H/h
- ▶ por hache o por be (fig., fam.) for one reason or another
- ▶ Llámele usted o llámale hache. (fam.) It boils/comes down to the same thing. Call it what you will (fam.)/like.

el hambre hunger
- ▶ A buen hambre no hay pan duro. (prov.) Hunger is the best sauce. (prov.)
- ▶ El hambre aguza el ingenio. (prov.) Necessity is the mother of invention. (prov.)

▶ ser más listo que el hambre (fig.) to be as smart as they come, to be [as] bright as a button (fig.), to be very sharp/clever, to be razor-sharp (fam.), to be [as] sharp as a razor

▶ el hambre de tres semanas o de lobo (fam.) ravenous hunger

▶ se juntaron el hambre y las ganas de comer (hum.) they're two of a kind, they're as bad as each other, one is as bad as the other

▷ hambre (comerse/roerse los **codo**s de ~)

▷ hambre (estar **muerto** de ~)

▷ hambre (más **cornada**s da el ~)

la harina flour

▶ ser harina de otro costal (fig.) to be a horse of a different or of another color (fig.), to be quite another or quite a different story (fam.), to be another or a different kettle of fish (fam.)

el hato bundle [of clothes]

▶ andar/ir con el hato a cuestas (fig.) to live out of a suitcase (fig.), to be often away, to often move

▷ hato (ser un ~ de **nervios**)

el hazmerreír (fam.) figure of fun

▶ ser el hazmerreír de la ciudad o de la gente to be the laughing stock of the city, to be the laughing stock

la hebra thread

▶ pegar la hebra (fig., fam.) to start or strike up a conversation, to get chatting (fam.)

hecho done, finished

▶ hecho y derecho upright (fig.), [fully] grown, fully fledged, real, accomplished, complete, out-and-out, inveterate ◆ *Es un hombre hecho y derecho. He's a real man. He's every inch a man. He's an upright man.* ◆ *Es un cirujano hecho y derecho. He's a fully fledged surgeon.* ◆ *Es un jugador hecho y derecho. He's an inveterate gambler.* ◆ *Es un granuja hecho y derecho. He's an out-and-out rogue.* ◆ *Es una mentirosa hecha y derecha. She's an out-and-out or an accomplished liar.*

▶ Lo hecho, hecho está. A lo hecho, pecho. What's done is done. What's done can't be undone. It's no use crying over spilt milk. (prov.)

el hecho deed

▶ el hecho consumado fait accompli ◆ *Lo pusieron/colocaron ante un hecho consumado. They confronted him with a fait accompli.*

▷ hecho (del **dicho** al ~ hay mucho trecho)

▷ hecho (**dicho** sin ~ no trae provecho)

helado frozen

▶ quedarse helado (fig.) to freeze [with fear/horror] (fig.), to be petrified or paralyzed with fear/horror (fig.), to be scared stiff (fam.)

▷ helar (helársele a alg. la **sangre** [en las venas])

▷ henchir el **baúl**

la herida wound, injury

▶ renovar la herida (fig.) to open up or reopen an old wound/sore (fig.) ◆ *Dile que cierre el pico. Está renovando la herida. Tell him to pipe down. He's reopening an old wound.*

▶ hurgar en la herida (fig.) to turn the knife in the wound (fig.), to rub salt in[to] the wound (fig.) ◆ *Juan se siente muy abatido porque ha perdido mucho dinero al póquer. Paco está hurgando en la herida diciendo cuánto ganaron los otros jugadores. Juan is feeling miserable about losing a lot of money at poker, and Paco is rubbing salt into the wound by saying how much the other gamblers won.*

▶ tocar [a alg.] en la herida (fig.) to touch on a sore spot/point (fig.), to hit a raw nerve (fig.) ◆ *Guárdate de mencionar el nombre de su ex esposa. Es mejor no tocar en la herida. Be careful not to mention his ex-wife's name. It's best not to touch on a sore point.*

▶ respirar por la herida (fig.) (by a careless remark): to reveal one's true feelings, to reveal one's secret thoughts

herir to wound, to hurt, to injure

▶ herir la vista o el oído (fig.) to offend/hurt the/one's eye[s]/ear[s] ◆ *Este color hiere la vista. This color offends the eye or hurts your eyes.*

▶ herir el suelo con el pie (fig.) to stamp one's foot

▶ como herido por el/un rayo (fig.) thunderstruck (fig.), stunned (fig.) ◆ *Me quedé como herido por un rayo cuando lo supe. I was thunderstruck when I heard about it or when I found out about it.*

▷ hermano (ser **primo** ~ de o ser primos ~s)

▷ hermoso (no **pecar** de ~)

herniarse to rupture o.s.

▶ no herniarse (fig., pop.) not to strain/kill (fam.) o.s. ◆ *¡Cuidado, no te vayas a herniar! (iron.) Mind you don't strain or kill yourself! (iron.)*

Herodes Herod

▶ ir de Herodes a Pilatos (fig.) (a) to run/chase from pillar to post (fig.) (b) to jump out of the frying pan into the fire ◆ *Había tantas formalidades burocráticas. Tuve que ir de Herodes a Pilatos para obtener los papeles. It was red tape all the way. I had to run from pillar to post to get the [identity] papers. ◆ Atracó un banco para pagar sus deudas. Fue de Herodes a Pilatos. He held up a bank to pay [off] his debts. He jumped out of the frying pan into the fire.*

▷ herradura (dar una en el **clavo** y ciento en la ~)

el herrero blacksmith

▶ En casa de herrero, cuchillo de palo. (prov.) The shoemaker's son always goes barefoot. (prov.)

la hiel gall, bile

▶ echar/sudar la hiel (fig.) to work very hard, to slog away (fam., Br.E.), to slave/sweat away (fam.), to slog/sweat one's guts out (fam., Br.E.), to work one's butt off (fam., Am.E.), to work one's tail off (fam.), to keep one's nose to the grindstone (fig.) ◆ *Les hice sudar la hiel. I made them work their butts off. I gave them a [good] run for their money. I kept their noses to the grindstone. (fig.)*

▶ no tener hiel (fig.) to be very sweet-tempered, to have a sweet/peaceful nature

▷ hiel (no hay **miel** sin ~)

▷ hiel (ser una **paloma** sin ~)

la hierba grass

▶ la hierba (fig., fam.) (marijuana): hash/pot (fam.), grass/weed/shit (sl.), tea (sl., Am.E.)

▶ oír/sentir/ver crecer la hierba (fig.) to hear the grass grow (fig.), to see through a millstone (fig.)

▶ pisar alguna mala hierba (fig., fam.) to have a bad day

▶ Mala hierba nunca muere. (prov.) Ill weeds grow apace. (prov.) A bad penny always turns up. (prov.) The devil looks after his own. (prov.)

▶ ... y otras hierbas (fam., hum.) . . . and so on/forth, et cetera ◆ *Compramos pan, queso, vino y otras hierbas. We bought bread, cheese, wine, and so on.*

el hierro iron

▶ quitar hierro a algo to draw the teeth of s.th. (fam.), to take the edge off s.th. (fig.)

▶ llevar hierro a Vizcaya (fig.) to carry coals to Newcastle (fig.) ◆ *Llevarle hielo a un esquimal es como llevar hierro a Vizcaya. Taking ice to an Eskimo is like carrying coals to Newcastle.*

▶ El que a hierro mata, a hierro muere. (prov.) He who lives by the sword, dies by the sword. (prov.)

▶ Al hierro caliente batir de repente. (prov.) Strike while the iron is hot. (prov.) Make hay while the sun shines. (prov.)

▷ hierro (a **fuego** y ~)

▷ hierro (**machacar** en ~ frío)

el hígado liver

▶ sacar el hígado por la boca (fig.) to run for all one is worth (fam.)

▶ echar los hígados (fig.) to slog one's guts out (fam., Br.E.) ▷ echar/sudar la **hiel**

▶ recalentarse los hígados (fig.) to flare up vehemently (fig.)

▶ tener hígados (fig., fam.) to have courage, to have gumption (fam.), to have guts (fam.), to have pluck (fig.), to have bottle (fam., Br.E.)

el higo fig

▶ el higo (pop.) (vagina) ▷ el conejo

▶ [no] importar a alg. un higo (fig.) not to give/care two hoots (fam.) ▷ no importar a alg. un **ardite**

▶ estar hecho un higo (fig.) to be all crumpled

▶ de higos a brevas (fam.) very rarely, once in a blue moon (fam.) ◆ *Vamos a verlos de higos a brevas. We go and see them once in a blue moon.*

la higuera fig tree

▶ estar en la higuera (fig., fam.) to have one's head in the clouds, to be away with the fairies (fam.), to be remote from it all (fig.), to be miles away (fig.), to have one's mind on other things, to be daydreaming

la hija daughter

▶ Tal madre tal hija. (prov.) Like mother like daughter. (prov.) The apple doesn't fall far from the tree. (prov.)

▷ hija (las ~s de **Eva**)

el hijo son

▶ Tal padre tal hijo. (prov.) Like father like son. (prov.). The apple doesn't fall far from the tree. (prov.)

▶ cada/cualquier hijo de vecino (fam.) everybody, every mother's son ◆ *Eso lo sabe cada hijo de vecino. Everybody knows that.*

▶ como cada/cualquier hijo de vecino (fam.) like everyone else, like the next man ◆ *Tienes que hacer cola como cualquier hijo de vecino. You have to queue up like everyone else.* ◆ *Yo tengo derechos como cada hijo de vecino. I've rights like everyone else.*

▷ hijo (los **vicio**s son los ~s del ocio)

hilar to spin

▶ hilar delgado o muy fino (fig.) (a) to be very pedantic or meticulous or particular or strict or demanding (b) to split hairs

la hilaza [spun] yarn

▶ descubrir la hilaza (fig., fam.) (a) to show [o.s. in] one's true colors (fig.) (b) to find out [about it] ◆ *Nunca se sabe qué piensa ese tío. No descubre la hilaza. You can never tell what that guy is thinking. He doesn't show his true colors.* ◆ *No creo que descubran la hilaza. I don't think they'll find out about it.*

el hilo thread

▶ colgar/pender o estar colgado/pendiente de un hilo (fig.) to hang or be hanging by a thread/hair (fig.) ◆ *El futuro de la firma pende de un hilo. The firm's future hangs by a thread.* ◆ *Su vida pendía o estaba pendiente de un hilo. His/her life was hanging by a thread or by a hair.*

▶ cortar el hilo de la conversación (fig.) to interrupt the conversation

▶ perder el hilo o cortársele a alg. el hilo (fig.) to lose the thread (fig.) ◆ *Perdió o se le cortó el hilo de la conversación. He lost the thread of the conversation.*

▶ tomar el hilo (fig.) to pick up the thread (fig.)

▶ pegar el hilo (fam.) to start or strike up a conversation, to get chatting (fam.)

▶ mover los hilos (fig.) to control, to be at the controls (fig.), to call the shots (fig.), to pull the strings (fig.) ◆ *Conocemos a quienes mueven los hilos. We know who's at the controls. We know who's calling the shots.* ◆ *Interés personal a menudo mueve los hilos de su política. Self-interest often controls their policy.*

▶ contar algo del hilo al ovillo (fam.) to tell s.th. without omitting a single detail, to tell s.th. down to the last detail ◆ *Nos lo contó todo del hilo al ovillo. He told us all about it without omitting a single detail.*

▶ Por el hilo se saca el ovillo. (fig.) It's just a question of putting two and two together.

▷ hilo (tener el **alma** en un ~)

el hincapié act of getting a firm footing

▶ hacer hincapié en algo (fig.) (a) to insist on s.th. (b) to dwell on s.th. (fig.), to stress s.th., to emphasize s.th., to lay/put [special/particular] emphasis on s.th. ◆ *Haremos especial hincapié en las grandes ventajas de este plan. We'll put special emphasis on the great advantages of this plan.*

hincar to thrust/drive [in]

▶ hincar el diente [a/en algo] (fig., fam.) (a) (eating): to dig in[to s.th.] (fam.), to sink one's teeth into s.th. (fam.) (b) to get/sink one's teeth into s.th. (fig., fam.), to tackle s.th. ◆ *Hincó el diente. He dug in.* ◆ *Estoy impaciente por hincar el diente en ese pastel de manzana. I can't wait to sink my teeth into that apple pie.* ◆ *Es una tarea que constituye un reto. Me perezco por hincarle el diente. This is a challenging task. I'm itching to get my teeth into it.*

▶ hincar el pico (fig., fam.) to bite the dust (fam.) ▷ **cascar**[la]

la hincha (fam.)

▶ tener hincha a alg. to have a grudge against s.o. ▷ tener a alg. **atravesado** ◆ *Le tengo hincha a él. I can't stand him.*

hinchar to blow up, to pump up, to inflate

▶ hinchar el perro (fig.) to lay it on thick (fam.), to exaggerate grossly

▶ hinchar a alg. (pop.) to get/make s.o. pregnant, to knock s.o. up (sl.)

▶ estar hinchada (pop.) (be pregnant): to have a bun in the oven (sl.)

▶ hincharse de plata/dinero (fig., fam.) to make a fortune, to make a mint/pile (fam.), to rake it in (fig., fam.), to make money hand over fist (fam.)

▶ hincharse (fig.) to puff o.s. up (fig.), to act big (fam.)

hipar to hiccup

▶ hipar por algo (fig., fam.) to be very keen on s.th., to long/yearn for s.th.

el hipo hiccup[s]

▶ tener hipo por algo (fig.) to have a craving for s.th.

▶ tener hipo con alg. (fig.) to have a grudge against s.o.

▶ quitar el hipo a alg. (fig., fam.) to leave s.o. speechless (fig.), to take s.o.'s breath away, to be a shock to s.o. (fig.) ◆ *Su grosería nos quitó el hipo. His rudeness left us speechless.*

▶ que quita el hipo (fig., fam.) breathtaking[ly], great (fam.), fantastic (fam.) ▷ cojonudo (a). ◆ *Tiene una esposa que quita el hipo. His wife is breathtakingly beautiful or is a breathtaking beauty.*

la historia history

▶ ser de historia (fig.) to be s.o. with a past, to have a bad reputation, to be notorious ◆ *Es una mujer de historia. She's a woman with a past.*

el hito boundary post/mark

▶ marcar un hito (fig.) to mark a milestone (fig.), to be a landmark (fig.), to be a landmark decision/discovery/etc. (fig.) ◆ *El descubrimiento de la teoría de la relatividad marcó un hito. The discovery of the theory of relativity was a milestone. The theory of relativity was a landmark discovery.*

▶ mirar a alg. de hito en hito to stare/gaze at s.o.

el hocico snout, muzzle

▶ el hocico (fig., fam.) face, mug (sl.)

▶ quitar los hocicos a alg. (fig., pop.) (threat): to put s.o.'s face out of joint (fam.), to smash s.o.'s face/head in (fam.) ◆ *Si lo dices otra vez, te voy a quitar los hocicos. If you say it once more, I'm going to put your face out of joint.*

▶ meter el hocico en algo (fig., fam.) to poke one's nose into s.th. (fig., fam.)

▷ hocico (dar a alg. con la **puerta** en los ~s)

la hoja leaf

▶ poner a alg. como hoja de perejil (fig.) to badmouth s.o. (fam.), not to have a good word to say about s.o., to run s.o. down (fig.), to slam s.o. (fam.), to slag s.o. off (fam., Br.E.), to pull s.o. to pieces (fam.), to tear s.o. to bits/pieces/shreds (fig., fam.) ◆ *Los críticos pusieron al escritor como hoja de perejil. The critics slammed the writer.*

▶ doblar/volver la hoja (fig.) (a) to change the subject (b) to change one's mind, not to keep one's promise (c) to turn over a new leaf (fig.) ◆ *Decidió volver la hoja y prometió que en lo sucesivo no volvería a cometer los mismos errores. He decided to turn over a new leaf and promised henceforth never to make the same mistakes again.*

▶ Eso o la cosa no tiene vuelta de hoja. (fig.) There's no doubt about it. There are no two ways about it. That's the way it is. There's no gainsaying it.

▷ hoja (**temblar** como una ~)

▷ hojaldre (quitar la ~ al **pastel**)

▷ hojuela (ser **miel** sobre ~s)

el hombre man

▶ hacerse el hombre (fam.) to try to act tough

▶ ser el hombre del día (fig.) to be the man of the moment

▶ ser muy hombre o todo un hombre to be a real man, to be every bit a man

▶ El hombre propone y Dios dispone. Man proposes and God disposes.

▶ Hombre pobre todo es trazas. (prov.) Necessity is the mother of invention. (prov.)

▶ Hombre prevenido vale por dos. (prov.) Forewarned is forearmed. (prov.)

▶ De hombre a hombre no va nada. (prov.) Basically it all depends on [good] luck or on the circumstances.

▷ hombre (no sólo de **pan** vive el ~)

▷ hombre (ser ~ de pelo en **pecho**)

▷ hombre (ser un ~ con toda la **barba**)

▷ hombro (echarse la **maleta** al ~)

▷ hombro (estar/andar **manga** por ~)

▷ hombro (**hurtar** el ~)

la hondura depth

▶ meterse en honduras (fig., fam.) to get into deep water (fig.), to get out of one's depth (fig.)

el hongo fungus, mushroom

▶ el hongo (fam.) bowler [hat], derby (Am.E.)

▶ aparecer o brotar o darse como hongos (fig.) to spring up or shoot up like mushrooms (fig.), to mushroom (fig.) ◆ *Hoteles y casinos aparecen como hongos en Las Vegas.* Hotels and casinos are springing up like mushrooms in Las Vegas.

▶ más solo que un hongo all alone, all on one's tod (fam., Br.E.), as lonely as a cloud (hum.) ◆ *Se sentía más solo que un hongo.* He was/felt as lonely as a cloud.

la hora hour, time

▶ a buenas horas, mangas verdes (fig.) to lock the barn door after the horse is stolen (fig., Am.E.), to lock/shut the stable door after the horse has bolted/gone (fig., Br.E.)

▶ a la hora de la verdad (fig.) at the moment of truth, when it comes down to it, when the chips are down (fam.) ◆ *A la hora de la verdad les faltó valor para eso.* At the moment of truth they didn't have the courage for it. ◆ *A la hora de la verdad nunca se puede contar con él.* When it comes down to it, you can never count on him.

▶ dar la hora [y quitar los cuartos] (fig., fam.) to be very good, to be excellent, to be great/super (fam.) ◆ *Esto da la hora y quita los cuartos.* This is great.

▷ horca (▷ **caudino**: pasar por las ~s caudinas)

▷ horchata (tener **sangre** de ~ en las venas)

la horizontal horizontal position

▶ la horizontal (fig., pop.) woman who has the oldest profession in the world, prostitute

▶ tomar la horizontal (fig., fam.) to [go and] recline (fam.)

la horma form, mold

▶ encontrar la horma de su zapato (fig., fam.) (a) to find/meet one's match (b) to find just what one wanted, to find the very thing

la hormiga ant

▶ ser una hormiga (fig.) to be very industrious, to be very hard-working

el horno oven

▶ ¡No está el horno para bollos! (fam.) (to joke/ask/etc.): This isn't the right moment! This is the wrong moment! This is a bad time!

▶ ¡Qué horno! (fig., fam.) What a sweltering/stifling heat!

el horror horror, dread

▶ divertirse horrores (fam.) to have a marvelous/tremendous time

▶ decir horrores de algo/alg. to tell horror stories about s.th./s.o., to say awful or terrible things about s.th./s.o. ◆ *Nos dijeron horrores de su viaje a Méjico.* They told us horror stories about their trip to Mexico. ◆ *Siempre dice horrores de su suegra.* He always says awful things about his mother-in-law.

▷ hortelano (ser [como] el **perro** del ~[, ...])

▷ hostia (hacer un **pan** como unas ~s)

hoy today

▶ Hoy por mí, mañana por tí. (fam.) You scratch my back and I'll scratch yours. (fig.)

▷ hoy (no dejes para **mañana** lo que puedes hacer ~)

el hoyo grave

▶ estar con un pie en el hoyo (fig.) to have one foot in the grave (fig.) ◆ *Mi abuelo tiene 92 años. Está con un pie en el hoyo.* My grandfather is 92 years old. He has one foot in the grave.

huérfano orphaned

▶ huérfano de (fig., fam.) bereft of (fig.), without ◆ *huérfano de esperanza* bereft of hope ◆ *huérfano de razón* bereft of reason ◆ *huérfano de enchufes* without connections or useful contacts

el hueso bone

▶ ¡A otro perro con ese hueso! (fam.) Tell that to the marines! (fam., Am.E.) Pull the other one! (fam., Br.E.)

▶ pinchar/dar en hueso (fam.) to find s.th. a hard nut to crack (fig.), to be a tough assignment ◆ *Con eso pinchamos en hueso.* We found that a hard nut to crack.

▶ ser un hueso duro de roer (fig., fam.) to be a hard nut to crack (fig.), to be a tough one (fam.), to be a braintwister ◆ *Este problema se las trae. Es un hueso duro de roer.* This is a difficult problem. It's a hard nut to crack.

▶ darle a alg. un hueso duro de roer (fig., fam.) to give s.o. a hard nut to crack (fig.) ◆ *El profesor nos dio un hueso duro de roer.* The teacher gave us a hard nut to crack.

▶ no dejar hueso sano a alg. (fig.) not to have a good word to say about s.o.

▶ estar en los huesos to be a bag of bones (fam.), to be all skin and bone (fam.), to be nothing but skin and bone (fam.)

▶ arrojar hasta los huesos (fam.) to be as sick as a parrot (fam., Br.E.), to spew one's guts out (sl.) ◆ *Todos [nosotros] arrojamos hasta los huesos. We were all as sick as parrots.*

▶ estar calado/mojado hasta los huesos to be soaked to the skin, to be wet through, to be soaking/dripping wet, to be drenched, not to have a dry stitch on one (fam.)

▶ mojarse hasta los huesos (fam.) to get soaked to the skin, to get wet through, to get soaking/dripping wet, to get drenched

▶ tener los huesos molidos (fig.) to be completely shattered (fam.) ▷ estar hecho **cisco**

▶ dar con los/sus huesos en el santo suelo (fam.) to fall flat on one's face, to fall in a sprawling

▶ dar con los/sus huesos en la cárcel (fam.) to land in prison/jail (fam.), to end up or finish up in prison/jail

▷ hueso (ser de **carne** y ~)

▷ hueso (ser un/estar hecho un **costal** de ~s)

la huéspeda landlady

▶ no contar con la huéspeda (fig.), echar la cuenta sin la huéspeda (fig.) to reckon without one's host (fig.), to get one's sums wrong

el huevo egg

▶ los huevos (vulg.) (testicles) ▷ las **canicas**

▶ costar un huevo (vulg.) to cost a tidy sum ▷ costar una **burrada**

▶ costar un huevo [+ infinitivo] (vulg.) to be one hell of a job [to + infinitive] (fam.), to have such a sweat [to + infinitive] (fam.), to be a real sweat (fam.) ◆ *Costó un huevo. It was one hell of a job. It was a real sweat.* ◆ *Me costó un huevo terminarlo. I had such a sweat to finish it.*

▶ [no] importar a alg. un huevo (vulg.) not to give a fuck/shit (vulg.) ◆ *Esto me importa un huevo. I don't give a fuck about this.*

▶ tener huevos (vulg.) to have balls (vulg.), to have guts (fam.), to have bottle (fam., Br.E.), to have pluck (fig.), to have gumption (fam.), to have courage

▶ parecerse como un huevo a otro to be as like as two peas [in a pod]

▶ parecerse como un huevo a una castaña (fig.) to be as different as night and day

(Am.E.)/as chalk and cheese (Br.E.) (fam.), not to look in the least bit alike ◆ *Sus hermanos se parecen como un huevo a una castaña. Her brothers don't look in the least bit alike.*

▶ vender/comprar algo a huevo (fam.) to sell/buy s.th. for peanuts (fam.), to sell/buy s.th. very cheap

▶ saber un huevo de algo (fam.) to know a lot about s.th. ◆ *Sabe un huevo de vinos. He knows a lot about wine.*

▷ huevo (buscar **pelos** al ~)

▷ huevo (**cacarear** y no poner ~s)

▷ huevo (matar la **gallina** de los ~s de oro)

▷ huevo (no se puede hacer **tortillas** sin romper ~s)

▷ huevo (¡**Sal** quiere el ~!)

▷ huevo (ser **largo** como pelo de ~)

▷ huevo (ser [un ~] duro de **pelar**)

▷ huir (El **gato** escaldado del agua fría huye.)

▷ huir de la[s] **ceniza**[s] y caer/dar en la[s] brasa[s]

▷ huir del **fuego** y caer en las brasas

▷ huir del **toro** y caer en el arroyo

el humo smoke

▶ tomar la del humo (fam.) to take to one's heels, to beat it (sl.)

▶ hacerse humo (fig.) to vanish/disappear into thin air or without trace, to make o.s. scarce (fam.)

▶ bajar los humos a alg. (fig.) to cut s.o. down to size (fig.), to take s.o. down a peg or two (fig.), to squelch s.o. (fig., fam., Am.E.)

▶ subírsele a alg. los humos a la cabeza (fig., fam.) to become [very] stuck-up (fam.), to become [very] high and mighty (fam.) ◆ *Se le subieron los humos a la cabeza a ella. She became very stuck-up.*

▶ subírsele a alg. el humo a las narices (fig., fam.) to get furious, to get mad (fam.) ◆ *Se me subió el humo a las narices. I got furious.*

▷ humo (donde **fuego** se hace, ~ sale)

▷ humor (estar de un ~ de **perros**)

hurtar to steal

▶ hurtarle el cuerpo a algo to dodge s.th. (blow/etc.) ◆ *El torero le hurtó el cuerpo a la cornada. The bullfighter dodged the thrust (bull's horns).*

▶ hurtar el hombro (fig.) (especially work): to skive off (fam., Br.E.), to shirk ◆ *Cada vez que teníamos mucho que hacer, ese tío hurtaba el hombro.* Whenever we had a lot to do, that guy shirked.

la husma (hunt): scent

▶ andar a la husma (fig.) to be/go snooping around (fam.)

▶ andar a la husma de algo (fig.) to be/go prying [secretly] into s.th., to be looking [secretly] into s.th. ◆ *El investigador privado sigue andando a la husma de ese asunto.* The private detective continues looking secretly into that matter.

I

▷ iceberg (la **punta** del ~)

la idea idea

▶ no tener ni la más remota o pálida idea de algo (fam.) not to have the foggiest [idea] about s.th., not to have the faintest idea about s.th., not to know beans about s.th. (sl., Am.E.), not to know one end of s.th. from the other

▷ idiota (la **caja** ~)

▷ ido (estar ~ de la **cabeza**)

▷ iglesia (**casarse** por detrás de la ~)

▷ iglesia (no **comulgar** en la misma ~)

▷ iglesia (ser más pobre que una **rata** [de ~])

la ignorancia ignorance

▶ Ignorancia no quita pecado. (prov.) Ignorance of the law is no excuse/defense. (prov.)

▷ impaciencia (**rabiar/reventar** de ~)

impepinable (adj., fam.) certain, for sure (fam.), inevitable, undeniable, there's no getting away [from that] (fam.) ◆ *Eso es impepinable. That's for sure. That's the way it is. There's no getting away from that.*

▷ importar (no ~ a alg. un **ardite**)

▷ importar ([no] ~ a alg. un **bledo/comino/ higo/huevo/pepino/pimiento/pito/rábano**)

▷ importar ([no] ~ a alg. una **puñeta**)

▷ incapaz (ser ~ de matar una **mosca**)

incrustarse to embed itself

▶ incrustársele algo a alg. en la memoria (fig.) s.th. engraves/stamps itself [firmly] on s.o.'s memory (fig.) ◆ *Se me ha incrustado esa idea en la memoria. That idea has stamped itself or is stamped firmly on my memory.* ◆ *Sus palabras se me han incrustado en la memoria. His words have engraved themselves on my memory.*

el infierno hell

▶ vivir/estar en el quinto infierno (fig., fam.) to live/be at the back of beyond ▷ vivir/estar donde **Cristo** dio las tres voces

▶ mandar a alg. al infierno (fig.) to tell s.o. to go to hell (fam.) ◆ *Yo que tú la mandaría al infierno. If I were you, I'd tell her to go to hell.*

▷ infierno (quien por su **gusto** padece, vaya al ~ a quejarse)

la ínfula infula

▶ darse ínfulas (fig.) to get on one's high horse (fig.)

▶ tener muchas ínfulas (fig.) to think a lot of o.s., to give o.s. airs, to be on one's high horse (fig.)

▶ tener ínfulas de ... (fig.) to fancy o.s. as ... (fam.) ◆ *Tiene ínfulas de escritor. He fancies himself as a writer.* ◆ *Siempre ha tenido ínfulas de genio. He's always fancied himself as a genius.*

▷ ingenio (el **hambre**/la **necesidad** aguza el ~)

▷ ingenuo (**pecar** de ~)

la ingratitud ingratitude

▶ De ingratitudes está el mundo lleno. (prov.) Desert and reward seldom keep company. (prov.)

el ingrato ingrate

▶ De ingratos está el mundo lleno. (prov.) Desert and reward seldom keep company. (prov.)

▷ inocencia (lavarse las **manos** [en ~])

la instancia authority

▶ en última instancia (fig., fam.) if [the] worst comes to [the] worst, if all else fails, as a last resort ◆ *En última instancia podríamos vender la casa. As a last resort we could sell the house.*

▷ insulto (soltar una **andanada**/un **rosario** de ~s a alg.)

la inyección injection

▶ La industria necesita una inyección financiera. (fig.) The industry needs an injection of funds/money. (fig.) The industry needs a shot in the arm. (fig., fam.)

▶ Lo que dijeron supuso una inyección de optimismo para nosotros. (fig.) What they said was a boost to our optimism. What they said was a shot in the arm for us. (fig., fam.)

ir to go

▶ ser el no va más (fam.) to be the ultimate, to be absolutely brilliant (fam., Br.E.), to be the [very] last word, to be the best/greatest thing since sliced bread (fam.) ◆ *Esto es el no va más. This is absolutely brilliant.* ◆ *el no va más en computadoras the ultimate in computers, the last word in computers*

▶ creerse el no va más to think one is the cat's pajamas (Am.E.) or pyjamas (Br.E.) or whiskers (fam.), to think one is the bee's knees (fam.), to think one is the greatest (fam.)

▷ ir (▷ **venir**: no me va ni me viene)

▷ ir (ni ~ ni **venir**)

la irrisión derisive laughter

▶ ser la irrisión de la cuidad (fig.) to be the laughing stock of the city

▷ izquierdo (levantarse con el **pie** ~)

▷ izquierdo (ser un **cero** a la izquierda)

▷ izquierdo (tener [mucha] **mano** izquierda)

J

el jabón soap
- ▶ dar un jabón a alg. **(fig.)** to give s.o. a [good] telling-off or dressing-down **(fam.)**, to tell s.o. off **(fam.)**, to dress s.o. down **(fam.)**
- ▶ dar jabón a alg. **(fig.)** to soft-soap s.o. **(fam.)**

la jabonadura soaping
- ▶ dar una jabonadura a alg. **(fig.)** to give s.o. a [good] telling-off or dressing-down **(fam.)**, to tell s.o. off **(fam.)**, to dress s.o. down **(fam.)**

jabonar to soap
- ▶ jabonar a alg. **(fig., fam.)** to give s.o. a [good] telling-off or dressing-down **(fam.)**, to tell s.o. off **(fam.)**, to dress s.o. down **(fam.)**

el jacarero **(fam.)** wag, cheerful type, amusing person

el jaez harness
- ▶ ser del mismo jaez **(fig.)** to be tarred with the same brush **(fam., pej.)**. ◆ *Son todos del mismo jaez. They're all tarred with the same brush. They're all as bad as each other.*
- ▶ gente de ese jaez **(fig.)** people of that ilk/sort/kind (pej.) ◆ *Yo no me trato con gente de ese jaez. I don't associate/mix with people of that ilk/sort.*

la jai **(pop.)** bird **(sl., Br.E.)**, chick **(fam., Am.E.)**, doll **(fam.)**

el jaleo cheering and clapping (to encourage the dancers)
- ▶ el jaleo **(fig., fam.)** (a) racket **(fam.)**, row **(fam.)**, ruckus **(fam., Am.E.)** (b) mess **(fig.)**, muddle ◆ *armar [un] jaleo to kick up a racket/row* ◆ *Ayer se armó un jaleo de mil demonios. There was a terrible ruckus/a hell of a row yesterday.* ◆ *¡Qué jaleo! What a mess! What a muddle!* ◆ *armarse alg. un [tremendo] jaleo to be [totally] wrong/mistaken, to be way out **(fam.)**, to be [way] off base (fig., Am.E.)* ◆ *Se armaron un tremendo jaleo con los cálculos. They were way out in their calculations.*

el jamón ham
- ▶ ¡Y un jamón [con chorreras]! **(fig., fam.)** (a) My foot! **(fam.)** Get away! **(fam., Br.E.)** Come off it! **(fam.)** (b) You're hopeful! **(fam.)** [That's] out of the question! ◆ *Dice que gana 100.000 dólares al año. ¡100.000 dólares y un jamón [con chorreras]! He says he earns $100,000 a year. Get away! Come off it! $100,000 my foot!*
- ▶ estar algo/alg. jamón **(fam., Esp.)** s.th.: to be great/fantastic **(fam.)**, to be splendid, to be delicious; s.o.: to be great **(fam.)**, to be dishy **(sl.)**, to be a dish **(fam.)**, to be attractive **(fig.)** ◆ *Este plato está jamón. This is a delicious meal.* ◆ *Esa chica está jamón That girl is a dish.*

el jarabe syrup
- ▶ jarabe de pico **(fig., fam.)** hot air **(fam.)**, empty/hollow promises **(fig.)**, mere words ◆ *Lo que dicen no es más que jarabe de pico. They just make hollow promises.* ◆ *Su hermano es puro jarabe de pico. His brother is full of hot air.*
- ▶ dar jarabe a alg. **(fig., fam.)** to butter s.o. up **(fam.)**

el jarope **(fam.)** syrup
- ▶ el jarope **(fig., fam.)** nasty drink **(fig.)**, brew **(fam.)**, concoction

la jarra pitcher **(Am.E.)**, jug **(Br.E.)**
- ▶ en jarras with arms akimbo
- ▶ ponerse en jarras to put one's hands on one's hips

el jarro pitcher **(Am.E.)**, jug **(Br.E.)**
- ▶ echar un jarro de agua fría a alg. **(fig.)** to bring s.o. down to earth with a bump **(fig.)**
- ▶ caer/sentar como un jarro de agua fría **(fam.)** to come as a complete shock **(fig.)**, to come as a nasty surprise, to come like a or be a bombshell **(fig.)**, to go down like a lead balloon **(fam., Br.E.)** ◆ *El resultado de las elecciones cayó como un jarro de agua fría. The election results came like a bombshell.* ◆ *Esa noticia me sentó como un jarro de agua fría. That piece of news came as a complete shock to me.*
- ▷ jarro (al **catarro**, con el ~)

Jesús Jesus
▶ ¡Hasta verte, Jesús mío! (fam.) Cheers! (fam.) Down the hatch! (fam.) Bottoms up! (fam.)

la jeta thick lip
▶ la jeta (pop.) (a) trap (sl.), gob (sl., Br.E.) (b) mug (sl.), dial (sl., Br.E.) ◆ *¡No asomes la jeta por aquí! Don't you dare show your mug around here!*
▷ jeta (**pelar** la ~)
▷ Job (tener más **paciencia** que ~)

joder [a alg.] (vulg.) to fuck [s.o.] (vulg.), to shag [s.o.] (vulg., Br.E.) ▷ **follar** [a alg.]
▶ joder algo (fam./vulg.) to screw s.th. up ▷ **escoñar** algo
▶ estar jodido (vulg.) to be up the creek (fam.) or up shit creek (vulg.) [without a paddle]
▶ ¡Que se/etc. joda/etc.! (vulg.) He/etc. knows/etc. what he/etc. can do! (fam.) ◆ *¡Que te jodas! You know what you can do! Get stuffed! (vulg.)*
▶ no tener ni una jodida peseta (vulg.) not to have one bloody (sl., Br.E.) peseta in one's pocket

la jota name of the letter J/j
▶ no saber ni jota de algo (fam.) not to have the foggiest [idea] about s.th., not to have the faintest idea about s.th., not to have a clue about s.th. (fam.), not to know the first thing about s.th., not to know beans about s.th. (sl., Am.E.), not to know one end of s.th. from the other ◆ *No sabe ni jota de literatura. He doesn't have a clue about literature.* ◆ *No sabe ni jota de computadoras. He doesn't know one end of a computer from the other.*

Juan John
▶ Juan Español (fig.) average Spaniard
▶ Juan Pérez (fig.) man in the street, John Q Public (Am.E.), man on the Clapham omnibus (fam., Br.E.)
▶ Juan Lanas (fig.) henpecked husband (fam.), wimp (fam.)
▶ Juan Palomo (fig.) (a) person who looks after Number One (fam.) (b) loner, lone wolf (fam.)

el jubileo jubilee
▶ parece que hay jubileo aquí/allí (fig., fam.) it's like Piccadilly Circus around here or there (fig.)

Judas Judas
▶ un judas (fig.) traitor, snake in the grass (fig.) ◆ *Algún judas se chivó contra nosotros. Some snake in the grass sneaked on us.*

el juego play, game
▶ jugar/hacer un doble juego (fig.) to play a double game
▶ conocerle/verle a alg. el juego (fig.) to see through or know s.o.'s little game (fam.), to know what s.o. is up to (fam.), to be wise to s.o. (fam.) ◆ *Le conozco/veo el juego a ella. I see through her little game. I know what she's up to.*
▶ tomar algo a juego (fig.) not to take s.th. seriously ◆ *Toman todo a juego. They don't take anything seriously.*
▶ estar en juego (fig.) to be at stake (fig.) ◆ *Mucho está en juego. There's a lot at stake.*
▶ poner algo en juego (fig.) to bring s.th. into play (fig.), to bring s.th. (influence/etc.) to bear, to stake s.th. (fig.) ◆ *Puso en juego una fortuna para adquirir ... He staked a fortune on acquiring . . .*
▶ no dejar entrar en juego a alg. (fig.) not to give s.o. a chance
▶ Desgraciado en el juego, afortunado en amores. (prov.) De malas en el juego, de buenas en amores. (prov.) Unlucky at cards, lucky in love. (prov.)

la juerga (fam.) [very] merry/good time, shindig (fam.), spree (fam.), binge (fam.), carousal
▶ estar de juerga to be partying, to have a merry/good time, to be on a spree/binge
▶ ir de juerga to go out partying, to go out for a merry/good time, to go on a spree/binge, to go on a blind (sl., Br.E.)
▶ correrse una juerga to have a ball (fam., Am.E.), to have a great time (fam.), to live it up, to have a real spree/binge, to whoop it up (fam.), to make whoopee (fam.) ◆ *Anoche nos corrimos una juerga. We had a real binge last night.*
▶ tomar algo a juerga (fam.) not to take s.th. seriously ◆ *Toman todo a juerga. They don't take anything seriously.*

el jueves Thursday
▶ no ser cosa del otro jueves (fam.) to be nothing special, to be nothing to write home about (fig.), to be nothing out of the ordinary, to be nothing exciting ◆ *El espectáculo*

no fue cosa del otro jueves. The show was nothing out of the ordinary.
▷ jueves (en la **semana** de tres ~/que no tenga ~)

la jugada (game): move
▶ hacer una mala jugada a alg. (fig.) to play a dirty/nasty trick on s.o. (fig.)

jugar to play, to gamble
▶ jugarse la vida (fig.) to risk one's life, to risk one's neck (fam.)
▶ jugarse el todo por el todo (fig.) to go to extremes, to go the whole hog (fam.), to shoot the works (fam.), to risk everything
▶ jugársela (fig.) (a) to stick one's neck out (fam.) (b) to be unfaithful
▶ jugársela a alg. (fig.) to do the dirty on s.o. (sl., Br.E.), to do it on s.o. (fam., Br.E.) ◆ *¡Nos la han jugado! They've done it on us!*
▷ jugar (o jugamos todos o se rompe la **baraja**)
▷ jugar a **cartas** vistas
▷ jugar al **gato** y al ratón con alg.
▷ jugar con el **fuego**
▷ jugar con/a dos **barajas**
▷ jugar hasta la **camisa**
▷ jugar la última **carta**
▷ jugar un doble **juego**
▷ jugar una mala **partida**/una **pieza** a alg.
▷ jugarse (~lo todo a una [sola] **carta**)
▷ jugarse el **pellejo**/el **pescuezo**/el **tipo**/la **vida**

el jugo juice
▶ el jugo (fig.) pith (fig.), essence (fig.), substance (fig.)
▶ sacar el jugo a algo/alg. (fig.) to get the essence/substance out of s.th., to get the most out of s.th./s.o., to make the most of s.th., to get everything one can out of s.o., to get the best out of s.o. ◆ *Le he sacado el jugo a este libro. I've got the substance out of this book.* ◆ *Le sacamos el jugo al buen tiempo que hizo allí. We made the most of the fine weather there.* ◆ *Les saca el jugo a sus empleados. He gets everything he can or as much as he possibly can out of his employees.*

el juguete toy
▶ ser un juguete de las olas (fig.) to be a plaything of the waves, to be at the mercy of the waves
▶ ser juguete de los caprichos de alg. (fig.) to be [like] putty in s.o.'s hands (fig.) ◆ *Ella tiene a él montado en las narices. Es juguete de los caprichos de él. She lets him do with her what he likes. She's putty in his hands.*
▶ ser un juguete en manos de alg. (fig.) to be a puppet in the hands of s.o. (fig.) ◆ *El presidente no es más que un juguete en manos de los magnates de la industria. The president is merely a puppet in the hands of the industrial magnates.*
▷ juicio (▷ **talón**: tener el ~ en los talones)
▷ juicio (estar en **tela** de ~)
▷ juicio (poner algo en **tela** de ~)

la jumera (fam.) drunkenness
▶ papar una jumera (pop.) to get drunk ▷ **cocerse** (a)
▷ jungla (la **ley** de la ~)

la jupa (Méjico y América Central) gourd
▶ la jupa (fig., fam.) nut (sl.) ▷ la **cebolla**
▶ darse una jupa (pop., Esp.) to slave/sweat away (fam.) ▷ echar/sudar la **hiel**

jurar to swear
▶ tenérsela jurada a alg. (fig., fam.) to have it in for s.o. (fam.) ◆ *Nos la tiene jurada. He has it in for us.*
▶ jurárselas a alg. (fam.) to vow vengeance against s.o. ◆ *Se las juré a ellos. I vowed vengeance against them.*
▷ jurar como un **carretero**
▷ jurar por lo más **sagrado**

la justicia justice
▶ no hacer justicia a alg. (fig.) ◆ *Nunca se le ha hecho justicia como artista. He has never received due recognition as an artist.* ◆ *Este retrato no le hace justicia a ella. This portrait doesn't do her justice.*
▷ justicia (doblar la **vara** de la ~)

K

el kanguro kangaroo
► el/la kanguro/kangura (fig., Esp.) baby-sitter ◆ *Hace de kangura dos veces por semana. She baby-sits twice a week.*

el kirie [eleison] kyrie eleison
► cantar el kirie (fig., fam.) to beg for mercy

L

la labia (fam.) articulacy, fluency
▶ tener mucha labia to have the gift of [the] gab (fam.)

el labio lip
▶ estar pendiente de los labios de alg. (fig.) to hang on s.o.'s lips (fig.), to hang on s.o.'s every word
▷ labio (▷ **sombrear**: ya le sombrea el ~ superior a alg.)
▷ labio (dejar a alg. con la **miel** en los ~s)
▷ labio (echar **candado** a los ~s)
▷ labio (estar aún con la **leche** en los ~s)

labrar to shape
▶ labrarse un porvenir to carve out a future for o.s. (fig.)

la ladilla crab louse
▶ pegarse como una ladilla a alg. (fig., fam.) to cling to s.o. like a leech/limpet (fig., fam.)

el lado side
▶ dejar algo a un lado o de lado (fig.) to leave s.th. aside, to omit s.th., to skip s.th. (fig.), to pass over s.th.
▶ dar de lado a alg. (fig.) to ignore/disregard s.o., to give s.o. the cold shoulder (fig.), to turn one's back on s.o. (fig.)
▶ ponerse del/al lado de alg. (fig.) to side with s.o., to stand up for s.o.
▷ ladrar a la **luna**
▷ ladrón (la **capa** [de ladrones])
▷ ladrón (la **ocasión** hace al ~)
▷ ladrón (ser más ~ que una **urraca**)

la ladronera den of thieves/robbers
▶ la ladronera (fam., hum.) money box

el lagarto big lizard
▶ el lagarto (fig.) fox (fig.), sly dog (fig., fam.), sly fellow
▶ ¡Lagarto, lagarto! (fig.) Touch wood! (Br.E.) Knock on wood! (Am.E.)

la lágrima tear
▶ llorar a lágrima viva to sob one's heart out, to cry one's eyes out
▶ llorar/derramar lágrimas de cocodrilo (fig.) to weep/shed crocodile tears (fig.) ◆ *Ella*

derramó lágrimas de cocodrilo cuando le dio a su jefe un infarto y se quedó en el sitio. Lo odiaba como a la peste. She shed crocodile tears when her boss dropped dead of a heart attack. She hated his guts.
▶ arrancarle a alg. lágrimas to bring tears to s.o.'s eyes, to be moved to tears (by) ◆ *La película nos arrancó lágrimas. We were moved to tears by the film.*
▶ beberse las lágrimas (fig.) to hold back one's tears, to fight back/down one's tears
▶ Lo que no va en lágrimas, va en suspiros. It's six of one and half a dozen of the other. (fig.) ◆ *¿Lo haremos ahora o más tarde? Lo que no va en lágrimas, va en suspiros. Shall we do it now or later? It's six of one and half a dozen of the other.*
▶ una lágrima de aguardiente (fig., fam.) drop of brandy/liquor
▷ lágrima (ser el **paño** de ~s de alg.)
▷ lamentar (más vale **prevenir** que ~)

el/la lameplatos (fam.) (a) toady (b) sponger (fam.), scrounger (fam.)

la lámpara lamp
▶ atizar la lámpara (fig., fam.) to have another drink, to hoist another one (sl., Am.E.), to fill up the glasses

la lana wool
▶ la lana (fam., Méjico) (money): dough (sl., Am.E.), bread (sl.), sugar (sl.), brass/dosh/ lolly (sl., Br.E.), wampum (sl., Am.E.)
▶ cardarle la lana a alg. (fig., fam.) to rap s.o. over the knuckles (fig.), to give s.o. a good telling-off or ticking-off (Br.E.) or dressing-down (fam.)
▶ ir por lana y volver esquilado o trasquilado (fig.) to get caught in one's own trap (fig.), to be hoist by/with one's own petard (fig.)
◆ *Comió la comida envenenada que fue para su esposo. Fue por lana y volvió trasquilado. She was hoist by her own petard when she ate the poisoned food that was meant for her husband.*
▷ lana (unos cardan la ~ y otros tienen/llevan/cobran la **fama**)

la lanza lance
▶ romper una lanza por algo/alg. (fig.) to stick one's neck out for s.th./s.o. (fam.), to take up the cudgels for s.th./s.o. (fig.)
▷ lanza (las **cañas** se vuelven ~s)

la lapa limpet
▶ pegarse como una lapa a alg. (fig., pop.) to cling to s.o. like a leech/limpet (fig., fam.)

largar to let loose, to let go
▶ largar a alg. (fig., fam.) (a) to ditch/dump s.o. (fam.), to drop/jilt s.o., to give s.o. the bird (fam.) (b) to fire s.o. (fam.) ▷ dar el **bote** a alg.
▶ largarse (fig., fam.) to vamoose (fam., hum., Am.E.), to beat it (sl.), to hop it (fam.), to clear off (fam.), to sling one's hook (sl., Br.E.) ◆ *¡Lárgate! Beat it!*
▶ largarse con viento fresco (fig., fam.) to beat it at once (sl.), to clear off at once (fam.)

largo long
▶ ser más largo que un día sin pan (fam.) (a) (person): to be a beanpole (fig., fam., hum.) (b) (s.th.): to be very long, to be as long as your arm (fam.) (c) to take forever (fam.), not to half take a long time (fam., Br.E.) ◆ *Su hermano es más largo que un día sin pan. His brother is a beanpole.* ◆ *La lista es más larga que un día sin pan. The list is as long as your arm.* ◆ *Esto sí que es más largo que un día sin pan. This is really taking forever. It doesn't half take a long time.*
▶ ser largo de manos (fig.) to be free with one's hands, to be quick to lash out
▶ ser largo de uñas (fig., fam.) to be light-fingered (fam.), to be a thief, to have sticky fingers (fam.)
▶ ser largo como pelo de huevo (fam.) to be very stingy/miserly
▶ a lo largo y a lo ancho de throughout [the length and breadth of], all over ◆ *a lo largo y a lo ancho de España throughout the length and breadth of Spain* ◆ *Hubo manifestaciones a lo largo y a lo ancho del país. There were demonstrations throughout the country or all over the country.*
▶ a lo largo y a lo lejos as far as the eye can see ◆ *A lo largo y a lo lejos no había bicho viviente. There wasn't a living soul as far as the eye could see.*

▶ a la corta o a la larga sooner or later ◆ *A la corta o a la larga [se] llevará su merecido. Sooner or later he'll get his just deserts.*
▷ largo (ser más ~ que una **cuaresma**)
▷ largo (tener las **manos** largas)

la lata can, tin. (Br.E.)
▶ dar la lata a alg. (fig., fam.) to get on s.o.'s nerves (fam.), to get on s.o.'s wick (fam., Br.E.), to bend s.o.'s ear (fam., Am.E.), to annoy s.o.

el latigazo lash, crack of a whip
▶ atarse/pegarse un latigazo (fam.) to hoist one (sl., Am.E.), to have a drink

el latín Latin
▶ saber [mucho] latín (fig., fam.) to be [very/pretty] sharp, to be wised up (fam., Am.E.)

el laurel laurel
▶ dormirse sobre los/sus laureles (fig.) to rest on one's laurels (fig.) ◆ *Sigue haciendo grandes cosas. Nunca se ha dormido sobre sus laureles. He keeps doing great things. He has never rested on his laurels.*

el/la lavacaras (fig., fam.) sycophant, toady, creep (fam.), bootlicker (fam.)
▷ lavar la **cara** a alg.
▷ lavar los **trapos** sucios ante el mundo entero/en casa

el lazo snare, lasso
▶ caer en el lazo (fig.) to fall/walk into the trap (fig.)

la leche milk
▶ estar aún con la leche en los labios (fig.) to be still wet behind the ears (fig.), to be still as green as a pea (fig., fam.), to be still young and inexperienced
▶ haber mamado algo [ya] en/con la leche (fig.) to have learned/learnt s.th. from the cradle (fig.), to have learned/learnt s.th. at one's mother's knee (fig.) ◆ *Lo ha mamado ya con la leche. He's already learned it at his mother's knee.*
▶ pedir leche a las cabrillas to ask the impossible
▶ la leche (pop.) (a) semen, spunk (vulg., Br.E.) (b) slap in the face
▶ pegar una leche a alg. to paste s.o. one (sl.), to land s.o. one (fam.)

▶ tener mala leche to have bad/evil intentions, to have a nasty/spiteful nature or disposition, to be a nasty piece of work (fam.), to be a bastard (fam.)

▶ estar de mala leche (vulg.) to be in a foul/stinking mood (fam.)

▷ leche (**blanco** y en botella, ~)

▷ leche (buscar **pelos** en la ~)

la lechera milkmaid, dairymaid

▶ la cuenta de la lechera (fig.) simple-minded reasoning

▶ hacer las cuentas de la lechera (fig.) to count one's chickens before they're hatched (fig.) ◆ *Aunque no está [absolutamente] seguro de que herede todo ese dinero, ya está haciendo grandes planes para el futuro. No hagas las cuentas de la lechera. Although he's not [absolutely] sure whether he'll inherit all that money, he's already making big plans for the future. Don't count your chickens before they're hatched.*

▷ lecho de **rosa**s (la vida no es un ~)

▷ lecho de **rosa**s ([no] estar/dormir sobre un ~)

▷ lechón (hasta la **perra** le/etc. parirá lechones)

la lechuga lettuce

▶ estar como una lechuga (fig., fam.) to be/look a picture of health (fig., fam.), to be bright-eyed and bushy-tailed (fam., hum.)

▶ estar fresco/fresquito como una lechuga (fam.) to be/feel as fresh as a daisy

▶ ser más fresco que una lechuga (fam.) to be very fresh (Am.E.)/cheeky, to be a cheeky monkey/devil (fam.), to be as bold as brass (fam.), to have a lot of nerve (fam.)

▶ la lechuga (fam., Esp.) 1000-peseta bill (Am.E.) or note (Br.E.)

▷ lechuga (entre **col** y col, ~)

▷ lejos (a lo **largo** y a lo ~)

▷ lejos (**llegar** ~)

la lengua tongue, language

▶ tener una lengua viperina o de víbora/de serpiente/de escorpión/de hacha (fig., fam.) to have a vicious/wicked tongue, to have a sharp tongue (fig.)

▶ tener la lengua gorda (fig., fam.) to be drunk

▶ soltar la lengua (fig.) to spill the beans (sl.)

▶ desatar/soltar la lengua a alg. (fig.) to make s.o. talk, to get s.o. to talk, to loosen s.o.'s tongue (fig.)

▶ tirar de la lengua a alg. (fig.) to draw/sound s.o. out (fig.), to winkle everything out of s.o. (fig., Br.E.), to drag everything/it out of s.o. (fam.) ◆ *Siempre hay que tirarle de la lengua. You always have to drag/winkle everything out of him.*

▶ pegársele a alg. la lengua al paladar (fig.) s.o. can't say a word ◆ *Se me pegó la lengua al paladar. I couldn't say a word.*

▶ morderse la lengua (fig.) to bite one's lip (fig.), to hold one's tongue (fig.), to pull [one's] punches (fig., sl.). ◆ *Tenía ganas de decirles cuatro verdades, pero me mordí la lengua. I felt like giving them a piece of my mind, but I held my tongue.*

▶ no morderse la lengua (fig.) not to mince one's words (fig.), not to pull [one's] punches (fig., sl.) ◆ *La puse a caldo. No me mordí la lengua. I told her what I thought of her. I didn't pull my punches or any punches.*

▶ irse de la lengua, írsele a alg. la lengua (fig., fam.) to be a slip of the tongue (fig.), to slip out (fig.), to let the cat out of the bag ◆ *Queríamos que fuese una sorpresa, pero desgraciadamente se fue de la lengua. We meant it to be a surprise, but unfortunately he let the cat out of the bag.* ◆ *Se me fue la lengua. It was a slip of the tongue.* ◆ *No debiera haberlo dicho pero se me fue la lengua. I shouldn't have said it but it [just] slipped out.*

▶ con la lengua fuera (fig.) with one's tongue hanging out (fig., fam.) ◆ *Llegué a la parada de autobuses con la lengua fuera. By the time I got to the bus stop my tongue was hanging out.*

▶ andar en lenguas (fig., fam.) to be the subject of gossip, to be the talk of the town

▶ llevar/traer a alg. en lenguas (fig.) to gossip about s.o.

▶ hacerse lenguas de algo/alg. (fig., fam.) to praise s.th./s.o. to the skies, to rave about s.th./s.o.

▷ lengua (▷ **nacer**: nació alg. con la ~ fuera)

▷ lengua (no tener **frenillo/pelo**s/**pepita** en la ~)

▷ lengua (tener algo en la **punta** de la ~)

▷ lengua (tener **pelos** en la ~)

▷ lento (ser más ~ que una **tortuga**)

la leña firewood
- ▶ dar leña a alg. (fig.), cargar de leña a alg. (fig.) to give s.o. a good going-over (sl.), to let s.o. have it (fam.) ▷ arrimar **candela** a alg.
- ▶ llevar leña al monte (fig.) to carry coals to Newcastle (fig.) ◆ *Llevarle hielo a un esquimal es como llevar leña al monte. Taking ice to an Eskimo is like carrying coals to Newcastle.*
- ▷ leña (echar ~ al **fuego**)

el leño log
- ▶ dormir como un leño (fig.) to sleep like a log (fam.)
- ▷ león (la **tajada** del ~)
- ▷ león (más vale ser **cabeza** de ratón que cola de ~)

la leona lioness
- ▶ la leona (pop.) porter, concierge

Lepe
- ▶ saber más que Lepe (fig., fam.) to be a walking encyclopedia (hum.), to be pretty/really smart

la letra letter
- ▶ tener mucha letra menuda (fig., fam.) to be very smart, to be as sly as they come (fam.)
- ▶ tener letras (fig., fam.) to be educated
- ▶ poner cuatro letras (fam.) to drop a few lines
- ▶ decir a una las cuatro letras (fam.) to call a woman a slut/whore
- ▶ La letra con sangre entra. (prov.) Spare the rod and spoil the child. (prov.) No pains, no gains. (prov.) There's no royal road to learning. (prov.)
- ▷ letra (al **pie** de la ~)

el/la levantacoches car thief
- ▷ levantar **cabeza**
- ▷ levantar **cabeza** (no ~)
- ▷ levantar el **vuelo**
- ▷ levantarse con las **gallina**s

el levante (fam.) (man or woman): easy/quick conquest (fig.), easy/quick pick-up (fam.)
- ▶ salir de levante to go out trying to pick s.o. up (fam.), to go out on the pick-up (fam.), to go out on the make (Am.E.) or on the pull (Br.E.) (sl.), to go out looking for talent (fam., Br.E.)
- ▶ hacer un levante a alg. to pick s.o. up (fam.)

la ley law
- ▶ Hecha la ley, hecha la trampa. (fam.) Every law has its loophole. (fig.)
- ▶ la ley de la jungla/selva (fig.) law of the jungle, jungle law
- ▶ la ley del más fuerte [principle of] might is right
- ▶ con todas las de la ley (fam.) proper[ly], real, duly, thorough[ly], carefully, fairly (win/etc.) ◆ *Lo ha hecho con todas las de la ley. He's done it properly/thoroughly.* ◆ *una comida con todas las de la ley a real/proper meal*
- ▷ ley (la **necesidad** carece de ~)

liar to bind, to tie [up]
- ▶ liarlas o liárselas (fam.) (a) to beat it (sl.) (b) to kick the bucket (fam.) ▷ **cascar**[la]
- ▷ liar el **petate**/los **bártulos**

librar to rescue, to free
- ▶ salir bien/mal librado de algo (fig.) to come out of s.th. well/badly
- ▶ salir bien librado (fig.) to get off lightly, to be lucky there
- ▶ ¡De buena me he/nos hemos/etc. librado! I/we/etc. got off lightly! I/we/etc. got lucky there! Talk about luck! That was close!
- ▷ libre (ser ~ como el **aire/viento**)

el libro book
- ▶ ahorcar/colgar los libros (fig.) to give up or quit (Am.E.) studying
- ▶ hacer libro nuevo (fig.) to turn over a new leaf (fig.) ◆ *Decidió hacer libro nuevo y prometió que en lo sucesivo no volvería a cometer los mismos errores. He decided to turn over a new leaf and promised henceforth never to make the same mistakes again.*
- ▶ perder los libros (fig.) to lose the knack or one's touch (fam.) ◆ *Recientemente ha tenido dificultad para explicarse con sencillez. Parece que ha perdido los libros. Recently he's had difficulty [in] explaining things simply. He seems to have lost his touch.*

la licencia (military): discharge, leave
- ▶ dar la licencia a alg. (pop.) to give s.o. his marching orders (fam.) ▷ dar el **bote** a alg.
- ▷ líder (ser un ~ con toda la **barba**)

la liebre hare
▶ levantar la liebre (fig.) to blow the gaff (fam., Br.E.), to let the cat out of the bag
▶ Donde/cuando menos se piensa, salta la liebre. Things often happen when you least expect them to. Life is full of surprises.
▷ liebre (▷ **corrido**: ser una ~ corrida)
▷ liebre (dar a alg. **gato** por ~)

la liendre nit
▶ cascarle/machacarle a alg. las liendres (fig., pop.) to give s.o. a sound thrashing (fam.)
  ▷ arrimar **candela** a alg.
▷ ligero (ser ~ de **cascos**)

el ligón (fam.) man who tries to pick/chat up women (fam.), wolf (fig., fam.), womanizer

la ligona (fam.) woman who can be picked up or chatted up easily (fam.), easy lay (sl.), to be one man after another with a woman, woman who will go with anybody, woman who always has a new man in tow (fig.)

la lima file
▶ comer como una lima (fig.) to eat greedily
  ▷ comer/mascar a dos **carrillos**

el limón lemon
▶ los limones (fig., fam.) (breasts): knockers (sl.), tits (fam.), boobs (fam.), hooters (sl., Am.E.)
▷ limonada (no ser ni **chicha** ni ~)
▷ limosna (alzarse/salirse con el **santo** y la ~)
▷ limpiar algo solamente por donde ve la **suegra**
▷ limpiar solamente lo que ve la **suegra**
▷ limpio (no ser **trigo** ~)
▷ limpio como una **patena**
▷ lince (tener **ojos** de ~)

el lirón dormouse
▶ dormir como un lirón (fig.) to sleep like a baby (fig.), to sleep like a log (fam.)

liso smooth, even
▶ ser lisa (fig., pop.) to be flat-chested ▷ ser de **Castellón de la Plana**
▷ listo (ser más ~ que el **hambre**)

la liza tournament field
▶ entrar en liza (fig.) to enter the arena (fig.)
  ◆ *Otro candidato entró en liza. Another candidate entered the arena.*

la llaga open wound
▶ renovar la[s] llaga[s] (fig.) to open up or reopen an old wound/sore (fig.), to open up or reopen old wounds/sores (fig.) ◆ *Dile que cierre el pico. Está renovando las llagas. Tell him to pipe down. He's opening up old wounds.*
▷ llaga (poner el **dedo** en la ~)

la llama flame
▶ salir de las llamas y caer en las brasas (fig.) to jump out of the frying pan into the fire ◆ *Atracó un banco para pagar sus deudas. Salió de las llamas y cayó en las brasas. He held up a bank to pay [off] his debts. He jumped out of the frying pan into the fire.*

llegar to arrive
▶ llegar a las manos (pop.) to come to blows ◆ *Llegaron a las manos. They came to blows.*
▶ llegar lejos (fig.) to go far [in life] (fig.)
▶ no llegar a tanto (fig.) not to get quite that bad, not to come to that ◆ *No llegó a tanto. It didn't get quite that bad.* ◆ *No creo que llegue a tanto. I don't think [that] it'll come to that.*
▷ llenarse la **barriga**/el **buche**/el **vientre**

llevar to carry, to wear, to lead
▶ llevar a alg. un/etc. año (fig.) to be one/ etc. year older than s.o. ◆ *Mi hermano me lleva cinco años. My brother is five years older than I.*
▶ llevar a alg. la cabeza (fig.) to be taller than s.o. by a head
▶ llevarse bien/mal con alg. to get or not to get along/on (Br.E.) with s.o. ◆ *Se llevan mal con el jefe. They don't get along with the boss.*
▶ llevarse todo por delante (fig.) to liven/hot (fam.) things up ◆ *Se llevó todo por delante en la última fiesta. He livened things up at the last party.*
▷ llevarse la **mar** de bien

llorar to weep
▶ Quien no llora no mama. (prov.) If you don't ask you don't get.
▷ llorar (me entraban unas **ganas** locas de ~)

▷ llorar a moco tendido/a **moco** y baba
▷ llorar como una **Magdalena**
▷ llorar con un **ojo**
▷ llorar **lágrimas** de cocodrilo

llover to rain

▶ llover sobre mojado (fig.) to be [struck by] one disaster after another, to be one [tragic] blow after another, on top of all or to cap it all (fig.) or to crown it all (fig.) or to add insult to injury or to make matters worse s.th. else happens ◆ *A ese pobre diablo le llueve sobre mojado. It's one tragic blow (fig.) after another for that poor devil.* ◆ *Eso fue llover sobre mojado. That capped/crowned it all.* ◆ *... y luego llovió sobre mojado. . . . and on top of all that s.th. else happened. . . . and to add insult to injury s.th. else happened. . . . and to make matters worse s.th. else happened.* ◆ *Siempre llueve sobre mojado. (prov.) It never rains but it pours. (prov.)*

▶ Nunca llueve a gusto de todos. (fig.) (a) One man's meat is another man's poison. (b) You can't please everybody. You can't please all the people all of the time.

▶ escuchar/oír como quien oye llover (fig.) to refuse to listen [to s.o.], turn a deaf ear [to s.o./s.th.], to pay no attention [to what s.o. says] ◆ *Oí lo que dijo como quien oye llover. I turned a deaf ear to what she said. I paid no attention to what she said.* ◆ *Me escuchaba como quien oye llover. He didn't listen to me. He refused to listen to me. He paid no attention to what I said.* ◆ *Estoy continuamente diciéndole que vaya al médico pero es como quien oye llover. I keep telling him to see his doctor or to go to the doctor's but it runs off him like water off a duck's back/but it's [like] water off a duck's back. (fam.)*

▶ Ha llovido mucho desde entonces. A lot of water has flowed under the bridge since then.

▷ llover (venir como llovido del **cielo**)

▷ llover a **cántaros/chorros/cubos/mares/torrentes**

el lobo wolf

▶ un viejo lobo de mar (fig.) old salt (fam.), old sea dog (fig.)

▶ un lobo con piel de cordero/oveja (fig.) wolf in sheep's clothing (fig.) ◆ *Ten cuidado con el director. Parece que no le cabe el corazón en el pecho, pero es un lobo con piel de cordero. Beware of the manager. He seems to be the very soul of kindness, but he's a wolf in sheep's clothing.*

▶ gritar ¡al lobo! (fig.) to cry wolf (fig.) ◆ *No grites ¡al lobo! con demasiada frecuencia. Nadie vendrá. Don't cry wolf too often. Nobody/none will come.*

▶ desollar/dormir el lobo (fam.) to sleep it off (fam.), to sleep off a hangover (fam.)

▶ arrojar a alg. a los lobos (fig.) to throw s.o. to the wolves/dogs (fig.) ◆ *La comisión jurídica exigió una explicación. El Ministro de Defensa le cargó el muerto al general y lo arrojó a los lobos. The Judiciary Committee was demanding an explanation. The Secretary of Defense passed the buck to the general and threw him to the wolves.*

▷ lobo (el **hambre** de ~)
▷ lobo (encomendar las **oveja**s al ~)
▷ lobo (haber visto las **oreja**s del ~)
▷ lobo (meterse en la **boca** del ~)
▷ lobo (ser ~s de una misma **camada**)
▷ lobo (ver las **oreja**s del ~)

loco mad

▶ estar/ser loco de atar o de remate (fam.) to be stark raving/staring mad (fam.), to be completely crazy or nuts (fam.), to be as mad as a hatter (Br.E.), to be as mad as a March hare (fam.)

▶ Es para volverse loco. (fig., fam.) It's enough to drive you mad/crazy. (fam.)

▶ Está loca por la música. (fam.) She's an easy lay. (sl.)

▶ Cada loco con su tema. (fam.) To each his own. Horses for courses. (fam., Br.E.)

▷ loco (de **cuerdo** y ~ todos tenemos un poco)
▷ loco (estar [~] como un **cencerro**)
▷ loco (estar más ~ que una **cabra**)
▷ loco (los **niño**s y los ~s dicen las verdades)

▷ lodo (cerrar algo a **piedra** y ~)
▷ lodo (sacar el **pie** del ~ a alg.)

la longaniza long, spicy pork sausage

▶ atar perros con longaniza (fig.) to court disaster (fig.), to play with fire (fig.) ◆ *Corrió un gran riesgo. Parece que le gusta atar perros con longaniza. He took a big risk. He seems to like playing with fire.*

▶ Allí tampoco atan los perros con longaniza[s]. (prov.) It's the same the whole world over. People elsewhere in the world don't live in the land of milk and honey either. (fig.)

el loquero (fam., hum.) funny farm (fam., hum.), loony bin (fam., hum.), nuthouse (fam.)

el lucero bright star
▶ quitarle al lucero del alba (fig.) not to mince one's words (fig.), to speak one's mind ◆ *Habló en plata. Le quitó al lucero del alba. He spoke bluntly. He didn't mince his words.*

▷ luchar a **brazo** partido

lucir to shine
▶ lucir en sus/los estudios (fig.) to be a brilliant (fig.) or an outstanding student, to shine at one's studies (fig.)

lucirse to distinguish o.s., to excel
▶ lucirse (iron.) to show o.s. up, to make a fool of o.s. ◆ *¡Te has lucido! A fine thing you've done! (iron.) You've really excelled yourself! (iron.) What a mess you've made of it! (fig.) You've made a real fool of yourself!*

▷ lugar (hacer[se] su/una **composición** de ~)

▷ lumbre (estar al **amor** de la ~)

la luna moon
▶ la luna de miel (fig.) honeymoon
▶ estar en la luna (fig., fam.) to have one's head in the clouds, to be away with the fairies (fam.), to be remote from it all (fig.), to be miles away (fig.), to have one's mind on other things, to be out to lunch (fam., Am.E.), to be daydreaming, to be woolgathering (fam.)
▶ vivir en la luna (fig., fam.) to have one's head in the clouds, to be living in cloud-cuckoo-land, to be living in never-never land, to be living in a dream/fantasy world
▶ pedir la luna (fig.) to ask the impossible
▶ mirar la luna (fig.) to gawp (fam., Br.E.), to gawk (fam.)
▶ ladrar a la luna (fig.) to talk to a brick wall (fig., fam.), to waste one's breath ◆ *No está escuchando. Es como ladrarle a la luna. He isn't listening. It is like talking to a brick wall [with him].*

▶ quedarse a la luna de Valencia (fig.) to be left empty-handed, to come away empty-handed, to be disappointed, to be left in the lurch (fig.), to be left high and dry (fig.)
▶ dejar a alg. a la luna de Valencia (fig.) to leave s.o. empty-handed, to disappoint s.o., to leave s.o. in the lurch (fig.), to leave s.o. high and dry (fig.) ◆ *Me dejaron a la luna de Valencia y tuve que hacerlo todo yo. They left me in the lurch and I had to do it all myself.*
▶ estar de buena/mala luna (fig.) to be in a good/bad mood
▶ tener sus lunas (fig.) to have strange/peculiar ideas
▷ luna (poner a alg. en/por o levantar a alg. a/hasta los **cuernos** de la ~)

la luz light
▶ dar luz verde a algo (fig.) to give s.th. the green light (fig.) or the go-ahead ◆ *Dieron luz verde al proyecto. They gave the plan the green light or the go-ahead.*
▶ ser de pocas luces o ser corto de luces o tener pocas luces (fig., fam.) to be pretty dim (fam., Br.E.), to be dim-witted (fam.), not to be very bright (fig.), not to be the brightest bulb in the chandelier (fig.), to be one sandwich short of a picnic (hum.), to be a few cards shy of a full deck (hum.), to be two bricks shy of a load (hum.)
▶ sacar algo a luz (fig.) (a) (book/etc.): to bring out, to publish (b) (secret or scandal/etc.): to bring to light (fig.)
▶ salir a luz (fig.) (a) (book/etc.): to come out, to be published (b) (secret or scandal/etc.): to become known, to come to light (fig.) ◆ *El lío acaba de salir a luz. The affair has just come to light.*
▶ Hay luz al final del túnel. (fig.) There is light at the end of the tunnel. (fig.) There is a bright spot on the horizon. (fig.) There is a glimmer of hope. (fig.)
▶ meter/poner la luz bajo el celemín (fig.) to hide one's light under a bushel (fig.) ◆ *No la subestimes. Tiene muchos talentos, pero pone la luz bajo el celemín. Don't underestimate her. She has many talents, but she hides her light under a bushel.*

LL

Las palabras que empiezan por "ll" aparecen bajo la letra L en su correspondiente orden alfabético.

Words beginning with "ll" are listed at the appropriate alphabetical position under letter L.

M

machacar to beat (meat/etc.), to pound, to crush

▶ machacar (fig., fam.) to cram (fam.), to swot (fam., Br.E.), to bone up (fam.)

▶ machacar algo (fig., fam.) to cram s.th. (fam.), to swot up [on] s.th. (fam., Br.E.), to mug up [on] s.th. (fam., Br.E.), to bone up on s.th. (fam.)

▶ machacar [en/sobre] algo (fig., fam.) to harp on [about] s.th. (fig., fam.), to go/keep on about s.th. ◆ *Sigue machacando en ese asunto.* He's still harping on about that matter.

▶ machacar en hierro frío (fig., fam.) to labor in vain, to waste one's time, to be a waste of time, to be a wasted effort, to flog a dead horse (fig., fam.) ◆ *Hablarle de aumentar los sueldos es como machacar en hierro frío. Talking to him about increasing the salaries is like flogging a dead horse or is a complete waste of time.*

▶ machacar a alg. (fig., fam.) (in debate; opponent): to crush s.o. (fig.), to flatten s.o. (fam.), to tear s.o. to bits/pieces/shreds (fig., fam.) ◆ *Uno de los candidatos a la presidencia machacó a los otros. One of the presidential candidates flattened the others.*

▶ machacar algo a alg. (fig., fam.) to drum s.th. into s.o. or into s.o.'s head (fig.) ◆ *Machácales lo que tienen que hacer. Drum into them or into their heads what they have to do.*

▶ machacársela (vulg., Esp.) (to masturbate) ▷ tocar la **campana**

la madera wood

▶ la madera (pop., Esp.) cops (fam.), fuzz (sl.), pigs (sl.), filth (sl., Br.E.), heat (sl., Am.E.)

▶ tener madera de ... (fig.) to have the makings of . . . ◆ *Tiene madera de actriz. She has the makings of an actress.*

▶ ser de la misma madera (fig.) to be made of the same stuff (fig.), to be two of a kind

la madre mother, riverbed

▶ como su madre le/lo/la echó al mundo (fig., fam.) in his/her birthday suit (hum.),

stark naked (fam.) ◆ *Cuando era joven iba a nadar como mi madre me echó al mundo. When I was young, I [often] went swimming in my birthday suit.*

▶ ciento y la madre (fig.) whole crowd of people ◆ *Hubo allí ciento y la madre. A whole crowd of people was there. The world and his wife were there. (fam., Br.E.)*

▶ salirse de madre (fig.) to kick over the traces (fig.), to lose all self-control

▷ madre (ahí está la ~ del **cordero**)

▷ madre (**Cristo** y la ~)

▷ madre (desde el **vientre** de su/etc. ~)

▷ madre (el **ocio**/la **ociosidad** es la ~ de todos los vicios)

▷ madre (ser más **feo** que pegar a la ~)

▷ madre (tal ~ tal **hija**)

madrugar to get up early

▶ madrugar [a alg.] (fig., fam.) (a) to jump the gun (fig.) (b) to beat s.o. to it, to get in first (fam.), to steal a march on s.o.

▶ A quien madruga, Dios le ayuda. (prov.) The early bird catches the worm. (prov.) God helps those who help themselves.

▷ maduro (está madura la **breva**)

▷ maestro (la **baza** maestra)

▷ maestro (la **necesidad** hace ~s)

Magdalena Magdalen, Madeleine

▶ llorar como una Magdalena (fig.) to weep bitterly, to cry one's eyes out, to sob one's heart out

mal; el mal bad[ly], evil, harm

▶ poner mal a alg. to run s.o. down (fam.)

▶ no estar nada mal (fam.) ◆ *Ganar mucho dinero no estaría nada mal. I wouldn't mind making a lot of money.*

▶ menos mal thank goodness, it's a good thing . . . ◆ *¡Menos mal! Thank goodness!* ◆ *¡Menos mal que no fuimos! Thank goodness we didn't go! It's a good thing [that] we didn't go!*

▶ estar/andar mal de algo to be short of s.th., to be low on s.th., to be almost out of s.th. ◆ *Estamos mal de dinero. We're short of money/cash. We're hard up. (fam.)*

▶ Si haces mal, espera otro tal. (prov.) An eye for an eye [and a tooth for a tooth]. (prov.)

▶ No hay mal que por bien no venga. (prov.) Every cloud has a silver lining. (prov.) It may be a blessing in disguise. It's an ill wind that blows nobody any good.

▶ Bien vengas mal, si vienes solo. (prov.) It never rains but it pours. (prov.)

▶ Mal de muchos, consuelo de todos. (prov.) (a) What's bad for s.o. may be a consolation for s.o. else. (b) We're all in the same boat. (fig.)

▷ mal (▷ **pensar**: piensa ~ y acertarás)

▷ mal (atajar el ~ de **raíz**)

▷ mal (estar ~ de la **cabeza/chaveta**)

▷ mal (**llevarse** ~ con alg.)

▷ mal (no hay **bien** ni ~ que cien años dure)

Málaga Malaga

▶ salir de Málaga y entrar en Malagón (fig., fam.) to jump out of the frying pan into the fire ◆ *Atracó un banco para pagar sus deudas. Salió de Málaga y entró en Malagón. He held up a bank to pay [off] his debts. He jumped out of the frying pan into the fire.*

▷ Malagón (salir de **Málaga** y entrar en ~)

el malaleche (fam., Esp.) nasty piece of work (fig., fam.)

el/la malapata (fam.) unlucky person

el/la malaúva (fam.) nasty piece of work (fig., fam.)

la maleta suitcase

▶ el maleta (fig., fam.) (a) bungler (b) (sports): poor player, rabbit (fam., Br.E.) (c) clumsy/poor bullfighter (d) ham [actor] (fam.)

▶ hacer la maleta (fig., fam.) to pack one's bags/things [and go] (fam.), to pack up [and go] (fam.), to [pull] up sticks (Br.E.) or stakes (Am.E.) (fig., fam.)

▶ echarse la maleta al hombro (fig.) to emigrate (from one's home country)

▷ malla (**deslizar**se por [entre] las ~s)

malo bad

▶ Más vale malo conocido que bueno por conocer. (prov.) Better the devil you know than the devil you don't [know]. (prov.)

▶ En las malas se conoce a los amigos. (prov.) A friend in need is a friend indeed. (prov.)

▷ malo (▷ **bueno**: por las buenas o por las malas)

la malva mauve

▶ estar criando malvas (fig., fam.) to be pushing up daisies (fam., hum.), to be dead

la mamada suck (at breast)

▶ hacerle una mamada a alg. (vulg.) to do a blow job on s.o. (vulg.), to suck s.o. off (vulg.), to give s.o. head (vulg., Am.E.)

▷ mamar (▷ **nacer**: nació alg. mamando el oficio)

la manaza great big hand

▶ ser un manazas (fam.) to have two left hands (fig.), to be all thumbs, to be a clumsy oaf/sort (fam.), to be clumsy

la mancha spot, stain

▶ extenderse o propagarse o difundirse como una mancha de aceite (fig.) to spread like wildfire (fig.) ◆ *El rumor se extendió como una mancha de aceite. The rumor spread like wildfire.*

el mandamás (fam.) big boss, big noise (sl.), top dog (fam.), big shot (fam.), bigwig (fam.)

el mandamiento order, command

▶ los cinco mandamientos (fig., fam.) fingers

la mandanga (pop.) (marijuana): hash/pot (fam.), grass/shit/weed (sl.), tea (sl., Am.E.)

la mandíbula jaw

▶ reír[se] a mandíbula batiente (fig., fam.) to laugh one's head off (fam.)

el mandil apron

▶ pegarle algo a alg. como un mandil a una vaca (hum.) s.th. doesn't suit s.o. at all, s.th. looks awful on s.o. ◆ *Esta camisa te pega como un mandil a una vaca. This shirt doesn't suit you at all. This shirt looks awful on you.*

▷ manera (hay muchas ~s de matar **pulga**s)

la manga sleeve

▶ tener manga ancha (fig.), ser de manga ancha (fig.) to be too lenient, to be overindulgent

▶ guardarse un as en la manga (fig.) to keep an ace up one's sleeve (fig.), to have an ace in the hole (fam., Am.E.) ◆ *Hasta ahora no ha conseguido encontrar una solución a este problema. No te preocupes. Siempre se guarda un as en la manga. So far, she hasn't had any success in finding a solution to this problem. Don't worry. She always keeps an ace up her sleeve.*

▶ traer algo en/por la manga (fig.) (a) to have s.th. up one's sleeve (fig.), to have a shot in the/one's locker (fam., Br.E.) (b) to pull s.th. out of a/the hat/bag (fig.), to come up with s.th. just like that, to give an off-the-cuff answer/speech/etc. ◆ *Ha traído el discurso en la manga. He's given an off-the-cuff speech.* ◆ *Trajo una respuesta genial en la manga. He came up with a brilliant answer just like that.*

▶ sacarse algo de la manga (fig.) (a) to make s.th. up [off the top of one's head] (b) to pull s.th. out of a/the hat/bag (fig.), to come up with s.th. just like that ◆ *Acaba de sacárselo de la manga. He's just made it up [off the top of his head].* ◆ *Se sacó la solución del problema de la manga. He pulled the solution to the problem out of a hat.*

▶ estar/andar manga por hombro (fig.) to be in a state of chaos, to be chaotic, to be [all] at sixes and sevens (fam.), to be topsy-turvy (fam.), to be in a [complete] mess (fig.) ◆ *En esta casa todo está manga por hombro. Everything is topsy-turvy in this house. This house is in a mess.* ◆ *En aquel país todo anda manga por hombro. Everything is in a state of chaos in that country.*

▶ hacer mangas y capirotes de algo (fig.) to rush s.th./things

▶ hacer mangas y capirotes de alg. (fig.) to ignore s.o. completely, to cut s.o. dead (fam.)

▷ manga (a buenas **horas**, ~s verdes)

▷ manga (ser más **corto** que las ~s de un chaleco)

la manita little hand
▶ tener manitas de plata/oro (fig.) to have very talented/artistic/skillful hands

la mano hand
▶ estar en la mano (fig.) to be obvious
▶ bajar la mano (fig.) to drop the price
▶ untar la mano a alg. (fig., fam.) to grease s.o.'s palm (fig., fam.), to bribe s.o.
▶ robar algo a alg. a mano airada (fam.) to rob s.o. of s.th. with violence
▶ caerse de las manos (libro/etc.) (fig.) (book/etc.): to be impossible (fig.), to be boring

▶ darse las manos (fig.) to make [it] up (with s.o.), to reconcile (with s.o.) ◆ *Finalmente se dieron las manos. They were finally reconciled.*

▶ lavarse las manos [en inocencia] (fig.) to wash one's hands of it (fig.)

▶ irsele a alg. la mano (fig.) to strike ◆ *Se le fue la mano. He/she struck.*

▶ mudar de manos (fig.) to change hands (fam.)

▶ estar con una mano atrás y otra [a]delante (fig.) to be stone-broke (fam., Am.E.), not to have a penny to one's name (fam.)

▶ salir con una mano atrás y otra [a]delante (fig.) not to get anywhere, to get nowhere

▶ tener las manos largas (fig.) (a) to be light-fingered (b) to be free with one's hands, to be quick to lash out

▶ tener [mucha] mano izquierda [con alg.] (fig., fam.) to have [got] a way with s.o., to know [very well] how to handle s.o. or how to manage, to know what's what [where s.o. is concerned] (fam.), to be [very] sly/crafty ◆ *Tiene mano izquierda con las mujeres. He's got a way with women. He knows what's what where women are concerned.* ◆ *Ella tiene mucha mano izquierda. She knows very well how to manage. She's very crafty.*

▶ venir a alg. a la[s] mano[s] (fig.) to [just] fall/drop into s.o.'s lap (fig.) ◆ *No le va a venir a las manos. It won't fall into his lap.*

▶ darle a alg. la/una mano y se toma el brazo (fig.) give s.o. an inch and he'll take a yard/mile (fig.) ◆ *Le das la mano y se toma el brazo. Give him an inch and he'll take a mile.*

▶ Una mano lava la otra. (prov.) You scratch my back and I'll scratch yours. (prov.)

▶ Muchas manos en un plato hacen mucho garabato. (prov.) Muchas manos en la olla echan el guiso a perder. (prov.) Too many cooks spoil the broth. (prov.)

▷ mano (coger a alg. con las ~s en la **masa**)
▷ mano (darle a alg. el **pie** y se toma la ~)
▷ mano (en buenas ~s está el **pandero**)
▷ mano (**llegar** a las ~s)
▷ mano (llevarse las ~s a la **cabeza**)
▷ mano (**morir** a ~ airada)
▷ mano (ser un **juguete** en ~s de alg.)
▷ manojo (ser un ~ de **nervio**s)

la manta blanket
▶ la manta (fig., fam.) good hiding (fam.)

▶ liarse la manta a la cabeza (fig.) to throw/cast caution to the wind[s] (fig.), to press on regardless

▶ tirar de la manta (fig.) to let the cat out of the bag, to give the game/show away (fam.); (s.th. embarrassing): to reveal (fig.), to bring to light (fig.), to take the lid off (fig., fam.) ◆ *Tiró de la manta para revelar el escándalo.* He took the lid off the scandal. ◆ *No creo que tiren de la manta.* I don't think they'll reveal it.

▶ a manta (fig.) in abundance, plenty of, galore ◆ *Hay frutas a manta.* There are fruits galore.

la manteca fat

▶ la manteca (fam.) (money): dough (sl., Am.E.), bread (sl.), sugar (sl.), brass/dosh/lolly (sl., Br.E.), wampum (sl., Am.E.)

la manzana apple

▶ la manzana de la discordia (fig.) apple of discord, bone of contention

▶ Una manzana podrida echa un ciento a perder. (prov.) One bad apple can spoil the whole barrel. (prov.) The rotten apple spoils the barrel. (prov.)

▶ A diario una manzana es cosa sana. (prov.) An apple a day keeps the doctor away. (prov.)

▷ manzana (estar más sano que una ~)

▷ maña (donde hay **gana**, hay ~)

mañana tomorrow

▶ No dejes para mañana lo que puedes hacer hoy. (prov.) Don't put off till tomorrow what you can do today. (prov.)

▷ mañana (de la **noche** a la ~)

▷ mañana (**hoy** por mí, ~ por tí)

el mapamundi world map

▶ el mapamundi (fig., fam.) bottom (fam.), backside (fam.), behind (fam., euph.), posterior (euph.), butt (fam., Am.E.), bum (fam., Br.E.)

el mar ocean, sea

▶ Quien no se arriesga no pasa la mar. (prov.) Nothing ventured, nothing gained. (prov.)

▶ arar en el mar (fig.) to labor in vain, to waste one's time, to be a waste of time, to be a wasted effort, to flog a dead horse (fig., fam.) ◆ *Hablarle de aumentar los sueldos es*

como arar en el mar. Talking to him about increasing the salaries is like flogging a dead horse or is a complete waste of time.

▶ hacer un mar con un vaso de agua (fig.) to make a mountain out of a molehill (fig.)

▶ la mar de (fig., fam.) ◆ *la mar de cosas* loads of things *(fam.)* ◆ *tener la mar de dinero* to have heaps/piles of money *(fam.)* ◆ *ser la mar de guapo* to be awfully pretty *(fam.)* ◆ *ser la mar de tonto* to be no end of a fool *(fam.)* ◆ *tener la mar de prisa* to be in a great hurry/rush, to be in a mortal hurry *(fam.)* ◆ *creerse la mar de listo* to think one is the cat's pajamas (Am.E.) or pyjamas (Br.E.) or whiskers *(fam.)*, to think one is the bee's knees *(fam.)*, to think to be very smart/clever ◆ *estar la mar de contento* to be terribly pleased/glad/happy ◆ *llevarse la mar de bien* to get on like a house on fire *(fam.)*, to be great pals/buddies *(fam.)*

▶ divertirse la mar to enjoy o.s. tremendously, to have a grand/great time (fam.), to have a whale of a time (fam.)

▶ sudar a mares (fig.) to sweat buckets/streams (fam.), to be dripping with sweat

▶ llover a mares (fig.) to rain in torrents, to come down in buckets/sheets, to rain cats and dogs, to be pouring [down or with rain], to be bucketing down (Br.E.), the floodgates of heaven open (fig.) ◆ *Ayer llovió a mares.* The floodgates of heaven opened yesterday. It rained in torrents or cats and dogs yesterday.

▷ mar (▷ **cagar**: ¡Me cago en la ~!)

▷ mar (echar **agua** en el ~)

▷ mar (estar hecho un **brazo** de ~)

▷ mar (ser una **gota** de agua en el ~)

la maravilla marvel, wonder

▶ a las mil maravillas (to go/run/etc.): marvelously, beautifully, extremely well, wonderfully [well], swimmingly (fig.), like clockwork (fig.), like a bomb (fam., Br.E.), like a dream (fam.), (to go) great guns (fam.), (to work) a treat (fig.) ◆ *Todo marcha a las mil maravillas.* Everything in the garden is lovely. Everything's hunky-dory. *(fam.)* ◆ *Todo fue a las mil maravillas.* It all went swimmingly or like clockwork or like a dream. ◆ *Todo ha salido a las mil maravillas.* Everything has turned out wonderfully. Everything worked a treat. ◆ *Manitas de Plata toca a las mil maravillas.* Manitas de Plata plays marvelously.

▷ marea (contra **viento** y ~)

la margarita daisy, pearl oyster
► deshojar la margarita (fig.) to play "she loves me, she loves me not"
► echar margaritas a los puercos (fig., fam.) to cast pearls before swine (fig.) ◆ *No se interesan por vino. Servirles un Burdeos es como echar margaritas a los puercos. They don't care about wine. To serve them a Bordeaux is like casting pearls before swine.*

la marica magpie
► el marica (fam.) (gay): queer/fairy/faggot (sl., pej.), pansy (fam., pej.), queen (sl.), poof[ter] (sl., pej., Br.E.), fag (sl., pej., Am.E.), arse bandit (vulg., Br.E.)

Maricastaña (fam.)
► año de/tiempo[s] de/días de Maricastaña donkey's years ago/old (fam.), [very] long ago, [in/from] the year dot (fam.), out of/with the Ark (fam.), prehistoric (fig., hum.), very old-fashioned ◆ *En tiempos de o en los días de Maricastaña fabricaron mejores coches. They made better cars donkey's years ago or in the year dot.* ◆ *Tienen un televisor del año de Maricastaña. They have a television [set] that is out of the Ark/that is donkey's years old. They have a prehistoric television [set].* ◆ *Este traje es/viene del tiempo de Maricastaña. This suit is from the year dot. This suit looks as if it came out of the Ark. This suit is really old-fashioned.*

el maricón (pop.) (gay): queer/fairy/faggot (sl., pej.), pansy (fam., pej.), queen (sl.), poof[ter] (sl., pej., Br.E.), fag (sl., pej., Am.E.), arse bandit (vulg., Br.E.)

el marinero seaman, sailor
► el marinero de agua dulce (fig.) landlubber (fam.)

la mariposa butterfly
► el mariposa (fam., euph.) (gay): queer/fairy/faggot (sl., pej.), pansy (fam., pej.), queen (sl.), poof[ter] (sl., pej., Br.E.), fag (sl., pej., Am.E.), arse bandit (vulg., Br.E.)

las marmellas (pop.) (breasts): knockers (sl.), tits (fam.), boobs (fam.), hooters (sl., Am.E.)

marras (fam.)
► de marras said, in question, agreed, you-know-who, that you/etc. know all about ◆ *el día de marras the agreed day* ◆ *el problema de marras same old problem* ◆ *Lo hizo el individuo de marras. The said individual did it. You-know-who did it.*

Martín ▷ San Martín

la masa dough, paste
► coger a alg. con las manos en la masa (fig.) to catch s.o. red-handed, to catch s.o. in the act, to catch s.o. with his hand in the cookie jar (fig.) ◆ *Lo cogieron con las manos en la masa. He was caught with his hand in the cookie jar.* ◆ *Estaba robando el contenido de la hucha de su hermano cuando la madre entró en el cuarto. Lo cogió con las manos en la masa. He was plundering his brother's piggy bank when the mother entered the room. She caught him red-handed.*

la máscara mask
► quitarse la máscara (fig.) to drop the mask (fig.), to show [o.s. in] one's true colors ◆ *Nunca se sabe qué piensa ese tío. No se quita la máscara. You can never tell what that guy is thinking. He doesn't show his true colors.*
► quitarle la máscara a alg. (fig.) to unmask s.o. (fig.), to expose s.o.

la mata shrub, bush
► ser más tonto que una mata de habas (fam.) to be as thick as they come (fam.)
▷ ser más tonto que **Carracuca**

el mátalas callando (fam.) sly sort (fam.), smooth type (fam.), wolf in sheep's clothing (fig.)
▷ matanza (**cebar**se en la ~)

matar to kill
► matarlas callando (fig.) to be insidious, to go about things slyly or on the quiet (fam.), to be a wolf in sheep's clothing (fig.) ◆ *Las mata callando. He goes about things slyly.* ◆ *Ten cuidado con el director. Parece que no le cabe el corazón en el pecho, pero las mata callando. Beware of the manager. He seems to be the very soul of kindness, but he's a wolf in sheep's clothing.*
▷ matar (el que a **hierro** mata, a hierro muere)
▷ matar (ser incapaz de ~ una **mosca**)
▷ matar a alg. a **fuego** lento/a **pedrada**s
▷ mayo (venir como **agua** de ~)
▷ mazo (a **Dios** rogando y con el ~ dando)

la meada (pop., vulg.) piss (vulg.)
▶ echar una meada to take/have (Br.E.) a leak (sl., hum.), to have a slash (sl., Br.E.), to have a piss (vulg.)

mear (pop., vulg.) to piss (vulg.), to have a piss (vulg.), to have a slash (sl., Br.E.)
▶ mearse (fam.) to wet o.s.
▶ mearse [de risa] (fam.) to wet o.s. laughing, to pee (fam.) or piss (vulg.) o.s. laughing
▷ Meca (andar de la **Ceca** a la ~)

la mecha wick, fuse
▶ aguantar [la] mecha (fig., fam.) to grin and bear it [patiently}, to stand the gaff (fam., Am.E.)
▶ a toda mecha (fam.) in a great hurry, like greased lightning (fam.), like the clappers (fam., Br.E.) ◆ *Salió a toda mecha de la casa. He left the house like greased lightning.* ◆ *Corrió a toda mecha. He went like the clappers.*
▷ medianoche (entre **gallos** y ~)
▷ medida (**colmar** la ~)
▷ Méjico (el **unto** de ~)

la melena mane
▶ soltarse la melena (fig.) to drop all scruples, to drop all restraint

la mella notch
▶ hacer mella en/a alg. (fig.) to make an impression on s.o.

el melón melon
▶ el melón (fig., fam.) nut (sl.) ▷ la cebolla
▶ estrujarse el melón (fig., fam.) to rack one's brains (fig.)
▶ un melón (fig., fam.) idiot ▷ un [pedazo de] **alcornoque**

la melopea (fam., Esp.) drunkenness
▶ coger una melopea to get canned (sl., Br.E.), to get tight (fam.) ▷ **cocer**se (a)

menda (pop.) I, yours truly (fam., hum.), muggins (fam., Br.E.) ◆ *Lo ha hecho el/la menda. I did it. Yours truly did it.* ◆ *¿Y quién tuvo que pagar? El/la menda. And who had to pay? Yours truly. Muggins here.*

menear to shake
▶ Peor es meneallo. (fig.) Mejor es no meneallo. (fig.) Más vale no meneallo. (fig.) It's best to leave that alone. It's best not to touch on that. It's best not to stir [all] that

up. (fig.) Let sleeping dogs lie. ◆ *No vuelvas a sacar ese mal asunto. Más vale no meneallo. Don't bring that nasty business up again. Let sleeping dogs lie.*
▷ menear (si le/etc. meanean, da **bellota**s)
▷ menear el **bigote/esqueleto**
▷ menear el **bulto/zarzo** a alg.

el meneo shake
▶ dar un meneo a alg. (fig., fam.) (a) to thrash s.o., to give s.o. a thrashing (b) to give s.o. a dressing-down (fam.), to give s.o. a telling-off (fam.)

mentir to lie
▶ mentir más que hablar o más que la Gaceta (fig.) to lie through one's teeth (fam.)
▷ mentir con toda la **barba/boca**
▷ mentir más que un **sacamuelas**
▷ mentir por los **codos**
▷ mentir que se las pela (▷ **pelar**)
▷ mentira (ser un **costal** de ~s)
▷ mentira (ser una ~ de **padre** y muy señor mío)
▷ mentira (ser una **solemne** ~)
▷ mentirosa (ser una ~ de siete **suela**s)
▷ merecer una **estatua**

la merluza hake
▶ coger una merluza (fig., pop.) to get canned (sl., Br.E.), to get tight (fam.) ▷ **cocer**se (a)

un merluzo (fam., pej.) idiot, bonehead (fam., Am.E.) ▷ un [pedazo de] **alcornoque**

el/la metepatas (fam.) person who is always putting his foot in it (fam.), person who is always dropping a clanger (sl.), person who is always making gaffes, person who has foot-in-mouth disease (fam., hum.) ◆ *Es una metepatas. She's always putting her foot in it. She has foot-in-mouth disease.*

meter to put/place (in/into)
▶ meterse alg. donde no le llaman to poke one's nose into other people's business ◆ *¡No te metas donde no te llaman! Mind your own business!*
▶ estar metido para dentro (fig.) to be introverted, to be introspective, to be reserved (fig.)
▶ estar [muy] metido en algo (a) to be [very/deeply] involved in s.th. (b) to be [very] involved in s.th., to be mixed up (fig.)

or caught up in s.th. ◆ *Están muy metidos en política. They're very involved in/with politics.* ◆ *Está muy metido en ese asunto. He's deeply involved in that matter. He's mixed up in that affair.*
► estar muy metido con alg. (fig.) to be deeply involved with s.o., to be well in with s.o.

el mico long-tailed monkey
► dar mico a alg. (fig., fam.) to stand s.o. up (fam.)
► correr un mico (fam.) to be/feel ashamed [of o.s.]

▷ miedo (**caerse** [muerto] de ~)
▷ miedo (**cagar**se/**ciscar**se de ~)
▷ miedo (dar un **susto** al ~)
▷ miedo (estar **muerto** de ~)
▷ miedo (**morir**se de ~)

la miel honey
► No hay miel sin hiel. (prov.) There's no rose without a thorn. (prov.)
► hacerse de miel (fig.) to be excessively kind
► ser miel sobre hojuelas (fig., fam.) to be wonderful, to be marvelous, to be fantastic, to be even better [than s.o. expected], to be almost too much of a good thing ◆ *¡Es miel sobre hojuelas! It's really marvelous! It's better still!* ◆ *Es una gran casa y el sitio es miel sobre hojuelas. It's a magnificent house and its location is even better than we expected.*
► dejar a alg. con la miel en los labios (fig.) to snatch s.th. away from under s.o.'s nose ◆ *Quise conseguir ese trabajo, pero un tío me dejó con la miel en los labios. I wanted to get that job, but a guy snatched it away from under my nose.*
► quedarse con la miel en los labios (fig.) to come close to success without attaining it; close, but no cigar (sl.)
► las mieles del triunfo (fig.) sweets of victory/success (fig.) ◆ *Saboreamos las mieles del triunfo. We savored the sweets of victory. (fig.)*
▷ miel (la **dedada** de ~)
▷ miel (la **luna** de ~)

la mierda shit (vulg.)
► la mierda (pop., Esp.) (marijuana): shit/grass/weed (sl.), hash/pot (fam.), tea (sl., Am.E.)
► mandar a alg. a la mierda (vulg.) to tell s.o. to go to hell (fam.), to tell s.o. to piss off (vulg.), to tell s.o. to screw himself (vulg.)

la miga crumb
► tener [su] miga (fig.) to be more in/to it than meets the eye, not to be easy, to have its difficulties ◆ *Esto tiene su miga. There's more in this than meets the eye. This isn't easy.*
► hacer buenas/malas migas con alg. (fig.) to get along/on well/badly with s.o., to hit it off with s.o./not to hit it off with s.o.
► estar hecho migas (fig.) to be shattered (fam., Br.E.) ▷ estar hecho **cisco**

mil thousand
► Preso por mil, preso por mil quinientos. (fam.) In for a penny, in for a pound. (Br.E.) In for a dime, in for a dollar. (Am.E.)
► a las mil y quinientas (fam.) very late, terribly late (fam.) ◆ *Llegó a las mil y quinientas. He arrived terribly late.*
▷ mina de **oro**
▷ mirada (**acaparar** todas las ~s)

la miranda
► estar de miranda (pop.) to be idle, to stand idly by while others are working

mirar to look at, to watch
► mirar bien/mal a alg. (fig.) [not] to like s.o., to dislike s.o.
► de mírame y no me toques (fig., fam.) very delicate, very fragile ◆ *Esta figurilla de porcelana es de las de mírame y no me toques. This porcelain figurine is very delicate/fragile. You only have to look at this porcelain figurine and it breaks. (fig.)*

la miseria destitution, poverty, want
► vender algo por una miseria (fig.) to sell s.th. for a song (fig., fam.)
► cobrar/ganar una miseria (fig.) to work for peanuts (fam.), to earn a pittance
▷ mistar (sin **chistar** ni ~)

mixto mixed
► el mixto (fam.) match

la mocada (pop.) blowing one's nose
► echar una mocada to blow one's nose

mocar (pop.) to blow one's nose
► mocarse to blow one's nose

el mochuelo little owl
► cada mochuelo a su olivo everyone to his place ◆ *Ya es muy tarde, ¡cada mochuelo a su olivo! It's very late now. Let's all go home!*

▶ cargar con el mochuelo (fig., fam.) to be left holding the bag (Am.E.) or the baby (Br.E.) (fam.), to [have to] carry the can (fam., Br.E.), to get landed with it (fam.)

▶ cargar el mochuelo a alg. (fig., fam.) (a) to pass the buck to s.o. (fig., fam.), to pin the blame on s.o., to leave s.o. holding the bag (Am.E.) or the baby (Br.E.) (fam.) (b) to lumber (Br.E.) or land or saddle s.o. with s.th. (fam.), to unload s.th. on [to] s.o. (fam.) (c) to frame s.o. [up] (fam.), to pin s.th. (crime/etc.) on s.o. ◆ *Me cargaron el mochuelo y se fueron a la playa.* They lumbered me with the job/etc. and went to the beach. ◆ *Los bofias colocaron pruebas para poder cargar el mochuelo a ese pobre diablo.* The cops planted evidence, so that they could frame that poor devil or pin the crime on that poor devil.

el moco snot (vulg.), nasal mucus

▶ caérsele a alg. el moco (fig., fam.) to be [still] a [real] greenhorn ◆ *Se le cae el moco a él.* He's still a real greenhorn.

▶ llorar a moco tendido o a moco y baba (fam.) to sob one's heart out, to cry one's eyes out, to sob/cry uncontrollably

▶ sorberse los mocos (fig., fam.) to sniffle

▶ quitar los mocos a alg. (fig., pop.) to bash s.o.'s face in (fam.), to put s.o.'s face out of joint (sl.) ◆ *Si vuelves a hacerlo, te voy a quitar los mocos.* If you do it again, I'll put your face out of joint.

▶ no saber ni siquiera quitarse los mocos (fig., pop.) to be as thick as they come (fam.)
▷ ser más tonto que **Carracuca**

el moco de pavo caruncle (turkey)

▶ no ser moco de pavo (fig., fam.) not to be sneezed/sniffed at (fam.), not to be just a small thing, to be no mean feat (fam.), to be no chickenfeed (sl.), not to be peanuts (fam.) ◆ *Gana cien mil dólares al año, que no es moco de pavo.* He earns one hundred thousand dollars a year, which is no chickenfeed. ◆ *Ganó una medalla de oro, que no es moco de pavo.* He won a gold medal, which isn't just a small thing or which is no mean feat.

el moho mold, rust

▶ no criar moho (fig., fam.) to be always on the go or on the jump (fam.), not to let the grass grow under one's feet

▶ no dejar criar moho a alg. (fig., fam.) to keep s.o. on the go, to keep s.o. on the jump (fam.), to keep s.o. on the trot (fig., fam., Br.E.)

▶ no dejar criar moho a algo (fig., fam.) to use s.th. up quickly
▷ moho (**piedra** movediza, el ~ no la cobija)
▷ mojado (estar ~ hasta los **huesos/tuétanos**)

mojar to wet

▶ mojar (fig., fam.) (success/etc.): to celebrate with a drink ◆ *¡Esto hay que mojarlo!* This calls for a drink! This calls for a celebration!

▶ no mojarse (fig., fam.) to keep out of it

▶ mojar en algo (fig., fam.) (a) to participate in s.th., to dabble in s.th. (fig.) (b) to meddle in s.th.
▷ mojarse hasta el **alma**/los **huesos**
▷ molino (**agua** pasada no mueve ~)
▷ molino (llevar el **agua** a su ~)
▷ molino ([no] **comulgar** con ruedas de ~)
▷ molino (**tragar**[se]las como ruedas de ~)

la mollera crown of the head

▶ la mollera (fig., fam.) sense, brains (fig.)
▶ ser duro de mollera (fig.) to be pigheaded
▶ ser cerrado de mollera (fig.) to be pretty dim (fam.), to be a bit dense (fig.)

la mona female monkey

▶ la mona (fig., fam.) drunkenness
▶ coger/pillar una mona (fam.) to get canned (sl., Br.E.), to get tight (fam.) ▷ **cocerse** (a)
▶ dormir la mona (fam.) to sleep off a hangover (fam.), to sleep it off (fam.)
▶ Aunque la mona se vista de seda, mona se queda. (prov.) Fine feathers don't make fine birds. (prov.) You can't make a silk purse out of a sow's ear. (prov.)

mondo clean, pure

▶ mondo y lirondo (fig., fam.) plain, plain and simple ◆ *Nos dijo la verdad monda y lironda.* He told us the plain truth.

la moneda coin

▶ pagar a alg. con/en la misma moneda (fig.) to pay s.o. back in his own coin (fig.) or in kind, to give s.o. tit for tat, to fight fire with fire (fig.)

[los] monises (fam.) (money): dough (sl., Am.E.), bread (sl.), sugar (sl.), brass/dosh/lolly (sl., Br.E.), wampum (sl., Am.E.)
▷ monje (el **hábito** [no] hace al ~)

115

el mono monkey
▶ El último mono es el que se ahoga. (prov.) Devil take the hindmost. (prov.) Every man for himself [and the devil take the hindmost]. (prov.)
▶ ser el último mono (fam.) to be a [complete] nobody (fig., pej.), to be the lowest of the low (pej.), to be the low man on the totem pole (fig., Am.E.)
▶ tener monos en la cara (fig.) to look conspicuous or ridiculous ◆ No me mirarías más ni que tuviera monos en la cara. You couldn't have stared at me more if I had come from another planet or from the moon.
▶ el mono (fam.) cold turkey (sl.), withdrawal pains/symptoms ◆ Está con el mono. He's suffering withdrawal symptoms. He's gone cold turkey.
▷ mono (aburrirse como un ~)
▷ montaña (prometerle a alg. ~s de oro)
▷ monte (creer que todo el ~ es orégano)
▷ monte (la cabra siempre tira al ~)
▷ monte (no todo el ~ es orégano)
▷ monte (tirar al ~)

el montón heap, pile
▶ ser del montón (fig., fam.) to be a nonentity, to be just an ordinary person, to be nothing special
▶ salirse del montón (fig., fam.) to be exceptional, to stand out from the crowd (fig.), to be s.th. special ◆ Ese escritor se sale del montón. That's an exceptional writer.

el monumento monument
▶ un monumento [nacional] (fig., fam.) (girl/woman): smasher (fam.), looker (fam.), stunner (fam.), very pretty girl/woman

moñarse (fam.) to get canned (sl., Br.E.), to get tight (fam.) ▷ cocerse (a)

el moño (hair): bun, topknot
▶ estar hasta el moño de algo (fam., Esp.) to have had it up to here with s.th. (fam.)
▷ estar hasta [más allá de] la coronilla de algo
▶ tirarse de los moños (mujeres) (fig.) (women): to be at each other, to be at each other's or at one another's throats (fam.), to be at loggerheads ◆ Aquellas vecinas se tiran siempre de los moños. Those neighbors are constantly at each other's throats.

▶ ponerse moños (fig., fam.) to puff o.s. up (fig.), to act big (fam.), to act the big shot (fam.)
▶ quitar moños a alg. (fig., fam.) to take/bring s.o. down off his high horse (fam.)

la morada home, stay
▶ la eterna morada (fig.) hereafter, [great] beyond

morado violet
▶ ponerse morado de algo (fig., fam., Esp.) to drink gallons of s.th. (fig., fam.), to stuff o.s. with s.th. (fam.), to gorge o.s. on s.th. ◆ Se puso morada de dulces. She stuffed herself with sweets. ◆ Nos pusimos morados de sangría. We drank gallons of sangría.
▶ pasarlas moradas (fig., fam.) to have a rough/tough time [of it] ◆ Las pasamos moradas. We had a tough time.

la morcilla blood sausage
▶ ¡Que te den morcilla! (fig., fam.) Get stuffed! (vulg., Br.E.) Go to hell! (fam.)
▷ morder el polvo
▷ morder [el] polvo (hacer ~ a alg.)

morir to die
▶ morir a mano airada (fam.) to die a violent death
▶ morir vestido (fig., fam.) not to die a natural death, not to die of natural causes
▶ ser para morirse de risa (fig.) to be a hoot (fam., Br.E.), to be a [real] scream (fam.), to be hilariously funny ◆ Era para morirse de risa. It was a scream. You just died laughing. (fig., fam.)
▶ morirse de envidia (fig.) to be green with envy (fig.), to be eaten up with envy
▶ morirse de vergüenza (fig.) to nearly die of shame (fam.)
▶ morirse de miedo (fig.) to be half-dead with fear/fright (fam.)
▶ morirse del susto (fig.) to get the fright of one's life, to be frightened or scared out of one's wits, to jump out of one's skin
▷ morir (de casi no se muere nadie)
▷ morir (el que a hierro mata, a hierro muere)
▷ morir (mala hierba nunca muere)
▷ morir (no ~ de cornada de burro)
▷ morir al pie del cañón
▷ morir como chinches
▷ morir con las botas puestas

el moro Moor
- ▶ ¡Hay moros en la costa! (fam.) Careful, there are people listening!
- ▶ no hay moros en la costa (fam.) the coast is clear (fig., fam.) ◆ *Ya podéis salir, no hay moros en la costa. You can come out now, the coast is clear.*
- ▷ moro (prometerle a alg. el **oro** y el ~)
- ▷ moro (querer el **oro** y el moro)

el morral nosebag
- ▶ el morral (fig., fam.) lout

morrearse (pop.) to have a good old snog (fam., Br.E.), to neck (fam.), to spoon (hum.)

el morro snout
- ▶ beber a morro (fam.) to drink straight from the bottle, to drink straight from the spring/ etc.
- ▶ tener un morro que se lo pisa (fam., hum.) to have got a real or a lot of nerve (fam.) ◆ *Ese tío tiene un morro que se lo pisa. That guy's got a real nerve.*
- ▶ ¡Qué morro tienes! (fam.) You've got a nerve! (fam.) You've got some nerve! (fam.) You've got a cheek! (fam., Br.E.)
- ▶ torcer el morro (fam.) to look sour (fig.) or cross (fam.)
- ▶ estar de morro[s] (fam.) to be in a bad mood
- ▶ estar de morro[s] con alg. (fam.) to be cross with s.o. (fam.), to be in a bad mood with s.o.
- ▶ hinchar los morros a alg. (pop.) to bash s.o.'s face in (fam.), to put s.o.'s face out of joint (sl.) ◆ *Si vuelves a hacerlo, te voy a hinchar los morros. If you do it again, I'll put your face out of joint.*

la mosca fly
- ▶ la mosca (fig., fam.) (money): dough (sl., Am.E.), bread (sl.), sugar (sl.), brass/dosh/ lolly (sl., Br.E.), wampum (sl., Am.E.)
- ▶ aflojar/soltar la mosca to cough up (fam.), to fork out (fam.), to stump up (fam., Br.E.)
- ▶ la mosca muerta (fig.) hypocrite
- ▶ las moscas blancas (fig., fam.) snowflakes
- ▶ hacer una mosca (fig.) to make a typing error, to make a typo (fam.)
- ▶ ser incapaz de matar una mosca (fig.) s.o. wouldn't harm/hurt a fly (fig.), s.o. wouldn't say boo to a goose (fam., Br.E.)

- ▶ matar moscas a cañonazos (fig.) to break a butterfly on the wheel (fig.)
- ▶ estar con o tener la mosca detrás de la oreja (fam.) to be on one's guard, to be suspicious, to be wary
- ▶ cazar moscas (fam.) to do useless things
- ▶ papar moscas (fig., fam.) to gape, to gawk (fam.), to gawp (fam., Br.E.), to stand around gaping
- ▶ mandar a alg. a capar moscas (fam.) to tell s.o. to go to hell (fam.) or to go to blazes (sl.) ◆ *La mandó a capar moscas. He told her to go to hell.*
- ▶ no se siente/oye [ni] una mosca (fig., fam.) it's [as] quiet/silent as the grave, there's [a] deathly silence (fig., fam.) ◆ *Dentro no se sentía/oía ni una mosca. Inside it was as silent as the grave. Inside there was [a] deathly silence. Inside you could have heard a pin drop. The place was like a grave.*
- ▶ poder oír volar una mosca (fig., fam.) ◆ *Había tanto silencio que se hubiera podido oír volar una mosca. It was so quiet you could have heard a pin drop.*
- ▶ ¿Qué mosca te/etc. ha picado? (fam.) What's eating/biting you/etc.? (fam.) What's bugging you/etc.? (fam., Am.E.) What's got into you/etc.? (fam.) What's wrong with you/etc.? ◆ *¿Qué mosca le habrá picado? I wonder what's eating him or what's got into him or what's wrong with him.*
- ▶ se asan las moscas (fam.) it's damn[ed]/ darn[ed] hot (fam.) ◆ *Ayer se asaron las moscas. It was darned hot yesterday.*
- ▶ por si las moscas (fam.) just in case, just to be on the safe side ◆ *Tráete un impermeable por si las moscas. Bring a raincoat just in case.*
- ▷ mosca (en **boca** cerrada no entran ~s)

mosquearse (fig., fam.) to go off in a huff, to get/go into a huff, to get the knock (sl.), to take offense

la mosquita
- ▶ la mosquita muerta (fam.) hypocrite
- ▶ hacerse la o parecer una mosquita muerta to look as if butter wouldn't melt in one's mouth

la mostaza mustard
- ▶ subírsele a alg. la mostaza a las narices (fig., fam.) to get furious, to get mad (fam.)

♦ *Se me subió la mostaza a las narices. I got furious.*

▷ mosto (al **probar** se ve el ~)

la moza girl
▶ la moza de partido (fam.) prostitute
▶ una buena moza (fam.) good-looking/ handsome girl

mu moo! (cow)
▶ no decir ni mu (fam.) not to say/breathe a word, not to open one's mouth, to button [up] one's lip/mouth (fig., fam.) ♦ *No dijeron ni mu en toda la tarde. They didn't say a single word all afternoon.*

▷ mu (habló el **buey** y dijo ~)
▷ mucho (muchos **poco**s hacen un ~)

mudarse [de casa] to move [house]
▶ mudarse clandestinamente (tenant): to shoot the moon (fam.)

▷ mudo (estar ~ como una **tumba**)

el mueble piece of furniture
▶ sacar muebles (fig., fam.) to pick one's nose
▶ ser un mueble de la casa (fig., fam.) (person): to be one of the fixtures (fam.)

la muerte death
▶ de mala muerte (fig., fam., pej.) miserable (pej.), lousy (fam., pej.) ♦ *un pueblo de mala muerte a dump/hole [of a town] (fig., fam., pej.), a miserable place ♦ un trabajo de mala muerte a lousy job*
▶ cada muerte de obispo (fam., América Latina) very rarely, once in a blue moon (fam.) ♦ *Nos hacen una visita cada muerte de obispo. They pay us a visit once in a blue moon.*

▷ muerte (dar un **susto** de ~ a alg.)

muerto; el muerto dead; dead person
▶ estar más muerto que mi abuela o que una piedra (fam.) to be stone-dead (fam.), to be as dead as a doornail (fam.), to be as dead as mutton (fam.)
▶ estar muerto [de cansancio] (fig., fam.) to be dead tired (fam.), to be dog-tired (fam.)
▶ estar muerto de envidia (fig.) to be green with envy (fig.)
▶ estar muerto de vergüenza (fig.) to nearly die of shame (fam.)
▶ estar muerto de miedo (fig.) to be half-dead with fear/fright (fam.), to be in a blue funk (fam., Br.E.)

▶ estar muerto de sed (fig.) to be dying of thirst (fig.), to have a raging thirst, to be parched (fam.)
▶ estar muerto de hambre (fig.) to be starving (fam.), to be dying of hunger (fig.)
▶ el muerto de hambre (fig., fam.) pauper
▶ contarle a alg. con los muertos (fig.) to have written s.o. off
▶ hacerse el muerto (fig.) to pretend to be dead, to play dead, to play possum (fam.)
▶ cargar el muerto a alg. (fig., fam.) to leave s.o. holding the baby (Br.E.) or the bag (Am.E.) (fam.), to pass the buck to s.o. (fig., fam.), to pin the blame on s.o.

▷ muerto (**callar**[se] como un ~)
▷ muerto (**punto** ~)
▷ muerto (quedarse [~] como un **pajarito**)

la mui (pop., Esp.) tongue, mouth
▶ irse de la mui to talk (fam.), to sing (sl.), to squeal (sl.), to spill the beans (sl.) ♦ *No se fue de la mui. He didn't sing. He didn't spill the beans.*
▶ darle a la mui to gas (fam.), to yack (fam.), to yap (fam.)
▶ achantar la mui to shut one's trap (sl.), to pipe down (fam.), to belt up (fam., Br.E.) ♦ *¡Achanta la mui! Shut your trap! Pipe down! Belt up!*

▷ mujer (tener que **ver** con una ~)
▷ mujer (una ~ de **armas** tomar/de **historia**)
▷ mujer (una ~ **señora**)

el mundo world
▶ este pícaro mundo (fam.) this wicked world
▶ hablar de este mundo y del otro (fig., fam.) to talk about everything under the sun (fam.)
▶ desde que el mundo es mundo since time began ♦ *Es así desde que el mundo es mundo. It's been that way since time began.*
▶ no ser nada/cosa del otro mundo (fam.) to be nothing to write home about (fig.), to be nothing special or exceptional or extraordinary ♦ *Este libro no es nada del otro mundo. This book is nothing special.*
▶ mandar a alg. al otro mundo (fig., fam.) to send s.o. to glory (fam.), to do s.o. in (fam.)
  ▷ **cargar**se a alg. (a)
▶ echarse al mundo to take to/up prostitution
▶ como Dios lo/etc. trajo al mundo (fig.), tal como vino/etc. al mundo (fig.) as naked as the day s.o. was born, starkers (fam., hum., Br.E.), stark naked (fam.) ♦ *Estuvo allí como*

Dios la trajo al mundo. She stood there as naked as the day she was born.

▶ A beber y a tragar, que el mundo se va a acabar. Eat, drink and be merry, for tomorrow we die. (fig.)

▷ mundo (como su **madre** le/lo/la echó al ~)

▷ mundo (de **ingratitud**es está el ~ lleno)

▷ mundo (el ~ es un **pañuelo**)

▷ mundo (el **ombligo** del ~)

▷ mundo (lavar los **trapo**s sucios ante el ~ entero)

la musa muse

▶ soplar la musa a alg. (fig., fam.) to be inspired ◆ *Nos ha soplado la musa. We're inspired.*

la musaraña speck floating in the eye

▶ las musarañas (fig., fam.) spots before one's eyes

▶ estar mirando a las musarañas to be staring vacantly, to be mooning [about/around]

▶ estar pensando en las musarañas to be woolgathering (fig., fam.), to be daydreaming

el museo museum

▶ ser algo/alg. [una] pieza de museo (fig., fam.) s.th./s.o.: to be a museum piece (fig., fam.) ◆ *Su cámara es una pieza de museo. His camera's a museum piece.*

▷ musgo (**piedra** movediza no coge ~)

la música music

▶ la música enlatada (fam.) canned music (fam.)

▶ la música ratonera (fam.) (music): caterwauling (fig.)

▶ música celestial (iron.) hot air (sl.), empty/hollow promises ◆ *Su hermano es pura música celestial. His brother is full of hot air.* ◆ *Lo que dicen no es más que música celestial. They just make hollow promises.*

▶ dar música a un sordo (fig.) to preach in the wilderness (fig.), to be a voice crying in the wilderness (fig.), to talk at deaf ears (fig.), to talk to the winds (fig.) ◆ *Nadie estaba escuchando. Diste música a un sordo. Nobody was listening. You were talking at deaf ears. You were a voice crying in the wilderness.*

▶ bailar al compás de la música de alg. (fig.) to dance to s.o.'s tune (fig.) ◆ *Siempre baila al compás de la música de su madre. Debería aprender a campar por sus respetos. She always dances to her mother's tune. She should learn to act independently.*

▶ irse con la música a otra parte (fig., fam.) to go somewhere else ◆ *¡Vámonos con la música a otra parte! Let's go somewhere else! Let's get out of here!* ◆ *¡Vete con la música a otra parte! Clear/push off! (fam.) Get out! (fam.) Take your troubles elsewhere! Sell it elsewhere! (fam.)*

▶ Me suena a música de caballitos. (fig.) I think I've heard that one before. It sounds all too familiar.

▷ música (▷ **loco**: está loca por la ~)

▷ música (por fuera no rompe un **plato**, pero tiene la ~ por dentro)

N

nacer to be born
- ► nacerse (costura) (fig.) (seam): to fray, to split
- ► Nadie nace enseñado. (prov.) Everyone has to learn. We all have to learn.
- ► no nació alg. ayer (fig., fam.) s.o. wasn't born yesterday (fig.), to be nobody's fool ◆ *¡Pero yo no nací ayer! Do you think I was born yesterday?!*
- ► nació alg. cansado o con la lengua fuera (fig., fam., hum.) s.o. was born lazy/idle (hum.), to be a born lazybones (fam.), lazy is s.o.'s middle name (fig., hum.) ◆ *Creo que aquellos tíos nacieron cansados. I reckon those guys were born lazy.*
- ► nació alg. de cabeza (fig., fam.) s.o. was born unlucky, to be an unlucky person
- ► nació alg. de pie[s] (fig., fam.) s.o. was born lucky, to be a lucky person
- ► nació alg. tarde (fig., fam.) not to be exactly a shining/leading light (fig., fam.)
- ► nació alg. para [ser] matemático/etc. s.o. was born to be a mathematician/etc., to be a brilliantly talented/gifted mathematician/ etc.
- ► nació alg. mamando el oficio (fig.) s.o. was born to the trade
- ▷ nacer (unos nacen con **estrella** y otros nacen estrellados)

nada nothing
- ► ¡Nada de eso! (fam.) No dice! (sl., Am.E.) [That's] out of the question!
- ► No sé nada de nada. Search me! (fam.)
- ► ¡No te digo nada! (fig., fam.) You have no idea! That's absolutely nothing yet!
- ► quedar en nada to fizzle out (fig.), not to get to or reach first base (fig., fam.), to come to nothing ◆ *El proyecto quedó en nada. The plan fizzled out. The plan didn't [even] reach first base.* ◆ *Había interés pero todo quedó en nada. There was some interest but it all came to nothing.*
- ▷ nada (no quedar a **deber** ~)
- ▷ nada (o **césar** o ~)
- ▷ nada (o **todo** o ~)

nadar to swim
- ► [nadar y] guardar la ropa (fig., fam.) to hedge one's bets (fig.), to take no chances,

to play it safe, to try to please everybody, to act very cautiously
- ► querer nadar y guardar la ropa (fig., fam.) to want to have it both ways, to want to have one's cake and eat it [too] (fig.)
- ► nadar entre dos aguas (fig.) (a) to act diplomatically or cautiously, to try to please everybody (b) to be undecided, to sit on the fence (fig.) ◆ *Muchos votantes nadan entre dos aguas. A lot of voters are [still] undecided.*
- ► Nadar y nadar, y a la orilla ahogar. (prov.) To come close to one's goal (fig.) without reaching it. To come close to success without attaining it. Close, but no cigar. (sl.)
- ▷ nadar en la **abundancia**

nadie nobody
- ► ser un don Nadie (fig.) to be a nobody (fam., pej.), to be a [walking] zero (fam., pej., Am.E.)

la naja spectacled cobra
- ► darse de naja (pop.) to beat it (sl.), to clear/push off (fam.)

najarse (pop.) to beat it (sl.), to clear/push off (fam.)
- ▷ nalga (tener **cara** de ~s)

la nana grandma/granny (fam.)
- ► del año de/en el año de la nana (fam.) donkey's years ago ▷ año de **Maricastaña**

las napias (pop.) (nose): beak/hooter (fam., hum.), conk (sl., Br.E.), snout (fam.), schnozzle (fam., Am.E.)

Napoleón Napoleon
- ► soy Napoleón si ... (fig., fam.) I'll eat my hat if . . . (fig., fam.) ◆ *Si llegan con puntualidad, yo soy Napoleón. If they arrive on time, I'll eat my hat.*

los napoleones (fig., fam.) [pair of] long-johns

la naranja orange
- ► mi media naranja (fig., fam.) my better half (fam.)
- ► ¡Naranjas! (pop.) ¡Naranjas chinas! (pop.) ¡Naranjas de la China! (pop.) (a) Nonsense! Rubbish! (fam., Br.E.) Garbage! (fam.,

Am.E.) (b) No way! (fam.) Not on your life! (fam.)

la nariz nose

▶ ¡Narices! (fam.) (a) Nonsense! Rubbish! (fam., Br.E.) Garbage! (fam., Am.E.) (b) No way! (fam.) (c) Damn [it]! (fam.)

▶ estar hasta las narices de algo (fam.) to be fed up with s.th. (fam.) ▷ estar hasta [más allá de] la **coronilla** de algo

▶ asomar las narices (fam.) to show up (fam.), to turn up (fig.)

▶ tocarse las narices (fig., fam.) to slack (fam.), to be idle, to stand idly by

▶ algo me da en la nariz (fig., fam.) I have a feeling, I get the feeling ◆ *Me da en la nariz que no les gusta. I've a feeling that they don't like it. I get the feeling they don't like it.*

▶ tener una nariz de primera (fig., fam.) to have a [very] good nose (fig.), to have [very] good instincts ◆ *Tiene una nariz de primera para estas cosas. He has a very good nose for things like this.*

▶ tener narices de perro perdiguero (fig.) to have a very good nose (fig.)

▶ en mis/etc. propias o mismísimas narices (fam.) from right under my/etc. nose, from under my/etc. very nose, from right in front of me/etc. ◆ *Le robaron el coche en sus mismísimas narices. They stole his car from under his very nose.* ◆ *Nos robaron el coche en nuestras propias narices. They stole our car from right in front of us or from right under our noses.*

▶ meter las narices en algo (fam.) to poke one's nose into s.th. (fam.) ◆ *Ella mete las narices en todo. She pokes her nose into everything.*

▶ dar de narices contra algo to bang one's face/head on s.th. ◆ *Dio de narices contra la puerta. He banged his face on the door. He walked/ran smack into the door.* ◆ *Dio de narices contra el suelo. He landed on his nose. He fell flat on his face.*

▶ caerse/dar de narices [en/contra el suelo] (literal) to land on one's nose, to fall flat on one's face (literal), to fall headlong/flat

▶ darse de narices (fig., fam.) to fall flat on one's face (fig., fam.) ◆ *Echó los consejos de sus amigos en saco roto e invirtió mucho dinero en ese proyecto. Se dio de narices. He cast his friends' advice to the winds and invested a lot of money in that project. He fell flat on his face.*

▶ romper las narices a alg. (fam.) to smash s.o.'s face in (fam.)

▶ hinchar las narices a alg. (fam.) to get up s.o.'s nose (fam.), to get on s.o.'s nerves or wick (Br.E.) (fam.)

▶ hinchársele a alg. las narices (fam.) to blow one's top (sl.) ▷ salirse de sus **casillas** ◆ *Se me hincharon las narices. I hit the roof.*

▶ tener a alg. agarrado/cogido por las narices (fig.) to keep s.o. on a [very] tight rein (fig.)

▶ tener a alg. montado en las narices (fig.) (a) to let s.o. do with one what s.o. likes. (b) to be fed up [to the back teeth] with s.o. (fam.) ◆ *Ella tiene a él montado en las narices. She lets him do with her what he likes.*

▶ no ver más allá de sus narices (fig.) s.o. can't see further than or beyond the end of his nose (fig.), to have very narrow horizons (fig.) ◆ *No ve más allá de sus narices. She can't see further than the end of her nose.*

▶ meter algo a alg. por las narices (fig., fam.) to shove s.th. under s.o.'s nose (fig.) ◆ *Nos lo metió por las narices. He shoved it under our noses.*

▶ de narices (fam.) very [well], jolly well (fam., Br.E.), really, great (fam.) ◆ *ser guapo de narices to be very pretty, to be pretty and then some (fam.)* ◆ *dormir de narices to sleep jolly well, to sleep very well.* ◆ *ser un problema de narices to be a really tricky problem* ◆ *La fiesta está de narices. It's a great party.*

▷ nariz (dar a alg. con la **puerta** en las narices)

▷ nariz (dejar a alg. con un **palmo** de narices)

▷ nariz (hacer un **palmo** de narices a alg.)

▷ nariz (quedarse con un **palmo** de narices)

▷ nariz (**refregar** algo a alg. [por las narices])

▷ nariz (subírsele a alg. el **humo**/la **mostaza** a las narices)

▷ nariz de **zanahoria**

▷ nariz respingona (▷ **respingón**)

la narizota (pop.) big nose

el/la narizotas (fam.) person with a big nose, big nose (person)

el naso (fam.) big conk (sl., Br.E.), big nose
▷ nata (la **flor** y ~)

la naturaleza nature

▶ La costumbre es otra o segunda naturaleza. (prov.) Man is a creature/slave of habit.

la navaja penknife
▶ la navaja (fig., fam.) sharp/evil tongue
▷ navaja (estar en el **filo** de la ~)
▷ nave (**quemar** las ~s)

la navidad Christmas
▶ contar muchas navidades (fig., fam.) to be old

el nazareno Nazarene
▶ estar hecho un nazareno (fig., fam.) to have taken some beating, to have taken a bad beating

la necesidad necessity
▶ La necesidad carece de ley. (prov.) Necessity knows no law. (prov.)
▶ La necesidad hace maestros o aguza el ingenio. (prov.) Necessity is the mother of invention. (prov.)
▶ La necesidad tiene cara de hereje. (prov.) Beggars cannot be or must not be choosers. (prov.)
▶ hacer de la necesidad virtud to make a virtue of necessity
▶ hacer sus necesidades (euph.) to relieve o.s., to do one's business (fig.)
▷ necio (a **palabras**/**pregunta**s necias oídos sordos)

la negra black woman, negress
▶ tocarle a alg. la negra (fig.) to have bad luck
▶ perseguir a alg. la negra o tener la negra (fig.) to have a streak/run of bad luck

negro black
▶ poner negro a alg. (fam.) to make s.o. cross
▷ sacar a alg. de sus **casillas**
▶ ponerse negro (fam.) to cut up rough (fam., Br.E.), to get cross (fam.)
▶ verse negro para hacer algo (fam.) to have a tough time doing s.th. ◆ *Me vi negro para terminar este trabajo. I had a tough time finishing this job.*
▶ vérselas negras con algo (fam.) to be a real uphill struggle ◆ *Nos las estamos viendo negras con este trabajo. This job is a real uphill struggle.*
▶ pasarlas negras (fam.) s.o.'s bad luck doesn't let up, to be dogged by bad luck (fig.), to have a rough/tough time [of it] (fam.), to go through a bad or a rough or an unlucky patch (Br.E.) ◆ *Las pasamos negras. We were dogged by bad luck.*

▶ tener el alma negra [como el carbón] (fam.) to have a [very] bad/guilty conscience
▶ estorbarle a alg. lo negro (fig.) (a) not to like reading, not to like to read (b) s.o. can't read ◆ *Todavía le estorba lo negro a él. He still can't read.*
▷ negro (estar tan lejos como lo **blanco** de lo ~)
▷ negro (hacer de lo **blanco** ~)
▷ negro (la **oveja** negra)
▷ negro (no distinguir lo **blanco** de lo ~)
▷ negro (ser el **garbanzo** ~ [de la familia])
▷ negro (volver en **blanco** lo ~)

el negro black
▶ trabajar como un negro (fig., fam.) to work like a slave (fig.) ▷ echar/sudar la **hiel**
▶ ¡No somos negros! (fig., fam.) We won't stand for it/that! You/etc. can't do that to us! We won't take that lying down! (fig.)
▶ el negro [literario] (fig.) ghostwriter

el nervio nerve
▶ tener nervios (fig., fam.) to be nervous, to have stage fright
▶ tener nervios de acero (fig.) to have nerves of steel (fig.)
▶ tener los nervios de punta (fam.) to have one's nerves on edge (fig.), to be all keyed up (fig.), to be all tensed up, to have butterflies in the/one's stomach (fig.)
▶ ser un hato/manojo de nervios (fig.) to be a bundle/bag of nerves (fam.)
▶ alterar/crispar los nervios a alg. (fig.), poner los nervios de punta a alg. (fam.) to get on s.o.'s nerves or wick (Br.E.) (fam.), to put s.o.'s nerves on edge, to jar/grate on s.o.'s nerves, to get under s.o.'s skin (fam.) ◆ *Su risa me crispó los nervios o me puso los nervios de punta. His laugh got/jarred on my nerves or put my nerves on edge.*
▷ nervio (tener los ~s a **flor** de piel)

el nido nest
▶ el nido de polvo (fig.) dust collector/trap (fam.) ◆ *Había muchos nidos de polvo en su galería de arte. There were a lot of dust collectors in his art gallery.*
▶ manchar el propio nido (fig.) to foul one's own nest (fig.)
▶ caer del nido (fig.) to come down/back to earth with a bump (fig.)
▶ caerse de un nido (fig., fam.) to be still very green (fig., fam.), to be still as green as a pea

(fig., fam.), to be still a bit wet behind the ears (fig.), to be so naive, to be dreadfully innocent ◆ *Se ha caído de un nido. He's still very green.*

la nieve snow
▶ la nieve (fig., pop.) (cocaine): snow (sl.), coke (sl.)

el niño child
▶ alegrarse/estar como [un] niño con zapatos nuevos (fig., fam.) to be like a child with a new toy, to be like a dog with two tails (fam., Br.E.), to be as pleased as Punch (fig.), to be tickled pink (fam.)
▶ Los niños y los locos dicen las verdades. (prov.) Children and fools tell the truth. (prov.)

[los] nipos (pop., Esp.) (money): dough (sl., Am.E.), bread (sl.), sugar (sl.), brass/dosh/lolly (sl., Br.E.), wampum (sl., Am.E.)

la noche night
▶ la noche blanca o toledana o vizcaína (fig.) sleepless night
▶ pasar la noche en blanco to have a sleepless night, not to sleep a wink all night (fam.), not to get a wink of sleep all night (fam.)
▶ de la noche a la mañana (fig.) overnight (fig.), from one day to the next (fig.) ◆ *Cambiaron de opinión de la noche a la mañana. They changed their minds from one day to the next.*
▶ hacer noche de algo (fig.) to steal s.th., to walk off with s.th. (fam.)
▶ hacerse noche (fig.) to disappear, to vanish
▷ noche (de ~ todos los **gato**s son pardos)
▷ noche (no tener más que el **pan** y la ~)

el nombre name
▶ llamar las cosas por su nombre (fig.) to call a spade a spade (fig.)
▶ no tener nombre (fig.) to be outrageous, to be scandalous, to be incredible (fig.), to be unspeakable, to be despicable, to be beyond belief (fam.), to be an absolute scandal (fam.), to be an incredible cheek (fam., Br.E.) ◆ *Lo que le has dicho a tu amigo no tiene nombre. What you've said to your friend is unspeakable or outrageous.* ◆ *Su falta de escrúpulos no tiene nombre. His unscrupulousness is beyond belief.*

la nota footnote, note
▶ forzar la nota (fig.) to exaggerate [grossly], to lay it on [too] thick (fam.)
▶ dar la nota (fig., fam.) to make a spectacle of o.s.
▶ el nota (fam., Esp.) [conspicuous] bloke (fam.)
▶ ser un notas (fam.) to be an odd fellow, to be an odd fish (fam.), to be an oddball (fam.)

el novillo young bull
▶ el novillo (fig., fam.) cuckold
▶ hacer novillos (fig.) to play truant (Br.E.), to play hooky (fam.)

la nube cloud
▶ una nube (fig., fam.) vast amount, multitude, crowd, swarm, cloud (fig.), storm (fig.) ◆ *Había una nube de gente. There was a large crowd.* ◆ *En ese pantano había nubes de mosquitos. There were swarms/clouds of mosquitoes in that swamp.* ◆ *Desencadenaron una nube de indignación o de protestas. They triggered/unleashed a storm of indignation or protest.*
▶ una nube de verano (fig.) (a) bagatelle, trifle, little/minor thing (b) s.th. short-lived, flash in the pan (fig.), nine days' wonder ◆ *No te enfades por cada nube de verano. Don't get worked up about every little thing.* ◆ *El interés en el caso no fue más que una nube de verano. The interest in the case was just a nine days' wonder. The interest in the case turned out to be very short-lived.*
▶ pasar como una nube de verano (fig.) (passion/enthusiasm/anger/etc.): to be short-lived, to blow over quickly (fig.), to be a flash in the pan (fig.) ◆ *Su cólera pasó como una nube de verano. His rage blew over quickly.* ◆ *Su entusiasmo pasó como una nube de verano. His enthusiasm was a flash in the pan or was short-lived.*
▶ estar mirando a las nubes to be staring into space
▶ andar por o estar en las nubes (fig., fam.) to have one's head in the clouds, to be away with the fairies (fam.), to be remote from it all (fig.), to be miles away (fig.), to have one's mind on other things, to be daydreaming
▶ andar por o vivir en las nubes (fig., fam.) to have one's head in the clouds, to be living in cloud-cuckoo-land, to be living in never-never land, to be living in a dream/fantasy world

▶ estar por las nubes (fig., fam.) to be prohibitive, to be astronomical (fig.), to be very steep (fig., fam.), to be sky-high (fig.), to be soaring (fig.), to be out of sight (fig., fam., Am.E.) ◆ *Aquí los precios están por las nubes. Prices are astronomical here.* ◆ *El alquiler está por las nubes. The rent is very steep.*

▶ levantar a alg. hasta o poner a alg. por las nubes (fig.) to praise s.o. to the skies, to heap praise on s.o. (fig.), to sing s.o.'s praises ◆ *El propietario de ese restaurante de postín en la esquina levanta al nuevo jefe de cocina hasta las nubes. The owner of that plush restaurant at the corner praises his new chef to the skies.*

▷ nuca (tener **ojos** en la ~)

el nudo knot

▶ cortar el nudo gordiano (fig.) to cut the Gordian knot (to force a solution) (fig.)

▷ nudo (tener un/hacérsele a alg. un ~ en la **garganta**)

la nueva piece of news

▶ coger a alg. de nuevas (fig.) to take s.o. by surprise

▶ hacerse de nuevas (fig.) to act surprised, to pretend to be surprised, to pretend not to have heard/known anything [about it]

▷ nueve (dar a alg. con los **ochos** y los ~s)

nuevo new, fresh

▶ No hay nada nuevo bajo el sol/las estrellas. (fig.) There's nothing new under the sun. (fig.)

▶ ponerle a alg. la cara nueva (fig., fam.) to give s.o. a few hefty clips (fam.) or boxes round the ears, to give s.o. a thick ear (fam.), to give s.o. a good hiding (fam.)

▷ nuez (mucho **ruido** y pocas nueces)

el número number

▶ montar un número (fig., fam.) to put on a show (fig., fam.)

▷ nunca (más vale **tarde** que ~)

el nuncio nuncio

▶ ¡Díselo o cuéntaselo al nuncio! (fig., fam., hum.) Tell that to s.o. else! Tell that to the marines! (fam., Am.E.)

▶ ¡Que lo haga el nuncio! (fig., fam., hum.) Get s.o. else to do it!

ñangué (fam., Andes)

▶ Lo mismo es ñangá que ñangué. It's six of one and half a dozen of the other. (fig.) ◆ *¿Lo haremos ahora o más tarde? Lo mismo es ñangá que ñangué. Shall we do it now or later? It's six of one and half a dozen of the other.*

▶ en [los] tiempos de ñangué in the dim and distant past ▷ tiempos de **Maricastaña**

el ñiquiñaque (fam.) (a) worthless individual, nobody (fig., pej.) (b) [useless] rubbish/junk (fam.)

la ñoña (vulg.; en algunos países latinoamericanos) crap (vulg.), shit (vulg.), turd (vulg.)

la ñorda (pop., Esp.) crap (vulg.), shit (vulg.), turd (vulg.)

O

el obispo bishop
▶ trabajar para el obispo (fig., fam.) to work for nothing

la obra work, deed
▶ ser obra de romanos (fig.) to be a great feat, to be a huge or mammoth work/task, to be a labor of Hercules
▶ Obras son amores, que no buenas razones. (prov.) Actions speak louder than words. (prov.)

la oca goose, dice game
▶ ¡Esto es la oca! (fig., fam.) This is the tops! (fam.) This is incredible! This is amazing!

la ocasión opportunity
▶ coger/asir la ocasión por los cabellos o por los pelos (fig., fam.) to seize the opportunity, to jump at the chance (fam.)
▶ A la ocasión la pintan calva. (fam.) You have to jump at the chance. (fam.) You have to strike while the iron is hot. (prov.) You have to make hay while the sun shines. (prov.) It's an offer one can't refuse.
▶ La ocasión hace al ladrón. (prov.) Opportunity makes the thief. (prov.)

ocho eight
▶ dar a alg. con los ochos y los nueves (fig., fam.) to tell s.o. a few home truths, to give s.o. a piece of one's mind (fam.)

el ocio idleness
▶ El ocio es la madre de todos los vicios. (prov.) Idleness is the root of all evil. (prov.) Vices are born of idleness. (prov.) An idle brain is the devil's workshop. (prov.) The devil finds work for idle hands. (prov.)
▷ ocio (los **vicio**s son los hijos del ~)

la ociosidad idleness
▶ La ociosidad es la madre de todos los vicios. (prov.) Idleness is the root of all evil. (prov.) Vices are born of idleness. (prov.) An idle brain is the devil's workshop. (prov.) The devil finds work for idle hands. (prov.)
▷ ocultar la **caca**
▷ ocultar los **trapo**s sucios

▷ ocupado (estar tan ~ como un **oso** que está en hibernación)
▷ oficial de **cuchara**

el oficio trade
▶ ser del oficio (fig., fam.) to be a whore, to be a hooker (sl., Am.E.), to be on the game (fam., Br.E.), to walk/work the streets (fam.)
▶ no tener ni oficio ni beneficio (fig.) to have no profession, to be out of work, to be idle
▶ sin oficio ni beneficio (fig.) without a profession/job, out of work ♦ *Es un vago sin oficio ni beneficio. He's a lazy bum. (fam., pej., Am.E.) He's a good-for-nothing layabout. (fam., pej., Br.E.)*
▷ oficio (▷ **nacer**: nació alg. mamando el ~)

el oído sense of hearing, [inner] ear
▶ decir algo al oído de alg. to whisper s.th. in s.o.'s ear, to whisper s.th. to s.o.
▶ Dicho al oído. (fig.) Between you and me.
▶ ¡Oído al parche! (fam.) Watch out! (fam.) Look out! (fam.)
▶ hacer/prestar oídos sordos [a algo] (fig.) to turn a deaf ear [to s.th.] (fig.), to take no notice [of s.th.]
▶ prestar/dar oídos a alg./algo to give/lend an ear to s.o./s.th. (fig.), to listen to what s.o. has to say, to pay attention to s.th., to take notice of s.th.
▶ ser todo oídos to be all ears
▶ aplicar el oído to listen carefully
▶ aguzar el oído (fig.) to prick up one's ears (fig.)
▶ entrarle a alg. por un oído y salirle por el otro (fig.) to go in one ear and [come] out [of] the other (fig.) ♦ *Lo que dijiste me entró por un oído y me salió por el otro. What you said went in one ear and came out the other.*
▶ ser un regalo para los oídos to be a treat for the ears ♦ *La música fue un regalo para los oídos. The music was a treat for the ears.*
▶ regalarle a alg. el oído (fig.) to flatter s.o.
▶ llegar a oídos de alg. to come to the attention/notice of s.o.
▶ no poder dar crédito a sus oídos not to believe one's ears ♦ *No podía dar crédito a mis*

oídos cuando lo oía. I couldn't believe my ears when I heard it.

▷ oído (a **palabra**s/**pregunta**s necias ~s sordos)

▷ oído (**herir** el ~)

el ojeo battue

▶ irse a ojeo de algo/alg. (fig., fam.) to be on the hunt for s.th. (fig., fam.), to chase after s.th. (fig.), to be out to + infinitive ◆ *Se iba a ojeo de trabajo. He was on the hunt for a job. He was job-hunting.* ◆ *Se va a ojeo de marido. She's out to get herself a husband.*

el ojete eyelet

▶ el ojete (fig., pop., Esp.) arsehole (vulg., Br.E.), asshole (vulg., Am.E.)

el ojo eye

▶ el ojo overo (fig., fam.) glass eye

▶ estar [con] ojo avisor to be on one's guard (fig.), to be on the alert

▶ estar con cien ojos (fig.) to be extremely alert or suspicious or wary

▶ avivar el/[los] ojo[s] (fig.) to be [on the] alert, to keep one's eyes open (fig.), to keep one's eyes peeled/skinned (fam.), to take care

▶ dormir con los ojos abiertos (fig., fam.) to be extremely alert

▶ tener ojo clínico (fig.) to be a keen observer

▶ tener ojos de águila/lince (fig.) to have eyes like a hawk (fig.)

▶ tener un ojo a la funerala (fig., fam.) to have a black eye, to have a shiner (fam.)

▶ tener ojos de besugo (fig., fam.) to be goggle-eyed (fam.), to have bulging eyes ◆ *Se quedaron mirando con ojos de besugo. They stood watching goggle-eyed.*

▶ tener ojos en la nuca (fig.) to have eyes in the back of one's head (fig.) ◆ *El jefe siempre siente qué está pasando. Parece que tiene ojos en la nuca. The boss always senses what is going on. He seems to have eyes in the back of his head.*

▶ poner los ojos en blanco to roll one's eyes

▶ no pegar ojo (fig.) not to sleep a wink (fam.) ◆ *No pegué ojo en toda la noche. I didn't sleep a wink all night.*

▶ llorar con un ojo (fig.) to weep/shed [a few] crocodile tears (fig.), to squeeze a tear (fig.) ◆ *Ella lloró con un ojo cuando su jefe se jubiló. Lo tenía atravesado. She wept a few crocodile tears when her boss retired. She couldn't stand him.*

▶ costar un ojo de la cara (fig., fam.) to cost an arm and a leg (fam.) ▷ costar una **burrada**

▶ estar hasta los ojos en algo (fig.) to be up to one's eyes/eyeballs in s.th. (debt or trouble or work/etc.) (fig.)

▶ recrear los ojos en algo, regalarse los ojos con algo to feast one's eyes on s.th. ◆ *Nos regalamos los ojos con su belleza. We feasted our eyes on her beauty.*

▶ comer con los ojos (fig.) s.o.'s eyes are too big for or are bigger than his stomach, to take more than one can eat ◆ *No pudieron comer la mitad de la comida que pidieron. Comieron con los ojos. They couldn't eat half of the food they ordered. Their eyes were bigger than their stomachs.*

▶ echar el ojo a alg./algo (fig.) to have one's eyes on s.o./s.th., to covet s.o./s.th.

▶ comerse a alg. con los ojos (fig.) to devour s.o. with one's eyes (fig.)

▶ irsele a alg. los ojos tras algo/alg. (fig.) to devour s.th./s.o. with one's eyes (fig.), to long/crave for s.th., to eye s.o. up (fam.), s.o. can't keep his eyes off s.o. ◆ *Al pobre chico se le van los ojos tras los helados. The poor boy is craving for an ice cream.* ◆ *Se le iban los ojos tras la chica. He couldn't keep his eyes off the girl. He devoured the girl with his eyes.*

▶ entrar a alg. por el ojo derecho (fig., fam.) to think a lot of s.o. ◆ *Entra a la gente por el ojo derecho. People think a lot of him/her.*

▶ mirar algo/a alg. con otros ojos (fig.) to look at s.th./s.o. through different eyes, to look at s.th./s.o. differently

▶ saltársele/salírsele a alg. los ojos de las órbitas (fig.) s.o.'s eyes pop out of their sockets or out of his head (fig.), s.o.'s eyes stand out on stalks (fig.) ◆ *Los ojos se te saltaban de las órbitas. Your eyes were popping out of their sockets. Your eyes were standing out on stalks.*

▶ salirle algo a alg. a los ojos (fig.) one can tell just by looking at s.o. or just by the look on s.o.'s face ◆ *La mala conciencia te sale a los ojos. One/I/we can tell just by looking at you that you have a bad conscience.*

▶ no saber uno dónde tiene los ojos (fig., fam.) to be blind (fig.), to be very stupid or clumsy ◆ *¿Pero no sabes dónde tienes los ojos? Are you really that blind?*

▶ quebrarse los ojos (fig., fam.) (reading/ etc.): to strain one's eyes excessively, to ruin one's eyes

▶ ser el ojo derecho de alg. (fig.) (a) to be s.o.'s right-hand man (b) to be in s.o.'s confidence (c) to be highly cherished by s.o., to be the apple of s.o.'s eye (fig.)

▶ Ojos que te vieron ir. (fig., fam.) That opportunity/chance won't come again. I won't see you or the money/etc. again.

▶ [poder/saber] hacer algo con los ojos cerrados (fig.) [to be able] to do s.th. with one's eye's closed (fig.), [to be able] to do s.th. blindfold (fig.), [to be able] to do s.th. standing on one's head or with one arm/hand tied behind one's back (fig.), [to be able] to do s.th. in a breeze (fam., Am.E.) ◆ *Lo hizo con los ojos cerrados. He did it blindfold. He did it in a breeze.* ◆ *Lo puedo/podría hacer con los ojos cerrados. I'm able to/I could do it blindfold or with one arm tied behind my back.*

▶ cerrar los ojos a algo (fig.) to close/shut one's eyes to s.th. (fig.)

▶ tener/traer a alg. entre ojos (fig.) to look askance at s.o. (fig.), to have it in for s.o. (fam.), to loathe s.o.

▶ mirar con ojos de sobrino (fig., fam., Colombia) to put on an innocent air, to look innocent, to have an innocent expression on one's face

▶ meterse por el ojo de una aguja (fig., fam.) s.o. always wants to be in on everything (fam.), to be very obtrusive or importunate, to be very pushy (fam.) ◆ *Siempre se mete por el ojo de una aguja. He always wants to be in on everything. He's always got to be in on everything.*

▶ a ojo de buen cubero (fig.) at a glance, at a rough guess, roughly, by guesswork ◆ *A ojo de buen cubero diría que ... At a glance or at a rough guess I'd say that . . .*

▶ en un abrir y cerrar de ojos in the twinkling of an eye (fig.), in a flash, before you can say Jack Robinson (fam.) ◆ *Todo pasó en un abrir y cerrar de ojos. It was all over in a flash.* ◆ *El ciervo había desaparecido en el bosque en un abrir y cerrar de ojos. In the twinkling of an eye, the deer had disappeared into the woods.*

▶ Ojos que no ven, corazón que no siente. (prov.) Out of sight, out of mind. (prov.)

What the eye doesn't see, the heart doesn't grieve over. (prov.)

▶ Ojo por ojo, diente por diente. (prov.) An eye for an eye [and a tooth for a tooth]. (prov.)

▷ ojo (echar **fuego** por los ~s)
▷ ojo (echar **tierra** a los ~s de alg.)
▷ ojo (echarse **tierra** a los ~s)
▷ ojo (encajar/caer como **pedrada** en ~ de boticario)
▷ ojo (hacer caer la **venda** de los ~s a alg.)
▷ ojo (hacérsele a alg. **candelillas** los ~s)
▷ ojo (meter a alg. los **dedos** por los ~s)
▷ ojo (no parecerse ni en el **blanco** de los ~s)
▷ ojo (tener **sangre** en el ~)
▷ ojo (tener una **venda** en los ~s)
▷ ojo (venir como **pedrada** en ~ de boticario)
▷ ola (ser un **juguete** de las ~s)
▷ oler a **chamusquina**/a **cuerno** quemado/a **gloria**/a **rayos**/a **tigre**
▷ oler el **poste**
▷ olerse la **tostada**

el olivo olive tree

▶ Olivo y aceituno, todo es uno. (fig., fam.) It's six of one and half a dozen of the other. (fig.)

▷ olivo (cada **mochuelo** a su ~)

la olla pot

▶ la olla de grillos (fig., fam.) madhouse (fig.), mad hatter's tea party (hum.), complete chaos ◆ *Esto parece una olla de grillos. It's like a madhouse in here.*

▶ tener la cabeza como una olla de grillos (fig., fam.) s.o.'s head is spinning (fig.)

▶ No hay olla sin tocino. (fig., fam.) There's no icing on the cake. (fig.)

▷ olla (muchas **manos** en la ~ echan el guiso a perder)
▷ olmo (no se le puede pedir **peras** al ~)
▷ olmo (pedir **peras** al ~)
▷ olvido (**relegar** algo al ~)

el ombligo navel

▶ el ombligo del mundo (fig.) center of the universe (fig.) ◆ *Dicen que París es el ombligo del mundo. Paris is said to be the center of the universe.*

▶ encogérsele a alg. el ombligo (fig.) to get the wind up (sl.), to get cold feet (fig., fam.)

▶ meter a alg. el ombligo para dentro (fam.) to put the wind up s.o. (fam., Br.E.), to give s.o. a [nasty] fright

once eleven

▶ tomar las once (fig.) to have a mid-morning snack

▶ estar a las once (fig., fam.) to be crooked, to be out of kilter (sl.) ◆ *Tu corbata está a las once. Your tie is crooked.* ◆ *El cuadro está a las once. The picture on the wall is out of kilter.*

▶ tener la cabeza a las once (fig., fam.) to be totally confused, to have a throbbing headache

▶ estar a las once y cuarto (pop.) to be crazy, to be nuts (fam.), to be off one's nut (fam., Br.E.)

onceno eleventh

▶ el onceno: [no estorbar] (fig., fam.) eleventh commandment: don't disturb

la onda wave

▶ estar en onda (fig., fam.) to be high (on drugs) (fam.)

▶ estar en la onda (fig., fam.) (a) (fashion/ etc.): to be in (s.th.) (fam.), to be with it (s.th.) (sl.), to be trendy (s.th./s.o.), to be hip (s.o.) (sl.) (b) to be [bang] up to date (fam.), to be in the picture (fam.), to be in the swim (fig.), to be on the ball (fam.), to be with it (sl.), to be hip to s.th. (sl.) ◆ *Este peinado está en la onda. This hairstyle is in/is with it.* ◆ *Siempre lleva vestidos que están muy en la onda. He's a very trendy dresser. He's very hip.* ◆ *Estamos en la onda de lo que ocurre. We're up to date with what's going on. We're hip to what's going on.*

▶ estar fuera de onda (fig., fam.) to be behind the times

▶ captar la onda (fig., fam.) (a) to understand, to get it (fam.), to twig it (fam.), to get the point (b) to get the hang of it (fam.)

▶ perder la onda (fig., fam.) to lose the knack or one's touch (fam.) ◆ *Recientemente ha tenido dificultad para explicarse con sencillez. Parece que ha perdido la onda. Recently he's had difficulty [in] explaining things simply. He seems to have lost his touch.*

la opinión opinion

▶ casarse con su opinión (fig.) to insist on one's opinion

▷ opinión (▷ el **sabio**: es de sabios cambiar de ~)

▷ opinión (estar **caballero** en su ~)

el opio opium

▶ dar el opio a alg. (fig., fam.) to captivate s.o. (fig.), to enchant s.o. (fig.), to bewitch s.o., to make an impression on s.o.

la órbita orbit

▶ poner a alg. en órbita (fig.) (a) to launch s.o. (artist/etc.) (b) (alcohol/drugs): to make s.o. high (fam.), to send s.o. on a trip (sl.)

el orégano oregano

▶ No todo el monte es orégano. (prov.) Life isn't all a bowl of cherries. (fig.) You've got to take the rough with the smooth. (fig.)

▶ creer que todo el monte es orégano to think everything is plain sailing (fig.)

la oreja ear

▶ planchar/chafar la oreja (fam.) to sleep, to kip (fam.), to have a kip (fam.), to get a bit of or some shut-eye (fam.)

▶ descubrir la oreja (fig.) to show [o.s. in] one's true colors (fig.), to reveal one's true nature ◆ *Nunca se sabe qué piensa ese tío. No descubre la oreja. You can never tell what that guy is thinking. He doesn't show his true colors.*

▶ tener a alg. de la oreja (fig., fam.) to keep s.o. on a tight rein (fig.)

▶ mojar la oreja a alg. (fig., fam.) to start squabbling or arguing with s.o., to be trying to pick an argument or a fight with s.o., to insult s.o.

▶ aguzar las orejas (fig.) to prick up one's ears (fig.)

▶ bajar las orejas (fig., fam.) to climb down (fig., fam.)

▶ ver las orejas del lobo (fig., fam.) to be in great danger

▶ haber visto las orejas del lobo (fig., fam.) to have escaped from great danger, to have got off lightly [this time], to have been lucky [this time]

▶ con las orejas gachas (fig.) with one's tail between one's legs (fig.), ashamed, embar-

rassed ◆ *Se fue con las orejas gachas. He slinked off with his tail between his legs.*
▷ oreja (echarle a alg. la **pulga** detrás de la ~)
▷ oreja (estar con/tener la **mosca** detrás de la ~)
▷ oreja (**sonreír** de ~ a ~)
▷ oreja (un **vino** de una ~/de dos ~s)
▷ oreja (**ventilar**le a alg. las ~s)
▷ orgullo (no caber en el **pellejo** de ~)
▷ original (ser más ~ que el **pecado**)

la orilla shore
▶ la otra orilla (fig.) hereafter, great beyond

el oro gold
▶ la mina de oro (fig.) gold mine (fig., fam.), money-spinner (fam., Br.E.)
▶ apalear oro (fig., fam.) to be raking it in (fig., fam.), to be rolling in money (fig., fam.)
▶ guardar algo como oro en paño to guard s.th. with one's life, to treasure s.th. [as if it were gold (Am.E.) or gold dust (Br.E.)]
▶ prometerle a alg. montañas de oro o el oro y el moro to promise s.o. the moon/earth ◆ *Nos prometieron el oro y el moro, pero sólo pagaron una miseria. They promised us the moon, but only paid a pittance.*
▶ querer el oro y el moro to want to have one's cake and eat it [too] (fig.), to want one's bread buttered on both sides (fig.)
▶ poner a alg. de oro y azul (fam.) to lay into s.o. (verbally) (fam.), to lambast[e] s.o. (fig.), to heap insults on s.o.
▶ como un oro (fig., fam.) spick-and-span (fam.), like spanking new (fam.) ◆ *Le gusta tener la casa como un oro. She likes to keep her house spick-and-span.*
▶ valer alg./algo su peso en oro (fig.), valer algo tanto oro como pesa (fig.) s.o./s.th.: to be worth one's/its weight in gold (fig.) ◆ *Mi secretaria vale su peso en oro. My secretary is worth her weight in gold.*

▶ No es oro todo lo que reluce. (prov.) All that glitters is not gold. (prov.)
▷ oro (adorar el **becerro** de ~)
▷ oro (el **pimpollo** [de ~])
▷ oro (ser **bueno** como el ~)
▷ oro (tener **manitas** de ~)
▷ oro (tener un **pico** de ~)

el oso bear
▶ hacer el oso (fig., fam.) (a) to act/play the fool, to clown about/around (b) to make a fool of o.s., to make a laughing stock of o.s.
▶ estar tan ocupado como un oso que está en hibernación (hum.) to be [as] busy as a hibernating bear (hum.) ◆ *Dice que está muy ocupado. ¡Muy ocupado, mi abuela! Está tan ocupado como un oso que está en hibernación. He says he's very busy. Very busy, my foot! He's as busy as a hibernating bear.*
▷ oso (vender la **piel** del ~ antes de cazarlo)

¡Oste! Shoo!
▶ sin decir oste ni moste (fig., fam.) without saying a word, without so much as a word ◆ *Salió del cuarto sin decir oste ni moste. He left the room without saying a word.*
▷ ostra (**aburrirse** como una ~)
▷ otorgar (▷ **callar**: quien calla otorga)

la oveja sheep
▶ la oveja negra (fig.) black sheep (fig.)
▶ apartar las ovejas de los cabritos (fig.) to separate the sheep from the goats (fig.), to separate the wheat/grain from the chaff (fig.)
▶ encomendar las ovejas al lobo (fig.) to ask for trouble
▶ Cada oveja con su pareja. (prov.) Birds of a feather flock together. (prov.)
▷ oveja (un **lobo** con piel de ~)
▷ overo (**ojo** ~)
▷ ovillo (contar algo del **hilo** al ~)
▷ ovillo (por el **hilo** se saca el ~)

P

la paciencia patience
- ▶ tener más paciencia que Job o que un santo (fig.) to have the patience of Job or of a saint (fig.)
- ▶ tener una paciencia angelical o de benedictino (fig.) to have the patience of Job or of a saint (fig.)
- ▶ ¡Paciencia y barajar! [Let's] wait and see! Don't give up!
- ▷ paciencia (poder hacer perder la ~ a un **santo**)
- ▷ paciencia (**revestirse** de ~)
- ▷ paciencia (tener la ~ de un **chino**)
- ▷ paciencia (**tentar** la ~ a alg.)

Paco (fam.) affectionate name for Francisco
- ▶ ya viene/vendrá el tío Paco con la rebaja (fig., fam.) this won't last forever, it's too good to last

padre (adj., fam.) huge, tremendous (fam.) ◆ *un susto padre an awful fright* ◆ *un escándalo padre a huge scandal, a full-blown scandal* ◆ *un éxito padre a terrific success*
- ▷ padre (pegarse la **vida** ~)

el padre father
- ▶ de padre y muy señor mío (fig., fam.) proper (fam.), decent (fam.), tremendous (fam.), terrible, terrific (fam.), almighty (fam.) ◆ *Le dieron una paliza de padre y muy señor mío. He took a terrible beating. He took a bashing and a half. (fam., Br.E.) He took the father and mother of a thrashing. (fam.) They beat the living daylights out of him. (fam.) They beat him black and blue. (fam.)* ◆ *Es una mentira de padre y muy señor mío. It's a great big lie. (fam.) It's a whopping great lie. (fam.)* ◆ *Cogí una mona de padre y muy señor mío. I drank myself silly. (fam.)*
- ▷ padre (tal ~ tal **hijo**)

el padrenuestro Lord's Prayer
- ▶ querer enseñar el padrenuestro al cura (fam.) to try to teach one's grandmother to suck eggs (fam.) ◆ *¿Le estás queriendo enseñar el padrenuestro al cura? Are you trying to teach your grandmother to suck eggs?*

- ▶ en menos que se reza un padrenuestro (fig.) before you can say Jack Robinson (fam.), in next to no time ◆ *Estoy allí en menos que se reza un padrenuestro. I'll be there before you can say Jack Robinson.*

el paganini
- ▶ ser el paganini (fig., fam., hum.) to be the one who pays, to be the one who has to pay, to foot the bill

el pagano heathen
- ▶ ser el pagano (fig., fam., hum.) to be the one who pays, to be the one who has to pay, to foot the bill

pagar to pay
- ▶ Quien o el que la hace la paga. (fig., fam.) One must bear/face the consequences. As you make your bed, so you must lie in it. (prov.)
- ▶ pagarse con algo (fig., fam.) to be content with s.th.
- ▶ pagarse de algo (fig., fam.) to show off s.th., to brag/boast about s.th.
- ▶ pagarse de sí mismo (fig., fam.) to be sold on o.s. (fig.), to be conceited, to be smug, to be full of o.s.
- ▶ ¡[Ya] me las pagarás! (fig.) You'll pay for this! (fig.) Just you wait! (fam.)
- ▶ ¡[Ya] me las pagarás con creces! (fig.) You'll pay for this in spades! (fig., fam., Am.E.)
- ▷ pagar (▷ **tocar**: ¡Tocan a ~!)
- ▷ pagar a toca **teja**
- ▷ pagar el **pato**
- ▷ pagar la **primada**
- ▷ pagar los **platos**/**vidrios** rotos

la página page
- ▶ saltar a las primeras páginas (fig.) to make/hit the headlines

la paja straw
- ▶ hacerse una paja (fig., pop.) (to masturbate) ▷ tocar la **campana**
- ▶ hacerse una paja mental (fig., pop.) to indulge in mental masturbation (fig.), to unnecessarily lose sleep over s.th.
- ▶ ver la paja en el ojo ajeno y no la viga en el propio (fig.) to see the mote in one's

neighbor's or in s.o. else's eye and not the beam in one's own (fig.)

▶ no dormirse en las pajas (fig.) not to pass up or miss any opportunity

▶ por un quítame allá esas pajas (fig.) over [absolutely] nothing, over some tiny thing, over some trifle ◆ *Riñeron por un quítame allá esas pajas. They squabbled or quarreled or argued over some trifle.*

▷ paja (apartar/separar el **grano** de la ~)

▷ pajar (buscar una **aguja** en un ~)

la pájara (fig., pej.) sly/crafty woman, scheming bitch (sl., pej.).

el pajarito baby bird

▶ el pajarito (fam.) penis of children, weeny (fam., Am.E.), willy (fam., Br.E.)

▶ comer como un pajarito (fig.) to eat like a bird (fig.)

▶ quedarse [muerto] como un pajarito (fig., fam.) to die peacefully, to fade away

▶ me lo dijo un pajarito (fig., fam.) a little bird told me (fig., fam.)

el pájaro bird

▶ el pájaro (pop.) (penis) ▷ el calvo

▶ ser un pájaro gordo (fig.) to be a bigwig (fam.), to be a big shot (fam.), to be a big cheese (fam.), to be a big wheel (fam.)

▶ ser un pájaro raro (fig.) to be a strange customer (fam.), to be an odd character, to be an odd/queer fish (fam.)

▶ ser un pájaro de cuenta (fig., fam.) to be a dangerous person, to be a nasty piece of work (fig., fam.), to be a bad lot (fam.), to be a nasty type (fam.), to be a wily bird (fam.), to be an unpleasant character

▶ ha volado el pájaro (fig.) the bird has flown (fig.)

▶ matar dos pájaros de un tiro (fig.) to kill two birds with one stone (fig.)

▶ Más vale pájaro en mano que ciento volando. (prov.) A bird in the hand is worth two in the bush. (prov.)

▷ pájaro (a **vista** de ~)

▷ pájaro (tener ~s en la **cabeza**)

▷ pájaro (tener la **cabeza** a ~s)

▷ pájaro (tener la **cabeza** llena de ~s)

▷ pala (el **cabe** de ~)

la palabra word

▶ beberle a alg. las palabras (fig.) to hang on s.o.'s lips (fig.), to hang on s.o.'s every word

▶ coger a alg. la palabra to take s.o. at his word, to keep s.o. to his word

▶ A palabras necias oídos sordos. (prov.) Don't take notice of the stupid things people say.

▷ palabra (**acaparar** la ~)

▷ palabra (al buen **entendedor**, pocas ~s [le bastan])

▷ palabra (estar **colgado** de las ~s de alg.)

▷ paladar (pegársele a alg. la **lengua** al ~)

▷ pálido (no tener ni la más pálida **idea** de algo)

la palinodia palinode

▶ cantar la palinodia (fam.) to recant, to make a public recantation

la palma palm (tree), palm (of one's hand)

▶ llevarse la palma to carry off the palm (fig.), to take the cake (fig.), to triumph, to win

▶ untar la palma a alg. (fig., fam.) to grease s.o.'s palm (fig., fam.), to bribe s.o.

▶ conocer algo como la palma de la mano (fig.) to know s.th. like the back of one's hand (fig.) ◆ *Conozco la ciudad como la palma de la mano. I know the city like the back of my hand.*

palmado

▶ estar palmado (fig., fam.) to be flat broke (fam.), to be stone-broke (fam., Am.E.), to be skint (fam., Br.E.)

palmarla (pop.) to cash/hand in one's chips (fam., hum.) ▷ **cascar**[la]

el palmo span

▶ palmo a palmo (fig.) slowly, step by step, inch by inch, little by little ◆ *Lo exploramos palmo a palmo. We explored it inch by inch.*

▶ hacer un palmo de narices a alg. (fam.) to thumb one's nose at s.o. (fam.)

▶ quedarse con un palmo de narices (fam.) to come away empty-handed, to end up with nothing

▶ dejar a alg. con un palmo de narices (fam.) to disappoint s.o. greatly, to take the wind out of s.o.'s sails (fam.) ◆ *Siempre se jactaba de ser un hacha para el ajedrez hasta que mi hermanito se lo comió crudo. Eso sí que lo dejó con un palmo de narices. He was always boasting about being a genius at chess until my kid brother beat him hollow. That really took the wind out of his sails.*

▶ conocer algo a palmos (fig.) to know s.th. very well ◆ *Conoce el terreno a palmos. He knows the terrain/ground very well. He knows every inch of the terrain/ground.*

el palo stick
▶ De tal palo, tal astilla. (prov.) The apple doesn't fall far from the tree. (prov.) Like father like son. (prov.) A chip off the old block.
▶ estar del mismo palo (fig.) to be in cahoots (fam.), to be hand in glove
▶ dar un palo a alg. (fig.) to criticize s.o. severely, to give s.o. a [real] roasting (fam.), to take s.o. to task (fig.)
▶ dar palos de ciego (a) to lash out blindly/wildly (b) to grope in the dark (fig.)
▶ andar a palos (fig., fam.) to be [always] squabbling, to fight like cat and dog (fig.)
▶ meter un palo en la rueda o palos en las ruedas [de alg.] (fig.) to put a spoke in s.o.'s wheel (fig., fam., Br.E.), to throw a spanner (Br.E.) or a monkey wrench (Am.E.) in[to] the works (fam.) ◆ *Me metió un palo en la rueda. He put a spoke in my wheel.* ◆ *Casi echó nuestros planes por el suelo cuando de repente se rajó. Él sí que metió palos en las ruedas. He almost ruined our plans when he suddenly backed out. He really threw a monkey wrench into the works.*
▶ aplicar una política del palo y la zanahoria (fig.) to apply a carrot-and-stick policy or a policy of the carrot and the stick (fig.) ◆ *El gobierno aplicó una política del palo y la zanahoria para cambiar la opinión del pueblo. The government applied a policy of the carrot and the stick in order to change the people's opinion.*
▶ a palo seco (fig.) ◆ *whisky a palo seco straight whisk[e]y* ◆ *beber a palo seco to drink without having anything to eat* ◆ *Me lo dijeron a palo seco. They told me straight out (Br.E.) or outright.* ◆ *Lo desmintió a palo seco. He flatly denied it.* ◆ *Pagaron los veinte dólares a palo seco. They paid the twenty dollars and not a cent more.*
▷ palo (hay **gusto**s que merecen ~s)
▷ palo (la **ene/pata** de ~)
▷ palo (sacar **agua** de un ~ seco)

la paloma pigeon
▶ palomas (waves): white horses
▶ la paloma (fig., pop.) streetwalker, prostitute

▶ ser una paloma sin hiel (fig.) to be a (fig.), to be very sweet-tempered, to h sweet/peaceful nature

el palomar pigeon loft
▶ alborotar el palomar (fig., fam.) to ca commotion

el palomino young pigeon
▶ el palomino (fig., fam.) brown spot (in underwear), skidmark (fig., fam., hum.)
▶ un palomino atontado (fig., pop.) id
▷ un [pedazo de] **alcornoque**

la palotada whack (with a stick)
▶ no dar palotada (fig., fam.) (a) not to do stroke of work (b) to get nothing right, s.c can't do a thing right

el pálpito (fam.) feeling, presentiment, hunch (fam.)
▶ darle a alg. el pálpito o tener el pálpito de que ... to have a feeling or a hunch that ..., s.th. tells s.o. that ... ◆ *Me da el pálpito o tengo el pálpito de que aquí hay gato encerrado. I have a feeling/hunch that there's something wrong here.*

el pan bread
▶ llamar al pan, pan y al vino, vino (fig.) to call a spade a spade (fig.)
▶ ser más bueno que el pan (fam.) (well-behaved): to be as good as gold
▶ hacer un pan como unas hostias (fig., fam.) to muck it [all] up (sl.), to make a hash/botch of s.th./things (fig., fam.)
▶ repartir algo como pan bendito (fig., fam.) to be extremely tight or tight-fisted with s.th. (fam.)
▶ ganarse el pan (fam.) to earn/make a living, to earn one's daily bread (fam.), to earn one's bread and butter (fam.), to earn one's crust (fam.)
▶ venderse como el pan o como pan caliente (fig.) to sell like hotcakes (fig.) ◆ *Estos libros se venden como pan caliente. These books sell/go like hotcakes.*
▶ ser el pan [nuestro] de cada día (fig.) to be a daily event, to be an everyday occurrence, to happen every day ◆ *Estas manifestaciones son el pan de cada día o se han convertido en el pan nuestro de cada día. These demonstrations are an everyday occurrence or have become a daily event.*

► ser pan comido **(fam.)** to be as easy as pie (sl.), to be a piece of cake (fam.), to be a breeze (fam., Am.E.), to be dead easy (fam.), to be like shooting fish in a barrel (fig., Am.E.) ▷ ser **coser** y cantar

► no tener más que el pan y la noche (fam.) to be very poor, to be as poor as a church mouse (fig.)

► no caérsele a alg. el pan (fig., fam.) to be dying of impatience (fig.), s.o. can hardly wait ◆ *El libro será publicado pronto. No se me cae el pan. The book will be published soon. I can hardly wait (for it to be published). I'm dying of impatience.*

► A falta de pan, buenas son tortas. (prov.) Any port in a storm. (prov.) Beggars cannot or must not be choosers. (prov.)

► Pan con pan, comida de tontos. (prov.) A change is a good thing. Variety is the spice of life. (prov.)

► No sólo de pan vive el hombre. (prov.) Man cannot live by bread alone. (prov.)

► Con pan y vino se anda el camino. (prov.) Things don't/never seem so bad after a good meal.

▷ pan (▷ **comer:** con su/etc. ~ se/etc. lo coma/etc.)

▷ pan (a buen **hambre** no hay ~ duro)

▷ pan (comprar/vender algo por un **pedazo** de ~)

▷ pan (**Dios** da ~ a quien no tiene dientes.)

▷ pan (ser más **largo** que un día sin ~)

▷ pan (ser **tortas** y ~ pintado)

▷ pan (ser un **pedazo** de ~)

▷ pan (tener **cara** de ~)

pancho calm

► quedarse/estar tan pancho (fam.) to remain/be perfectly calm ▷ quedarse/estar tan **campante**

el pandero tambourine

► en buenas manos está el pandero (fig., fam.) s.th./it is in good hands

el panorama panorama

► ¡Vaya un panorama! (fam.) That's a fine look-out! (iron.)

el pantalón pants (Am.E.), trousers (Br.E.)

► llevar los pantalones (fig.) to wear the pants/trousers (fig.) ◆ *La madre lleva los pantalones en nuestra casa. The mother wears the trousers in our house.*

la panza belly, paunch (fam.)

► la panza de burra (fig., fam.) grey (Br.E.) or gray (Am.E.) sky (especially during snowy weather)

► la panza de burro (fig., fam.) overhang (climbing)

► echar panza (fam.) to start to get a paunch (fam.), to put on weight

el pañal nappy, diaper (Am.E.)

► estar aún/todavía en pañales (fig.) to be still in its infancy (fig.) ◆ *Este proyecto está aún en pañales. This project is still in its infancy.*

el paño cloth

► ser del paño (fam.) to be an expert, to be well up in s.th., to know one's oats (fam., Am.E.)

► conocer el paño (fig., fam.) to know what's what (fam.), to be on the ball (fam.), to know what/who one is dealing with

► acudir al paño (fig.) to take the bait (fig.), to walk into the trap (fig.)

► Hay paño que cortar. (fig.) There's enough of it.

► ser un paño de lágrimas (fig.) to be a helpful soul

► ser el paño de lágrimas de alg. (fig.) to be a shoulder for s.o. to cry on

► aplicar paños calientes (fig.) to take half measures (fig.), to do things in half measures (fig.) or by halves, to apply ineffective remedies

► no andarse con paños calientes (fig.) not to do things in half measures (fig.) or by halves, not to go in for half measures (fig.)

► en paños menores (fig., fam., hum.) in one's undies (fam., hum.), in one's shirt, in one's negligee

el pañuelo handkerchief

► El mundo es un pañuelo. (fig., fam.) It's a small world.

la papa (América Latina) potato

► no entender ni papa (fam.) not to understand a word [of it]

► no saber ni papa de algo (fam.) not to know beans about s.th. (sl., Am.E.)

la papalina (fam.) roaring drunkenness (fam.)

► coger una papalina to get roaring drunk (fam.), to drink o.s. silly (fam.)

el papel paper
- ▶ no fumar más que papel (fig., fam.) to smoke cigarettes only
- ▶ no poder coger algo ni con papel de fumar (fig., fam., Esp.) s.o. wouldn't touch s.th. with a bargepole or ten-foot pole (fig.)
- ▶ el papel todo lo aguanta (fig.) rubbish (Br.E.) or garbage (Am.E.) that ends up on paper (fig., fam.)
- ▶ no ser más que papel mojado (fig., fam.) to be a scrap of paper (fig.), to be a worthless bit of paper (fig.), not to be worth the paper [s.th. is written on] (fig.), to be useless ◆ *Este contrato no es más que papel mojado. This contract is just a worthless bit of paper. This contract isn't worth the paper it's written on.*
- ▶ venir a alg. con papeles (fig., fam.) to play up to s.o., to soft-soap s.o. (fam.)
- ▶ hacer [un] buen papel (fig.) to make a good impression, to behave [well], to prove one's worth (fig.), to show what one can do, to put up a good/etc. performance/etc. ◆ *Anoche hiciste muy buen papel. You made a very good impression last night.* ◆ *Nuestro equipo hizo un buen papel en el torneo. Our team put up a good performance in the tournament. The players in/on our team showed what they can do.*
- ▶ jugar/desempeñar un papel (fig.) to play a role (fig.), to play a part ◆ *Ella desempeña un papel importante en la empresa. She plays an important role in the company. She's a key player in the company.*

la papeleta bit/slip of paper
- ▶ tocarle a alg. una papeleta difícil (fig.) to face a difficult job, to face a tough one (fam.)

la papilla pap, baby food
- ▶ estar hecho papilla (fig., fam.) to be completely shattered (fam., Br.E.), to be dog-tired (fam.) ▷ estar hecho **cisco**
- ▶ hacer papilla a alg. (fig., fam.) (a) to beat s.o. to a pulp (fig.), to make mincemeat of s.o. (fig.) (b) to come down on s.o. like a ton of bricks (fam.)

el paquete package, parcel
- ▶ el paquete (fam.) (motorcycle): pillion passenger/rider
- ▶ ir de paquete (fam.) to ride on the back (of a motorcycle), to ride pillion

- ▶ cargar con el paquete (fam., Esp.) to [have to] carry the can (fam., Br.E.)
- ▶ meter un paquete a alg. (fig., fam.) to give s.o. a rocket (fig., fam., Br.E.), to tear a strip off s.o. (fam.)
- ▶ dejar a alg. con el paquete (fam.) to get/make s.o. pregnant, to get s.o. in the family way (fam.), to knock s.o. up (sl.)

parado motionless
- ▶ quedarse parado (fig.) to be [utterly] bewildered, to be [completely] floored (fam.), s.o.'s jaw drops (fam.)
- ▶ no quedarse ahí parado (fig.) not to leave it at that
- ▶ mal parado in pretty bad shape, in a bad way ◆ *Salieron mal parados del accidente. They were in pretty bad shape after the accident.*
- ▷ paraíso (como **Adán** en el ~)

parar to stop
- ▶ ¿Adónde quieres/etc. ir a parar? (fig.) What are you/etc. getting or driving (fig.) at?
- ▶ ¿Adónde vamos a parar? (fig.) Where's it all going to end?
- ▶ No sabemos en qué va a parar todo esto. We don't know where all this is going to end.
- ▷ parar (no ~se en **barra**s)
- ▷ parar (sin ~se en **barra**s)

el parche sticking plaster
- ▶ pegar un parche a alg. (fig., fam.) to put one/it over on s.o. (fam.), to cheat s.o., to swindle s.o., to con s.o. (fam.)
- ▷ pardo (de noche todos los **gato**s son ~s)
- ▷ parecerse (no ~ ni en el **blanco** de los ojos)
- ▷ parecerse como dos **gota**s de agua/un **huevo** a otro/un **huevo** a una castaña

la pared wall
- ▶ Las paredes oyen. Walls have ears.
- ▶ entre sus cuatro paredes (fig.) within one's own four walls (at home) (fig.) ◆ *He pasado el día entre mis cuatro paredes. I've spent the day within my own four walls or at home.*
- ▶ vivir pared por medio to live next door
- ▶ ponerse más blanco que la pared to go as white as a sheet/ghost
- ▶ hablar a la pared (fig., fam.) to talk to a brick wall (fig., fam.) ◆ *No está escuchando. Es como hablar a la pared. He isn't listening. It is like talking to a brick wall [with him].*

▶ subirse por las paredes (fig.) to go up the wall (fig., fam.), to go off at the deep end (fam.), to go spare (fam., Br.E.) ▷ salirse de sus **casillas**

▶ hacer a alg. subirse por las paredes (fig.) to drive s.o. up the wall (fig., fam.) ▷ sacar a alg. de sus **casillas** ◆ *Esto me hace subirme por las paredes. This drives me up the wall.*

▶ ser [como] para subirse por las paredes (fig.) to be enough to drive you up the wall (fig., fam.), to be enough to drive you spare (fam., Br.E.), to be enough to drive you mad/crazy (fam.) ◆ *Era para subirse por las paredes. It was enough to drive you up the wall.*

▶ hasta la pared de enfrente (fig., fam.) to an extremely high degree, completely, loads/heaps/piles of (fam.), crowds of, root and branch (fig.) ◆ *Había gente hasta la pared de enfrente. There were crowds/loads of people [there].* ◆ *Tiene dinero hasta la pared de enfrente. He has heaps/piles of money.* ◆ *Erradicaron la peste hasta la pared de enfrente. They eradicated the plague root and branch.*

▷ pared (dar con la **cabeza** en las ~es)
▷ pared (estar entre la **espada** y la ~)
▷ pared (poner a alg. entre la **espada** y la ~)

el paredón thick wall
▶ mandar a alg. al paredón (fam.) to put s.o. up against a wall (fam.), to put s.o. before a firing squad
▶ ¡Al paredón con él/etc.! (fam.) Put him/etc. up against the wall [and shoot him/etc.]! Shoot him/etc.!

la pareja pair, couple
▶ correr parejas o andar de pareja (fig.) to go hand in hand (fig.), to go together, to keep pace, to be on a par ◆ *Su ansia de poder corre parejas con su falta de escrúpulos. His lust for power is on a par with or is matched by his ruthlessness.*

▶ hacer una buena/bonita pareja to make a lovely couple
▷ pareja (cada **oveja** con su ~)

paripé
▶ hacer el paripé (fam.) to show off, to put on an act (fig., fam.), to put on a show (fig., fam.)

parir to give birth
▶ poner a alg. a parir (fig., fam.) (a) to drive s.o. into a corner (fig.), to put the screws on s.o. (fig., fam.) (b) to badmouth s.o. (fam.), to backbite s.o., to criticize s.o. behind his back, to slag s.o. off (fam., Br.E.) (c) to piss s.o. off (vulg.)

el parné (pop.) (money): dough (sl., Am.E.), bread (sl.), sugar (sl.), brass/dosh/lolly (sl., Br.E.), wampum (sl., Am.E.)

la parra vine tendril
▶ subirse a la parra (fig., fam.) (a) to think one is important, to get bigheaded (b) to go up the wall (fig., fam.), to hit the roof (fig., fam.), to go spare (fam., Br.E.) ▷ salirse de sus **casillas**

el párrafo paragraph
▶ echar un párrafo [con alg.] (fig., fam.) to have a chat [with s.o.], to chat [with s.o.], to chew the fat or the rag (Am.E.) (fam.)
▶ tener que echar un párrafo o un parrafito aparte con alg. (fig., fam.) to have a bone to pick with s.o., to have a crow to pluck with s.o. ◆ *Tenemos que echar un párrafo aparte. We have a bone to pick with each other.*
▶ párrafo aparte (fig.) to change the subject

la parte part
▶ dar su parte al fuego (fig.) to shed some ballast (fig.)
▶ llevarse la mejor parte (fig.) to come off best, to come out on top
▷ parte (no tener **arte** ni ~ en algo)

la partida game
▶ jugar una mala partida a alg. (fig.) to play a dirty/nasty trick on s.o. (fig.)

el parto birth
▶ un parto difícil (fig.), el parto de los montes (fig.) tough job (fam.) ◆ *Ha sido un parto difícil. It was a tough job. It was tough going.* ◆ *¡El parto de los montes! Tough job!*

el pasaporte passport
▶ dar [el] pasaporte a alg. (fig., fam.) to give s.o. the pink slip (Am.E.), to give s.o. his cards (Br.E.) ▷ dar el **bote** a alg.

pasaportear a alg. (fam.) to put a bullet through s.o.'s head (fam.), to bump s.o. off (sl.), to knock s.o. off (sl.) ▷ **cargarse** a alg. (a)

pasar to cross, to pass [through], to go past
▶ poder pasar sin algo (fig.) s.o. can manage/do/live without s.th.
▶ no poder pasar sin alg. (fig.) s.o. can't live without s.o.
▶ no poder pasar a alg. (fig., fam.) s.o. can't stand s.o.
▶ no pasar de ser ... to be nothing else but ..., to be just ... ◆ *Lo que dice no pasa de ser una excusa barata. What he says is nothing else but a poor excuse.*
▶ pasar por (fig.) to be considered to be, to pass for, to take for ◆ *Ella pasa por tonta. She is considered to be stupid.* ◆ *Podrían pasar por hermanos. They could be taken for brothers. They could pass for brothers.*
▷ pasar (▷ **morado/negro/puto**: ~las moradas/negras/putas)
▷ pasar (~lo **cañón/chachi/pipa**)
▷ pasar (~lo de **rechupete**)
▷ pasar de **castaño** oscuro
▷ pasar un **trago** amargo

el pasar livelihood
▶ tener su/un buen pasar to make a decent living, to be well off

la Pascua (de Resurrección) Easter
▶ estar [contento] como o más contento que unas pascuas (fig., fam.) to be as pleased as Punch, to be tickled pink (fam.), to be as happy as a clam/lark (fam., Am.E.), to be as happy as a sandboy/as Larry (fam., Br.E.)
▶ tener cara de pascuas to be beaming all over one's face, to be all smiles
▶ hacer la pascua a alg. (fig., fam.) to annoy s.o., to harass s.o., to bug s.o. (fam., Am.E.)
▶ de Pascuas a Ramos (fig.) very rarely, once in a blue moon (fam.) ◆ *Nos hacen una visita de Pascuas a Ramos. They pay us a visit once in a blue moon.*

el paseante walker, stroller
▶ el paseante en corte (fig., fam.) loafer (fam.), idler

el paseo walk, stroll
▶ no va a ser un paseo (fig., Esp.) it won't be a walkover (fam.), it won't be a doddle (Br.E.), it's not going to be easy
▶ mandar a alg. a paseo (fig., fam.) to tell s.o. to get lost (fam.) or to go to hell (fam.) or to go to blazes (sl.), to tell s.o. where to go (fam.), to send s.o. about his business, to send s.o. packing (fig.), to give s.o. the brush-

off (fam.) ◆ *Yo que tú la mandaría a paseo. If I were you, I'd send her packing.*
▶ ¡Vete a paseo! (fig., fam.) Go to hell! (fam.) Go to blazes! (sl.) Get lost! (fam.)
▶ dar el paseo a alg. (fig., Esp.) to shoot and kill s.o., to bump s.o. off (sl.)

el pasmarote (fam.) halfwit, idiot, dummy (fam., Am.E.) ◆ *¡No te quedes ahí como un pasmarote! Don't just stand there like an idiot!*

el paso step, way
▶ a pasos agigantados (fig.) by leaps and bounds (fig.), with giant strides (fig.) ◆ *Las ganancias aumentaron a pasos agigantados. The profits increased by leaps and bounds.* ◆ *La informática sigue avanzando a pasos agigantados. Computer science is still advancing by leaps and bounds. Giant strides are still being made in computer science.*
▶ dar los primeros pasos (fig.) to take one's first steps (fig.), to start out (fam., Am.E.) ◆ *Da los primeros pasos como escritor. He's taking his first steps as a writer.*
▶ marcar el paso (fig.) to mark time (fig.), not to get anywhere, to get nowhere
▶ salir al paso de algo (fig.) to nip s.th. in the bud (fig., fam.), to strangle s.th. at birth (fig., fam.), to forestall s.th.
▶ salir al paso a/de alg. (fig.) (a) to make concessions toward[s] s.o. (b) to confont s.o.
▶ seguir los pasos de alg. (fig.) to follow s.o.'s example, to follow in s.o.'s footsteps (fig.), to tread in s.o.'s steps (fig.) ◆ *El hijo siguió los pasos de su padre. The son followed his father's example.*
▶ volver sobre sus pasos (fig.) to retract
▶ El primer paso es el que cuesta. (prov.) Nothing's easy to start off with.
▷ paso (a ~ de **buey/tortuga**)

la pasta dough, paste
▶ la pasta (fig., fam.) (money): dough (sl., Am.E.), bread (sl.), sugar (sl.), brass/dosh/lolly (sl., Br.E.), wampum (sl., Am.E.)
▶ soltar la pasta to cough up (fam.), to fork out (fam.), to stump up (fam., Br.E.)
▶ la pasta gansa (fig., fam.) big money

el pastel pie, cake
▶ descubrir el pastel (fig., fam.) (a) to smell a rat (fig.), to get onto s.th. (fam.), to get wise to s.th. (fam.) (b) to take the lid off s.th.

(fig., fam.), to expose s.th. (fig.), to give the game or show away (fam.), to blow the gaff (fam., Br.E.), to let the cat out of the bag ◆ *Se le descubrió el pastel.* *He was found out. Somebody saw through his little game. His little game was found out. The lid was taken off his operation.*
▶ quitar la hojaldre al pastel (fig.) to [try to] expose s.th. (fig.)

la pastilla tablet
▶ a toda pastilla (fam., Esp.) [at] full lick (fam.), full-belt (sl.), at top speed, flat out (fam.), full blast (fam.) ◆ *Trabajan a toda pastilla. They're working flat out.* ◆ *Íbamos a toda pastilla. We were driving/going flat out or full-belt or at top speed or at full lick.* ◆ *Pusieron la música a toda pastilla. They put the music on full blast.* ◆ *Subió el volumen de la radio a toda pastilla. He turned the radio up full blast.*

el pasto pasture, fodder
▶ ser pasto de algo (fig.) ◆ *El edificio fue pasto de la llamas. The building was engulfed in flames or was destroyed by fire.* ◆ *Su hermana es pasto de la murmuración. His sister is the subject of gossip. His sister sets tongues wagging. (fam.)* ◆ *El escándalo fue pasto de la prensa amarilla. The scandal was just what the tabloids were waiting for.*
▶ a todo pasto (fam.) ◆ *beber a todo pasto to drink to excess* ◆ *comer a todo pasto to eat until one is fit to burst (fam.), to eat until one is [as] full/tight as a tick (fam.)* ◆ *Comí y bebí a todo pasto. I ate and drank to my heart's content.* ◆ *fumar a todo pasto to smoke like a chimney (fig.)*

la pata paw
▶ la pata (fig., pop., hum.) hand, paw (fam.), mitt (sl., Am.E.), leg/foot (person), leg (chair/table/etc.)
▶ la pata de palo (fam.) wooden leg
▶ ir a la pata chula (fig., pop.) to limp
▶ tener mala pata (fam.) to have bad luck, to be unlucky
▶ tener buena pata (fam.) to be lucky
▶ meter la pata (fig., fam.) to put one's foot in it (fam.), to put one's foot in one's mouth (fam., Am.E.), to blot one's copybook (fam.), to step out of line (fig.), to make a blunder, to make a boob (sl.), to show o.s. up

▶ estirar la pata (fig., fam.) to kick the bucket (fam.) ▷ **cascar**[la]
▶ a pata (fam.) on foot
▶ patas de gallo (fig.) crow's feet (wrinkles at the corner of the eyes)
▶ estar patas arriba (fig., pop.) to be stone-dead (fam.), to be as dead as a doornail (fam.), to be as dead as mutton (fam.)
▶ patas arriba (fig., fam.) upside down, topsy-turvy, in a complete mess (fig.), a[n absolute] shambles (fig.) ◆ *Tiene toda la casa patas arriba. His house is in a complete mess or is an absolute shambles.*
▶ salir/quedar pata[s] (fig.) to draw even, to tie, to end in a tie/draw

la patada kick
▶ dar la patada a alg. (fam.) (a) to ditch s.o. (sl.), to dump s.o. (fam.), to jilt s.o., to drop s.o., to give s.o. the bird (fam.) (b) to give s.o. the boot (fam.) ▷ dar el **bote** a alg.
▶ dar a alg. una patada en el culo (pop.) to kick s.o. up the backside (fam.)
▶ echar a alg. a patadas (fam.) to kick s.o. out ◆ *Lo echaron del bar a patadas. He got kicked out of the bar.*
▶ tratar a alg. a patadas (fig.) to treat s.o. [very] badly/rudely, to treat s.o. like dirt (fam.)
▶ a patadas (fig., fam.) in abundance, galore ◆ *Había frutas a patadas. There were fruits galore.*

el patán (fam.) rustic, yokel
▶ el patán (fig., fam.) lout, yob (fam., Br.E.), boor (fig.)

la patata potato
▶ la patata (fig., fam.) watch, fob watch
▶ una patata caliente (fig.) hot potato (fig.), hot issue
▶ ser una patata (fam., Esp.) to be a dud (fam.), to be a lemon (fam.)
▶ no entender ni patata (fam.) not to understand a word [of it]
▶ no saber ni patata de algo (fam.) not to know beans about s.th. (sl., Am.E.)

patear a alg. (pop.) to boo s.o., to give s.o. the bird (fam.)

la patena paten
▶ limpio como una patena (fig.) spick-and-span (fam.), squeaky clean (fam.), as bright/clean as a new pin (fig.), like a new

pin (fig.), spotless ◆ *Tiene la casa limpia como una patena. She keeps her house spick-and-span.*

▷ patita (poner a alg. de ~s en la **calle**)

el pato duck

▶ [tener que] pagar el pato (fig., fam.) to [have to] foot the bill, to [have to] carry the can (fam., Br.E.), to [have to] take the rap (sl., Am.E.), to be left holding the baby (Br.E.) or the bag (Am.E.) (fam.), to [have to] take the blame, to get the blame ◆ *Ella pagó el pato. She footed the bill.*

▶ estar hecho un pato (fig., fam.) to be soaked to the skin, to be wet through, to be soaking/dripping wet, to be drenched, not to have a dry stitch on one (fam.)

paular (fam.)

▶ sin paular ni maular without a word, without so much as a word ◆ *Lo aceptaron sin paular ni maular. They took it without a word.*

la pava (pop.) dog/fag end (fam., Br.E.), cigarette butt/end

la pava turkey (hen)

▶ vivir/estar como pava en corral (fig.) to live/be in clover (fig.), to be as snug as a bug in a rug (fam.)

la pavesa little particle of burning soot

▶ estar hecho una pavesa (fig., fam.) to be very weak

el pavipollo young turkey

▶ un pavipollo (fig., fam.) twit (fam., Br.E.), idiot

el pavo turkey (cock)

▶ comer pavo (fig., fam.) to be a wallflower (a girl that is not attractive and therefore is not asked to dance) (fig., fam.) ◆ *Estaba comiendo pavo. Nobody asked her to dance.*

▶ subírsele a alg. el pavo o ponerse hecho un pavo (fig., fam.) to blush like a beetroot (fam., Br.E.), to blush like a lobster (fig.), to go [bright] red

▶ un pavo (pop., Esp.) one duro (5-peseta coin)

▷ pavo (la **edad** del ~)

▷ paz (dejar la **fiesta** en ~)

la pe name of the letter P/p

▶ de pe a pa (fam.) from A to Z ▷ de **cabo** a cabo

la pea (pop.) drunkenness

▶ coger una pea to get legless (fam., Br.E.)
▷ **cocerse** (a)

el pecado sin

▶ ser más original que el pecado (fig., fam.) to be more than imaginative

▶ sería un pecado no ... (fam.) it would be a sin (fig.) or a crime (fam.) not to . . . , it would be such a pity not to . . . ◆ *Sería un pecado no hacerlo. It would be a sin not to do it.* ◆ *Sería un pecado no aprovecharlo. It would be such a pity not to make use of it.*

▶ de mis pecados (fam.) damned (fam.), wretched ◆ *este coche de mis pecados this wretched car of mine* ◆ *estas cuentas de mis pecados these damned bills*

▷ pecado (**ignorancia** no quita ~)
▷ pecado (ser más **feo** que el ~)

pecar to sin

▶ pecar de + adj. (fig.) to be [far/much] too + adj. ◆ *pecar de generoso to be far too generous* ◆ *pecar de confiado to be too gullible* ◆ *pecar de ingenuo to be very naïve* ◆ *pecar de tonto to be as thick as they come* ◆ *no pecar de guapo to be anything but pretty or handsome, not to be exactly what you might call pretty or handsome*

▶ Nunca se peca por demasiado cuidado. One can't be too careful.

▷ pecar por **exceso**

el pecho chest, breast

▶ no caberle algo a alg. en el pecho (fig.) s.o. can't keep s.th. to himself, s.o. can't keep s.th. under his hat (fam.) ◆ *No les cabía el secreto en el pecho. They couldn't keep the secret to themselves.*

▶ no quedarse con nada en el pecho (fig., fam.) to talk (fam.), to blab (fam.), to spit it all out (fig.), to spill the beans (sl.)

▶ no pudrírsele a alg. nada o las cosas en el pecho (fig., fam.) s.o. can't keep anything to himself, s.o. can't keep anything [a] secret, s.o. can't keep mum (fam.), s.o. can't keep his mouth shut (fam.) ◆ *No se le pudren las cosas en el pecho a ella. She can't keep anything to herself. She can't keep anything a secret.*

▶ quedarse con algo entre pecho y espalda (fig.) to keep s.th. back

▶ echarse algo entre pecho y espalda (fam.) to drink s.th. down, to eat s.th. right up
▷ echarse algo al **coleto** (a), (b)

▶ descubrir/abrir el pecho a alg. (fig.) to pour one's heart out to s.o., to unbosom o.s. to s.o.

▶ tomar algo a pecho[s] (fig.) to take s.th. to heart, to take s.th. seriously

▶ ¡Pecho al agua! (fig.) Courage! Chin up! (fam.)

▶ a pecho descubierto (fig.) intrepidly, undauntedly, boldly ◆ *Se abalanzaron a pecho descubierto sobre el enemigo.* They threw *themselves intrepidly upon the enemy.*

▶ ser hombre de pelo en pecho (fig., fam.) to be a real man, to be some guy (fam.)

▷ pecho (a lo **hecho**, ~)

▷ pecho (darse con un **canto** en los ~s)

▷ pecho (no caberle a alg. el **corazón** en el ~)

▷ pecho (poner el **puñal** en el ~ a alg.)

el pedal pedal

▶ hundir el pedal to floor it (fam., Am.E.), to put one's foot down hard (fam.), to step on it (fam.), to go/drive at top speed, to go/drive flat out (fam.)

el pedazo piece

▶ el pedazo del alma o del corazón o de las entrañas (fig., fam.) one's darling, one's love
◆ *pedazo de mi alma o de mi corazón o de mis entrañas* my darling, my love

▶ ser un pedazo de pan (fig., fam.) to be very good-natured, to be terribly nice (fam.)

▶ comprar algo por un pedazo de pan (fig.) to buy s.th. for a song (fig., fam.)

▶ vender algo por un pedazo de pan (fig.) to sell s.th. for a song (fig., fam.)

▶ trabajar por un pedazo de pan (fig., fam.) to work for peanuts (fam.), to work for a mere pittance

▶ estar hecho pedazos (fig., fam.) to be completely shattered (fam., Br.E.) ▷ estar hecho **cisco**

▷ pedazo (**caerse** [a ~s] de viejo)

▷ pedazo de **alcornoque/atún/gloria**

el pedo (pop.) fart (vulg.)

▶ soltar/tirar[se] un pedo to fart (vulg.), to let off [a fart] (fam., Br.E.)

▶ el pedo (fam.) (a) drunkenness (b) trip (drug-induced) (sl.)

▶ agarrar[se] un pedo to get drunk ▷ **cocerse** (a)

▶ estar/andar pedo (a) (on drugs): to be high (fam.), to be on a trip (sl.), to be out of one's head (sl.), to be stoned (sl.) (b) (drunk): to be sloshed (fam.), to be plastered (fam.), to be stoned (sl.), to be out of one's head (sl.)

la pedorrera (vulg.) string of farts (vulg.)

▶ soltar una pedorrera to let off a string of farts

la pedrada throw of a stone

▶ caer/sentar como una pedrada (fig., fam.) to take it very ill, to go down very badly (fig.)
◆ *La cosa le sentó como una pedrada al jefe.* The boss took it very ill. The affair went *down very badly with the boss.*

▶ encajar/caer como pedrada en ojo de boticario (fig., fam.) to be a perfect fit/match

▶ venir como pedrada en ojo de boticario (fig., fam.) to be just what s.o. needs/needed, to be just what the doctor ordered (fig., fam.)
◆ *El dinero me vino como pedrada en ojo de boticario.* The money was just what I *needed.*

▶ matar a alg. a pedradas to stone s.o. to death

Pedro Peter

▶ como Pedro por/en su casa (fig., fam.) quite uninhibitedly, as if one owned the place ◆ *Se pasea por nuestro jardín como Pedro por su casa.* He walks around in our *garden as if he owned the place.* ◆ *Esa hembra entró como Pedro en su casa.* That fe*male came in as if she owned the place. That female came in quite uninhibitedly.*

▷ Pedro Botero (las **caldera**s de ~)

la pega pitching, coat of pitch

▶ saber a la pega (fig., fam.) to have been brought up badly, s.o.'s manners betray or reveal a bad upbringing (fig.)

pegar to stick

▶ no pegar (fig.) (a) not to make sense, not to add up (fig.) (b) not to go together ◆ *No pega.* It doesn't make sense. It doesn't add up.
◆ *Estos colores no pegan.* These colors don't *go together.* ◆ *Esta corbata no pega con tu chaqueta. This tie doesn't go with your jacket.*
◆ *El vino tinto no pega con una fondue. Red wine doesn't go [well] with a fondue.*

▶ pegársela a alg. (fig., fam.) (a) to cuckold s.o., to deceive s.o., to be unfaithful to s.o., to cheat on s.o. (fam., Am.E.) (b) to double-

cross s.o., to trick s.o., to take s.o. for a ride (fam.), to cheat s.o., to do s.o. down (fam., Br.E.) ◆ *Se la pega a su marido. She's cheating on her husband.*
▷ pegar (no ~ ni con **cola**)
▷ pegar (ser más **feo** que ~ a Dios/a la madre)
▷ pegarse como una **lapa** a alg.

pelado bald, bare, shorn
▶ [el] veinte/etc. pelado (fig.) exactly twenty/ etc., twenty/etc. as a round number
▶ estar pelado (fig., fam.) to be broke (fam.), to be skint (fam., Br.E.) ◆ *Salieron pelados del casino. They lost their shirts at the casino. (fig.)*
▶ dejar pelado a alg. (fig., fam.) to fleece s.o. (fig.), to milk s.o. (fig.)

el pelaje [thick] hair
▶ tener el pelaje de la dehesa (fig.) to betray (fig.) one's rustic/humble origins

pelar to cut the hair, to shear
▶ ser [un huevo] duro de pelar (fig., fam.) to be a hard nut to crack (fig.), to be a brain-twister (fam.), to be a tough one (fam.), to be a tough job (fam.)
▶ pelársela (vulg.) (to masturbate) ▷ tocar la **campana**
▶ pelar la jeta (pop.) to be pretty strong stuff (fam.) ▷ pasar de **castaño** oscuro ◆ *Eso pela la jeta. That's pretty strong stuff.*
▶ hacer un frío que pela (fig., fam.) to be [absolutely] freezing (fam.), to be freezing cold (fam.), to be cold enough to freeze the balls off a brass monkey (fam., Br.E.), to be brass monkey weather (sl., Br.E.), not to be half cold (fam., Br.E.)
▶ ... que se las pela (fig., fam.) ◆ *Corre que se las pela. He runs like the wind. (fam.) He runs like nobody's business. (fam.)* ◆ *Miente que se las pela. She lies through her teeth. (fam.) She lies like nobody's business. (fam.)* ◆ *Bailan que se las pelan. They're dancing wildly and untiringly. They're dancing like nobody's business. (fam.)*
▶ pelárselas por algo (fig., fam.) to crave for s.th., to drool over s.th. (fig.), to be very much after s.th.
▷ pelar (corre un **gris** que pela)

pelechar to grow hair/feathers
▶ no pelechar (fig.) not to get anywhere, to get nowhere

la película film
▶ contar su película a alg. (fam.) to pour one's heart out to s.o.
▶ de película (fig., fam.) fantastic (fam.), incredible (fig.), absolutely wonderful, dream ... (fig.) ◆ *Viven en una casa de película. They live in a dream house.* ◆ *Anoche ocurrió algo de película. Something incredible happened last night.*
▷ peligro (▷ **abocar a**: verse abocado a un ~)

el pelillo small hair
▶ echar pelillos a la mar (fig., fam.) to bury the hatchet (fig.), to make it up
▶ [no] pararse en pelillos (fig.) [not] to waste one's time on little things, [not] to stick at trifles, [not] to split hairs

el pellejo pelt, wineskin
▶ no caber en el pellejo (fig., fam.) to be very fat, to be [as] fat as a pig/sow (fam.)
▶ no caber en el pellejo de alegría (fig., fam.) to be bursting with joy (fig.), to be beside o.s. with joy (fig.)
▶ no caber en el pellejo de orgullo (fig., fam.) to be bursting [at the seams] with pride (fig.)
▶ salvar el pellejo (fig., fam.) to save one's skin/neck (fam.), to save one's bacon (fam., hum.), to save one's life
▶ salvar el pellejo a alg. (fig., fam.) to save s.o.'s skin/neck (fam.), to save s.o.'s bacon (fam., hum.), to save s.o.'s life
▶ jugarse el pellejo (fig., fam.) to risk one's neck (fam.), to risk one's life
▶ no tener más que el pellejo (fam.) to be all skin and bone (fam.)
▶ No quisiera estar en su pellejo. (fam.) I wouldn't like to be in his shoes. (fam.)
▶ mudar el pellejo (fig., fam.) to change, to change one's life
▶ dar/soltar el pellejo (fam.) to die, to lose one's life
▶ estar hecho un pellejo (fig., fam.) to be blind drunk (fam.) ▷ estar hecho un **cesto**

pellizcar to pinch
▶ pellizcar los céntimos (fig., fam.) to count every penny, to be very stingy

el pelo hair
▶ agarrarse o asirse a un pelo (fig., fam.) to clutch at straws, to clutch at any opportunity
▶ cortar un pelo en el aire (fig.) to be too clever by half (fam., Br.E.)

▶ dar a alg. para el pelo (fig., fam.) to beat s.o. up, to give s.o. a thrashing

▶ estar a medios pelos (fig., fam.) to be tipsy, to be tiddly (fam., Br.E.), to be sozzled (sl., Br.E.), to be half-seas over (fam.)

▶ echar buen pelo (fig., fam.) to be coming along [again], to be getting on fine [again], to be getting on one's feet again (fig.)

▶ tener el pelo de la dehesa (fig.) to betray (fig.) one's rustic/humble origins

▶ no tener un pelo de tonto (fig., fam.) to be no fool, to be nobody's fool, there are no flies on s.o. (fam.)

▶ tener pelos en el corazón (fig., fam.) to have no heart (fig.)

▶ tener pelos en la lengua (fig., fam.) to be a tough one (fam.), to be a bitch (woman, sl.)

▶ no tener pelos en la lengua (fig., fam.) not to mince one's words (fig.), to shoot from the hip (fig., fam.), to be very outspoken ◆ *Habla en plata. No tiene pelos en la lengua.* He speaks bluntly. He doesn't mince his words. He shoots from the hip.

▶ soltarse el pelo (fig.) to drop all scruples, to drop all restraint

▶ ponerle o ponérsele a alg. los pelos de punta ◆ *Esa escena me puso los pelos de punta.* That scene made my hair stand on end or made my hair curl. (fam.) That was a spine-chilling scene. That scene gave me the heebie-jeebies or the willies. (fam.) ◆ *Se me pusieron los pelos de punta.* My hair stood on end. I got the willies. (fam.)

▶ tomarle el pelo a alg. (fig., fam.) to pull s.o.'s leg (fam.), to take the mickey out of s.o. (fam., Br.E.), to have s.o. on (fam.), to put s.o. on (fam., Am.E.), to rag s.o. (fam., Br.E.), to chip s.o. (fam.), to have a lark with s.o. (fam., Br.E.), to tease s.o.

▶ no tocar un pelo [de la ropa] a alg. (fig.) not to harm or hurt a hair on s.o.'s head, not to lay a finger on s.o.

▶ no ver el pelo a alg. (fam.) not to see hide nor hair of s.o. (fam.) ◆ *Hace mucho que no le veo el pelo.* I haven't seen hide nor hair of him for a long time. ◆ *Ya no se le ve el pelo por aquí.* You never see him around here any more.

▶ ¡Se le/etc. va a caer el pelo! (fig., fam.) He's/etc. in for it! (fam.) He/etc. won't know what's hit him/etc.! (fam.) ◆ *¡Se te va a caer el pelo!* You're in for it [now]!

▶ venirle a alg. al pelo (fig., fam.) to be just what s.o. needs/needed, to be just what the doctor ordered (fig., fam.) ◆ *El dinero me vino al pelo.* The money was just what I needed.

▶ andar al pelo (fig., fam.) to get/be at each other, to be at loggerheads, to fight, to squabble

▶ ser capaz de contar los pelos al diablo (fig., fam.) to be as sly as they come (fam.)

▶ buscar pelos en la sopa/leche o al huevo (fig., fam.) to have/find s.th. to grouse about, to have/find s.th. to gripe or bellyache about (fam.), to have/find s.th. to criticize ◆ *Siempre le busca pelos al huevo.* He always has something to grouse about or to criticize.

▶ traer algo por los pelos (fig.) to be far-fetched (fig.) ◆ *Me parece un poco traído por los pelos.* I think it's a bit far-fetched. ◆ *Lo has traído por los pelos.* It (what you've said) is far-fetched.

▶ con [todos sus] pelos y señales in great detail, in minute detail, down to the last detail, with chapter and verse (fig.) ◆ *Me lo contó con todos sus pelos y señales.* He told it to me down to the last detail. ◆ *La describieron con pelos y señales.* They gave a very detailed description of her.

▶ por un pelo (fig.), por los pelos (fam.) by a hair's breadth (fam.), by the skin of one's teeth (fam.), only just, [very] nearly, (to be saved) by the bell (fig.), (to be/have) a close/narrow shave (fig., fam.) or a close call (fam.) ◆ *[Nos] escapamos por un pelo.* We escaped by a hair's breadth. We had a narrow escape. We had a close shave. ◆ *Nos salvamos por los pelos.* We escaped by a hair's breadth or by the skin of our teeth. We were saved by the bell. ◆ *No perdí el tren por los pelos.* I very nearly missed the train. I caught the train by the skin of my teeth. I only just caught the train in time. ◆ *Por un pelo me atropellan.* I just missed being run over by the skin of my teeth. ◆ *Aprobaron el examen por los pelos.* They just scraped (fig.) through the exam.

▷ pelo (coger/asir la **ocasión** por los ~s)
▷ pelo (cuando las **ranas** críen ~)
▷ pelo (estar hasta la **punta** de los ~s/del ~ de alg./algo)
▷ pelo (**gente** de ~)
▷ pelo (¡Hasta que/cuando las **ranas** críen ~!)

▷ pelo (ser hombre de ~ en **pecho**)
▷ pelo (ser **largo** como ~ de huevo)

la pelota ball
▶ devolver la pelota a alg. (fig.) to turn the tables on s.o.
▶ La pelota está en el tejado. (fig., fam.) It's all up in the air. (fig.) The situation is unresolved. Nothing has been decided.
▶ La pelota sigue en el tejado. (fig., fam.) It's still all up in the air. (fig.) The situation is still unresolved. Nothing has been decided yet.
▶ las pelotas (pop.) (testicles) ▷ las **canicas**
▶ hinchar las pelotas a alg (vulg.) to get on s.o.'s tits (vulg., Br.E.), to get up s.o.'s nose (fam.)
▶ en pelota[s] (fig., pop.) stark naked (fam.), starkers (fam., hum., Br.E.), not to have a stitch on (fam.)

la pelotilla little ball
▶ hacer la pelotilla a alg. (fig., fam.) to suck up to s.o. (sl.), to toady to s.o., to brownnose s.o. (sl., Am.E.), to ingratiate o.s. with s.o.

el pelotillero (fig., fam.) arse-licker (vulg.), crawler (fig.), creep (fam.), toady, bootlicker (fam.), yes-man (pej.)

la peluca wig
▶ echar una peluca a alg. (fig., fam.) to give s.o. a dressing-down or a tongue-lashing or a roasting (fam.), to give s.o. a ticking-off or a wigging (fam., Br.E.)

el peluquín small wig
▶ ¡Ni hablar del peluquín! (fig., fam.) It's out of the question!
▷ pelusa (**gente** de ~)

la pena trouble, toil, grief
▶ pasar las penas del purgatorio (fig.) to go through hell
▶ sin pena ni gloria (fig.) mediocre, ordinary, undistinguished ◆ *Fue un partido sin pena ni gloria. It was a mediocre game.* ◆ *Cada uno de ellos pasó por la universidad sin pena ni gloria. Each of them had an undistinguished university career.* ◆ *Su última película pasó por las carteleras sin pena ni gloria. His last movie came and went almost unnoticed.*

▶ a duras penas with great/utmost difficulty, only just, hardly, scarcely, just barely ◆ *A duras penas llegó a la meta. Only with the utmost difficulty he reached the finishing line.* ◆ *Aprobó el examen a duras penas. He just scraped (fig.) through the exam.* ◆ *Te oí a duras penas. I could hardly/scarcely hear you.*

el penalty penalty [kick]
▶ casarse de penalty (fam., Esp.) (girl): to have a shotgun wedding (fam.)
▷ pender de un **cabello/hilo**
▷ pendiente (tener **cuentas** ~s con alg.)

el pendón (fig., fam.) floozie (fam.), slag (sl., pej., Br.E.), slut (fam.)

Penélope Penelope
▶ tejer la tela de Penélope (fig.) to live in a fool's paradise
▷ pensamiento (el ~ no conoce/tiene **barreras**)

pensar to think
▶ ¡Ni pensarlo! (fig., fam.) Forget it! No way! (fam.) Not on your life! (fam.)
▶ Piensa mal y acertarás. If you think the worst, you won't be far wrong.
▶ el día menos pensado one day when you/etc. least expect it, when least expected
▷ pensar (más vale un "**por si acaso**" que un "¿quién pensara?")

el penseque (fam.) thoughtless error
▶ ¡A penseque lo ahorcaron! (fig., fam.) Better [to be] safe than sorry! (prov.)
▷ pensión de **tapujo**

la peña rock
▶ dormir como una peña (fig.) to sleep like a log (fam.)

peor worse
▶ ponerse en lo peor (fig.) to prepare for the worst

Pepa (fam.) familiar form of Josef[in]a
▶ ¡Viva la Pepa! To hell (fam.)/blazes (sl.) with everybody else or with the work/etc.!

Pepe (fam.) familiar form of José
▶ ponerse como un Pepe (fig., fam.) to have a great time (fam.)

el pepino cucumber
▶ el pepino (fig., fam.) unripe melon

► pepinos (fig., fam.) bullets
► [no] importar a alg. un pepino (fig., fam.) not to give/care two hoots (fam.) ▷ no importar a alg. un **ardite**

la pepita pip
► no tener pepita en la lengua (fig., fam.) (a) to talk a mile a minute (fam., Am.E.), to talk nineteen to the dozen (fam., Br.E.) (b) not to mince one's words (fig.), to be outspoken

la pera pear
► del año de/en el año de la pera (fam.) donkey's years ago (fam.) ▷ año de **Mari-castaña**
► saber de qué lado caen las peras (fig.) to know which way the cat jumps (fig.) or which way the cookie crumbles (fam., Am.E.) or which way the wind is blowing (fig.)
► [esperar a] ver de qué lado caen las peras (fig.) to [wait and/to] see which way the cat jumps (fig.) or which way the cookie crumbles (fam., Am.E.) or which way the wind is blowing (fig.)
► poner a alg. las peras a cuarto to give s.o. a piece of one's mind
► no quisiera partir peras con alg. (fig., fam.) s.o. is a tough customer (fam.) ◆ *No quisiera/quisiéramos partir peras con él. He's a tough customer.*
► pedir peras al olmo to ask the impossible
► No se le puede pedir peras al olmo. (prov.) You can't make a silk purse out of a sow's ear. (prov.)
▷ pera (de **uva**s a ~s)

el percebe barnacle
► un percebe (fig., fam.) idiot ▷ un [pedazo de] **alcornoque**

la percha perch
► tener buena percha (fig., fam.) to have a good build/physique; (woman): to have a good figure

perder to lose
► llevar las de perder, salir perdiendo (fig.) to [be bound to] lose, to come off a loser, to come off worst, to lose out (fam.) ◆ *Lleva las de perder. He's bound to lose.* ◆ *No discutas con ellos porque llevas las de perder. Don't argue with them because you'll lose or come off a loser.* ◆ *Salimos perdiendo. We lost out. We came off worst.*

▷ perder la **chaveta**
▷ perder la **chaveta** por alg.
▷ perder la **onda/tramontana**
▷ perder los **libros**
▷ perder **terreno**

la pérdida loss
► no tener pérdida (fig., fam.) to be very easy to find, s.o. can't miss it ◆ *La calle no tiene pérdida. The street is very easy to find. You can't miss it.*

perdidizo (fam.) [seemingly] not to be found
► hacerse el perdidizo to make o.s. scarce (fam.), to slip/sneak away

perdido lost
► ser un caso perdido (fam.) to be a hopeless case (fam.)
► ser un borracho perdido (fam.) to be a hardened boozer (fig., fam.), to be an out-and-out drunkard, to be an inveterate drinker
► De perdidos, al agua/río. (fam.) In for a penny, in for a pound. (Br.E.) In for a dime, in for a dollar. (Am.E.)
► estar perdido por alg./algo to be head over heels in love with s.o. (fam.), to be smitten with s.o. (fam.), to be mad or crazy or wild about s.o./s.th. (fam.)
► estar o ponerse perdido de algo (fig., fam.) ◆ *Estás perdido de suciedad. You're covered in dirt. You're dirt all over.* ◆ *Te has puesto perdido de polvo. You've got covered in dust. You're totally dust-covered.* ◆ *Te has puesto la chaqueta perdida de tinta o de suciedad. You've got ink all over your jacket. Your jacket is thick with dirt.*
▷ perdido (estar más ~ que **Carracuca**)

perecer to die, to perish
► perecerse de risa (fig.) to die laughing (fig.)
► perecerse de envidia (fig.) to be dying of envy (fig.), to be eaten up with envy, to be green with envy (fig.)
► perecerse por algo (fig.) to be mad/crazy about s.th. (fam.), to crave for s.th., to long for s.th., to pine for s.th., to be dying for s.th. (fig.)
► perecerse por + infinitivo (fig.) to be dying/itching to + infinitive (fig.), to be champing at the bit to + infinitive (fig.), to long to + infinitive, to love + gerund ◆ *Me perezco por hacerlo. I'm dying to do it. I'd love doing*

it. ◆ *Se perecía por verla. He was dying/ longing to see her.*

el perejil parsley
▶ huir del perejil y dar en el berenjenal (fig., fam.) to jump out of the frying pan into the fire ◆ *Atracó un banco para pagar sus deudas. Huyó del perejil y dio en el berenjenal. He held up a bank to pay [off] his debts. He jumped out of the frying pan into the fire.*
▶ perejiles (fig., fam.) (a) frills (fig.), trimmings, fancy bits (fam., Br.E.), fripperies (fig.), buttons and bows (b) handles to one's name (fam.), extra titles
▷ perejil (poner a alg. como **hoja** de ~)

el perigallo double chin, dewlap (fam.)
▶ el perigallo (fig., fam.) (person): beanpole (fig., fam., hum.)

la perilla pear-shaped ornament
▶ venir de perilla[s] (fig., fam.) to be just what s.o. needs/needed, to come in very handy (fam.) ◆ *El dinero me vino de perillas. The money was just what I needed.*

el periódico newspaper
▶ el periódico amarillo (fig.) sensational or gutter or yellow newspaper
▶ ser periódico de ayer (fig.) to be old news, to be old hat (fam.)

el periodicucho (fam.) (newspaper): rag (fam., pej.)

peripatética (fig., fam.)
▶ ser una peripatética to be on the game (fam.), to walk/work the streets, to be a prostitute

peripuesto (fam.)
▶ estar peripuesto to be dressed up to the nines (fam.), to be in one's glad rags (fam., Br.E.), to be in one's Sunday best (fam.)

la perla pearl
▶ de perlas (fig., fam.) (to be) just what s.o. needs/needed, (to come in) very handy (fam.), (to come) just right, (to suit) perfectly or down to the ground, (to go) perfectly or very well ◆ *El dinero me vino de perlas. The money was just what I needed.* ◆ *El martes me vendría de perlas. Tuesday would suit me down to the ground.* ◆ *Todo marchó de perlas. Everything went perfectly. Everything went very well.*
▷ Pero Botero (las **caldera**s de ~)

el pero objection
▶ ¡No hay pero que valga! There's no buts about it! No buts!

la perra female dog
▶ la perra chica (fig., fam., Esp.) 5-céntimo coin
▶ la perra gorda (fig., fam., Esp.) 10-céntimo coin
▶ costar unas perras (fig., fam.) to cost a few coppers (fam.), to cost a few bucks (fam., Am.E.), to cost a few quid (fam., Br.E.)
▶ no tener [ni] una perra (fig., fam.) to be flat broke (fam.), to be stone-broke (fam., Am.E.)
▶ hasta la perra le/etc. parirá lechones (fam.) he's/etc. always damned lucky (fam.)

la perrada (fig., fam.) dirty trick (fig., fam.)
▶ hacer una perrada a alg. to play a dirty/ nasty trick on s.o. (fig., fam.)

el perro dog
▶ el perro salchicha (fam.) dachshund, sausage dog (fam., Br.E.)
▶ ser [un] perro viejo (fig., fam.) to be an old hand, to be an old fox (fig.), to be a cunning old devil (fam.)
▶ tratar a alg. como a un perro (fig.) to treat s.o. like dirt (fig.)
▶ dar perro a alg. (fam.) to keep s.o. waiting
▶ darse a perros (fam.) to get hopping mad (fam.), to get livid (fam., Br.E.), to get terribly angry
▶ echar los perros a alg. (fig., fam.) (a) to take drastic action against s.o. (b) to come down on s.o. like a ton of bricks (fam.)
▶ meter los perros en danza (fig.) to set the cat among the pigeons
▶ hacer tanta falta como los perros en misa, ser como perro en misa (a) to be very/ wholly out of place (b) to be like a fifth wheel (fig., fam.)
▶ irle a alg. como a los perros en misa (fig.) not to have an easy time of it (fam.), to have a terrible time of it (fam.)
▶ Le conocen hasta los perros. Everybody knows him.
▶ de perros (fam.) ◆ *la vida de perros (fig., fam.) the dog's life (fig.)* ◆ *estar de un humor de perros to be in a foul/stinking mood (fig.), to be in a very bad mood, to be like a bear with a sore head (fam.)* ◆ *Hace un tiempo de perros. The weather's foul (fig.) or lousy (fam.)*

145

or terrible. ◆ *hacer un frío de perros to be [absolutely] freezing (fam.), to be freezing cold (fam.), to be cold enough to freeze the balls off a brass monkey (fam., Br.E.), to be brass monkey weather (sl., Br.E.), not to be half cold (fam., Br.E.)*

▶ A perro flaco no le faltan pulgas. (prov.) It never rains but it pours. (prov.)

▶ Muerto el perro, se acabó la rabia. (prov.) The best way to solve a problem is to attack the root cause of it.

▶ Perro ladrador, nunca buen mordedor o poco mordedor. (prov.) Perro que ladra no muerde. (prov.) A barking dog never bites. (prov.) His/etc. bark's worse than his/etc. bite. (fig.)

▶ ser [como] el perro del hortelano[, que ni come la berza ni la deja comer] to be a dog in the manger ◆ *Aunque el vestido le está demasiado ancho, no se lo da a su hermana. Es como el perro del hortelano. Although this dress is too big/wide for her, she doesn't let her sister have it. She's a dog in the manger.* ◆ *Tiene una entrada para ir al teatro, pero no puede ir. Si no fuese como el perro del hortelano, me la daría. He has a ticket for the theater, but he can't go. If he were not a dog in the manger, he would give it to me.*

▷ perro (▷ **nariz**: tener narices de ~ perdiguero)

▷ perro (¡A otro ~ con ese **hueso**!)

▷ perro (Allí tampoco atan los ~s con **longaniza.**)

▷ perro (atar ~s con **longaniza**)

▷ perro (cual el **dueño**, tal el ~)

▷ perro (**hinchar** el ~)

▷ perro (tener **carne** de ~)

el Perú Peru

▶ el Perú (fig.) gold mine (fig., fam.), money-spinner (fam., Br.E.), moneymaker

▶ valer algo/alg. un Perú (fig., fam.) (a) s.th.: to be invaluable, to be worth a fortune (b) s.o.: to be worth one's weight in gold (fig.) ◆ *Mi secretaria vale un Perú. My secretary is worth her weight in gold.*

▷ pesar lo **suyo**

▷ pescado (no ser **carne** ni ~)

pescar to fish

▶ pescar en aguas turbias (fig.) to fish in troubled waters (fig.)

▶ no saber uno lo que se pesca (fig., fam.) not to have a clue what it's [all] about (fam.), to have no idea what it's [all] about

▶ pescarse un marido (fig., fam.) to get or hook (fam.) o.s. a husband

▷ pescar (~las al **vuelo**)

▷ pescar (No se pescan **truchas** a bragas enjutas.)

▷ pescar al **candil**

▷ pescar el **bulto** a alg.

▷ pescar en **río** revuelto

▷ pescar una **trucha**

el pescuezo neck, scruff of the neck

▶ jugarse el pescuezo (fig., fam.) to risk one's neck (fam.)

▶ retorcer el pescuezo a alg. (fam.) to wring s.o.'s neck (fam.) ◆ *¡Cierra el pico, o te retuerzo el pescuezo! Shut your trap, or I'll wring your neck!*

la peseta peseta

▶ A quien cuida la peseta nunca le falta un duro. (prov.) Look after the pennies and the pounds will look after themselves or will take care of themselves.

▶ cambiar la peseta (fig., fam.) to vomit, to throw up (fam.), to blow one's cookies/lunch (sl.), to feed the fishes (seasick person) (fam.)

▷ peseta (¡**Salud**, amor y ~s!)

la pesetera (pop.) cheap tart (sl.), cheap hooker (sl., Am.E.), cheap prostitute

el peso weight

▶ quitársele a alg. un [gran] peso de encima (fig.) to be a [heavy/real] load off s.o.'s mind (fig.) ◆ *Se me quitó un gran peso de encima. That was a heavy load off my mind.*

▶ quitarle a alg. un [gran] peso de encima (fig.) to take a [heavy/real] load off s.o.'s mind (fig.)

▶ no estar en su peso (fig., fam.) to be under the weather (fam.)

▷ peso (**caerse** de/por su propio ~)

el pesquis (fam.) common sense, horse sense (fam.), know-how, nous (fam.) ◆ *Tiene mucho pesquis. He has a lot of nous.* ◆ *No tiene pesquis. He's dumb. (fam., Am.E.)* ◆ *Si tuvieran un poco más pesquis ... If they had a bit more common/horse sense . . .*

la pestaña eyelash
- ► quemarse las pestañas (fig., fam.) to study/work far into the night, to burn the midnight oil, to cram (fam.), to swot (fam., Br.E.), to bone up (fam.)

el pestazo (fam.) [horrible] stink/pong (fam., Br.E.)/stench
- ▷ peste (▷ **cebar**: se ceba la ~)

la petaca (pop.) (a) hip flask (b) bed, sack (sl.), kip (sl.)
- ► irse a la o echarse en la petaca to hit the sack, to hit the hay (sl., Am.E.)
- ► hacerle la petaca a alg. to make s.o. an apple-pie bed (fam., Br.E.)

petar (fam.)
- ► No me peta ir al cine. I don't [really] feel like going to the cinema.
- ► Si te peta. If you feel like it.

el petardo firecracker
- ► el petardo (fig., argot, Esp.) joint (sl.), spliff (sl., Br.E.), marijuana cigarette
- ► el petardo (fig., fam.) swindle, fraud
- ► pegar un petardo a alg. (fig., fam.) to cheat s.o., to con s.o. (fam.), to pull a fast one on s.o. (sl.), to tap s.o. for money (with the intention of not paying it back)

el petate (fam.) baggage
- ► liar el petate (fig., fam.) (a) to pack one's bags/things [and go] (fam.), to pack up [and go] (fam.), to [pull] up sticks (Br.E.) or stakes (Am.E.) (fig., fam.) (b) to kick the bucket (fam.) ▷ **cascar**[la]

el pez fish
- ► un pez gordo (fig., fam.) big fish (fig.), bigwig (fam.), big shot (fam.), big cheese (fam.), big noise (sl.), fat cat (fig., fam. Am.E.), top nob (sl., Br.E.), big wheel (fam.)
- ► estar/sentirse como el pez en el agua (fig.) to be in one's element, to feel completely at home (fam.), to feel really great, to feel on top of the world (fam.)
- ► estar pez en algo (fam.) to know nothing at all about s.th., not to know the first thing about s.th., not to know beans about s.th. (sl., Am.E.), not to have a clue about s.th. (fam.) ◆ *Está pez en matemáticas. He doesn't have a clue when it comes to mathematics.*

- ► salga pez o salga rana (fig., fam.) as luck will have it, on the off-chance
- ▷ pez (por la **boca** muere el ~)
- ▷ pez (**reírse** de los peces de colores)

la pezuña hoof
- ► la pezuña (fig., pop.) hand, paw (fam.)
- ► meter la pezuña (fig., pop.) to put one's foot in it ▷ meter la **pata**

la pica pike
- ► poner una pica en Flandes (fig.) to bring off s.th. very difficult, to bring off a coup, to achieve a signal success
- ► poder pasar por las picas de Flandes (fig.) to be [absolutely] perfect, to be beyond all criticism, to stand up to the severest criticism

el picadero riding-school
- ► el picadero (fig., fam.) bachelor pad (fam.), trouble-free digs (fam., Br.E.), apartment used for sexual encounters, love nest

el picadillo minced meat
- ► hacer picadillo a alg. (fig., fam.) (a) to make mincemeat of s.o. (fig.), to beat s.o. to a pulp (fig.) (b) to give s.o. a severe dressing-down (fam.)

el picador horse-breaker
- ► tener la cabeza más dura que un picador (fig., fam.) to be pigheaded, to be stubborn

picar to prick, to sting
- ► picar [más] alto (fig., fam.) to aim high[er] (fig.)
- ▷ picar (quien se pica, **ajos** come)
- ▷ picar que rabia (▷ **rabiar**)

la picha (vulg.) (penis) ▷ el calvo

pichi (adj., pop.) elegant, smart, posh (fam.)

el pichón young pigeon
- ► el pichón (fig., fam.) darling, honey/hon (fam., Am.E.)
- ► la pichona (fam.) darling, honey/hon (fam., Am.E.), sweetie (fam.) ◆ *Sí, pichona. Yes, darling. Yes, sweetie.*
- ▷ Picio (ser más **feo** que ~)

el pico peak, beak, bill
- ► costar un pico (fam.) to cost a tidy sum ▷ costar una **burrada**
- ► irse de/a picos pardos (fam.) (a) to go out on the town (fam.), to spend a night on the

tiles (fam., Br.E.), to go out for a good time (b) to be unfaithful (to one's husband/wife/etc.), to two-time (one's husband/wife) (fam.)

▶ a las diez/etc. y pico (fam.) just after 10/etc.

▶ el pico (fig., fam.) trap (sl.), mouth ◆ *abrir el pico to talk, to open one's mouth* ◆ *cerrar el pico to shut one's mouth/trap, to pipe down (fam.), to belt up (fam., Br.E.)* ◆ *¡Cierra el pico! Shut your trap! Pipe down! Belt up!* ◆ *darle al pico to talk a lot* ◆ *darse el pico to kiss, to have a good old snog (fam., Br.E.)* ◆ *tener buen pico to have the gift of [the] gab* ◆ *tener un pico de oro to be silver-tongued, to be very eloquent* ◆ *perderse por el pico to harm o.s. by saying too much, to talk too much*

▷ pico (**hincar** el ~)
▷ pico (**jarabe** de ~)

la picota pillory
▶ poner a alg. en la picota (fig.) to pillory s.o. (fig.)

la picotada peck
▶ la picotada (fam.) (drug injection): shot (sl.), fix (sl.)

el picotazo peck
▶ el picotazo (fam.) (drug injection): shot (sl.), fix (sl.)

el pie foot
▶ levantarse con el pie izquierdo o salir con mal pie (fig., fam.) to get up on the wrong side of the bed (fam., Am.E.), to get out of bed on the wrong side (fam., Br.E.)

▶ no estirar los pies más de lo que da la frazada (fam., Cono Sur) to cut one's coat according to one's cloth (Br.E.), to go easy on the sugar (fig.)

▶ buscar cinco/tres pies al gato (fig., fam.) (a) to ask/look for trouble (b) to split hairs, to quibble

▶ cojear del mismo pie (fig., fam.) to have the same faults, to be tarred with the same brush (fam., pej.), to be two of a kind

▶ saber de qué pie cojea alg. (fig., fam.) to know s.o.'s faults or weakness[es], to know s.o.'s weak point[s] or spot[s]

▶ tomar pie de algo (fig.) to use s.th. as an excuse or as a pretext

▶ dar pie para/a (fig.) to give rise to, to give cause for

▶ darle a alg. el pie y se toma la mano (fig.) give s.o. an inch and he'll take a yard/mile (fig.) ◆ *Le das el pie y se toma la mano. Give him an inch and he'll take a yard.* ◆ *Dales el pie y se tomarán la mano. Give them an inch and they'll take a mile.*

▶ no dar pie con bola (fam.) to do everything wrong, s.o. can't get a thing right, to be no good at anything

▶ caer de pies (fig.) to fall/land on one's feet (fig.), to get out or emerge unscathed

▶ hacer algo con los pies (fig.) to bungle s.th., to botch s.th. [up] (fam.), to make a mess or a botch of s.th. (fig.) ◆ *una carta escrita con los pies a very poorly written letter*

▶ sacar los pies del plato o de las alforjas (fig., fam.) (a) to go one's own way (fig.), to go off on a different tack (fig.) (b) to abandon all restraint, to kick over the traces (fig.)

▶ sacar a alg. con los pies adelante (fig., fam.) to bury s.o.

▶ sacar el pie del lodo a alg. (fig., fam.) to get s.o. out of a jam/fix (fam.), to get s.o. off the hook (fam.)

▶ estar al pie del cañón (fig., fam.) to be ready for battle (fig.), to be ready to act

▶ morir al pie del cañón (fig., fam.) to die in harness (fig.), to die with one's boots on (fig.) ◆ *Dice que prefiere morir al pie del cañón a morir en la cama. He says he prefers dying with his boots on to dying in bed.*

▶ al pie de la letra (fig.) literally, word for word, to the letter, exactly ◆ *Lo repitió todo al pie de la letra. He repeated it all word for word.*

▶ a pie juntillo (fig.) (believe/etc.): firmly, absolutely ◆ *Lo cree a pie juntillo. He firmly believes it.*

▶ no tener pies ni cabeza (fig., fam.) to make no sense whatsoever, there's no rhyme or reason [to s.th.], s.o. can't make head[s] or tail[s] of s.th. (fam.), to be absurd, to be ridiculous ◆ *Para mi/nosotros esto no tiene pies ni cabeza. I/we can't make head or tail of it.* ◆ *Esta decisión no tiene pies ni cabeza. There's no rhyme or reason to this decision.* ◆ *Este argumento no tiene pies ni cabeza. This argument is pointless/absurd.*

▶ tener los pies [bien puestos] en/sobre la tierra (fig.) to have both/one's feet [firmly] on the ground (fig.)

▶ tener un pie en dos zapatos (fig.) to have two/several irons in the fire or strings to one's bow (fig.)

▶ ser pies y manos de alg. (fig.) to be s.o.'s right-hand man (fig.)

▶ vestirse por los pies (fam., hum.) to be a man ♦ ¿Quién es? Se viste por los pies. Who is it? It's a man.

▶ andar con pies de plomo (fig.) to go about it very warily or carefully or cautiously, to tread (fig.) or proceed very warily or carefully or cautiously

▶ arrastrar los pies (fig., fam.) to be old and frail

▶ estar siempre con un pie en el aire (fam.) to be always on the go or on the jump (fam.)

▶ poner pies en polvorosa (fig.) to take to one's heels, to turn tail (fig.), to beat it (sl.), to do a bunk (fam., Br.E.), to skedaddle (fam.)

▶ ¿Pies, para qué os quiero? (fig., fam.) Let's get out of here! (fam.)

▷ pie (▷ nacer: nació alg. de ~[s])

▷ pie (caérsele a alg. el alma a los ~s)

▷ pie (estar con un ~ en el estribo/hoyo)

▷ pie (herir el suelo con el ~)

▷ pie (tener un ~ en la tumba)

la piedra stone

▶ arrojar/tirar la primera piedra (fig.) to cast the first stone (fig.)

▶ no dejar piedra para mover (fig.) to leave no stone unturned (fig.), to do everything in one's power

▶ cerrar algo a piedra y lodo (fig.) to firmly lock s.th., to shut s.th. all up

▶ tirar piedras a su o sobre el propio tejado (fig.) to foul one's own nest (fig.), to cut off one's nose to spite one's face

▶ Eso sería tirar piedras a su o sobre el propio tejado. (fig.) People who live in glass houses should not throw stones. (fig.)

▶ Piedra movediza, el moho no la cobija. (prov.) Piedra movediza no coge musgo. (prov.) A rolling stone gathers no moss. (prov.)

▶ pasar a una mujer por la piedra (pop., vulg.) to screw a woman (vulg.) ▷ calzar[se] a alg.

▶ sacar la piedra (pop., vulg.) (to have an orgasm): to come (fam.); (man): to shoot off (vulg., Br.E.)

▷ piedra (callar[se] como una ~)

▷ piedra (estar a [un] tiro de ~)

▷ piedra (estar más muerto que una ~)

▷ piedra (sacar agua de las ~s)

la piel skin

▶ dar la piel (fig., fam.) to die

▶ dejarse la piel (fig.) to give one's all ▷ echar/sudar la hiel

▶ ser de la piel del diablo (fig., fam.) (child): to be very unruly, to be difficult to keep under control (fam.), to be a little monster/devil (fam.), to be a holy terror (fam.)

▶ vender la piel del oso antes de cazarlo (fig.) to count one's chickens before they're hatched (fig.) ♦ Aunque no está [absolutamente] seguro de que herede todo ese dinero, ya está haciendo grandes planes para el futuro. No vendas la piel del oso antes de cazarlo. Although he's not [absolutely] sure whether he'll inherit all that money, he's already making big plans for the future. Don't count your chickens before they're hatched.

▷ piel (a flor de ~)

▷ piel (un lobo con ~ de cordero/oveja)

la pierna leg

▶ estirar la pierna más larga que la sábana (fig.) not to cut one's coat according to one's cloth (Br.E.), not to go easy on the sugar (fig.)

▶ dormir a pierna suelta (fam.) to sleep the sleep of the just/dead, to sleep soundly

▶ salir por piernas (fam.) to take to one's heels, to leg it (fam.)

▶ ser un piernas (fam., pej.) to be a nobody (fig.), to be a dead loss (fig., fam.), to be a washout (fam.)

la pieza piece

▶ una buena pieza (fig., fam., iron.) nasty customer (fig., fam.), troublemaker, villain, rogue

▶ jugar una pieza a alg. (fig., fam.) to play a dirty/nasty trick on s.o. (fig., fam.)

▶ quedarse de una pieza (fig., fam.) to be [left] speechless, to be struck dumb, to be struck all of a heap (fam.), to be knocked sideways or for a loop (Am.E.) or for six (Br.E.) (fam.), to be dumbfounded, to be flabbergasted (fam.), to be like a dying duck [in a thunderstorm] (fam.), to be completely taken aback (fig.) ◆ *Al oírlo nos quedamos de una pieza. We were struck all of a heap or knocked sideways or completely taken aback when we heard it.*

▶ dejar a alg. de una pieza (fig., fam.) to strike s.o. dumb, to strike s.o. all of a heap (fam.), to knock s.o. sideways or for a loop (Am.E.) or for six (Br.E.) (fam.), to floor s.o. (fam.)

la pifia miscue
▶ la pifia (fig., fam.) blunder, bloomer (fam., Br.E.), goof (fam., Am.E.), boob (fam.), boo-boo (fam.), clinker (sl., Am.E.)
▶ dar una pifia to blunder, to goof, to make a bloomer/boob

pifiar (fig., fam.) to blunder, to goof, to make a bloomer/boob

la pija (pop.) (penis) ▷ el calvo

el pijo (pop.) (penis) ▷ el calvo

la pila drinking trough
▶ ser más bruto que la pila de un pozo (fig., pop.) to be as thick as two short planks (fam.) ▷ ser más tonto que **Carracuca**
▷ Pilatos (ir de **Herodes** a ~)

la píldora pill
▶ píldoras (fam.) bullets ◆ *Frieron al traidor a píldoras. They riddled the traitor with bullets.*
▶ tragar la píldora (fig., fam.) to fall for it (fam.), to be taken in (fam.)
▶ dorar la píldora (fig.) to sweeten or sugar or sugar-coat the pill (fig.) ◆ *No dores la píldora. Dímelo con toda franqueza. Don't sweeten the pill. Give it to me straight or tell me straight out.*
▷ pillar a alg. en **bolas/bragas**
▷ pillar una **mona/zorra**
▷ pillarse los **dedos**

la piltra (pop.) bed, kip (sl.), sack (sl.)
▶ irse a la o echarse en la piltra to hit the sack (fam.), to hit the hay (fam., Am.E.)

el pimiento pepper
▶ [no] importar a alg. un pimiento (fig., fam.) not to give/care two hoots (fam.) ▷ no importar a alg. un **ardite**

el pimpampúm (fam.) shooting gallery

el pimpollo shoot, bud
▶ el pimpollo [de oro] (fig., fam.) bonny child

pinchar to prick
▶ ni pinchar ni cortar (fig.) (a) to be neither fish nor fowl (fig.), to be neither one thing nor the other (b) not to have any say, not to have any clout (fig.), to cut no ice (fam.) ◆ *Ella aquí ni pincha ni corta. She doesn't have any say [in what goes on] here. She cuts no ice here.*
▶ pincharse (fam.) (drug): to shoot up (sl.), to jack up (sl.), to give o.s. a fix/shot (sl.), to give o.s. a jab (sl., Br.E.)

la pinga (pop.) (penis): ▷ el calvo

el pingajo shred
▶ estar hecho un pingajo (fig., fam.) to be completely shattered (fam., Br.E.) ▷ estar hecho **cisco**

pinganitos (fam.)
▶ estar en pinganitos to be well up, to be well-placed socially

el pino pine [tree]
▶ hacer el pino to do a handstand or headstand, to stand on one's head
▶ plantar un pino (fig., pop.) (to relieve o.s.): to do one's business (fig., fam.), to take a dump (vulg.)
▶ vivir/estar en el quinto pino (fig.) to live/be at the back of beyond ▷ vivir/estar donde **Cristo** dio las tres voces

pintado painted, colorful
▶ el más pintado (fig., fam.) cleverest, craftiest, best ◆ *Eso podría pasarle al más pintado. That could happen to the cleverest [of us] or to anybody.* ◆ *Lo hizo como el más pintado. He did it with the or as well as the best.*
▶ no poder ver a alg. ni pintado (fig., fam.) s.o. can't stand s.th. ▷ tener a alg. **atravesado**
▶ venir/sentar [a alg.] que ni pintado o como pintado (fig., fam.) to come at just the right time, to fit/suit [s.o.] to a T ▷ venir/sentar [a alg.] como **anillo** al dedo (a), (b)

pintar to paint
▶ no pintar nada (fig., fam.) to have no say, not to have any say, not to have any clout (fig.), not to count, to cut no ice (fam.) ◆ *Ella aquí no pinta nada. She doesn't have any say [in what goes on] here. She doesn't count here.*

▶ pintarse uno solo o pintárselas solo para algo (fig., fam.) to be a dab hand at s.th. (fam., Br.E.), to be an expert at/in s.th., to be red hot on s.th. (fam.), to be an ace . . . , to be very well suited for s.th. ◆ *Se pinta él solo para los deportes. He's an ace athlete.* ◆ *Él se las pinta solo para las matemáticas. He's an ace mathematician. He's an out-standing mathematician.*

▶ ¿Qué diablo te pintas tú/etc. por aquí? (fam.) What the devil/hell are you/etc. up to here? (fam.) ◆ *¿Qué diablo se pinta él por aquí? What the devil is he up to here?*

▶ No es tan feo el diablo como le pintan. (prov.) It's not as bad as all that. It's nothing to get upset about.

pintiparado (fam.)

▶ venir [que ni] pintiparado (fig.) to come just right, to be just what s.o. needs/needed, to be just what the doctor ordered (fig., fam.)

Pinto y Valdemoro (Esp.)

▶ estar entre Pinto y Valdemoro (fam., Esp.) (a) s.o. can't make up his mind, to be in two minds (b) to be tipsy, to be tiddly (fam., Br.E.), to be sozzled (sl., Br.E.)

la pintura painting

▶ ser una pintura (fig.) to be lovely[-looking]

▶ no poder ver algo o a alg. ni en pintura (fig., fam.) s.o. can't stand the sight of s.o. (fam.), to hate s.o.'s guts (fam.) ▷ tener algo o a alg. **atravesado** ◆ *No puedo ver el queso de cabra ni en pintura. I can't stand goat cheese.*

▷ pinza (**sacar** algo a alg. con ~s)

el piñón pine seed, pine nut

▶ una boquita de piñón (fig., fam.) pretty girl, sweet girl (fam.)

▶ estar a partir un piñón [con alg.] (fig., fam.) to be very thick with s.o. (fam.), to be bosom pals or buddies [with s.o.] (fam.), to be as thick as thieves ◆ *Ella está a partir un piñón con él. She's very thick with him. She's bosom pals with him.* ◆ *Juan y Pepe están a partir un piñón. Juan and Pepe are the best of buddies or are bosom buddies or are as thick as thieves.*

el pío cheep, chirp

▶ no decir ni pío (fig., fam.) not to hear a peep out of or from s.o. (fam.), not to say/breathe a word, not to open one's mouth, to keep one's mouth shut, to keep mum (fam.), to

button [up] one's lip/mouth (fig., fam.) ◆ *¡De eso no digas ni pío! You keep your mouth shut about that!* ◆ *Se fueron sin decir ni pío. They went off without a word.* ◆ *No dijeron ni pío en toda la tarde. I/we didn't hear a peep from them all afternoon.*

la pipa pipe

▶ la pipa (pop.) pistol, rod (sl., Am.E.)

▶ tener mala pipa (euph.) to have bad intentions ▷ tener mala **leche**

▶ pasarlo pipa (fam.) to have a great/fantastic time (fam.), to have a whale of a time (fam.), to have high jinks (fam.)

pirarse, pirárselas (fam.) to beat it (sl.), to clear out/off (fam.), to make o.s. scarce (fam.), to cut class (fam.)

piripi (fam.)

▶ estar piripi to be merry (fam.), to be tipsy (fam.)

piro (pop.)

▶ darse el piro to beat it (sl.), to split (sl.), to clear off/out (fam.)

el piropo compliment

▶ ser un piropo ambulante (fig., fam.) (woman): to be very pretty, to be a beauty

pisar to tread

▶ pisar a alg. (fig., pop.) to bang s.o. (vulg.) ▷ **calzar**[se] a alg.

▶ pisar algo/a alg. (fig., fam.) to steal s.th./s.o. (fig.), to pinch s.th./s.o. (sl., Br.E.) ◆ *Me pisaron la idea. They stole/pinched my idea.* ◆ *José le pisó la novia a su amigo. José pinched his friend's girl.* ◆ *pisar la clientela a alg. to steal/pinch s.o.'s clientele or customers*

el pisotón stamp on the foot

▶ dar el pisotón (fig.) (reporter/etc.): to bring off a scoop (sl.), to get a beat on (sl., Am.E.)

la pista track, trail

▶ la pista falsa (fig.) red herring (fig.) ◆ *Es una pista falsa. It's a red herring. He's/they're/etc. [just] trying to draw/take the people's attention away from the actual/real issue.*

el pisto type of Spanish dish

▶ el pisto (fig., fam.) bad food, swill (fig., pej.), muck (fig., fam.)

▶ el pisto (fam.; Méjico, América Central, Andes) (money): dough (sl., Am.E.), bread

(sl.), sugar (sl.), brass/dosh/lolly (sl., Br.E.), wampum (sl., Am.E.)
► darse pisto (fig., fam.) to swank (fam., Br.E.), to show off, to put on the dog (fam., Am.E.)
▷ pistola (sentarle algo a alg. como a un santo **cristo** un par de ~s)

el pistón piston
► los pistones (pop.) (testicles) ▷ las **canicas**

pistonudo (fam.) great (fam.) ▷ cojonudo (a)

la pitada whistle
► dar una pitada (fig., fam.) to step out of line (fig.)

pitar to whistle
► pitar (fig., fam.) to work [well], to go off well ◆ *Esto no pita. This doesn't work.* ◆ *Pitó. It went off well.*
► pitar (fig.) to let fly (fig.), to let rip (fam.)
► salir pitando (fig., fam.) to beat it (sl.), to clear/push off (fam.), to make off very quickly

la pítima (fam.) drunkenness
► coger una pítima to get plastered (fam.) ▷ **cocerse** (a)

el pito whistle
► el pito (fig., pop.) (penis): ▷ el **calvo**
► tocarse el pito (fig., fam.) to twiddle one's thumbs (fig., fam.), to do sod all (sl., Br.E.), to do damn all (fam.), to do sweet f.a. (fam.), to be bone-idle (fam.)
► no tocar pito en algo (fam.) to have nothing to do with s.th. ◆ *No toqué pito en eso. I had nothing to do with that.*
► [no] importar a alg. un pito (fig., fam.) not to give/care two hoots (fam.) ▷ no importar a alg. un **ardite**
► no valer un pito (fig., fam.) not to be worth a bean (fam.) ▷ no valer un **ardite**
► Cuando pitos flautas, cuando flautas pitos. It's something different every time. First it's this, then it's that.
► Cuando no es por pitos, es por flautas. If it isn't one thing it's another.
► hoy le da a a alg. por pitos y mañana por flautas s.o. doesn't know what he wants

pitorrearse (fam., Esp.)
► pitorrearse de alg. to pull s.o.'s leg (fam.), to tease s.o., to take the mickey out of s.o. (fam., Br.E.), to make fun of s.o.

la plancha (fig., fam.) gaffe, blunder, boob (fam.), boo-boo (fam.), goof (fam., Am.E.), clinker (sl., Am.E.)
► tirarse una plancha to put one's foot in it (fam.), to drop a clanger/brick (fam., Br.E.)

plantar to plant
► plantar la carrera (fig., fam.) to quit college/university, to quit one's profession, to quit one's career
► plantar o dejar plantado a alg. (fig., fam.) to ditch s.o. (fam.), to jilt s.o., to stand s.o. up (fam.), to leave s.o. in the lurch (fig.), to leave s.o. high and dry (fig.) ◆ *Plantó a su novio. She ditched her boyfriend.* ◆ *Como me dejaron plantado, tuve que hacerlo todo yo. Since they left me high and dry or in the lurch, I had to do it all myself.*
▷ plantar a alg. en la **calle**
▷ plantar un **pino**

el plantón seedling
► dar un plantón a alg. (fig., fam.) to stand s.o. up (on a date) (fam.) ◆ *La convidé a cenar y me dio un plantón. I invited her to dinner but she stood me up or she didn't show up.*
► estar cansado del plantón (fig., fam.) to be tired of the endless/long wait

la plata silver
► hablar en plata (fig.) to speak bluntly (fig.), to speak frankly ◆ *hablando en plata[, ...] to put it bluntly[, . . .]*
► como una plata (fig., fam.) spick-and-span (fam.), squeaky clean (fam.), as bright/clean as a new pin (fig.), like a new pin (fig.), spotless
▷ plata (como una **tacita** de ~)
▷ plata (**hinchar**se de ~)
▷ plata (la **Tacita** de Plata)
▷ plata (tener **manita**s de ~)
▷ platillo (a **bombo** y ~)

el plato plate, dish
► Del plato a la boca se pierde la sopa. (prov.) There's many a slip 'twixt cup and lip. (prov.)
► no ser plato de su gusto (fig.) not to be s.o.'s cup of tea (fam., Br.E.), not to like it/s.th.

♦ *No es plato de mi gusto. It's not exactly my cup of tea.*

▶ ser plato de segunda mesa (fig.) to be a second-rater, to be second-best, to play second fiddle (fig.)

▶ comer en un mismo o en el mismo o del mismo plato (fig., fam.) to be inseparable, to get on like a house on fire (fam.), to be great pals/buddies (fam.), to be hand in glove ♦ *Comen en un mismo plato. They're inseparable.*

▶ no/nunca haber roto un plato [en su vida] (fig., fam.) ♦ *Parece que ella nunca ha roto un plato. She looks as if butter wouldn't melt in her mouth. (fam.)* ♦ *Tiene cara de no haber roto un plato en su vida. He looks as if butter wouldn't melt in his mouth. (fam.)*

▶ Por fuera no rompe un plato, pero tiene la música por dentro. (fam.) Still waters run deep. (prov.)

▶ [tener que] pagar los platos rotos (fig., fam.) to [have to] carry the can (fam., Br.E.), to [have to] take the rap (sl., Am.E.)

▶ nada entre dos platos (fig., fam.) nothing much, a little/minor thing, a trifle ♦ *¿Qué pasó? Nada entre dos platos. What happened? Nothing much.*

▷ plato (muchas **mano**s en un ~ hacen mucho garabato)

▷ plato (sacar los **pie**s del ~)

la plazoleta small square

▶ comprar algo a plazoletas (fam., hum.) to buy s.th. on the never-never (fam., hum., Br.E.), to pay for s.th. in instal[l]ments

el plomo lead, fuse

▶ nadar como un plomo (fam.) to swim like a brick (fam.)

▶ ser algo/alg. un plomo (fig., fam.) s.th./s.o.: to be deadly boring (fam.), to be a bore, to be a drag (sl.); s.th.: to be as exciting as watching [the] paint dry (hum.); s.o.: to be a pain in the neck (fam.) ♦ *Este libro es un plomo. This book is deadly boring. This book is about as exciting as watching the paint dry.* ♦ *Ese tío es un plomo. That guy is a pain in the neck.* ♦ *¡Qué plomo! What a drag!*

▶ fundírsele a alg. los plomos (fig., Esp.) to blow a fuse (fig., sl., hum.), to blow/pop one's cork (sl.), to blow one's top (sl.), to go through or hit the roof (fig., fam.)

▷ plomo (andar con **pie**s de ~)

la pluma feather

▶ Más fuerte es la pluma que la espada. (prov.) The pen is mightier than the sword. (prov.)

▶ echar buena pluma (fig., fam.) to shape up nicely ▷ echar buen **pelo**

▶ el pluma (pop., Esp.) (gay): queer/fairy/faggot (sl., pej.), pansy (fam., pej.), queen (sl.), poof[ter] (sl., pej., Br.E.), fag (sl., pej., Am.E.), arse bandit (vulg., Br.E.)

▶ las plumas (fig., fam.) bed ♦ *Están todavía en las plumas. They're still in bed.*

▶ adornarse con plumas ajenas (fig.) to adorn o.s. with borrowed plumes (fig.), to take credit for what s.o. else has done

▶ escribir/anotar [algo] a vuela pluma to write [s.th.] [down] quickly or without much thought, to jot s.th. down ♦ *Estaba escribiendo a vuela pluma. He was writing quickly.* ♦ *He anotado unas ideas a vuela pluma. I've jotted down a few ideas.*

el plumero bunch of feathers

▶ se le ve el plumero a alg. (fig., fam.) you can see what s.o. is up to (fam.)/is after/is really thinking ♦ *Se te ve el plumero. One/I/we can see what you're up to.*

▷ pobre (ser más ~ que una **rata** [de iglesia])

la pobreza poverty

▶ Pobreza no es vileza. (prov.) Poverty is not a crime. (prov.) Poverty is no sin. (prov.)

poco little

▶ Muchos pocos hacen un mucho. (prov.) Look after the pennies and the pounds will look after themselves or will take care of themselves.

▶ Quien poco tiene, poco teme. (prov.) He who has nothing has nothing to lose.

poder can, to be able to

▶ a más no poder ♦ *gritar a más no poder to scream/shout at the top of one's voice or lungs* ♦ *reír[se] a más no poder to roar with laughter* ♦ *comer a más no poder to eat to excess, to eat until one is fit to burst, to eat until one is [as] full/tight as a tick (fam.)* ♦ *correr a más no poder to run like crazy/hell (fam.), to run hell for leather (fam.), to run for all one is worth (fam.), to run as fast as one can* ♦ *trabajar a más no poder to work flat out (fam.), to go at it hammer and tongs (fam.)* ♦ *ganar dinero a más no poder to*

make pots/piles/stacks of money (fam.) ◆ *ser terco a más no poder to be utterly/extremely obstinate, to be as obstinate as they come* ◆ *ser desmañado/torpe a más no poder to be very awkward, to be [as] awkward as a cow on a crutch or as a cow on roller skates (hum.)* ◆ *ser feo a más no poder to be as ugly as sin/hell (fam.), to be incredibly ugly* ◆ *ser tonto a más no poder to be as dumb as they come (fam., Am.E.), to be a complete idiot* ◆ *ser algo aburrido a más no poder s.th.: to be deadly boring (fam.), to be as exciting as watching [the] paint dry (hum.)* ◆ *gustarle a alg. leer a más no poder to be passionately fond of reading*
▷ poder (**querer** es ~)

podrido rotten, bad
▶ estar podrido de dinero (fam.) to be stinking/filthy rich (fam.)

la polca polka
▶ del año de/en el año de la polca (fam.) donkey's years ago ▷ año de **Maricastaña**

el poli (fam.) cop (fam.), copper (fam.), pig (sl.)

la poli (fam.) cops (fam.), fuzz (sl.), pigs (sl.), filth (sl., Br.E.), heat (sl., Am.E.)

la polilla moth
▶ la polilla (jerga del hampa) cops (fam.), fuzz (sl.), pigs (sl.), filth (sl., Br.E.), heat (sl., Am.E.)

el polizonte (fam.) cop (fam.), copper (fam.), pig (sl.)

la polla young hen, pullet
▶ la polla (fig., fam.) young girl, chick (sl.), bird (sl., Br.E.)
▶ la polla (fig., pop.) (penis) ▷ el calvo

el pollo chicken
▶ el pollo (fig., fam.) young man/lad, boy
▶ el pollo (vulg.) (thick sputum): gob (fam.), spittle
▶ tener calentura de pollo (fig., fam.) to pretend to be ill/sick, to sham ill

la polvareda dust cloud
▶ levantar una polvareda (fig., fam.) to kick up or raise a dust (fig.), to cause a stir, to cause a commotion

el polvo dust, powder
▶ el polvo (fam.) (cocaine/heroin): stuff (sl.)

▶ sacudir el polvo a alg. (fig., fam.) to beat s.o. up (fam.) ▷ arrimar **candela** a alg.
▶ hacer polvo a alg. (fig., fam.) (a) to take it out of s.o., to wear s.o. out (fig.), to shatter s.o. (fam.) (b) (in a debate; opponent): to flatten s.o. (fam.), to slam s.o. (fam.), to crush s.o. (fig.), to tear s.o. to pieces/shreds (fig., fam.), to wipe the floor with s.o. (fig.) ◆ *Uno de los candidatos a la presidencia hizo polvo a los otros. One of the presidential candidates flattened the others.*
▶ estar hecho polvo (fig., fam.) to be totally worn out (fig.) ▷ estar hecho **cisco**
▶ morder el polvo (fig., fam.) (to die): to bite the dust (fig., fam.)
▶ hacer morder [el] polvo a alg. (fig., fam.) to crush s.o. (fig.), to humiliate s.o.
▶ echar un polvo (fig., pop.) to have a screw (vulg.), to get a/one's leg over (sl., Br.E.) ▷ echar un **casquete**
▷ polvo (el **nido** de ~)

la pólvora gunpowder
▶ no haber inventado la pólvora (fig., fam.) not to be exactly an Einstein, s.o. won't set the world or the Thames (Br.E.) on fire (fam.)
▶ gastar la pólvora en salvas (fig.) to waste one's [time and] energy
▷ pólvora (propagarse como un **reguero** de ~)
▷ pólvora (tirar con ~ del **rey**)
▷ polvorosa (poner **pie**s en ~)

el pompis (fam.) bottom (fam.), backside (fam.), behind (fam., euph.), posterior (euph.), butt (fam., Am.E.), bum (fam., Br.E.)
▷ poncho (vivir/estar donde el **diablo** perdió el ~)

pontifical pontifical
▶ estar/ponerse de pontifical (fig., fam.) to be in one's glad rags (fam., Br.E.), to put on one's glad rags (fam., Br.E.)

la popa stern
▶ la popa (fig., fam.) behind (fam., euph.), backside (fam.), bottom (fam.), posterior (euph.), butt (fam., Am.E.), bum (fam., Br.E.)

por si acaso just in case
▶ Más vale un "por si acaso" que un "¿quién pensara?" (prov.) Better [to be] safe than sorry. (prov.)

la porra club, cudgel, truncheon
- la porra (fig., pop.) (penis) ▷ el calvo
- un agente de la porra (fig., fam.) policeman
- mandar a alg. a la porra (fig., fam.) to send s.o. packing (fig.) ◆ *Yo que tú la mandaría a la porra. If I were you, I'd send her packing.*
- ¡Vete a la porra! (fig., fam.) Go to hell! (fam.) Go to blazes! (sl.) You know what you can do! (fam.)
▷ porrazo (de **golpe** y ~)

la porreta leek
- en porreta[s] (fig., fam.) starkers (fam., hum., Br.E.), stark naked (fam.), in the raw (fam.) ◆ *Cuando era joven iba a nadar en porretas. When he was young, he [often] went swimming in the raw.*

el porro (fam., Esp.) joint (sl.), spliff (sl., Br.E.), marijuana cigarette

▷ porvenir (**labrar**se un ~)
▷ porvenir (**sonreír**le a alg. el ~)

el poso sediment, deposit
- hasta los posos (fig.) [down] to the last drop. ◆ *Apuró el cáliz hasta los posos. He drank/drained the cup down to the last drop.*

el poste post, pillar
- serio como un poste (fig., fam.) deadly serious, dead serious (fam.)
- dar poste a alg. (fig., fam.) to keep s.o. waiting [for] an excessively or unduly long time, to keep s.o. hanging about
- oler el poste (fig., fam.) to sense/scent danger, to smell a rat (fig.)

el postín (fam.) (a)showing-off, swank (fam., Br.E.), pompousness, pompous behavior (b) luxury, poshness (fam.), elegance ◆ *darse postín to swank (fam., Br.E.), to show off, to think one is important* ◆ *Ayer cenamos en un restaurante de postín. We had dinner in a posh (fam.) or a plush (sl.) or a smart or an elegant restaurant yesterday.* ◆ *una modista de postín an expensive dressmaker*

el postre dessert
- llegar a los postres (fig.) to come too late, to come after everything is over

potable drinkable
- potable (fig., fam.) reasonable, bearable, passable (fig.) ◆ *precios potables reasonable prices* ◆ *un trabajo potable a bearable job* ◆

una persona potable a bearable/passable person

el pote earthenware pot
- darse pote (fig., fam.) to swank (fam., Br.E.), to show off, to think one is important
- a pote (fig., fam.) galore (fam.), in plenty, pots of (fam.), heaps of (fam.) ◆ *ganar dinero a pote to make pots of money* ◆ *beber a pote to drink an awful lot, to be a heavy drinker*

Potosí Potosí (famous silver mining town in Bolivia)
- valer algo/alg. un Potosí (fig.) (a) s.th.: to be invaluable, to be worth a fortune (b) s.o.: to be worth one's weight in gold (fig.) ◆ *Mi secretaria vale un Potosí. My secretary is worth her weight in gold.*

la potra filly
- tener potra (fig., fam.) to be lucky, to be in luck, to be jammy (fam., Br.E.)

el potro colt, rack (torture)
- tener a alg. en el potro (fig.) to keep s.o. in suspense, to keep s.o. on tenterhooks (fig.), to keep s.o. on pins and needles (fig., Am.E.) ◆ *¡Dímelo ahora! ¡No me tengas en el potro más tiempo! Tell me now. Don't keep me on tenterhooks any longer!*
- poner a alg. en el potro (fig.) to torment s.o. (fig.), to harass s.o.

el poyetón (fam.)
- sentarse en el poyetón to be left on the shelf (fig.), not to get a man

el pozo well
- ser un pozo sin fondo (fig., fam.) to be [like] a bottomless pit (fig., fam.) ◆ *Es un pozo sin fondo. It's a bottomless pit. It's never ending.*
- ser un pozo de ciencia (fig.) to be immensely learned
- caer en el pozo airón (fig.) to fall/sink into oblivion for good, to disappear for good
▷ pozo (ser más bruto que la **pila** de un ~)
▷ pozo ([todo] mi/etc. o el gozo en el/un ~)

predicar to preach
- predicar en el desierto (fig.) to preach in the wilderness (fig.), to be a voice crying in the wilderness (fig.), to talk at deaf ears (fig.), to talk to the winds (fig.) ◆ *Nadie estaba escuchando. Predicaste en el desierto. Nobody*

was listening. You were a voice crying in the wilderness. You were talking at deaf ears.

▶ predicar con el ejemplo to set a good example, to practice what one preaches, to put one's money where one's mouth is (fam.)

▷ predicar (▷ **subirse**: subírsele algo a alg. a ~)

▷ pregonar algo a los cuatro **vientos**

▷ pregonero (dar un **cuarto** al ~)

la pregunta question

▶ andar/estar a la cuarta pregunta (fig., fam.) to be flat broke (fam.), to be stone-broke (fam., Am.E.), to be down to one's last penny (Br.E.) or nickel (Am.E.) (fam.)

▶ dejar a alg. a la cuarta pregunta (fig., fam.) to fleece s.o. (fig.), to milk s.o. (fig.)

▶ A preguntas necias oídos sordos. Ask a silly question, get a silly answer.

▶ Cuál la pregunta, tal la respuesta. You get what you give.

▷ pregunta (**asar/freír** a alg. a ~s)

la prenda pledge

▶ la prenda (fig., fam.) treasure (fig.), love, darling, sweetheart ◆ *Sí, prenda. Yes, darling.*

▶ soltar prenda (fig., fam.) to commit o.s. rashly

▶ no soltar prenda (fig., fam.) to avoid committing o.s., to be very uncommunicative, to be buttoned up (fig., fam.), not to say a word, to give nothing away, to play/keep one's cards close to one's chest (fig.) ◆ *Aunque lo interrogaron horas y horas, no soltó prenda. Although they grilled him for hours and hours, he gave nothing away.*

▶ no dolerle prendas a alg. (fig.) to meet one's obligations [on time]

la prensa press

▶ la prensa amarilla o del corazón (fig.) gutter/yellow press, trashy weeklies

▶ tener buena/mala prensa (fig.) to have a good/bad press (fig.)

▷ preso por **mil**, preso por mil quinientos

prestar to lend

▶ prestar atención a alg./algo (fig.) to give/lend an ear to s.o./s.th. (fig.), to pay attention to s.th.

▷ prestar **oídos** a alg./algo

▷ prestar **oídos** sordos [a algo]

▷ prestar **salud**

la pretensión aspiration

▶ andar en pretensiones (fam.) to be looking for a wife

prevenir to prevent

▶ Más vale prevenir que curar. (prov.) Prevention is better than cure. (prov.) An ounce of prevention is worth a pound of cure. (prov.) Better [to be] safe than sorry. (prov.)

▶ Más vale prevenir que lamentar. (prov.) Better [to be] safe than sorry. (prov.)

la primada (fam.) piece of stupidity, silly mistake

▶ pagar la primada to have to pay for one's stupidity/naivety

primer[o] first

▶ El primer venido, primer servido. First come, first served.

la primera (de cambio) first of exchange

▶ a las primeras de cambio (fig., fam.) suddenly, unexpectedly, at the first best opportunity, as soon as I/etc. turned my/etc. back, before you know where you are ◆ *Se largó a las primeras de cambio. He did a bunk at the first best opportunity.*

el primo cousin

▶ el primo (fig., fam.) fool, patsy (sl., Am.E.), mug (sl., Br.E.), sucker (sl.), dupe

▶ hacer el primo (fig., fam.) to be [easily] taken in (fam.), to be [easily] taken for a ride (fam.), to be [easily] conned (fam.)

▶ venirle a una mujer el primo de América (fam.) to start one's period ◆ *Le vino el primo de América a su hermana. His sister started her period.*

▶ ser primo hermano de o ser primos hermanos (fig., fam.) (s.th./things): to be/look very much like, to be very similar to, to be/look extraordinarily alike ◆ *Tu vestido es primo hermano del que yo tengo. Your dress looks very much like mine. Your dress is very similar to the one I have.* ◆ *La música folklórica de Galicia y la música tradicional de Escocia son primas hermanas. The folk[loric] music in Galicia and the traditional music in Scotland are extraordinarily alike.*

el primor skill

▶ ... que es un primor (fig., fam.) . . . that it is a delight, beautifully ◆ *Canta que es un primor. She sings in a way that is a delight to hear. She sings like an angel.*

▶ ser un primor (a) to be a [real] masterpiece, to be a brilliant feat (b) to be charming, to be delightful ◆ *Su última novela fue un primor. His last novel was a masterpiece.* ◆ *Tus hijas son un primor. Your daughters are charming girls.*

el príncipe prince

▶ vivir como un o a lo príncipe (fig.) to live like a lord/king (fig.), to live in grand style, to live on a grand scale
▶ el príncipe azul (fig.) Prince Charming (fig.)
▶ el príncipe encantado (especialmente iron.) Prince Charming (fig.)

pringar to dip in fat
▶ pringarla (pop.) (a) to mess it up (fig.), to botch it up (fam.), to make a boob (fam.), to make a blunder, to drop a brick/clanger (fam., Br.E.) (b) to kick the bucket (fam.) ▷ cascar[la]
▶ pringar[las] (fig., fam.) to sweat one's guts out (fam.) ▷ echar/sudar la **hiel**
▶ pringarse algo (fig., fam.) to embezzle s.th., to swipe s.th. (sl.), to pinch s.th. (sl., Br.E.), to walk off with s.th.
▶ O nos pringamos todos, o ninguno. (fig., fam.) Either we all carry the can or none of us does. (fam., Br.E.)
▷ prisa (▷ **vestir**: vísteme despacio, que estoy de ~/que tengo ~)

probar to try
▶ Al probar se ve el mosto. (prov.) The proof of the pudding is in the eating. (prov.)
▷ problema (atajar el ~ de **raíz**)

la procesión procession

▶ andarle/irle a alg. la procesión por dentro (fig.) not to show one's feelings, to keep one's troubles or worries to o.s., not to show one's anger, to be a deep (fam.) or quiet one
▶ La procesión va por dentro. (fig.) Still waters run deep. (prov.) There is more in/to this than meets the eye.
▷ procesión (no se puede **repicar** y estar en la ~)
▷ procesión (querer tocar las **campanas** y asistir a la ~)

prodigar to squander, to waste
▶ prodigar algo a alg. (fig.) to heap (fig.) or lavish s.th. on s.o. ◆ *Nos prodigaron las alabanzas. They heaped praise on us.*

la prójima (fam.) loose woman (fig.)

el pronto (fam.) sudden impulse, sudden fit (of temper/etc.) (fig.), sudden notion or feeling ◆ *Me dio un pronto. Suddenly it came over me.* ◆ *Le dio un pronto y me tiró el libro. He had a sudden fit of temper/rage and threw the book at me.* ◆ *En uno de sus prontos me tiró el libro. In one of his fits of rage or bouts of anger he threw the book at me.* ◆ *Le dio un pronto y echó todos los planes por tierra. He had a sudden notion to put paid (Br.E.) to all plans.* ◆ *En un pronto echó todos los planes por tierra. On a sudden impulse he put paid (Br.E.) to all plans.*
▶ tener prontos de enojo to have a quick temper, to be quick-tempered

propinar to tip, to give a tip
▶ propinar algo a alg. (fig., fam.) ◆ *Le propiné una paliza o un puntapié o una bofetada. I dealt/gave him a beating or a kick or a slap in the face.* ◆ *Le propinaron unas cuantas almendras o píldoras. They shot him several times.* ◆ *El polizonte me propinó una multa. The cop gave me a fine. The cop fined me.*

la prosa prose

▶ la prosa (fig., fam.) verbiage, talkativeness
▶ gastar mucha prosa to talk a lot
▷ provecho (**dicho** sin hecho no trae ~)

la púa tooth (comb)

▶ saber cuántas púas tiene un peine (fig., fam.) to be clever, to be sly, to be crafty

el púcher (pop.) pusher (sl.), dealer

el puchero cooking pot

▶ el puchero (fig., fam.) ballot box
▶ el puchero (fig.) daily bread (fam.) ◆ *Apenas ganan para el puchero. They hardly earn enough to eat.*
▶ ganarse el puchero to earn/make a living, to earn one's daily bread or one's bread and butter or one's crust (fam.)
▶ meter la cabeza en un puchero (fig.) to have blinkers (Br.E.) or blinders (Am.E.) on (fig.), to be blinkered (fig.), not to want to see/accept that one is on the wrong track (fig.)
▶ hacer pucheros (fig.) to screw up one's face (fig.), to pout, to make a weepy face

pudrirse to rot
▶ pudrirse en la cárcel (fig., fam.) to rot in jail (fig.)

▶ ¡Que se pudra! (fam.) It serves him/her right! Let him/her rot! (fam.) He/she can go to hell! (fam.)

▶ ¡Y tú que te pudras! (fam.) And you can go to hell! (fam.)

▶ pudrirse de aburrimiento (fig., fam.) to [nearly] die of boredom (fig.) ◆ *Nos pudrimos de aburrimiento. We nearly died of boredom.* ◆ *Te vas a pudrir de aburrimiento en aquel pueblo. You'll die of boredom in that village.*

el puente bridge

▶ un día puente (fig.) a day off work between two public holidays

▶ hacer puente (fig.) to take an extra day or extra days off work between two public holidays, to take a long weekend

▶ tender un puente (fig.) to build bridges (fig.), to offer a compromise

▶ tender puentes de plata a alg. (fig.) to lean/bend over backwards to make it easy for s.o., to make it as easy as possible for s.o.

▷ puente (ha corrido/pasado mucha **agua** bajo el ~)

▷ puerco (a cada ~ le llega su **San Martín**)

▷ puerco (echar **margarita**s a los ~s)

la puerta door

▶ estar a la puerta o en puertas (fig.) to be just around the corner (fig.), to be imminent ◆ *La navidad está a la puerta. Christmas is just around the corner.*

▶ cerrar todas las puertas a alg. (fig.) to close [off] all avenues to s.o. (fig.)

▶ enseñar/mostrar la puerta a alg. (fig.) to show s.o. the [way to the] door

▶ dar a alg. con la puerta en la cara o en los hocicos o en las narices (fig., fam.) to slam/shut the door in s.o.'s face

▶ echar las puertas abajo (fig., fam.) to knock like crazy, to lean on the doorbell (fig.)

▶ quedarse por/a puertas (fig.) to become desperately poor

▶ tener todas las puertas abiertas (fig.) to be welcomed with open arms everywhere (fig.)

▶ llamar a la puerta de alg. (fig.) to ask s.o. for help

▷ puerta (¡Por los **clavo**s de una ~ vieja!)

▷ puesto (tener el **corazón** bien ~)

▷ puesto (tener la **cabeza** bien puesta)

▷ puesto (tener los **pies** [bien ~s] en/sobre la tierra)

la pulga flea

▶ echarle a alg. la pulga detrás de la oreja (fig.) to put ideas into s.o.'s head ◆ *Tiene problemas. Su hermano le echó la pulga detrás de la oreja. He's in trouble. His brother put ideas into his head.*

▶ hacer de una pulga un elefante o un camello (fig.) to make a mountain out of a molehill (fig.)

▶ tener malas pulgas (fig.) to be bad-tempered, to have a bad/violent temper, to have a or be on a short fuse (fam.), to have a nasty (fig.) nature

▶ no aguantar/sufrir pulgas (fig.) to stand no nonsense, not to suffer fools gladly

▶ buscar las pulgas a alg. (fig., fam.) to tease s.o., to needle s.o. (fam.), to wind s.o. up (fam., Br.E.), to put s.o. on (fam., Am.E.)

▶ sacudirse las pulgas (fig., fam., Esp.) to wash one's hands of it

▶ Hay muchas maneras de matar pulgas. (prov.) There's more than one way to skin a cat. (prov.)

▷ pulga (A **perro** flaco no le faltan ~s.)

el pulpo octopus

▶ poner a alg. como un pulpo (fig., fam.) to give s.o. a good thrashing (fam.) ▷ arrimar **candela** a alg.

el pulso pulse

▶ el pulso firme (fig.) steady hand

▶ tomar el pulso a alg. (fig.) to sound s.o. out (fig.)

▶ tomar el pulso a algo (fig.) to sound s.th. out (fig.), to gauge s.th. (fig.) ◆ *Tomamos el pulso a la opinión pública. We sounded out public opinion.*

▶ echar un pulso to arm wrestle

▶ quedarse sin pulso[s] (fig.) to be frightened or scared out of one's wits (fam.), to be petrified or paralyzed with fear/horror (fig.)

▶ ganar[se] algo a pulso (fig.) to [really] earn s.th. (fig.), to work hard for s.th., to get s.th. the hard way ◆ *Lo ha ganado a pulso. He's really earned it. He's worked hard for it.*

la punta [sharp] end, tip, point

▶ la punta del iceberg (fig.) tip of the iceberg (fig.)

▶ acabarse en punta (fig., fam.) to die

▶ estar de punta con alg. (fig.) to have fallen out with s.o., to be at odds with s.o.

▶ tener de punta a alg. (fig.) to be at daggers drawn with s.o. (fig., Br.E.)

▶ tener algo en la punta de la lengua (fig.) to have s.th. on the tip of one's tongue (fig.)

▶ estar/ir/ponerse de punta en blanco (fig., fam.) to be/get dressed up to the nines (fam.) ▷ estar/ponerse de veinticinco alfileres

▶ estar hasta la punta de los pelos o del pelo de alg./algo (fam.) to be fed up to the back teeth with s.o. (fam.), to be utterly fed up with s.o./s.th. (fam.), to be sick and tired of s.o./s.th. (fam.) ▷ estar hasta [más allá de] la coronilla de algo

▶ a punta pala (fig., fam.) plenty of, galore, tons of (fam.), by the ton (fam.), by the score (fam.), scores of (fam.), loads or heaps or piles or stacks of (fam.), no end of (fam.), in spades (fam., Am.E.) ◆ *Tiene dinero a punta pala. He's got loads of money.* ◆ *Nos causaron molestias a punta pala. They caused/ gave us no end of trouble. They caused/gave us trouble in spades.*

▷ punta (de ~ a **cabo**)

▷ punta (poner los **nervio**s de ~ a alg.)

▷ punta (ponerle/ponérsele a alg. los **pelos** de ~)

▷ punta (tener los **nervio**s de ~)

la puntilla (bullfight): short dagger (for administering or giving the coup de grâce); nib (of fountain pen)

▶ dar la puntilla a alg. (fig., fam.) to finish s.o. off ◆ *Eso les dio la puntilla. That finished them off.*

▶ dar la puntilla a algo (fig., fam.) to put an end to s.th. ◆ *Dieron la puntilla a esas maquinaciones. They put an end to these machinations.*

▶ de puntillas on tiptoe, very quietly ◆ *Entraron de puntillas en el cuarto para no despertar a los niños. They tiptoed into the room so as not to wake the children.* ◆ *Entraron de puntillas en el cuarto de los niños. They entered the children's room very quietly.*

▶ ponerse de puntillas (fig., fam.) to stubbornly insist on one's opinion

el punto point, dot

▶ el punto flaco (fig.) sore/weak point (fig.), weak spot (fig.)

▶ el punto muerto (fig.) deadlock (fig.) ◆ *llegar a un punto muerto to reach deadlock* ◆ *salir del punto muerto to break the deadlock*

▷ punto (contar algo con ~s y **coma**s)

el puñal dagger

▶ poner el puñal en el pecho a alg. (fig.) to hold a gun/pistol to s.o.'s head (fig.) ◆ *El gángster le puso el puñal en el pecho a ella para que firmase el contrato. The gangster held a gun to her head so that she signed the contract.*

la puñalada stab, dagger thrust

▶ coser a alg. a puñaladas (fig.) to carve s.o. up (fam.), to stab s.o. repeatedly, to stab away at s.o.

▶ dar una puñalada trapera a alg. (fig.) to stab s.o. in the back (fig.), to play a dirty/nasty trick on s.o. (fig.)

la puñeta (vulg.) masturbation

▶ hacer la puñeta (to masturbate) ▷ tocar la **campana**

▶ mandar a alg. a hacer la puñeta (fig., pop.) to tell s.o. to go to hell (fam.), to tell s.o. to get stuffed (vulg.) ◆ *Lo mandó a hacer la puñeta. She told him to get stuffed.*

▶ ¡Vete a la puñeta! (fig., pop.) Get stuffed! (vulg.) Go to hell! (fam.)

▶ ¡Es la puñeta! (fig., pop.) It's bloody disgusting! (sl., Br.E.)

▶ ¡No me hagas la puñeta! (fig., pop.) Leave me alone!

▶ ¿Qué puñetas estás/etc. haciendo aquí? (fig., pop.) What the devil/hell are you/etc. doing here? (fam.)

▶ [no] importar a alg. una puñeta (fig., pop.) not to give a shit/fuck (vulg.) ◆ *Esto me importa una puñeta. I don't give a fuck about this.*

▶ vivir/estar en la quinta puñeta (fig., pop.) to live/be at the back of beyond ▷ vivir/estar donde **Cristo** dio las tres voces

el puño fist

▶ tener a alg. en un puño (fig., fam.) to have s.o. under one's thumb (fig.), to have s.o. on a string (fig.)

▶ meter a alg. en un puño (fig., fam.) (a) to intimidate s.o., to cow s.o. (b) to bring s.o. under control

▶ estar con el alma en un puño (fig., fam.) to be scared to death (fam.)

► apretar los puños (fig.) to struggle hard
► creer algo a puño cerrado (fig.) to believe s.th. blindly
► decir mentiras como puños (fig.) to tell whopping great lies (fam.)
▷ puño (**tragar**[se]las como ~s)

el puré purée
► el puré (fig.) peasouper (thick fog) (fam.)
► estar hecho puré (**fam.**) to be knackered (sl., Br.E.) ▷ estar hecho **cisco**
► hacer puré a alg. (fig., fam.) to make mincemeat of s.o. (fig., fam.)

la puta (pop.) whore (fam.)
► irse de putas (pop.) to whore [around] or go whoring [around] (fam.)

puto (pop.) damn (fam.), goddam[n] (sl., Am.E.), bloody (sl., Br.E.) ◆ *No tiene ni puta idea.* He doesn't have a goddamn clue. ◆ *No nos hizo ni puto caso.* He completely *bloody ignored us. He didn't take the damnedest bit of notice of us.*
► pasarlas putas (pop.) to have a terrible time, to have a really lousy time (fam.), to have a bloody awful time (sl., Br.E.)

que (added meaning)
▶ yo que tú/Ud. if I were you ◆ *Yo que tú no iría. If I were you I wouldn't go.*
▷ quebrarse la **cabeza**

quedarse to remain
▶ quedarse con alg. (fig., fam.) (a) to deceive s.o., to cheat s.o., to take s.o. for a ride (fam.) (b) to pull s.o.'s leg (fam.), to have s.o. on (fam.) (c) to bore s.o. to death (fam.), to bore the pants off s.o. (fam.)

quemar to burn [up]
▶ quemar las naves (fig.) to burn one's boats (fig.), to burn one's bridges [behind one] (fig.) ◆ *Porque le soltó una andanada de insultos al banquero no se le permitió volver a entrar en ese banco. Quemó las naves. Because he unleashed a volley of abuse at the banker he wasn't allowed to enter that bank again. He burned his boats.*
▶ quemar etapas (fig.) to make rapid progress (fig.)
▷ quemar el **caucho**
▷ quemar el último **cartucho**
▷ quemarse las **ceja**s

la quemazón burning
▶ la quemazón (fig.) intense heat

querer to want, to wish
▶ Querer es poder. (prov.) Where there's a will, there's a way. (prov.)
▶ ser un poeta/etc., no así como quiera not to be [just] any old poet/etc. (fam.) ◆ *Es un hombre de ciencia, no así como quiera. He isn't just any old scientist.*

el queso cheese
▶ los quesos (fig., pop., hum.) feet, smelly feet, cheesy feet (fam.)
▶ dársela a alg. con queso (pop., Esp.) to fool s.o. (fam.), to put one/it over on s.o. (fam.), to pull a fast one on s.o. (sl.) ◆ *Nos la dio con queso. He put one over on us.* ◆ *A mí no me la das con queso. You can't fool me. I'm not going to fall for that. (fam.)*

el quicio door hinge
▶ sacar a alg. de quicio (fig.) to drive s.o. crazy (fam.), to get s.o. worked up, to get on s.o.'s nerves or wick (Br.E.) (fam.), to get on s.o.'s tits (vulg., Br.E.), to get under s.o.'s skin (fam.), to rub s.o. up the wrong way (fig., fam.)

el quid (fam.) key point, crux, core, nub (fam.)
▶ dar en el quid to hit the nail on the head (fig.)
▶ este es el quid that's what it's all about
▶ el quid de la cuestión o de la cosa o del asunto es que ... the crux/nub of the matter is that . . . , the key point is that . . .

el quiebro dodge
▶ dar el quiebro a alg. (fig., fam.) to shake s.o. off (fig.), to dodge s.o.

quilar [a alg.] (pop., Esp.) to screw [s.o.] (vulg.) ▷ **follar** [a alg.]

el quilo chyle
▶ sudar el quilo (fig., fam.) to slog/sweat one's guts out (fam., Br.E.) ▷ echar/sudar la **hiel**

la quina cinchona bark
▶ [tener que] tragar quina (fig.) [to have] to swallow the bitter pill (fig.), [to have] to put up with it, [to have] to take it, to suppress or stifle one's anger ◆ *El padre tragó quina cuando pusieron a su hijo a la sombra por asesinato. The father swallowed the bitter pill when his son was put in clink for murder.* ◆ *Me insultaron y tuve que tragar quina. They insulted me and I had to take it.*

quince fifteen
▶ dar quince y raya/falta a alg. (fig.) to be streets ahead of s.o. (fam.), to be more than a match for s.o., to beat s.o. hollow (fam.), to run rings around s.o. (fam.) ▷ **comerse** crudo a alg. ◆ *Nos dan quince y raya en el diseño. They are streets ahead of us in design.*

Quintín ▷ San Quintín

▷ quinto (vivir/estar en la quinta **puñeta**)
▷ quinto **cielo** (estar en el ~)
▷ quinto **infierno/pino** (vivir/estar en el ~)

quisque (fam.)
- todo/cada quisque every man jack of them (fam.) ▷ todo **bicho** viviente
- como cada/todo quisque like everyone else, like the next man
- ni quisque not a living soul, not a sod (sl., Br.E.) ◆ *No había ni quisque en la calle. There wasn't a living soul in/on the street.*

la quisquilla (fam.) little/minor thing, trifle, triviality

el quitamiedos (fam.) (safety appliance): handrail, safety rope, etc.

el/la quitamotas (fam.) toady, creep (fam.)

el quitapenas (fam.) problem solver, gun, pistol, rod (sl., Am.E.), knife, chiv (sl.), alcohol

quitar to take away, to remove
- ni quitar ni poner (fam.) to have no say, not to have any say, not to have any clout (fig.), not to count, to cut no ice (fam.) ◆ *Ella aquí ni quita ni pone. She doesn't have any say [in what goes on] here. She or her opinion doesn't count around here.*
- quitar algo de en medio to get s.th. out of the way (fig.), to get rid of s.th.
- quitar a alg. de en medio (fig.) to get rid of s.o. (euph.), to kill s.o. ▷ **cargar**se a alg. (a)
- quitarse algo/a alg. de encima to shake s.th./s.o. off (fig.), to get rid of s.th./s.o., to steer clear of s.th./s.o. (fig.)
- ¡Quítate de ahí o de en medio! (fam.) Get out of here! Off with you! Beat it! (sl.) Get lost! (fam.) Push off! (fam.)
- quitarse del alcohol to give up drinking, to go on the [water] wag[g]on (fam.)
- quitarse del tabaco to give up smoking
- esto/eso no quita que ... this/that doesn't mean that . . . ◆ *Esto no quita que él tenía la culpa. This doesn't mean it wasn't his fault.* ◆ *Yo ataco el problema así, eso no quita que se pueda atacarlo de otra manera. I tackle the problem like this but that doesn't mean that there aren't other ways of tackling it.*
- quitando ... (fam.) except [for] . . . , apart/ aside from . . . ◆ *Quitando a los más jóvenes todos pueden venir. They can all come except for the very youngest ones.* ◆ *Quitando la sopa cené bien. Apart from the soup I had a good dinner.*
- ▷ quitar (por un quítame allá esas **pajas**)

el quite parry (fencing)
- estar al quite (fig.) to be on hand [to help s.o.], to be ready [to go to s.o.'s aid]

R

el rábano radish

▶ [no] importar a alg. un rábano (fig., fam.) not to give/care two hoots ▷ no importar a alg. un **ardite**

▶ tomar el rábano por las hojas (fig.) to put the cart before the horse (fig.), to get hold of the wrong end of the stick (fig., fam.), to bark up the wrong tree (fig.)

el rabel (fam.) behind (fam., euph.), backside (fam.), bottom (fam.), posterior (euph.), butt (fam., Am.E.), bum (fam., Br.E.)

▷ rabia (muerto el **perro**, se acabó la ~)

rabiar to rage, to rave

▶ a rabiar (fig., fam.) incredibly (fig.), terribly (fam.), like mad (fam.), like crazy (fam.) ◆ *Aplaudieron a rabiar. They applauded like mad.* ◆ *Me gusta a rabiar. I'm terribly fond of it.*

▶ rabiar de impaciencia (fig., fam.) to be burning with impatience (fig.)

▶ rabiar por algo (fig.) to be very keen on s.th., to long for s.th., to be dying for s.th. (fam.)

▶ rabiar por + infinitivo (fig.) to be itching/dying to + infinitive (fam.), to be champing at the bit to + infinitive (fig.) ◆ *Rabiaba por conocerte. He was itching to meet you.*

▶ picar que rabia (fig., fam.) to be terribly hot (fam.) ◆ *La salsa pica que rabia. The sauce is terribly hot.*

el rabo tail

▶ el rabo (vulg.) (penis) ▷ el calvo

▶ Aún falta/queda el rabo por desollar. (fig.) The main difficulty or the most difficult part is yet/still to come. The worst is yet/still to come.

▶ irse con el rabo entre las piernas/patas (fig.) to slink off or go away with one's tail between one's legs (fig.)

▶ asir algo por el rabo (fig., fam.) to go about s.th. the wrong way

▶ rabos de gallo (fig.) cirrus [cloud]

▷ rabo (de **cabo** a ~)

la rabona

▶ hacer rabona (fig., fam.) to play truant (Br.E.) or hooky (fam., Am.E.)

▶ hacer rabona a alg. (fam.) to stand s.o. up (fam.)

la raíz root

▶ atajar el mal o el problema de raíz (fig.) to strike at the root of the evil/problem (fig.)

▶ arrancar algo de raíz (fig.) to eradicate s.th. root and branch (fig.), to root s.th. out completely (fig.) ◆ *Arrancaron la peste de raíz. They eradicated the plague root and branch.*

▶ cortar algo de raíz (fig.) *to nip s.th. in the bud (fig.), to scotch a rumor (fig.)* ◆ *Había problemas en el vestuario, pero el entrenador los cortó de raíz. There was trouble in the locker room, but the coach nipped it in the bud.* ◆ *Cortaron el rumor de raíz. They scotched the rumor.*

▶ echar raíces (fig.) to put down roots (fig.), to settle down ◆ *No quiero echar raíces aquí. I don't want to put down roots here. I don't want to settle down here.*

la raja crack, slit, splinter, slice (bread/etc.)

▶ la raja (vulg.) (vagina) ▷ el conejo

▶ hacerse rajas (fig., fam.) to nearly kill o.s. (with work/etc.) (fam.) ◆ *Ayer estuve hecho cisco. Me hice rajas. I was completely shattered yesterday. I nearly killed myself.*

▶ sacar raja (fig., fam.) to get a rake-off (fam.), to make a haul/killing (fam.)

rajarse to crack, to split

▶ rajarse de risa (fig., fam.) to split one's sides laughing or with laughter (fig.), to crack up (fam., Am.E.), to crease up (fam., Br.E.), to kill o.s. laughing (fam.), to be in stitches (fam.)

▶ rajarse por (fig., fam.) to nearly kill o.s. + gerund (fam.), to put everything one has into s.th. ◆ *Me rajé por este ensayo. I nearly killed myself getting this essay done.*

▶ rajarse (fig., fam.) to climb down (fig.), to back out (fam.), to pull out (fig.), to chicken out (fam.) ◆ *No podimos ir porque se rajaron. We couldn't go because they chickened out.*

el rallo grater

▶ la cara de rallo (fig., fam.) pockmarked face

la rama branch
▶ andarse por las ramas (fig.) (a) to beat about/around the bush (fig.) (b) to get bogged down in details (fig.) ◆ *No se anduvo por las ramas. He didn't beat about the bush. He laid it on the line. (fam.)*
▶ asirse a las ramas (fig.) to make lame (fig.) excuses

la rana frog
▶ la rana (vulg.) (vagina) ▷ el conejo
▶ la rana (pop.) (gay): queer/fairy/faggot (sl., pej.), pansy (fam., pej.), queen (sl.), poof[ter] (sl., pej., Br.E.), fag (sl., pej., Am.E.), arse bandit (vulg., Br.E.)
▶ ¡Hasta que/cuando las ranas críen pelo! (fig., fam.) Pigs might fly! (iron.) Till hell freezes over! (fam.) If I never see you again it will be too soon! (hum.)
▶ cuando las ranas críen pelo (fig., fam.) when pigs learn to fly (iron.), in a month of Sundays (fam.), in a coon's age (sl., Am.E.), never ◆ *Pagarán cuando las ranas críen pelo. They'll pay when pigs learn to fly. They'll never pay.* ◆ *A este paso terminarán el trabajo cuando las ranas críen pelo. At this rate they'll never finish the job or they won't finish the job in a coon's age.*
▶ no ser rana (fig.) to be no fool, to know one's stuff (fam.)
▶ salir/ser alg./algo rana (fam.) (a) person/s.th.: to turn out to be or be a washout (fam.) or a dead loss (fig., fam.) or a failure or a big disappointment (b) s.th.: to turn out to be or be a letdown (fam.)
▷ rana (el **unto** de ~)
▷ rana (salga **pez** o salga ~)

el rancho (military/prison/etc.): food, mess, communal meal
▶ hacer rancho aparte (fig.) to isolate o.s., to keep to o.s., to go one's own way, to form one's own little clique (in life or at a party/etc.)

el rapapolvo squib (firework)
▶ echar un rapapolvo a alg. (fam.) to rap s.o. over the knuckles (fig.), to give s.o. a [good] ticking-off or wigging (fam., Br.E.), to give s.o. a [good] dressing-down/telling-off/talking-to (fam.)
▶ recibir un rapapolvo (fig.) to get a rap over the knuckles (fig.)

el rapaterrones (pop.) country yokel/bumpkin (pej.), hick (fam., pej., Am.E.), cornball (fam.)
▷ raro (ser un **pájaro** ~)

rascar to scratch
▶ llevar/tener qué rascar (fig., fam.) to chew on that (fig.), not to get over that/it easily (fig.) ◆ *Llevará qué rascar durante mucho tiempo. He'll/she'll be chewing on that for a while to come.*
▶ rascar el violín (fig., fam.) to scrape/saw away at the violin (fam.)
▶ rascar la guitarra (fig., fam.) to strum away at the guitar
▶ rascarse para adentro (fam.) to line one's [own] pockets, to look after Number One (fam.)
▶ no tener tiempo ni para rascarse (fig., fam.) not to have [got] a minute
▷ rascar (el **comer** es como el ~, todo es cuestión de empezar)
▷ rascar[se] el **bolsillo**

el rasero strickle
▶ medirlo todo o medirlos a todos por el mismo rasero (fig.) to lump everything together (fig.), to lump them all together (fig.)
▶ No se puede medirlo todo o medirlos a todos por el mismo rasero. (fig.) You can't just lump everything together. (fig.) You can't just lump them all together.

rasgar to tear up
▶ rasgarse las vestiduras (fig) to throw up one's hands [in horror], to tear one's hair [out] (fig.)

la raspa beard
▶ tender la raspa (fig., pop.) to hit the sack (fam.), to hit the hay (fam., Am.E.)

la rata rat
▶ la rata de biblioteca (fig., fam.) bookworm (fig.)
▶ ser más pobre que una rata [de iglesia] (fig.) to be as poor as a church mouse (fig.)

el rato while
▶ saber un rato [largo] de algo (fam.) to know a [hell/heck of a] lot about s.th. (fam.) ◆ *Saben un rato largo de literatura. They know a heck of a lot about literature.*

el ratón mouse
- ► el ratón de biblioteca (fig., fam.) bookworm (fig.)
- ▷ ratón (cuando el **gato** duerme, bailan los ratones)
- ▷ ratón (cuando el **gato** va a sus devociones, bailan los ratones)
- ▷ ratón (jugar al **gato** y al ~ con alg.)
- ▷ ratón (más vale ser **cabeza** de ~ que cola de león)

la raya line, boundary
- ► hacer raya (fig.) to have a profound impact, to be outstanding (fig.) ♦ *Hizo raya en matemáticas. He was an outstanding mathematician.*
- ► echar raya a alg. (fig.) to take s.o. on ♦ *No hay quien le eche raya a él. Nobody can take him on. Nobody can beat him.*
- ► pasar de la raya (fig.) to go too far (fig.), to overstep or overshoot the mark
- ► tener/mantener a alg. a raya to keep/hold s.o. in check (fig.), to keep s.o. at bay, to keep s.o. under control
- ► poner a alg. a raya to put s.o. in his place
- ▷ raya (¡**Cruz** y ~!)
- ▷ raya (dar **quince** y ~ a alg.)

rayado (record): scratched
- ► sonar como un disco rayado (fig.) to be harping on the same old theme every time (fig.), to be the same old story every time (fig.)

el rayo lightning
- ► el rayo de esperanza (fig.) glimmer of hope (fig.), bright spot on the horizon (fig.)
- ► echar rayos y centellas (fig., fam.) to be fuming (fig., fam.), to be seething [with rage] (fig.), to be wild with rage (fam.)
- ► saber a rayos (pop.) to taste awful/foul
- ► oler a rayos (pop.) to smell awful/foul
- ► ¡Que mal rayo le/etc. parta! (fig., pop.) He/etc. can go to hell! (fam.) Damn him/etc.! (fam.)
- ▷ rayo (▷ **herir**: como herido por el/un ~)
- ▷ razón (**huérfano** de ~)
- ▷ razón (**obras** son amores, que no buenas razones)

el real old Spanish coin (worth 25 céntimos)
- ► un real sobre otro (fig.) down to the last penny or cent (Am.E.)

- ► estar sin un real o no tener [ni] un real (fam.) to be stone-broke (fam., Am.E.) ▷ estar sin un **cuarto** o no tener [ni] un cuarto

el real army camp
- ► [a]sentar el real o sus reales (fig., fam.) to settle down, to establish o.s.
- ▷ rebaja (ya viene/vendrá el tío **Paco** con la ~)

la rebatiña scramble
- ► andar a la rebatiña de algo (fam.) to argue/quarrel over s.th., to scramble for s.th. (fig.)

rebosar to overflow
- ► rebosar de salud (fig.) to be brimming/bursting with health (fig.)
- ► rebosar de alegría o de entusiasmo (fig.) to be bubbling over with joy or with enthusiasm (fig.)
- ► rebosar de ternura (fig.) to be overflowing with tenderness or with affection (fig.)
- ► rebosar en dinero (fig.) to have pots of money (fam.), to be loaded (sl.)
- ▷ rebuznar (quien nace **burro** muere rebuznando)

recalar (port): to steer for, to head for
- ► recalar en (fig., fam.) to land [up] at, to show up at, to turn up at (fig.), to end up at ♦ *Recaló en casa de ella. He ended up at her house/place.*

recetar to prescribe
- ► recetar largo (fig., fam.) to have a long wish list, to come up with a lot of wishes

rechupete (fam.) ♦ *una comida de rechupete delicious meal, yummy meal (fam.), scrumptious meal (fam.)* ♦ *una mujer de rechupete gorgeous woman, tasty (Br.E.) or yummy woman (fig., fam.), real smasher (fam.)* ♦ *pasarlo de rechupete to have a great/fine time (fam.)* ♦ *Aquí todo marcha de rechupete. Everything's going wonderfully well here. Everything's going marvelously or fantastically here. (fam.)*

recibir to receive
- ► tocarle a alg. recibir (fig., fam.) to be in for it ♦ *Mañana te toca[rá] recibir. You'll be in for it tomorrow.*

el reclamo decoy, [mating/bird] call
- ► acudir al reclamo (fig.) to take the bait (fig.), to walk into the trap (fig.)

el recorrido overhaul
▶ dar un [buen] recorrido a alg. (fig., fam.) (a) to give s.o. a [good] going-over (fig.), to give s.o. a [sound] beating (b) to give s.o. a [good] going-over (fig.), to give s.o. a [good] wigging (fam., Br.E.)

la recua train (of pack animals)
▶ con toda la recua (fig., fam.) with the whole family, with the whole clan (fig.), with the whole caboodle (sl.) ◆ *Llegaron con toda la recua. They came with the whole clan in tow.*

el recuelo second brew
▶ el recuelo (fig., fam.) thin coffee, thin brew (pej.)

la red net
▶ caer en la red (fig.) to fall/walk into the trap (fig.)

la redada catch, haul
▶ coger una buena redada (fig., fam.) to make a big haul (fig.)

el redaño mesentery
▶ tener redaños (fig., fam.) to have gumption (fam.), to have pluck (fig.), to have guts (fam.), to have balls (vulg.), to have bottle (sl., Br.E.)

el redil fold
▶ volver al redil (fig.) to return to the fold (fig.)

redondear to round [off]
▶ redondearse (fig., fam.) to get rich/wealthy, to line one's pockets, to feather one's nest (fig.)
▷ redondo (**caerse ~**)

refregar to rub
▶ refregar algo a alg. [por las narices] (fig., fam.) to rub s.o.'s nose in s.th. (fig., fam.), to rub s.th. in (fig., fam.) ◆ *¡Acaba ya de refregármelo! Now stop rubbing it in [all the time]!* ◆ *Yo sé que cometí un error. No me lo refriegues constantemente por las narices. I know that I made a mistake. Don't constantly rub my nose in it.*

la regadera sprinkler, watering can
▶ estar como una regadera (fig., fam.) to be [completely] crazy, to be as mad as a hatter (Br.E.)

▷ regalarle a alg. el **oído**
▷ re\`galo (ser un ~ para los **oído**s)

regar to water, to irrigate
▶ regar una comida con vino (fig., fam.) to have wine with a meal, to accompany a meal with wine, to wash down a meal with wine
▶ regar a una mujer (fig., vulg.) to screw a woman (vulg.) ▷ **calzar**[se] a alg.

regentar (hotel/etc.): to run, to manage
▶ regentar (fig., fam.) to boss about (fam., Br.E.), to boss around (fam.)

el registro register
▶ tocar todos los registros (fig., fam.) to pull out all the stops (fig.), to leave no stone unturned (fig.)
▶ salir por otro registro (fig., fam.) to take a tougher line

el reguero trickle
▶ propagarse como un reguero de pólvora (fig.) to spread like wildfire (fig.) ◆ *El rumor se propagó como un reguero de pólvora. The rumor spread like wildfire.*

reír to laugh [at]
▶ Quien o el que ríe último, ríe mejor. (prov.) He who laughs last laughs longest or loudest. (prov.)
▶ reírse a solas o para sus adentros to laugh up one's sleeve
▶ reírse de los peces de colores (fam.) not to give/care a damn (fam.), s.o. couldn't care less (fam., Br.E.) ◆ *Me río de los peces de colores. I don't give a damn. I couldn't care less.*
▷ reír (~le a alg. la[s] **gracia**[s])
▷ reír (al **freír** será el ~)
▷ reír (ande yo **caliente** y ríase la gente)
▷ reír[se] a **carcajada**s/a **mandíbula** batiente/a más no **poder**
▷ reír[se] como un **descosido**
▷ reja (meter **aguja** para sacar ~)
▷ relámpago (salir del **trueno** y dar con el ~)

el relance throwing back, relaunch
▶ de relance (fig., pop.) [in] cash ◆ *Pagamos de relance. We paid cash.*

relegar to relegate
▶ relegar algo al olvido (fig.) to banish (fig.) s.th. from one's mind, to consign s.th. to oblivion

el reloj clock, watch
▶ ir/marchar como un reloj (fig., fam.) to go like clockwork (fig.) ◆ *Todo va como un reloj. Everything's going like clockwork.*

relucir to shine
▶ sacar a relucir algo (fig., fam.) to come out with s.th. (fam.) ◆ *¡Sácalo a relucir! [Come on,] out with it!*

remar to row
▶ remar (fig., fam.) to toil [and moil], to struggle [hard] ▷ echar/sudar la **hiel**

rematado (fig., fam.) utter, absolute, complete, out-and-out, no end of (fam.), to the core (fig.) ◆ *disparates rematados utter/absolute nonsense* ◆ *Es un tonto rematado. He's no end of a fool. (fam.) He's an utter fool. He's an absolute or a complete idiot.* ◆ *Es un estafador rematado. He's an out-and-out cheat. He's a cheat to the core.*
▷ remate (estar/ser **loco** de ~)

el remediavagos (fam.) mnemonic aid

el remedio remedy
▶ ser peor el remedio que la enfermedad (fig.) to be a case of the solution being worse than the problem
▶ No hay [más] remedio. (fig., fam.) It can't be helped. There's no help for it. There's no other way. (fig.) There's no way around it. (fig.)
▶ ni para un remedio not for love [n]or money ◆ *No se podía encontrar ni para un remedio. It couldn't be had for love or money.* ◆ *No encontramos una vivienda ni para un remedio. We couldn't find a flat or an apartment (Am.E.) for love nor money.*

el remo oar
▶ el remo (fam.) (erect penis): hard-on (vulg.)
▶ tomar el remo (fig.) to take charge, to take over

remojar to soak
▶ remojar (fig., fam.) (success/etc.): to celebrate with a drink ◆ *¡Esto hay que remojarlo! This calls for a drink! This calls for a celebration!*

el remolque tow, towing
▶ hacer algo a remolque (fig., fam.) to do s.th. unwillingly or reluctantly ◆ *Lo hicieron a remolque. They did it reluctantly. They had to be pushed to do it.*
▶ llevar a remolque a alg. (fig., fam.) to drag s.o. along (fig.) ◆ *Siempre tenemos que llevarlo a remolque. We always have to drag him along [with us].*

el remoquete punch (in the face)
▶ el remoquete (pop.) nickname
▶ dar remoquete a alg. (fig., fam.) to make snide/cutting remarks at s.o.
▷ remoto (no tener ni la más remota **idea**)

el renacuajo tadpole
▶ el renacuajo (fig., fam., pej.) little squirt (pej.), shrimp (fig., fam.), runt (fig., pej.), shorty (fam.)

la renta income, interest
▶ vivir de renta (fig., deportes) (sports): to play for time, to run out the clock, not to risk anything

el renuncio (card game): revoke
▶ coger a alg. en un renuncio (fig., fam.) to give the lie to s.o., to catch s.o. lying, to catch s.o. out, to catch s.o. in a fib

la repesca (fam.) (school): repeat exam

repescar a alg. (fam.) to give s.o. (who failed the exam) a second chance to pass the exam

repicar to ring, to peal
▶ No se puede repicar y estar en la procesión. (prov.) You can't be in more than one place at the same time.

repiquetear to ring, to peal
▶ repiquetearse (fig., fam.) to exchange insults, to slag each other or one another off (sl., Br.E.)

requete... (fam.) ◆ *Lo has hecho requetebién. You've done it brilliantly. (fig.) You've done it extremely well.* ◆ *Esta película es requetemala. This film is terrible/awful.* ◆ *una mujer requeteguapa an awfully/extraordinarily pretty woman* ◆ *La muchacha llevó una requetesuperminifalda. The girl wore an ultrashort miniskirt.* ◆ *Eso lo tenemos requeteoídos. We've heard that time and [time] again.* ◆ *Lo tendré requetepensado. I'll think it over thoroughly.* ◆ *Esto lo tengo muy requetepensado. I've thought this over very thoroughly.*

requilorios (fam.) ado, fuss
▶ no andarse con requilorios not to waste any time ▷ la **chiquita**: no andarse con/en chiquitas

el requisito requirement
▶ con todos sus requisitos (fig., fam.) with all the trimmings (fig.)

la resaca (fam.) (after drinking): hangover (fam.) ◆ *Tengo resaca. Pues échate un trago [de alcohol] que así se cura. I have a hangover. Have/try a hair of the dog [that bit you]. (fam.)*

el resbalón slip
▶ dar un resbalón (fig.) to slip up (fam.), to put one's foot in it (fam.), to commit a faux pas

el rescoldo hot ashes
▶ el rescoldo (fig., fam.) pangs/pricks of conscience (fig.), scruples
▶ avivar el rescoldo [de algo] to stir up the dying embers (fig.), to rekindle s.th. (fig.)

resollar to breathe heavily
▶ resollar (fig., fam.) to give a sign of life ◆ *Hace mucho tiempo que no resuellan. It's a long time since we/I heard from them. They have given no sign of life for a long time.*

el resorte spring
▶ tocar todos los resortes (fig., fam.) to mobilize all one's influential friends, to use all one's influence, to pull all the strings [one can] (fig.), to do everything in one's power ◆ *Tocaron todos los resortes para llegar a ver al presidente. They pulled all the strings they could to get to see the president.*
▷ respeto (**campar** por sus ~s)

respingar (horse): to shy, to buck
▶ respingar (fig., fam.) (skirt/dress/etc.): to ride up, to fit poorly, to be baggy

respingón (animal): stubborn
▶ la nariz respingona (fig.) snub nose, turned-up nose

respirar to breathe
▶ no respirar (fig., fam.) to say absolutely nothing, not to breathe a word
▶ no dejar respirar a alg. (fig.) not to give s.o. a minute's rest, to keep s.o. constantly on the go, to keep s.o. on his toes, to badger s.o. (fig.)

▶ no tener tiempo ni de respirar (fig.) to hardly have time to breathe (fig.)
▷ respuesta (cuál la **pregunta**, tal la ~)

el resquicio crack
▶ el resquicio (fig., fam.) good opportunity/opening, chance

el resto rest
▶ echar el resto (fig.) to shoot one's bolt (fig.), to go all out (fam.), to do one's utmost, to make an all-out or a supreme effort ◆ *Eché el resto. I shot my bolt. I went all out.* ◆ *Echamos el resto por ayudarles. We did our utmost to help them.*
▶ para los restos (fig., fam.) forever, for good, for keeps (fam.) ◆ *Si vuelve a ganar la copa, se la queda para los restos. If he wins the cup again, it's his for keeps.*

el resuello heavy breathing
▶ meter a alg. el resuello en el cuerpo (fig., fam.) (a) to put the wind up s.o. (fam., Br.E.), to give s.o. a [nasty] fright (b) to take s.o. down a peg or two (fig.)

el retortero twist
▶ andar/ir al retortero (fig., fam.) to be constantly on the go or on the jump (fam.), to be running about (Br.E.) or around nonstop, to bustle about
▶ traer a alg. al retortero (fig., fam.) not to give s.o. a minute's rest, to keep s.o. constantly on the go or on the jump (fam.)

revenir to shrink
▶ revenirse (fig., fam.) to give in, to give way

reventar to burst
▶ reventar de risa (fig., fam.) to split one's sides laughing or with laughter, to burst out laughing
▶ reventar de envidia (fig., fam.) to be bursting with envy
▶ reventar de impaciencia o de curiosidad (fig., fam.) to be bursting with impatience or with curiosity
▶ reventar por + infinitivo (fig., fam.) to be dying/itching to + infinitive (fam.), to be champing at the bit to + infinitive (fig.) ◆ *Revienta por verla. He's dying to see her.*
▶ reventar[se] (fig., pop.) to kick the bucket (fam.) ▷ **cascar**[la]
▶ reventarse (fig., fam.) to work o.s. to death (fig., fam.) ▷ echar/sudar la **hiel**

▶ estar reventado (fig., fam.) to be completely beat (fam., Am.E.) ▷ estar hecho **cisco**

revestirse to put on one's vestments
▶ revestirse de paciencia (fig.) to arm o.s. with patience
▶ revestirse de valor (fig.) to arm o.s. with courage, to pluck up or screw up or muster up [one's] courage (fig.), to screw o.s. up to do s.th. ◆ *Se revistieron de valor y fueron a hablarle al jefe.* They plucked up courage and went to speak to the boss.

el revientacajas (pop.) safecracker (fam.)

el revientapisos (pop.) burglar, house-breaker

revolcar to knock down/over
▶ revolcar a alg. (fig., fam.) (opponent): to tear to pieces/shreds (fig., fam.), to wipe the floor with (fam.) ◆ *Los revolcó en el último debate.* He wiped the floor with them in the last debate.

revolcarse to roll about (Br.E.), to roll around
▶ revolcarse en algo (fig., fam.) to harp on [about] s.th. (fig., fam.)
▶ revolcarse de la risa (fam.) to roll around laughing or with laughter, to roll in the aisles [with laughter]

el rey king
▶ en tiempos del rey que rabió o del rey Wamba (fig., fam.) donkey's years ago
▷ tiempos de **Maricastaña**
▶ ser del tiempo del rey que rabió o del rey Wamba (cuento/chiste/etc.) (fig., fam.) (custom/story/joke/etc.): to be out of the Ark (fig.), to be old chestnuts (fam.), to be old hat (fam.)
▶ Hablando del rey de Roma [y él que se asoma o por la puerta asoma]. Speak/talk of the devil [and he's sure to appear]. Talk of angels!
▶ no temer rey ni roque to know no fear
▶ no quitar ni poner rey (fig.) not to interfere, to remain neutral
▶ tirar con pólvora del rey (fig.) to work with s.o. else's or with other people's means
▷ rey (en tierra de **ciego**s el tuerto es ~)
▷ rey (**sota**, caballo y ~)
▷ rey (tratar/atender a alg. a **cuerpo** de ~)

rezar (text): to read, to run
▶ [no] rezar con (fig., fam.) [not] to apply to, [not] to be s.o.'s thing (fam.), [not] to like, [not] to appeal to, to be in or out of keeping with, to be right up s.o.'s alley (Am.E.) or street (Br.E.) (fam.) ◆ *Esto reza conmigo. This appeals to me. I like this. This is right up my alley/street.* ◆ *Eso no reza con nosotros. That doesn't apply to us.* ◆ *Su estilo de vida no reza con su creencia. His lifestyle is out of keeping with his belief.*
▷ rezar (en menos que se reza un **padrenuestro**)

la ricura (fam.) pretty girl

la rienda rein
▶ dar rienda suelta a algo (fig.) to give free rein to s.th. (fig.), to let off steam (fig.) ◆ *Dio rienda suelta a su imaginación. He gave free rein to his imagination. He let his imagination run free or run wild.* ◆ *Di rienda suelta a mi ira. I let off steam.*
▶ llevar/tener las riendas (fig.) to have things under control, to be in charge, to be in control
▶ aflojar las riendas (fig.) to loosen/slacken the reins (fig.), to let up (fam.)
▶ sujetar/templar las riendas (fig.) to tighten the reins (fig.)
▶ tomar/coger/empuñar las riendas (fig.) to take charge

el rigor severity, toughness
▶ ser el rigor de las desdichas (fig., fam.) to be buffeted by fate

el riñón kidney
▶ tener el riñón bien cubierto (fig.) to be well heeled (fam.)
▶ costar un riñón (fig., fam.) to cost a bomb (fam., Br.E.) ▷ costar una **burrada**
▶ echar los riñones (fig., fam.) to slog/sweat one's guts out (fam., Br.E.), to work o.s. to death (fig., fam.) ▷ echar/sudar la **hiel**
▶ tener riñones (fig., fam.) to have courage, to have gumption (fam.), to have guts (fam.), to have pluck (fig.), to have bottle (sl., Br.E.)

la riñonada kidney stew
▶ costar una riñonada (fig., fam.) to cost a bomb (fam., Br.E.) ▷ costar una **burrada**

el río river
▶ pescar en río revuelto (fig.) to fish in troubled waters (fig.)

▶ A río revuelto, ganancia de pescadores. (prov.) There's good fishing in troubled waters. It's an ill wind that blows nobody any good.

▶ Cuando el río suena, agua lleva o piedras trae. (prov.) Where there's smoke, there's fire. (prov.) There's no smoke without fire. (prov.)

▷ río (de **perdidos**, al ~)

▷ río (no llegar la **sangre** al ~)

el ripio filler, padding (fig.)

▶ no perder ripio (fam.) to miss nothing of what is going on or of what is being said, not to miss any opportunity, not to miss a trick

▶ meter ripio (fam.) to blather (fam.), to drivel (Br.E.), to talk nonsense

la risa laughter, laugh

▶ tomarse algo a risa (fam.) to take/treat s.th. as a joke, to laugh s.th. off, not to take s.th. seriously ♦ *Todo se lo toma a risa. He takes everything as a joke. He doesn't take anything seriously.*

▷ risa (**descoyuntarse/desternillarse** de ~)

▷ risa (**mearse** [de ~])

▷ risa (**perecerse/rajarse/reventar** de ~)

▷ risa (**revolcarse** de la ~)

▷ risa (ser para **morir**se de ~)

▷ robar algo a alg. a **mano** airada

el robo robbery, theft

▶ ser un robo (fig., fam.) to be daylight robbery (fig., fam.), to be a rip-off (fam.)

rodado

▶ venir rodado (fig., fam.) to be just what s.o. needs/needed, to come at just the right time ♦ *El dinero me vino rodado. The money came at just the right time.*

rodar to roll

▶ echarlo todo a rodar (fig., fam.) (a) to mess it all up (fig.), to spoil everything, to gum up the works (fam.) (b) to chuck it all in/up (fam., Br.E.), to throw everything overboard (fig.)

▶ echar a rodar los proyectos de alg. (fig.) to queer s.o.'s pitch (fam., Br.E.), to spike s.o.'s guns (fig., Br.E.), to thwart s.o.'s plans

Rodríguez Rodríguez (a last name)

▶ estar de rodríguez (fig., fam.) to be a grass widower (hum.)

▷ roer (darle a alg. un **hueso** duro de ~)

▷ roer (ser un **hueso** duro de ~)

▷ roer los **zancajo**s a alg.

▷ roerse los **codo**s de hambre

▷ rojo (ponerse ~ como un **cangrejo**)

▷ rojo (ponerse más ~ que una **amapola**)

▷ Roma (hablando del **rey/ruin** de ~ [y ...])

romper to break

▶ ¡Rompe de una vez! (fig., pop.) [Come on,] out with it! Spit it out! (fam.)

▷ romper el **bautismo**/las **bolas**/los **cascos**/la **crisma** a alg.

▷ romper una **lanza** por algo/alg.

▷ romperse los **cascos**/los **codos**/la **crisma**/el **culo**

▷ roncar como un **tronco**

rondar to patrol

▶ rondar por los cuarenta/etc. (fig., fam.) to be about/around 40/etc.

roñoso mangy, dirty

▶ roñoso (fig., fam.) stingy, miserly, tight (fam.)

▶ no dejarse llamar roñoso (pop.) to be generous, s.o. doesn't want it to be said that he's stingy

la ropa clothes

▶ ¡Hay ropa tendida! (fig., fam.) Be careful what you say, we can be heard or walls have ears!

▶ tentarse la ropa (fig.) to think [it over] long and hard [before doing anything]

▶ La ropa sucia se lava en casa. (fig.) You shouldn't wash your dirty linen in public. (fig.)

▷ ropa ([**nadar** y] guardar la ~)

▷ ropa (querer **nadar** y guardar la ~)

el roque (chess): castle, rook

▶ estar roque (fig., fam.) to be fast asleep

▶ quedarse roque (fig., fam.) to fall soundly asleep

▷ roque (no temer **rey** ni ~)

la rosa rose

▶ No hay rosa[s] sin espinas. (prov.) There's no rose without a thorn. (prov.)

▶ verlo todo de color de rosa (fig.) to see everything/things or the world through rose-tinted spectacles (Br.E.) or through rose-colored glasses (Am.E.) (fig.), to be ridiculously optimistic

▶ la vida no es un lecho de rosas (fig.) life isn't [all/always] a bed of roses (fig.)

▶ estar/dormir sobre un lecho de rosas (fig.) s.o.'s life is a bed of roses (fig.)

▶ no estar/dormir sobre un lecho de rosas (fig.) s.o.'s life is no bed of roses (fig.)

el rosario rosary

▶ acabar como el rosario de la aurora (fig.) to come to a bad end, to end in disaster

▶ un rosario de (fig.) [whole] series of, [whole] string or catalogue of (fig.) ◆ *Nos soltaron un rosario de insultos. They hurled a string of insults at us.*

la rosca thread, ring-shaped roll

▶ pasarse de rosca (fig., fam.) (a) to flip one's lid (fam.), to go ape (fam., Am.E.) (b) to go too far (fig.), to overdo it (fig.), to go over the top (fig., fam.) ◆ *Ahora sí que te has pasado de rosca. Now you've really gone too far.*

▶ hacer la rosca a alg. (fig., fam.) to butter s.o. up (fam.), to soft-soap s.o. (fam.), to play up to s.o.

▶ hacer la rosca [de galgo] (fig., fam.) to get a bit of or some shut-eye (fam.), to hit the hay (fam., Am.E.), to hit the sack (fam.)

▶ hacer la rosca (dog/cat/etc.): to curl up; (snake): to coil up

▶ hacerse una rosca (person): to curl up into a ball

▶ comerse una rosca (fam.) to make it [with a woman] (sl.)

▶ no comerse una rosca [con] (fam.) to get absolutely nowhere [with], not to get anywhere [with] ◆ *No se come una rosca con las mujeres.* He gets absolutely nowhere with women. He never gets anywhere with women.

▶ tirarse una rosca (fam., Esp., universidad) to plough (sl., Br.E., university)

la rosquilla ring-shaped pastry (type of doughnut)

▶ venderse como rosquillas (fig.) to sell like hotcakes (fig.)

▶ no saber a rosquilla (fig., fam.) to be no picnic (fam.), to be no bed of roses (fig.)

▷ rostro (**vestir** el ~ de alegría/gravedad)

el roto hole (in a dress/etc.)

▶ No/nunca falta un roto para un descosido. (prov.) Birds of a feather flock together.

(prov.) You can always find a companion in misfortune.

rozar to touch

▶ rozar los cuarenta/etc. (fig.) to be about/around 40/etc.

▶ rozar [con] algo (fig.) to border/verge on s.th. (fig.), to be next door to s.th. (fig.) ◆ *Eso roza la frescura. That borders on cheek.* ◆ *Eso ya roza con el delirio. That is verging on madness. That's next door to madness.*

▶ rozarse con alg. (fig., fam.) to rub shoulders with s.o. (fig.), to hobnob with s.o.

la rubia blonde

▶ la rubia de frasco/bote (fam.) peroxide blonde (fam.)

▶ la rubia (fig., fam.) peseta (coin)

el Rubicón Rubicon

▶ pasar/atravesar el Rubicón (fig.) to cross the Rubicon (fig.)

la rueda wheel

▶ ir/marchar sobre ruedas (fig.) to run on oiled wheels (fig.), to go/run smoothly, to go swimmingly (fig.), to go like clockwork (fig.), to come on a treat (fig.) ◆ *Todo marcha sobre ruedas. Everything's going smoothly. Everything's coming on a treat. Everything's hunky-dory. (fam.)*

▷ rueda (**comulgar** con ~s de molino)

▷ rueda (meter un **bastón/palo** en la ~ o bastones/palos en las ~s [de alg.])

▷ rueda (no **comulgar** con ~s de molino)

▷ rueda (**tragar**[se]las como ~s de molino)

el ruido noise

▶ Mucho ruido y pocas nueces. (prov.) Much ado about nothing.

▶ quitarse de ruidos (fig.) to keep out of trouble

▷ ruido (▷ **taladrar**: ser un ~ que taladra [los oídos])

el ruin mean person

▶ Hablando del ruin de Roma [y él que se asoma o por la puerta asoma]. Speak/talk of the devil [and he's sure to appear]. Talk of angels!

la ruina ruin

▶ las ruinas (fig., fam.) leftovers

▷ ruso (la **cafetera** [rusa])

S

la sábana sheet (bed)
- ▶ la sábana (pop., Esp.) 1000-peseta bill (Am.E.) or note (Br.E.)
- ▶ pegársele a alg. las sábanas (fig., fam.) to be bad about getting up, to oversleep ◆ *Otra vez se les han pegado las sábanas. They have overslept again.*
- ▶ ponerse más blanco que una sábana to go as white as a sheet/ghost
- ▷ sábana (estirar la **pierna** más larga que la ~)

el sabañón chilblain
- ▶ comer como un sabañón (fig., fam.) to eat like a horse (fam.)
- ▶ comer más que un sabañón (fig., fam.) to be a glutton

saber to taste
- ▶ saber a más (fig.) to hope there's more where that came from (fam.), to taste excellent
- ▷ saber (no ~ a **rosquilla**)
- ▷ saber a **gloria/rayo**s

saber to know
- ▶ saberlas todas o muy largas (fig., fam.) to know every trick in the book (fam.), to be as sly as they come (fam.)
- ▶ no saber de sí (fig., fam.) s.o. can't take/have a breather (fam.), to be snowed under with work (fig.)
- ▶ ¡Si lo sabré yo! I know it only too well! Don't I know it!
- ▶ ¡Qué sé yo! How should I know! Search me! (fam.)
- ▶ y qué sé yo (fam.) (after enumerations): and many other things, and what not, and who knows what else (fam.) ◆ *Tiene cinco coches, dos yates, tres casas y qué sé yo. He has five cars, two yachts, three houses and who knows what else.*
- ▶ el señor no sé cuántos (fam.) Mr. What's-his-name (fam.), Mr. So-and-so (fam.)
- ▷ saber (▷ **gastar**: ya ~ cómo las gasta alg.)
- ▷ saber [mucho] **latín**
- ▷ saber (no ~ a qué **santo** encomendarse)
- ▷ saber (no ~ ni **jota/papa/patata** de algo)
- ▷ saber (no ~ [ni] la **cartilla**)

- ▷ saber algo al **dedillo**/de buena **tinta**
- ▷ saber cuántas son **cinco**
- ▷ saber de qué **pie** cojea alg.
- ▷ saber la **biblia** en verso
- ▷ saber más que **Briján/Lepe/siete**
- ▷ saber un **rato** [largo] de algo

el saber knowledge
- ▶ El saber no ocupa lugar. (prov.) One can never know too much.

la sabiduría wisdom, knowledge
- ▶ la sabiduría no llega a más to be at one's wits' end, to be at a complete loss as to what to do [next] ◆ *Mi sabiduría no llega a más. I'm at my wits' end.*

sabio wise
- ▶ ser más sabio que Salomón (fig.) to be wiser than Solomon (fig.), to be as wise as an owl (fam.)

el sabio wise/learned man
- ▶ Es de sabios el callar. (prov.) A still tongue makes a wise head. (prov.)
- ▶ Es de sabios cambiar de opinión. (prov.) Only a fool never changes his mind. (prov.)

el sablazo slash with a sword
- ▶ dar un sablazo a alg. (fig., fam.) to tap (Am.E.) or touch (Br.E.) s.o. for money (fam.), to hit on s.o. for money (fam., Am.E.)
- ▶ vivir de sablazos (fig., fam.) to live by sponging (fam.)

el sabor taste, flavor
- ▶ dejar a alg. [con] mal sabor de boca (fig.) to leave a bad or nasty taste in one's mouth (fig.) ◆ *Ese asunto del divorcio me dejó con mal sabor de boca. That divorce business left a bad taste in my mouth.*
- ▷ sacacorcho (**sacar** algo a alg. con ~s)

el sacamantas (fam.) tax collector

el/la sacamuelas (fam., hum.) tooth-puller (fam.)
- ▶ mentir más que un sacamuelas (fam.) to tell huge lies, to lie through one's teeth (fam.)

▶ hablar más que un sacamuelas (fam.) s.o. wouldn't stop talking ▷ hablar más que una **cotorra**

sacar to take out, to pull out
▶ sacar algo a alg. con pinzas o con sacacorchos o con tirabuzón (fig., fam.) *to drag/winkle (Br.E.) s.th. out of s.o. (fig.)* ◆ *Tuvimos que sacarles la verdad con pinzas. We had to drag/winkle the truth out of them.* ◆ *No pudimos sacarle el secreto ni con tirabuzón. We couldn't drag the secret out of him. He kept mum.* ◆ *No se lo van a sacar ni con sacacorchos. Wild horses won't drag it out of him. He'll keep mum.*
▶ sacar a alg. de un apuro (fam.) to get s.o. out of a jam/fix (fam.), to get s.o. out of a tight spot (fam.), to bail s.o. out (fig.)
▷ sacar a alg. de las **garras** de alg.
▷ sacar a alg. de sus **casillas**
▷ sacar el **jugo** a algo/alg.
▷ sacar **tajada**
▷ sacarse algo de la **manga**

el saco sack
▶ el saco (pop.) 1000-peseta bill (Am.E.) or note (Br.E.)
▶ medio saco (pop.) 500-peseta bill (Am.E.) or note (Br.E.)
▶ echar algo en saco roto (fig., fam.) to cast s.th. to the winds, to ignore s.th., to disregard s.th. ◆ *Echaron mis consejos en saco roto.* They cast my advice to the winds.
▶ no echar algo en saco roto (fig., fam.) to take s.th. to heart, to heed s.th. ◆ *No echaron mis consejos en saco roto.* They took my advice to heart.
▷ sacristán (los **dineros** del ~ cantando se vienen y cantando se van)
▷ sacudir el **bulto/polvo** a alg.
▷ sacudir el **yugo**

sagrado holy
▶ jurar por lo más sagrado [que ...] to swear by all that is holy [that . . .], to swear to God [that . . .], to swear black and blue [that . . .] (fam.) ◆ *Juro por lo más sagrado. I swear to God. Cross my heart and hope to die. (fam.)*

la sal salt
▶ la sal (fig.) (a) wit, wittiness, quick-wittedness (b) charm, grace[fulness] ◆ *Tiene mucha sal. He's a great wit. He's very amusing.* ◆ *¡Mira qué sal tiene para moverse!*

Look how gracefully she moves! She's a real mover! (fam.)
▶ deshacerse como la sal en el agua (plan/hopes/etc.): to go [quickly] up in smoke, to come [quickly] to nothing ◆ *Sus planes se deshicieron como la sal en el agua. His plans went quickly up in smoke.*
▶ ¡Sal quiere el huevo! (fig., fam.) He/she/etc. seeks recognition.
▷ sal (tomar algo con un **grano** de ~)
▷ salchicha (el **perro** ~)

salir to come out, to go out, to leave
▶ salir con alg. (fig.) to go [steady] with s.o. (fam.), to date s.o. (fam.)
▶ salir con algo (fig., fam.) to come out with s.th. (fam.)
▶ salir a volar (fig.) to become known to the public ◆ *Sus maquinaciones salieron a volar. Their machinations became known to the public.*
▶ salirle algo a alg. caro (fig.) to pay dearly for s.th. (fam.) ◆ *Esta bobada te va a salir cara. You'll pay dearly for the stupid thing you've done.*
▶ salir a alg. (fam.) to give s.o. the boot (fam.), to fire s.o. (fam.) ◆ *Les salieron. They were fired.*
▶ salirse del tema to digress from the subject, to wander from the point
▶ salga lo que salga/saliere come what may, whatever turns up, at all events, regardless of the consequences ◆ *Lo haremos, salga lo que salga. We'll do it, no matter how it turns out or regardless of the consequences.*
▷ salir (~sele a alg. los **ojo**s de las órbitas)
▷ salir algo **corriente** y moliente
▷ salir de **levante**
▷ salirse de sus **casillas**

la saliva saliva
▶ gastar saliva (fig.) to waste one's breath (fig.) ◆ *No puedes convencernos. No gastes saliva. You can't persuade us. You're wasting your breath.* ◆ *Nadie estaba escuchando. Gastaste saliva. Nobody was listening. You were wasting your breath.*
▶ tragar saliva (fig.) to swallow one's anger/feelings, to swallow hard (fig.)
▷ Salomón (ser más **sabio** que ~)

la salsa sauce
▶ la salsa de San Bernardo (fig.) hunger

▶ estar en su [propia] salsa (fig.) to be in one's element ◆ *Los niños salieron corriendo a retozar en la piscina. Allí están en su propia salsa.* The children dashed off for a romp in the swimming pool. There they are in their element[s].

▶ cocerse en su propia salsa (fig.) to stew in one's own juice (fig.)

▶ dejar a alg. cocer en su propia salsa (fig.) to let s.o. stew in his own juice (fig.) ◆ *Varias veces te he echado un cable. Esta vez te dejo cocer en tu propia salsa.* I've bailed you out several times. This time I let you stew in your own juice.

▶ poner a alg. hecho una salsa (fig., pop.) (a) to give s.o. a good thrashing (fam.) (b) to give s.o. a good roasting (fam.)

saltar to jump, to leap, to hop

▶ estar al que salte (fig., pop.) s.o. (girl/woman) can't find a man

▶ estar a la que salta (fig.) to watch out for an opportunity, to look for an opening, to wait for the right opportunity

▷ saltar (~sele a alg. los **ojos** de las órbitas)

▷ saltar a la **cara** a alg.

▷ saltar sobre la propia **sombra**

la salud health

▶ ¡Salud! (fam.) Cheers! Here's to you! Mud in your eye! (fam.)

▶ ¡Salud, amor y pesetas! (fam., Esp.) Here's to health, wealth and love! Mud in your eye! (fam.)

▶ beber a la salud de alg. (fam.) to drink to the health of s.o.

▶ vender/prestar salud (fam.) to be bursting/brimming with health (fig.), to be/look a picture of health (fig., fam.), to be in the pink (fig.)

▷ salud (**rebosar** de ~)

▷ salvar el **pellejo**

▷ salvar el **pellejo** a alg.

salvarse to save o.s.

▶ ¡Sálvese quien pueda! Every man for himself!

▷ salvarse en una **tabla**

▷ salvarse por el **canto** de un duro

el salvohonor (hum.) posterior (euph.), behind (fam., euph.), backside (fam.), bottom (fam.), butt (fam., Am.E.), bum (fam., Br.E.)

el sambenito (histórico) sanbenito

▶ echar el sambenito a alg. (fig.) to pass the buck to s.o. (fam.) ▷ cargar el **baúl** a alg.

▶ colgar el sambenito a alg. (fig.) to brand s.o. (fam.), to label s.o. (fig.) ◆ *Le colgaron el sambenito de comunista.* They branded him [as] a communist. ◆ *Me colgaron el sambenito de estafador.* They labeled me [as] a con man.

▷ San Bernardo (la **salsa** de ~)

▷ San Fernando (ir/venir en el **coche** de ~)

▷ San Francisco (ir/venir en el **caballo/coche** de ~)

sangrar to bleed

▶ estar sangrando algo (fig., fam.) (a) to be still very fresh, to be very new still (b) to be obvious

la sangre blood

▶ sudar sangre to sweat blood

▶ escupir sangre (fig., fam.) to lay/put much emphasis on one's being blue-blooded

▶ estar chorreando sangre algo (fig., fam.) to be still very fresh, to be very new still

▶ tener sangre blanca o sangre de horchata en las venas (fig., fam.) to be as cold as a fish (fig.), to be [as] cold as marble (fig.), to be stone cold (fam.)

▶ tener la sangre gorda (fig.) to be very phlegmatic

▶ tener sangre de chinches (fig., fam.) to be a real pest (fig.), to be an extremely annoying individual/person

▶ tener sangre en el ojo (fig., fam.) to want to get/take one's revenge, s.o. can't wait to get his own back (fam.), to bear a grudge

▶ no llegar la sangre al río (fig., fam.) ◆ *No creemos que llegue la sangre al río.* We don't think it'll be too disastrous. ◆ *No llegará la sangre al río.* It won't be or it isn't as bad as all that. ◆ *Afortunadamente no llegó la sangre al río.* Fortunately it wasn't too disastrous or [quite] that bad or as bad as all that.

▶ chupar la sangre a alg. (fig., fam.) to bleed s.o. [white/dry] (fam.), to suck s.o. dry (fig.), to exploit s.o. (fig.)

▶ bullirle a alg. la sangre en las venas (fig.) to be bursting with energy or with [youthful] vigor (fig.), to be full of energy or of [youthful] vigor

▶ subírsele a alg. la sangre a la cabeza (fig.) to see red, s.o.'s blood gets up (fig.)

▶ freír la sangre a alg. (fig.) to rile s.o. (fam.), to needle s.o. (fam.)

▶ encender/quemar la sangre a alg. (fig., fam.) to make s.o.'s blood boil (fig.), to infuriate s.o.

▶ helársele a alg. la sangre [en las venas] (fig.) s.o.'s blood runs cold or freezes (fig.) ◆ *Si te contase las cosas horribles que pasaron se te helaría la sangre. If I told you the horrible things that happened your blood would run cold.*

▶ bajársele a alg. la sangre a los talones (fig.) to be scared stiff (fam.), to be scared to death (fam.), to be petrified or paralyzed with fear/horror (fig.) ◆ *Se les bajó la sangre a los talones. They were scared stiff.*

▷ sangre (a **fuego** y ~)

▷ sangre (**cebar**se en la ~)

▷ sangre (la **letra** con ~ entra)

▷ sangre (no quedarle a alg. **gota** de ~ en las venas)

▷ sangre (poner algo a **fuego** y ~)

San Martín Saint Martin

▶ llegarle a alg. su San Martín (fig.) to meet one's Waterloo (fig.)

▶ A cada cerdo/puerco le llega su San Martín. (prov.) Everyone gets his comeuppance sooner or later. (fam.) Everyone gets his just deserts sooner or later. Everyone comes to his day of reckoning.

▷ San Miguel (encender una **vela** a ~ y otra al diablo)

sano healthy

▶ cortar por lo sano (fig.) to take drastic action or extreme measures, to strike right at the root of the trouble, to make a clean break (fig.)

▶ estar más sano que una manzana (fig.) to be as fit as a fiddle

San Quintín Saint Quentin

▶ costar la de San Quintín (fig.) to cost a bomb (fam., Br.E.) ▷ costar una **burrada**

▶ armar la de San Quintín (fig.) to kick up an almighty row (fam.), to kick up an incredible rumpus (fam.), to raise hell (fam.) ◆ *Se armó la de San Quintín. All hell broke loose. There was an almighty row.* ◆ *Se va a armar la de San Quintín. There will be an almighty row or an incredible rumpus.*

sanseacabó (fam.) [and] that's that, [and] that's the end of it ◆ *Lo harás así porque te lo digo yo y sanseacabó. You will do it like that because I say so and that's that.*

▷ Santa María (para alg. no hay más **Dios** [ni ~] que ...)

santísimo most holy

▶ hacer la santísima (fig., pop.) to kick up a row (fam.)

▶ hacer la santísima a alg. (fig., fam.) to drive s.o. up the wall (fam.), to drive s.o. spare (fam., Br.E.)

santo; el santo holy; saint

▶ todo el santo día (fig., fam.) all the livelong day, the whole livelong or blessed day, the whole day long ◆ *Estuvo nevando todo el santo día. It was snowing all the livelong day.*

▶ hacer su santa voluntad (fig., fam.) to do exactly as one pleases, to have one's [own] way [at all costs]

▶ dormirse como un santo to fall soundly asleep

▶ llegar y besar el santo (fig.) to pull it off at the first attempt (fam.)

▶ alzarse/salirse con el santo y la limosna/cera (fig., fam.) to clear off with the whole lot (fam.), to make off with the whole thing

▶ desnudar/desvestir a un santo para vestir otro to rob Peter to pay Paul ◆ *Quiere tomar un préstamo para pagar sus deudas. Eso equivaldría a desnudar a un santo para vestir otro. He wants to take out a loan to pay [off] his debts. That would be robbing Peter to pay Paul.*

▶ quedarse para vestir santos (fig., fam.) (girl/woman): to be left on the shelf (fig.)

▶ írsele a alg. el santo al cielo (fig.) to dry up (in speech/etc.) (fam.), to forget what one was about to say or do

▶ no saber a qué santo encomendarse (fam.) not to know which way to turn (fig., fam.), to be at one's wits' end, to be at the end of one's rope or one's tether (Br.E.) (fig.)

▶ tener el santo de espaldas (fam.) to have bad luck

▶ tener el santo de cara (fam.) to be lucky, to be in luck

▶ poder hacer perder la paciencia a un santo even a saint can lose his patience with s.o. ◆ *Ese tío podría hacer perder la paciencia a un santo. Even a saint could lose his patience with that guy.*

▶ No es santo de mi devoción. (fam.) He's/she's not my type. (fam.) He's/she's not my cup of tea. (fam., Br.E.)
▷ santo (**comer**se los ~s)
▷ santo (rogar a **Dios** por ~s mas no por tantos)
▷ santo (tener más **paciencia** que un ~)
▷ Santo Tomás (**una** y no más, ~)

el sapo toad
▶ echar sapos y culebras (fig., fam.) to eff and blind (fam., Br.E.), to curse and swear, to rant and rave
▶ pisar el sapo (fig.) to get up late

el saque serve or service (tennis)
▶ tener buen saque (fig., fam.) (a) to be a good trencherman, to eat heartily (b) (drinking): s.o. can really down the stuff (fam.)

el sarasa (pop.) (gay): queer/fairy/faggot (sl., pej.), pansy (fam., pej.), queen (sl.), poof[ter] (sl., pej., Br.E.), fag (sl., pej., Am.E.), arse bandit (vulg., Br.E.)
▷ sardina (arrimar el **ascua** a su ~)

la sargentona (fam.) tough mannish woman, butch (fam.)

la sarna scabies
▶ ser más viejo que la sarna (fig., fam.) to be as old as the hills (fig.), to be as old as Methuselah (fig.)

la sarta series
▶ una sarta de (fig., fam.) [whole] series of, [whole] string or catalogue of (fig.) ◆ *una sarta de mentiras a string/pack of lies* ◆ *una sarta de disparates a load/pack of nonsense or rubbish (Br.E.) (fam.)* ◆ *Nos soltaron una sarta de insultos. They hurled a string of insults at us.*

la sartén frying pan
▶ saltar/caer de la sartén y dar en la brasa to jump out of the frying pan into the fire ◆ *Atracó un banco para pagar sus deudas. Saltó de la sartén y dio en la brasa. He held up a bank to pay [off] his debts. He jumped out of the frying pan into the fire.*
▶ tener la sartén por el mango (fig., fam.) to have things under control, to be the boss (fig.)
▷ sastre (**cajón** de ~)

el Satán Satan
▶ darse a Satán (fig., fam.) to get terribly angry

el Satanás Satan
▶ darse a Satanás (fig., fam.) to get terribly angry

el sayo smock
▶ cortar un sayo a alg. (fig., fam.) to talk behind s.o.'s back (fig.), to gossip about s.o.
▷ sayo (hacer de su **capa** un ~)

seco dry
▶ estar más seco que una pasa (fig., fam.) to be very skinny, to be as thin as a rake (fig.)
▶ quedar seco (fig., fam.) to suddenly die, to drop dead
▶ dejar seco a alg. (fig., fam.) to kill s.o. stonedead (fam.)
▷ sed (**abrasarse** de ~)

la seda silk
▶ ir/marchar como una seda (fig., fam.) to go very smoothly, to go swimmingly (fig.), to go like a dream, to go like clockwork (fig.)
▶ estar como una seda (fig., fam.) to be very sweet-tempered, to be as meek as a lamb (fig.)
▶ hacer seda (fig., fam.) to sleep, to kip (fam.)
▷ seda (aunque la **mona** se vista de ~, mona se queda)
▷ seda (tratar a alg. con **guante** de ~)

las seguidillas (fig., fam.) diarrhea, runs (fam., Br.E.), trots (fam.), shits (vulg.), Montezuma's revenge (hum.)
▷ seguro (ser tan ~ como el **evangelio**)
▷ sello del **estómago**
▷ selva (la **ley** de la ~)

la semana week
▶ en la semana que no tenga jueves o de tres jueves (fig., fam.) when pigs learn to fly (iron.), in a month of Sundays (fam.), in a coon's age (sl., Am.E.), never ◆ *Pagarán en la semana que no tenga jueves. They'll pay when pigs learn to fly. They'll never pay.* ◆ *A este paso terminarán el trabajo en la semana de tres jueves. At this rate they'll never finish the job or they won't finish the job in a month of Sundays.*
▷ semana (el **hambre** de tres ~s)

sembrar to sow
▶ sembrar en la arena (fig.) to build on sand (fig.) ◆ *Esta inversión es demasiado insegura. No siembro en la arena. This investment is too insecure. I don't build on sand.*
▷ sembrar (▷ **cosechar**: se cosecha lo que se siembra)
▷ sembrar (**cosechar** lo que uno ha sembrado)

la senda path
▶ seguir la senda trillada (fig.) to keep to the beaten track (fig.)
▷ seno (criar la **víbora** en el ~)

sentado sitting
▶ estar bien sentado (fig., fam.) to be firmly in the saddle (fig.), to hold a good position
▶ dar algo por sentado (fig.) to take s.th. for granted, to assume s.th. ◆ *Están dando demasiado por sentado. They're taking too much for granted.*

sentar to suit, to fit
▶ sentar bien a alg. (fig., fam.) to serve s.o. right ◆ *Te sienta bien. It serves you right.*

el sentido sense, meaning
▶ el sexto sentido (fig., fam.) sixth sense (fig.)
▶ costar un sentido o los cinco sentidos (fig., fam.) to cost the earth (fig., fam., Br.E.)
▷ costar una **burrada**
▶ poner sus cinco sentidos en algo (fig.) to give one's whole/full attention to s.th. ◆ *Pongo mis cinco sentidos en el trabajo. My heart's in my work.*
▷ sentirse como **gallina** en corral ajeno
▷ señal (con [todos sus] **pelo**s y ~es)
▷ séptimo **cielo** (estar en el ~)
▷ sepultura (**genio** y figura hasta la ~)

señor (fam., adj.) ◆ *un señor vino a wonderful wine* ◆ *una mujer señora a real lady* ◆ *un coche muy señor a really posh car* ◆ *Comí en un restaurante muy señor. I ate in a really posh (fam.) or plush (sl.) restaurant. I ate in a very smart or elegant restaurant.* ◆ *Le dieron una señora paliza. They gave him a terrific or a really good hiding. They beat the living daylights out of him. (fam.) They beat him black and blue. (fam.) They knocked him into the middle of next week. (fam.)*

el señor gentleman, man
▶ a lo gran señor (fig., fam.) ◆ *vivir a lo gran señor to live like a lord/king (fig.)* ◆ *Ayer comimos a lo gran señor. We had an excellent/exquisite meal yesterday.* ◆ *Siempre se viste a lo gran señor. He's always dressed very smart or posh. (fam.)*

ser to be
▶ ser de lo que no hay (fam.) to be incredible (fam.), there's nothing like it ◆ *Esto es de lo que no hay. This is incredible.*
▶ ser muy de alg. (fam.) to be s.o. all over (fam.) ◆ *Eso es muy de ti. That's you all over.*
▶ un sí es no es (fam.) a [little] bit ◆ *Eres un sí es no es irrespetuoso. You're a little bit disrespectful.*
▶ O somos o no somos. (fig., fam.) We have to take action now (it's expected of us). We have to show who we are. (fam.)
▶ Ni están todos los que son, ni son todos los que están. (prov.) Appearances are deceptive. (prov.) You can't always go by appearances.

la serenata serenade
▶ dar la serenata a alg. (fig., fam.) to pester s.o., to get on s.o.'s nerves (fam.)
▷ serio como un **poste**

el sermón sermon
▶ echar un sermón a alg. (fig., fam.) to give s.o. a lecture (fam.), to give s.o. a talking-to (fam.) ◆ *Le eché un sermón por ser irrespetuoso. I gave him a lecture for being disrespectful.*
▷ serpiente (tener una **lengua** de ~)

el serrín sawdust
▶ tener la cabeza llena de serrín (fig., fam.) to have nothing but sawdust in one's head (fig., fam.), to be a blockhead (fam.), to be a numskull (fam.), to be soft in the head (fam.)

servir to serve
▶ para servirle [a usted] at your service
▶ no servir para descalzar a alg. (fig.) not to be a patch on s.o. (fam.), s.o. can't hold a candle to s.o. ◆ *No sirve para descalzar a su hermana. He can't hold a candle to his sister.*
▶ Al que le sirva que se lo ponga. (fig.) If the cap/shoe fits, wear it. (fig.)

el seso brain
▶ el seso (fig.) sense

▶ devanarse/torturarse los sesos (fig., fam.) to rack one's brains (fig., fam.)
▶ hacer perder el seso a alg. (fig., fam.) to turn s.o.'s head (fig.) ◆ *Esa chica hace perder el seso a cada joven. That girl turns every young man's head.*
▶ sorber los sesos a alg. (fig., fam.) ◆ *Esto me sorbe los sesos. This governs/dominates my [way of] thinking completely. (fig.)* ◆ *Sus preocupaciones les estaban sorbiendo los sesos. They were being consumed by their worries. (fig.)* ◆ *Esa chica le tiene sorbido los sesos. He's completely crazy about that girl. (fam.)*
▷ seso (▷ **cocer**: cocérsele a alg. los ~s)
▷ seso (la **cabeza** blanca y el ~ por venir)
▷ seso (levantarle a alg. la **tapa** de los ~s)
▷ seso (levantarse la **tapa** de los ~s)

la seta mushroom
▶ la seta (fig., pop.) (vagina) ▷ el conejo
▶ aparecer o brotar o darse como las setas (fig.) to spring/shoot up like mushrooms (fig.), to mushroom (fig.) ◆ *Hoteles y casinos aparecen como las setas en Las Vegas. Hotels and casinos are springing up like mushrooms in Las Vegas.*

sí yes
▶ un día sí y otro también (fam.) day in, day out
▶ un día sí y otro no every other day
▷ sí (▷ **ser**: un ~ es no es)

el sierrahuesos (fam., pej.) (bad surgeon): butcher (fig., pej.)

siete seven
▶ más que siete (fig., fam.) ◆ *comer más que siete* to pig out *(fam., Am.E.)*, to make a pig of o.s. *(fam.)* ◆ *beber más que siete* to drink like a fish *(fam.)* ◆ *hablar más que siete* to talk nineteen to the dozen *(fam., Br.E.)*, to talk a mile a minute *(fam., Am.E.)* ◆ *saber más que siete* to be very clever/smart, to be a real smart alec[k]/Alec[k] *(fam.)* or clever dick/Dick *(sl., Br.E.) (pej.)*, to be a know-[it-]all *(fam.)*, to be a wise guy *(fam.)*
▷ siete (de ~ **suela**s)
▷ siete (tener ~ **vida**s [como los gatos])

el siglo century
▶ ir con el siglo (fig.) to move with the time

la silla chair
▶ de silla a silla (fig., fam.) in private ◆ *¿Podemos hablar de silla a silla? Can we talk in private?*
▶ mover la silla para que caiga alg. (fig.) to pull the rug out from under s.o. (fig.) ◆ *Movieron la silla para que cayésemos. They pulled the rug out from under us.*

la sinhueso (fam., hum.) tongue
▶ darle a la sinhueso to gas (fam.), to yack (fam.), to yap (fam.), to shoot the breeze/bull (fam., Am.E.)
▶ soltar la sinhueso to shoot one's mouth off (fam.), to talk (fam.), to come out with it, to spill the beans (sl.), to spit it [all] out (fam.) ◆ *¡Suelta la sinhueso! [Come on,] out with it! Spit it out!*
▷ siniestro (a **diestro** y ~/a diestra y siniestra)

el sitio place
▶ dejar a alg. en el sitio (fam.) to kill s.o. on the spot
▶ quedarse en el sitio (fam.) to die on the spot, to die instantly, to drop dead ◆ *Tuvieron un accidente de automóvil y se quedaron en el sitio. They died on the spot or instantly in a car accident.* ◆ *Le dio un infarto [de miocardio] y se quedó en el sitio. She dropped dead of a heart attack.*
▶ poner a alg. en su sitio (fig., fam.) to put s.o. in his place (fig.), to cut s.o. down to size (fig.)
▶ poner las cosas en su sitio (fig.) to set the record straight
▶ tener que ir a un sitio (fig., euph.) s.o. must just [go and] pay a visit (euph., Br.E.) ◆ *Tengo que ir a un sitio. I must just go and pay a visit.*
▷ sitio (tener la **cabeza**/el **corazón** en su ~)

la soba kneading
▶ dar [una] soba a alg. (fig., fam.) (a) to give s.o. a beating, to give s.o. a walloping (fam.), to give s.o. a hiding (fam.) (b) to give s.o. a wigging (fam., Br.E.), to give s.o. a telling-off (fam.)

sobresaliente jutting out, projecting
▶ sobresaliente (fig.) outstanding (fig.), excellent
▶ sobresaliente con tres eses (fam., hum.) (exam): failed, flunked (fam., Am.E.)

▷ sobrino (mirar con **ojo**s de ~)

▷ sociedad (la **flor** y nata de la ~)

la sofrenada jerk on the reins

▶ la sofrenada (fig., fam.) ticking-off (fam., Br.E.), roasting (fam.)

sofrenar to rein back sharply

▶ sofrenar a alg. (fig., fam.) to give s.o. a ticking-off (fam., Br.E.), to give s.o. a roasting (fam.)

la soga rope

▶ estar con la soga al cuello (fig., fam.) to be in an awful or in a real jam/fix (fam.), to be in a very tight spot (fam.)

▶ traer/llevar la soga arrastrando (fig., fam.) to live in constant fear of punishment

▶ echar la soga tras el caldero (fig.) to throw in the towel/sponge (fig.), to throw in one's hand (fig.), to chuck it all in/up (fam., Br.E.), to throw good money after bad ◆ *Probemos al menos una vez más. Es demasiado prematuro echar la soga tras el caldero. Let's try at least one more time. It's too early/soon to throw in the towel.*

▶ dar soga a alg. (fig., fam.) (a) to make fun of s.o. (b) to encourage s.o. to talk, to let s.o. ride his hobby-horse (fig.)

▶ hablar de o mentar o nombrar la soga en casa del ahorcado (fig.) to say s.th. very/singularly inappropriate, to say s.th. that is quite uncalled-for

▶ No hay que hablar de o mentar o nombrar la soga en casa del ahorcado. (fig.) Don't talk of ropes in the house of a man who was hanged. (fig.) There's a time and a place for everything.

el sol sun

▶ de sol a sol from morning to/till evening, from sunrise to/till sunset

▶ salga el sol por Antequera o por donde quiera (fig.) whatever happens, come what may ◆ *Lo haré y salga el sol por donde quiera. I'll do it, whatever happens.*

▶ ser más claro que el sol (fig., fam.) to be as clear as daylight (fig.), to be as clear/plain as day, to be as plain as the nose on your face, to be as plain as a pikestaff (Br.E.) ◆ *Lo que dijo fue más claro que el sol. What he said was as clear as daylight.*

▶ arrimarse al sol que más calienta (fig., fam.) to be an opportunist, to climb on the bandwagon (fam.), to know which side one's bread is buttered (fig.)

▶ no dejar a alg. [ni] a sol ni a sombra (fig.) not to give s.o. a minute's rest or a moment's peace, to breathe down s.o.'s neck (fam.), to chase s.o. around

▶ meter a alg. donde no vea el sol (fig.) to clap s.o. in jail (fam.), to put s.o. in clink (sl.), to put s.o. in the slammer (sl.), to put s.o. behind bars (fig.), to put s.o. inside (fam.)

▷ sol (no hay nada **nuevo** bajo el ~)

solemne solemn

▶ solemne (fam.) ◆ *una solemne tontería an extremely stupid thing [to do]* ◆ *¡Qué solemne desfachatez! What an incredible cheek/nerve! (fam.)* ◆ *Es una solemne mentira. It's a downright/an absolute lie.* ◆ *Cometieron una solemne falta. They made a huge/terrible mistake.* ◆ *Dijo solemnes disparates. He talked utter nonsense. He made extremely stupid remarks.*

la soleta sole

▶ dar soleta a alg. (fig., fam.) to chuck/kick s.o. out (fam.)

▶ tomar soleta (fam.) to beat it (sl.), to clear off (fam.)

la solfa singing practice, solfa

▶ tocar la o dar una solfa a alg. (fig., fam.) to give s.o. a hiding or tanning or thrashing (fam.)

▶ poner algo en solfa (fig., fam.) to turn s.th. into ridicule, to make fun of s.th., to poke fun at s.th.

▶ poner a alg. en solfa (fig., fam.) to make s.o. look ridiculous, to hold s.o. up to ridicule/mockery, to make a monkey [out] of s.o. (hum.)

▷ solo (más ~ que un **hongo**)

la sombra shadow

▶ estar a la sombra (fig., fam.) to be in jail, to be in clink (sl.), to be in the slammer (sl.), to be in the can (sl., Am.E.), to be behind bars (fig.), to be inside (fam.), to do bird (sl., Br.E.), to do time (fam.) ◆ *Estuvo/pasó dos años a la sombra. He did two years bird. He did two years inside.*

▶ poner a alg. a la sombra (fig., fam.) to clap s.o. in jail (fam.) ▷ meter a alg. donde no vea el **sol**

▶ **tener buena sombra (fig., fam.)** (a) to be lucky (b) to be lik[e]able, to be nice, to make a good impression

▶ **tener mala sombra (fig., fam.)** (a) to be unlucky (b) to be an unpleasant character, to make a bad impression, to be a nasty piece of work (fig., fam.)

▶ **saltar sobre la propia sombra (fig.)** to overcome o.s.

▶ **desconfiar hasta de su sombra (fig.)** not to even trust one's own shadow, to be extremely distrustful ◆ *Desconfía hasta de su sombre. He doesn't even trust his own shadow.*

▶ **hacer sombra a alg. (fig.)** to put s.o. in the shade (fig.), to overshadow s.o. (fig.), to outshine s.o. (fig.), to upstage s.o. (fig.) ◆ *Uno de los jugadores de ajedrez hizo sombra a todos los otros. One of the chess players put all the others in the shade.*

▶ **ser la sombra de alg. (fig.)** to follow s.o. [around] like a shadow

▶ **no ser [ni] sombra de lo que era/etc. (fig.)** to be a [mere] shadow of one's former self (fig.) ◆ *No eres ni sombra de lo que eras. You're a mere shadow of your former self.*

▶ **ni sombra de (fig.)** ◆ *no tener ni sombra de vergüenza* not to have an ounce of shame (fig.), not to have the least bit of shame ◆ *no tener ni sombra de valor* not to have an ounce of courage (fig.), not to have the least bit of courage ◆ *Esto no tiene ni sombra de verdad. There's not a grain of truth in this. (fig.) This is absolutely false.*

▶ **sin sombra de duda** without a shadow of [a] doubt (fig.)

el sombrajo shelter from the sun

▶ **caérsele a alg. los palos del sombrajo (fig., fam.)** s.o.'s heart sinks [into his boots] ◆ *Se me cayeron los palos del sombrajo. My heart sank into my boots.*

▶ **hacer sombrajos (fig., fam.)** to block the light/sun, to stand in the light ◆ *¡No me hagas sombrajos! Get out of my/the light! Don't stand in my light!*

sombrear to shade

▶ **ya le sombrea el labio superior a alg. (fig., fam.)** the first down/fuzz is already appearing on s.o.'s upper lip ◆ *Ya te sombrea el labio superior. The first fuzz is already appearing on your upper lip.*

el son sound

▶ **bailar al son que le tocan a alg. (fig., fam.)** (a) to toe the line/mark (b) to adapt/adjust [o.s.] to the circumstances, to roll with the punches (fig.), to trim one's sails to the wind (fig.)

▶ **bailar a cualquier son (fig., fam.)** to be a weathercock (fig.), to be a fickle person, to change one's mind more often than one changes one's underwear (fig., fam., hum.)

▷ **son (hablar sin ton ni ~)**

sonreír to smile

▶ **sonreír de oreja a oreja** to grin like a Cheshire cat

▶ **sonreírle a alg. la suerte o la fortuna (fig.)** fortune smiles upon s.o. (fig.) ◆ *Me sonrió la fortuna. Fortune smiled upon me.*

▶ **sonreírle a alg. el porvenir (fig.)** to have a bright future [ahead] ◆ *El porvenir nos sonríe. We have a bright future.*

sonsacar to get by cunning

▶ **sonsacar algo a alg. (fig.)** to get/worm/coax s.th. out of s.o., to winkle s.th. out of s.o. (fig., Br.E.) ◆ *Es difícil sonsacarle la verdad. It's difficult to get/winkle the truth out of him.* ◆ *Le sonsacamos el secreto. We winkled/wormed the secret out of her.*

la soñación (fam.)

▶ **¡Ni por soñación!** Not on your life! No way! (fam.)

soñar to dream

▶ **¡Ni soñarlo! (fam.)** Not on your life! No way! (fam.) Fat chance! (sl., iron.)

▶ **soñar con + infinitivo (fig.)** to dream of + gerund (fig.) ◆ *Sueño con volver a España. I dream of going back to Spain.*

▶ **soñar con algo/alg.** to dream about s.th./s.o. ◆ *Sueño mucho contigo. I often dream about you.*

la sopa sop

▶ **estar hecho una sopa (fig., fam.)** (a) to be sopping or soaking or dripping wet, to be soaked to the skin (fam.) (b) to be drunk, to be plastered (fam.), to be sloshed (fam.), to be tight (fam.), to be smashed (sl.), to be canned (sl., Br.E.), to be legless (fam., Br.E.)

la sopa soup

▶ **comer la o vivir de la sopa boba (fig., fam.)** to scrounge one's meals (fam.), to live on/off

other people, to live at s.o. else's expense, to sponge a living (fam.)

▷ sopa (buscar **pelos** en la ~)

▷ sopa (del **plato** a la boca se pierde la ~)

la sopapina (fam.) series of slaps in the face
◆ *Le propiné una sopapina. I gave him a series of slaps in the face.*

soplar to blow up/away

▶ soplar algo [a alg.] (fig., fam.) (a) to pinch s.th. (sl., Br.E.), to swipe s.th. (sl.), to nick s.th. [from s.o.] (sl., Br.E.), to steal s.th. [from s.o.] (b) (to overcharge): to sting s.o. for s.th. (sl.) ◆ *Sopló mucho dinero. He stole a lot of money.* ◆ *Sopló la novia a su amigo. He pinched his friend's girl[friend].* ◆ *En ese restaurante me soplaron 500 pesetas. They stung me for 500 pesetas in that restaurant.*

▶ soplarse algo (fig., fam.) (a) (food): to wolf/bolt [down] (b) (beverage): to down (fam.), to knock back (fam., Br.E.) ◆ *Se sopló una docena de tortillas. He wolfed a dozen omelets or omelettes (Br.E.) down.* ◆ *Se sopló unos cuantos vasos de cerveza. He knocked a few glasses of beer back.*

▶ ¡Sopla! (fam.) Well I'm blowed! (fam.)

el soplo blow

▶ dar el/un soplo (fig., fam.) to tip off (fam.), to give a tip-off (fam.), to give a tip ◆ *¿Quién dio el soplo a la policía? Who gave the police a tip-off?* ◆ *Le dieron el soplo para un robo en una casa. They gave him a tip for a burglary.* ◆ *Nos dio un soplo para la carrera de caballos. He gave us a [hot] tip for the horse race.*

el soplón, la soplona (fam.) informer, canary (sl., Am.E.), stoolie (sl., Am.E.), stool pigeon (sl., Am.E.), grass (sl., Br.E.), nark (sl., Br.E.), telltale (sl., Br.E.), sneak (fam., Br.E.), tattletale (fam.)

▷ sorber los **vientos** por alg.

la sordina sound absorber

▶ a la sordina (fig., fam., adv.) on the quiet (fam.), by stealth ◆ *Salió a la sordina. He left on the quiet.*

el sordo, la sorda deaf person

▶ No hay peor sordo que el que no quiere oír. (prov.) There are none so deaf as those who will not listen. (prov.)

▷ sordo (a **palabras**/**preguntas** necias, oídos ~s)

▷ sordo (dar **música** a un ~)

▷ sordo (¡El **diablo** sea ~!)

▷ sordo (hacer/prestar **oídos** ~s [a algo])

▷ sordo (ser más ~ que una **tapia**)

la sota (card game): jack, knave

▶ la sota (fig., fam.) prostitute, whore, hooker (sl., Am.E.), floozie (sl., Am.E.), tart (sl.)

▶ sota, caballo y rey (fig., fam.) (food): always the same

▷ suave (quedarse más ~ que un **guante**)

subirse to climb, to go up

▶ subírsele algo (vino/etc.) a alg. a predicar (fig., fam.) (wine/etc.): to loosen s.o.'s tongue (fig.) ◆ *El alcohol se le subió a predicar. The alcohol loosened his tongue.*

▷ subirse al **campanario**

▷ subirse por las **paredes**

▷ subirse por las **paredes** (hacer a alg. ~)

▷ subírsele algo a alg. a la **cabeza**

sudar to sweat

▶ sudarlo (fam.) to sweat/stick it out (fam.)
◆ *Tienes que sudarlo hasta que te releven. You have to sweat it out until you're relieved.*

▷ sudar a **chorros**/**mares**

▷ sudar la **gota** gorda/la **hiel**/el **quilo**

▷ sudar **sangre**/**tinta**

▷ sudor (con el ~ de su/etc. **frente**)

el sueco Swede

▶ hacerse el sueco (fig., fam.) to pretend not to hear/see, to pretend not to understand, to act dumb (fam., Am.E.)

la suegra mother-in-law

▶ ¡Cuénteselo a su o cuéntaselo a tu suegra! (fig., fam.) Tell that to the marines! (fam., Am.E.) Pull the other one! (fam., Br.E.)

▶ limpiar algo solamente por donde ve la suegra o limpiar solamente lo que ve la suegra (fam., hum.) to give s.th. a lick and a promise (fam.), to clean [s.th.] [up] very superficially ◆ *Lo limpió solamente por donde vio la suegra. He gave it a lick and a promise.* ◆ *Siempre limpia solamente lo que ve la suegra. He always cleans up very superficially.*

▶ Suegra, ni aun de azúcar es buena. (prov.) A mother-in-law would be bitter even if she were made of sugar. (fig.)

la suela sole (shoe)

▶ no llegarle a alg. a la suela del zapato (fig.) s.o. can't hold a candle to s.o. (fig.), not to be

a patch on s.o. (fam.), not to be fit to tie s.o.'s shoelaces or bootlaces (fig.) ◆ *No le llega a la suela del zapato a su hermano. He can't hold a candle to his brother.*
▶ de siete suelas (fig., fam.) ◆ *Es un estafador de siete suelas. He's an out-and-out con man. (fam.) He's a real con man. (fam.)* ◆ *Es una mentirosa de siete suelas. She's an out-and-out liar. She's a real or downright or chronic liar.* ◆ *Es un cobarde de siete suelas. He's a real/stinking (fam.) coward.*

el suelo ground, floor
▶ arrastrar/poner algo o a alg. por los suelos (fig., fam.) to speak ill of s.th./s.o., to run s.th./s.o. down (fam.), to slander s.o.
▶ echar algo al o por el suelo (fig., fam.) to put paid to s.th. (Br.E.), to ruin s.th., to shatter s.th. (fig.), to knock s.th. on the head (fam.), to knock s.th. for six (fam., Br.E.) ◆ *Echaron el plan al suelo. They ruined the plan. They knocked the plan on the head.* ◆ *Eso echó nuestras esperanzas por el suelo. That shattered our hopes.*
▶ venirse al suelo (fig.) to fail, to be ruined
▶ echarse por los suelos (fig., fam.) to grovel (fig., Br.E.)
▶ estar por los suelos (fig., fam.) (a) to be dirt cheap (fam.), to be a dime a dozen, to be at rock bottom (price) (fig., fam.) (b) to be having or going through a real low (fig.), to be at or reach rock bottom (one's morale/spirits) (fig., fam.) ◆ *Los géneros estuvieron por los suelos. The goods were dirt cheap.* ◆ *Por el momento los precios están por los suelos. Prices are at rock bottom at the moment.* ◆ *Tenía la moral por los suelos. His morale reached rock bottom. He was having a real low.*
▷ suelo (dar con la **carga** en el ~)
▷ suelo (dar con los/sus **hueso**s en el santo ~)
▷ suelo (**herir** el ~ con el pie)
▷ sueñecito (**descabezar** un ~)
▷ sueño (**caerse** de ~)
▷ sueño (**defraudar** el ~)

la suerte luck, destiny, lottery ticket
▶ ¡Buena suerte! Good luck! Break a leg! (fam., hum.)
▶ La suerte está echada. (fig.) The die is cast. (fig.)
▷ suerte (**sonreír**le a alg. la ~)

el surco furrow
▶ echarse al o en el surco (fig., fam.) (a) to knock off [work] (fam.), to think one has done enough (b) to give up ◆ *Ya se echó en el surco a las tres de la tarde. He already knocked off work at three in the afternoon.*

el suspiro sigh
▶ recoger el postrer suspiro de alg. (fig.) to comfort s.o. or be at s.o.'s side at the hour of death
▷ suspiro (lo que no va en **lágrima**s, va en ~s)

sustentarse to sustain o.s.
▶ sustentarse del aire (fig.) to live on air (fig.)

el susto fright
▶ dar un susto de muerte a alg. to scare the living daylights out of s.o. (fam.), to scare the pants off s.o. (fam.), to scare s.o. silly (fam.)
▶ dar un susto al miedo (fig., fam.) to be as ugly as sin/hell (fam.), to be incredibly ugly
▶ no ganar para sustos (fam.) to have nothing but trouble ◆ *Este año no hemos ganado para sustos. We've had nothing but trouble this year.*
▷ susto (**morir**se del ~)
▷ susto (ser más **feo** que un ~ a medianoche)
▷ susto (un ~ **padre**)

suyo, suya his, hers
▶ aguantar lo suyo to put up with a lot
▶ pesar algo lo suyo s.th.: to weigh a ton (fam.)
▶ cada uno/cual tiene lo suyo (fig., fam.) nobody's perfect, we all have our little failings
▶ cada uno/cual a lo suyo it's best to mind one's own business, each to his own
▶ a cada uno/cual, lo suyo to each his own, horses for courses (fam., Br.E.)
▶ ir a lo suyo o a la suya to think only of o.s., to look after Number One (fam.)
▶ hacer de las suyas (fig., fam.) to be/get up to one's old or one's usual tricks, to be up to no good ◆ *Hizo una de las suyas. She was up to one of her old tricks. That was just like her.* ◆ *Han vuelto a hacer de las suyas. They're up to their old tricks again. They're up to no good again.*
▶ salirse con la suya (fam.) to get/have one's [own] way

T

▷ tabaco (**quitar**se del ~)

el tabanque treadle of the potter's wheel
▶ levantar el tabanque (fig., fam.) to pack one's bags/things [and go] (fam.)

la tabarra (fam.)
▶ dar la tabarra a alg. to get on s.o.'s nerves (fam.), to get on s.o.'s wick (fam., Br.E.), to annoy s.o., to bug s.o. (fam., Am.E.)

el tabique partition wall
▶ vivir tabique por medio (fam.) to live next door

la tabla board, plank
▶ hacer tabla rasa [de algo] (fig.) to wipe the slate clean (fig.), to make a clean sweep of s.th. (fig.)
▶ salvarse en una tabla (fig.) to escape by a hair's breadth, to have a narrow escape, to have a close shave (fig., fam.)

la tacita small cup
▶ la Tacita de Plata affectionate name for Cádiz
▶ como una tacita de plata (fig., fam.) spick-and-span (fam.), squeaky clean (fam.), as bright/clean as a new pin (fig.), like a new pin (fig.), spotless ◆ *Le gusta tener la casa como una tacita de plata. She likes to keep her house spick-and-span.* ◆ *Tiene su coche como una tacita de plata. He keeps his car spotless or as bright as a new pin.*

el taco (Esp.) swearword
▶ soltar tacos (fig., fam.) to use coarse (fig.) language, to swear

el tafanario (fam.) posterior (euph.), behind (fam., euph.), backside (fam.), bottom (fam.), butt (fam., Am.E.), bum (fam., Br.E.)

la tagarnina golden thistle
▶ la tagarnina (fig., fam.) (a) cheap/bad cigar, stinker (fam.) (b) cheap/bad tobacco, weed (sl.)

la tajada slice
▶ la tajada del león (fig.) lion's share

▶ sacar tajada (fig., fam.) to get a rake-off (fam.), to make a haul/killing (fam.), to get s.th. out of it, to take one's cut (fam.)

el tal, la tal this man/woman (s.o. mentioned/etc.)
▶ una tal (fig., euph.) a woman of that sort (prostitute) (euph.)
▶ ser tal para cual (fam.) to be two of a kind ◆ *Ambos/ambas son tal para cual. They [both] are two of a kind.* ◆ *Los dos hermanos son tal para cual. Both brothers are as bad as each other.*

taladrar to drill, to pierce
▶ ser un ruido que taladra los oídos (fig.) to be an ear-piercing or ear-splitting noise
▶ ser un ruido que taladra (fig.) to be a shattering noise (fig.)

la taleguilla small bag
▶ la taleguilla de la sal (fig., fam.) money for the daily expenses

el talón heel
▶ mostrar/levantar los talones (fig., fam.) to show a clean pair of heels (fam.), to take to one's heels
▶ pisar los talones a alg. (fig., fam.) to be [hot/hard] on s.o.'s heels (fam.), to dog s.o.'s heels
▶ pegarse a los talones de alg. (fig., fam.) to stick [hard] on s.o.'s heels (fam.)
▶ tener el juicio en los talones (fig., fam.) not to be exactly an Einstein (fam.), s.o. must have been at the back of the queue when they were handing brains out (hum.)
▷ talón (bajársele a alg. la **sangre** a los talones)

el tambor drum
▶ salir a tambor batiente (fig.) to come out/off with flying colors
▶ estar tocando el tambor (fig.) to dawdle away one's time, to waste one's time, not to get anywhere, to get nowhere

el tamboril tambourine
▶ tamboril por gaita (fig., fam.) six of one and half a dozen of the other (fam.) ◆ *¿Lo haremos ahora o más tarde? Da tamboril por*

gaita. Shall we do it now or later? It's six of one and half a dozen of the other.

el tamborilero drummer
▶ En casa del tamborilero todos son danzantes. (prov.) The apple doesn't fall far from the tree. (prov.) Like father like son. (prov.) Like mother like daughter. (prov.)

la tanda (work): shift, turn
▶ estar de tanda (fig., fam.) to be one's turn ◆ *Ahora estamos de tanda. Now it's our turn.*

la tangente tangent
▶ salir[se]/escapar[se]/irse por la tangente (fig., fam.) (a) to go off at a tangent (fig.) (b) to evade/dodge the issue, to give an evasive answer, to beat about/around the bush (fig.), to talk round the subject

el tanto goal (football/soccer)
▶ apuntarse un tanto (fig.) to notch up a [plus] point (fig., fam.)

la tapa lid
▶ levantarse la tapa de los sesos (fig., fam.) to blow one's brains out (fam.), to blow one's head off (fam.), to put a bullet through one's head
▶ levantarle a alg. la tapa de los sesos (fig., fam.) to blow s.o.'s brains out (fam.), to blow s.o.'s head off (fam.), to put a bullet through s.o.'s head

[el]/la tapaboca[s] (fig., pop.) slap [on the mouth]

el tapadillo veiling (women)
▶ de tapadillo (fig., fam.) on the quiet (fam.), stealthily, secretly ◆ *Salió de tapadillo. He left on the quiet.*
▶ pasar algo de tapadillo (fig., fam.) to smuggle s.th. through
▶ andar con tapadillos (fig., fam.) to have secrets

tapar to cover [up], to plug up
▶ tapar a una mujer (fig., pop.) to screw a woman (vulg.) ▷ **calzar[se]** a alg.
▶ tapar la boca a alg. (fig.) to shut s.o. up (fam.), to silence s.o.
▷ tapar la **caca**

el tapete table cover/cloth
▶ estar sobre el tapete (fig.) to be under discussion, to be up for discussion

▶ poner algo sobre el tapete (fig.) to put/bring s.th. up for discussion ◆ *Pusimos ese asunto sobre el tapete. We put that matter up for discussion.*
▶ quedar sobre el tapete (fig.) not to be brought/put up for discussion, not to be brought up ◆ *Eso quedó sobre el tapete. That wasn't brought up.*

la tapia mud wall
▶ ser más sordo que una tapia (fig., fam.) to be stone-deaf (fam.), to be as deaf as a post (fam.)

el tapón stopper, plug
▶ el tapón (fig., fam.) short, chubby person
▶ Al primer tapón, zurrapa[s]. (prov.) Everyone has to learn. Well, the first shot was a failure. (fig.)

el tapujo cover[ing]
▶ la pensión de tapujo (fig., fam.) short-time hotel/motel (fam.)
▶ andar con tapujos (fig.) to be very secretive, to be involved in some shady (fam.) or dubious business
▶ sin tapujos (fig.) unvarnished (fig.), plain, aboveboard, openly, honestly ◆ *Me dijo la verdad sin tapujos. He told me the plain/unvarnished truth.* ◆ *Me lo echaron en cara sin tapujos. They said it openly to my face.*

la tarántula tarantula
▶ estar picado de la tarántula (fig., fam.) to have VD (venereal disease)

la tarasca carnival dragon
▶ la tarasca (fig., fam.) (woman): battleax[e] (fam.), shrew, virago, termagant, old bag (fam., pej.), old hag (pej.)

tarde late
▶ Más vale tarde que nunca. (prov.) Better late than never. (prov.)
▷ tarde (▷ **nacer**: nació alg. ~)
▷ tarde (nunca es ~ si la **dicha** es buena)

la tarja tally
▶ beber sobre tarja (fig.) to drink on credit, to drink on tick (fam., Br.E.)

el tarugo (fig., fam.) backhander (fam.)

el tate (fam.) (marijuana): hash/pot (fam.), grass/shit/weed (sl.), tea (sl., Am.E.)

el taxi taxi
- el taxi (fig., pop.) prostitute, streetwalker, hooker (sl., Am.E.), tart (sl.)

el taxista taxidriver
- el taxista (pop.) pimp (fam.)

el tebeo comic (for children)
- ser más conocido que el tebeo (fig., fam.) everybody knows him/etc., to be known everywhere

la tecla key
- dar en la tecla (fig., fam.) to hit the nail on the head (fig.)
- dar en la tecla de + infinitivo (fig., fam.) to fall into the habit of + gerund ◆ *Dio en la tecla de levantarse muy temprano. He fell into the habit of getting up very early. He has/had a thing about getting up very early.*
- tocar todas las teclas (fig., fam.) to pull out all the stops (fig.), to leave no stone unturned (fig.)
- no quedarle a alg. ninguna tecla por tocar (fig., fam.) there's nothing else left for s.o. to try, to have tried every avenue (fig.) or approach

teclear algo (fam.) to manage s.th., to wangle s.th. (fam.); (problem): to approach from various angles (fig.)

la teja [roofing] tile
- pagar a toca teja (fig., Esp.) to pay on the nail (fam.), to pay cash
▷ tejado (la **pelota** está/sigue en el ~)
▷ tejado (tirar **piedra**s a su o sobre el propio ~)

la tela fabric
- la tela (pop.) (money): dough (sl., Am.E.), bread (sl.), sugar (sl.), brass/dosh/lolly (sl., Br.E.), wampum (sl., Am.E.)
- sacudir/soltar la tela to cough up (fam.), to fork out (fam.), to stump up (fam., Br.E.)
- poner algo en tela de juicio (fig.) to question s.th., to call s.th. into question, to cast doubt on s.th.
- estar en tela de juicio (fig.) (success; s.th. to be the case or to be true): to be uncertain
- haber tela que cortar (fam.), haber tela para rato (fam.) to be a long job, to have a lot of work on one's hands, there's plenty of material (fig.), to be broad or endless (subject/topic/etc.), to be lots to talk about ◆ *Hay tela que cortar. There's still lots to talk about.*
- ◆ *Voy a tener tela para rato. It's going to be a long job. I'm going to have a lot of work on my hands.*
- llegarle a alg. a las telas del corazón (fig., fam.) to hurt/wound s.o. deeply (fig.)
▷ tela (tejer la ~ de **Penélope**)

la telaraña cobweb
- mirar las telarañas (fig., fam.) to have one's head in the clouds
- tener telarañas en los ojos (fig., fam.) to be blind (fig.), not to have [got] eyes in one's head (fig.)
- sacudirse las telarañas (fig., fam.) to blow the cobwebs away (fig.), to clear one's mind

temblar to tremble, to shake
- temblar como una hoja o como un azogado o como un flan (fig.) to shake like a leaf/jelly (fig.), to tremble all over
- dejar un vaso o una botella temblando (fig., fam.) to almost empty a glass/bottle, to use most of a bottle ◆ *Dejó la botella temblando. He almost emptied the bottle.*
- Un vaso o una botella está temblando. (fig., fam.) A glass/bottle is almost empty (after a swig or after pouring wine/etc.). ◆ *La botella está temblando. The bottle is almost empty.*
▷ temblarle a alg. las **carne**s

el tembleque (fam.) shaking
- tener un tembleque to have the shakes (fam.), to have the heebie-jeebies (fam.)
- entrarle a alg. tembleques o un tembleque to start shaking/trembling, to begin to shake/tremble, to get the shakes (fam.)
▷ tempestad (quien siembra **viento**s recoge ~es)
▷ témpora (tomar/confundir el **culo** por las ~s)

ten (fam.)
- ir con mucho ten con ten to go about it very/extremely carefully

las tenazas pliers
- no poder coger algo o a alg. ni con tenazas (fig., fam.) s.o. wouldn't touch s.th./s.o. with a bargepole or ten-foot pole (fig.) ◆ *Ese novelón no puedo coger ni con tenazas. I wouldn't touch that pulp novel with a bargepole.*

tentar to tempt
- ▶ tentar a Dios o al diablo to tempt fate/providence
- ▶ tentar la paciencia a alg. (fig., fam.) to get on s.o.'s nerves (fam.), to get on s.o.'s wick (fam., Br.E.)

la teología theology
- ▶ no meterse en teologías (fig., fam.) not to talk about things one doesn't know anything about ◆ *No te metas en teologías. Don't talk about things you don't know anything about.*
- ▷ terco (ser ~ a más no **poder**)
- ▷ ternura (**rebosar** de ~)

el terreno ground, terrain
- ▶ pisar el terreno de alg. (fig.) to get under s.o.'s feet (fig., fam.)
- ▶ ganar terreno (fig.) to gain ground (fig.) ◆ *Están ganando terreno en su lucha por conseguir mejores condiciones laborales. They're gaining ground in their struggle for better working conditions.*
- ▶ perder terreno (fig.) to lose ground (fig.), to fall behind
- ▶ comerle el terreno a alg. (fig.) to surpass s.o., to outstrip s.o. (fig.)
- ▶ tantear/medir el terreno (fig.) to see how the land lies (fig.) ◆ *Su negocio no prospera allí. Debiera haber tanteado el terreno antes de abrirlo. His business doesn't prosper there. He should have seen how the land lies before he opened it.*
- ▶ minar el terreno a alg. (fig.) to undermine s.o.'s position (fig.), to cut the ground from under s.o.'s feet ◆ *Esperamos que no destroce otra vez la base de nuestro proyecto. Ya nos ha minado el terreno dos veces. We hope that he won't destroy the foundation of our plan again. He's already cut the ground from under our feet two times.*
- ▶ preparar el terreno a alg./algo (fig.) to pave the way for s.o./s.th. (fig.), to prepare the ground for s.th. (fig.)

el terrón clod/lump [of earth]
- ▶ destripar terrones (fig., pop.) to slog away (fam., Br.E.) ▷ echar/sudar la **hiel**

la tetorra (pop.) big breasts, big boobs (fam.), big tits (fam.), bazookas (sl., hum., Am.E.)

la tía aunt
- ▶ ¡No hay tu tía! (fig.) No chance! (fam.) No way! (fam.) Nothing doing! (fam.)
- ▶ quedar[se] para tía (fig., fam.) to be an old maid (fam.)
- ▷ tiempo (~[s] de **Maricastaña**)
- ▷ tiempo (en ~s del **rey** que rabió/del rey Wamba)
- ▷ tiempo (en [los] ~s de **ñangué**)
- ▷ tiempo (hacer un ~ de **perros**)
- ▷ tiempo (no tener ~ ni para **rascar**se)
- ▷ tiempo (**tirar**se ~ haciendo algo)

la tierra earth
- ▶ besar la tierra (fig., fam.) to fall flat/headlong
- ▶ en toda/cualquier tierra de garbanzos (fig., fam.) everywhere, all over
- ▶ estar comiendo tierra (fig., fam.) to be pushing up [the] daisies (fam., hum.), to have bitten the dust (fam.)
- ▶ echar tierra sobre/a algo (fig.) (a) to cover s.th. up (fig.), to hush s.th. up (b) to forget about s.th., to put s.th. behind one, to let the dust settle on s.th. (fig.)
- ▶ echar tierra a los ojos de alg. (fig., fam.) to throw dust in s.o.'s eyes (fig.) ◆ *Me echó tierra a los ojos y acabó vendiéndome el reloj más caro. He threw dust in my eyes and I ended up buying the most expensive watch.*
- ▶ echarse tierra a los ojos (fig., fam.) to cut off one's nose to spite one's face
- ▶ poner tierra por medio (fig., fam.) to make a quick getaway (fam.), to clear off/out (fam.)
- ▶ tragarse la tierra a alg. (fig.) to disappear from or vanish off the face of the earth ◆ *Parecía que se los hubiera tragado la tierra. It was as if they'd vanished off the face of the earth or as if the earth had swallowed them up.*
- ▶ sacar algo de debajo de la tierra (fig., fam.) to go to great trouble to get s.th.
- ▷ tierra (aunque se junten el **cielo** y la ~)
- ▷ tierra (dar con la **carga** en ~)
- ▷ tierra ([re]mover **cielo** y ~)
- ▷ tierra (tener los **pies** [bien puestos] en/sobre la ~)

tieso stiff
- ▶ ¡Tente tieso! (fig.) Keep your chin up! (fam.) Keep your pecker up! (fam., Br.E.)
- ▶ tieso como un ajo (fig., pop.) as stiff as a poker/ramrod (fam.), bolt upright

▶ quedarse tieso (fig., fam.) to kick the bucket (fam.) ▷ **cascar**[la]

▶ dejar tieso a alg. (fig., pop.) to bump s.o. off (sl.) ▷ **cargar**se a alg. (a)

▶ tenerlas tiesas [con/a alg.] (fig.) to stubbornly defend one's opinion [against s.o.], to put up a firm resistance [to s.o.]

el tiesto flowerpot

▶ mear fuera del tiesto (fig., pop.) to talk round the issue/subject

el tigre tiger

▶ oler a tigre (fam., Esp.) to smell of sweat, to pong (sl., Br.E.)

la[s] tijera[s] scissors

▶ ser una buena tijera (fig., fam.) (a) to be a big eater (b) to be a scandalmonger, to be a backbiter

el tilín tinkle

▶ hacer tilín a alg. (fig., fam.) to appeal to s.o., to like, to be s.o.'s thing (fam.), to be right up s.o.'s alley (Am.E.) or street (Br.E.) (fam.) ◆ *Nos hace tilín. We like it. It's right up our alley/street.* ◆ *No me hizo tilín. It didn't appeal to me. It wasn't my thing.*

▷ timón (dar un **golpe** de ~)

el tinglado shed

▶ el tinglado (fig., fam.) (a) joint (sl.), business (b) intrigue, plot

▶ montar un tinglado to set up in business

▶ armar un tinglado to lay a plot

▶ conocer el tinglado to see through it, to see [through] s.o.'s little game

la tinta ink

▶ sudar tinta (fig., fam.) to slave/sweat away (fam.) ▷ echar/sudar la **hiel**

▶ hacerle sudar tinta a alg. (fig., fam.) to keep s.o.'s nose to the grindstone (fig.), to give s.o. a [good] run for his money

▶ saber algo de buena tinta (fig.) to know s.th. on good authority, to be straight from the horse's mouth (fam.) ◆ *Es verdad. Lo sabemos de buena tinta. It's true. It's straight from or we heard it straight from the horse's mouth.*

▶ [re]cargar las tintas (fig.) to exaggerate

el tintero inkpot

▶ dejar algo o quedársele algo a alg. en el tintero (fig.) to clean forget about s.th. ◆ *Lo*

dejé o se me quedó en el tintero. I clean forgot about it.

la tintura dye

▶ la tintura (fig., fam.) smattering ◆ *Tiene tintura de español. He has a smattering of Spanish.*

el tiovivo merry-go-round (Br.E.), carousel (Am.E.)

▶ dar más vueltas que un tiovivo (fig., fam.) to run/chase from pillar to post (fig.) ◆ *Había tantas formalidades burocráticas. Tuve que dar más vueltas que un tiovivo para obtener los papeles. It was red tape all the way. I had to chase from pillar to post to get the [identity] papers.*

la tipeja (fam., pej.) bitch (sl., Br.E.; vulg., Am.E.), nasty piece of work (fig., fam.)

el tipejo (fam., pej.) (a) bastard (sl.), bad lot (fam.), nasty piece of work (fig., fam.) (b) odd sort, queer fish (fam.), strange customer (fam.)

el tipo type, figure, physique

▶ no ser su/etc. tipo (fig., fam.) not to be his/etc. type (fam.) ◆ *Ella no es mi tipo. She's not my type.*

▶ mantener el tipo (fam.) to put on a brave face

▶ jugarse el tipo (fig.) to risk one's neck (fam.)

el tira y afloja (fig.) tug-of-war (fig.) ◆ *Un tira y afloja precedió a la firma del pacto. A tug-of-war preceded the signing of the treaty.*

▷ tirabuzón (**sacar** algo a alg. con ~)

tirar to throw, to pull, to shoot

▶ tirar algo por la ventana (fig.) to play ducks and drakes with s.th. (fig.), to squander s.th. ◆ *Tira su dinero por la ventana. He's playing ducks and drakes with his money.*

▶ tirarse a una mujer (pop.) to lay a woman (sl.), to knock a woman off (sl., Br.E.) ▷ **calzar**[se] a alg.

▶ tirarse a muerto (fig., fam.) to play the fool/clown

▶ tirarse tiempo o un año/etc. haciendo algo (fig., fam.) to spend time or a year/etc. doing s.th., to take s.o. time or a year/etc. to do s.th. ◆ *Me he tirado el día escribiendo. I've spent the day writing.* ◆ *Me tiré dos años escribiendo este libro. I spent two years writ-*

ing this book. It took me two years to write this book. ◆ *Se tiraron mucho tiempo haciéndolo. They spent a lot of time doing it. It took them a lot of time to do it.*

▶ no tirar algo a alg. (fig., fam.) s.th. doesn't wash with s.o. (fam.) ◆ *Esta excusa no me tira. This excuse doesn't wash with me.*

▶ tirar (fig., fam.) to last [out] ◆ *Estos zapatos tirarán otro verano. These shoes will last another summer.*

▶ a todo tirar (fig.) at best, at the most ◆ *Me queda gasolina para 10 kms a todo tirar. I have only enough petrol (Br.E.) or gas (Am.E.) for 10 kms at the most.*

▶ ir tirando (fig., fam.) to manage (fam.), to get by/along, to keep going, to keep one's head above water (fig.)

▶ tirar al monte (fig., fam.) to be homesick

▶ tirar por un camino (fig.) to tread a path (fig.), to adopt a course (fig.) ◆ *Ha llegado la hora o el momento de tirar por el camino de la moderación. It's time to tread the path of moderation.*

▶ tirar una foto (fam.) (to take a photograph): to take a shot (fam.)

▶ tirar más allá del blanco (fig.) to overshoot the mark (fig.), to go over the top (fig., fam.)

el tiro throw, shot

▶ estar a [un] tiro de piedra (fig.) to be only a stone's throw away (fig.) ◆ *Nuestra casa estaba a un tiro de piedra de la costa. Our house was only a stone's throw away from the coast.*

▶ un tiro al azar (fig.) a shot in the dark (fig.) ◆ *¿Sabías de verdad la contestación o es que fue un tiro al azar? Did you really know the answer or was it a shot in the dark?*

▶ saber por dónde van los tiros (fig.) to know which way the wind is blowing (fig.) or which way the cat jumps (fig.) or which way the cookie crumbles (fam., Am.E.)

▶ [esperar a] ver por dónde van los tiros (fig.) to [wait and/to] see which way the wind is blowing (fig.) or which way the cat jumps (fig.) or which way the cookie crumbles (fam., Am.E.)

▶ salirle a alg. el tiro por la culata (fig., fam.) to backfire [s.th.] on s.o. (fig.), to boomerang [s.th.] on s.o. (fig.), to be hoist by/with one's own petard (fig.) ◆ *Le salió a ella el tiro por la culata cuando comió la comida envenenada que fue para su esposo. She*

was hoist by her own petard when she ate the poisoned food that was meant for her husband.

▶ sentarle algo a alg. como un tiro (fig., fam.) (a) to really disagree with s.o. (food), to upset s.o.'s stomach (food), to really upset s.o. (fig.), to really bother s.o. (b) (dress/etc.): not to suit s.o. at all, to look awful on s.o. ◆ *El embutido me sienta como un tiro. The sausage really disagrees with me.* ◆ *Les sentó como un tiro que no los invitásemos. It really upset/bothered them that we didn't invite them.* ◆ *Este vestido te sienta como un tiro. This dress doesn't suit you at all. This dress looks awful on you.*

▶ estar/andar a tiros con alg. (fig., fam.) to be at daggers drawn with s.o. (fig., Br.E.)

▷ tiro (**coser/freír** a alg. a ~s)

▷ tiro (**matar dos pájaro**s de un ~)

el tirón pull, tug

▶ de un tirón (fig.) in one go, at a single or at one sitting (fig.), without a break, at a stretch, straight off/through ◆ *Leí el libro de un tirón. I read the book at a single sitting or in one go or straight through.* ◆ *Trabajamos 15 horas de un tirón. We worked 15 hours at a stretch or without a break.* ◆ *Apuró su vaso de un tirón. He emptied his glass in one go.*

▶ Ni a tirones me/nos sacan de aquí. (fig., fam.) Wild horses couldn't drag me/us away from here.

la tirria (fam.) dislike, grudge

▶ tener tirria a alg. to have a grudge against s.o.

el títere marionette, puppet

▶ no dejar/quedar títere con cabeza (fig., fam.) to wreck the place (fam.), to break up everything in sight, to spare nobody ◆ *No dejaron títere con cabeza. They wrecked the place. They broke up everything in sight.* ◆ *No quedó títere con cabeza. The place was wrecked. Nothing remained intact or in one piece. Nobody was spared. Nobody came through or escaped [it] unscathed.* ◆ *Tras el reajuste ministerial no quedó títere con cabeza. Nobody escaped the cabinet reshuffle unscathed.*

la toalla towel

▶ arrojar/tirar la toalla (fig.) to throw in the towel/sponge (fig.), to pick up one's marbles (fig., fam., Am.E.) ◆ *Probemos al menos una vez más. Es demasiado prematuro arro-*

jar la toalla. Let's try at least one more time. It's too early/soon to throw in the towel.

▷ tocado (estar ~ de la **cabeza**)

tocar to touch, to play, to ring
▶ tocársela (pop., Esp.) (to masturbate) ▷ tocar la **campana**
▶ tocárselas (fig., fam.) to beat it (sl.), to clear off (fam.), to take to one's heels
▶ ¡Tocan a pagar! o ¡A pagar tocan! (fig., fam.) It's time to pay up!
▶ Tocan a matar. (fig., fam.) This is where we get down to serious business.

▷ tocino (no hay **olla** sin ~)

todo everything, all
▶ O todo o nada. (prov.) All or nothing.
▷ todo (**jugar**se el ~ por el ~)
▷ toledano (la **noche** toledana)

tomar to take
▶ tomarla con alg. (fam.) to pick a quarrel or an argument with s.o.
▶ tenerla tomado con alg. (fam.) to have it in for s.o. (fam.), to have a down on s.o. (fam., Br.E.) ◆ *La tienen tomado conmigo. They have a down on me.*
▶ ¡Toma! (fig., fam.) Fancy that! There/here you are!
▶ Más vale un toma que dos te daré. (prov.) A bird in the hand is worth two in the bush. (prov.)

el tomate tomato
▶ el tomate (fig., fam.) hole in the heel (sock/stocking)
▶ ponerse como un tomate to turn as red as a beet (fam., Am.E.) ▷ ponerse como una **amapola**
▶ poner a alg. el culo como un tomate to give s.o. a good thrashing/hiding (fam.)
▶ tener [mucho] tomate (fig., fam.) to be [really] tough (fig.), to be a [very] tough one (fig.), to be a [real] stinker (fam.) ◆ *Este trabajo tiene mucho tomate. This job is a real stinker.*

ton (fam.)
▶ sin ton ni son for no reason at all, for no apparent or particular reason, without rhyme or reason ◆ *Le dieron el bote sin ton ni son. They gave him the boot for no apparent reason.* ◆ *Tomó una decisión sin ton ni son. He made a decision without rhyme or reason.* ◆ *Se rieron sin ton ni son. They*

laughed for no reason at all. ◆ *hablar sin ton ni son to talk through one's hat (fam.)*

el tono tone
▶ darse tono (fig.) to talk big (fam.), to put on airs, to put on the dog (fam., Am.E.), to fancy o.s. (fam.) ◆ *Ese tío sí que se da tono. That guy doesn't half fancy himself. (fam., Br.E.)*
▶ decírselo a alg. en todos los tonos (fig., fam.) to tell s.o. or try telling s.o. or try to get it across to s.o. every way imaginable or every way one can think of ◆ *Se lo he dicho a ella en todos los tonos. I've told her every way imaginable.*

▷ tontería (una **solemne** ~)

tonto stupid, dumb (fam., Am.E.)
▶ ser tonto del bote/de capirote (fam.) to be a complete idiot, to be a prize idiot (fam.), to be as dumb (Am.E.) or as thick as they come (fam.), to be no end of a fool (fam.)
▶ estar como tonto en vísperas (fam.) to be at a complete loss as to what to do [next]
▶ a tontas y a locas without rhyme or reason, without thinking, haphazardly, blindly, wildly ◆ *Habló a tontas y a locas. He talked without rhyme or reason.* ◆ *Lo hicieron a tontas y a locas. They did it without thinking. They did it any old how. (Br.E.)* ◆ *repartir golpes a tontas y a locas to lash/hit out blindly/wildly*
▷ tonto (la **caja** tonta)
▷ tonto (no tener un **pelo** de ~)
▷ tonto (**pan** con pan, comida de ~s)
▷ tonto (**pecar** de ~)
▷ tonto (ser ~ a más no **poder**)
▷ tonto (ser la **mar** de ~)
▷ tonto (ser más ~ que **Abundio**/que **Carracuca**/que una **mata** de habas)

el tope top, end, limit
▶ estar hasta los topes de algo (fig., fam.) to be utterly fed up with s.th. (fam.) ▷ estar hasta [más allá de] la **coronilla** de algo

el topo mole
▶ ser más ciego que un topo (fig.) to be [as] blind as a bat (fam.)

el toque touch
▶ dar el último/[los últimos] toque[s] a algo (fig.) to add/put the finishing touch[es] to s.th. ◆ *Dio los últimos toques a su novela. He put the finishing touches to his novel.*

▷ torcer (no dar su **brazo** a ~)

▷ torcido (**cabeza** torcida)

la tormenta storm

▶ una tormenta en un vaso de agua (fig.) storm in a teacup (fig., Br.E.), tempest in a teapot (fig., Am.E.)

la torna return

▶ volver las tornas a alg. (fig.) to turn the tables on s.o., to give s.o. tit for tat, to pay s.o. back in kind or in his own coin (fig.)

▶ Se han vuelto las tornas. (fig.) Now the tide has turned. (fig.) It's all changed. It's a different story now. Now the boot's on the other foot. (fig., Br.E.) Now the shoe's on the other foot. (fig., Am.E.) It's a whole new ball game now. (fig., fam.)

▷ tornaboda (no hay **boda** sin ~)

el tornillo screw

▶ faltarle a alg. un tornillo o tener flojos los tornillos (fig., fam.) to have a screw loose (fam.), to have rocks in one's head (sl., Am.E.), not to be all there (fam.) ◆ *Le falta un tornillo a él. He's not all there.*

▶ apretar los tornillos a alg. (fig.) to put the screws on s.o. (fig., fam.), to put the pressure on s.o. (fig.), to apply pressure on s.o. (fig.)

el toro bull

▶ ¡Ahora van a soltar al toro! (fig., fam.) Here we go! This is it now!

▶ huir del toro y caer en el arroyo (fig.) to jump out of the frying pan into the fire ◆ *Atracó un banco para pagar sus deudas. Huyó del toro y cayó en el arroyo. He held up a bank to pay [off] his debts. He jumped out of the frying pan into the fire.*

▶ coger el toro por los cuernos (fig.) to take the bull by the horns (fig.), to grasp the nettle (fig.) ◆ *Nos vimos enfrentados a un grave problema. Cogimos el toro por los cuernos y lo solucionamos. We were faced with a serious problem. We took the bull by the horns and solved it.*

▶ echar/soltar el toro a alg. (fig.) to give s.o. a severe wigging (Br.E.) or dressing-down (fam.)

▶ pillar el toro a alg. (fig.) (argument): to get s.o. into a corner (fig.)

▶ Hay toros y cañas. (fig.) All hell is let loose. (fam.) ◆ *Hubo toros y cañas. All hell was let loose.* ◆ *Habrá toros y cañas. All hell will be let loose.*

▶ ¡Ciertos son los toros! It had to happen! It was bound to happen!

▷ toro (andar/verse en los **cuernos** del ~)

▷ toro (dejar a alg. en las **astas** del ~)

▷ toro (ser un ~ **corrido**)

▷ toro (ver los ~s desde la **barrera**)

▷ torpe (ser ~ a más no **poder**)

el torrente torrent

▶ llover a torrentes to rain in torrents, to come down in buckets/sheets, to rain cats and dogs, to be pouring [down or with rain], to be bucketing down (Br.E.), the floodgates of heaven open (fig.) ◆ *Ayer llovió a torrentes. It rained in torrents yesterday. It was pouring yesterday. The floodgates of heaven opened yesterday.*

la torta cake, pie

▶ ser tortas y pan pintado (fam.) to be child's play (fig.), to be a cinch (sl.) ◆ *Esto es tortas y pan pintado. This is child's play.*

▶ pegar una torta a alg. (fig., fam.) to paste s.o. one (sl.), to land s.o. one (fam.), to give s.o. a thick ear (fam.), to give s.o. a wallop (fam.)

▷ torta (a falta de **pan**, buenas son ~s)

el tortazo (pop.) punch

▶ pegarse un tortazo (fig.) to have a bad accident (esp. car accident)

la torti (pop., Esp.) lesbian, dyke/dike (sl.)

la tortilla omelet (Am.E.), omelette (Br.E.)

▶ cambiar/volver la tortilla a alg. (fig.) to turn the tables on s.o.

▶ dar la vuelta a la tortilla (fig.) to change the situation completely

▶ Se ha vuelto la tortilla. (fig.) Now the tide has turned. (fig.) ▷ se han vuelto las **torna**s

▶ No se puede hacer tortillas sin romper huevos. (prov.) You can't make an omelet without breaking eggs. (prov.)

▶ hacer algo/a alg. [una] tortilla (fig., fam.) to smash s.th. to pieces, to beat s.o. up

▶ hacer una tortilla (fam.) to have lesbian intercourse

la tortillera (fig., pop.) lesbian, dyke/dike (sl.)

la tórtola turtledove

▶ la tórtola (fig., fam.) woman who is head over heels in love, lovebird

el tórtolo male turtledove
▶ el tórtolo (fig., fam.) man who is head over heels in love, lovebird

la tortuga turtle, tortoise
▶ ser [más lento que] una tortuga (fig.) to be [as] slow as or slower than molasses [in January] (fig., Am.E.), to be [such] a slowcoach (Br.E.) or slowpoke (Am.E.) (fam.) ◆ *Es más lento que una tortuga. He's slower than molasses in January. He's such a slowpoke.*
▶ a paso de tortuga (fig.) at a snail's pace (fig.), [as] slow as or slower than molasses [in January] (fig., Am.E.) ◆ *Allí hay una cola de coches que se extiende hasta 10 millas. Se puede ir sólo a paso de tortuga. There's a 10-mile traffic jam. You can only drive at a snail's pace. The traffic is as slow as molasses in January.* ◆ *Estoy impaciente esperando las noticias. El tiempo parece pasar a paso de tortuga. I'm anxiously awaiting the news. Time seems to be moving at a snail's pace.*
▷ torturarse los **sesos**

toser to cough
▶ toser fuerte (fig., fam.) to swank (fam., Br.E.), to show off
▶ A ése no hay quien le tosa. (fig.) Nobody can take him on. Nobody can compete with him. He's in a class by himself or of his own.
▶ A mí no me tose nadie. (fig.) I'm not taking anything/that from anybody. I'll not stand for that.

la tostada toast
▶ olerse la tostada (fig., fam.) to smell a rat (fig., fam.) ◆ *Se olía la tostada. You could smell a rat. I/we smelled a rat.*
▶ hacer una tostada de años (fam.) ages ago (fam.) ◆ *Hace una tostada de años que no lo veo. It's [been] ages since I saw him. I haven't seen him for ages.*
▶ dar/pegar una tostada a alg. (fig., fam.) to put one/it over on s.o. (fam.), to cheat s.o.

tostar to toast, to roast, to brown
▶ tostarse [al sol] (fig., fam.) to sunbathe, to tan, to brown, to get a tan, to get brown

la traba fetter, shackle
▶ poner trabas a alg. (fig.) to shackle s.o. (fig.), to put a spoke in s.o.'s wheel (fig., fam., Br.E.)
▷ trabajar a más no **poder**/a todo **vapor**
▷ trabajar como un **buey/negro**

▷ trabajar para el **obispo**
▷ trabajar por un **pedazo** de pan

el trabajo work
▶ El trabajo es el encanto de la vida. (prov.) Work sweetens life. (fig.)
▷ trabajo (no hay **atajo** sin ~)

traer to bring
▶ traer y llevar [a alg.] (fig., fam.) to gossip [about s.o.]
▶ traérselas (fig., fam.) ◆ *Este problema se las trae. This is a difficult problem.* ◆ *El asunto se las trae. It's a tough one. (fig.) It's a sticky business. (fig., fam.)* ◆ *El trabajo se las traía. It was a difficult or tough (fig.) job. The job was tough going. (fam.)* ◆ *El examen realmente se las traía. The exam was really tough. (fig.)* ◆ *Hace un calor que se las trae. This heat is too much of a good thing. This is an unbearable heat.*

las tragaderas (fam.) gullet
▶ tener buenas tragaderas (fig., fam.) (a) to be a big eater (b) to be very gullible, to swallow anything (fig.) (c) to put up with a lot, to be excessively tolerant

el/la tragaldabas (fam.) glutton, greedy-guts (hum., Br.E.)

el tragantón, la tragantona (fam.) glutton, greedy-guts (hum., Br.E.), guzzler (fam., Br.E.)

el/la tragaperras (fam.) slot machine, one-armed bandit (fam.)

tragar to swallow
▶ no poder tragar a alg. (fig., fam.) s.o. can't stand s.o., s.o. can't stomach s.o. (fig.)
▶ tragarlo (fig., fam.) to lie down under it (fig.), to take it lying down (fig.) ◆ *Lo tragó. He lay down under it.* ◆ *Ésta no la tragamos. We won't take this lying down.*
▶ tragárselas (fig., fam.) to put up with anything
▶ tragar[se]las como puños (fig., fam.) to swallow anything (fig.), to buy anything (sl., Am.E.) ◆ *Las tragará como puños. He'll swallow anything.* ◆ *Se las tragó como puños. He bought it, the whole ball of wax. (fam, Am.E.)*
▶ tragar[se]las como ruedas de molino (fig., fam.) to swallow anything hook, line and sinker (fig.) ◆ *Inventaron un cuento para*

explicar por qué habían faltado al colegio. El profesor se las tragó como ruedas de molino. They made up a story about why they had been absent from school. The teacher swallowed it hook, line and sinker.
▷ tragar **quina/saliva**
▷ tragarse la **tierra** a alg.

el trago sip, swig (fam.)
► atizarse un trago (pop.) to hoist one (sl., Am.E.), to have a swig (fam.), to have a drink
► pasar un trago amargo (fig.) to have a hard/rough time, to go through a bad/rough patch (Br.E.)
► ser un trago amargo (fig.) to be a bitter pill [to swallow] (fig.), to be an awful or a bad experience, to be a cruel/terrible blow (fig.) ◆ *Fue un trago amargo para él cuando su hija murió de una sobredosis de heroína.* It was a bitter pill for him to swallow when his daughter ODed on heroin.
► quedarle a alg. todavía el trago más amargo (fig.) the worst [of it] is yet/still to come ◆ *Me/nos quedaba todavía el trago más amargo.* The worst of it was still to come.

el tragón, la tragona (fam.) glutton, greedy-guts (hum., Br.E.), guzzler (fam., Br.E.)

el traje suit, dress
► cortar un traje a alg. (fig., fam.) to gossip about s.o.
► cortar trajes (fig., fam.) to gossip
▷ traje (en ~ de **Adán/Eva**)

la tramontana north wind
► perder la tramontana (fig., fam.) to lose one's head

la trampa trap
► hacer trampa[s] (fig., fam.) to cheat, to swindle, to be on the fiddle (fam., Br.E.) ◆ *Hicieron trampa con los votos.* They fiddled the voting. (fam., Br.E.) They juggled with the votes. (fig.)
► las trampas (fig., fam.) debt ◆ *estar comido de trampas* to be up to one's ears/eyeballs in debt (fam.), to be in Queer Street (fam., Br.E.)
▷ trampa (hecha la **ley**, hecha la ~)

el trance critical juncture
► a todo trance (fig.) at all costs (fig.), at any cost (fig.), whatever happens ◆ *Hay que evi-*

tarlo a todo trance. It must be avoided at all costs.

el tranco big step, stride
► en dos trancos (fig.) in two shakes [of a lamb's tail] (fam., Am.E.), in two or in a couple of ticks (fam., Br.E.), before you can say Jack Robinson (fam.) ◆ *Estoy allí en dos trancos.* I'll be there in two shakes/ticks or before you can say Jack Robinson.

el tranquillo (fig.) knack
► coger el tranquillo a algo to get the knack of s.th., to get the hang of s.th. (fam.)

la trapaza swindle, fiddle (fam., Br.E.)
► el bachiller Trapazas (fig., fam.) crook, swindler, racketeer, schemer, shyster (sl., Am.E.)
▷ trapito (los **trapos**/~s de cristianar)

el trapo rag
► los trapos/trapitos de cristianar (fig., fam.) one's Sunday best (fam.), one's glad rags (fam., Br.E.) ◆ *Se puso los trapitos de cristianar.* He put on his Sunday best.
► poner a alg. como un trapo (fig.) (a) (debate): to flatten s.o. (fam.), to tear s.o. to pieces or to shreds or to bits (fig., fam.) (b) (to scold): to give s.o. a [good] dressing-down (fam.), to haul s.o. over the coals (fig.)
► lavar los trapos sucios ante el mundo entero (fig.) to wash one's dirty linen in public (fig.)
► lavar los trapos sucios en casa (fig.) not to wash one's dirty linen in public (fig.)
► Los trapos sucios se lavan en casa. (fig.) You shouldn't wash your dirty linen in public. (fig.)
► sacar los trapos [sucios] a relucir (fig.) to bring out the skeletons in the closet (Am.E.) or in the cupboard (Br.E.) (fig.), to tell [a lot of] home truths ◆ *Temen que la comisión investigadora saque todos los trapos a relucir.* They fear that the investigating committee will bring out all the skeletons in the cupboard or will reveal all their [little] secrets.
► ocultar los trapos sucios (fig.) to sweep it under the carpet (Br.E.) or under the rug (fig.)
► soltar el trapo (fig., fam.) (a) to burst out laughing (b) to burst out crying, to burst into tears
► hablar de trapos (fig., fam.) to talk about clothes/fashion

► gastar una barbaridad en trapos (fig., fam.) to spend an awful lot on clothes

► navegar a todo trapo (fig., fam.) to make an all-out effort, to make a supreme effort

trasconejar algo (fig., fam.) to mislay/misplace s.th., to lose s.th.

trasero back, rear, hind

► el trasero (fam.) behind (fam., euph.), backside (fam.), bottom (fam.), posterior (euph.), butt (fam., Am.E.), bum (fam., Br.E.)

traspintarse (fig., fam.) to turn out [very] differently or things turn out [very] differently [than one thinks/expects]

el traspontín (fam.) backside (fam.), behind (fam., euph.), bottom (fam.), posterior (euph.), butt (fam., Am.E.), bum (fam., Br.E.)

▷ trasquilar (ir por **lana** y volver trasquilado)

la trastienda back room of a shop

► la trastienda (fig., fam.) backside (fam.), behind (fam., euph.), bottom (fam.), posterior (euph.), butt (fam., Am.E.), bum (fam., Br.E.)

► tener mucha trastienda (fig., fam.) to be very crafty, to be as sly as they come (fam.)

el trasto household utensil

► el trasto (fig., fam.) good-for-nothing

► los trastos (fam.) things, stuff (fam.), goods and chattels (fam., Br.E.) ◆ *¿Tienes tus trastos? Have you got [all] your things [together]?*

► tirar los trastos (fig., fam.) to chuck the whole thing (fam.), to chuck it all in/up (fam., Br.E.)

► tirarse los trastos a la cabeza (fig., fam.) to have a blazing or a flaming [marital] row (fig., fam.)

▷ tratar a alg. a coces (▷ **coz**)
▷ tratar a alg. a **cuerpo** de rey
▷ tratar a alg. a **patada**s/**zapatazo**s
▷ tratar a alg. como a un **perro**

trece thirteen

► mantenerse/seguir en sus trece (fig., fam.) to stick to one's guns (fig.), to hold/stand one's ground (fig.), to stand firm (fig.), to stick firmly to one's opinion

▷ trecho (del **dicho** al hecho hay mucho ~)

la tremolina (fig., fam.) row (fam.), rumpus (fam.), ruckus (fam.), commotion ◆ *Ayer se armó la/una tremolina. It was chaos yesterday. There was one hell of a row yesterday. There was a terrible rumpus yesterday.*

el tren train

► estar como un tren (fig., fam., Esp.) to have a great figure, to be hot stuff (fam.), to look terrific (fam.), to have stunning good looks

► vivir a todo tren (fig.) to live on the fat of the land, to live high on the hog (fam., Am.E.), to live in grand style, to live a luxurious lifestyle, to live like a king (fig.)

la trena (pop.) jail, prison, clink (sl., Br.E.), can (sl., Am.E.), slammer (sl.), jug (sl.), nick (sl., Br.E.)

► estar en la trena to be in prison ▷ estar a la **sombra**

tres three

► como [que] tres y dos son cinco (fig., fam.) as sure as eggs is/are eggs (fam., Br.E.), as sure as sure can be, as sure as the day is long (Am.E.), as sure as night follows day (Br.E.) ◆ *Fue ella, como que tres y dos son cinco. As sure as eggs is eggs, it was she.*

► ni a la de tres (fig., fam.) not possibly, on no account, by no or not by any manner of means, not for the life of one (fam.) ◆ *No puedo convencerla ni a la de tres. I cannot possibly persuade her. I cannot persuade her for the life of me.*

▷ tres (en un **dos** por ~)
▷ tres (no ver ~ en un **burro**)

el trigo wheat

► el trigo (fig., fam.) (money): dough (sl., Am.E.), bread (sl.), sugar (sl.), brass/dosh/lolly (sl., Br.E.), wampum (sl., Am.E.)

► no ser algo/alg. trigo limpio (fig., fam.) (a) (s.th.): to be dishonest, to be fishy (fam.), to be dubious, not to be kosher (fig.), not to be aboveboard (b) (s.o.): not to be trustworthy, to be dishonest, to be a shady customer (fam.), to be a fly-by-night (fam.)

trinar to trill, to warble

► estar alg. que trina (fig., fam.) to be hopping mad (fam.) ▷ estar hecho un **basilisco** ◆ *Tu amigo está que trina. Your friend's hopping mad.*

193

la tripa intestine
▶ echar tripa (fig., fam.) to start to get a paunch (fam.), to put on weight
▶ sacar la tripa de mal año (fam.) to eat one's fill, to eat well
▶ hacer una tripa a alg. (fig., pop.) to get/ make s.o. pregnant, to get s.o. in the family way (fam.), to knock s.o. up (sl.)
▶ echar las tripas (fig., fam.) to spew one's guts out (sl.), to throw up violently
▶ revolver las tripas a alg. (fig., fam.) to turn s.o.'s stomach (fig.), to make s.o.'s stomach turn (fig.), to make s.o. sick to his stomach (fig.), to make s.o. [want to] puke (fam.) ◆ *Esto me revuelve las tripas. This makes me sick to my stomach.*
▶ sacar las tripas a alg. (fig., fam.) to fleece s.o. of everything (fig.), to milk s.o. dry (fig.)
▶ hacer de tripas corazón (fig.) (a) to pluck up (fig.) or screw up [one's] courage (b) to make a virtue of necessity (c) to grasp the nettle (fig.), to grin and bear it (fam.)
▶ tener malas tripas (fig.) to be cruel

la tripita diminutive of tripa
▶ salir con [una] tripita (fig., fam.) to get pregnant

el triunfo triumph, trump
▶ echar un triunfo (fig.) to play one's trump card (fig.)
▶ tener todos los triunfos [en la mano] (fig.) to hold all the trumps (fig.)
▷ triunfo (las **miel**es del ~)

la trompa trunk (elephant)
▶ la trompa (fig., fam.) (a) big nose, big conk (sl., Br.E.), big hooter (fam., hum.) (b) drunkenness
▶ estar trompa to be plastered (fam.), to be sloshed (fam.), to be tight (fam.), to be smashed (sl.)
▶ coger[se] una trompa to get plastered (fam.), to get tight (fam.)

el trompo spinning top
▶ ponerse como un trompo (fig., fam.) to stuff o.s. (fam.), to eat to bursting point
▶ roncar como un trompo (fig.) to snore heavily, to saw wood (fig., hum.)

el troncho stalk
▶ el troncho (pop.) (penis) ▷ el calvo

el tronco trunk (tree)
▶ dormir como un tronco (fam.) to sleep like a log (fam.)
▶ dormirse o quedarse dormido como un tronco (fam.) to go out like a light (fig., fam.)

el trotacalles (fam., pej.) loafer, bum (fam., pej., Am.E.)

la trotacalles (fam.) (a) loafer, bum (fam., pej., Am.E.) (b) streetwalker, prostitute

la trotaconventos (fig., fam.) procuress, go-between

el trote trot
▶ para todo trote (fig., fam.) for everyday use ◆ *Zapatos para todo trote. Shoes for everyday use.*
▶ andar a trote corto (fig.) (walking): to mince
▶ ya no estar para esos trotes (fig.) to be too old for that [sort of thing], not to be up to that [sort of thing] any more ◆ *Ya no estamos para esos trotes. We're not up to that sort of thing any more.*

la trucha trout
▶ pescar una trucha (fig., fam.) to get soaked to the skin
▶ No se pescan truchas a bragas enjutas. (prov.) No pains, no gains. (prov.)

el trueno thunder
▶ salir del trueno y dar con el relámpago to jump out of the frying pan into the fire

la tuerca (mechanics): nut
▶ tener una tuerca floja (fig.) to have a screw loose (fam.), to have rocks in one's head (sl., Am.E.), not to be all there (fam.) ◆ *Tiene una tuerca floja. He's not all there.*
▶ apretar las tuercas a alg. (fig.) to put the screws on s.o. (fig.), to put the pressure on s.o. (fig.), to apply pressure on s.o. (fig.)
▷ tuerto (en tierra de **ciego**s el ~ es rey)

el tuétano marrow
▶ estar mojado hasta los tuétanos (fig., fam.) to be soaked to the skin, to be wet through, to be soaking/dripping wet, to be drenched, not to have a dry stitch on one (fam.)
▶ estar enamorado hasta los tuétanos (fig., fam.) to be head over heels in love ◆ *Está enamorado hasta los tuétanos de ella. He's head over heels in love with her.*

▶ ser español/etc. hasta los tuétanos (fig., fam.) to be a Spaniard/etc. to the core (fig.) or through and through

el tufo stink

▶ tener muchos tufos (fig., fam.) to be very conceited, to be [as] conceited as a barber's cat (fam.), to think no end of o.s. (fam.)

la tumba grave

▶ tener un pie en la tumba (fig.) to have one foot in the grave (fig.) ◆ *Mi abuelo tiene 92 años. Está con un pie en la tumba. My grandfather is 92 years old. He has one foot in the grave.*

▶ cavar su propia tumba (fig.) to dig one's own grave (fig.)

▶ estar mudo como una tumba o ser [como] una tumba (fig.) to be [as] silent as the grave, to keep absolutely quiet, to shut up like a clam (fam.), to keep one's mouth shut (fam.)

▶ correr/lanzarse a tumba abierta (fam.) to go at full lick (fam.), to go like the clappers (fam., Br.E.), to go/drive flat out (fam.)

tumbar to knock down, to knock to the ground

▶ tumbar a alg. (fig., fam.) to waste s.o. (sl., Am.E.) ▷ **cargar**se a alg. (a)

▶ tumbar a una mujer (fig., fam.) to lay a woman (sl.), to knock a woman off (sl., Br.E.) ▷ **calzar**[se] a alg.

▶ beber hasta tumbar a alg. (fig.) to drink s.o. under the table

la tunda shearing

▶ pegar una tunda a alg. (fig., fam.) to give s.o. a [good] hiding/thrashing (fam.)

▷ túnel (hay luz al final del ~)

el tupé toupee

▶ el tupé (fig., fam.) cheek (fam.), nerve (sl.) ◆ *Tuvo el tupé de volver a asomar la jeta por aquí. He had the nerve to show his face around here again.*

▷ turco (**cabeza** de ~)

la tutía zinc oxide preparation

▶ [Contra eso] no hay tutía. (fig., fam.) There's no cure for that [yet].

U

▷ Úbeda (irse por los **cerros** de ~)

último last
▶ ir vestido a la última (fam.) to be dressed in the latest fashion/style ◆ *Siempre va vestida a la última. She's always dressed in the latest style.*
▶ tomar la última (fam.) to have one for the road (fam.) ◆ *Vamos a tomar la última. ¡Barman! Let's have one for the road. Bartender!*
▶ estar en las últimas (fam.) (a) to be at death's door, to be breathing one's last (b) to be on one's last legs (fam.), to be on one's beam-ends (fam., Br.E.), to be broke (fam.)
▶ estar en las diez de últimas (fam.) to be on one's last legs (fam.), to be on one's beam-ends (fam., Br.E.)
▶ hacer las diez de últimas (fam.) not to reach one's goal (fig.), to queer one's own pitch (fam., Br.E.), to damage one's own cause
▷ último (▷ **reír**: quien ríe ~, ríe mejor)
▷ último (dar el ~ **golpe** a algo)
▷ último (dar el ~/[los ~s] **toque**[s] a algo)
▷ último (en última **instancia**)
▷ último (hasta la última **gota**)
▷ último (jugar la última **carta**)

una one
▶ Una no es ninguna. (prov.) Once doesn't count. (prov.)
▶ Una y no más, Santo Tomás. (fam., Esp.) Never again.
▷ untar el **carro**/la **mano**/la **palma** a alg.

el unto (animal) fat
▶ el unto de Méjico o de rana (fig., fam.) backhander (fam.), bribe [money]

la uña nail (fingernail/toenail)
▶ vivir de la uña (pop.) to live from/by stealing, to make one's living from/by stealing
▶ ser uña y carne (fig.) to be inseparable, to be as thick as thieves (fam.), to be hand in glove
▶ tener algo en la uña (fam.) to have a good grip on s.th. (fig.), to have complete command of s.th. (fig.), to have got the hang of s.th. (fam.), to know s.th. very well

▶ empezar a afilarse las uñas (fig.) to start work, to set to work, to roll up one's sleeves (fig.)
▶ dejarse las uñas en algo (fig., fam.) to work one's fingers to the bone at s.th. (fig.), to work very hard at s.th., to break one's back doing s.th. (fig.)
▶ caer en las uñas de alg. (fig.) to fall into s.o.'s clutches (fig.)
▶ enseñar/mostrar las uñas (fig.) to show one's claws/teeth (fig.)
▶ estar de uñas con alg. (fam.) to be at daggers drawn with s.o. (fig., Br.E.)
▷ uña (ser **largo** de ~s)

el/la uñetas (fam.) thief, light-fingered person (fam.)

el urdemalas (fam.) schemer

la urraca magpie
▶ ser una urraca (fig., fam.) to hoard [up] anything, to be a hoarder, to be a squirrel (fig., fam.), to be a pack rat (fig., fam., Am.E.), to be a magpie (fig., fam., Br.E.)
▶ hablar más que una urraca (fig., fam.) to be a real chatterbox (fam.)
▶ ser más ladrón que una urraca (fig., fam.) to steal anything one can get one's hands on, to steal anything that isn't nailed down (fig.) ◆ *Es más ladrona que una urraca. She'll steal anything she can get her hands on.*

la uva grape
▶ estar hecho una uva (fig., fam.) to be [completely] sloshed (fam.) ▷ estar hecho un **cesto**
▶ estar de buena/mala uva (fig., fam.) to be in a good or in a bad/foul mood
▶ tener mala uva (fig., fam.) to be nasty (fig.) ▷ tener mala **leche**
▶ entrar a por uvas (fig.) to take the plunge (fig.) ◆ *Estoy a punto de entrar a por uvas. I'm on the point of taking the plunge. I'm about to take the plunge.*
▶ de uvas a peras (fam.) very rarely, once in a blue moon (fam.) ◆ *Nos hacen una visita de uvas a peras. They pay us a visit once in a blue moon.*

V

la vaca cow
- ▶ estar como una vaca (fig., fam.) to be a barrel (fig., fam.), to be a tub of lard (fig., fam.), to be a fatso (sl.), to be very fat
- ▶ ser la vaca de la boda (fig.) to be the milch cow (fig.), to be the backer
- ▶ las vacas gordas/flacas (fig.) fat (fig.) or boom years, lean years (fig.) ◆ *Han llegado los años de las vacas flacas para la industria del automóvil. The lean years have begun for the automobile/car industry.*
- ▶ pasar las vacas gordas (fig.) to have a great/grand time [of it], to have the time of one's life
- ▷ vaca (pegarle algo a alg. como un **mandil** a una ~)
- ▷ vago (ser más ~ que la **chaqueta** de un guardia)
- ▷ Valencia (dejar a alg. a la **luna** de ~)
- ▷ valer (hombre **prevenido** vale por dos)
- ▷ valer (más vale pecar por **exceso** que por defecto)
- ▷ valer (más vale **prevenir** que curar/lamentar)
- ▷ valer (más vale ser **cabeza** de ratón que cola de león)
- ▷ valer (más vale un **"por si acaso"** que un ¿quién pensara?)
- ▷ valer (no ~ un **ardite/cojón/comino/pito**)
- ▷ valer alg./algo su peso en **oro**
- ▷ valer algo tanto **oro** como pesa
- ▷ valer algo/alg. un **Perú/Potosí**
- ▷ valiente (darse **aires** de ~)
- ▷ valiente (lo **cortés** no quita lo ~)
- ▷ valor (**revestirse** de ~)

el vapor steam
- ▶ a todo vapor (fig.) at full steam (fig.), [at] full tilt, at full speed, flat out (fam.), hammer and tongs (fam.) ◆ *Trabajan a todo vapor. They're working at full steam. They're working flat out. They're going at it hammer and tongs.* ◆ *El proyecto va a todo vapor. The project is going full steam ahead.* ◆ *Íbamos a todo vapor. We were going flat out. We were going at full tilt/speed.*

la vara stick, wand, pike
- ▶ medirlo todo o medirlos a todos con la misma vara (fig.) to lump everything together (fig.), to lump them all together (fig.)
- ▶ No se puede medirlo todo o medirlos a todos con la misma vara. (fig.) You can't just lump everything together. (fig.) You can't just lump them all together. (fig.)
- ▶ doblar la vara de la justicia (fig.) to pervert justice
- ▶ picar de vara larga (fig., fam.) to play it safe
- ▶ tomar varas (fig., fam.) (woman): to like to try to get friendly with men
- ▷ vara (meterse en **camisa** de once ~s)

la vareta small pole, lime twig
- ▶ echar varetas o una vareta (fig., fam.) to make insinuations, to make an insinuation
- ▶ estar/irse de varetas (fig., fam.) to have diarrhea

Vargas
- ▶ ¡Averígüelo Vargas! (fam.) Heaven only knows!
- ▷ variedad (en la ~ está el **gusto**)
- ▷ vaso (▷ **temblar**: dejar un ~ temblando)
- ▷ vaso (▷ **temblar**: un ~ está temblando)
- ▷ vaso (gafas de **culo** de ~)
- ▷ vaso (la **gota** que desborda/colma el ~)
- ▷ vaso (un **culo** de ~)
- ▷ vaso de agua (**ahogarse** en un ~)
- ▷ vaso de agua (hacer un **mar** con un ~)
- ▷ vaso de agua (una **tormenta** en un ~)
- ▷ vecino (cada/cualquier **hijo** de ~)

vegetar (plant): to grow
- ▶ vegetar (fig.) to vegetate (fig., pej.), to live like a cabbage (Br.E.) or like a vegetable (fig., fam.)

el vejestorio (fam., pej.) (a) [piece of] old junk (fam.), old relic (fam.), old crock (fam., Br.E.) (b) old crock (fam., Br.E.), old relic (fam.), old dodderer (fam.)

la vejez old age
- ▶ A la vejez, viruelas. (prov.) There's no fool like an old fool. (prov.) Fancy that happening at his/etc. age!

la vela sail, candle
- ▶ a toda vela (fig.) [at] full tilt ▷ a todo **va-por**
- ▶ levantar velas (fig.) to leave
- ▶ recoger velas (fig.) to give in/up, to draw in one's horns (fig.), to throw in the towel/sponge (fig.) ◆ *Probemos al menos una vez más. Es demasiado prematuro recoger velas.* Let's try at least one more time. It's too early/soon to give in/up.
- ▶ estar a la vela (fig.) to be ready
- ▶ estar a dos velas (fig., fam.) to be broke (fam.)
- ▶ estar entre dos velas (fig., fam.) to be tipsy, to be merry, to be tiddly (fam., Br.E.), to be half-seas over (fam.)
- ▶ tender las velas (fig.) to seize the opportunity
- ▶ las velas (fig., fam.) snot (that runs down from the nose) (fam./vulg.)
- ▶ encender una vela a San Miguel o a Dios y otra al diablo (fig.) to want to have it both ways
- ▶ tener una vela encendida por si la otra se apaga (fig.) to have another iron in the fire (fig.), to have another string to one's bow (fig.)
- ▶ ... vela en este entierro (fig., fam.) ◆ *¿Quién te ha dado vela en este entierro?* Who asked for your opinion? What business is it of yours? Who asked you to poke your nose in? (fig.) ◆ *Nadie te ha dado vela en este entierro.* You've got no business being here. ◆ *No se les dará vela en este entierro.* They will have no say or will not be given any say in this matter. ◆ *Aunque no tenemos vela en este entierro ...* We know that nobody asked for our opinion or that this is none of our business, but ...
- ▶ derecho como una vela (fig.) as straight as a ramrod, bolt upright
- ▶ estar entre cuatro velas (fig.) to be in the coffin

la veleta weather vane
- ▶ ser un/una veleta (fig.) to be a weathercock (fig.) ▷ bailar a cualquier **son**

el velo veil
- ▶ descorrer el velo sobre algo (fig.) to unveil/uncover s.th. (fig.), to reveal s.th. (fig.) ◆ *Descorrieron el velo sobre el secreto.* They unveiled the secret.

- ▶ correr/echar un velo sobre algo (fig.) to draw a veil over s.th. (fig.), to shroud s.th. (fig.)

la vena vein
- ▶ tener vena de ... (fig.) to have/show a talent for ..., to have the makings of ... (fig.) ◆ *Tiene vena de escritor.* He shows a talent for writing. He has the makings of a writer.

vencer to defeat, to conquer
- ▶ Vine, vi y vencí. (prov.) I came, I saw, I conquered. (Latin: veni, vidi, vici)
- ▶ darse por vencido to give in/up, to cry/say uncle (fam., Am.E.)

la venda bandage
- ▶ tener una venda en los ojos (fig.) to be blind (fig., fam.) ◆ *Cree que es sincera. Debe [de] tener una venda en los ojos.* He thinks/believes that she's sincere. He must be blind.
- ▶ caérsele a alg. la venda de los ojos (fig.) scales fall from s.o.'s eyes (fig.) ◆ *De repente se le cayó la venda de los ojos.* Suddenly the scales fell from his eyes.
- ▶ hacer caer la venda de los ojos a alg. (fig.) to open s.o.'s eyes (fig.), to remove the scales from s.o.'s eyes (fig.) ◆ *Ella no se daba cuenta de qué estaba pasando allí. Tuve que hacer caerle la venda de los ojos.* She didn't realize what was going on there. I had to open her eyes.

vender to sell
- ▶ vender a alg. (fig.) to sell s.o. down the river (betray) (fig., fam.)
- ▷ vender algo a **huevo**
- ▷ vender algo por un **pedazo** de pan
- ▷ vender **salud**
- ▷ venderse como **rosquilla**s

venir to come
- ▶ ni ir ni venir (fig.) to be undecided ◆ *Ni va ni viene.* He's/she's undecided.
- ▶ venir a menos (fig.) to come down in the world (fig.), to become impoverished ◆ *Es un aristócrata venido a menos.* He's an impoverished aristocrat.
- ▶ venir ancho algo a alg. (fig.) not to be up to s.th. (fam.), s.th. is too much for s.o. ◆ *Les viene muy ancho el cargo.* They're not up to the job at all. The job is way too much for them.

▶ No me va ni me viene. (fam.) It's/that's no skin off my nose. (fam.)

▷ ventana (**tirar** algo por la ~)

▷ ventana (tirar la **casa** por la ~)

ventilar to air

▶ ventilarle a alg. las orejas (fig., fam.) to box s.o.'s ears

ver to see

▶ tener que ver con una mujer (pop.) to have a relationship or an affair with a woman

▶ no tener nada que ver con algo to have nothing to do with s.th. ◆ *No tengo nada que ver con ese banco. I have nothing to do with that bank.*

▶ vérselas con alg. (fig.) to have to deal with s.o., to be in trouble with s.o. ◆ *Tendrán que vérselas con nosotros como se atrevan a maltratarte. They'll have us to deal with or be in trouble with us if they dare to ill-treat you.*

▶ tener que verse y desearse para hacer algo (fig., fam.) to take s.o. a great effort to do s.th., to have such a struggle or sweat (fam.) to do s.th. ◆ *Tuve que verme y desearme para hacer esto. It took me a great effort to do this.*

▶ verlas venir (fig., fam.) to see s.th. coming ◆ *Las veíamos venir, por eso tomamos precauciones. We saw it coming, so we took precautions.*

▶ no haberlas visto [nunca] más gordas (fig., fam.) to have never heard of it

▶ ni quien tal vio (fam.) (intensifies a negative) ◆ *No lo hice yo ni quien tal vio. I really didn't do it. ◆ No fue ella ni quien tal vio. It was really not she.*

▶ [Allí] donde fueres haz como vieres o lo que vieres. (prov.) When in Rome, do as the Romans [do]. (prov.)

▷ ver (no ~ tres en un **burro**)

▷ verano (pasar como una **nube** de ~)

▷ verano (una **golondrina** no hace ~)

▷ verano (una **nube** de ~)

▷ veras (entre **bromas** y ~)

▷ veras (mezclar **bromas** con ~)

la verdad truth

▶ decirle a alg. cuatro verdades o las verdades del barquero (fig.) to tell s.o. a few home truths, to give s.o. a piece of one's mind

▷ verdad (a la **hora** de la ~)

▷ verdad (los **niños** y los locos dicen las ~es)

verde green

▶ poner verde a alg. (fig., fam.) to give s.o. a good wigging (Br.E.) or dressing-down (fam.), to call s.o. all the names under the sun

▶ ¡Están verdes! (prov.) [It's] sour grapes! (fig.)

▷ verde (el **viejo** ~)

el verde green

▶ el verde (pop.) 1000-peseta bill (Am.E.) or note (Br.E.)

▶ darse un verde (fig., fam.) to relax [for a change], to take it easy or have a breather [for a change] (fam.)

la verdulería fruit and vegetable store, greengrocer's [shop] (Br.E.)

▶ la verdulería (fig., fam.) dirty joke

▶ decir verdulerías to tell dirty jokes, to talk smut (fig.)

la vereda footpath

▶ meter/poner a alg. en vereda (fig.) to put s.o. [back] on the straight and narrow

la vergüenza shame

▶ caérsele a alg. la cara de vergüenza s.o. is/feels so ashamed [of himself], he just wants the earth to open and swallow him up or he just wants to curl up and die (fam.) ◆ *Se me cayó la cara de vergüenza. I was so ashamed, I just wanted the earth to open and swallow me up/I just wanted to curl up and die.*

▷ vergüenza (estar **muerto** de ~)

▷ vergüenza (**morir**se de ~)

▷ verso (contar/saber la **biblia** en ~)

▷ vestidura (**rasgar**se las ~s)

vestir to dress

▶ vestir el rostro de gravedad (fig.) to put on a serious expression

▶ vestir el rostro de alegría (fig.) to put on a joyful expression

▶ irse al cielo vestido y calzado (fig., fam.) to be sure to go to heaven ◆ *Ella se irá al cielo vestida y calzada. She's sure to go to heaven.*

▶ el mismo/la misma que viste y calza (fig., fam.) selfsame, very same ◆ *Soy el mismo que viste y calza. It's I[, and nobody else]. It's the selfsame. ◆ ¿Aquella mujer allí no es tu tía? [Es] la misma que viste y calza. Isn't that* woman your aunt over there? [It's] the very same. It sure is.

▶ Vísteme despacio, que estoy de prisa o que tengo prisa. (prov.) More haste, less speed! (prov.)

▷ vestir (▷ **último**: ir vestido a la última)

▷ vestirse a lo gran señor (▷ el **señor**)

▷ vestirse por la **cabeza**/por los **pies**

el viaje trip, journey

▶ estar de viaje (fig., fam.) (a) to be on a trip (sl.), to be spaced out (fam.), to be on drugs, to be high (fam.), to be stoned (sl.), to be out of one's head (sl.) (b) to be in the picture (fam.)

la víbora viper

▶ criar la víbora en el seno (fig.) to cherish a viper in one's bosom (fig.)

▷ víbora (tener una **lengua** de ~)

el vicio vice

▶ Los vicios son los hijos del ocio. (prov.) Vices are born of idleness. (prov.) Idleness is the root of all evil. (prov.) An idle brain is the devil's workshop. (prov.) The devil finds work for idle hands. (prov.)

▷ vicio (el **ocio**/la **ociosidad** es la madre de todos los ~s)

▷ victoria (**cantar** ~)

la vida life

▶ Así es la vida. That's the way the ball bounces. (fam., Am.E.) That's the way the cookie crumbles. (fam., Am.E.)

▶ tener siete vidas [como los gatos] (fig.) to have nine lives (fig.), to have as many lives as a cat (fig.)

▶ ganarse la vida (fam.) to earn/make a living, to earn one's daily bread (fam.), to earn one's bread and butter (fam.), to earn one's crust (fam.)

▶ jugarse la vida (fig.) to risk one's life, to risk one's neck (fam.)

▶ pegarse la vida padre (fam.) to live/have an easy life, to live the life of Riley (fig.)

▶ echarse a la vida (fig.) to take to/up prostitution

▶ ser de la vida (fig.) to be a prostitute

▷ vida (**enterrar**se en ~)

▷ vida (estar en la **flor** de la ~)

▷ vida (la ~ de **perros**)

▷ vida (la ~ no es un lecho de **rosas**)

el vidrio glass

▶ [tener que] pagar los vidrios rotos (fig., fam.) to [have to] take the responsibility, to [have to] carry the can (fam., Br.E.), to [have to] take the rap (sl., Am.E.)

▷ vieja (el **cuento** de ~s)

viejo; el viejo old; old man

▶ estar haciéndose viejo (fig., fam.) to avoid all work, to steer clear of all work (fig.) ◆ ¿Qué hace él? Se está haciendo viejo. What is he doing? He's avoiding all work.

▶ el viejo verde (fam.) dirty/randy old man (fam.), randy old goat (fig., fam.), old lecher

▷ viejo (**caerse** [a pedazos] de ~)

▷ viejo (ser más ~ que **Carracuca**/que la **sarna**)

▷ viejo (ser [un] **perro**/**zorro** ~)

el viento wind

▶ ser libre como el viento (fig.) to be [as] free as [the] air (fam.), to be footloose and fancy-free (fam.) ◆ No creo que mi hermano se case. Le gusta ser libre como el viento. I don't think that my brother will get married. He likes being footloose and fancy-free.

▶ papar viento (fig., fam.) to gape, to gawk (fam.), to gawp (fam., Br.E.), to stand around gaping

▶ beber los vientos (poético) to run like the wind (fig.)

▶ beber los vientos por algo (fig., fam.) to yearn/long for s.th.

▶ beber/sorber los vientos por alg. (fig., fam.) to be crazy/nuts about s.o. (fam.), to have a crush on s.o. (fam.), to be madly in love with s.o. (fam.)

▶ pregonar/proclamar algo a los cuatro vientos (fig.) to tell all and sundry about s.th., to shout s.th. from the rooftops (fig.)

▶ contra viento y marea (fig.) against all [the] odds, come what may, come hell or high water (fam.), through thick and thin (fam.) ◆ Triunfaron contra viento y marea. They triumphed/succeeded against all odds. ◆ luchar contra viento y marea para + infinitivo to fight against all the odds to + infinitive ◆ Defenderemos nuestros derechos contra viento y marea. We will defend our rights come hell or high water. ◆ apoyar a alg. contra viento y marea to stick by/to s.o. through thick and thin

▶ Quien siembra vientos recoge tempestades. (prov.) He who sows the wind will reap the whirlwind. (prov.)
▷ viento (**largarse** con ~ fresco)

el **vientre** belly
▶ llenarse el vientre (fam.) to stuff o.s. (fam.), to make a [real] pig of o.s. (fam.)
▶ sacar el vientre de mal año (fam.) to eat one's fill, to eat well
▶ servir al vientre (fig., fam.) to gormandize, to have a feast
▶ desde el vientre de su/etc. madre (fig.) from/since birth ◆ *Soy ciego desde el vientre de mi madre. I've been blind since birth. I was born blind.*

la **viga** beam
▶ estar contando las vigas (fig.) to be staring into space, to be gazing vacantly at the ceiling
▷ viga (ver la **paja** en el ojo ajeno y no la ~ en el propio)

la **vihuela** early form of the guitar
▶ tocar la vihuela (fig., fam.) to do nothing
▷ **cojón**: tocarse los cojones
▷ vileza (**pobreza** no es ~)

Villadiego place name
▶ tomar/coger las de Villadiego (fam.) to take to one's heels, to beat it quick (sl.)

vilo
▶ en vilo [up] in the air
▶ estar en vilo (fig.) to be left/kept in suspense

el **vinagre** vinegar
▶ poner cara de vinagre (fig., fam.) to make a sour face (fig.), to put on a sour expression (fig.)
▶ estar hecho un vinagre (fam.) to be hopping mad (fam.)

el **vino** wine
▶ ser un vino peleón (fig., fam.) to be [a] cheap/coarse wine, to be plonk (fam., Br.E.)
▶ ser un vino de una oreja (fam.) to be [an] excellent wine
▶ ser un vino de dos orejas (fam.) to be [an] absolutely wonderful wine, to be [a] divine wine (fig., fam.), to be [a] heavenly wine (fam.)
▶ bautizar/cristianizar el vino (fig., fam.) to water [down] the wine

▶ tener el vino agrio/alegre (fig., fam.) to get nasty (fig.) or merry after a few glasses of wine
▶ dormir el vino (fig.) to sleep it off (fam.), to sleep off a hangover (fam.)
▷ vino (con **pan** y ~ se anda el camino)
▷ vino (llamar al **pan**, pan y al ~, ~)
▷ vino (**regar** una comida con ~)
▷ vino (un **señor** ~)

la **viña** vineyard
▶ De todo tiene la o hay en la viña del Señor. (prov.) (a) It takes all kinds/sorts to make a world. (prov.) There's nowt so queer as folk. (prov., Br.E.) (b) We all have our little failings. Nobody's perfect.
▶ De mis viñas vengo. (fig., fam.) I've nothing to do with it/this. I've nothing to do with the/this matter. Search me! (fam.)
▷ violeta (el **erudito**/la **erudita** a la ~)
▷ violín (**rascar** el ~)
▷ virtud (hacer de la **necesidad** ~)
▷ viruela (a la **vejez**, ~s)

la **visión** vision
▶ ver visiones (fig., fam.) to be seeing things ◆ *No hay nadie en esta casa. Tú ves visiones. There's nobody in this house. You're seeing things.*
▶ estar como viendo visiones (fig., fam.) s.o. can't believe his eyes ◆ *En aquel momento estuve como viendo visiones. I couldn't believe my eyes at that moment.*
▷ víspera (estar como **tonto** en ~s)

la **vista** eyesight, look, view
▶ estar a la vista (fam.) to be obvious
▶ echar la vista encima a alg. (fam.) to see s.o. ◆ *Hace mucho tiempo que no les echo la vista encima. I haven't seen them for a long time.*
▶ comerse a alg. con la vista (fig., fam.) to devour s.o. with one's eyes (fig.) ◆ *Se la comía con la vista. He devoured her with his eyes.*
▶ a vista de pájaro bird's-eye view of ◆ *Desde los rascacielos se ve Nueva York a vista de pájaro. From the skyscrapers you get a bird's-eye view of New York.*
▷ vista (▷ **gordo**: hacer la ~ gorda)
▷ vista (**herir** la ~)

vivir to live
▶ Vivir y dejar vivir. (prov.) To live and let live. (prov.)
▶ No se vive más que una vez. (prov.) You only have one life to live. (prov.)
▷ vivir (no sólo de **pan** vive el hombre)
▷ vivir a **cuerpo** de rey/a lo gran señor (▷ el **señor**)/a todo **tren**
▷ vivir como **Dios** en Francia/**pava** en corral
▷ vivir como un **canónigo/príncipe**
▷ vivir de **gorra**/de la **uña**
▷ vivir donde **Cristo** dio las tres voces/etc.
▷ vivir donde el **diablo** perdió el poncho
▷ vivir en el quinto **infierno/pino**
▷ vivir en la **luna**/las **nubes**
▷ vivir en la quinta **puñeta**
▷ vivir **tabique** por medio

vivo alive, living
▶ afectar a alg. en lo más vivo (fig.) to affect s.o. [very] deeply ◆ *Su muerte nos afectó en lo más vivo. His death affected us very deeply.*
▶ llegar a o herir/tocar en lo más vivo a alg. (fig.) to cut s.o. to the quick (fig.), to hurt s.o. [very] deeply (fig.), to [really] touch/get s.o. on the raw (fig.) ◆ *Tus palabras le llegaron a o le/lo hirieron en lo más vivo. Your words cut him to the quick.*
▷ vivo (dejar a alg. en **cueros** [~s])
▷ vivo (en **cueros** [~s])
▷ vivo (herir a alg. en **carne** viva)
▷ vivo (llorar a **lágrima** viva)
▷ vivo (tener el **genio** ~)

el vivo, la viva (fig., fam.) sharp/smooth operator (fam.), crafty devil (fam.), sly one ◆ *Es un vivo. He's a smooth operator.*

▷ vizcaíno (la **noche** vizcaína)
▷ Vizcaya (llevar **hierro** a ~)

el voceras (fam.) bigmouth (fam.), loudmouth (fam.)

volcar to knock over, to tip over
▶ volcarse (fig., fam.) to do one's utmost, to go out of one's way (fig.), to lean/bend over backwards (fam.), to go all out (fam.) ◆ *Se volcó para ayudarnos. He did his utmost to help us.* ◆ *Nos volcamos por ella. We backed her up to the hilt.* ◆ *Me volqué por complacerlos. I went out of my way or leaned/leant over backwards to satisfy or please them.*
▷ voluntad (▷ **santo**: hacer su santa ~)

▷ voluntad (**ganar**se la ~ de alg.)
▷ voto (no tener ni **voz** ni ~)

la voz voice
▶ llevar la voz cantante (fig., fam.) to call the tune/shots (fig.) ▷ llevar la **batuta**
▶ No se oye más voz que la suya. (fig.) He's/she's talking big. (fam.) He's/she's bragging.
▶ tener voz en capítulo (fig.) to have a say (in a matter)
▶ no tener ni voz ni voto (fig.) to have no say or not to have any say (in a matter) ◆ *No tienen ni voz ni voto en esto. They have no say in this/the matter.*
▶ corre la voz [de] que ... (fig.) there is a rumor going [a]round that . . . , it is rumored that . . . , rumor has it that . . . , scuttlebutt has it that . . . (fam., Am.E.) ◆ *Corre la voz [de] que tiene un lío con ella. It is rumored that he has an affair with her. Scuttlebutt has it that he has an affair with her.*
▷ voz (vivir/estar donde **Cristo** dio las tres voces)

el vuelo flight
▶ cazarlas/cogerlas/pescarlas al vuelo (fig., fam.) to catch on immediately (fam.), to get (fam.) or grasp (fig.) or twig (sl., Br.E.) it at once, to be [very] quick on the uptake ◆ *Es muy listo. Siempre las coge al vuelo. He's very bright. He always catches on immediately.*
▶ alzar/levantar el vuelo (fig.) (a) to clear off (fam.) (b) (young person): to begin to stand on one's own two feet, to spread one's wings (fig.), to leave the parental nest (fig.)
▶ cortar los vuelos a alg. (fig.) to clip s.o.'s wings (fig.)
▷ vuelo (echar las **campanas** al ~)

la vuelta turn, revolution, lap, round, return
▶ poner a alg. de vuelta y media (fig., fam.) to give s.o. a piece of one's mind, to give s.o. a good telling-off or dressing-down (fam.)
▶ dar una vuelta a alg. (fig., fam.) to beat s.o. up, to give s.o. a [good] hiding (fam.)
▶ dar cien vueltas a alg. (fig., fam.) to be streets ahead of s.o. (fam.), to be miles better than s.o. (fam.), to run rings around s.o. (fam.) ▷ **comer**se crudo a alg. ◆ *Él les da cien vueltas a los otros estudiantes. He's streets ahead of the other students.* ◆ *Ella te*

dará cien vueltas bebiendo. She'll drink you under the table.

▶ coger las vueltas a alg. (fig., fam.) to know how to handle s.o.

▶ dar muchas vueltas a algo (fig.) to give s.th. a lot of thought

▶ andar[se] con vueltas (fig., fam.) to beat around/about the bush (fig.)

▶ guardar las vueltas (fig.) to be careful, to watch out, to be on one's guard

▶ No hay que darle vueltas. (fig.) That's the way it is. There are no two ways about it. There's no doubt or mistake about it.

▶ ser de muchas vueltas (fam.) to know a lot of tricks

▷ vuelta (dar ~s a la **almohada**)

▷ vuelta (dar la ~ a la **tortilla**)

▷ vuelta (dar más ~s que un **tiovivo**)

▷ vuelta (eso/la cosa no tiene ~ de **hoja**)

W

▷ Wamba (en tiempos del **rey** ~)

Y

la yacija [rough] bed
▶ ser de mala yacija (fig., fam.) to sleep badly, to be a restless sleeper

la yema yolk
▶ dar en la yema (fig.) to hit the nail on the head (fig.)

la yerba grass
▶ la yerba (fig., fam.) grass (sl.) ▷ la hierba

yerto stiff
▶ quedarse yerto (fig.) to be scared stiff (fam.), to be petrified or paralyzed with fear/horror (fig.)

el/la yonqui (fam.) junkie (fam.), drug addict

el yugo yoke
▶ sacudir el yugo (fig.) to throw off the yoke (fig.)

Z

la zaga (car/etc.): back part, rear
▶ no ir en zaga a alg. (fig.) to be just as or every bit as good as s.o. ◆ *Tienes un talento para los idiomas, y tu hermana no te va en zaga. You have a talent/gift for languages, and your sister is just as good.* ◆ *Él no le va en zaga a nadie. He is second to none.*
▶ quedarse a la zaga de o en zaga a alg. (fig.) to be behind s.o. ◆ *Se ha quedado muy a la zaga de su hermano. He's well behind his brother.*
▶ dejar en zaga a alg. (fig.) to leave s.o. behind, to outstrip s.o. (fig.)

zambullir to dip, to plunge
▶ zambullir a alg. en la cárcel (fig., pop.) to clap s.o. in jail (fam.) ▷ meter a alg. donde no vea el **sol**

Zamora Zamora
▶ No se ganó Zamora en una hora. (prov.) Rome was not built in a day. (prov.)

el/la zampabollos o **zampatortas** (fam.) glutton, greedy-guts (hum., Br.E.)

la zanahoria carrot
▶ la nariz de zanahoria (fig.) drinker's nose

la zanca leg (bird)
▶ la zanca (fig., fam.) [long] leg, matchstick leg (fig.)
▶ andar en zancas de araña (fig.) to make excuses

el zancajo heel
▶ darle al zancajo (fig., fam.) to take to one's heels
▶ roer los zancajos a alg. (fig.) not to have a good word to say about s.o., to pull s.o. to pieces (fig., fam.)
▶ no llegarle a alg. a los zancajos (fig.) s.o. can't hold a candle to s.o. (fig.), not to be a patch on s.o. (fam.), not to be fit to tie s.o.'s shoelaces or bootlaces (fig.) ◆ *No le llega a los zancajos a su hermano. He can't hold a candle to his brother.*

el zanco stilt
▶ andar/estar en zancos (fig., fam.) to be in a good/high position (fig.), to have gone up the social ladder (fig.)

la zanguanga (fam.) fictitious illness
▶ hacer la zanguanga to malinger, to swing the lead (fam., Br.E.)

el zapatazo blow with a shoe
▶ tratar a alg. a zapatazos (fig.) to treat s.o. very badly/rudely, to treat s.o. like dirt (fam.)

el zapatero shoemaker
▶ ¡Zapatero, a tus zapatos! (prov.) Stick to your last! (prov.) Stick to what you know!

el zapato shoe
▶ saber dónde aprieta el zapato (fig.) to know where the shoe pinches (fig.), to know where the problem lies or the problems lie
▶ No quisiera estar en sus zapatos. (fam.) I wouldn't like to be in his shoes. (fam.)
▶ estar como tres en un zapato (fig.) to be packed in like sardines (fig.)
▷ zapato (alegrarse como un **niño** con ~s nuevos)
▷ zapato (encontrar la **horma** de su ~)
▷ zapato (hasta los **gatos** quieren ~s)
▷ zapato (no llegarle a alg. a la **suela** del ~)
▷ zapato (tener un **pie** en dos ~s)
▷ zapato (¡**Zapatero**, a tus ~s!)

el zarandillo small sieve
▶ el zarandillo (fig., fam.) live wire (fig.), [very] active person
▶ traer/llevar a alg. como un zarandillo (fig.) to keep s.o. on the go

la zarpa paw
▶ echar la zarpa a algo (fig., fam.) to grab s.th., to get/lay hold of s.th., to get one's hands on s.th., to swipe s.th. (sl.)

zarpar to weigh anchor
▶ zarpar con rumbo desconocido (fig.) to go for/on a jaunt [through the countryside]

el zarzo canework, wattle
▶ menear el zarzo a alg. (fig., fam.) to give s.o. a hiding/tanning (fam.)

la zorra vixen
- ▶ la zorra (fig., fam.) prostitute, whore, tart (sl.), hooker (sl., Am.E.)
- ▶ la zorra (fam.) drunkenness
- ▶ pillar una zorra to get drunk, to get tight (fam.), to get canned (sl., Br.E.)

la zorrera foxhole
- ▶ la zorrera (fig., fam.) smoky/frowsy/fuggy (fam. Br.E.)/stuffy room or pad

el zorro fox (dog fox)
- ▶ el zorro (fig.) sly/crafty person
- ▶ ser [un] zorro viejo (fig.) to be an old fox (fig.), to be a cunning old devil (fam.)
- ▶ estar hecho unos zorros (fam.) to be completely done in/up (fam.) ▷ estar hecho **cisco**
- ▷ zorro (ser más **corrido** que un ~ viejo)

zullarse (pop.) (a) to shit o.s. (vulg.) (b) to fart (vulg.), to let off [a fart] (fam., Br.E.)

zumbar to drone, to hum, to buzz
- ▶ zumbarle a alg. los cuarenta/etc. años (fig., fam.) to be close to forty/etc. [years of age]
- ◆ *Ya le zumban los cincuenta. He's already close to fifty.*
- ▶ zumbarse a una mujer (fig., fam.) to bang a woman (vulg.), to knock a woman off (sl., Br.E.) ▷ **calzar**[se] a alg.
- ▶ zumbársela (fig., fam.) (to masturbate) ▷ tocar la **campana**

zurdo left-handed
- ▶ no ser zurdo (fig., fam.) not to be stupid, to be no fool

la zurra tanning
- ▶ dar una zurra a alg. (fig., fam.) to give s.o. a tanning/hiding (fam.)
- ▷ zurrapa (al primer **tapón**, ~[s])
- ▷ zurrar la **badana** a alg.

English-Spanish Dictionary and Index

This dictionary and index provides the Spanish equivalents for over 8,000 English expressions. Each Spanish equivalent is cross-referenced to a more complete treatment, often including an example sentence, in the main Spanish-English Idiomatic Dictionary; the appropriate headword is indicated in bold, whenever it is not the first word of the expression. For a more complete explanation of conventions and abbreviations used in this index, consult the Introduction.

A

A (from ~ to Z) de **cabo** a cabo/rabo o de
punta a cabo; desde la **cruz** hasta la
fecha; de **pe** a pa

aback (be completely taken ~) quedarse **frío**;
quedarse de una **pieza**

ablaze (s.o.'s eyes are ~ with anger/indignation)
echar **fuego** por los ojos

to be ablaze with desire abrasarse en deseo

to be about (have no idea/not to have a clue what it's
[all] about) no saber uno lo que se pesca
(▷ **pescar**)

to be about 40/etc. rondar por/rozar los cuarenta/
etc.

to be above s.o.'s head ser **chino** algo para alg.

aboveboard sin **tapujos**

aboveboard (not to be ~) no ser **trigo** limpio

absence (be conspicuous by one's ~) brillar alg. por
su **ausencia**

to be absent from s.th. **fumar**se algo

the absentee is always [in the] wrong ausente sin
culpa, ni presente sin disculpa

absolute por los cuatro **costados**; rematado;
solemne

absolutely a **pie** juntillo

absorbed (become ~ in s.th.) **cebar**se/**enfrascar**se
en algo

to be absurd no tener **cabo** ni cuerda/**pie**s ni
cabeza

absurd answers (give ~) irse por los **cerros** de
Úbeda

abundance (in ~) a **granel/manta/patada**s

abuse (heap ~ on s.o.) poner a alg. como un
Cristo

to accept (not to want to ~ that one is on the wrong
track) meter la cabeza en un **puchero**

accident (have a bad ~) pegarse un **tortazo**

to accompany a meal with wine regar una comida
con vino

accomplished hecho y derecho

account (have ~s/an ~ to settle with s.o.) tener
cuentas pendientes con alg.

account (give a blow-by-blow ~ [of s.th.]) contar la
biblia en verso; contar algo con puntos y
comas

account (on no ~) ni a la de **tres**

accounting (there's no ~ for taste) sobre **gusto**s
no hay nada escrito/para cada gusto se
pintó un color

accounting (there's no ~ for taste!) hay **gusto**s
que merecen palos

ace (be an ~ . . .) ser un **hacha** [en/para algo];
pintarse uno solo/pintárselas solo para
algo

ace (be/come within an ~ of) [por] el **canto** de un
duro

ace (have an ~ in the hole) guardarse un as en la
manga

ace (keep an ~ up one's sleeve) guardarse un as
en la **manga**

aces (hold all the ~) llevar/tener [todas] las de
ganar

aches and pains **gotera**s

act (catch s.o. in the ~) coger a alg. en el **garlito/**
con las manos en la **masa**

act (get in on the ~) meter su **cuchara**

act (perform a skillful balancing ~) bailar en la
cuerda floja

act (put on an ~) hacer el **paripé**

act (stupid ~) la burrada

to act (be ready to ~) estar al **pie** del cañón

to act as if nothing had happened quedarse/estar
tan **campante/fresco/pancho**

to act big darse **aires** de grandeza; echar de
bolina; ponerse como una gallina **clueca**;
darse **charol**; hinchar**se**; ponerse **moño**s

to act diplomatically/cautiously nadar entre dos
aguas; [nadar y] guardar la ropa

to act dumb hacerse el **sueco**

to act freely hacer de su **capa** un sayo

to act high and mighty darse **aires** de grandeza;
pintar la **cigüeña**

to act independently campar por sus respetos

to act on one's own hook campar por sus respetos

to act surprised hacerse de **nueva**s

to act the big shot darse **aires** de grandeza; echar
de **bolina**; pintar la **cigüeña**; ponerse
como una gallina **clueca**; darse **charol**;
alzar/levantar el **gallo**; ponerse **moño**s

to act the buffoon/fool hacer el **gracioso/oso**

to act the elegant/refined man/woman meterse a
finolis

to act tough ([try to] ~) darse **aires** de valiente;
hacerse el **hombre**

action (a person who is all talk and no ~) el/la
cantamañanas

action (be all talk [and no ~]) cacarear y no poner
huevos; írsele a alg. la **fuerza** por la boca

action (take drastic ~ [against s.o.]) sin pararse en
barras (example); echar los **perro**s a alg.;
cortar por lo **sano**

action (we have to take ~ now) o somos o no
somos (▷ **ser**)

actions (everyone must bear/face the consequences
of his ~) quien por su **gusto** padece, vaya
al infierno a quejarse

actions speak louder than words del **dicho** al
hecho hay mucho trecho; dicho sin hecho
no trae provecho; **obra**s son amores, que
no buenas razones
active person ([very] ~) el zarandillo
actor (ham ~) el maleta
to adapt [o.s.] to the circumstances bailar al **son**
que le tocan a alg.
to add up (not to ~) no **pegar**
addict (drug ~) el/la yonqui
to adjust [o.s.] to the circumstances bailar al **son**
que le tocan a alg.
ado (much ~ about nothing) mucho **ruido** y
pocas nueces
ado (without much ~) sin **alharaca**s ni
bambollas
to adore s.o. mirarse en alg. como en un **espejo**
to adorn o.s. with borrowed plumes adornarse con
plumas ajenas
to adulate s.o. lavar la **cara** a alg.
advantage (shamelessly take ~ of s.th.) ponerse las
botas
advantage (turn things to one's ~) llevar el **agua** a
su molino
advantage (work things to one's own ~) arrimar el
ascua a su sardina
advantages (get ~) enchufarse
adventurous (be more ~!) ¡nadie muere de
cornada de burro!
affair (come in on an ~) tomar **carta**s en un
asunto
affair (have an ~ [with a woman]) echar una **cana**
al aire; tener que **ver** con una mujer
affair ([love] ~) el apaño
affair (get involved in a nasty ~) meterse en un
fregado
affairs (poke one's nose into other people's ~)
meterse en **camisa** de once varas
to affect s.o. [very] deeply afectar a alg. en lo más
vivo
affected (be deeply ~ by s.th.) llegarle algo a alg.
al **alma**
affection (be overflowing with ~) rebosar de
ternura
to be aflame with desire abrasarse en deseo
afloat (keep/stay ~) mantenerse a **flote**
after (just ~ 10/etc.) a las diez/etc. y **pico**
after all al fin y al **cabo**
to be after s.th. pelárselas por algo (▷ **pelar**)
to be after s.th. (you can see what s.o. is after) se le
ve el **plumero** a alg.
against (be up ~ s.o.) habérselas con alg.
(▷ **haber**)
age (awkward ~) la **edad** burral/ingrata/del pavo
age (be close to forty/etc. years of ~) **zumbar**le a
alg. los cuarenta/etc. años
age (fancy that happening at his/etc. ~!) a la **vejez**,
viruelas

age (in a coon's ~) en las **Calendas** griegas;
cuando meen las **gallinas**; cuando las
ranas críen pelo; en la **semana** que no
tenga jueves/de tres jueves
age (lie about one's ~) quitarse/restarse **años**
ages ago hacer una **tostada** de años
ago (donkey's years/[very] long ~) año de/
tiempo[s] de/días de **Maricastaña**; del año
de/en el año de la **nana**; en [los] tiempos
de **ñangué**; del año de o en el año de la
pera/polca; en tiempos del **rey** que
rabió/del rey Wamba
to agree to everything decir **amén** a todo
to agree with a nod afirmar con el **gesto**
to agree with s.o. hacer **coro** con alg.
agreed de **marras**
agreement (nod in ~) afirmar con el **gesto**
aid (be ready to go to s.o.'s ~) estar al **quite**
to aim high (even the most ordinary people ~)
hasta los **gatos** quieren zapatos
to aim high[er] picar [**más**] alto
air (be [as] free as [the] ~) ser libre como el **aire/
viento**
air (be up in the ~) estar en el **aire**
air (build castles in the ~) hacer **castillo**s en el
aire
air (clear the ~) aclarar las cosas
air (disappear/vanish into thin ~) desaparecer
por [el] **escotillón**; hacerse **humo**
air (hot ~) jarabe de pico; música celestial
air (it's [still] all up in the ~) la **pelota** está/sigue
en el tejado
air (live on ~) sustentarse del aire
air (put on an innocent ~) mirar con **ojos** de
sobrino
airs (give o.s. [grand] ~) darse **aires** de grandeza;
tener muchas **ínfulas**
airs (put on ~) alzar/levantar el **gallo**; darse
tono
aisles (roll in the ~ [with laughter]) revolcarse de
la risa
akimbo (with arms ~) en **jarra**s
alcohol (as a problem solver) el quitapenas
alert (be extremely ~) dormir con los **ojos**
abiertos; estar con cien **ojos**
alert (be [on the] ~) estar [con] **ojo** avisor; avivar
el/[los] **ojo**[s]
alike (be/look extraordinarily ~) ser **primo**
hermano de o ser primos hermanos
alike (not to look ~ at all) parecerse como un
huevo a una castaña
alive (skin s.o. ~) **comer**[se] a alg. vivo
all (give one's ~) dejarse la **piel**
all (know ~ about s.th.) estar al **cabo** de algo/de
la calle
all (stake one's ~) poner toda la **carne** en el
asador
all (that's ~ there is) no hay más **cera** que la que
arde

all (when ~ is said and done) al fin y al **cabo**

all and sundry (tell ~ [about it/s.th.]) dar un **cuarto** al pregonero; pregonar/proclamar algo a los cuatro **vientos**

to be all in (exhausted) estar hecho una braga (▷ **bragas**); estar/quedar hecho **cisco**; tener los **huesos** molidos; estar hecho **migas/papilla/pedazos**; estar hecho un **pingajo**; estar hecho **polvo/puré**; estar reventado (▷ **reventar**); estar hecho unos **zorros**

all of a sudden de buenas a primeras (▷ **bueno**); de **golpe** y porrazo

all or nothing o **césar** o nada; o **todo** o nada

all out (go ~ [to + infinitive]) batirse el **cobre** por + infinitivo; echar el **resto**; **volcar**se

all out (work ~ to + infinitive) batirse el **cobre** por + infinitivo

all over a lo **largo** y a lo ancho de; en toda/cualquier **tierra** de garbanzos

all over (be s.o. ~) ser muy de alg.

all over (be/get dirt/etc. ~) estar o ponerse **perdido** de algo

all over (tremble ~) temblarle a alg. las **carnes**; temblar como una hoja/un azogado/un flan

all right (during the day pious Annie, during the night a bit of ~) de día **beata**, de noche gata

alley (be right up s.o.'s ~) rezar con; hacer **tilín** a alg.

all-out effort (make an ~) echar el **resto**; navegar a todo **trapo**

almighty de padre y muy señor mío (▷ **el padre**)

almost [por] el **canto** de un duro

alone (all ~) más solo que un **hongo**

alone (it's best to leave that ~) peor es meneallo o mejor es no meneallo o más vale no meneallo (▷ **menear**)

alone (leave me ~!) ¡no me hagas la **puñeta**!

altar (lead s.o. to the ~) llevar a una al **altar**

alternative (there's no ~) no hay más **cáscara**s

to amaze s.o. dejar **bizco** a alg.

to be amazed quedarse **bizco**

amazing bestial; chachi; cojonudo; dabute[n]/dabuti; que quita el **hipo**; pistonudo

to be amazing ser un/de **alucine**

amazing (this is ~!) ¡esto es la **oca**!

ambitious (even the most ordinary people are ~) hasta los **gatos** quieren zapatos

amount (a vast ~) una nube

amusing (be very ~) la sal (example)

amusing person el jacarero

and so on/forth ... y otras **hierbas**

angel (sing like an ~) ... que es un **primor** (example)

angels (talk of ~!) hablando del **rey/ruin** de Roma [y él que se asoma o por la puerta asoma]

anger (not to show one's ~) andarle/irle a alg. la **procesión** por dentro

anger (s.o.'s eyes blaze/are ablaze with ~) echar **fuego** por los ojos

anger (suppress/stifle one's ~) tragar **bilis**; morder/tascar el **freno**; tragar **quina**

anger (swallow one's ~) tragar **saliva**

anger (take one's ~ out on s.o.) **cebar**se en alg.

anger (vent one's ~ on s.o.) descargar la **bilis** en/contra alg.; **cebar**se en alg.

angles (approach from various ~) teclear algo

angry (be terribly ~) estar hecho un **basilisco**; estar alg. que brinca (▷ **brincar**); echar **chispas**; estar alg. que trina (▷ **trinar**)

angry (force o.s. not to get ~) tragar **bilis**

angry (get terribly ~) ponerse como un **basilisco**; exaltársele a alg. la **bilis**; ponerse hecho un **demonio**; darse a **perros/Satán**

to announce (suddenly [and unexpectedly] ~ s.th.) descolgarse con algo

to annoy s.o. buscar las **cosquillas**/dar la **lata**/hacer la **pascua**/dar la **tabarra** a alg.

annoying individual/person el/la chinche

annoying individual/person (be an extremely ~) tener **sangre** de chinches

answer (ask a silly question, get a silly ~) a **preguntas** necias oídos sordos

answer (give an evasive ~) salir[se]/escapar[se]/irse por la **tangente**

answers (give absurd/ridiculous/silly ~) irse por los **cerros** de Úbeda

antiquated ideas (a man who has ~) el carroza

antique (walking ~) una antigualla

any old (not to be [just] ~ poet/etc.) ser un poeta/etc., no así como quiera (▷ **querer**)

any old how a tontas y a locas (▷ **tonto**) (example)

anyone can see that lo ve un **ciego**

anything (be no good at ~) no dar **pie** con bola

anything (buy ~: believe) **tragar**[se]las como puños

anything (do ~) agarrarse a un **clavo** ardiendo

anything (do ~ to . . .) vender el **alma** al diablo (example)

anything (fall for ~) comulgar con ruedas de molino

anything (I'm not taking ~ from anybody) a mí no me tose nadie (▷ **toser**)

anything (not for ~ in the world) aunque se junten el **cielo** y la tierra

anything (not to be worth ~) no valer un **ardite**/**comino/pito**

anything (not to let ~ get in one's way) no ponérsele a alg. nada por **delante** anything (not to want to have ~ more to do with s.th./s.o.) echar la **bendición** a algo/alg.

anything (not [to want] to have ~ to do with it) ver los toros desde la **barrera**

anything (put up with ~) aguantar **carro**s y carretas; tragárselas (▷ **tragar**)

anything (swallow ~) comulgar con ruedas de molino; tener buenas **creederas**/ **tragaderas**; **tragar**[se]las como puños

anything (swallow ~ hook, line and sinker) **tragar**[se]las como ruedas de molino

anything (without having [had] ~ to do with it) sin **comer**lo ni beberlo

anywhere (neither here nor ~) ni aquí/acá ni en la **China**

anywhere (not to get ~) salir con una **mano** atrás y otra [a]delante; marcar el **paso**; no **pelechar**; estar tocando el **tambor**

anywhere (not to get ~ [with]) no comerse una **rosca** [con]

apart from . . . quitando ... (▷ **quitar**)

apartment (used for sexual encounters) el picadero

ape (go ~: go crazy) perder la **chaveta**; pasarse de **rosca**

ape (go ~: lose temper) ponerse como un **basilisco**

appeal (have a special ~) tener **duende**

to appeal to s.o. rezar con; hacer **tilín** a alg.

to appeal to s.o. (not to ~) no **rezar** con

appearances are deceptive ni están todos los que son, ni son todos los que están (▷ **estar**); el **hábito** no hace al monje

appetizing (look ~) estar algo diciendo cómeme (▷ **comer**)

to applaud ironically reírle a alg. la[s] **gracia**[s]

apple (an ~ a day keeps the doctor away) a diario una **manzana** es cosa sana

apple (one bad ~ can spoil the whole barrel) una **manzana** podrida echa un ciento a perder

apple (the rotten ~ spoils the barrel) una **manzana** podrida echa un ciento a perder

the apple doesn't fall far from the tree de tal **costilla**, tal astilla; en casa del **gaitero** todos son danzantes; de casta le viene al **galgo** ser rabilargo; tal padre tal **hijo**; de tal **palo**, tal astilla; en casa del **tamborilero** todos son danzantes

apple of discord la **manzana** de la discordia

apple of s.o.'s eye (be the ~) ser el **ojo** derecho de alg.

apple-pie bed (make s.o. an ~) hacerle la **petaca** a alg.

to apply to ([not] to ~) [no] **rezar** con

approach (have tried every ~) no quedarle a alg. ninguna **tecla** por tocar

to approach from various angles teclear algo

apron strings (be tied to s.o.'s ~) estar bajo la **férula** de alg.

arena (enter the ~) entrar en **liza**

to argue (one can ~ about this) sobre esto no hay nada escrito (▷ **escribir**)

to argue (start arguing with s.o.) mojar la **oreja** a alg.

to argue back and forth andar al **daca** y toma/en **dares** y tomares/en **dimes** y diretes

to argue over s.th. andar a la **rebatiña** de algo

argument (be trying to pick an ~ with s.o.) mojar la **oreja** a alg.

argument (pick an ~ with s.o.) **tomar**la con alg.

argument (this is open to ~) sobre esto no hay nada escrito (▷ **escribir**)

arguments (protracted and idle/pointless/ unresolvable ~) discusiones bizantinas (▷ **bizantino**)

Ark (be out of the ~) ser del tiempo del **rey** que rabió/del rey Wamba

Ark (it's out of/it went out with the ~) una antigualla

Ark (out of/with the ~) año de/tiempo[s] de/días de **Maricastaña**; del año de/en el año de la **nana**; en [los] tiempos de **ñangué**; del año de o en el año de la **pera/polca**; en tiempos del **rey** que rabió/del rey Wamba

arm ([be able] to do s.th. with one ~ tied behind one's back) [poder/saber] hacer algo con los **ojo**s cerrados

arm (be as long as your ~) ser más **largo** que un día sin pan

arm (cost an ~ and a leg) costar una **burrada**/un **dineral**/un **huevo**/un **ojo** de la cara/un **pico**/un **riñón**/una **riñonada**; costar la de San **Quintín**; costar un **sentido** o los cinco sentidos

arm (not to let s.o. twist one's ~) no dar su **brazo** a torcer

arm (the industry needs a shot in the ~) la industria necesita una **inyección** financiera

arm (what they said was a shot in the ~ for us) lo que dijeron supuso una **inyección** de optimismo para nosotros

to arm o.s. with courage/patience revestirse de valor/paciencia

to arm wrestle echar un **pulso**

arms (be welcomed with open ~ everywhere) tener todas las **puerta**s abiertas

arms (watch with one's ~ crossed) estar/quedarse con los **brazo**s cruzados

arms (with ~ akimbo) en **jarra**s

to be around 40/etc. rondar por/rozar los cuarenta/etc.

to arouse s.o.'s curiosity hacer **cosquillas** a alg.

arrangement ([provisional/temporary] ~) la componenda

to arrest s.o. llevar a alg. **codo** con codo; echar la **garra**/el **guante** a alg.

arse el culo

arse (pain in the ~) el/la chinche

arse (s.o. can't tell his ~ from his elbow) tomar/ confundir el **culo** por las témporas

arse bandit (gay) el canco/marica/maricón/ mariposa/pluma; la rana; el sarasa

arsehole el ojete

arse-licker el pelotillero

articulacy la labia

artist (hot-air ~) el farolero/la farolera

artistic hands (have ~) tener **manita**s de plata/ oro

ashamed con las **oreja**s gachas

ashamed [of o.s.] (be/feel ~) correr un **mico**

ashamed (s.o. is/feels so ~ [of himself], he just wants the earth to open and swallow him up/ he just wants to curl up and die) caérsele a alg. la cara de **vergüenza**

aside (leave s.th. ~) dejar algo a un **lado**/de lado

aside from . . . quitando ... (▷ **quitar**)

to ask (all you have to do is ~) pide por esa **boca**

to ask (if you don't ~ you don't get) quien no llora no mama (▷ **llorar**)

to ask (just ~) pide por esa **boca**

to ask the impossible pedir **leche** a las cabrillas; pedir la **luna**; pedir **peras** al olmo

askance (look ~ at s.o.) tener/traer a alg. entre **ojos**

asking (for the ~) a pedir de **boca**

asleep (be fast ~) estar **roque**

asleep (fall soundly ~) quedarse **roque**; dormirse como un **santo**

asleep (s.o. can't fall ~) dar vueltas a la **almohada**

ass el culo

ass (pain in the ~) el/la chinche

ass (s.o. can't tell his ~ from his elbow) tomar/ confundir el **culo** por las témporas

ass peddler el chapero

asshole el ojete

assignment (be a tough ~) pinchar/dar en **hueso**

assignment (take on a dangerous/risky ~) poner el **cascabel** al gato

to assume s.th. dar algo por **sentado**

to be astounded quedarse **bizco**

to be astronomical andar/estar por las **nube**s

atmosphere (clear the ~) aclarar las cosas

atom (not an ~ of) ni **chispa** de

to attack s.o. violently poner a alg. como **chupa** de dómine

to attack s.th. dar **caña** a algo

to attain (come close to success without ~ing it) quedarse con la **miel** en los labios; nadar y nadar, y a la orilla ahogar

attempt (pull it off at the first ~) llegar y besar el **santo**

attendance (dance ~ on s.o.) bailar el **agua** a alg.

attention (be the center/focus of ~) estar algo/alg. en [el] **candelero**

attention (bring s.th./s.o. into the center of ~) poner algo/a alg. en [el] **candelero**

attention (come to the ~ of s.o.) llegar a **oído**s de alg.

attention (give one's whole/full ~ to s.th.) poner sus cinco **sentido**s en algo

attention (occupy everybody's ~) acaparar la atención [de todos]

attention (pay ~ to s.th.) prestar/dar **oído**s a algo; prestar atención a algo

attention (pay no ~ [to what s.o. says]) escuchar/ oír como quien oye **llover**

attention (try to draw/take the people's ~ away from the actual/real issue) la **pista** falsa (example)

attentions (lavish ~ on s.o.) tratar/atender a alg. a **cuerpo** de rey

to be attractive estar alg. **jamón**

authority (be in a position of ~) estar alg. en [el] **candelero**

authority (know s.th. on good ~) saber algo de buena **tinta**

avenue (have tried every ~) no quedarle a alg. ninguna **tecla** por tocar

avenues (close [off] all ~ to s.o.) cerrar todas las **puerta**s a alg.

average Spaniard Juan Español

to avoid all work estar haciéndose **viejo**

away (be miles ~) estar en **Babia**/en las **Batueca**s/en **Belén**/en la **higuera**; estar en la **luna**; andar por o estar en las **nube**s

away (be often ~) andar/ir con el **hato** a cuestas

to be away with the fairies estar en **Babia**/en las **Batueca**s/en **Belén**/en la **higuera**; estar en la **luna**; andar por o estar en las **nube**s

awesome bestial; chachi; cojonudo; dabute[n]/ dabuti; que quita el **hipo**; pistonudo

awful (smell/taste) oler/saber a **demonio**s/**rayo**s

awful (s.th. looks ~ on s.o.) sentarle algo a alg. como a un santo **cristo** un par de pistolas; pegarle algo a alg. como un **mandil** a una vaca; sentarle algo a alg. como un **tiro**

awful experience (be an ~) ser un **trago** amargo

awful things (say ~ about s.th./s.o.) decir **horror**es de algo/alg.

awful[ly] padre (example); requete...

to be awfully pretty la **mar** de

awkward (be very ~ or [as] ~ as a cow on a crutch/ on roller skates) a más no **poder**

awkward age la **edad** burral/ingrata/del pavo

B

baby (be left holding the ~) cargar con el
mochuelo; [tener que] pagar el **pato**

baby (leave s.o. holding the ~) cargar el **baúl/
blanco/mochuelo/muerto** a alg.; echar el
sambenito a alg.

baby (sleep like a ~) dormir como un **bendito/
lirón**

babymachine la coneja

to baby-sit el/la canguro/cangura (example); el/
la kanguro/kangura (example)

baby-sitter el/la canguro/cangura; el/la
kanguro/kangura

bachelor pad el picadero

back (as soon as I/etc. turned my/etc. ~) a las
primeras de cambio

back (break one's ~ doing s.th.) dejarse las **uñas**
en algo

back (criticize s.o. behind his ~/talk behind s.o.'s
~) poner a alg. a **parir**; cortar un **sayo** a
alg.

back (give the shirt off one's ~) dar hasta la
camisa; dar la **capa**

back (have a monkey on one's ~) quedar **colgado**

back (put one's ~ into it) batir[se] el **cobre**

back (ride on the ~ [of a motorcycle]) ir de
paquete

back (stab s.o. in the ~) dar una **puñalada**
trapera a alg.

back (turn one's ~ on s.o.) dar de **lado** a alg.

back (you scratch my ~ and I'll scratch yours) hoy
por mí, mañana por tí; una **mano** lava la
otra

back and forth (argue ~) andar al **daca** y toma/
en **dares** y tomares/en **dimes** y diretes

back marker (be the ~) ser el **farolillo** rojo

back number una antigualla

back of beyond (live/be at the ~) vivir/estar donde
Cristo dio las tres voces/etc. o donde el
diablo perdió el poncho; vivir/estar en el
quinto **infierno/pino** o en la quinta
puñeta

to back down apearse de su **burro**

to back out rajarse

to back s.o. up to the hilt **volcar**se (example)

to backbite s.o. poner a alg. a **parir**

backbiter (be a ~) ser una buena **tijera**

backbone (have no ~) doblar el **espinazo**

backer (be the ~) ser la **vaca** de la boda

to backfire on s.o. salirle a alg. el **tiro** por la
culata

backhander el tarugo; el **unto** de Méjico/rana

backside (buttocks) el culo; donde la **espalda**
pierde su honesto nombre; el

mapamundi/pompis; la popa; el rabel/
salvohonor/tafanario/trasero/traspontín; la
trastienda

backside (kick s.o. up the ~) dar a alg. una
patada en el culo

backside (sit on one's ~) tocarse los cojones
(▷ **cojón**); tocar la **vihuela**

backwards (lean/bend over ~) andar/bailar de
coronilla; **volcar**se

backwards (lean/bend over ~ to make it easy for
s.o.) tender **puentes** de plata a alg.

backwards and forwards (know s.th. ~) saber algo
al **dedillo**

bacon (save one's/s.o.'s ~) salvar el **pellejo**; salvar
el **pellejo** a alg.

bad (be as ~ as each other) se juntaron el **hambre**
y las ganas de comer; ser **tal** para cual

bad ([be] begin[ning] to look ~) ir tomando algo
mal **cariz**; ponerse algo **feo**

bad (it's not as ~ as all that) no es tan feo el
diablo como le pintan (▷ **pintar**)

bad (it's not that ~) ni tanto ni tan **calvo**

bad (not to be as ~ as all that/[quite] that ~) no
llegar la **sangre** al río

bad (not to get that ~) no **llegar** a tanto

bad (one is as ~ as the other) se juntaron el
hambre y las ganas de comer

bad (things don't/never seem so ~ after a good
meal) con **pan** y vino se anda el camino

bad (what's ~ for s.o. may be a consolation for s.o.
else) mal de muchos, consuelo de todos

bad cigar/tobacco la tagarnina

bad end (come to a ~) acabar como el **rosario** de
la aurora

bad experience (be a ~) ser un **trago** amargo

bad job el buñuelo

bad lot el tipejo

bad lot (be a ~) ser un **pájaro** de cuenta

bad luck (be dogged by ~) pasarlas negras
(▷ **negro**)

bad luck (have ~) tocarle a alg. la **china/negra**;
tener mala **pata**; tener el **santo** de
espaldas

bad luck (have a streak/run of ~) perseguir a alg.
la **negra**/tener la negra

bad luck (s.o.'s ~ doesn't let up) pasarlas negras
(▷ **negro**)

bad patch (go through a ~) pasarlas negras
(▷ **negro**); pasar un **trago** amargo

bad time (this is a ~!) ¡no está el **horno** para
bollos!

to badger s.o. no dejar **respirar** a alg.

badly (come out of s.th. ~) salir mal librado de algo (▷ **librar**)

badly (treat s.o. very ~) tratar a alg. a coces (▷ **coz**)/a **patada**s/a **zapatazo**s

to badmouth s.o. poner a alg. como **hoja** de perejil/a **parir**

to be bad-tempered tener malas **pulga**s

bag (be left holding the ~) cargar con el **mochuelo**; [tener que] pagar el **pato**

bag (leave s.o. holding the ~) cargar el **baúl/blanco/mochuelo/muerto** a alg.; echar el **sambenito** a alg.

bag (let the cat out of the ~) irse de la **lengua**/írsele a alg. la lengua; levantar la **liebre**; tirar de la **manta**; descubrir el **pastel**

bag (old ~) la tarasca

bag (pack one's ~s [and go]) liar los **bártulo**s; hacer la **maleta**; liar el **petate**; levantar el **tabanque**

bag (pull s.th. out of a/the ~) traer algo en/por la **manga**; sacarse algo de la **manga**

bag (s.o. who couldn't fight his way out of a paper ~) el/la gallina

bag (s.th. is in the ~) tener algo en el **bote**

bag of bones (be a ~) ser un/estar hecho un **costal** de huesos; quedarse en el **chasis**; estar en los **hueso**s

bag of nerves (be a ~) ser un hato/manojo de **nervio**s

bagatelle una **nube** de verano

to be baggy (pants/etc.) respingar

to bail s.o. out echar un **cable** a alg.; sacar a alg. de un apuro

bait (swallow/take the ~) morder el **cebo**; acudir al **paño/reclamo**

baker's dozen la **docena** del fraile

to be balanced on a knife-edge estar en el **filo** de la navaja

balancing act (perform a skillful ~) bailar en la **cuerda** floja

bald (be as ~ as a billiard ball/a coot/a cue ball) estar como [una] **bola** de billar

ball (▷ **balls**)

ball (be on the ~) estar en la **onda**; conocer el **paño**

ball (carry the ~) cortar el **bacalao**; llevar la **batuta**; llevar/ponerse los calzones (▷ **calzón**); ser el amo del o dirigir el **cotarro**; llevar la **voz** cantante

ball (have a ~) correrse una **juerga**

ball (that's the way the ~ bounces) así es la **vida**

ball game (it's a whole new ~ now) se han vuelto las **torna**s; se ha vuelto la **tortilla**

ball game (that's a different ~) eso es otro cantar (▷ **el cantar**)

ball of wax (be utterly fed up with the whole ~) estar hasta [más allá de] la **coronilla** de algo (example)

ball of wax (buy it, the whole ~) **tragar[se]**las como puños (example)

to ball it/s.th./things up cagar algo; **cagar**la; escoñar/joder algo

to ball [s.o.] (have sex [with s.o.]) pasar a una por las **armas**; **calzar**[se]/**cargar**se a alg.; echar un **casquete**; **cepillar**[se] a una; poner un **clavo** a una; follar/joder [a alg.]; pasar a una mujer por la **piedra**; pisar a alg.; echar un **polvo**; quilar [a alg.]; regar/tapar/**tirar**se/tumbar/**zumbar**se a una mujer

ballast (shed some ~) dar su **parte** al fuego

balloon (go down like a lead ~) caer/sentar como un **jarro** de agua fría

ballot box el puchero

balls (be cold enough to freeze the ~ off a brass monkey) hacer un frío de cojones (▷ **cojón**)/que pela (▷ **pelar**); de **perro**s

balls (have ~) tener cojones (▷ **cojón**); tener **huevo**s/**redaño**s

balls (testicles) las **bola**s/**canica**s; los cataplines; los cojones (▷ **cojón**); los **conejo**s/**huevo**s; las **pelota**s; los pistones (▷ **pistón**)

to balls it/s.th./things up cagar algo; **cagar**la; escoñar/joder algo

to ballyhoo s.th. dar **bombo** a algo; a **bombo** y platillo (example)

ballyhooed (much-~) cacarear algo (example)

baloney (load of ~) el **cuento** chino

bananas (drive s.o. ~) traer de **culo** a alg.

band [of thieves] la camada

bandit (arse ~: gay) el canco/marica/maricón/mariposa/pluma; la rana; el sarasa

bandit (one-armed ~) el/la tragaperras

bandwagon (climb on the ~) arrimarse al **sol** que más calienta

to bang one's face/head on s.th. dar de narices contra algo (▷ **nariz**)

to bang [s.o.] (have sex [with s.o.]) pasar a una por las **armas**; **calzar**[se]/**cargar**se a alg.; echar un **casquete**; **cepillar**[se] a una; poner un **clavo** a una; follar/joder [a alg.]; pasar a una mujer por la **piedra**; pisar a alg.; echar un **polvo**; quilar [a alg.]; regar/tapar/**tirar**se/tumbar/**zumbar**se a una mujer

banger (old ~: car) la antigualla (example); la cafetera [rusa]

to banish s.th. from one's mind relegar algo al olvido

bar (▷ **bars**)

bar (go from one ~ to another) andar/ir de **chateo**

bar (singles ~) el **bar** de ligue/alterne

barber's cat (be [as] conceited as a ~) tener muchos **tufo**s

barefaced lie (tell a ~) con toda la **barba**; mentir con toda la **boca** barefoot (the shoemaker's son always goes ~) en casa de **herrero**, cuchillo de palo

barely (just ~) a duras **pena**s

bargain (both/all sides are driving a hard ~) batirse el **cobre**

bargepole (s.o. wouldn't touch s.th./s.o. with a ~) no poder coger algo ni con **papel** de fumar; no poder coger algo/a alg. ni con **tenazas**

bark (his/etc. ~'s worse than his/etc. bite) perro ladrador, nunca buen mordedor/poco mordedor o perro que ladra no muerde

to bark up the wrong tree tomar el **rábano** por las hojas

barn door (lock the ~ after the horse is stolen) asno muerto, la cebada al rabo; a buenas **hora**s, mangas verdes

barrage (ask s.o. a ~ of questions) a **granel**

barrage (hurl a ~ of insults at s.o.) soltar un **chaparrón** de insultos a alg.

barrel (as round as a ~) estar hecho una **botija**

barrel (be a ~) estar como una **vaca**

barrel (be like shooting fish in a ~) ser **coser** y cantar; ser **pan** comido

barrel (be over a ~) estar con el **agua** al cuello

barrel (have s.o. over a ~) tener a alg. con el **agua** al cuello

bars (be behind ~) estar a la **sombra**/en la **trena**

bars (be put behind ~) ponerse el **capuchón**

bars (do the ~) andar/ir de **chateo**

bars (put s.o. behind ~) meter a alg. donde no vea la **sol**; poner a alg. a la **sombra**; zambullir a alg. en la cárcel

base (be [way] off ~) el jaleo (example)

base (not to get to/reach first ~) quedar en **nada**

to bash s.o.'s face in quitar los **mocos** a alg.; hinchar los **morros** a alg.

to bash s.o.'s head in romper los **cascos**/la **crisma** a alg.

bashing (take a ~ and a half) de padre y muy señor mío (▷ **el padre**) (example)

bastard el cabrón/cagachín/tipejo

bastard (be a ~) tener mal **café**; tener mala **leche/pipa/uva**

bat (be [as] blind as a ~) no ver tres en un **burro**; ser más ciego que un **topo**

bat (go on a ~) andar/ir de **chateo**

bat (right off the ~) de buenas a primeras (▷ **bueno**)

bat (run like a ~ out of hell) ir como **alma** que lleva el diablo

to bat (not to ~ an eyelash/eyelid) quedarse/estar tan **campante/fresco/pancho**

bats (have ~ in one's/the belfry) estar mal de la **azotea**; no estar bueno de la **cabeza** o estar ido/mal/tocado de la cabeza o tener pájaros en la cabeza; estar como una **cabra/cafetera**; estar [loco] como un

cencerro; estar **chalado**; estar mal de la **chaveta**; estar **chiflado**

to batten down the hatches atrancar las **escotillas**

battle (be a pitched/tough ~) batirse el **cobre**

battle (be ready for ~) estar al **pie** del cañón

battle (win the ~) ganar la batalla

battle-ax[e] una mujer de **arma**s tomar; la cascarrabias/tarasca

bay (keep s.o. at ~) tener/mantener a alg. a **raya**

bay tree (flourish like the green ~) crecer como la **espuma**

bazookas (big breasts) la tetorra

to be (here/there you are!) ¡toma! (▷ **tomar**)

to be (we have to show who we are) o somos o no somos (▷ **ser**)

to be it (this is it now!) ¡ahora van a soltar al **toro**!

beak (nose) el asa; las napias

beam (see the mote in one's neighbor's/in s.o. else's eye and not the ~ in one's own) ver la **paja** en el ojo ajeno y no la viga en el propio

to beam all over one's face tener cara de **pascua**s

beam-ends (be on one's ~) andar/ir con el **culo** a rastras; estar en las últimas/en las diez de últimas (▷ **último**)

bean (head) la calabaza/cebolla/chaveta/cholla/ coca; el coco/güiro/güito; la jupa; el melón

bean (not to be worth a ~) no valer un **ardite/ comino/pito**

bean (not to have a ~) estar sin/no tener **blanca**; estar sin un/no tener [ni] un **cuarto/real**

bean (not to know ~s about s.th.) ni **chispa** de; no tener ni la más remota/pálida **idea** de algo; no saber ni **jota/papa/patata** de algo; estar **pez** en algo

bean (spill the ~s) cantar; vaciar el **costal**; desembuchar; soltar la **lengua**; irse de la **mui**; no quedarse con nada en el **pecho**; soltar la **sinhueso**

beanpole (be a ~: person) ser más **largo** que un día sin pan

beanpole (person) el aleluya; la caña; el espárrago/gansarón/perigallo

bear (be [as] busy as a hibernating ~) estar tan ocupado como un **oso** que está en hibernación

bear (be like a ~ with a sore head) de **perro**s

to bear (bring s.th. to ~) poner algo en **juego**

bear (each of us has his cross to ~) cada uno lleva su **cruz**

to bear (s.o. can't ~ s.o.) caerle **gordo** a alg.

to bear a grudge tener **sangre** en el ojo

bearable potable

beard (the bloke/guy with the ~) el barbas

to beard the lion in his den entrar en el cubil de la **fiera**

beat (▷ dead-beat)

beat (get a ~ on) dar el **pisotón**

to be beat (exhausted) estar hecho una braga
· (▷ **bragas**); estar/quedar hecho **cisco**;
tener los **huesos** molidos; estar hecho
migas/papilla/pedazos; estar hecho un
pingajo; estar hecho **polvo/puré**; estar
reventado (▷ **reventar**); estar hecho unos
zorros

to beat about/around the bush andar en/andarse
con **floreos**; andarse por las **ramas**;
salir[se]/escapar[se]/irse por la **tangente**;
andar[se] con **vueltas**

to beat about/around the bush (not to ~) no
andarse con/en chiquitas (▷ la **chiquita**);
no andarse con **requilorios**

beat it! ¡quítate de ahí/de en medio! (▷ **quitar**)

to beat it ahuecar el **ala**; darse el **bote**; sacar el
bulto; apretar las **calzaderas**; tomar la del
humo; **largar**se; **liar**las o liárselas; darse
de **naja**; najarse; poner **pies** en polvorosa;
pirarse o pirárselas; darse el **piro**; salir
pitando (▷ **pitar**); tomar **soleta**; tocárselas
(▷ **tocar**)

to beat it at once **largar**se con viento fresco

to beat it quick tomar/coger las de **Villadiego**

to beat s.o. at/in s.th. ganar a alg. en algo

to beat s.o. black and blue de padre y muy señor
mío (▷ **el padre**) (example); señor

to beat s.o. hollow cascar a alg.; **comer**se a alg.
crudo; dar **quince** y raya/falta a alg.; dar
cien **vuelta**s a alg.

to beat s.o. to a pulp hacer **papilla/picadillo** a
alg.

to beat s.o. to it madrugar a alg.

to beat s.o. up zurrar la **badana** o menear/
sacudir el **bulto** a alg.; arrimar **candela**/dar
caña/medir las **costillas**/sentar las
costuras a alg.; dar **leña** o cargar de leña a
alg.; cascarle/machacarle a alg. las
liendres; dar a alg. para el **pelo**; sacudir el
polvo a alg.; poner a alg. como un **pulpo**;
hacer a alg. [una] **tortilla**; dar una **vuelta** a
alg.

to beat the living daylights out of s.o. de padre y
muy señor mío (▷ **el padre**) (example);
señor

beaten track (keep to the ~) seguir la **senda**
trillada

beating (give s.o. a ~) dar **caña** a alg.; dar un
[buen] **recorrido**/[una] **soba** a alg.

beating (take a bad/terrible ~) estar hecho un
nazareno; de padre y muy señor mío (▷ **el
padre**) (example)

beautifully a las mil **maravilla**s; ... que es un
primor

beauty (be a ~) ser un **piropo** ambulante

beauty (real ~) un buen **bocado**

beaver (vagina) la almeja; el bacalao/beo/bollo/
chocho/conejo/coño/higo; la raja/rana/
seta

bed la petaca/piltra; las **plumas**

bed (as you make your ~, so you must lie in it)
como uno se lo guisa, así se lo come
(▷ **guisar**); quien o el que la hace la paga
(▷ **pagar**)

bed (get out of ~ on the wrong side/get up on the
wrong side of the ~) levantarse con el **pie**
izquierdo o salir con mal pie

bed (go to ~ early) acostarse con las **gallina**s

bed (make s.o. an apple-pie ~) hacerle la **petaca** a
alg.

bed (you've/etc. made your/etc. ~, now you/etc.
must lie in/on it) guisárselo y comérselo
(▷ **guisar**)

bed of roses (be no ~) no saber a **rosquilla**

bed of roses (life isn't [all/always] a ~) la vida no
es un lecho de **rosas**

bed of roses (s.o.'s life is a ~) pasársela en **flor**es;
estar/dormir sobre un lecho de **rosas**

bed of roses (s.o.'s life is no ~) no estar/dormir
sobre un lecho de **rosas**

bee (have a ~ in one's bonnet) tener algo metido
entre **ceja** y ceja

bee's knees (think one is the ~) creerse el no va
más (▷ **ir**); la **mar** de

beet (turn as red as a ~) ponerse como una o
más rojo que una **amapola**; ponerse como
un **cangrejo** asado o rojo como un
cangrejo; ponerse como un **tomate**

beetroot (blush like a/go as red as a ~) ponerse
como una o más rojo que una **amapola**;
ponerse como un **cangrejo** asado o rojo
como un cangrejo; subírsele a alg. el **pavo**
o ponerse hecho un pavo; ponerse como
un **tomate**

to befuddle s.o.'s brain comer el **coco** a alg.

beggars cannot or must not be choosers a quien
dan no escoge (▷ **dar**); la **necesidad** tiene
cara de hereje; a falta de **pan**, buenas son
tortas

beginner (be no ~) haber sido **cocinero** antes
que fraile

beginning (from ~ to end) de **cabo** a cabo/rabo
o de punta a cabo; desde la **cruz** hasta la
fecha; de **pe** a pa

to behave [well] hacer [un] buen **papel**

behavior (pompous ~) el postín

behind (buttocks) donde la **espalda** pierde su
honesto nombre; el mapamundi/pompis;
la popa; el rabel/salvohonor/tafanario/
trasero/traspontín; la trastienda

to be behind s.o. quedarse a la **zaga** de o en
zaga a alg.

to be behind the times estar fuera de **onda**

behind (fall ~) perder **terreno**

behind (leave s.o. ~) dejar en **zaga** a alg.

behind (put s.th. ~ one) echar **tierra** sobre/a
algo

belief (be beyond ~) no tener **nombre**

to believe (not to ~ one's ears) no poder dar crédito a sus **oído**s

to believe (not to know what to ~) no saber a qué **carta** quedarse

to believe (s.o. can't ~ his eyes) estar como viendo visiones (▷ **visión**)

to believe it (would you ~!) ser de lo que no hay (▷ **haber**)

to believe s.th. blindly creer algo a **puño** cerrado

bell (be saved by the ~) por un **pelo**/los pelos

to bell the cat poner el **cascabel** al gato

to bellyache about (have/find s.th. to ~) buscar **pelo**s en la sopa/leche o al huevo

belongings los bártulos

belt (tighten one's ~) apretarse el **cinturón**

to belt one or a few down alzar/empinar el **codo**; mojarse el **garguero**; mojar/refrescar el **gaznate**

to belt up echar el **cierre**; achantar la **mui**; cerrar el **pico**

bend (be round the ~) estar mal de la **azotea**; no estar bueno de la **cabeza** o estar ido/mal/tocado de la cabeza o tener pájaros en la cabeza; estar como una **cabra/cafetera**; estar [loco] como un **cencerro**; estar **chalado**; estar mal de la **chaveta**; estar **chiflado**

bend (drive s.o. round the ~) llevar de **cabeza** a alg.; sacar a alg. de sus **casillas**; traer de **culo** a alg.; poner **negro** a alg.; hacer a alg. subirse por las **pared**es

to bend over backwards andar/bailar de **coronilla**; **volcar**se

to bend over backwards to make it easy for s.o. tender **puentes** de plata a alg.

to bend s.o.'s ear dar la **lata** a alg.

beneath ([not] to be ~ s.o.['s dignity]) [no] caérsele a alg. los **anillo**s

bereft of huérfano de

berserk (go ~) ponerse hecho un **demonio**

to be beside o.s. with joy no caber en sí de alegría; no caberle a alg. el **corazón** en el pecho; no caber en el **pellejo** de alegría

to be besotted with s.o./s.th. caérsele a alg. la **baba** con/por alg./algo

the best el más **pintado**; la **flor** y nata

best (at ~) a todo **tirar**

best (be the ~ of) ser la **gala** de

best (be the ~ that money can buy) ser la flor de la **canela**

best (be the very ~) ser la flor de la **canela**

best (come off ~) llevarse la mejor **parte**

best (cream off the ~) chuparse [una] buena **breva**

best (do one's level ~) emplearse a **fondo**

best (everybody does their ~) cada uno estornuda como Dios le ayuda (▷ **estornudar**)

best (get the ~ out of s.o.) sacar el **jugo** a alg.

best (have the ~ of both worlds) comer a dos **carrillo**s

best (that's the ~ I/we can do) no hay más **cera** que la que arde

best thing (be the ~ since sliced bread) ser el no va más (▷ **ir**)

bet (hedge one's ~s) [nadar y] guardar la ropa

to bet (you can ~ your life/your bottom dollar on that) apostaría la **cabeza**

to bet (you can ~ your life/your bottom dollar [that] . . .) apostar[se] la **cabeza**/el **cuello** a que ...

to bet s.o. anything he likes [that] . . . apostar[se] la **cabeza**/el **cuello** a que ...

to betray one's humble/rustic origins tener el **pelaje/pelo** de la dehesa

better (be even ~ [than s.o. expected]) ser **miel** sobre hojuelas

better (be miles ~ than s.o.) dar cien **vuelta**s a alg.

better (get the ~ of s.o.) **ganar**le la batalla a alg.

better (think ~ of it) apearse de su **burro**

better time (s.th. couldn't have come at a ~) venir como **agua** de mayo/como **anillo** al dedo; venir como llovido/llegar como caído del **cielo**; venir que ni **pintado**/como pintado

between you and me dicho al **oído**

bewildered (be [utterly] ~) quedarse **parado**

to bewitch s.o. dar el **opio** a alg.

beyond (live/be at the back of ~) vivir/estar donde **Cristo** dio las tres voces/etc. o donde el **diablo** perdió el poncho; vivir/estar en el quinto **infierno/pino** o en la quinta **puñeta**

beyond (the great ~) la eterna **morada**; la otra **orilla**

to be beyond a joke pasar de **castaño** oscuro; pelar la jeta

to be beyond all criticism poder pasar por las **pica**s de Flandes

to be beyond belief no tener **nombre**

to bicker andar al **daca** y toma/en **dares** y tomares/en **dimes** y diretes

bickering dimes y diretes

bicycle la burra

biff on the head la coca; el cocotazo

big (act ~) darse **aire**s de grandeza; echar de **bolina**; ponerse como una gallina **clueca**; darse **charol**; **hinchar**se; ponerse **moño**s

big (great ~) de los **bueno**s (example); de padre y muy señor mío (▷ **el padre**) (example)

big (important/etc.) de muchas **campanilla**s

big (talk ~) echar de **bolina**; escupir por el **colmillo**; darse **tono**; no se oye más **voz** que la suya

big boobs la tetorra

big boss el mandamás

big cheese[s] un gran **bonete**; gente gorda; un **pez** gordo big eater (be a ~) ser una buena **tijera**; tener buenas **tragaderas**

big fish un **pez** gordo

big flashy car el cochazo

big money la **pasta** gansa

big names gente de alto **copete**

big noise un gran **bonete**; el mandamás; un **pez** gordo

big noise (be a ~) tener muchas **campanilla**s

big shot (act the ~) darse **aires** de grandeza; echar de **bolina**; pintar la **cigüeña**; ponerse como una gallina **clueca**; darse **charol**; alzar/levantar el **gallo**; ponerse **moño**s

big shot (be a ~) tener muchas **campanilla**s; ser un **pájaro** gordo

big shot[s] un gran **bonete**; gente de alto **copete**; gente gorda; el mandamás; un **pez** gordo

big wheel (be a ~) tener muchas **campanilla**s; ser un **pájaro** gordo

big wheel[s] un gran **bonete**; gente gorda; un **pez** gordo

bigheaded (get ~) subirse a la **parra**

bigmouth el/la bocazas; el farolero/la farolera; el voceras

bigwig (be a ~) tener muchas **campanilla**s; ser un **pájaro** gordo

bigwig[s] un gran **bonete**; gente de alto **copete**; gente gorda; el mandamás; un **pez** gordo

bike la burra

bill ([have to] foot the ~) ser el **paganini/pagano**; [tener que] pagar el **pato**

bill of goods (sell s.o. a ~) dar a alg. **gato** por liebre

billfold la chicharra

billiard ball (be as bald as a ~) estar como [una] **bola** de billar

bin (loony ~) el loquero

binge la juerga

binge (be/go on a ~) estar/ir de **juerga**

binge (have a real ~) correrse una **juerga**

binge (of eating) la comilona

bird (a ~ in the hand is worth two in the bush) más vale **pájaro** en mano que ciento volando; más vale un toma que dos te daré (▷ **tomar**)

bird (a little ~ told me) me lo dijo un **pajarito**

bird (be a wily ~) ser un **pájaro** de cuenta

bird (do ~) estar a la **sombra**/en la **trena**

bird (eat like a ~) comer como un **gorrión/pajarito**

bird (girl) la jai/polla

bird (give s.o. the ~: to boo) patear a alg.

bird (give s.o. the ~: in a relationship) largar a alg.; dar la **patada** a alg.

bird (the ~ has flown) ha volado el **pájaro**

bird (the early ~ catches the worm) a quien madruga, Dios le ayuda (▷ **madrugar**)

birds (be for the ~) ser para el o pal **gato**

birds (fine feathers don't make fine ~) aunque la **mona** se vista de seda, mona se queda

birds (fine feathers make fine ~) el **hábito** hace al monje

birds (kill two ~ with one stone) matar dos **pájaros** de un tiro

birds (want to kill two ~ with one stone) querer ir por **atún** y a ver al duque

to be birds of a feather ser lobos de una misma **camada**

birds of a feather flock together Dios los cría y ellos se juntan; cada **oveja** con su pareja; no/nunca falta un **roto** para un descosido

bird's-eye view (a ~ of) a **vista** de pájaro

birth (from/since ~) desde el **vientre** de su/etc. madre

birth (strangle s.th. at ~) salir al **paso** de algo

birthday suit (in one's ~) en traje de **Adán**/como Adán en el paraíso; en traje de **Eva**; como su **madre** le/lo/la echó al mundo

biscuit (take the ~) pasar de **castaño** oscuro; colmar la medida; pelar la jeta

bit (▷ **bits**)

bit (a little ~) un sí es no es (▷ **ser**)

bit (be champing at the ~ to + infinitive) **perecer**se/rabiar/reventar por + infinitivo

bit (be every ~ a man) ser muy **hombre**/todo un hombre

bit (do one's ~) aportar/poner su **grano** de arena

bit (not the least ~ of) ni **chispa/sombra** de

bit of all right (during the day pious Annie, during the night a ~) de día **beata**, de noche gata

bitch (be a ~: woman) tener **pelos** en la lengua

bitch (be a mean son of a ~) ser un mal **bicho**

bitch (scheming ~) la pájara

bitch (son of a ~) el cabrón; el cagachín

bitch (woman) la tipeja

bite (have ~) tener **garra**

bite (his/etc. bark's worse than his/etc. ~) perro ladrador, nunca buen mordedor/poco mordedor o perro que ladra no muerde

bite (not to have a ~ to eat) comerse/roerse los **codos**

to bite (once bitten twice shy) de los escarmentados nacen los avisados (▷ **escarmentar**); el **gato** escaldado del agua fría huye

to bite (what's biting you/etc.?) ¿qué **mosca** te/etc. ha picado?

to bite off (don't ~ or you can ~ more than you can chew) quien mucho abarca, poco aprieta (▷ **abarcar**)

to bite off more than one can chew meterse en **camisa** de once varas

to bite s.o.'s head off la bronca (example)

to bite the dust (die) **cascar**[la]; hincar el pico; morder el **polvo**

to bite the dust (have bitten the dust) estar comiendo **tierra**

bits (be thrilled to ~ with s.th.) caérsele a alg. la **baba** con/por algo

bits (fancy ~) **perejil**es

bits (naughty ~) las **alegría**s

bits (put in one's [own] two ~) meter **baza** [en]; escupir en **corro**; echar su **cuarto** a espadas; meter su **cuchara**

bits (tear s.o. to ~) poner a alg. como un **guiñapo**/como **hoja** de perejil; machacar a alg.; poner a alg. como un **trapo**

bits (tear s.th. to ~) hacer algo **cisco**

bitter (take the ~ with the sweet) tomar las duras con las maduras (▷ **duro**)

bitter pill (be a ~ [to swallow]) ser un **trago** amargo

bitter pill ([have to] swallow the ~) [tener que] tragar **quina**

bitterness (drain/drink the cup of ~ [down] to the last drop) apurar el **cáliz** de cicuta/de [la] amargura/de dolor hasta las heces

bittersweet entre **dulce** y amargo

to blab (reveal) írsele a alg. la **burra**; cantar; vaciar el **costal**; no quedarse con nada en el **pecho**

blabbermouth el/la **bocazas**

black (look ~/as ~ as thunder) tener **cara** de pocos amigos

black (make out that white is ~) hacer de lo **blanco** negro/volver en blanco lo negro

black and blue (beat s.o. ~) de padre y muy señor mío (▷ **el padre**) (example); señor

black and blue (swear ~ [that ...]) jurar por lo más **sagrado** [que ...]

black and white (have it in ~) **carta**[s] canta[n]

black eye (have a ~) tener un **ojo** a la funerala

black sheep la **oveja** negra

black sheep (be the ~ [of the family]) ser el **garbanzo** negro [de la familia]

blame (get/[have to] take the ~) [tener que] pagar el **pato**

blame (pin the ~ on s.o.) cargar el **baúl/blanco** a alg.; endiñar algo a alg. (example); cargar el **mochuelo/muerto** a alg.; echar el **sambenito** a alg.

blank (s.o.'s mind goes ~/is a ~) quedarse en **blanco**

blanket (be a wet ~) aguar la **fiesta**

blarney el **camelo**

blast (full ~) a toda **pastilla**

to blather meter **ripio**

to blaze (s.o.'s eyes ~ with anger/indignation) echar **fuego** por los ojos

blazes (go to ~!) ivete a espulgar un **galgo**/a **paseo**/a la **porra**!

blazes (tell s.o. to go to ~) mandar a alg. al **diablo**/a capar **moscas**/a **paseo**

blazes (to ~ with everybody else or with work/etc.!) iviva la **Pepa**!

blazing [marital] row (have a ~) tirarse los **trastos** a la cabeza

to bleed s.o. [dry/white] dejar a alg. en **calzoncillos**/en **cueros** [vivos]; dejar esquilmado a alg. (▷ **esquilmar**); chupar la **sangre** a alg.

blessed day (the whole ~) todo el **santo** día

blessing (it may be a ~ in disguise) no hay **mal** que por bien no venga

to be blind no saber uno dónde tiene los **ojos**; tener **telarañas**/una **venda** en los ojos

blind (be [as] ~ as a bat) no ver tres en un **burro**; ser más ciego que un **topo**

blind (go on a ~) ir de **juerga**

blind (in the country of the ~ the one-eyed man is king) en tierra de **ciegos** o en el país/reino de los ciegos el tuerto es [el] rey

to be blind drunk estar cocido (▷ **cocer**) (example)

blind eye (turn a ~ [to s.th.]) hacer la vista gorda [a algo] (▷ **gordo**)

blinders (have ~ on) llevar las **anteojeras** puestas; meter la cabeza en un **puchero**

blindfold ([be able] to do s.th. ~) [poder/saber] hacer algo con los **ojos** cerrados

blindly a tontas y a locas (▷ **tonto**)

blindly (believe s.th. ~) creer algo a **puño** cerrado

blindly (lash out ~) dar **palos** de ciego

to be blinkered llevar las **anteojeras** puestas; meter la cabeza en un **puchero**

blinkers (have ~ on) meter la cabeza en un **puchero**

block (a chip off the old ~) de tal **costilla**, tal astilla; de casta le viene al **galgo** ser rabilargo; de tal **palo**, tal astilla

block (knock s.o.'s ~ off) romper el **bautismo**/la **crisma** a alg.

blockhead un [pedazo de] **alcornoque/atún**; un bombero; un[a] **cabeza** de corcho; una calabaza; un alma de **cántaro**; un ceporro/ melón/merluzo; un **palomino** atontado; un percebe

blockhead (be a ~) tener la cabeza llena de **serrín**

bloke ([conspicuous] ~) el **nota**

the bloke with the beard el **barbas**

blonde (peroxide ~) la **rubia** de frasco/bote

blood (be out for s.o.'s ~) buscar el **bulto** a alg.

blood (make s.o.'s ~ boil) encender/quemar la **sangre** a alg.

blood (s.o.'s ~ freezes or runs cold) helársele a alg. la **sangre**

blood (s.o.'s ~ gets up) subírsele a alg. la **sangre** a la cabeza blood (sweat ~) sudar la **gota** gorda; sudar **sangre**

blood (try to get ~ out of a stone) sacar **agua** de las piedras/de un palo seco

bloody puto

bloody (completely ~) puto (example)

bloody (not to have one ~ peseta in one's pocket) no tener ni una jodida peseta (▷ **joder**)

bloody (that's none of your ~ business!) ¿qué **coño** te importa?

bloody awful time (have a ~) puto (example)

to be bloody cold/hot hacer un frío/calor de cojones (▷ **cojón**)

bloomer la pifia

bloomer (make a ~) dar una **pifia**, pifiar

to blot one's copybook meter la **pata/pezuña**

blow (be a cruel/terrible ~) ser un **trago** amargo

blow (be dealt an endless stream of ~s/ the ~s come thick and fast) a **granel**

blow (be one [tragic] ~ after another) llover sobre mojado

blow (come to ~s) llegar a las manos

to blow a fuse fundírsele a alg. los **plomo**s

to blow hot and cold dar una de **cal** y otra de arena

to blow it **cagar**la

to blow it (now we've blown it!) ¡la hemos fastidiado! (▷ **fastidiar**); ¡estamos **fresco**s!

blow job (do a ~ on s.o.) hacerle una **mamada** a alg.

blow me! ¡**caracol**es!; ¡**cáscara**[s]!

to blow one's brains out/head off levantarse la **tapa** de los sesos

to blow one's cookies/lunch cambiar la **peseta**

to blow one's cool/cork/stack/top (▷ **cool; cork; stack; top**)

to blow one's nose echar una **mocada**; mocar; **mocarse**

to blow one's own horn/trumpet no necesitar **abuela**; darse **bombo**; echarse/tirarse **flores**

to blow over quickly pasar como una **nube** de verano

to blow s.o. away freír a alg.; dejar **frito** a alg.

to blow s.o.'s brains out/head off levantarle a alg. la **tapa** de los sesos

to blow s.th. **fumar**se algo

to blow s.th. for a lark estar hasta las **ceja**s/el **coco**/[más allá de] la **coronilla** de algo; estar **frito** de algo; estar hasta el **gorro**/el **moño**/las narices (▷ **nariz**)/la **punta** de los pelos o del pelo/los **topes** de algo

to blow the gaff levantar la **liebre**; descubrir el **pastel**

to blow up (get angry) ponerse como un **basilisco**; exaltársele a alg. la **bilis**; ponerse hecho un **demonio**

blow-by-blow account (give a ~ [of s.th.]) contar la **biblia** en verso; contar algo con puntos y **coma**s

blowed (well I'm ~!) ¡**cáscara**[s]!; ¡sopla! (▷ **soplar**)

blow-out (feast/meal) la comilona

blow-out (have a ~) ponerse las **bota**s

blue (out of the ~) de buenas a primeras (▷ **bueno**)

blue funk (be in a ~) **cagar**se/**ciscar**se de miedo (examples); estar **muerto** de miedo

blue moon (once in a ~) de **higo**s a brevas; cada **muerte** de obispo; de **Pascua**s a Ramos; de **uva**s a peras

blue-blooded (lay/put much emphasis on one's being ~) escupir **sangre**

blues (have the ~) tener la/estar con la **depre**

blunder la pifia/plancha

blunder (make a ~) meter la **pata/pezuña**; **pringar**la

to blunder dar una **pifia**, pifiar

bluntly (speak ~) hablar en **plata**

bluntly (to put it ~[, . . .]) hablando en **plata**[, ...]

to blurt out s.th. írsele la **boca** a alg.; descolgarse con algo

to blush like a beetroot ponerse como una o más rojo que una **amapola**; ponerse como un **cangrejo** asado o rojo como un cangrejo; subírsele a alg. el **pavo** o ponerse hecho un pavo; ponerse como un **tomate**

to blush like a lobster ponerse como un **cangrejo** asado o rojo como un cangrejo; subírsele a alg. el **pavo** o ponerse hecho un pavo

to blush to the roots of one's hair ponerse de mil **color**es

to blush [with shame] salírsele/subírsele a alg. los **color**es

board (be [as] flat as a ~) ser de **Castellón de la Plana**; ser lisa (▷ **liso**)

board the boat before it sails/has set sail camarón que se duerme, se lo lleva la corriente

to boast [about s.th.] cacarear algo; darse **charol**; **pagar**se de algo

boasting (be just or nothing but empty ~) cacarear y no poner huevos

boat (board the ~ before it sails/has set sail) camarón que se duerme, se lo lleva la corriente

boat (don't miss the ~) camarón que se duerme, se lo lleva la corriente

boat (push the ~ out) echar/tirar la **casa** por la ventana

boat (we're all in the same ~) mal de muchos, consuelo de todos

boats (burn one's ~) quemar las naves

bogey la albondiguilla

bogged down in details (get ~) andarse por las **rama**s

to **boil** (make s.o.'s blood ~) encender/quemar la **sangre** a alg.

to **boil down to** (it boils down to the same thing) llámele usted o llámale **hache**

bold (be as ~ as brass) tener más **cara** que espalda; ser más fresco que una **lechuga**

boldly a **pecho** descubierto

boldly (say s.th. quite ~) decir algo tan **fresco**

bollocking (give s.o. a terrific ~) la bronca (example)

bollocks (testicles) las **bolas/canicas**; los cataplines; los cojones (▷ **cojón**); los **conejos/huevos**; las **pelotas**; los pistones (▷ **pistón**)

bolt (have shot one's ~) haber quemado su último **cartucho**

bolt (shoot one's ~) echar el **resto**

to **bolt** [down] (food) **soplar**se algo

bolt upright tieso como un ajo; derecho como una **vela**

bomb (cost a ~) costar una **burrada**/un **dineral**/un **huevo**/un **ojo** de la cara/un **pico**/un **riñón**/una **riñonada**; costar la de **San Quintín**; costar un **sentido** o los cinco sentidos

bomb (like a ~) a las mil **maravillas**

bomb (make a ~) hacer su **agosto**

to **bombard** s.o. with questions freír a alg. a preguntas; a **granel**

bombshell (come like a/be a ~) caer/sentar como un **jarro** de agua fría

bonce (head) la calabaza/cebolla/chaveta/cholla/coca; el coco/güiro/güito; la jupa; el melón

bone (be a bag of ~s) ser un/estar hecho un **costal** de huesos; quedarse en el **chasis**; estar en los **huesos**

bone (be all or nothing but skin and ~) ser un/estar hecho un **costal** de huesos; quedarse en el **chasis**; estar en los **huesos**; no tener más que el **pellejo**

bone (be close to the ~) pasar de **castaño** oscuro; pelar la jeta

bone (have a ~ to pick with s.o.) tener **cuentas** pendientes con alg.; tener que echar un **párrafo**/parrafito aparte con alg.

bone of contention la **manzana** de la discordia

to **bone up** [on s.th.] quemarse las **cejas**; romperse los **codos**; empollar [algo]; machacar [algo]; quemarse las **pestañas**

bonehead un merluzo

to be **bone-idle** ser más **vago** que la **chaqueta** de un guardia; tocarse el **pito**

to **bonk** [s.o.] (have sex [with s.o.]) pasar a una por las **armas**; **calzar**[se]/**cargar**se a alg.; echar un **casquete**; **cepillar**[se] a una; poner un **clavo** a una; follar/joder [a alg.]; pasar a una mujer por la **piedra**; pisar a alg.; echar un **polvo**; quilar [a alg.]; regar/

tapar/**tirar**se/tumbar/**zumbar**se a una mujer

to be **bonkers** estar **chalado/chiflado**

bonkers (go ~) perder la **chaveta**

bonny child el pimpollo [de oro]

boo (s.o. wouldn't say ~ to a goose) ser incapaz de matar una **mosca**

to **boo** s.o. patear a alg.

boob la pifia/plancha

boob (make a ~) meter la **pata/pezuña**; dar una **pifia**, pifiar; **pringar**la

boob tube (TV) la **caja** boba/idiota/tonta

boo-boo el golpe de **bombero**; la pifia/plancha

boobs (big ~) la tetorra

boobs (breasts) las **aldabas**; los **cántaros**/**globos**/limones (▷ **limón**); las marmellas

booger la albondiguilla

book (out-of-date [and worthless] ~) una antigualla

bookworm la **rata**/el **ratón** de biblioteca

boom years las **vacas** gordas

to **boomerang** [s.th.] on s.o. salirle a alg. el **tiro** por la culata

boondocks (live/be [way] out in the ~) vivir/estar donde **Cristo** dio las tres voces/etc. o donde el **diablo** perdió el poncho; vivir/estar en el quinto **infierno/pino** o en la quinta **puñeta**

boonies (live/be [way] out in the ~) vivir/estar donde **Cristo** dio las tres voces/etc. o donde el **diablo** perdió el poncho; vivir/estar en el quinto **infierno/pino** o en la quinta **puñeta**

boor el patán

boost (what they said was a ~ to our optimism) lo que dijeron supuso una **inyección** de optimismo para nosotros

boot (die with one's ~s on) morir con las **botas** puestas/al **pie** del cañón

boot (give s.o. the ~) dar el **bote** a alg.; echar/despedir a alg. con **cajas** destempladas; echar a alg. a la **calle**/poner a alg. de patitas en la calle; plantar a alg. en la **calle**; largar a alg.; dar la **licencia**/[el] **pasaporte**/la **patada** a alg.; salir a alg.

boot (lick s.o.'s ~s) lavar la **cara** a alg.

boot (now the ~'s on the other foot) se han vuelto las **tornas**; se ha vuelto la **tortilla**

to **boot** s.o. out dar el **bote** a alg.; echar/despedir a alg. con **cajas** destempladas; echar a alg. a la **calle**/poner a alg. de patitas en la calle; plantar a alg. en la **calle**; largar a alg.; dar la **licencia**/[el] **pasaporte**/la **patada** a alg.

bootlaces (not to be fit to tie s.o.'s ~) no llegarle a alg. a la **suela** del zapato/a los **zancajos**

bootlicker el/la lavacaras; el pelotillero

bootstraps (pull o.s. up by one's [own] ~) a **cuerpo** gentil (example)

boozer el cuero; la espita/esponja

to border on s.th. rozar [con] algo

bore el/la chinche

bore (be a ~) ser algo/alg. un **plomo**

to bore (be [deadly] boring) caerse de las **mano**s; ser algo/alg. un **plomo**; a más no **poder**

to bore (it's boring) no tiene **garra**

to bore s.o. to death quedarse con alg.

to bore the pants off s.o. quedarse con alg.

to be bored to death/tears aburrirse como una ostra/una almeja/un mono

boredom ([nearly] die of ~) pudrirse de aburrimiento

born (some are ~ under a lucky star and some are ~ seeing stars) unos nacen con **estrella** y otros nacen estrellados

born idle/lazy (s.o. was ~) nació alg. cansado o con la lengua fuera (▷ **nacer**)

born lazybones (be a ~) nació alg. cansado o con la lengua fuera (▷ **nacer**)

born lucky/unlucky (s.o. was ~) nació alg. de pie[s]/de cabeza (▷ **nacer**)

born to be a mathematician/etc. (s.o. was ~) nació alg. para [ser] matemático/etc. (▷ **nacer**)

born to the trade (s.o. was ~) nació alg. mamando el oficio (▷ **nacer**)

born yesterday (s.o. wasn't ~) no **comulgar** con ruedas de molino; no chuparse el **dedo**; no nació alg. ayer (▷ **nacer**)

borrowed plumes (adorn o.s. with ~) adornarse con **pluma**s ajenas

bosom (cherish a viper in one's ~) criar la **víbora** en el seno

to be bosom buddies/pals [with s.o.] estar a partir un **piñón** [con alg.]

boss (be the ~) cortar el **bacalao**; llevar la **batuta**; llevar/ponerse los calzones (▷ **calzón**); ser el amo del o dirigir el **cotarro**; tener la **sartén** por el mango; llevar la **voz** cantante

boss (big ~) el mandamás

to boss about/around regentar

botch el buñuelo

botch (make a ~ of s.th./things) cagar algo; hacer un **pan** como unas hostias; hacer algo con los **pies**

to botch s.th./it [up] escoñar/joder algo; hacer algo con los **pies**; pringar**la**

botched job el buñuelo

botch-up el buñuelo

to bother s.o. sentarle algo a alg. como un **tiro**

bothered (not to know why one ~) ser para el o pal **gato**

bottle (a ~ is almost empty) una botella está temblando (▷ **temblar**)

bottle (almost empty a/use most of a ~) dejar una botella temblando (▷ **temblar**)

bottle (have ~) tener cojones (▷ **cojón**); tener **hígados/huevos/redaños**; tener riñones (▷ **riñón**)

bottle (hit the ~) darle a la **botella**

bottom (buttocks) el culo; donde la **espalda** pierde su honesto nombre; el mapamundi/pompis; la popa; el rabel/salvohonor/tafanario/trasero/traspontín; la trastienda

bottom (get to the ~ of it/s.th.) tomar la **corriente** desde la fuente

bottom (have got/gotten to the ~ of s.th.) estar al **cabo** de algo/de la calle

bottom (the ~ falls out of s.o.'s world) caérsele a alg. la **casa** encima/a cuestas

bottom dollar (you can bet your ~ on that) apostaría la **cabeza**; son **haba**s contadas

bottom dollar (you can bet your ~ [that] . . .) apostar[se] la **cabeza**/el **cuello** a que ...

bottomless pit (be [like] a ~) ser un **pozo** sin fondo

bottom-of-the-table team (be the ~) ser el **farolillo** rojo

bottoms up! ¡hasta verte, **Cristo/Jesús** mío!

bouncer el apagabroncas

to be bound to lose llevar las de **perder**/salir perdiendo

bounds (by leaps and ~) a **paso**s agigantados

bouts of anger el pronto (example)

bow (have more than one or another string to one's ~) comer a dos **carrillos**; tener una **vela** encendida por si la otra se apaga

bow (have two/several strings to one's ~) tener un **pie** en dos zapatos

to bow down doblar/bajar la **cerviz**

to bow to the inevitable besar la **cruz**

bowl of cherries (life isn't all a ~) no todo el monte es **orégano**

bowler [hat] el hongo

box ([goggle] ~: TV) la **caja** boba/idiota/tonta

box round the ears la chuleta

to box s.o.'s ears ventilarle a alg. las orejas

boxes round the ears (give s.o. a few hefty ~) ponerle a alg. la cara nueva (▷ **nuevo**)

boy el pollo

boy (rent ~) el chapero

boy (whipping ~) un[a] **cabeza** de turco

to brag [about s.th.] darse **bombo**; cacarear algo; darse **charol**; escupir por el **colmillo**; echarse/marcarse un **farol**; alzar/levantar el **gallo**; pagar**se** de algo; no se oye más **voz** que la suya

braggadocio (be just or nothing but ~) cacarear y no poner huevos

braggart el farolero/la farolera

brain (an idle ~ is the devil's workshop) el **ocio**/la **ociosidad** es la madre de todos los vicios; los **vicios** son los hijos del ocio

to brain o.s. romperse la **crisma**

to brain s.o. romper el **bautismo** a alg.

brains (blow one's/s.o.'s ~ out) levantarse la **tapa** de los sesos; levantarle a alg. la **tapa** de los sesos

brains (intelligence) la cholla; el coco; la mollera

brains (rack one's ~) quebrarse/romperse la **cabeza**; darse de **cabezadas**; romperse los **cascos**; comerse el **coco**; estrujarse el **melón**; devanarse/torturarse los **sesos**

brains (s.o. must have been at the back of the queue when they were handing ~ out) ser más tonto que **Abundio**; si le/etc. menean, da **bellotas**; ser más tonto que **Carracuca**; ser más **cerrado** que un cerrojo; ser más **corto** que las mangas de un chaleco; ser más tonto que una **mata** de habas; no saber ni siquiera quitarse los **mocos**; ser más bruto que la **pila** de un pozo; tener el juicio en los talones (▷ **talón**)

braintwister (be a ~) ser un **hueso** duro de roer; ser [un huevo] duro de **pelar**

to brainwash s.o. comer el **coco** a alg.

brainwork (kill o.s. with ~) romperse los **cascos**

branch (saw off one's own ~) matar la **gallina** de los huevos de oro

to brand s.o. colgar el **sambenito** a alg.

brass (be as bold as ~) tener más **cara** que espalda; ser más fresco que una **lechuga**

brass (money) el barro; el **calé** o calés; la china; [los] **cuartos**; la guita/lana/manteca; [los] monises; la mosca; [los] nipos; el parné; la pasta; el pisto; la tela; el trigo

brass (top ~) gente de alto **copete**

brass farthing (not to be worth a ~) no valer un **ardite/comino/pito**

brass farthings (not to have two ~ to rub together) no tener ni para unas **alpargatas**; estar sin/no tener **blanca**; no tener qué llevarse a la **boca**/donde **caerse** muerto; estar sin un/no tener [ni] un **cuarto/real**

brass monkey (be cold enough to freeze the balls off a ~) hacer un frío de cojones (▷ **cojón**)/ que pela (▷ **pelar**); de **perros**

to be brass monkey weather hacer un frío que pela (▷ **pelar**); de **perros**

brass tacks (get [straight] down to ~) no andarse con/en chiquitas (▷ la **chiquita**); ir al **grano**; no andarse con requilorios

brave face (put on a ~) mantener el **tipo**

brazenly (say s.th. quite ~) decir algo tan **fresco**

bread (be the best/greatest thing since sliced ~) ser el no va más (▷ **ir**)

bread (cast one's ~ [up]on the waters) hacer [el] **bien** sin mirar a quién

bread (daily ~) el **puchero**

bread (earn one's daily ~) ganarse los **fríjol**es/los **garbanzo**s/el **pan**/el **puchero**/la **vida**

bread (know which side one's ~ is buttered) arrimarse al **sol** que más calienta

bread (man cannot live by ~ alone) no sólo de **pan** vive el hombre

bread (money) el barro; el **calé** o calés; la china; [los] **cuartos**; la guita/lana/manteca; [los] monises; la mosca; [los] nipos; el parné; la pasta; el pisto; la tela; el trigo

bread (want one's ~ buttered on both sides) querer el **oro** y el moro

bread and butter (earn one's ~) ganarse los **fríjol**es/los **garbanzo**s/el **pan**/el **puchero**/la **vida**

breadline (be on the ~) no tener qué llevarse a la **boca**; comerse/roerse los **codos**

break (lucky ~) la bolichada/breva; el **cabe** de pala

break (make a clean ~) cortar por lo **sano**

break (make a clean ~ with s.th. [and start again]) hacer **borrón** y cuenta nueva

break (without a ~) de un **tirón**

break a leg! ¡buena **suerte**!

to break up (marriage/etc.) irse al **cuerno**; **escoñar**se

to break up (spy ring/etc.) desvertebrar algo

to break up everything in sight no dejar/quedar **títere** con cabeza

breaker's yard (be ready for the ~) estar algo para el **arrastre**

breasts (big ~) la tetorra

breasts (boobs; hooters; knockers; tits) las **aldaba**s; los **cántaros**/globos/limones (▷ **limón**); las marmellas

breath (take s.o.'s ~ away) quitar el **hipo** a alg.

breath (waste one's ~) ladrar a la **luna**; gastar **saliva**

to breathe (hardly have time to ~) no tener tiempo ni de **respirar**

to breathe (not to ~ a word) no decir esta **boca** es mía; no descoser la **boca**; coserse la **boca**; callar[se] como un muerto/una piedra; echar **candado** a la boca/a los labios; no decir ni **mu/pío**; no **respirar**

to breathe down s.o.'s neck no dejar a alg. [ni] a **sol** ni a sombra

to breathe one's last estar en las últimas (▷ **último**)

breather (have a ~) darse un **verde**

breather (s.o. can't have/take a ~) no **saber** de sí

breathtaking[ly] que quita el **hipo**

breeze (be a ~) ser una **breva**; ser **coser** y cantar; ser **pan** comido

breeze ([be able] to do s.th. in a ~) [poder/saber] hacer algo con los **ojos** cerrados

breeze (shoot the ~) cascar; darle a la **sinhueso**

brevity is the soul of wit lo **bueno**, si breve, dos veces bueno

brew ([thin] ~) el jarope/recuelo

to brew (there's trouble ~ing) oler a **chamusquina**

bribe el **unto** de Méjico/rana

to bribe s.o. untar el **carro**/la **mano**/la **palma** a alg.

brick (be as thick as a ~) ser más tonto que **Abundio**; si le/etc. menean, da **bellotas**; ser más tonto que **Carracuca**; ser más **cerrado** que un cerrojo; ser más **corto** que las mangas de un chaleco; ser más tonto que una **mata** de habas; no saber ni siquiera quitarse los **mocos**; ser más bruto que la **pila** de un pozo

brick (drop a ~) tirarse una **plancha**; **pringar**la

brick (swim like a ~) nadar como un **plomo**

brick wall (talk to a ~) ladrar a la **luna**; hablar a la **pared**

bricks (be like a cat on hot ~) estar en/sobre **ascuas**

bricks (be two ~ shy of a load) ser de pocas luces/corto de luces o tener pocas luces (▷ **luz**)

bricks (come down on s.o. like a ton of ~) soltar la/una **andanada** a alg.; zurrar la **badana** a alg.; la bronca (example); dar una **calada** a alg.; soltar/decir cuatro **fresca**s a alg.; hacer **papilla**/echar los **perro**s a alg.

bridge (a lot of water has flowed under the ~ [since then]) ha corrido/pasado mucha **agua** bajo el puente; ha llovido mucho desde entonces (▷ **llover**)

bridge (be water under the ~) ser **agua** pasada

bridges (build ~) tender un **puente**

bridges (burn one's ~ [behind one]) quemar las naves

bright (as ~ as a new pin) limpio como una **patena**; como una **plata**/una **tacita** de plata

bright (be [as] ~ as a button) ser más listo que el **hambre**

bright (not to be very ~) ser de pocas luces/corto de luces o tener pocas luces (▷ **luz**)

bright spot on the horizon el **rayo** de esperanza

bright spot on the horizon (there is a ~) hay **luz** al final del túnel

brightest . . . (the ~) la **flor** y nata (example)

to be bright-eyed and bushy-tailed estar como una **lechuga**

to be brill ser un/de **alucine**

brilliant (be [absolutely] ~) ser un/de **alucine**; ser el no va más (▷ **ir**)

brilliant mathematician (be a ~) ser un **hacha** [en/para algo] (example)

brilliant student (be a ~) lucir en sus/los estudios

brilliant[ly] bestial; cañón; chachi; cojonudo; dabute[n]/dabuti; que quita el **hipo**; pistonudo; requete...

brilliantly gifted/talented mathematician/etc. (be a ~) nació alg. para [ser] matemático/etc. (▷ **nacer**)

to be brimming with health rebosar de salud; vender/prestar **salud**

to bring off a coup poner una **pica** en Flandes

to bring off a scoop dar el **pisotón**

to bring off s.th. very difficult poner una **pica** en Flandes

to bring o.s. to do s.th. sacar **fuerza**s de flaqueza

to bring out (book/etc.) sacar algo a **luz**

to bring s.o. down off his high horse quitar **moño**s a alg.

to bring s.o. down to earth with a bump echar un **jarro** de agua fría a alg.

to bring s.o. up as mommy's/mummy's boy/darling guardar/tener o criar a alg. entre algodones (▷ **algodón**)

to bring s.th. up for discussion poner algo sobre el **tapete**

to bring up (have been brought up badly) saber a la **pega**

to bring up (not to ~ any more: s.th. negative) dejar la **fiesta** en paz

to bring up (not to be brought up [for discussion]) quedar sobre el **tapete**

bristling with cuajado de; erizado de

to be broad (subject/etc.) haber **tela** que cortar/para rato

to broadcast s.th. ([boastfully] ~) cacarear algo

broke (be [flat] ~) estar sin/no tener **blanca**; estar sin un/no tener [ni] un **cuarto**; andar/ir con el **culo** a rastras; estar **palmado**/**pelado**; no tener [ni] una **perra**; andar/estar a la cuarta **pregunta**; estar sin un/no tener [ni] un **real**; estar en las últimas (▷ **último**); estar a dos **velas**

broke (be stone-~) estar con una **mano** atrás y otra [a]delante; estar **palmado**; no tener [ni] una **perra**; andar/estar a la cuarta **pregunta**

broth (too many cooks spoil the ~) muchas **mano**s en un plato hacen mucho garabato o muchas manos en la olla echan el guiso a perder

brother (everyone and his ~) todo **bicho** viviente; Cristo y la madre/todo Cristo; todo/cada **quisque**

brow (by the sweat of one's ~) con el sudor de su/etc. **frente**

brown (get ~) **tostar**se [al sol]

to brown (tan) **tostar**se [al sol]

brown spot (in the underwear) el **palomino**

to brownnose s.o. hacer la **pelotilla** a alg.

brush (be as daft as a ~) ser más tonto que **Abundio**

brush-off (give s.o. the ~) dar **calabaza**s a alg.; mandar a alg. a **paseo**

to be bubbling over with enthusiasm/joy rebosar de entusiasmo/alegría

buck (cost a few ~s) costar unas **perra**s

buck (pass the ~ to s.o.) cargar el **baúl/blanco/ mochuelo/muerto** a alg.; echar el **sambenito** a alg.

bucket (kick the ~) irse al otro **barrio**; liar los **bártulos**; **cascar**[la]; diñarla; quedarse **frío/frito**; pelar **gallo**; **guiñar**la; hincar el pico; **liar**las o liárselas; palmarla; estirar la **pata**; liar el **petate**; **pringar**la; **reventar**[se]; quedarse **tieso**

to be bucketing down a **cántaros** (example); llover a **chorros/cubos/mar**es**/torrentes**

buckets (come down in ~) a **cántaros** (example); llover a **chorros/cubos/mar**es**/torrentes**

buckets (sweat ~) sudar a **chorros**/la **gota** gorda/a **mar**es

bud (nip s.th. in the ~) segar en **flor**; salir al **paso** de algo; cortar algo de **raíz**

budding writer/etc. (be a ~) ser un escritor/etc. en **ciernes**

buddy (be bosom/great buddies) la **mar** de; estar a partir un **piñón** [con alg.]; comer en un/ el o del mismo **plato**

buff el forofo

buff (in the ~) en traje de **Adán**/como Adán en el paraíso; en **carnes** [vivas]; en **cueros** [vivos]; en traje de **Eva**

to be buffeted by fate ser el **rigor** de las desdichas

buffoon (act/play the ~) hacer el **gracioso**

bug (be as snug as a ~ in a rug) estar en su[s] **gloria**[s]; vivir/estar como **pava** en corral

to bug (what's ~ging you/etc.?) ¿qué **mosca** te/etc. ha picado?

to bug s.o. hacer la **pascua**/dar la **tabarra** a alg.

bugger (do ~ all) tocarse los cojones (▷ **cojón**); tocar la **vihuela**

to bugger s.th. up escoñar/joder algo

build (have a good/great/fantastic ~) estar como un **camión**; tener buena **percha**

to build bridges tender un **puente**

to build castles in the air/in Spain hacer **castillos** en el aire

to build on sand hacer **castillos** de arena; sembrar en la arena

to build s.o. up poner a alg. en [el] **candelero**

bulb (not to be the brightest ~ in the chandelier) ser de pocas luces/corto de luces o tener pocas luces (▷ **luz**)

bulging eyes (have ~) tener **ojos** de besugo

bull (lie/nonsense) el camelo; el **cuento** chino

bull (like a ~ in a china-shop) como un **burro/ caballo/elefante** en una cacharrería

bull (shoot the ~) cascar; darle a la **sinhueso**

bull (sweat like a ~) sudar la **gota** gorda

bull (take the ~ by the horns) acometer algo de **frente**; coger el **toro** por los cuernos

bull (work like a ~) trabajar como un **buey**

bullet (put a ~ through s.o.'s/one's head) pasaportear a alg.; levantarle a alg. la **tapa**

de los sesos; levantarse la **tapa** de los sesos

bullets **almendra**s; **pepino**s; **píldoras**

bullets (riddle s.th./s.o. with ~) dejar algo/a alg. como un **colador**; coser/freír a alg. a tiros/ balazos

bullfighter (clumsy/poor ~) el maleta

bull's-eye (score a ~) dar en el **blanco**; dar en la **diana**/hacer diana

bum (be a lazy ~) sin **oficio** ni beneficio (example)

bum (buttocks) el culo; donde la **espalda** pierde su honesto nombre; el mapamundi/ pompis; la popa; el rabel/salvohonor/ tafanario/trasero/traspontín; la trastienda

bum (person) el/la trotacalles

to bum around ir por o correr la **gandaya**

bump (bring s.o. down to earth with a ~) echar un **jarro** de agua fría a alg.

bump (come down/back to earth with a ~) caer del **nido**

to bump s.o. off **cargar**se/cascar/**cepillar**[se] a alg.; dar **cuenta** de alg.; freír a alg.; dejar **frito** a alg.; mandar a alg. al otro **mundo**; pasaportear a alg.; dar el **paseo** a alg.; quitar a alg. de en medio; dejar **tieso** a alg.; tumbar a alg.

bumpkin (country ~) el rapaterrones

bun (have a ~ in the oven) estar hinchada (▷ **hinchar**)

bunch (the whole ~ [of them]) el ganado

bunch of no-gooders la camada

bundle of nerves (be a ~) ser un hato/manojo de **nervios**

to bungle s.th. hacer algo con los **pies**

bungler el maleta

bunk (do a ~) ahuecar el **ala**; poner **pies** en polvorosa

bureaucrat (minor ~) el chupatintas

burglar el reventapisos

to burn one's bridges [behind one]/one's boats quemar las naves

to burn one's fingers pillarse los **dedos**

to burn the midnight oil quemarse las **ceja**s/ **pestañas**

to be burning with impatience rabiar de impaciencia

to be burning with love abrasarse de amores

to burst (eat until one is fit to ~) a todo **pasto**; a más no **poder**

to burst into tears soltar el **trapo**

to burst out crying soltar el **trapo**

to burst out laughing soltar la **carcajada**; soltar el **chorro** [de la risa]; reventar de risa; soltar el **trapo**

to be bursting [at the seams] with pride no caber en el **pellejo** de orgullo

bursting point (eat to ~) ponerse como un **trompo**

to be **bursting with curiosity/envy/impatience**
reventar de curiosidad/envidia/
impaciencia

to be **bursting with energy/[youthful] vigor** bullirle
a alg. la **sangre** en las venas

to be **bursting with health** rebosar de salud;
vender/prestar **salud**

to be **bursting with joy** no caberle a alg. el
corazón en el pecho; no caber en el
pellejo de alegría

to **bury (have one's head buried in one's work)** no
levantar/alzar **cabeza**

to **bury one's head in the sand** esconder/meter la
cabeza bajo el ala

to **bury o.s. in s.th. enfrascar**se en algo

to **bury s.o.** sacar a alg. con los **pies** adelante

bush (beat about/around the ~) andar en/andarse
con **floreos**; andarse por las **ramas**;
salir[se]/escapar[se]/irse por la **tangente**;
andar[se] con **vuelta**s

bush (not to beat about/around the ~) no andarse
con/en chiquitas (▷ la **chiquita**); no
andarse con **requilorios**

bush (women's pubic hair) el felpudo

to be **bushed (exhausted)** estar hecho una braga
(▷ **bragas**); estar/quedar hecho **cisco**;
tener los **huesos** molidos; estar hecho
migas/papilla/pedazos; estar hecho un
pingajo; estar hecho **polvo/puré**; estar
reventado (▷ **reventar**); estar hecho unos
zorros

bushel (hide one's light under a ~) meter/poner la
luz bajo el celemín

bushy-tailed (be bright-eyed and ~) estar como
una **lechuga**

business el tinglado

business (be a fishy ~) oler a **cuerno** quemado

business (be a sticky ~) traérselas (▷ **traer**)

business (be involved in some shady/dubious ~)
andar con **tapujo**s

business (be the ~) bestial

business (dance/lie/run like nobody's ~) ... que se
las pela (▷ **pelar**)

business (do one's ~) echar una **carta** al correo;
hacer sus **necesidad**es; plantar un **pino**

business (get involved in a nasty ~) meterse en
un **fregado**

business (get [straight] down to ~) no andarse
con/en chiquitas (▷ la **chiquita**); ir al
grano; no andarse con **requilorios**

business (it's best to mind one's own ~) cada uno/
cual a lo **suyo**

business (mind one's own ~) meterse en sus
calzones (▷ **calzón**)

business (mind your own ~!) meterse alg. donde
no le llaman (example)

**business (poke one's nose into other people's ~)
meter**se alg. donde no le llaman

business (send s.o. about his ~) mandar a alg. a
paseo

business (set up in ~) montar un **tinglado**

business (tell everyone one's private ~) dar un
cuarto al pregonero

**business (that's none of your bloody/goddam[n]
~!)** ¿qué **coño** te importa?

business (this is where we get down to serious ~)
tocan a matar (▷ **tocar**)

**business (we know that this is none of our ~,
but . . .)** ... vela en este entierro

business (what ~ is it of yours?) ... vela en este
entierro

business (you've got no ~ being here) ... vela en
este entierro

business is business la **cuenta** es cuenta

to **bust a gut** batir[se] el **cobre**

to **bustle about** andar/ir al **retortero**

busy (be [as] ~ as a hibernating bear) estar tan
ocupado como un **oso** que está en
hibernación

but (no ~s!) ¡no hay **pero** que valga!

but (there are no ~s about it!) ¡no hay **pero** que
valga!

butch (shrew) una mujer de **armas** tomar; la
sargentona

butcher (bad surgeon) el sierrahuesos

butt (buttocks) el culo; donde la **espalda** pierde
su honesto nombre; el mapamundi/
pompis; la popa; el rabel/salvohonor/
tafanario/trasero/traspontín; la trastienda

butt (cigarette ~) la pava

butt (sit on one's ~) tocarse los cojones
(▷ **cojón**); tocar la **vihuela**

butt (work one's ~ off) trabajar como un **buey**;
dar el **callo**; romperse los **cuerno**s/el **culo**;
echar/sudar la **hiel**; echar los **hígado**s;
darse una **jupa**; trabajar como un **negro**;
dejarse la **piel**; pringar[las]; sudar el **quilo**;
remar; **reventar**se; echar los riñones
(▷ **riñón**); destripar terrones (▷ **terrón**);
sudar **tinta**

to **butt in [on]** meter **baza** [en]

to **butt into or in on [a/the conversation/etc.]** meter
baza en; escupir en **corro**; meter su
cuchara

butter (look as if ~ wouldn't melt in one's mouth)
hacerse la/parecer una **mosquita** muerta;
no/nunca haber roto un **plato** [en su vida]

to **butter s.o. up** hacer la **barba**/hacer
carantoñas/dar **coba**/hacer **fiestas**/dar
jarabe/hacer la **rosca** a alg.

butterfly (break a ~ on the wheel) matar **moscas** a
cañonazos

butterfly (have butterflies in the/one's stomach)
tener los **nervios** de punta

buttocks las **cachas**

buttocks (▷ backside; behind; bottom; bum; butt;
posterior)

button (be [as] bright as a ~) ser más listo que el **hambre**

to button [up] one's lip/mouth no decir ni **mu/pío**

to be buttoned up (s.o.) no soltar **prenda**

to be buttoned up (s.th.) tener algo en el **bote**

buttons and bows **perejil**es

to buy anything (believe) **tragar**[se]las como puños

to buy s.th. for a song comprar algo por un **pedazo** de pan

to buy s.th. for peanuts comprar algo a **huevo**

to buy s.th. on the never-never comprar algo a **plazoleta**s

bygones (let ~ be ~) [hacer] **borrón** y cuenta nueva

by-your-leave (without so much as a ~) sin decir **agua** va

C

cabbage (live like a ~) vegetar

caboodle (with the whole ~) con toda la **recua**

to cadge andar/vivir de **gorra**

Cádiz (affectionate name for ~) la Tacita de Plata (▷ **tacita**)

cahoots (be in ~) estar del mismo **palo**

Cain (raise ~) armar la de **Dios** es Cristo; armar la gorda (▷ **gordo**)

cake (be a piece of ~) ser una **breva**; ser **coser** y cantar; ser **pan** comido

cake (take the ~) llevarse la **gala**; llevar[se] el **gato** al agua; llevarse la **palma**

cake (there's no icing on the ~) no hay **olla** sin tocino

cake (want to have one's ~ and eat it [too]) querer ir por **atún** y a ver al duque; querer **nadar** y guardar la ropa; querer el **oro** y el moro

caked with cuajado de

cakes (sell like hot ~) venderse como el **pan**/como pan caliente; venderse como **rosquillas**

calends (on the Greek ~) en las **Calendas** griegas

calf (worship the golden ~) adorar el **becerro** de oro

call (be/have a close ~) [por] el **canto** de un duro; por un **pelo**/los pelos

to call (nature ~s) echar una **carta** al correo (example)

to call (this ~s for a celebration/drink!) ¡esto hay que **mojar**lo/**remojar**lo!

to call s.o. all the names under the sun poner a alg. como un **Cristo**; poner **verde** a alg.

to call s.th. into question poner algo en **tela** de juicio

to call the shots cortar el **bacalao**; llevar la **batuta**; llevar o ponerse los calzones (▷ **calzón**); ser el amo del o dirigir el **cotarro**; mover los **hilos**; llevar la **voz** cantante

to call the tune cortar el **bacalao**; llevar la **batuta**; llevar/ponerse los calzones (▷ **calzón**); ser el amo del o dirigir el **cotarro**; llevar la **voz** cantante

call it what you like/will llámele usted o llámale **hache**

to be callous estar curado de **espanto**

calm (remain/be perfectly ~) quedarse/estar tan **pancho**

camel's back (the straw that/which breaks the ~) la **gota** que desborda/colma el vaso

can (either we all carry the ~ or none of us does) o nos pringamos todos, o ninguno (▷ **pringar**)

can ([have to] carry the ~) tocarle a alg. la **china**; cargar con el **mochuelo**/**paquete**; [tener que] pagar el **pato**/los **plato**s rotos/los **vidrio**s rotos

can (jail/prison) la trena

can (jail/prison: be in the ~) estar a la **sombra**/en la **trena**

can (jail/prison: be put in the ~) ponerse el **capuchón**

canapé el sello del **estómago**

canard el **cuento** chino

canary (informer) el chivato/la chivata; el soplón/la soplona

candle (s.o. can't hold a ~ to s.o.) no **servir** para descalzar a alg.; no llegarle a alg. a la **suela** del zapato/a los **zancajos**

to be canned estar hecho un **cesto**; estar cocido (▷ **cocer**); estar hecho una **cuba**/un **cuero**/un **pellejo**/una **sopa**/una **uva**

canned (get ~) cogerse una **castaña**; **cocer**se; papar una **jumera**; coger una **melopea**/**merluza**; coger/pillar una **mona**; moñarse; coger una **pea**; agarrar[se] un **pedo**; coger una **pítima**; pillar una **zorra**

canned music la **música** enlatada

cantankerous person el/la cascarrabias

cap (if the ~ fits, wear it) quien o el que se pica, **ajos** come; al que le sirva que se lo ponga (▷ **servir**)

to cap it all s.th. else happens llover sobre mojado

to captivate s.o. dar el **opio** a alg.

car (big flashy/luxury flash/really posh/whacking great ~) el cochazo; señor

card (play one's last [trump] ~) jugar la última **carta**; quemar el último **cartucho**

cards (be a few ~ shy of a full deck) ser de pocas luces/corto de luces o tener pocas luces (▷ **luz**)

cards (fold up/collapse like a house of ~) derrumbarse como un **castillo** de naipes

cards (give s.o. his ~) dar [el] **pasaporte** a alg.

cards (lay/put one's ~ on the table) jugar a **carta**s vistas; poner las **carta**s boca arriba

cards (play/keep one's ~ close to one's chest) no soltar **prenda**

cards (unlucky at ~, lucky in love) desgraciado en el **juego**, afortunado en amores o de malas en el juego, de buenas en amores

care (take ~) avivar el/[los] **ojo**[s]

care (take ~ of o.s.) arreglárselas (▷ **arreglar**) (example); componérselas (▷ **componer**) (example)

to care (a fat lot I ~!) ¡tal día hará un **año**!

to care (I don't ~ a damn!) ¡tal día hará un **año**!

to care (not to ~ a monkey's/a rap/a [tinker's] damn or cuss/two hoots) no importar a alg. un **ardite**; [no] importar a alg. un **bledo/ comino/higo/pepino/pimiento/pito/ rábano**; reírse de los peces de colores

to care less (I couldn't ~ what other people say/ think) ande yo **caliente** y ríase la gente

to care less (s.o. couldn't ~) no importar a alg. un **ardite**; [no] importar a alg. un **bledo/ comino/higo/pepino/pimiento/pito/ rábano**; reírse de los peces de colores

to be careful guardar las **vueltas**

careful (be ~ what you say, walls have ears/we can be heard!) ¡hay **ropa** tendida!

careful (one can't be too ~) nunca se peca por demasiado cuidado (▷ **pecar**)

careful, there are people listening! ¡hay **moros** en la costa!

carefully con todas las de la **ley**

carefully (go about it or proceed/tread very ~) andar con **pies** de plomo; ir con mucho **ten** con ten

carefully (listen ~) aplicar el **oído**

to caress s.o. hacer **fiestas** a alg.

carousal la juerga

carpet (roll out the red ~/give s.o. the red-~ treatment) echar/tirar la **casa** por la ventana

carpet (sweep it under the ~) ocultar los **trapos** sucios

carrot and the stick (apply a policy of the ~) mezclar **bromas** con veras; dar una de **cal** y_otra de arena; aplicar una política del **palo** y la zanahoria

carrot-and-stick policy (apply a ~) mezclar **bromas** con veras; dar una de **cal** y otra de arena; aplicar una política del **palo** y la zanahoria

to carry on (know exactly how s.o. carries on) **gastar**las

cart (put the ~ before the horse) tomar el **rábano** por las hojas

to carve out a future for o.s. **labrar**se un porvenir

to carve s.o. up coser a alg. a **puñalada**s

case (just in ~) por si las **moscas**

cash (count one's ~) consultar con el **bolsillo**

cash ([in] ~) de **relance**

cash (pay ~) pagar a toca **teja**

to cast one's bread [up]on the waters hacer [el] **bien** sin mirar a quién

to cast the first stone arrojar/tirar la primera **piedra**

castles (build ~ in the air/in Spain) hacer **castillos** en el aire

cat (at night all ~s are gray/grey) de noche todos los **gato**s son pardos

cat (be a fat ~) tener muchas **campanillas**

cat (be [as] conceited as a barber's ~) tener muchos **tufos**

cat (be like a ~ on hot bricks/on a hot tin roof) estar en/sobre **ascuas**

cat (bell the ~) poner el **cascabel** al gato

cat (fat ~[s]) gente gorda; un **pez** gordo

cat (fight like ~ and dog) andar a **palos**

cat (grin like a Cheshire ~) sonreír de oreja a oreja

cat (have as many lives as a ~) tener siete **vidas** [como los gatos]

cat (it's enough to make a ~ laugh) no hay tales **borregos/carneros/cordero**s

cat (know which way the ~ jumps) saber de qué lado caen las **peras**/por dónde van los **tiros**

cat (let the ~ out of the bag) irse de la **lengua**/ írsele a alg. la lengua; levantar la **liebre**; tirar de la **manta**; descubrir el **pastel**

cat (rain ~s and dogs) a **cántaros** (example); llover a **chorros/cubos/mares/torrente**s

cat (set the ~ among the pigeons) meter los **perros** en danza

cat (there's more than one way to skin a ~) hay muchas maneras de matar **pulgas**

cat (there's no room to swing a ~) no caber ni un **alfiler**; estar de **bote** en bote

cat (think one is the ~'s pajamas/pyjamas/ whiskers) creerse el no va más (▷ **ir**); la **mar** de

cat ([wait and/to] see which way the ~ jumps) [esperar a] ver de qué lado caen las **peras**/por dónde van los **tiros**

cat (when the ~'s away, the mice will play) cuando el **gato** duerme, bailan los ratones; cuando el **gato** va a sus devociones, bailan los ratones

cat and mouse (play ~ with s.o.) jugar al **gato** y al ratón con alg.

catalogue (a [whole] ~ of) un **rosario** de; una **sarta** de

cat-and-mouse game (play a ~ with s.o.) jugar al **gato** y al ratón con alg.

to catch (▷ **caught**)

to catch on immediately cazarlas/cogerlas/ pescarlas al **vuelo**

to catch on to s.th. calzar/diquelar/guipar algo

to catch s.o. (at it or doing s.th.) coger a alg. en el **garlito**

to catch s.o. in a fib coger a alg. en un **renuncio**

to catch s.o. in the act coger a alg. en el **garlito**/ con las manos en la **masa**

to catch s.o. lying coger a alg. en un **renuncio**

to catch s.o. on the hop pillar a alg. en **bolas**/ **bragas**

to catch s.o. out coger a alg. en un **renuncio**

to catch s.o. red-handed pillar a alg. en **bolas**; coger a alg. en el **garlito**/con las manos en la **masa** to catch s.o. with his hand in the cookie jar coger a alg. con las manos en la **masa**

to catch s.o. with his pants/trousers down pillar a alg. en **bola**s/**bragas**

to catch up with (your lies will always ~ you in the end) antes se coge al **embustero** que al cojo

caterwauling (music) la **música** ratonera

cat-lick (give o.s. a ~) lavarse a lo **gato**

caught (get ~ in one's own trap) ir por **lana** y volver esquilado/trasquilado

to be caught between the devil and the deep blue sea estar entre la **espada** y la pared/entre dos **fuego**s

caught up (get/be ~ in it/s.th.) meterse en o estar/andar metido en [la] **danza**; estar [muy] metido en algo (▷ **meter**)

cause (damage one's own ~) hacer las diez de últimas (▷ **último**)

cause (give ~ for) dar **pie** para/a

cause (the best way to solve a problem is to attack the root ~ of it) muerto el **perro**, se acabó la rabia

causes (not to die of natural ~) morir vestido

caution (cast/throw ~ to the wind[s]) liarse la **manta** a la cabeza

cautiously (act [very] ~) nadar entre dos aguas; [nadar y] guardar la ropa

cautiously (go about it or proceed/tread very ~) andar con **pies** de plomo

to celebrate [prematurely] echar las **campanas** al vuelo

to celebrate with a drink mojar; remojar

celebration (this calls for a ~!) ¡esto hay que **mojar**lo/**remojar**lo!

cent (down to the last ~) un **real** sobre otro

cent (not to be worth a red ~) no valer un **ardite**/ **comino**/**pito**

cent (not to have a red ~ to one's name) no tener ni para unas **alpargata**s; estar sin/no tener **blanca**; no tener qué llevarse a la **boca**/ donde **caerse** muerto; estar sin un/no tener [ni] un **cuarto**/**real**

cent (put in one's two ~s[' worth]) meter **baza** [en]; escupir en **corro**; echar su **cuarto** a espadas; meter su **cuchara**

center of attention (be the ~ or bring s.th./s.o. into the ~) estar algo/alg. o poner algo/a alg. en [el] **candelero**

center of the universe el **ombligo** del mundo

céntimo (5-~ coin) la **perra** chica

céntimo (10-~ coin) la **perra** gorda

certain impepinable

cert (be a dead ~) ser tan seguro como el **evangelio**

certain (be absolutely/dead ~) ser tan seguro como el **evangelio**

certain something (have that ~) tener **duende**

certainly! ¡no faltaba/faltaría más! (▷ **faltar**)

certainly not! ¡ni en **copla**s!; ¡no faltaba/faltaría más! (▷ **faltar**)

certainty (it's a ~) son **haba**s contadas

chaff (separate the wheat/grain from the ~) apartar/separar el **grano** de la paja; apartar las **oveja**s de los cabritos

chalk and cheese (be as different as ~) estar tan lejos como lo **blanco** de lo negro/no parecerse ni en el blanco de los ojos; parecerse como un **huevo** a una castaña

challenge (take up the ~) recoger el **guante**

to be champing at the bit to + infinitive **perecer**se/ rabiar/reventar por + infinitivo

chance el resquicio

chance (a fat ~ you've/etc. got) no caerá esa **breva**

chance (fat ~!) ¡ni **soñar**lo!

chance (give s.o. a second ~ to pass the exam) repescar a alg.

chance (jump at the ~) coger/asir la **ocasión** por los cabellos/pelos

chance (no ~!) ¡no hay tu **tía**!

chance (not to give s.o. a ~) no dejar entrar en **juego** a alg.

chance (that ~ won't come again) **ojo**s que te vieron ir

chance (unexpected ~) el **cabe** de pala

chance (you have to jump at the ~) a la **ocasión** la pintan calva

chance piece of good luck la breva; el **cabe** de pala

chances (take no ~) [nadar y] guardar la ropa

chandelier (not to be the brightest bulb in the ~) ser de pocas luces/corto de luces o tener pocas luces (▷ **luz**)

change (a ~ is a good thing) entre **col** y col, lechuga; **pan** con pan, comida de tontos

change of direction (make a [radical] ~) dar un **golpe** de timón

to change (chop and ~) dar una de **cal** y otra de arena

to change (it's all ~d) se han vuelto las **tornas**; se ha vuelto la **tortilla**

to change (keep changing one's job/etc.) ser [un] **culo** de mal asiento

to change [one's life] mudar el **pellejo**

to change one's mind more often than one changes one's underwear bailar a cualquier **son**; ser un[a] **veleta**

to change sides cambiar de/la **chaqueta**

to be chaos la tremolina (example)

chaos (be in a state of ~) estar/andar **manga** por hombro

chaos (complete ~) la **olla** de grillos

to be chaotic estar/andar **manga** por hombro

chaperon[e] la carabina; el **dragón** de seguridad

chaperon[e] (go [along] as/play ~) hacer/ir de **carabina**

chapter and verse (with ~) con [todos sus] **pelos** y señales

character (be a nasty ~) ser un mal **bicho**

character (be an odd ~) ser un **pájaro** raro

character (be an unpleasant ~) ser un **pájaro** de cuenta; tener mala **sombra**

charge (be in ~) llevar/tener las **riendas**

charge (take ~) empuñar el **bastón**; tomar el **remo**; tomar/coger/empuñar las **riendas**

charm la sal

charm (have ~) tener **duende**

charm (turn on the old ~) andar en/andarse con **floreos**

to be charming ser un **primor**

to chase after s.th. irse a **ojeo** de algo

to chase s.o. around no dejar a alg. [ni] a **sol** ni a sombra

chat (have a ~ [with s.o.]) echar un **párrafo** [con alg.]

to chat cascar

to chat (get ~ting) pegar la **hebra**/el **hilo**

to chat [with s.o.] echar un **párrafo** [con alg.]

to chat up (a woman who can be chatted up easily) la ligona

to chat up women (a man who tries to ~) el ligón

chattels (goods and ~) los bártulos; los **trastos**

to chatter cascar

chatterbox la cotorra

chatterbox (be a ~) hablar más que una **cotorra**/que un **sacamuelas**/que una **urraca**

cheap (be dirt ~) estar por los **suelos**

cheap (sell/buy s.th. very ~) vender/comprar algo a **huevo**

cheap cigar/tobacco la tagarnina

cheap hooker/prostitute/tart la pesetera

cheap wine (be [a] ~) ser un **vino** peleón

to cheat hacer **trampa**[s]

to cheat on s.o. meter/poner [los] **cuerno**s a alg.; pegársela a alg. (▷ **pegar**)

to cheat s.o. dar la **castaña** a alg.; pegar un **parche** a alg.; pegársela a alg. (▷ **pegar**); pegar un **petardo** a alg.; quedarse con alg.; dar/pegar una **tostada** a alg.

check (keep/hold s.o. in ~) tener/mantener a alg. a **raya**

cheek (be an incredible ~) no tener **nombre**

cheek (be the height of ~) pasar de **castaño** oscuro; pelar la jeta

cheek (impudence) el tupé

cheek (¡what an incredible ~!) solemne

cheek (you've got a ~!) ¡qué **morro** tienes!

cheeks (have chubby ~) tener **cara** de nalgas

cheeky (be very ~) ser más fresco que una **lechuga**

cheeky (get ~ [with s.o.]) subirse a las **barba**s de alg.; ponerse **flamenco**

cheeky devil (be a ~) tener más **cara** que espalda; ser más fresco que una **lechuga**

cheeky monkey (be a ~) ser más fresco que una **lechuga**

cheerful type el jacarero

cheers! ¡hasta verte, **Cristo/Jesús** mío! ¡salud!

cheese (be a big ~) tener muchas **campanillas**; ser un **pájaro** gordo

cheese (be as different as chalk and ~) estar tan lejos como lo **blanco** de lo negro/no parecerse ni en el blanco de los ojos; parecerse como un **huevo** a una castaña

cheese (big ~[s]) un gran **bonete**; gente gorda; un **pez** gordo

to be cheesed off with s.o. estar hasta las **ceja**s de alg.; estar **frito** de alg.

to be cheesed off with s.th. estar hasta las **cejas**/el **coco**/[más allá de] la **coronilla** de algo; estar **frito** de algo; estar hasta el **gorro**/el **moño**/las narices (▷ **nariz**)/la **punta** de los pelos o del pelo/los **topes** de algo

cheesy feet los **queso**s

to cherish (be highly ~ed by s.o.) ser el **ojo** derecho de alg.

cherry (life isn't all a bowl of cherries) no todo el monte es **orégano**

Cheshire cat (grin like a ~) sonreír de oreja a oreja

chest (play/keep one's cards close to one's ~) no soltar **prenda**

chestnuts (be old ~) ser del tiempo del **rey** que rabió/del rey Wamba

chestnuts (old ~) una antigualla

chestnuts (to pull s.o.'s ~ out of the fire for him) sacar las **castaña**s del fuego a alg.

to chew on that llevar/tener qué **rascar**

to chew the fat/rag echar un **párrafo**

chick (girl) la jai/polla

to be chicken no morir de **cornada** de burro

chicken (count one's ~s before they are hatched) cantar victoria; hacer las cuentas de la **lechera**; vender la **piel** del oso antes de cazarlo

chicken (coward) el/la gallina

to chicken out rajarse

chickenfeed (be no ~) no ser **grano** de anís; no ser **moco de pavo**

child (be like a ~ with a new toy) alegrarse/estar como [un] **niño** con zapatos nuevos

child (bonny ~) el **pimpollo** [de oro]

child (spare the rod and spoil the ~) la **letra** con sangre entra

children and fools tell the truth los **niño**s y los locos dicen las verdades

child's play (be ~) ser una **breva**; ser **coser** y cantar; ser **pan** comido; ser **tortas** y pan pintado

to chime in escupir en **corro**; meter su **cuchara**

to chime in with s.o. hacer **coro** con alg.

chimney (smoke like a ~) fumar como un **carretero**/una **chimenea**; a todo **pasto** chin (keep your ~ up!) ¡tente **tieso**!

chin up! ¡pecho al agua!

china-shop (like a bull in a ~) como un **burro**/**caballo**/**elefante** en una cacharrería

to be Chinese to s.o. ser **chino** algo para alg.

chip (cash/hand in one's ~s: to die) palmarla

chip (when the ~s are down) a la **hora** de la verdad

chip off the old block de tal **costilla**, tal astilla; de casta le viene al **galgo** ser rabilargo; de tal **palo**, tal astilla

to chip s.o. tomarle el **pelo** a alg.

chipper (be very ~) estar [alegre] como unas **castañuelas**

chirpy (be very ~) estar [alegre] como unas **castañuelas**

chiv (knife: as a problem solver) el quitapenas

to be chock-a-block no caber ni un **alfiler**; estar de **bote** en bote

choice (there's no ~) no hay más **cáscaras**

to choke up tener un nudo en la **garganta**/hacérsele a alg. un nudo en la garganta

to choke [with] or be choked [with] tener un nudo en la **garganta**/hacérsele a alg. un nudo en la garganta

to chop and change dar una de **cal** y otra de arena

chronic liar (be a ~) ser un **costal** de mentiras; de siete **suelas**

chubby (short, ~ person) el tapón

chubby cheeks (have ~) tener **cara** de nalgas

to be chubby-cheeked tener **cara** de nalgas

chuck (give s.o. the ~) dar el **bote** a alg.; echar/despedir a alg. con **cajas** destempladas; echar a alg. a la **calle**/poner a alg. de patitas en la calle; plantar a alg. en la **calle**; largar a alg.; dar la **licencia**/[el] **pasaporte**/la **patada** a alg.

to chuck it all in/up dar con la **carga** en tierra/en el suelo o echarse con la carga; mandar algo al **cuerno**/a tomar por **culo**/al **diablo** (examples); echarlo todo a **rodar**; echar la **soga** tras el caldero; tirar los **trastos**

to chuck s.o. out dar el **bote** a alg.; echar/despedir a alg. con **cajas** destempladas; echar a alg. a la **calle**/poner a alg. de patitas en la calle; plantar a alg. en la **calle**; largar a alg.; dar la **licencia**/[el] **pasaporte**/la **patada** a alg.; dar soleta a alg.

to chuck s.th. in/up mandar algo al **cuerno**/a tomar por **culo**/al **diablo**

to chuck the whole thing dar con la **carga** en tierra/en el suelo o echarse con la carga; mandar algo al **cuerno**/a tomar por **culo**/al **diablo** (examples); tirar los **trastos**

church mouse (be as poor as a ~) no tener ni para unas **alpargatas**; no tener qué llevarse a la **boca**/donde **caerse** muerto; no tener más

que el **pan** y la noche; ser más pobre que una **rata** [de iglesia]

churchy type la beata

churchy type (be a ~) **comer**se los santos

cigar (bad/cheap ~) la tagarnina

cigar (close, but no ~) quedarse con la **miel** en los labios; nadar y nadar, y a la orilla ahogar

cigarette (marijuana ~) el petardo/porro

cigarette butt/end la pava

cigarettes (smoke ~ only) no fumar más que **papel**

cinch (be a ~) ser una **breva**; ser **coser** y cantar; ser **pan** comido; ser **torta**s y pan pintado

Circe la **castigadora**

circles (move in high ~) codearse con los de **arriba**

circumstances (adapt/adjust [o.s.] to the ~) bailar al **son** que le tocan a alg.

circumstances (basically it all depends on the ~) de **hombre** a hombre no va nada

circumstances (consider one's financial ~) consultar con el **bolsillo**

cirrocumuli cabrillas

cirrus [cloud] **rabo**s de gallo

clam (be as happy as a ~) estar [alegre] como unas **castañuelas**; estar [contento] como o más contento que unas pascuas (▷ **Pascua**)

clam (shut up like a ~) callar[se] como un muerto/una piedra; estar mudo como una **tumba**/ser [como] una tumba

clan (with the whole ~) con toda la **recua**

clanger (drop a ~) cagarla; tirarse una **plancha**; pringarla

clanger (person who is always dropping a ~) el/la metepatas

to clap s.o. in jail meter a alg. donde no vea el **sol**; poner a alg. a la **sombra**; zambullir a alg. en la cárcel

Clapham omnibus (the man on the ~) Juan Pérez

clappers (go like the ~) ir como **alma** que se lleva el diablo; a toda **mecha**; correr/lanzarse a **tumba** abierta

class (cut ~) pirarse o pirárselas

class (he's in a ~ by himself/of his own) a ése no hay quien le tosa (▷ **toser**)

class[es] (belong to the upper ~) codearse con los de **arriba**

claws (show one's ~) enseñar/mostrar las **uñas**

clean (as ~ as a new pin) limpio como una **patena**; como una **plata**/una **tacita** de plata

clean (come ~ [about s.th.]) cantar de plano; desembuchar [algo]

clean (squeaky ~) limpio como una **patena**; como una **plata**/una **tacita** de plata

to clean s.o. out dejar a alg. en **cueros** [vivos]; dejar esquilmado a alg. (▷ **esquilmar**)

to clean [s.th.] [up] superficially limpiar algo
solamente por donde ve la **suegra** o
limpiar solamente lo que ve la suegra
clear (be as ~ as crystal/as day/as daylight/as
vodka) estar más claro que el **agua**; ser
más claro que el **sol**
clear (steer ~ of all work) estar haciéndose **viejo**
clear (steer ~ of s.th./s.o.) **quitar**se algo/a alg. de
encima
clear (the coast is ~) no hay **moros** en la costa
clear off! irse con la **música** a otra parte
(example)
to clear off (go/leave) sacar el **bulto**; **largar**se;
darse de **naja**; najarse; pirarse o
pirárselas; darse el **piro**; salir pitando
(▷ **pitar**); tomar **soleta**; poner **tierra** por
medio; tocárselas (▷ **tocar**); alzar/levantar
el **vuelo**
to clear off at once **largar**se con viento fresco
to clear off with the whole lot alzarse/salirse con
el **santo** y la limosna/cera
to clear one's mind sacudirse las **telarañas**
to clear the air/atmosphere aclarar las cosas
clergyman (be a ~) vestirse por la **cabeza**
cleric (be a ~) vestirse por la **cabeza**
clerk (petty ~) el cagatintas/chupatintas
clever (be too ~ by half) cortar un **pelo** en el aire
clever (be [very] ~) saber más que **Briján**; ser
más listo que el **hambre**; tener mucha
letra menuda; saber cuántas **púas** tiene
un peine; saber más que **siete**
clever (think to be very ~) la **mar** de
clever dick/Dick (be a real ~) más que **siete**
cleverest (the ~) el más **pintado**
to climb a tree (go ~!) ¡anda a **bañar**te!; ¡vete a
freír **buñuelos/espárragos**!
to climb a tree (tell s.o. to go ~) mandar a alg. a
freír **buñuelos**/al **cuerno**/a freír
espárragos/a hacer **gárgaras**
to climb down apearse de su **burro**; cantar la
gallina; bajar las **orejas**; rajarse
to cling to s.o. agarrarse a los faldones de alg.
(▷ **faldón**)
to cling to s.o. like a leech/limpet pegarse como
una **ladilla/lapa** a alg.
clink (be in ~) estar a la **sombra**/en la **trena**
clink (be put in ~) ponerse el **capuchón**
clink (jail/prison) la trena
clink (put s.o. in ~) meter a alg. donde no vea el
sol; poner a alg. a la **sombra**; zambullir a
alg. en la cárcel
clinker (gaffe) la pifia/plancha
clip round the ears la chuleta
to clip s.o.'s wings cortar las **alas**/los **vuelos** a
alg.
clips round the ears (give s.o. a few hefty ~)
ponerle a alg. la cara nueva (▷ **nuevo**)
clique (form one's own little ~) hacer **rancho**
aparte

cloak-and-dagger film/etc. una película/etc. de
capa y espada
clobbering (give s.o. a ~) zurrar la **badana** o
menear/sacudir el **bulto** a alg.; arrimar
candela/dar **caña**/medir las **costillas**/
sentar las **costuras** a alg.; dar **leña** o
cargar de leña a alg.; cascarle/machacarle
a alg. las **liendres**; sacudir el **polvo** a alg.;
poner a alg. como un **pulpo**
clock (at 6 o'~ sharp/on the nose) a las seis
clavadas (▷ **clavado**)
clock (run out the ~) vivir de **renta**
clockwork (go/run like ~) ir que grana
(▷ **granar**); a las mil **maravillas**; ir/marchar
como un **reloj**/sobre **ruedas**/como una
seda
clod un [pedazo de] **alcornoque/atún**; un[a]
cabeza de corcho; una calabaza; un alma
de **cántaro**; un ceporro/melón/merluzo;
un **palomino** atontado; un percebe
clogs (pop one's ~) irse al otro **barrio**; **cascar**[la];
diñarla; quedarse **frío/frito**; pelar **gallo**;
guiñarla; hincar el pico; **liar**las o liárselas;
palmarla; estirar la **pata**; liar el **petate**;
pringarla; **reventar**[se]; quedarse **tieso**
close (that was ~!) ¡de buena me he/nos hemos/
etc. librado! (▷ **librar**)
close, but no cigar quedarse con la **miel** en los
labios; nadar y nadar, y a la orilla ahogar
close shave (be/have a ~) [por] el **canto** de un
duro; por un **pelo**/los pelos; salvarse en
una **tabla**
close to a **flor** de
close to (come ~ one's goal without reaching it/
success without attaining it) quedarse con la
miel en los labios; nadar y nadar, y a la
orilla ahogar
close to (come very ~) [por] el **canto** de un duro
to be close to forty/etc. [years of age] **zumbar**le a
alg. los cuarenta/etc. años
to be close to the bone pasar de **castaño** oscuro;
pelar la jeta
to close one's eyes [to s.th.] hacer la vista gorda [a
algo] (▷ **gordo**); cerrar los **ojos** a algo
to close s.th. firmly/tight/securely cerrar algo a **cal**
y canto
cloth (cut one's coat according to one's ~) no
estirar los **pies** más de lo que da la
frazada
cloth (give up the ~) ahorcar/colgar los **hábitos**
cloth (not to cut one's coat according to one's ~)
estirar la **pierna** más larga que la sábana
clothes (spend an awful lot on ~) gastar una
barbaridad en **trapos**
clothes (talk about ~) hablar de **trapos**
clothes do not make the man el **hábito** no hace al
monje
clothes make the man el **hábito** hace al monje
cloud una nube

cloud (as lonely as a ~) más solo que un **hongo**

cloud (cirrus ~) **rabo**s de gallo

cloud (every ~ has a silver lining) no hay **mal** que por bien no venga

cloud nine (be on ~) estar en el séptimo/quinto **cielo**; estar en su[s] **gloria**[s]

cloud-cuckoo-land (be living in ~) tener la **cabeza** llena de pájaros; vivir en la **luna**; andar por o vivir en las **nubes**

clouds (cotton-wool/fleecy ~) cabrillas

clouds (have one's head in the ~) estar en **Babia**/ en las **Batuecas**/en **Belén**/en la **higuera**; estar/vivir en la **luna**; andar por o estar/ vivir en las **nubes**; mirar las telarañas

clout (not to have any ~) ni **pinchar** ni cortar; no **pintar** nada; ni **quitar** ni poner

clover (live/be in ~) vivir como **Dios** en Francia; vivir/estar como **pava** en corral

clown (play the ~) **tirar**se a muerto

to clown about/around hacer el **oso**

clue (not to have a ~ [about s.th.]) no distinguir lo **blanco** de lo negro; oír **campana**s y no saber dónde; no saber [ni] la **cartilla**; no saber ni **jota** de algo; estar **pez** en algo

clue (not to have a ~ what it's [all] about) no saber uno lo que se pesca (▷ **pescar**)

to be clumsy ser un **manazas**; no saber uno dónde tiene los **ojos**

clumsy bullfighter el maleta

clumsy oaf/sort (be a ~) ser un **manazas**

to clutch at straws/at any opportunity agarrarse a un **clavo** ardiendo; agarrarse/asirse a un **pelo**

clutches (fall into s.o.'s ~) caer en las **garra**s/ **uña**s de alg.

clutches (free s.o. from s.o.'s ~) sacar a alg. de las **garra**s de alg.

coals (carry ~ to Newcastle) echar **agua** en el mar; llevar **hierro** a Vizcaya/**leña** al monte

coals (haul s.o. over the ~) soltar la/una **andanada** a alg.; zurrar la **badana**/dar una **calada** a alg.; poner a alg. como un **trapo**

coarse language (use ~) soltar **tacos**

coarse wine (be [a] ~) ser un **vino** peleón

coast (the ~ is clear) no hay **moros** en la costa

coat (cut one's ~ according to one's cloth) no estirar los **pies** más de lo que da la frazada

coat (not to cut one's ~ according to one's cloth) estirar la **pierna** más larga que la sábana

to coax s.th. out of s.o. sonsacar algo a alg.

cobwebs (blow the ~ away) sacudirse las **telarañas**

cocaine (coke; snow; stuff) la blanca; el Charly; la coca/nieve; el polvo

cock el arma/asunto/bolo/calvo/canario/ chorizo/cimbel; la gurrina; el pájaro; la picha/pija; el pijo; la pinga; el pito; la polla/porra; el rabo/troncho

cock of the roost/walk el gallito

to cock it/s.th./things up cagar algo; **cagar**la; escoñar/joder algo

cock-and-bull story el **cuento** chino

cockcrow (at ~) al **canto** del gallo

cock-teaser la calientapollas

to coddle s.o. [in his childhood] guardar/tener o criar a alg. entre algodones (▷ **algodón**); criar a alg. en **estufa**

coffee (black ~ with a dash of brandy) el carajillo

coffee (thin ~) el recuelo

coffin (be in the ~) estar entre cuatro **velas**

to cohabit casarse por detrás de la iglesia

to coil up (snake) hacer la **rosca**

coin (5-céntimo ~) la **perra** chica

coin (10-céntimo ~) la **perra** gorda

coin (pay s.o. back in his own ~) pagar a alg. con/ en la misma **moneda**; volver las **torna**s a alg.

coincidence (be a lucky ~) sonar la **flauta** [por casualidad]

coke (cocaine) la blanca; el Charly; la coca/nieve

cold (be [as] ~ as a fish/as marble) tener **sangre** blanca/de horchata en las venas

cold (be bloody/damn[ed] ~) hacer un frío de cojones (▷ **cojón**)

cold (be freezing ~) hacer un frío que pela (▷ **pelar**); de **perros**

cold (be stone ~) tener **sangre** blanca/de horchata en las venas

cold (leave s.o. out in the ~) dejar a alg. **colgado**

cold (not to be half ~) hacer un frío que pela (▷ **pelar**); de **perros**

cold (s.o.'s blood runs ~) helársele a alg. la **sangre**

cold (the wind is [as] ~ as a witch's caress) corre un **gris** que pela

cold (when you have a ~, drink some booze/have a toddy) al **catarro**, con el jarro

to be cold enough to freeze the balls off a brass monkey hacer un frío de cojones (▷ **cojón**)/que pela (▷ **pelar**); de **perros**

cold feet (get ~) quedarse **frío**; encogérsele a alg. el **ombligo**

cold print (have it in ~) **carta**[s] canta[n]

cold shoulder (give s.o. the ~) dar de **lado** a alg.

cold turkey el mono

cold wind (there's a ~ [blowing]) hace un **gris**

to collapse in a heap caerse redondo

to collapse like a house of cards derrumbarse como un **castillo** de naipes

collar (get hot under the ~) perder los **estribos**

to collar s.o. coger/pescar el **bulto** a alg.

collection (motley ~) cajón de sastre

collection (take a ~) echar un **guante**

collector (dust ~) el **nido** de polvo

colors (come off/out with flying ~) salir a **tambor** batiente colors (show [o.s. in] one's true ~) quitarse la **careta**; enseñar el **cobre**; quitarse el **embozo**; descubrir la **hilaza**; quitarse la **máscara**; descubrir la **oreja**

colossal bestial; cojonudo; garrafal

comb (go through/over s.th with a fine-tooth ~) pasar algo por la **criba**

to come (easy ~, easy go) los **dinero**s del sacristán cantando se vienen y cantando se van; lo ganado por lo gastado (▷ **ganar**)

to come (first ~, first served) el **primer** venido, primer servido

to come (have an orgasm) **correr**se; sacar la **piedra**

to come (I came, I saw, I conquered) vine, vi y vencí (▷ **vencer**)

to come (not to ~ to s.th.) **fumar**se algo

to come (not to ~ to that) no **llegar** a tanto

to come (not to know any more whether one is coming or going) no saber dónde volver la **cabeza**

to come (see s.th. coming) **ver**las venir

to come (the main difficulty or the most difficult part or the worst [of it] is yet/still to ~) aún falta/queda la **cola**/el **rabo** por desollar; quedarle a alg. todavía el **trago** más amargo

to come after everything is over llegar a los **postre**s

to come again (that opportunity/chance won't ~) **ojos** que te vieron ir

to come along [again] echar buen **pelo**/buena **pluma**

to come at a better time (s.th. couldn't have ~) venir como **agua** de mayo/como **anillo** al dedo; venir como llovido/llegar como caído del **cielo**; venir que ni **pintado**/como pintado

to come at just the right time venir como **agua** de mayo/como **anillo** al dedo; venir como llovido/llegar como caído del **cielo**; venir que ni **pintado**/como pintado; venir **rodado**

to come clean [about s.th.] cantar de plano; desembuchar [algo]

to come down in buckets/sheets a **cántaro**s (example); llover a **chorro**s/**cubo**s/**mar**es/**torrente**s

to come down in the world venir a menos

to come down on s.o. like a ton of bricks soltar la/una **andanada** a alg.; zurrar la **badana** a alg.; la bronca (example); dar una **calada** a alg.; soltar/decir cuatro **fresca**s a alg.; hacer **papilla**/echar los **perro**s a alg.

to come down to (it comes down to the same thing) llámele usted o llámele **hache**

to come down to (when it comes down to it) a la **hora** de la verdad

to come down/back to earth with a bump caer del **nido**

to come from (hope there's more where that came from) saber a más

come hell or high water contra **viento** y marea

to come in on an affair tomar **carta**s en un asunto

to come in very handy venir de **perilla**[s]; de **perla**s

to come just right de **perla**s; venir [que ni] **pintiparado**

to come like manna from heaven venir como llovido/llegar como caído del **cielo**

to come off a loser llevar las de **perder**/salir perdiendo

to come off best llevarse la mejor **parte**

come off it! ¡y un **jamón** [con chorreras]!

to come off [very] well pescar una buena **breva**

to come off worst llevar las de **perder**/salir perdiendo

to come out (book/etc.) salir a **luz**

to come out of s.th. badly/well salir bien/mal librado de algo (▷ **librar**)

to come out on top llevarse la mejor **parte**

to come out with s.th./it (▷ also: **out with it!**) descolgarse con algo; sacar a **relucir** algo; salir con algo; soltar la **sinhueso**

to come over s.o. pronto (example)

to come straight out [with s.th.] no andarse con/en chiquitas (▷ la **chiquita**); no andarse con **requilorios**

to come to nothing irse al **cuerno**; **escoñar**se; quedar en **nada**; deshacerse como la **sal** en el agua

to come too late llegar a los **postre**s

to come up with s.th. just like that traer algo en/por la **manga**; sacarse algo de la **manga**

come what may salga lo que salga/saliere (▷ **salir**); salga el **sol** por Antequera/por donde quiera; contra **viento** y marea

comeuppance (everyone gets his ~ sooner or later) a cada cerdo/puerco le llega su **San Martín**

comfort (crumb of ~) la **dedada** de miel

comfort (I dress for ~, not for other people) ande yo **caliente** y ríase la gente

to comfort s.o. at the hour of death recoger el postrer **suspiro** de alg.

command (be in ~) cortar el **bacalao**; llevar la **batuta**; llevar/ponerse los calzones (▷ **calzón**); ser el amo del o dirigir el **cotarro**; llevar la **voz** cantante

command (have complete ~ of s.th.) tener algo en la **uña**

command (take ~) empuñar el **bastón**

commandment (11th ~: don't disturb) el **onceno**: [no estorbar]

to commit o.s. (avoid committing o.s.) no soltar **prenda**

to commit o.s. rashly soltar **prenda**

to be common knowledge andar algo de **boca** en boca (example); andar en **copla**s

common sense el pesquis

commotion la tremolina

commotion (cause a ~) alborotar el **palomar**; levantar una **polvareda**

companion in misfortune (you can always find a ~) no/nunca falta un **roto** para un descosido

company (desert and reward seldom keep ~) de **ingratitud**es/**ingrato**s está el mundo lleno

company (you can judge a person by the ~ he keeps) dime con quién andas y te diré quién eres (▷ **decir**)

to compete (nobody can ~ with him) a ése no hay quien le tosa (▷ **toser**)

competitor (be a ~) ser de la otra **acera**

to complain [about] despotricar [contra]

complete hecho y derecho; rematado

complete (be [as good as] ~) no faltar un **cabello** a algo

complete idiot (be a ~) a más no **poder**; ser **tonto** del bote/de capirote

completely hasta la **pared** de enfrente

completely bloody puto (example)

complicated (be [very] ~) tener **bigote**/tres pares de bigotes; tener algo muchos **entresijos**

compliments (pay s.o. [pretty] ~) echar **flor**es a alg.

compromise la componenda

compromise (offer a ~) tender un **puente** con el camelo

to con (be [easily] ~ned) hacer el **primo**

to con s.o. dar [el] **camelo**/la **castaña** a alg.; dar a alg. **gato** por liebre; pegar un **parche**/**petardo** a alg.

con man (be an out-and-out/a real ~) de siete **suelas**

conceited (be [as] ~ as a barber's cat) tener muchos **tufos**

conceited (be [very] ~) **pagar**se de sí mismo; tener muchos **tufos**

concessions (make ~ towards s.o.) salir al **paso** a/de alg.

concierge la leona

conclusions (draw ~) atar/unir **cabos**

concoction el jarope

condom (French letter; johnny; rubber) el calcetín/globo; la goma

confession (make a full ~) cantar de plano

confidence (be in s.o.'s ~) ser el **ojo** derecho de alg.

confidence (propose a vote of ~) plantear la cuestión de **gabinete**

confidence/confident (▷ **over~**)

confirmed por los cuatro **costados**

to confront s.o. plantar **cara** a alg.; salir al **paso** a/de alg.

confused (be totally ~) tener la cabeza a las **once**

conk (head) la calabaza/cebolla/chaveta/cholla/coca; el coco/güiro/güito; la jupa; el melón

conk (nose) el asa; las napias

conk (nose: big ~) el naso; la trompa

connection (good ~) el enchufe

connections (without ~) huérfano de enchufes

to conquer (I came, I saw, I ~ed) vine, vi y vencí (▷ **vencer**)

conquest (easy/quick ~) el levante

conscience (have a [very] bad/guilty ~) tener el alma negra [como el carbón] (▷ **negro**)

conscience (pangs/pricks of ~) el rescoldo

conscience (with a clear ~ you sleep well) la mejor **almohada** es una conciencia tranquila

consent (silence gives/implies ~) quien calla otorga (▷ **callar**)

consequences (everyone must bear/face the ~ of his actions) quien por su **gusto** padece, vaya al infierno a quejarse

consequences (have [grave] ~) tener/traer **cola**

consequences (one must bear/face the ~) quien o el que la hace la paga (▷ **pagar**)

consequences (regardless of the ~) salga lo que salga/saliere (▷ **salir**)

to be considered to be pasar por

to consign s.th. to oblivion relegar algo al olvido

consolation (what's bad for s.o. may be a ~ for s.o. else) mal de muchos, consuelo de todos

conspicuous (look ~) tener **mono**s en la cara

conspicuous bloke el nota

to be conspicuous by one's absence brillar alg. por su **ausencia**

constitution (have an iron ~) tener **carne** de perro

to be consumed by one's worries sorber los **seso**s a alg.

to be consumed with envy comer a alg. la envidia

contact (break off ~ with people) **enterrar**se en vida

contact (useful ~) el enchufe

contacts (use of ~ to obtain advantages/favors) el enchufismo

contacts (without useful ~) huérfano de enchufes

content (to one's heart's ~) a pedir de **boca**; a todo **pasto**

to be content with s.th. **pagar**se con algo

to contradict (not to dare to ~ s.o.) llevar el **genio** a alg.

to contrive to + infinitive arreglárselas/componérselas para + infinitivo (▷ **arreglar**/**componer**)

control (be difficult to keep under ~) ser de la **piel** del diablo

control (be in ~) llevar/tener las **rienda**s

control (bring s.o. under ~) meter a alg. en **cintura**/**costura**; meter a alg. en un **puño**

control (get/keep s.o. under ~) tirar de la **cuerda** a alg.; tener/mantener a alg. a **raya** control (have things under ~) llevar/tener las **rienda**s; tener la **sartén** por el mango

to control mover los **hilo**s

controls (be at the ~) mover los **hilo**s

conversation (butt into or in on/join in the ~) escupir en **corro**

conversation (interrupt the ~) cortar el **hilo** de la conversación

conversation (start a/strike up a ~) pegar la **hebra**/el **hilo**

cook (too many ~s spoil the broth) muchas **mano**s en un plato hacen mucho garabato o muchas manos en la olla echan el guiso a perder

to be cooked up **cocer**se

cookie (know which way the ~ crumbles) saber de qué lado caen las **pera**s/por dónde van los **tiro**s

cookie (that's the way the ~ crumbles) así es la **vida**

cookie ([wait and/to] see which way the ~ crumbles) [esperar a] ver de qué lado caen las **pera**s/por dónde van los **tiro**s

cookie jar (catch s.o. with his hand in the ~) coger a alg. con las manos en la **masa**

cookies (blow one's ~) cambiar la **peseta**

cool (. . . as ~ as a cucumber) quedarse/estar tan **campante/fresco/pancho**

cool (blow/lose one's ~) ponerse como un **basilisco**; exaltársele a alg. la **bilis**; subirse al **campanario**; salirse de sus **casilla**s; ponerse hecho un **demonio**; perder los **estribo**s; hinchársele a alg. las narices (▷ **nariz**); subirse por las **pared**es/a la **parra**

cool (say s.th. as ~ as you please) decir algo tan **fresco**

cool it! ¡para el **carro**!; ¡echa el **freno**, Ma[g]daleno!

to cool one's heels estar en/sobre **ascua**s; estar [como] en **brasa**s

coon (in a ~'s age) en las **Calenda**s griegas; cuando meen las **gallina**s; cuando las **rana**s críen pelo; en la **semana** que no tenga jueves/de tres jueves

coot (be as bald as a ~) estar como [una] **bola** de billar

cop (policeman) el **bofia/poli/polizonte**

to cop it ganársela (▷ **ganar**)

to cop out [of it] escurrir/escapar/huir el **bulto**

copper (policeman) el **bofia/poli/polizonte**

coppers (cost a few ~) costar unas **perra**s

cops (police) la **bofia/madera/poli/polilla**

to copy s.th. illegally fusilar algo

copybook (blot one's ~) meter la **pata/pezuña**

core (be a Spaniard/etc. to the ~) ser español/etc. hasta los **tuétano**s

core (essential part) el quid

core (to the ~) por los cuatro **costado**s; rematado

cork (blow/pop one's ~) ponerse como un **basilisco**; exaltársele a alg. la **bilis**; subirse al **campanario**; salirse de sus **casilla**s; ponerse hecho un **demonio**; hinchársele a alg. las narices (▷ **nariz**); subirse por las **pared**es/a la **parra**; fundírsele a alg. los **plomo**s

cornball el rapaterrones

corner (be just around the ~) estar a la **puerta**/en puertas

corner (disappear around the ~) dar [el] **esquinazo**

corner (drive s.o. into a ~) poner a alg. entre la **espada** y la pared; poner a alg. a **parir**

corner (get s.o. into a ~) pillar el **toro** a alg.

cost (at all ~s/any ~) por **fas** o por nefas; a todo **trance**

to cost a few bucks/coppers/quid costar unas **perra**s

to cost an arm and a leg/a bomb/the earth/a fortune/a packet/a pretty penny/a tidy sum costar una **burrada**/un **dineral**/un **huevo**/un **ojo** de la cara/un **pico**/un **riñón**/una **riñonada**; costar la de **San Quintín**; costar un **sentido** o los cinco sentidos

to cotton on to s.th. guipar algo

cotton wool (wrap s.o. [up] in ~) guardar/tener o criar a alg. entre algodones (▷ **algodón**)

cotton-wool clouds cabrillas

to cough up rascar[se] el **bolsillo**; aflojar/soltar la **china/mosca**; soltar la **pasta**; sacudir/soltar la **tela**

to count (not to ~: person) no **pintar** nada; ni **quitar** ni poner

to count (once doesn't ~) una no es ninguna

to count every penny pellizcar los céntimos

to count one's cash consultar con el **bolsillo**

to count one's chickens before they are hatched cantar victoria; hacer las cuentas de la **lechera**; vender la **piel** del oso antes de cazarlo

counter (under the ~) bajo **cuerda**/por debajo de cuerda

counting on one's fingers la **cuenta** de la vieja

country bumpkin/yokel el rapaterrones

coup (bring off a ~) poner una **pica** en Flandes

couple (make a lovely ~) hacer una buena/bonita **pareja**

courage! ¡pecho al agua!

courage (arm o.s. with ~) revestirse de valor

courage (have ~) tener **hígado**s/**huevo**s; tener riñones (▷ **riñón**)

courage (muster/pluck/screw/summon up [one's] ~) sacar **fuerza**s de flaqueza; revestirse de valor; hacer de **tripa**s corazón

courage (not to have an ounce/the least bit of ~) ni **sombra** de

course (adopt a ~) tirar por un camino

course (alter ~ [radically]) dar un **golpe** de timón

course (let things take their ~) dejar que ruede la **bola**

course (of ~!) ¡no faltaba/faltaría más! (▷ **faltar**)

courses (horses for ~) cada **loco** con su tema; a cada uno/cual, lo **suyo**

to court disaster atar perros con **longaniza**

to court s.o. arrastrar el **ala** a alg.

cover (from ~ to ~) de **cabo** a cabo/rabo o de punta a cabo; de **pe** a pa

to cover s.th. up ocultar/tapar la **caca**; echar **tierra** sobre/a algo

covered in (be/get ~ dirt/etc.) estar o ponerse **perdido** de algo

covered with cuajado de

to covet s.o./s.th. echar el **ojo** a alg./algo

cow (be [as] awkward as a ~ on a crutch/on roller skates) a más no **poder**

cow (be the milch ~) ser la **vaca** de la boda

cow (wait till the ~s come home) esperar sentado

to cow s.o. meter las **cabras** en el corral a alg.; meter a alg. en un **puño**

coward el/la gallina

coward (be a [real/stinking] ~) no morir de **cornada** de burro; de siete **suelas**

coward (don't be [such] a ~!) ¡nadie muere de **cornada** de burro!

crack of dawn (at the ~) al **canto** del gallo

crack of dawn (get up at the ~) levantarse con las **gallinas**

to crack one's head open romperse la **crisma**

to crack s.th. up dar **bombo** a algo

to crack up (burst out laughing) descoyuntarse/ desternillarse/rajarse de risa

to be cracked estar **chiflado**

crackerjack (be a ~ [at s.th.]) ser un **hacha** [en/ para algo]

crackers (be [completely] ~) estar [loco] como un **cencerro**

cradle (have learned/learnt s.th. from the ~) haber mamado algo [ya] en/con la **leche**

craftiest (the ~) el más **pintado**

crafty (be [very] ~) tener muchas **camándulas**/ **carlancas**; tener mucha **trastienda**

crafty devil el vivo/la viva

crafty person el zorro

crafty woman la pájara

to cram [s.th.] quemarse las **cejas**; romperse los **codos**; empollar [algo]; machacar [algo]; quemarse las **pestañas**

crap la ñoña/ñorda

crap (have/take a ~) cagar; plantar la **estaca**; hacer de lo **gordo**

to crave for s.th. írsele a alg. los **ojos** tras algo; pelárselas por algo (▷ **pelar**); perecerse por algo

craving (have a ~ for) tener **hipo** por algo

crawling with cuajado de

crawler el pelotillero

to be crazy estar mal de la **azotea**; no estar bueno de la **cabeza** o estar ido/mal/ tocado de la cabeza o tener pájaros en la cabeza; estar como una/más loco que una **cabra**; estar como una **cafetera**; estar [loco] como un **cencerro**; estar **chalado**; estar mal de la **chaveta**; estar **chiflado**; estar/ser **loco** de atar/remate; estar a las **once** y cuarto; estar como una **regadera**

to be crazy (we're all a little ~ in one way or another) de **cuerdo** y loco todos tenemos un poco

to be crazy about s.th./s.o. (enthusiastic) beber los **aires** por algo/alg.; caérsele a alg. la **baba** con/por alg./algo; estar **chalado/chiflado** por alg.; ser **forofo** de algo/alg.; estar **perdido** por alg./algo; **perecerse** por algo; sorber los **sesos** a alg.; beber/sorber los **vientos** por alg.

crazy (drive s.o. ~) llevar de **cabeza** a alg.; sacar a alg. de sus **casillas**; es para volverse **loco**; poner **negro** a alg.; hacer a alg. subirse por las **paredes**; ser [como] para subirse por las **paredes**; sacar a alg. de **quicio**

crazy (go ~ [about s.o.]) perder la **chaveta** [por alg.]

crazy (knock like ~) echar las **puertas** abajo

crazy (like ~) como el/un **diablo**; a más no **poder**; a **rabiar**

crazy (run like ~) como el **diablo**; correr como **gato** por ascuas; a más no **poder**

crazy idea el golpe de **bombero**

cream (elite) la **flor** y nata

cream (skim the ~ off) chuparse [una] buena **breva**

to cream off the best chuparse [una] buena **breva**

to crease up descoyuntarse/desternillarse/rajarse de risa

creature of habit (man is a ~) la costumbre es otra/segunda **naturaleza**

credit (drink on ~) beber sobre **tarja**

credit (some do [all] the work and others get [all] the ~/one does [all] the work and the other [one] gets [all] the ~) unos cardan la lana y otros tienen/llevan/cobran la **fama**

credit (take ~ for what s.o. else has done) adornarse con **plumas** ajenas

creek (be up the ~/up shit ~ [without a paddle]) estar jodido (▷ **joder**)

creep el/la lavacaras; el pelotillero; el/la quitamotas

to creep [into s.o.'s favor] chupar del **bote**

creeps (give s.o. or get the ~) ponerle o ponérsele a alg. [la] **carne** de gallina

crème de la crème la **flor** y nata

crème de la crème (be the ~) ser la flor de la **canela**

crib (for cheating in exam) la chuleta

to crib s.th. (plagiarize) fusilar algo

crime (it would be a ~ not to . . .) sería un **pecado** no ...

crime (poverty is not a ~) pobreza no es vileza

criticism (be beyond all ~/stand up to the severest ~) poder pasar por las **pica**s de Flandes

to criticize (have/find s.th. to ~) buscar **pelo**s en la sopa/leche o al huevo

to criticize s.o. behind his back poner a alg. a **parir**

to criticize s.o. severely dar un **palo** a alg.

to croak (die) irse al otro **barrio**; cascar[la]; diñarla; quedarse **frío/frito**; pelar **gallo**; **guiñar**la; hincar el pico; **liar**las o liárselas; palmarla; estirar la **pata**; liar el **petate**; **pringar**la; **reventar**[se]; quedarse **tieso**

to croak s.o. **cargar**se/cascar/**cepillar**[se] a alg.; freír a alg.; dejar **frito** a alg.; mandar a alg. al otro **mundo**; pasaportear a alg.; quitar a alg. de en medio; dejar **tieso** a alg.; tumbar a alg.

crock (old ~: car) la antigualla; la **cafetera** [rusa]; el vejestorio

crock (old ~: person) una antigualla; el carcamal/vejestorio

crocodile tears (weep/shed [a few] ~) llorar/ derramar **lágrima**s de cocodrilo; llorar con un **ojo**

cronyism el enchufismo

crook el bachiller Trapazas (▷ **trapaza**)

to be crooked (piece of clothing) estar a las **once**

cross (each of us has his ~ to bear) cada uno lleva su **cruz**

cross (get [very] ~) exaltársele a alg. la **bilis**; subirse al **campanario**; salirse de sus **casilla**s; hinchársele a alg. las narices (▷ **nariz**); ponerse **negro**; subirse por las **pared**es/a la **parra**

cross (look ~) torcer el **morro**

cross (make s.o. ~) sacar a alg. de sus **casilla**s; poner **negro** a alg.; hacer a alg. subirse por las **pared**es

cross look (have a ~ on one's face) tener **cara** de pocos amigos

cross my heart and hope to die jurar por lo más **sagrado** [que . . .] (example)

to cross swords with s.o. habérselas con alg. (▷ **haber**)

to cross the Rubicon pasar/atravesar el **Rubicón**

to be cross with s.o. estar de **morro**[s] con alg.

crow (eat ~) pedir **alafia**; doblar el **espinazo**

crow (have a ~ to pluck with s.o.) tener **cuenta**s pendientes con alg.; tener que echar un **párrafo**/parrafito aparte con alg.

crow (shout until one is [as] hoarse as a ~) desgargantarse

to crow about s.th. cacarear algo

crowd una nube

crowd (a whole ~ of people) ciento y la **madre**

crowd (attract/draw a ~) hacer **gente**

crowd (go along with/follow the ~) dejarse llevar de/por la **corriente**

crowd (stand out from the ~) salirse del **montón**

to crowd s.o. buscar el **bulto** a alg.

to be crowded out no caber ni un **alfiler**; estar de **bote** en bote

crowds of hasta la **pared** de enfrente

to crown it all s.th. else happens llover sobre mojado

crow's feet **pata**s de gallo

to be cruel tener malas **tripa**s

cruel blow (be a ~) ser un **trago** amargo

cruisemobile (flashy ~) el cochazo

crumb of comfort la **dedada** de miel

crumpled (be all ~) estar hecho un **higo**

crush (have a ~ on s.o.) estar **chalado/chiflado** por alg.; perder la **chaveta** por alg.; beber/ sorber los **viento**s por alg.

to crush s.o. machacar a alg.; hacer **polvo** a alg.; hacer morder [el] **polvo** a alg.

crust (belong to the upper ~) codearse con los de **arriba**

crust (earn one's ~) ganarse los **fríjol**es/los **garbanzo**s/el **pan**/el **puchero**/la **vida**

crust (upper ~) gente gorda

crutch (be [as] awkward as a cow on a ~) a más no **poder**

crux el quid

to cry (be a voice ~ing in the wilderness) clamar en el desierto; dar **música** a un sordo; predicar en el desierto

to cry (burst out ~ing) soltar el **trapo**

to cry (it's no use ~ing over spilt milk) lo **hecho**, hecho está/a lo hecho, pecho; agua pasada no mueve molino

to cry one's eyes out llorar a **lágrima** viva/como una **Magdalena**; llorar a **moco** tendido/a moco y baba

to cry out to heaven clamar al cielo

to cry uncle darse por vencido (▷ **vencer**)

to cry uncontrollably llorar a **moco** tendido/a moco y baba

to cry wolf gritar ¡al **lobo**!

crystal (be as clear as ~) estar más claro que el **agua**

to be crystal-clear estar más claro que el **agua**

cuckold el cornudo/novillo

to cuckold s.o. meter/poner [los] **cuerno**s a alg.; adornar la **frente** a alg.; pegársela a alg. (▷ **pegar**)

cucumber (. . . as cool as a ~) quedarse/estar tan **campante/fresco/pancho**

cudgels (take up the ~ for s.th./s.o.) defender algo a **capa** y espada; romper una **lanza** por algo/alg.

cue ball (be as bald as a ~) estar como [una] **bola** de billar

cunning old devil (be a ~) ser [un] toro **corrido/** [una] liebre corrida; ser [un] **perro/zorro** viejo

cunt (vagina) la almeja; el bacalao/beo/bollo/ chocho/conejo/coño/higo; la raja/rana/ seta

cup (there's many a slip 'twixt ~ and lip) del **dicho** al hecho hay mucho trecho; dicho sin hecho no trae provecho; del **plato** a la boca se pierde la sopa

cup of bitterness/sorrow (drain/drink the ~ [down] to the last drop) apurar el **cáliz** de cicuta/de [la] amargura/de dolor hasta las heces

cup of tea (he's/she's not my ~) no es **santo** de mi devoción

cup of tea (not to be s.o.'s ~) no ser **plato** de su gusto

cups (be in one's ~) estar cocido (▷ **cocer**)

cure (an ounce of prevention is worth a pound of ~) más vale **prevenir** que curar

cure (prevention is better than ~) más vale **prevenir** que curar

cure (there's no ~ for that [yet]) [contra eso] no hay **tutía**

curiosity (arouse/tickle s.o.'s ~) hacer **cosquillas** a alg.

curiosity (be bursting with ~) reventar de curiosidad

to curl (make s.o.'s hair ~) ponerle o ponérsele a alg. los **pelos** de punta

to curl up hacer la **rosca**

to curl up and die (s.o. is/feels so ashamed [of himself], he just wants to ~) caérsele a alg. la cara de **vergüenza**

to curl up into a ball hacerse una **rosca**

to curry favor [with s.o.] chupar del **bote**

curse (she has the ~ [of Eve]) está con la **cuenta**

to curse and swear echar **sapos** y culebras

cushy job el **bocado** sin hueso; el enchufillo

cushy job (a person who has a ~) el enchufado/la enchufada

cushy job (get [s.o.] a ~) enchufar a alg.; enchufarse

cuss (not to be worth a [tinker's] ~) no valer un **ardite/comino/pito**

cuss (not to give/care a [tinkers] ~) no importar a alg. un **ardite**; [no] importar a alg. un **bledo/comino/higo/pepino/pimiento/ pito/rábano**

customer (be a shady ~) no ser alg. **trigo** limpio

customer (be a strange ~) ser un **pájaro** raro

customer (be a/s.o. is a tough ~) ser de **armas** tomar; no quisiera partir **peras** con alg.

customer (nasty ~) una buena **pieza**

customer (strange ~) el tipejo

cut (take one's ~) sacar **tajada**

to cut and run **largar**se

to cut loose echar una **cana** al aire

to cut no ice ni **pinchar** ni cortar; no **pintar** nada; ni **quitar** ni poner

to cut o.s. off from the world **enterrar**se en vida

to cut s.o. dead hacer **mangas** y capirotes de alg.

to cut s.o. down to size bajar los **humos** a alg.; poner a alg. en su **sitio**

to cut s.o. to the quick herir a alg. en **carne** viva; llegar a o herir/tocar en lo más **vivo** a alg.

to cut up rough ponerse **negro**

cutting remarks (make ~ at s.o.) dar **remoquete** a alg.

D

dab hand (be a ~ at s.th.) **pintar**se uno solo/ pintárselas solo para algo

to dabble in s.th. mojar en algo

dachshund el **perro** salchicha

daft gil/gilí

daft (be as ~ as a brush) ser más tonto que **Abundio**

daggers (be at ~ drawn with s.o.) tener de **punta** a alg.; estar/andar a **tiro**s con alg.; estar de **uña**s con alg.

daily bread el puchero

daily bread (earn one's ~) ganarse los **fríjoles**/los **garbanzo**s/el **pan**/el **puchero**/la **vida**

daily event (be a ~) ser el **pan** [nuestro] de cada día

daisy (be pushing up [the] daisies) estar criando **malva**s/comiendo **tierra**

daisy (be/feel as fresh as a ~) estar fresco/ fresquito como una **lechuga**

to damage one's own cause hacer las diez de últimas (▷ **último**)

damn puto

damn (do ~ all) tocarse los cojones (▷ **cojón**)/el **pito**; tocar la **vihuela**

damn (I don't care/give a ~!) ¡tal día hará un **año**!

damn (I don't give a ~ what other people say/think) ande yo **caliente** y ríase la gente

damn (not to be worth a [tinker's] ~) no valer un **ardite/cojón/comino/pito**

damn (not to give a ~ about s.th./s.o.) **cagar**se en algo/alg.

damn (not to give/care a [tinkers] ~) no importar a alg. un **ardite**; [no] importar a alg. un **bledo/comino/higo/pepino/pimiento/ pito/rábano**; reírse de los peces de colores

damn him/etc.! ¡que mal **rayo** le/etc. parta!

damn [it]! ¡me cago en diez/en la mar! (▷ **cagar**); ¡caracole**s**!; ¡narices! (▷ **nariz**)

damned de mis **pecado**s

to be damn[ed] cold/hot hacer un frío/calor de cojones (▷ **cojón**)

to be damn[ed] heavy como el/un **diablo**

damn[ed] hot (it's ~) se asan las **mosca**s

damper (put a ~ on s.o.) aguar la **fiesta** (example)

to dance menear/mover el **esqueleto**

to dance attendance on s.o. bailar el **agua** a alg.

to dance like nobody's business ... que se las pela (▷ **pelar**)

to dance to s.o.'s tune llevar/seguir la **corriente** a alg.; bailar al compás de la **música** de alg.

to dance wildly and untiringly ... que se las pela (▷ **pelar**)

danger (be in great ~) estar en la **boca** del lobo; andar/verse en los **cuerno**s del toro; ver las **oreja**s del lobo

danger (be facing ~) abocar a

danger (have escaped from great ~) haber visto las **oreja**s del lobo

danger (scent/sense ~) oler el **poste**

danger (see ~ looming ahead) abocar a

dangerous (talking too much can be ~) por la **boca** muere el pez

dangerous assignment/job (take on a ~) poner el **cascabel** al gato

dangerous person (be a ~) ser un **pájaro** de cuenta

dark (be/grope in the ~) oír **campana**s y no saber dónde; dar **palo**s de ciego

dark (no-one will notice in the ~) de noche todos los **gato**s son pardos

darling el **pedazo** del alma/del corazón/de las entrañas; el pichón/la pichona; la prenda

darling ([little] ~) un pedazo de **gloria**

darn[ed] hot (it's ~) se asan las **mosca**s

to dash (my/etc. hopes are ~ed) [todo] mi/etc. o el **gozo** en el/un pozo

to dash along/through the street desempedrar la **calle**

date (be [bang] up to ~) estar en la **onda**

to date s.o. salir con alg.

daughter (like mother like ~) en casa del **gaitero** todos son danzantes; de casta le viene al **galgo** ser rabilargo; tal madre tal **hija**; en casa del **tamborilero** todos son danzantes

daughters (the ~ of Eve) las hijas de **Eva**

to dawdle away one's time estar tocando el **tambor**

dawn (at the crack of ~) al **canto** del gallo

dawn (get up at the crack of ~) levantarse con las **gallina**s

day (a ~ off work between two public holidays) un día **puente**

day (as naked as the ~ s.o. was born) como Dios lo/etc. trajo al **mundo** o tal como vino/etc. al mundo

day (as sure as the ~ is long/as night follows ~) como [que] **tres** y dos son cinco

day (at the end of the ~) al fin y al **cabo**

day (be as clear/plain as ~) ser más claro que el **sol**

day (be as different as night and ~) estar tan lejos como lo **blanco** de lo negro/no parecerse ni en el blanco de los ojos; parecerse como un **huevo** a una castaña

day (every other ~) un día **sí** y otro no

day (from one ~ to the next) de la **noche** a la mañana

day (happen every ~) ser el **pan** [nuestro] de cada día

day (have a bad ~) pisar alguna mala **hierba**

day (have an easy ~ of it) echar una **cana** al aire

day (have had one's ~) estar alg. para el **arrastre**

day (take an extra ~ or extra ~s off work between two public holidays) hacer **puente**

day (the whole ~ long) todo el **santo** día

day (the whole blessed/livelong ~ or all the livelong ~) todo el **santo** día

day in, day out un día **sí** y otro también

day of reckoning (everyone comes to his ~) a cada cerdo/puerco le llega su **San Martín**

daybreak (at ~) al **canto** del gallo

to be daydreaming estar en **Babia**/en las **Batuecas**/en **Belén**/en la **higuera**; estar en la **luna**; estar pensando en las **musarañas**; andar por o estar en las **nubes**

daylight (be as clear as ~) ser más claro que el **sol**

daylight (beat the living ~s out of s.o.) de padre y muy señor mío (▷ **el padre**) (example); señor

daylight (scare the living ~s out of s.o.) dar un **susto** de muerte a alg.

to be daylight robbery ser un **robo**

to be dead estar criando **malvas**

dead (be as ~ as a doornail/as mutton) estar más **muerto** que mi abuela/que una piedra; estar **patas** arriba

dead (be stone-~) estar más **muerto** que mi abuela/que una piedra; estar **patas** arriba

dead (cut s.o. ~) hacer **manga**s y capirotes de alg.

dead (drop ~) quedar **seco**; quedarse en el **sitio**

dead (play ~/pretend to be ~) hacerse el **muerto**

dead (sleep the sleep of the ~) dormir a **pierna** suelta

dead cert (be a ~) ser tan seguro como el **evangelio**

dead certain (be ~) ser tan seguro como el **evangelio**

dead easy (be ~) ser **pan** comido

to be dead on one's feet caerse de cansancio/sueño

dead loss el/la ablandabrevas/**berza**s

dead loss (be a ~) ser alg. una **calamidad**; ser [como o lo mismo que] la **carabina** de Ambrosio; ser un **cero** a la izquierda; no servir a **Dios** ni al diablo; ser un **piernas**; ser alg./algo **rana**

dead loss (turn out to be a ~) salir alg./algo **rana**

dead of night (in the or at ~) entre **gallo**s y medianoche

dead ringer (be a ~ for s.o.) ser **clavado** a alg./ser alg. clavado

to be dead tired estar **muerto** [de cansancio]

to be dead-beat (exhausted) estar hecho una braga (▷ **bragas**); estar/quedar hecho **cisco**; tener los **huesos** molidos; estar hecho **miga**s/**papilla**/**pedazo**s; estar hecho un **pingajo**; estar hecho **polvo**/**puré**; estar reventado (▷ **reventar**); estar hecho unos **zorros**

deadlock el **punto** muerto

deadlock (break the ~/reach ~) el **punto** muerto (examples)

to be deadly boring ser algo/alg. un **plomo**; a más no **poder**

dead[ly] serious serio como un **poste**

deaf (be as ~ as a post) ser más sordo que una **tapia**

deaf (be stone-~) ser más sordo que una **tapia**

deaf (there are none so ~ as those who will not listen) no hay peor **sordo** que el que no quiere oír

deaf ear (turn a ~ [to s.th.]) escuchar/oír como quien oye **llover**; hacer/prestar **oídos** sordos [a algo]

deaf ears (talk at ~) clamar en el desierto; dar **música** a un sordo; predicar en el desierto

deal (shady ~) la componenda

to deal (know who/what one is ~ing with) conocer a su **gente**; conocer el **paño**

to deal s.o. a beating/a kick or a slap in the face propinar algo a alg.

to deal with s.o. (have to ~) habérselas con alg. (▷ **haber**); vérselas con alg. (▷ **ver**)

dealer (drug ~) el **púcher**

dearly (pay ~ for s.th.) **salir**le algo a alg. caro

death (be at ~'s door) estar con la **candela** en la mano/con un pie en el **estribo**; estar en las últimas (▷ **último**)

death (be at s.o.'s side/comfort s.o. at the hour of ~) recoger el postrer **suspiro** de alg.

death (be bored to ~) aburrirse como una ostra/una almeja/un mono

death (be scared to ~) tener el **alma** en un hilo; caerse [muerto] de miedo; no llegarle a uno la **camisa** al cuerpo; estar con el alma en un **puño**; bajársele a alg. la **sangre** a los talones

death (be worried to ~) tener el **alma** en un hilo

death (bore s.o. to ~) quedarse con alg.

death (die a thousand ~s) pasar las de **Caín**

death (die a violent ~) morir a mano airada

death (not to die a natural ~) morir vestido

death (stone s.o. to ~) matar a alg. a **pedrada**s

death (work o.s. to ~) **reventar**se; echar los riñones (▷ **riñón**)

deathly silence (there's [a] ~) no se siente/oye [ni] una **mosca**

debt las **trampas**

debt (be up to one's ears/eyeballs in ~) las **trampas** (example)

debt (be up to one's neck in ~) estar con el **agua** al cuello

début/debut (make one's ~) vestir sus primeras **galas** de mujer

to deceive s.o. pegársela a alg. (▷ **pegar**); quedarse con alg.

decent de los **buenos**; de padre y muy señor mío (▷ **el padre**)

to decide (nothing has been ~d [yet]) la **pelota** está/sigue en el tejado

decision (stick to one's ~) tener **bigote**/tres pares de bigotes

decisions (make one's own ~) hacer de su **capa** un sayo

deck (be a few cards shy of a full ~) ser de pocas luces/corto de luces o tener pocas luces (▷ **luz**)

decked out (be all ~) estar de veinticinco **alfileres**; estar/ir de **punta** en blanco

deep end (go off at the ~) subirse al **campanario**/por las **pared**es

deep one (be a ~) tener alg. muchos **entresijos**; andarle/irle a alg. la **procesión** por dentro

deep water (get into ~) meterse en **honduras**

to deep-six s.o. **cargar**se/cascar/**cepillar**[se] a alg.; freír a alg.; dejar **frito** a alg.; mandar a alg. al otro **mundo**; pasaportear a alg.; quitar a alg. de en medio; dejar **tieso** a alg.; tumbar a alg.

defeat (suffer a humiliating ~) pasar por las horcas caudinas (▷ **caudino**)

to defend (fight tooth and nail to ~ s.th.) defender algo a **capa** y espada

to defend one's opinion [against s.o.] (stubbornly ~) tenerlas tiesas [con/a alg.] (▷ **tieso**)

to defend s.th. to the last ditch defender algo a **capa** y espada

defense (ignorance of the law is no ~) ignorancia no quita pecado

defense (put everything one has into the ~ of) defender algo a **capa** y espada

to defy s.o. plantar **cara** a alg.

degree (to an extremely high ~) hasta la **pared** de enfrente

to be dejected no levantar/alzar **cabeza**

delicate (very ~) de mírame y no me toques (▷ **mirar**)

delicious de **rechupete**

to be delicious estar algo **jamón**

delicious (taste ~) saber a **gloria**

delight (. . . that it is a ~) . . . que es un **primor**

delight (fiendish/malicious ~) el **gustazo**

to be delighted with s.th. caérsele a alg. la **baba** con/por algo

to be delightful ser un **primor**

delightful (look ~) estar algo diciendo cómeme (▷ **comer**)

to be demanding hilar delgado/muy fino

demon (be a ~ for s.th.) ser una **fiera** para/en algo

to demonstrate echarse a la **calle**

dense (be a bit ~) calzar poco; ser corto de **entendederas**/tener malas entendederas; ser cerrado de **mollera**

to deny (flatly ~ s.th.) a **palo** seco

to depend (basically it all ~s on [good] luck/on the circumstances) de **hombre** a hombre no va nada

to be depressed arrastrar el **ala**; no levantar/alzar **cabeza**

depression (dejection) la depre

depth (get out of one's ~) meterse en **hondura**s

derby (hat) el hongo

desert and reward seldom keep company de **ingratitud**es/**ingrato**s está el mundo lleno

deserts (everyone gets his just ~ sooner or later) a cada cerdo/puerco le llega su **San Martín**

to deserve it (punishment/etc.) calzárselos (▷ **calzar**)

desire (be ablaze/aflame with ~) abrasarse en deseo

to be despicable no tener **nombre**

to be destined [by fate] to + infinitive estar escrito (▷ **escribir**)

destitute (be utterly ~) comerse/roerse los **codo**s

to be destroyed by fire ser **pasto** de algo

detail ([tell s.th.] down to the last/in great/in minute ~) contar la **biblia** en verso; contar algo con puntos y **coma**s/del **hilo** al ovillo; con [todos sus] **pelo**s y señales

detail (tell s.th. without omitting a single ~) contar algo del **hilo** al ovillo

details (get bogged down in ~) andarse por las **ramas**

details (not to fuss about ~) no andarse con/en chiquitas (▷ la **chiquita**); no andarse con **requilorios**

to be detestable ser de mala **digestión**

to develop a thick skin criar **callos**

devil (be a cheeky ~) tener más **cara** que espalda; ser más fresco que una **lechuga**

devil (be a cunning old ~) ser [un] toro **corrido**/[una] liebre corrida; ser [un] **perro/zorro** viejo

devil (be a little ~) ser de la **piel** del diablo

devil (be [caught] between the ~ and the deep blue sea) estar entre la **espada** y la pared/entre dos **fuegos**

devil (better the ~ you know than the ~ you don't [know]) más vale **malo** conocido que bueno por conocer

devil (crafty ~) el vivo/la viva

devil (run/hurt like the ~) como el/un **diablo**

devil (sell one's soul to the ~) vender el **alma** al diablo

devil (speak/talk of the devil [and he's sure to appear]) hablando del **rey/ruin** de Roma [y él que se asoma o por la puerta asoma]

devil (the ~ as a moralizer) el **diablo** predicador

devil (what the ~ are you/etc. doing here or up to here?) ¿qué **demonios** estás/etc. haciendo aquí?; ¿qué diablo te pintas tú/etc. por aquí? (▷ **pintar**); ¿qué **puñetas** estás/etc. haciendo aquí?

the devil finds work for idle hands el **ocio**/la **ociosidad** es la madre de todos los vicios; los **vicios** son los hijos del ocio

the devil looks after his own mala **hierba** nunca muere

devil take the hindmost ¡el que venga detrás, que arree! (▷ **arrear**); el último **mono** es el que se ahoga

devil's workshop (an idle brain is the ~) el **ocio**/la **ociosidad** es la madre de todos los vicios; los **vicios** son los hijos del ocio

to devour s.th./s.o. with one's eyes írsele a alg. los **ojos** tras algo/alg.; comerse a alg. con los **ojos**/con la **vista**

to devour s.th. (book/etc.) echarse algo al **coleto**

dial (face) la jeta

diamond (be a rough ~ or a ~ in the rough) ser un **diamante** en bruto

diarrhea (have ~) estar/irse de **varetas**

diarrhea (runs; shits; trots; Montezuma's revenge) la cagalera; las seguidillas

dice (no ~!) ¡ni **hablar**!; ¡nada de eso!

dick el arma/asunto/bolo/calvo/canario/chorizo/cimbel; la gurrina; el pájaro; la picha/pija; el pijo; la pinga; el pito; la polla/porra; el rabo/troncho

Dick (every Tom, ~ and Harry) todo **bicho** viviente; Cristo y la madre/todo Cristo; todo/cada **quisque**

dickhead el/la gilipollas

die (the ~ is cast) la **suerte** está echada

to die irse al otro **barrio**; dar/soltar el **pellejo**; dar la **piel**

to die (be dying) estar con la **candela** en la mano

to die (be dying for s.th.) **perecer**se/rabiar por algo

to die (be dying of envy) **perecer**se de envidia

to die (be dying of hunger) estar **muerto** de hambre

to die (be dying of impatience) no caérsele a alg. el **pan**

to die (be dying of the heat) abrasarse de calor; **asar**se vivo

to die (be dying of thirst) abrasarse de sed; estar **muerto** de sed

to die (be dying to + infinitive) **perecer**se/rabiar/reventar por + infinitivo

to die (bite the dust; cash or hand in one's chips; croak; kick the bucket; peg out; pop off; pop one's clogs; snuff it) irse al otro **barrio**; liar los **bártulos**; acabársele a alg. la **candela**; cascar[la]; diñarla; quedarse **frío/frito**; pelar **gallo**; **guiñar**la; hincar el pico; **liar**las o liár**sel**as; palmarla; estirar la **pata**; liar el **petate**; **pringar**la; morder el **polvo**; **reventar**[se]; quedarse **tieso**

to die (eat, drink and be merry, for tomorrow we ~) dentro de cien **años** todos calvos; a beber y a tragar, que el **mundo** se va a acabar

to die (not to ~ a natural death/of natural causes) morir vestido

to die (s.o. is/feels so ashamed [of himself], he just wants to curl up and ~) caérsele a alg. la cara de **vergüenza**

to die (suddenly ~) quedar **seco**

to die a thousand deaths pasar las de **Caín**

to die a violent death morir a mano airada

to die in harness/with one's boots on morir con las **bota**s puestas/al **pie** del cañón

to die in the heat (nearly ~) abrasarse de calor

to die in the last ditch luchar hasta quemar el último **cartucho**

to die instantly quedarse en el **sitio**

to die laughing descoyuntarse/desternillarse de risa; ser para **morir**se de risa (example); **perecer**se de risa

to die like flies caer/morir como **chinches**

to die of boredom ([nearly] ~) pudrirse de aburrimiento

to die of shame (nearly ~) **morir**se de/estar **muerto** de vergüenza

to die on the spot quedarse en el **sitio**

to die peacefully quedarse [muerto] como un **pajarito**

different (be as ~ as chalk and cheese/as night and day) estar tan lejos como lo **blanco** de lo negro/no parecerse ni en el blanco de los ojos; parecerse como un **huevo** a una castaña

different (it's s.th. ~ every time) cuando **pitos** flautas, cuando flautas pitos

different (things would be very ~ if . . .) otro **gallo** cantaría o otro gallo me/etc. cantara si . . .

different matter (it would be quite a ~ if . . .) otro **gallo** cantaría o otro gallo me/etc. cantara si . . .

differently (look at s.th./s.o. ~) mirar algo/a alg. con otros **ojos**

difficult (be [very] ~) tener **bigote**/tres pares de bigotes

difficult (bring/pull off s.th. [very] ~) llevar[se] el **gato** al agua; poner una **pica** en Flandes

difficult (find s.th. [very] ~ [to + infinitive]) hacérsele algo a alg. [muy] **cuesta** arriba [+ infinitivo]

difficult (make things ~ for s.o.) poner **china**s a alg.

difficult job (be/face a [very] ~) necesitar **Dios** y [su] ayuda; tocarle a alg. una **papeleta** difícil; traérselas (▷ **traer**)

difficult part (the most ~ is yet/still to come) aún falta/queda la **cola**/el **rabo** por desollar

difficult problem traérselas (▷ **traer**)

difficult situation (be in a [very] ~) estar más perdido que **Carracuca**; estar entre la **espada** y la pared/entre dos **fuegos**

difficult task (face a very ~) necesitar **Dios** y [su] ayuda

difficult time (give s.o. a [very] ~) llevar/traer a alg. por la **calle** de la amargura

difficulty (have its difficulties) tener [su] **miga**

difficulty (the main ~ is yet/still to come) aún falta/queda la **cola**/el **rabo** por desollar

difficulty (with great/utmost ~) a duras **penas**

to dig in (eat) dar un buen **golpe** a la comida; hincar el diente

to dig one's own grave cavar su propia **tumba**

dignity ([not] to be beneath s.o.'s ~) [no] caérsele a alg. los **anillos**

to digress from the subject **salir**se del tema

digs (the trouble-free ~) el picadero

dike (lesbian) la bollera/torti/tortillera

dilemma (be in a ~) no saber a qué **carta** quedarse

dilemma (be on the horns of a ~) estar entre la **espada** y la pared/entre dos **fuegos**

diligently (pursue s.th. very ~) andar/bailar de **coronilla**

dim (be pretty ~) calzar poco; no tener dos **dedos** de frente; ser corto de **entendederas**/tener malas entendederas; ser de pocas luces/corto de luces o tener pocas luces (▷ **luz**); ser cerrado de **mollera**

dime (be a ~ a dozen) estar por los **suelos**

dime (in for a ~, in for a dollar) [una vez] puesto en el **burro**; preso por **mil**, preso por mil quinientos; de **perdidos**, al agua/río

to be dim-witted ser de pocas luces/corto de luces o tener pocas luces (▷ **luz**)

to dine (wine and ~ s.o.) tratar/atender a alg. a **cuerpo** de rey

diplomatically (act ~) nadar entre dos aguas

dipso el cuero; la espita/esponja

direction (make a [radical] change of ~) dar un **golpe** de timón

dirt (treat s.o. like ~) tratar a alg. a coces (▷ **coz**)/a **patada**s/como a un **perro**/a **zapatazo**s

to be dirt cheap estar por los **suelos**

dirty (do the ~ on s.o.) jugársela a alg. (▷ **jugar**)

dirty joke la verdulería

dirty jokes (tell ~) decir **verdulería**s

dirty linen (not to wash one's ~ in public) lavar los **trapo**s sucios en casa

dirty linen (wash one's ~ in public) lavar los **trapo**s sucios ante el mundo entero

dirty linen (you shouldn't wash your ~ in public) la **ropa** sucia se lava en casa; los **trapo**s sucios se lavan en casa

dirty old man el **viejo** verde

dirty trick (play a ~ on s.o.) hacer una **faena**/una mala **jugada** a alg.; jugar una mala **partida** a alg.; hacer una **perrada** a alg.; jugar una **pieza** a alg.; dar una **puñalada** trapera a alg.

dirty work (do s.o.'s ~ for him) sacar las **castañas** del fuego a alg.

to disagree with s.o. (food) sentarle algo a alg. como un **tiro**

to disappear hacerse **noche**

to disappear around the corner dar [el] **esquinazo**

to disappear for good caer en el **pozo** airón

to disappear from the face of the earth tragarse la **tierra** a alg.

to disappear into thin air hacerse **humo**

to disappear without trace desaparecer por [el] **escotillón**; hacerse **humo**

to disappoint s.o. dejar **fresco** a alg.; dejar a alg. a la **luna** de Valencia/con un **palmo** de narices

to be disappointed quedarse **fresco**/a la **luna** de Valencia

disappointment (turn out to be or be a big ~) salir/ser alg./algo **rana**

disaster (be heading for a ~) abocar a

disaster (be [struck by] one ~ after another) llover sobre mojado

disaster (court ~) atar perros con **longaniza**

disaster (end in ~) acabar como el **rosario** de la aurora

disaster (be a [complete] ~: person) como presidente/etc. es el acabóse (▷ **acabar**); ser alg. una **calamidad**

disastrous (not to be too ~) no llegar la **sangre** al río

discussion (be under/be up for ~) estar sobre el **tapete**

discussion (bring/put s.th. up for ~) poner algo sobre el **tapete**

discussion (not to be brought/put up for ~) quedar sobre el **tapete**

discussions (protracted and idle/pointless/ unresolvable ~) discusiones bizantinas (▷ **bizantino**)

disease (person who has foot-in-mouth ~) el/la metepatas

disgusting (incredibly ~) de **bigote**

disgusting (it's bloody ~!) ¡es la **puñeta**!

dish (be a ~) estar alg. **jamón**

dish (she's a real ~) está para comérsela (▷ **comer**)

disheartened (become ~) caérsele a alg. el **alma** a los pies

to be dishonest no ser algo/alg. **trigo** limpio

to be dishy estar alg. **jamón**

dislike la tirria

to dislike s.o. mirar mal a alg.

disorder (be in utter ~) cajón de sastre (example)

disposition (have a nasty/spiteful ~) tener mal **café**; tener mala **leche/pipa/uva**

to disregard s.o./s.th. dar de **lado** a alg.; echar algo en **saco** roto

to be disrespectful to s.o. subirse a las **barbas** de alg.

to dissipate s.th. **fumars**e algo

dissolute life (lead/live a ~) correr sin **freno**

distinguished de muchas **campanillas**

to distort things (truth/facts) hacer de lo **blanco** negro/volver en blanco lo negro

distrustful (be extremely ~) desconfiar hasta de su **sombra**

to disturb (11th commandment: don't ~) el **onceno**: [no estorbar]

disturbance (create a ~) echar a rodar los **bolos**

ditch (defend s.th. to the last ~) defender algo a **capa** y espada

ditch (die in the last ~) luchar hasta quemar el último **cartucho**

ditch (fight on to the last ~) luchar hasta quemar el último **cartucho**

to ditch s.o. largar a alg.; dar la **patada** a alg.; plantar o dejar plantado a alg.

to be divine ser un/de **alucine**; ser **canela** fina

divine (smell/taste ~) oler/saber a **gloria**

divine wine (be [a] ~) ser un **vino** de dos orejas

to divulge s.th. desembuchar algo

do (be a slap-up ~) haber **arroz** y gallo muerto

do (make ~ with a lick and a promise) lavarse a lo **gato**

to do (▷ done)

to do (a fine thing you've done!) lucirse (example)

to do (be at a [complete] loss as to what to ~ [next]) no saber como salir del **atranco**; la **sabiduría** no llega a más; estar como **tonto** en vísperas

to do (forget what one was about to ~) írsele a alg. el **santo** al cielo

to do (have nothing to ~ with s.th.) no tocar **pito** en algo; no tener nada que **ver** con algo

to do (have nothing whatsoever to ~ with a matter/with it) no tener **arte** ni parte en algo; no pegar ni con **cola**

to do (have to ~ with s.o.) habérselas con alg. (▷ **haber**)

to do (he/etc. knows/etc. what he/etc. can ~!) ¡que se/etc. joda/etc.! (▷ **joder**)

to do (I've nothing to ~ with it/this or with the/this matter) de mis **viñas** vengo

to do (know what one is ~ing) haber sido **cocinero** antes que fraile

to do (let s.o. ~ with one what s.o. likes) tener a alg. montado en las narices (▷ **nariz**)

to do (not to ~ a hand's turn) no dar **golpe**

to do (not to be at a loss as to what to ~) arreglárselas (▷ **arreglar**); componérselas (▷ **componer**)

to do (not to want to have anything more to ~ with s.th./s.o.) echar la **bendición** a algo/alg.

to do (not [to want] to have anything to ~ with it) ver los toros desde la **barrera**

to do (now you've [really] done it!) **hacer**la buena (example)

to do (show what one can ~) hacer [un] buen **papel**

to do (s.o. can ~ without s.th.) poder **pasar** sin algo

to do (that's the best I/we can ~) no hay más **cera** que la que arde

to do (without having [had] anything to ~ with it) sin **comer**lo ni beberlo

to do (you/etc. can't ~ that to us!) ¡no somos negros! (▷ **el negro**)

to do (you know what you can ~!) ¡vete a la **porra**!

to do anything agarrarse a un **clavo** ardiendo

to do anything to . . . vender el **alma** al diablo (example)

to do bird estar a la **sombra**/en la **trena**

to do bugger/damn/sod all tocarse los cojones (▷ **cojón**)/el **pito**; tocar la **vihuela**

to do enough (think one has done enough) echarse al o en el **surco**

to do everything wrong no dar **pie** con bola

to do [exactly] as one pleases campar por sus respetos; hacer de su **capa** un sayo; hacer su santa voluntad (▷ **santo**)

to do good to all alike hacer [el] **bien** sin mirar a quién

to do it (get s.o. else to ~!) ¡que lo haga el **nuncio**!

to do it (it's one thing to say s.th. and another to actually ~) del **dicho** al hecho hay mucho trecho; dicho sin hecho no trae provecho

to do it on s.o. jugársela a alg. (▷ **jugar**)

to do nothing echarse/tenderse/tumbarse a la **bartola**; estar/quedarse con los **brazos** cruzados; tocar la **vihuela**

to do nothing about s.th. dar **carpetazo** a algo

to do s.o. down pegársela a alg. (▷ **pegar**)

to do s.o. in mandar a alg. al otro **barrio**; **cargars**e/cascar/**cepillar**[se] a alg.; freír a alg.; dejar **frito** a alg.; mandar a alg. al otro **mundo**; pasaportear a alg.; quitar a alg. de en medio; dejar **tieso** a alg.; tumbar a alg.

to do s.th. for s.o.['s sake] hacer algo por **amor** de/a alg.

to do sweet f.a. tocarse los cojones (▷ **cojón**)/el **pito**; tocar la **vihuela**

to do the dirty on s.o. jugársela a alg. (▷ **jugar**)

to do things by halves/in half measures aplicar **paños** calientes

to do things by halves/in half measures (not to ~) no andarse con **paños** calientes

to do time estar a la **sombra**/en la **trena**
to do useless things cazar **moscas**
to do [very] well pescar una buena **breva**
to do what one likes with one's own things hacer de su **capa** un sayo
to do without quitarse algo de la **boca**
doctor (be just what the ~ ordered) venir como **agua** de mayo/como **anillo** al dedo; venir como llovido/llegar como caído del **cielo**; venir como **pedrada** en ojo de boticario; venirle a alg. al **pelo**; venir que ni **pintado**/como pintado; venir [que ni] **pintiparado**
dodderer (old ~) el vejestorio
doddle (be a ~) ser una **breva**; ser **coser** y cantar; ser **pan** comido
doddle (it won't be a ~) no va a ser un **paseo**
to dodge escurrir/escapar/huir el **bulto**
to dodge s.th./s.o. **hurtar**le el cuerpo a algo; dar el **quiebro** a alg.
to dodge the issue salir[se]/escapar[se]/irse por la **tangente**
dog (a barking ~ never bites) perro ladrador, nunca buen mordedor/poco mordedor o perro que ladra no muerde
dog (be like a ~ with two tails) alegrarse/estar como [un] **niño** con zapatos nuevos
dog (have/try a hair of the ~ [that bit you]) la resaca (example)
dog (it's better to be the head of a ~ than the tail of a lion) más vale ser **cabeza** de ratón que cola de león
dog (let sleeping ~s lie) peor es meneallo/mejor es no meneallo/más vale no meneallo (▷ **menear**)
dog (old sea ~) un viejo **lobo** de mar
dog (put on the ~) darse **pisto/tono**
dog (sausage ~) el **perro** salchicha
dog (sly ~) el lagarto
dog (the ~'s life) de **perros**
dog (throw s.o. to the ~s) arrojar a alg. a los **lobos**
dog (top ~) el mandamás
dog end la pava
dog in the manger (be a ~) ser [como] el **perro** del hortelano[, que ni come la berza ni la deja comer]
to dog s.o.'s heels pisar los talones a alg. (▷ **talón**)
to be dogged by bad luck pasarlas negras (▷ **negro**)
doggedly erre que erre
dogma (make s.th. into a ~) hacer **evangelio** de algo
dogsbody (be a/the [general] ~) servir lo mismo para un **barrido** que para un fregado
to be dog-tired estar hecho una braga (▷ **bragas**); caerse de cansancio/sueño; estar/quedar hecho **cisco**; tener los

huesos molidos; estar hecho **migas/papilla/pedazos**; estar hecho un **pingajo**; estar hecho **polvo/puré**; estar reventado (▷ **reventar**); estar hecho unos **zorros**
doll (girl) la jai
to doll [o.s.] up ponerse de veinticinco **alfileres**; emperejilar[se]/emperifollar[se]; ponerse de **punta** en blanco
to doll up (be all ~ed up) estar de veinticinco **alfileres**; estar/ir de **punta** en blanco
to doll up (get [all] ~ed up) ponerse de veinticinco **alfileres**; emperejilar[se]/emperifollar[se]; ponerse de **punta** en blanco
dollar (in for a dime, in for a ~) [una vez] puesto en el **burro**; preso por **mil**, preso por mil quinientos; de **perdidos**, al agua/río
dollar (you can bet your bottom ~ on that) apostaría la **cabeza**; son **habas** contadas
dollar (you can bet your bottom ~ [that] ...) apostar[se] la **cabeza**/el **cuello** a que ...
dollars to doughnuts (it's ~ [that] ...) apostar[se] la **cabeza**/el **cuello** a que ...
dolt un [pedazo de] **alcornoque/atún**; un[a] **cabeza** de corcho; una calabaza; un alma de **cántaro**; un ceporro/melón/merluzo; un **palomino** atontado; un percebe
to dominate s.o.'s [way of] thinking completely sorber los **sesos** a alg.
domination (be under s.o.'s ~) estar bajo la **férula** de alg.
done (be [as good as] ~) no faltar un **cabello** a algo
done (what's ~ can't be undone) lo **hecho**, hecho está/a lo hecho, pecho
done (what's ~ is ~) lo **hecho**, hecho está/a lo hecho, pecho
done (when all is said and ~) al fin y al **cabo**
to be done in/up (exhausted) estar hecho una braga (▷ **bragas**); estar/quedar hecho **cisco**; tener los **huesos** molidos; estar hecho **migas/papilla/pedazos**; estar hecho un **pingajo**; estar hecho **polvo/puré**; estar reventado (▷ **reventar**); estar hecho unos **zorros**
dong el arma/asunto/bolo/calvo/canario/chorizo/cimbel; la gurrina; el pájaro; la picha/pija; el pijo; la pinga; el pito; la polla/porra; el rabo/troncho
donkey (talk the hind legs off a ~) hablar como una **chicharra**; hablar más que una **cotorra**/un **sacamuelas**
donkey's years ago/old año de/tiempo[s] de/días de **Maricastaña**; del año de/en el año de la **nana**; en [los] tiempos de **ñangué**; del año de o en el año de la **pera/polca**; en tiempos del **rey** que rabió/del rey Wamba
to be doomed to fail/failure abocar a

door (be at death's ~) estar con la **candela** en la mano/con un pie en el **estribo**; estar en las últimas (▷ **último**)

door (be next ~ to s.th.) rozar [con] algo

door (live next ~) vivir **pared/tabique** por medio

door (lock the barn ~ after the horse is stolen) asno muerto, la cebada al rabo; a buenas **hora**s, mangas verdes

door (lock/shut the stable ~ after the horse has bolted/gone) asno muerto, la cebada al rabo; a buenas **hora**s, mangas verdes

door (show s.o. the [way to the] ~) enseñar/ mostrar la **puerta** a alg.

door (slam/shut the ~ in s.o.'s face) dar a alg. con la **puerta** en la cara/en los hocicos/en las narices

doorbell (lean on the ~) echar las **puerta**s abajo

doornail (be as dead as a ~) estar más **muerto** que mi abuela/que una piedra; estar **pata**s arriba

dope (stupid person) un [pedazo de] **alcornoque/atún**; un[a] **cabeza** de corcho; una calabaza; un alma de **cántaro**; un ceporro/melón/merluzo; un **palomino** atontado; un percebe

dopehead el/la grifota

dosh el barro; el **calé** o calés; la china; [los] **cuartos**; la guita/lana/manteca; [los] monises; la mosca; [los] nipos; el parné; la pasta; el pisto; la tela; el trigo

dot (at 6 on the ~/on the ~ of 6) a las seis clavadas (▷ **clavado**)

dot ([in/from] the year ~) año de/tiempo[s] de/ días de **Maricastaña**; del año de/en el año de la **nana**; en [los] tiempos de **ñangué**; del año de o en el año de la **pera/polca**; en tiempos del **rey** que rabió/del rey Wamba

to dote on a child caérsele a alg. la **baba** con/por alg.

dotted with cuajado de

to double-cross s.o. pegársela a alg. (▷ **pegar**)

to be double Dutch to s.o. ser **chino** algo para alg.

double game (play a ~) jugar con/a dos **baraja**s; jugar/hacer un doble **juego**

double-edged sword (be a ~) ser un arma de dos **filos**

doubt (cast ~ on s.th.) poner algo en **tela** de juicio

doubt (there's no ~ about it) son **habas** contadas; eso o la cosa no tiene vuelta de **hoja**; no hay que darle **vuelta**s

doubt (without a shadow of [a] ~) sin **sombra** de duda

dough (money) el barro; el **calé** o calés; la china; [los] **cuartos**; la guita/lana/ manteca; [los] monises; la mosca; [los] nipos; el parné; la pasta; el pisto; la tela; el trigo

down (be feeling ~) tener la/estar con la **depre**

down (do s.o. ~) pegársela a alg. (▷ **pegar**)

down (go ~ very badly) caer/sentar como una **pedrada**

down (have a ~ on s.o.) tenerla tomado con alg. (▷ **tomar**)

down (let s.o. ~) dejar **colgado** a alg.

down (run s.o. ~) traer en **boca**s a alg.; arrastrar a alg. por el **fango**; poner a alg. como un **guiñapo**/como **hoja** de perejil; poner **mal** a alg.; arrastrar/poner a alg. por los **suelo**s

down (run s.th. ~) arrastrar algo por el **fango**; arrastrar/poner algo por los **suelo**s

down (the first ~ is already appearing on s.o.'s upper lip) ya le sombrea el labio superior a alg. (▷ **sombrear**)

down the hatch! ¡hasta verte, **Cristo/Jesús** mío!

down to the last cent/penny un **real** sobre otro

to down s.th. echarse algo al **coleto**/entre **pecho** y espalda; **soplar**se algo

to down the stuff (s.o. can really ~) tener buen **saque**

downright solemne; de siete **suela**s

dowry (marry a woman without a ~) casarse con una mujer en **camisa**

dozen (baker's ~/long ~) la **docena** del fraile

dozen (it's six of one and half a ~ of the other) lo que no va en **lágrima**s, va en suspiros; lo mismo es ñangá que **ñangué**; olivo y aceituno, todo es uno; tamboril por gaita

drag (be a ~) ser algo/alg. una **castaña**/un **plomo**

drag (influence) el enchufe

to drag (wild horses couldn't ~ me/us away from here) ni a tirones me/nos sacan de aquí (▷ **tirón**)

to drag everything/it out of s.o. tirar de la **cuerda/ lengua** a alg.

to drag s.o. along llevar a **remolque** a alg.

to drag s.o.'s name through the mud/mire arrastrar a alg. por el **fango**

to drag s.th. out of s.o. sacar algo a alg. con pinzas/sacacorchos/tirabuzón

to be drained (exhausted) estar hecho una braga (▷ **bragas**); estar/quedar hecho **cisco**; tener los **hueso**s molidos; estar hecho **miga**s/**papilla/pedazos**; estar hecho un **pingajo**; estar hecho **polvo/puré**; estar reventado (▷ **reventar**); estar hecho unos **zorros**

drakes (play ducks and ~ with s.th.) tirar algo por la ventana

drastic action (take ~ [against s.o.]) sin pararse en **barras** (example); echar los **perros** a alg.; cortar por lo **sano**

drastic measures (take ~) sin pararse en **barras** (example)

draw (end in a ~) salir/quedar **pata**[s]

to draw even salir/quedar **pata**[s]

to draw s.o. out tirar de la **lengua** a alg.

dreadfully escandalosamente (▷ **escandaloso**)

dream . . . de **película**

dream (go like a ~) a las mil **maravilla**s; ir/ marchar como una **seda**

dream world (be living in a ~) tener la **cabeza** llena de pájaros; vivir en la **luna**; andar por o vivir en las **nube**s

to dream about s.th./s.o. soñar con algo/alg.

to dream of + gerund soñar con + infinitivo

to be drenched estar calado/mojado hasta los **hueso**s; estar hecho un **pato**; estar mojado hasta los **tuétano**s

drenched (get ~) mojarse hasta el **alma**/los **hueso**s

to dress for comfort (I ~, not for other people) ande yo **caliente** y ríase la gente

to dress s.o. down dar un **jabón**/una **jabonadura** a alg.; jabonar a alg.

dressed (be immaculately ~) estar hecho un **brazo** de mar

to be dressed in the latest fashion/style ir vestido a la última (▷ **último**)

to be dressed to kill estar de veinticinco **alfilere**s; estar hecho un **brazo** de mar; estar/ir de **punta** en blanco

to be dressed up to the nines estar de veinticinco **alfilere**s; estar hecho un **brazo** de mar; estar **peripuesto**; estar/ir de **punta** en blanco

dressed up to the nines (get ~) ponerse de veinticinco **alfilere**s/de **punta** en blanco

dressing-down (give s.o. a ~) soltar la/una **andanada** a alg.; zurrar la **badana**/dar una **calada** a alg.; poner a alg. a **caldo**; dar un **fregado**/un **jabón**/una **jabonadura** a alg.; jabonar a alg.; cardarle la **lana** a alg.; dar un **meneo** a alg.; echar una **peluca** a alg.; hacer **picadillo** a alg.; echar un **rapapolvo** a alg.; echar/soltar el **toro** a alg.; poner a alg. como un **trapo**; poner **verde** a alg.; poner a alg. de **vuelta** y media

drink (celebrate with a ~) mojar; remojar

drink (have a ~/a few ~s) alzar/empinar el **codo**; mojarse el **garguero**; mojar/refrescar el **gaznate**; atarse/pegarse un **latigazo**; atizarse un **trago**

drink (have another ~) atizar la **lámpara**

drink (nasty ~) el jarope

drink (this calls for a ~!) ¡esto hay que **mojar**lo/ **remojar**lo!

to drink darle a la **botella**

to drink (eat, ~ and be merry, for tomorrow we die) dentro de cien **año**s todos calvos; a beber y a tragar, que el **mundo** se va a acabar

to drink (give up ~ing) **quitar**se del alcohol

to drink (have s.th. to ~) echarse algo al **cuerpo**

to drink an awful lot como un **descosido** (example); a **pote** (example)

to drink gallons of s.th. ponerse **morado** de algo

to drink like a fish como un **descosido** (example); beber como una **esponja**; más que **siete**

to drink on credit/tick beber sobre **tarja**

to drink o.s. silly de padre y muy señor mío (▷ **el padre**) (example); coger una **papalina**

to drink s.o. under the table beber hasta **tumbar** a alg.; dar cien **vuelta**s a alg. (example)

to drink s.th. down echarse algo al **coleto**/entre **pecho** y espalda

to drink straight from the bottle/spring/etc. beber a **morro**

to drink to excess a todo **pasto**

to drink to the health of s.o. beber a la **salud** de alg.

to drink without having anything to eat a **palo** seco

drinker (be a heavy ~) beber como una **esponja**; a **pote** (example)

drinker's nose la nariz de **zanahoria**

drinking expedition (go on a ~) andar/ir de **chateo**

dripping (constant ~ wears away a stone) gota a gota se llena la bota

to be dripping wet estar calado/mojado hasta los **hueso**s; estar hecho un **pato**/una **sopa**; estar mojado hasta los **tuétano**s

dripping wet (get ~) mojarse hasta el **alma**/los **hueso**s

to be dripping with sweat sudar a **chorro**s/**mare**s

to drive at (what are you/etc. driving at?) ¿adónde quieres/etc. ir a **parar**?

to drive flat out conducir a toda **castaña**; quemar el **caucho**; a toda **pastilla** (example); hundir el **pedal**; correr/lanzarse a **tumba** abierta; a todo **vapor** (example); a toda **vela**

to drivel meter **ripio**

to drool over s.o./s.th. caérsele a alg. la **baba** con/por algo/algo; chuparse los **dedo**s [por algo]; pelárselas por algo (▷ **pelar**)

drop (be [just] a ~ in the ocean) ser una **gota** de agua en el mar

drop ([down] to the last ~) hasta los **poso**s

drop of brandy/liquor una **lágrima** de aguardiente

to drop (be ready to ~) caerse de cansancio/ sueño

to drop dead quedar **seco**; quedarse en el **sitio**

to drop like flies caer/morir como **chinche**s

to drop s.o. largar a alg.; dar la **patada** a alg.

to drop the price bajar la **mano**

drug addict el/la yonqui

drugs (be on ~) estar de **viaje**

drum (beat the ~ for s.th.) dar **bombo** a algo

to drum s.th. into s.o.['s head] machacar algo a alg.

to be **drunk to the gills** estar hecho un **cesto**/una **cuba**/un **cuero**/un **pellejo**/una **uva**

drunk (be [as] ~ as a lord/skunk) estar hecho un **cesto**/una **cuba**/un **cuero**/un **pellejo**/una **uva**

drunk (be [blind] ~) estar hecho un **cesto**; estar cocido (▷ **cocer**); estar hecho una **cuba**/un **cuero**; tener la **lengua** gorda; estar hecho un **pellejo**/una **sopa**/una **uva**

drunk (get ~) cogerse una **castaña**; **cocer**se; papar una **jumera**; coger una **melopea**/**merluza**; coger/pillar una **mona**; moñarse; coger una **pea**; agarrar[se] un **pedo**; coger una **pítima**; pillar una **zorra**

drunk (get roaring ~) coger una **papalina**

drunkard el **cuero**; la **espita/esponja**

drunkenness la **jumera/melopea/mona/pea**; el **pedo**; la **pítima/trompa/zorra**

drunkenness (roaring ~) la **papalina**

dry stitch (not to have a ~ on one) estar calado/mojado hasta los **huesos**; estar hecho un **pato**; estar mojado hasta los **tuétanos**

to dry up (in speech/etc.) írsele a alg. el **santo** al cielo

to be dubious no ser algo **trigo** limpio

dubious business (be involved in some ~) andar con **tapujos**

duck (be like a dying ~ [in a thunderstorm]) quedarse de una **pieza**

duck (be [like] or run off s.o. like water off a ~'s back) escuchar/oír como quien oye **llover** (example)

duck (take to s.th. like a ~ to water) encontrarse en seguida en su **elemento**

to duck out [of it] escurrir/escapar/huir el **bulto**

ducks and drakes (play ~ with s.th.) tirar algo por la ventana

dud (be a ~) ser una **patata**

duly con todas las de la **ley**

dumb gil/gilí

dumb (act ~) hacerse el **sueco**

dumb (be as ~ as they come) a más no **poder**; ser **tonto** del bote/de capirote

dumb (be struck ~) quedarse de una **pieza**

dumb (strike s.o. ~) dejar a alg. de una **pieza**

to dumbfound s.o. dejar **clavado** a alg.

to be dumbfounded quedarse **bizco**; quedarse de una **pieza**

dumbo un [pedazo de] **alcornoque/atún**; un[a] **cabeza** de corcho; una calabaza; un alma de **cántaro**; un ceporro/melón/merluzo; un **palomino** atontado; un percebe

dummy (fool) el/la **berzas/gilipollas**; el pasmarote

dump (of a town) de mala **muerte** (example)

dump (take a ~) plantar un **pino**

to dump s.o. largar a alg.; dar la **patada** a alg.

dumps (be down in the ~) arrastrar el **ala**; no levantar/alzar **cabeza**; tener la/estar con la **depre**

dupe el primo

durable de **cal** y canto

duro (5-peseta coin) un pavo

dust (bite the ~: to die) hincar el pico; morder el **polvo**

dust (have bitten the ~) estar comiendo **tierra**

dust (kick up/raise a ~) levantar una **polvareda**

dust (let the ~ settle on s.th.) echar **tierra** sobre/a algo

dust (throw ~ in s.o.'s eyes) meter a alg. los **dedo**s por los ojos; echar **tierra** a los ojos de alg.

dust collector/trap el **nido** de polvo

Dutch (be double ~ to s.o.) ser **chino** algo para alg.

Dutch (this beats the ~!) ¡[esto] es el acabóse! (▷ **acabar**)

dwarf el gorgojo

to dwell on s.th. hacer **hincapié** en algo

dyed-in-the-wool por los cuatro **costados**

dying embers (stir up the ~) avivar el **rescoldo**

dyke (lesbian) la **bollera/torti/tortillera**

E

each (to ~ his own) cada **loco** con su tema; a cada uno/cual, lo **suyo**

each and everyone of them todo **bicho** viviente; Cristo y la madre/todo Cristo; todo/cada **quisque**

each other (be/get at ~) tirarse de los **moños**; andar al **pelo**

each to his own cada uno/cual a lo **suyo**

ear (▷ **ears**)

ear (bend s.o.'s ~) dar la **lata** a alg.

ear (give s.o. a thick ~) ponerle a alg. la cara nueva (▷ **nuevo**); pegar una **torta** a alg.

ear (give/lend an ~ to s.o./s.th.) prestar/dar **oído**s a alg./algo; prestar atención a alg./algo

ear (go in one ~ and [come] out [of] the other) entrarle a alg. por un **oído** y salirle por el otro

ear (offend/hurt the/one's ~[s]) herir el oído

ear (turn a deaf ~ [to s.th.]) escuchar/oír como quien oye **llover**; hacer/prestar **oído**s sordos [a algo]

the early bird catches the worm a quien madruga, Dios le ayuda (▷ **madrugar**)

to earn (hardly ~ enough to eat) el puchero (example)

to earn a living/one's bread and butter/one's daily bread/one's crust ganarse los **fríjol**es/los **garbanzo**s/el **pan**/el **puchero**/la **vida**

to earn a pittance cobrar/ganar una **miseria**

to earn s.th. ganar[se] algo a **pulso**

ear-piercing/ear-splitting noise (be an ~) ser un ruido que taladra los oídos (▷ **taladrar**)

ears (be a treat for the ~) ser un regalo para los **oído**s

ears (be all ~) ser todo **oído**s

ears (be still wet behind the ~) llevar todavía el **cascarón** pegado al culo; estar aún con la **leche** en los labios; caerse de un **nido**

ears (be up to one's ~ in s.th.) andar/ir de **cabeza** con algo; estar metido hasta las **cacha**s en algo

ears (box/clip round the ~) la chuleta

ears (box s.o.'s ~) **ventilar**le a alg. las orejas

ears (give s.o. a few hefty boxes/clips round the ~) ponerle a alg. la cara nueva (▷ **nuevo**)

ears (not to believe one's ~) no poder dar crédito a sus **oído**s

ears (prick up one's ~) aguzar el **oído**/las **oreja**s

ears (talk at deaf ~) clamar en el desierto; dar **música** a un sordo; predicar en el desierto

ears (walls have ~) las **pared**es oyen

ears (walls have ~: be careful what you say, walls have ~!) ¡hay **ropa** tendida!

earth (bring s.o. down to ~ with a bump) echar un **jarro** de agua fría a alg.

earth (come down/back to ~ with a bump) caer del **nido**

earth (cost the ~) costar un **sentido** o los cinco sentidos

earth (disappear from/vanish off the face of the ~) tragarse la **tierra** a alg.

earth (it was as if the ~ had swallowed them up) tragarse la **tierra** a alg. (example)

earth (promise s.o. the ~) prometerle a alg. montañas de **oro** o el oro y el moro

earth (s.o. is/feels so ashamed [of himself], he just wants the ~ to open and swallow him up) caérsele a alg. la cara de **vergüenza**

earth (what on ~'s that?) ¿con qué se come eso? (▷ **comer**)

to ease up aflojar la **cuerda**

easy (be as ~ as falling off a log) ser **coser** y cantar; ser **pan** comido

easy (be as ~ as pie) ser una **breva**; ser **coser** y cantar; ser **pan** comido

easy (be dead ~) ser **pan** comido

easy (go ~ on the sugar) no estirar los **pie**s más de lo que da la frazada

easy (it's not going to be ~) no va a ser un **paseo**

easy (make it as ~ as possible for s.o.) tender **puente**s de plata a alg.

easy (make it/things ~ for s.o.) hacer el **caldo** gordo a alg.

easy (not to be ~) tener [su] **miga**

easy (not to go ~ on the sugar) estirar la **pierna** más larga que la sábana

easy (nothing's ~ to start off with) el primer **paso** es el que cuesta

easy (take it ~) echarse/tenderse/tumbarse a la **bartola**; darse un **verde**

easy come, easy go los **dinero**s del sacristán cantando se vienen y cantando se van; lo ganado por lo gastado (▷ **ganar**)

easy conquest/pick-up el levante

easy day (have an ~ of it) echar una **cana** al aire

easy lay la ligona

easy lay (she's an ~) está loca por la música (▷ **loco**)

easy life (live/have an ~) vivir como un **canónigo**; pegarse la **vida** padre

easy time (have an ~ of it) echarse/tenderse/tumbarse a la **bartola**

easy time (not to have an ~ of it) irle a alg. como a los **perro**s en misa

easy to find (be very ~) no tener **pérdida**

to eat (drink without having anything to ~) a **palo**
seco

to eat (hardly earn enough to ~) el puchero
(example)

to eat (have s.th. to ~) echarse algo al **cuerpo**

to eat (I'll ~ my hat if . . .) soy **Napoleón** si ...

to eat (take more than one can ~) comer con los
ojos

to eat (what's ~ing you/etc.?) ¿qué **mosca** te/etc.
ha picado?

to eat crow pedir **alafia**; doblar el **espinazo**

eat, drink and be merry, for tomorrow we die
dentro de cien **años** todos calvos; a beber
y a tragar, que el **mundo** se va a acabar

to eat greedily comer/mascar a dos **carrillos**;
ponerse como el chico del **esquilador**;
comer como una **lima**

to eat heartily tener buen **saque**

to eat humble pie pedir **alafia**; doblar el **espinazo**

to eat like a bird comer como un **gorrión/
pajarito**

to eat like a horse comer más que un **alguacil**;
llenarse la **andorga**; henchir el **baúl**;
comer/mascar a dos **carrillos**; ponerse
como el chico del **esquilador**; comer como
una **lima**/un **sabañón**

to eat one's fill sacar la **tripa**/el **vientre** de mal
año

to eat s.th. right up echarse algo al **coleto**/al
estómago/entre **pecho** y espalda

to eat to bursting point ponerse como un **trompo**

to eat to excess como un **descosido** (example); a
más no **poder**

to eat until one is [as] full/tight as a tick a todo
pasto; a más no **poder**

to eat until one is fit to burst a todo **pasto**; a más
no **poder**

to eat well sacar la **tripa**/el **vientre** de mal año

to be eaten up with envy comer a alg. la envidia;
morirse/perecerse de envidia

eater (be a big ~) ser una buena **tijera**; tener
buenas **tragaderas**

eating (the proof of the pudding is in the ~) al
freír será el reír; al **probar** se ve el mosto

eating is like scratching: once you start, you don't
want to stop or you can't stop el **comer** es
como el rascar, todo es cuestión de
empezar

edge (be all on ~) a **flor** de piel

edge (be on a razor's ~) estar en el **filo** de la
navaja

edge (have one's nerves on ~) tener los **nervios** de
punta

edge (put s.o.'s nerves on ~) alterar/crispar los
nervios a alg. o poner los nervios de
punta a alg.

edge (s.o.'s nerves are all on ~) a **flor** de piel

edge (take the ~ off s.th.) quitar **hierro** a algo

edgeways/edgewise (not to let anybody get a word
in ~) acaparar la palabra; no dejar meter
baza a nadie

edgeways/edgewise (not to let s.o. get a word in ~)
no dejar meter **baza** a alg.

to be educated tener **letras**

to eff and blind echar **ajos** [y cebollas]; darse a
todos los **demonios**; echar **sapos** y
culebras

effect (have heard s.th./noises to that ~) oír
campanas y no saber dónde

effort (be a wasted ~) azotar el **aire**; machacar
en hierro frío; arar en el **mar**

effort (make an all-out/a supreme/a tremendous ~)
batir[se] el **cobre**; echar el **resto**; navegar
a todo **trapo**

effort (take s.o. a great ~ to do s.th.) tener que
verse y desearse para hacer algo

effort (take s.o. a supreme ~ [to + infinitive])
costar **Dios** y ayuda a alg. [+ infinitivo]

egg (go fry an ~!) ¡anda a **bañarte**!; ívete a freír
buñuelos/espárragos!

egg (tell s.o. to go fry an ~) mandar a alg. a freír
buñuelos/al **cuerno**/a freír **espárragos**/a
hacer **gárgaras**

eggs (as sure as ~ is/are ~) como [que] **tres** y dos
son cinco

eggs (kill the goose that lays golden ~) matar la
gallina de los huevos de oro

eggs (put all one's ~ in one basket) poner toda la
carne en el asador; jugárselo todo a una
[sola] **carta**

eggs (try to teach one's grandmother to suck ~)
querer enseñar el **padrenuestro** al cura

eggs (you can't make an omelet without breaking
~) no se puede hacer **tortillas** sin romper
huevos

eight (have had one over the ~) estar hecho un
cesto/una **cuba**/un **cuero**/un **pellejo**/una
uva

Einstein (not to be exactly an ~) ser más tonto
que **Abundio**; si le/etc. menean, da
bellotas; ser más tonto que **Carracuca**; ser
más **cerrado** que un cerrojo; ser más
corto que las mangas de un chaleco; ser
más tonto que una **mata** de habas; no
saber ni siquiera quitarse los **mocos**; ser
más bruto que la **pila** de un pozo; no
haber inventado la **pólvora**; tener el juicio
en los talones (▷ **talón**)

either we all carry the can or none of us does o nos
pringamos todos, o ninguno (▷ **pringar**)

either we all do it/we all go/etc. or nobody does o
jugamos todos o se rompe la **baraja**

elbow (bend/lift one's ~) alzar/empinar el **codo**

elbow (s.o. can't tell his arse/ass from his ~)
tomar/confundir el **culo** por las témporas

elegance el postín

elegant pichi; el postín (example); señor

elegant man/woman (act/play the ~) meterse a **finolis**

element (be in one's ~) estar como **abeja** en flor; estar en su **elemento**/en su[s] **gloria**[s]; estar/sentirse como el **pez** en el agua; estar en su [propia] **salsa**

eleventh commandment: don't disturb el **onceno**: [no estorbar]

eleventh finger el **dedo** veintiuno

eloquent (be very ~) tener un **pico** de oro

else (and who knows what ~) y qué sé yo (▷ **saber**)

else (get s.o. ~ to do it!) ¡que lo haga el **nuncio**!

else (go somewhere ~) irse con la **música** a otra parte

else (like everyone ~) como cada/cualquier **hijo** de vecino; como todo/cada **quisque**

else (tell that to s.o. ~!) ¡díselo o cuéntaselo al **nuncio**!

elsewhere (sell it ~!) irse con la **música** a otra parte (example)

elsewhere (take your troubles ~!) irse con la **música** a otra parte (example)

embarrassed con las **orejas** gachas

embers (stir up the dying ~) avivar el **rescoldo**

to embezzle s.th. **pringar**se algo

to embolden s.o. dar **alas** a alg.

to emigrate echarse la **maleta** al hombro

emphasis (lay/put much ~ on one's being blue-blooded) escupir **sangre**

emphasis (lay/put [special/particular] ~ on s.th.) hacer **hincapié** en algo

to emphasize s.th. hacer **hincapié** en algo

empty (a bottle/glass is almost ~) una botella/un vaso está temblando (▷ **temblar**)

to empty (almost ~ a bottle/glass) dejar una botella/un vaso temblando (▷ **temblar**)

empty boasting (be just or nothing but ~) cacarear y no poner huevos

empty promises jarabe de pico; música celestial

empty-handed (be left/come away ~) quedarse **asperges**; chuparse el **dedo**; quedarse a la **luna** de Valencia/con un **palmo** de narices

empty-handed (leave s.o. ~) dejar a alg. a la **luna** de Valencia

to enchant s.o. dar el **opio** a alg.

to encourage s.o. dar **alas** a alg.

to encourage s.o. to talk dar **cuerda/soga** a alg.

encyclopedia (be a walking ~) saber más que **Lepe**

end ([and] that's the ~ of it!) sanseacabó

end (at the ~ of the day) al fin y al **cabo**

end (be at the ~ of one's rope/tether) no saber como salir del **atranco**; no saber a qué **santo** encomendarse

end (be no ~ of a fool) la **mar** de; ser **tonto** del bote/de capirote

end (cigarette/dog/fag ~) la pava

end (come to a bad ~) acabar como el **rosario** de la aurora

end (from beginning to ~) de **cabo** a cabo/rabo o de punta a cabo; desde la **cruz** hasta la fecha; de **pe** a pa

end (get hold of the wrong ~ of the stick) oír **campana**s y no saber dónde; tomar el **rábano** por las hojas

end (get the dirty/short ~ of the stick) tocarle a alg. bailar con la más fea (▷ **feo**)

end (go off at the deep ~) subirse al **campanario**/por las **pared**es

end (in the ~) al fin y al **cabo**

end (it's not the ~ of the world) más se perdió en **Cuba**

end (just not to come to an ~) ser una **gotera**

end (keep one's ~ up) **defender**se bien

end (make s.o.'s hair stand on ~/s.o.'s hair stands on ~) ponerle o ponérsele a alg. los **pelos** de punta

end (no ~ of) a **punta** pala; rematado

end (not to know one ~ of s.th. from the other) no tener ni la más remota/pálida **idea** de algo; no saber ni **jota** de algo

end (put an ~ to s.th.) dar la **puntilla** a algo

end (show up at the ~) llegar a los amenes (▷ **amén**)

end (that's the ~ of that!) ¡se acabó! (▷ **acabar**)

end (there's an ~ to everything) no hay **bien** ni mal que cien años dure

end (think no ~ of o.s.) tener muchos **tufos**

end (tie up loose ~s) atar/unir **cabo**s

end (your lies will always catch up with you in the ~) antes se coge al **embustero** que al cojo

to end (be never ~ing) ser un **pozo** sin fondo

to end (we don't know where all this is going to ~) no sabemos en qué va a **parar** todo esto

to end (where's it all going to ~?) ¿adónde vamos a **parar**?

to end in a tie/draw salir/quedar **pata**[s]

to end in disaster acabar como el **rosario** de la aurora

to end up at recalar en

to end up in jail/prison dar con los/sus **huesos** en la cárcel

to end up with nothing quedarse **asperges**; chuparse el **dedo**; quedarse con un **palmo** de narices

to be endless (topic/etc.) haber **tela** que cortar/para rato

energy (be full of/bursting with ~) bullirle a alg. la **sangre** en las venas

energy (waste one's ~) gastar la **pólvora** en salvas

English (in plain ~) en **cristiano**

English (say/tell s.th. in plain ~) hablar en **castellano** [puro y llano]; hablar en **cristiano**

to engrave (s.th. ~s itself [firmly] on s.o.'s memory) incrustársele algo a alg. en la memoria (▷ **incrustarse**)

engrossed (be totally ~ in one's work) no levantar/ alzar **cabeza**

engrossed (become ~ in s.th.) **cebar**se/ **enfrascar**se en algo

to be engulfed in flames ser **pasto** de algo

to enjoy o.s. immensely/tremendously ponerse las **botas**; divertirse la **mar**

to enjoy s.th. to the full ponerse las **botas**

enormous bestial; cojonudo; garrafal

enough (do just ~ to get by) cubrir el **expediente**

enough (it's ~ to drive you mad/crazy) es para volverse **loco**

enough (it's ~ to make a cat laugh) no hay tales **borregos/carneros/corderos**

enough (it's just ~ to live from hand to mouth) [lo] **comido** por [lo] servido

enough (leave well ~ alone) bueno está lo bueno [pero no lo demasiado]

enough (that's quite ~!) ¡cruz y raya!

enough (there's ~ of it) hay **paño** que cortar

enough is as good as a feast rogar a **Dios** por santos mas no por tantos; el mucho **dulce** empalaga

enough of that! ¡cruz y raya!

to be enough to drive you crazy/mad/spare/up the wall) ser [como] para subirse por las **pared**es

to be enough to make you weep ser una triste **gracia**

to entertain s.o. lavishly tratar/atender a alg. a **cuerpo** de rey

enthusiasm (be bubbling over with ~) rebosar de entusiasmo

enthusiast el forofo

envy (be bursting with ~) reventar de envidia

envy (be consumed with ~) comer a alg. la envidia

envy (be dying of ~) **perecer**se de envidia

envy (be eaten up with ~) comer a alg. la envidia; **morir**se/**perecer**se de envidia

envy (be green with ~) **morir**se de envidia; estar **muerto** de envidia; **perecer**se de envidia

envy (make s.o. green with ~) poner los **dientes** largos a alg.

to envy (not to ~ s.o.) no arrendarle la **ganancia** a alg.

to err is human quien o el que tiene **boca**, se equivoca

error (make a typing ~) hacer una **mosca**

error (persist in one's ~) no apearse de su **burro**

error (recognize one's ~) apearse de su **burro**

error (thoughtless ~) el penseque

escape (have a narrow ~) [por] el **canto** de un duro; por un **pelo**/los pelos; salvarse en una **tabla**

escape (have ~d from great danger) haber visto las **orejas** del lobo

to escape by a hair's breadth por un **pelo**/los pelos (examples); salvarse en una **tabla**

essence el jugo

essence (get the ~ out of s.th.) sacar el **jugo** a algo

to establish o.s. [a]sentar el **real** o sus reales

et cetera ... y otras **hierba**s

to evade the issue salir[se]/escapar[se]/irse por la **tangente**

evasive answer (give an ~) salir[se]/escapar[se]/ irse por la **tangente**

Eve (daughters of ~) las hijas de **Eva**

even (draw ~) salir/quedar **pata**[s]

even (get ~ with s.o.) ajustar **cuenta**s con alg.

evening (from morning to/till ~) de **sol** a sol

event (be a daily ~) ser el **pan** [nuestro] de cada día

events (at all ~) salga lo que salga/saliere (▷ **salir**)

every man for himself! ¡sálvese quien pueda! (▷ **salvarse**)

every man for himself [and the devil take the hindmost] ¡el que venga detrás, que arree! (▷ **arrear**); el último **mono** es el que se ahoga

everybody todo **bicho** viviente; Cristo y la madre/todo Cristo; cada/cualquier **hijo** de vecino; todo/cada **quisque**

everybody is talking about s.th. andar algo en **boca** de todos

everyday occurrence (be an ~) ser el **pan** [nuestro] de cada día

everyday use (for ~) para todo **trote**

everyone todo **bicho** viviente; Cristo y la madre/todo Cristo; todo/cada **quisque**

everyone (each and ~ of them) todo **bicho** viviente; Cristo y la madre/todo Cristo; todo/cada **quisque**

everyone (tell ~ one's private business) dar un **cuarto** al pregonero

everyone and his brother todo **bicho** viviente; Cristo y la madre/todo Cristo; todo/cada **quisque**

everyone else (like ~) como cada/cualquier **hijo** de vecino; como todo/cada **quisque**

everyone to his place cada **mochuelo** a su olivo

everything (get ~ one can out of s.o.) sacar el **jugo** a alg.

everything (know ~/about [absolutely] ~) saber la **biblia** en verso

everything (put ~ one has into s.th.) rajarse por

everything (put ~ one has into the defense of s.th.) defender algo a **capa** y espada

everywhere acá y en la **China**; en toda/ cualquier **tierra** de garbanzos

everywhere (be known ~) ser más conocido que el **tebeo**

evil (idleness is the root of all ~) el **ocio**/la
ociosidad es la madre de todos los vicios;
los **vicio**s son los hijos del ocio

evil intentions (have ~) tener mal **café**; venir con
las de **Caín**; tener mala **leche/pipa/uva**

exactly al **pie** de la letra

exactly (not to know ~) oír **campana**s y no saber
dónde

exactly twenty/etc. [el] veinte/etc. **pelado**

to exaggerate [re]cargar las **tinta**s

to exaggerate (don't ~) ni tanto ni tan **calvo**

to exaggerate [grossly] hinchar el perro; forzar la
nota

exam (give s.o. a second chance to pass the ~)
repescar a alg.

exam (repeat ~) la repesca

example (follow s.o.'s ~) seguir los **paso**s de alg.

example (set a good ~) predicar con el ejemplo

to excel o.s. (you've really ~led yourself!) lucirse
(example)

to excel s.o. at/in s.th. ganar a alg. en algo

excellent a lo gran señor (▷ **el señor**);
sobresaliente

to be excellent dar la **hora** [y quitar los cuartos]

excellent (taste ~) saber a más

excellent wine (be [an] ~) ser un **vino** de una
oreja

except [for] ... quitando ... (▷ **quitar**)

to be exceptional ser **canela fina**; salirse del
montón

exceptional (be nothing ~) no ser nada/cosa del
otro **mundo**

excess (drink to ~) a todo **pasto**

excess (eat to ~) como un **descosido** (example);
a más no **poder**

exchange (verbal ~) dimes y diretes

to exchange insults **repiquetear**se

excited (be all ~) echar las **campana**s al vuelo

exciting (be as ~ as watching [the] paint dry) ser
algo un **plomo**; a más no **poder**

exciting (be nothing ~) no ser cosa del otro
jueves

excuse (ignorance of the law is no ~) ignorancia
no quita pecado

excuse (use s.th. as an ~) tomar **pie** de algo

to excuse s.o. s.th. hacerle a alg. **gracia** de algo

excuses (make [lame] ~) andar en/andarse con
floreos; asirse a las **rama**s; andar en
zancas de araña

to exert o.s. batir[se] el **cobre**

to be exhausted estar hecho una braga
(▷ **bragas**); estar/quedar hecho **cisco**;
tener los **hueso**s molidos; estar hecho
migas/**papilla/pedazos**; estar hecho un
pingajo; estar hecho **polvo/puré**; estar
reventado (▷ **reventar**); estar hecho unos
zorros

to expect (one day when you/etc. least ~ it) el día
menos pensado (▷ **pensar**)

to expect (things often happen when you least ~
them to) donde/cuando menos se piensa,
salta la **liebre**

to expect (what did you/etc. ~ of him/etc.?) habló
el **buey** y dijo mu

expected (when least ~) el día menos pensado
(▷ **pensar**)

expedition (go on a drinking ~) andar/ir de
chateo

expense (go to enormous ~/spare no ~) echar/tirar
la **casa** por la ventana

expense (live at s.o. else's ~) andar/vivir de **gorra**;
comer la/vivir de la **sopa** boba

expenses (money for the daily ~) la **taleguilla** de
la sal

expensive (be shockingly ~) costar una **burrada/**
un **dineral**/un **huevo**/un **ojo** de la cara/un
pico/un **riñón**/una **riñonada**; costar la de
San Quintín; costar un **sentido** o los cinco
sentidos

expensive dressmaker el postín (example)

experience (be a terrible ~) ser pasar por las
horcas caudinas (▷ **caudino**)

experience (be an awful/a bad ~) ser un **trago**
amargo

expert (be an ~ [at/in s.th.]) ser del **paño**;
pintarse uno solo/pintárselas solo para
algo

expert (soi-disant ~) el **erudito**/la **erudita** a la
violeta

to explain (be good at ~ing things [away]) tener
buenas **explicaderas**

explanation (without so much as an ~) sin decir
agua va

to explode (be ready to ~) a **flor** de piel

to exploit s.o. chupar la **sangre** a alg.

to be exploited hacer el **canelo**

to expose s.o. quitarle la **careta/máscara** a alg.

to expose s.th. descubrir el **pastel**; quitar la
hojaldre al **pastel**

to express o.s. clearly hablar en **cristiano**

expression (have an innocent ~ on one's face) mirar
con **ojos** de sobrino

expression (put on a joyful ~) vestir el rostro de
alegría

expression (put on a serious ~) vestir el rostro de
gravedad

expression (put on a sour ~) poner cara de
vinagre

exquisite a lo gran señor (▷ **el señor**)

to be exquisite ser **canela** fina

extra titles **perejil**es

extraordinarily requete...

extraordinary (be nothing ~) no ser nada/cosa
del otro **mundo**

extreme measures (take ~) cortar por lo **sano**

extremely escandalosamente (▷ **escandaloso**);
solemne

to be extremely obstinate a más no **poder**

257

extremely well a las mil **maravillas**; requete...

extremes (go to ~) **jugar**se el todo por el todo

eye (▷ eyes)

eye (an ~ for an ~ [and a tooth for a tooth]) donde las dan, las toman (▷ **dar**); si haces **mal**, espera otro tal; ojo por ojo, diente por diente

eye (as far as the ~ can see) a lo **largo** y a lo lejos

eye (be or there is more in/to it/this than meets the ~) tener [su] **miga**; la **procesión** va por dentro

eye (be the apple of s.o.'s ~) ser el **ojo** derecho de alg.

eye (glass ~) el **ojo** overo

eye (have a black ~) tener un **ojo** a la funerala

eye (in the twinkling of an ~) en menos que canta un **gallo**; en un abrir y cerrar de **ojos**

eye (mud in your ~!) ¡salud!; ¡salud, amor y pesetas!

eye (offend/hurt the/one's ~[s]) herir la vista

eye (see the mote in one's neighbor's/in s.o. else's ~ and not the beam in one's own) ver la **paja** en el ojo ajeno y no la viga en el propio

eye (turn a blind ~ [to s.th.]) hacer la vista gorda [a algo] (▷ **gordo**)

eye (what the ~ doesn't see, the heart doesn't grieve over) **ojos** que no ven, corazón que no siente

eye (you can see that with half an ~) lo ve un **ciego**

to eye s.o. up írsele a alg. los **ojos** tras alg.

eyeballs (be up to one's ~ in s.th.) andar/ir de **cabeza** con algo; estar metido hasta las **cacha**s en algo; estar hasta los **ojos** en algo

eyelash (not to bat an ~) quedarse/estar tan **campante/fresco/pancho**

eyelid (not to bat an ~) quedarse/estar tan **campante/fresco/pancho**

eyes (all ~ are on s.o.) acaparar todas las miradas

eyes (be a sight for sore ~) dar **gusto** verlo

eyes ([be able] to do s.th. with one's ~ closed) [poder/saber] hacer algo con los **ojos** cerrados

eyes (be up to one's ~ in s.th.) andar/ir de **cabeza** con algo; estar metido hasta las **cacha**s en algo; estar hasta los **ojos** en algo

eyes (bring tears to s.o.'s ~) arrancarle a alg. **lágrima**s

eyes (close/shut one's ~ [to s.th.]) hacer la vista gorda [a algo] (▷ **gordo**); cerrar los **ojos** a algo

eyes (cry one's ~ out) llorar a **lágrima** viva/como una **Magdalena**; llorar a **moco** tendido/a moco y baba

eyes (devour s.th./s.o. with one's ~) írsele a alg. los **ojos** tras algo/alg.; comerse a alg. con los **ojos**/con la **vista**

eyes (feast one's ~ on s.th.) recrear los **ojos** en/regalarse los ojos con algo

eyes (have ~ in the back of one's head) tener **ojos** en la nuca

eyes (have ~ like a hawk) tener **ojos** de águila/lince

eyes (have bulging ~) tener **ojos** de besugo

eyes (have one's ~ on s.o./s.th.) echar el **ojo** a alg./algo

eyes (keep one's ~ open/peeled/skinned) avivar el/[los] **ojo**[s]

eyes (look at s.th./s.o. through different ~) mirar algo/a alg. con otros **ojos**

eyes (make sheep's ~ at s.o.) hacer **carantoña**s a alg.

eyes (not to have [got] ~ in one's head) tener **telaraña**s en los ojos

eyes (open s.o.'s ~) hacer caer la **venda** de los ojos a alg.

eyes (remove the scales from s.o.'s ~) hacer caer la **venda** de los ojos a alg.

eyes (roll one's ~) poner los **ojos** en blanco

eyes (ruin/strain one's ~) quebrarse los **ojos**

eyes (s.o. can't believe his ~) estar como viendo visiones (▷ **visión**)

eyes (s.o. can't keep his ~ off s.o.) írsele a alg. los **ojos** tras alg.

eyes (s.o.'s ~ are too big for/are bigger than his stomach) comer con los **ojos**

eyes (s.o.'s ~ blaze/are ablaze with anger/indignation) echar **fuego** por los ojos

eyes (s.o.'s ~ pop out of their sockets/out of his head) saltársele/salírsele a alg. los **ojos** de las órbitas

eyes (s.o.'s ~ stand out on stalks) saltársele/salírsele a alg. los **ojos** de las órbitas

eyes (spots before one's ~) las musarañas

eyes (the scales fall from s.o.'s ~) caérsele a alg. la **venda** de los ojos

eyes (throw dust in s.o.'s ~) meter a alg. los **dedo**s por los ojos; echar **tierra** a los ojos de alg.

F

f.a. (do sweet ~) tocarse los cojones (▷ **cojón**)/el **pito**; tocar la **vihuela**

fabulous[ly] cañón

face el hocico

face (bang one's ~ on s.th.) dar de narices contra algo (▷ **nariz**)

face (bash s.o.'s ~ in) quitar los **moco**s a alg.; hinchar los **morro**s a alg.

face (cut off one's nose to spite one's ~) escupir al cielo; tirar **piedra**s a su o sobre el propio tejado; echarse **tierra** a los ojos

face (fall flat on one's ~) dar con los/sus **hueso**s en el santo suelo; darse de narices (▷ **nariz**); caerse/dar de narices [en/contra el suelo] (▷ **nariz**)

face (feed/stuff one's ~) comer más que un **alguacil**; llenarse la **andorga**; apiparse; henchir el **baúl**; menear el **bigote**; comer/mascar a dos **carrillo**s; como un **descosido** (example); ponerse como el chico del **esquilador**; dar un buen **golpe** a la comida; comer como una **lima**

face (grotesque ~) la carantoña

face (have a round ~) tener **cara** de pan

face (have s.th. written all over one's ~) tener algo escrito en la frente/cara (▷ **escribir**)

face (make a sour ~) poner cara de **vinagre**

face (make a weepy ~) hacer **puchero**s

face (make/pull ~s) hacer **gesto**s

face ([old] hairy ~: person) el barbas

face (pockmarked ~) la cara de **rallo**

face (put on a brave ~) mantener el **tipo**

face (put s.o.'s ~ out of joint) quitar los **hocico**s/**moco**s a alg.; hichar los **morro**s a alg.

face (say s.th. to s.o.'s ~) decir algo en las **barba**s de alg.

face (screw up one's ~) hacer **puchero**s

face (slam/shut the door in s.o.'s ~) dar a alg. con la **puerta** en la cara/en los hocicos/en las narices

face (smash s.o.'s ~ in) romper el **bautismo**/la **crisma** a alg.; quitar los **hocico**s a alg.

face (ugly ~) la carantoña

to be **facing danger** abocar a

to **fade away** (die) quedarse [muerto] como un **pajarito**

fag (gay) el canco/marica/maricón/mariposa/pluma; la rana; el sarasa

fag end la pava

fagged out (get ~) calentarse la **cabeza**

faggot (gay) el canco/marica/maricón/mariposa/pluma; la rana; el sarasa

to **fail** (be doomed to ~) abocar a

to **fail** (if all else ~s) en última **instancia**

to **fail** (plan/etc.) **escoñar**se, venirse al **suelo**

to **fail** s.o. dar **calabaza**s a alg.; dejar **colgado** a alg.

failed (exam) sobresaliente con tres eses

failings (we all have our little ~) cada uno/cual tiene lo **suyo**; de todo tiene la/hay en la **viña** del Señor

failure (be a ~) ser alg./algo **rana**

failure (be doomed to ~) abocar a

failure (turn out to be a ~) salir alg./algo **rana**

failure (well, the first shot was a ~) al primer **tapón**, zurrapa[s]

faintest idea (not to have the ~ [about s.th.]) no distinguir lo **blanco** de lo negro; no saber [ni] la **cartilla**; no tener ni la más remota/pálida **idea** de algo; no saber ni **jota** de algo

fair (all the fun of the ~) habido y por **haber**

to be **fair to middling** no ser ni **fu** ni fa

fairly con todas las de la **ley**

fairy (be away with the fairies) estar en **Babia**/en las **Batuecas**/en **Belén**/en la **higuera**; estar en la **luna**; andar por o estar en las **nube**s

fairy (gay) el canco/marica/maricón/mariposa/pluma; la rana; el sarasa

fait accompli el hecho consumado (▷ el **hecho**)

fake jewel/gem[stone] un **culo** de vaso

fall guy un[a] **cabeza** de turco

to **fall apart** (s.th. is so old it is ~ing apart) caerse [a/en pedazos] de viejo

to **fall behind** perder **terreno**

to **fall flat on one's face** dar con los/sus **hueso**s en el santo suelo; darse de narices (▷ **nariz**); caerse/dar de narices [en/contra el suelo] (▷ **nariz**)

to **fall flat/headlong** caerse/dar de narices [en/contra el suelo] (▷ **nariz**); besar la **tierra**

to **fall for** (I'm not going to ~ that) dársela a alg. con **queso** (example)

to **fall for anything** comulgar con ruedas de molino

to **fall for it** tragar la **píldora**

to **fall for s.th.** írsele a alg. el **alma** tras algo

to **fall in a heap** caerse redondo

to **fall in a sprawling** dar con los/sus **hueso**s en el santo suelo

to **fall on one's feet** caer de **pie**s

to **fall out with s.o.** **esquinar**se con alg.

to **fall out with s.o.** (have ~en out with s.o.) estar de/en **esquina** con alg.; estar esquinado con alg. (▷ **esquinar**); estar de **punta** con alg.

to fall to pieces (s.th. is so old it is ~ing to pieces) caerse [a/en pedazos] de viejo

to fall through/flat irse al **cuerno**; **escoñar**se

false (be absolutely ~) ni **sombra** de

familiar (get too ~ with s.o.) subirse a las **barba**s de alg.

familiar (it sounds all too ~) me suena a **música** de caballitos

family (with the whole ~) con toda la **recua**

family way (get s.o. in the ~) dejar a alg. con el **paquete**; hacer una **tripa** a alg.

to be famished bestial (example)

fan el forofo

fan (be a real ~ of s.th./s.o.) ser **forofo** de algo/ alg.

fancy bits **perejil**es

to fancy o.s. darse **tono**

to fancy o.s. as ... tener **ínfula**s de ...

fancy that! ¡toma! (▷ **tomar**)

fancy that happening at his/etc. age! a la **vejez**, viruelas

fancy-free (be footloose and ~) ser libre como el **aire/viento**

fanfare (with great/much ~) a **bombo** y platillo

fanny (vagina) la almeja; el bacalao/beo/bollo/ chocho/conejo/coño/higo; la raja/rana/ seta

to be fantastic ser un/de **alucine**; ser **canela** fina; estar algo **jamón**; ser **miel** sobre hojuelas

fantastic time (have a ~) chachi (example); dabute[n]/dabuti (example); pasarlo **pipa**

fantastic[ally] bestial; de **bigote**; cañón; chachi; cojonudo; dabute[n]/dabuti; que quita el **hipo**; de **película**; pistonudo

fantastically (go ~) de **rechupete**

fantasy world (be living in a ~) tener la **cabeza** llena de pájaros; vivir en la **luna**; andar por o vivir en las **nubes**

far (as ~ as the eye can see) a lo **largo** y a lo lejos

far (go ~ [in life]) llegar lejos

far (go too ~) estirar la **cuerda**; pasar de la **raya**; pasarse de **rosca**

far (you can take things too ~) bueno está lo bueno [pero no lo demasiado]

to be far out ser un/de **alucine**

to be far-fetched traer algo por los **cabello**s/ **pelo**s

fare (monotonous ~) **azote**s y galeras

farm (funny ~) el loquero

fart el pedo

fart (let off a ~) soltar/tirar[se] un **pedo**; zullarse

fart (let off a string of ~s) soltar una **pedorrera**

fart (loud ~) el cuesco

fart (silent ~) el follón

fart (string of ~s) la pedorrera

to fart soltar/tirar[se] un **pedo**; zullarse

to fart silently **follar**se

farthing (not to be worth a [brass] ~) no valer un **ardite/comino/pito**

farthings (not to have two [brass] ~ to rub together) no tener ni para unas **alpargata**s; estar sin/no tener **blanca**; no tener qué llevarse a la **boca**/donde **caer**se muerto; estar sin un/no tener [ni] un **cuarto/real**

fashion (be dressed in the latest ~) ir vestido a la última (▷ **último**)

fashion (talk about ~) hablar de **trapo**s

fast (run as ~ as one can) a más no **poder**

fast (stand ~) no dar su **brazo** a torcer

fast (the blows came thick and ~) a **granel**

fast one (pull a ~ on s.o.) pegar un **petardo** a alg.; dársela a alg. con **queso**

fat (be [as] ~ as a pig/sow) estar hecho una **botija**; no caber en el **pellejo**

fat (be very ~) no caber en el **pellejo**; estar como una **vaca**

fat (chew the ~) echar un **párrafo**

fat (live on the ~ of the land) vivir a **cuerpo** de rey/a todo **tren**

fat (now the ~ is in the fire) armar la gorda (▷ **gordo**) (example)

fat cat (be a ~) tener muchas **campanilla**s

fat cat[s] gente gorda; un **pez** gordo

fat chance! ¡ni **soñar**lo!

fat chance (a ~ you've/etc. got) no caerá esa **breva**

fat lot (a ~ I care!) ¡tal día hará un **año**!

fat woman la foca

fat years las **vaca**s gordas

fate (be buffeted by ~) ser el **rigor** de las desdichas

fate (tempt ~) tentar a Dios/al diablo

to be fated to + infinitive estar escrito (▷ **escribir**)

father (like ~ like son) de tal **costilla**, tal astilla; en casa del **gaitero** todos son danzantes; de casta le viene al **galgo** ser rabilargo; tal padre tal **hijo**; de tal **palo**, tal astilla; en casa del **tamborilero** todos son danzantes

father and mother (take the ~ of a thrashing) de padre y muy señor mío (▷ **el padre**) (example)

fatso la foca

fatso (be a ~) estar hecho una **botija**; estar como una **vaca**

fatty (the ~) la foca

fault (through no ~ of one's own) sin **comer**lo ni beberlo

faults (have the same ~) cojear del mismo **pie**

faults (know s.o.'s ~) saber de qué **pie** cojea alg.

faux pas el desliz

faux pas (commit a ~) dar un **resbalón**

favor (creep [into s.o.'s ~]/curry ~ [with s.o.]) chupar del **bote**

favor (win s.o.'s ~) **ganar**se la voluntad de alg.

favorite subject/topic (he's/she's onto his/her ~
again) ha vuelto a la misma **canción/
cantilena**

favoritism el enchufismo

to fawn on s.o. hacer la **barba** a alg.; hacer
fiestas a alg.

fear (be half-dead with ~) **morir**se de miedo;
estar **muerto** de miedo

fear (be petrified/paralyzed with ~) no quedarle a
alg. **gota** de sangre en las venas; quedarse
helado; quedarse sin **pulso**[s]; bajársele a
alg. la **sangre** a los talones; quedarse
yerto

fear (know no ~) no temer **rey** ni roque

fear (live in constant ~ of punishment) traer/llevar
la **soga** arrastrando

feast la comilona

feast (be a real ~) haber **arroz** y gallo muerto

feast (enough is as good as a ~) rogar a **Dios** por
santos mas no por tantos; el mucho **dulce**
empalaga

feast (have a ~) servir al **vientre**

feast (she's a ~ for the eyes) está para comérsela
(▷ **comer**)

to feast one's eyes on s.th. recrear los **ojos** en/
regalarse los ojos con algo

feat (be a brilliant/great ~) ser **obra** de romanos;
ser un **primor**

feat (be no mean ~) no ser **moco de pavo**

to feather one's nest hacer su **agosto**; ponerse las
botas; chupar del **bote**; **redondear**se

to be featherbrained tener la **cabeza** a pájaros

feathers (fine ~ don't make fine birds) aunque la
mona se vista de seda, mona se queda

feathers (fine ~ make fine birds) el **hábito** hace al
monje

fed up (be utterly ~ with s.o.) estar hasta las
cejas/hasta la **punta** de los pelos o del
pelo de alg.

fed up (be [utterly] ~ with s.th.) estar hasta las
cejas/el **coco**/[más allá de] la **coronilla** de
algo; estar **frito** de algo; estar hasta el
gorro/el **moño**/las narices (▷ **nariz**)/la
punta de los pelos o del pelo/los **topes** de
algo

to be fed up to the back teeth with s.o. estar hasta
las **cejas** de alg.; estar **frito** de alg.; tener a
alg. montado en las narices (▷ **nariz**);
estar hasta la **punta** de los pelos/del pelo
de alg.

to be fed up to the back teeth with s.th. estar hasta
las **cejas**/el **coco**/el **cogote**/[más allá de]
la **coronilla** de algo; estar **frito** de algo;
estar hasta el **gorro**/el **moño**/las narices
(▷ **nariz**)/la **punta** de los pelos o del pelo/
los **topes** de algo

to feed one's face comer más que un **alguacil**;
llenarse la **andorga**; apiparse; henchir el
baúl; menear el **bigote**; comer/mascar a

dos **carrillos**; como un **descosido**
(example); ponerse como el chico del
esquilador; dar un buen **golpe** a la
comida; comer como una **lima**

to feed the fishes (vomit) cambiar la **peseta**

to feel completely at home/on top of the world/
really great estar como **abeja** en flor; estar/
sentirse como el **pez** en el agua

to feel like . . ./not to feel like . . . petar

to feel like a fish out of water/like a square peg in a
round hole estar/sentirse como **gallina** en
corral ajeno

to feel one's oats sentirse en la **cumbre**

to feel very/wholly out of place or very uneasy
estar/sentirse como **gallina** en corral
ajeno

to be feeling down/low tener la/estar con la
depre

feeling (have a ~ that . . .) darle a alg. el **pálpito**/
tener el pálpito de que ...

feeling (I get the/have a ~) algo me da en la **nariz**

feeling (sudden ~) el pronto

feelings (have ~ too) ser de **carne** y hueso

feelings (have the same ~ as other people) ser de
carne y hueso

feelings (not to show one's ~) andarle/irle a alg. la
procesión por dentro

feelings (reveal one's true ~) respirar por la
herida

feelings (swallow one's ~) tragar **saliva**

fellow (be an odd ~) ser un **notas**

fellow (sly ~) el lagarto

female (be a ~) vestirse por la **cabeza**

fence (receiver of stolen goods) la **capa** [de
ladrones]

fence (sit on the ~) estar entre dos **aguas**; ver los
toros desde la **barrera**; nadar entre dos
aguas

fib (catch s.o. in a ~) coger a alg. en un **renuncio**

fickle person (be a ~) bailar a cualquier **son**; ser
un[a] **veleta**

fiddle (be as fit as a ~) estar más **sano** que una
manzana

fiddle (be on the ~) hacer **trampa**[s]

fiddle (play first ~) cortar el **bacalao**; llevar la
batuta; llevar/ponerse los calzones
(▷ **calzón**); ser el amo del o dirigir el
cotarro; llevar la **voz** cantante

fiddle (play second ~) ser **plato** de segunda
mesa

fiddle (swindle/etc.) el apaño

to fiddle s.th. hacer **trampa**[s] (example)

field (play the ~) ir de **flor** en flor

fiend (be a ~ for s.th.) ser una **fiera** para/en algo

fiendish delight/glee el gustazo

fifth wheel (be/feel like a ~) sentirse de **carabina**;
hacer tanta falta como los **perros** en misa/
ser como perro en misa

fight la camorra

fight (be trying to pick a ~ with s.o.) mojar la **oreja** a alg.

fight (look for a ~) la bronca/camorra (examples)

fight (pick/start a ~) la camorra (example); mojar la **oreja** a alg.

to fight (quarrel) andar al **pelo**

to fight (s.o. who couldn't ~ his way out of a paper bag) el/la **gallina**

to fight back/down one's tears beberse las **lágrima**s

to fight bitterly luchar a **brazo** partido

to fight fire with fire pagar a alg. con/en la misma **moneda**

to fight like cat and dog andar a **palo**s

to fight on to the last ditch luchar hasta quemar el último **cartucho**

to fight tooth and nail [to defend s.th.] luchar a **brazo** partido; defender algo a **capa** y espada

fighting spirit tener **garra** (example)

figure (have a good/fantastic/great ~) estar como un **camión**; tener buena **percha**; estar como un **tren**

fill (eat one's ~) sacar la **tripa**/el **vientre** de mal año

to fill one's pants **cagar**se

to fill s.o.'s head [with s.th.] calentar la **cabeza** a alg.

to fill up the glasses atizar la **lámpara**

filth (dirt) la caca

filth (police) la bofia/madera/poli/polilla

to be filthy rich estar **podrido** de dinero

financial circumstances (consider one's ~) consultar con el **bolsillo**

to find (be very easy to ~) no tener **pérdida**

to find a way arreglárselas (▷ **arreglar**); componérselas (▷ **componer**)

to find just what one wanted encontrar/hallar la **horma** de su zapato

to find out [about it] descubrir la **hilaza**

to find s.th. [very] difficult/hard [to + infinitive] hacérsele algo a alg. [muy] **cuesta** arriba [+ infinitivo]

to find the very thing encontrar/hallar la **horma** de su zapato

fine de **rechupete**

fine (get on ~ [again]) echar buen **pelo**/buena **pluma**

fine (go ~) ir que chuta (▷ **chutar**)

fine (just ~) a pedir de **boca**

fine one (he's/she's a ~!) ¡menuda/buena **alhaja**!

fine thing (a ~ you've done!) lucirse (example)

fine time (have a ~) de **rechupete**

to fine s.o. propinar algo a alg.

finery (put on one's ~) ponerse de veinticinco **alfilere**s/de **punta** en blanco

fine-tooth comb (go through/over s.th with a ~) pasar algo por la **criba**

finger (eleventh ~) el **dedo** veintiuno

finger (not to lay a ~ on s.o.) no tocar un **pelo** [de la ropa] a alg.

finger (not to lift a ~) no dar **golpe**

finger (put one's ~ on the spot) poner el **dedo** en la llaga

finger (twist s.o. [a]round one's little ~) meterse a alg. en el **bolsillo**; llevar a alg. de un **cabello**

fingers los cinco **mandamiento**s

fingers (burn one's ~) pillarse los **dedo**s

fingers (counting on one's ~) la **cuenta** de la vieja

fingers (have sticky ~) ser **largo** de uñas

fingers (work one's ~ to the bone at s.th.) dejarse las **uña**s en algo

fingertip (have s.th. at one's ~s) saber algo al **dedillo**

finish (from start to ~) de **cabo** a cabo/rabo o de punta a cabo; de **pe** a pa

to finish s.o. off **cargar**se/cascar/**cepillar**[se] a alg.; freír a alg.; dejar frito a alg.; mandar a alg. al otro **mundo**; pasaportear a alg.; quitar a alg. de en medio; dejar **tieso** a alg.; tumbar a alg.

to finish up in jail/prison dar con los/sus **hueso**s en la cárcel

finished (be [as good as] ~) no faltar un **cabello** a algo

fire (add fuel to the ~) echar leña al **fuego**/apagar el fuego con aceite

fire (fight ~ with ~) pagar a alg. con/en la misma **moneda**

fire (get on like a house on ~) la **mar** de; comer en un/el o del mismo **plato**

fire (have more than one or another iron in the ~) comer a dos **carrillo**s; tener una **vela** encendida por si la otra se apaga

fire (have two/several irons in the ~) tener un **pie** en dos zapatos

fire (play with ~) jugar con el **fuego**; atar perros con **longaniza**

fire (the ~ is raging) se ceba el fuego (▷ **cebar**)

fire (there's no smoke without ~/where there's smoke, there's ~) donde **fuego** se hace, humo sale; cuando el **río** suena, agua lleva o piedras trae

fire (with ~ and sword) a **fuego** y hierro/sangre

to fire s.o. dar el **bote** a alg.; echar/despedir a alg. con **caja**s destempladas; echar a alg. a la **calle**/poner a alg. de patitas en la calle; plantar a alg. en la **calle**; largar a alg.; dar la **licencia**/[el] **pasaporte**/la **patada** a alg.; salir a alg.

fireplace (be/sit by the ~) estar al **amor** de la lumbre

fireside (be/sit by the ~) estar al **amor** de la lumbre

firing squad (put s.o. before a ~) mandar a alg. al **paredón**

firm de **cal** y canto
firm (stand ~) mantenerse/seguir en sus **trece**
firmly (believe/etc.) a **pie** juntillo
firmly (shut/close s.th. ~) cerrar algo a **cal** y canto
firmness (politeness and ~ aren't mutually exclusive) lo **cortés** no quita lo valiente
first (get in ~) madrugar
first (put o.s.~) barrer hacia/para dentro
first base (not to get to/reach ~) quedar en **nada**
first come, first served el **primer** venido, primer servido
first fiddle (play ~) cortar el **bacalao**; llevar la **batuta**; llevar/ponerse los calzones (▷ **calzón**); ser el amo del o dirigir el **cotarro**; llevar la **voz** cantante
first it's this, then it's that cuando **pitos** flautas, cuando flautas pitos
fish (be a queer ~) ser un **pájaro** raro
fish (be an odd ~) ser un **notas**/un **pájaro** raro
fish (be another/a different kettle of ~) ser **harina** de otro costal
fish (be [as] cold as a ~) tener **sangre** blanca/de horchata en las venas
fish (be like shooting ~ in a barrel) ser **coser** y cantar; ser **pan** comido
fish (be neither ~ nor fowl) no ser **carne** ni pescado; no ser ni **chicha** ni limonada/ni **fu** ni fa; ni **pinchar** ni cortar
fish (be/feel like a ~ out of water) estar/sentirse como **gallina** en corral ajeno
fish (big ~) un **pez** gordo
fish (drink like a ~) como un **descosido** (example); beber como una **esponja**; más que **siete**
fish (it's better to be a big ~ in a small pond than a small ~ in a big pond) más vale ser **cabeza** de ratón que cola de león
fish (that's [quite] another/a different kettle of ~) eso es otro cantar (▷ **el cantar**)
fish (this is a pretty kettle of ~!) meterse en un **berenjenal** (example)
to fish in troubled waters pescar al **candil**; pescar en aguas turbias; pescar en **río** revuelto
fishes (feed the ~: to vomit) cambiar la **peseta**
fishing (there's good ~ in troubled waters) a **río** revuelto, ganancia de pescadores
to be fishy no ser algo **trigo** limpio
fishy (smell/sound ~) oler a **camelo**/a **cuerno** quemado
fishy (there's s.th. ~ about it/this) oler a **camelo**/a **cuerno** quemado
fishy (there's s.th. ~ [going on] [here]) [aquí] hay **gallo** tapado/**gato** encerrado
fishy business (be a ~) oler a **cuerno** quemado
fit (be a perfect ~) encajar/caer como **pedrada** en ojo de boticario
fit (be as ~ as a fiddle) estar más **sano** que una manzana

fit (not to be ~ to tie s.o.'s bootlaces/shoelaces) no llegarle a alg. a la **suela** del zapato/a los **zancajo**s
fit (sudden ~ [of temper/etc.]) el pronto
to fit [s.o.] like a glove/to a T sentar [a alg.] como **anillo** al dedo/que ni **pintado** o como pintado
to fit poorly respingar
five (give me ~!) ¡choca esos **cinco**!
fix (be in an awful/a real ~) estar más perdido que **Carracuca**; estar con el **dogal**/la **soga** al cuello
fix (get o.s. into a ~) meterse en un **atolladero**/**berenjenal**; meterse en **camisa** de once varas
fix (get out of a ~) ponerse/salir a **flote**
fix (get s.o. into a [real] ~) poner a alg. en las **astas** del toro
fix (get/help s.o. out of a ~) sacar a alg. del **atolladero**; echar un **cable** a alg.; sacar el **pie** del lodo a alg.; sacar a alg. de un apuro
fix (give o.s. a ~) **chutar**se; **pinchar**se
fix (leave s.o. in a ~) dejar a alg. en las **astas** del toro
fix (of drug) el chute; la picotada; el picotazo
to fix s.o. up with a cushy job enchufar a alg. (example)
fixtures (be one of the ~: person) ser un **mueble** de la casa
to fizzle out quedar en **nada**
to be flabbergasted quedarse **bizco**; quedarse de una **pieza**
flames (add fuel to the ~) echar leña al **fuego**/apagar el fuego con aceite
flaming [marital] row (have a ~) tirarse los **trastos** a la cabeza
to flare up (get angry) ponerse como un **basilisco**; exaltársele a alg. la **bilis**; ponerse hecho un **demonio**
to flare up very quickly (tend to ~) a **flor** de piel
flash (in a ~) en un decir **amén**/un **credo**/un **dos** por tres; en menos que canta un **gallo**; en un abrir y cerrar de **ojos**
flash in the pan una **nube** de verano
flash in the pan (be a ~) pasar como una **nube** de verano
flashy car (big ~) el cochazo
flashy cruisemobile el cochazo
flask (hip ~) la petaca
flat (be [as] ~ as a board/pancake) ser de **Castellón de la Plana**; ser lisa (▷ **liso**)
flat (fall ~) caerse/dar de narices [en/contra el suelo] (▷ **nariz**); besar la **tierra**
flat (fall ~ on one's face) dar con los/sus **hueso**s en el santo suelo; darse de narices (▷ **nariz**); caerse/dar de narices [en/contra el suelo] (▷ **nariz**)
flat (fall ~: plan/etc.) irse al **cuerno**; **escoñar**se

to be flat broke estar sin/no tener **blanca**; estar sin un/no tener [ni] un **cuarto**; andar/ir con el **culo** a rastras; estar **palmado**; no tener [ni] una **perra**; andar/estar a la cuarta **pregunta**; estar sin un/no tener [ni] un **real**

flat out a toda **pastilla**; a todo **vapor**; a toda **vela**

flat out (drive/go ~) conducir a toda **castaña**; quemar el **caucho**; a toda **pastilla** (example); hundir el **pedal**; correr/lanzarse a **tumba** abierta; a todo **vapor** (example); a toda **vela**

flat out (work ~) a toda **pastilla** (example); a más no **poder**; a todo **vapor** (example); a toda **vela**

flat panic (be in a ~) estar con los cojones de corbata (▷ **cojón**)

to be flat-chested ser de **Castellón de la Plana**; ser lisa (▷ **liso**)

flatly deny s.th. a **palo** seco

to flatten s.o. machacar a alg.; hacer **polvo** a alg.; poner a alg. como un **trapo**

to flatter s.o. hacer la **barba** a alg.; hacer **carantoñas** a alg.; regalarle a alg. el **oído**

to fleece s.o. [of everything] dejar a alg. en **calzoncillos**/en **cueros** [vivos]; dejar esquilmado a alg. (▷ **esquilmar**); dejar **pelado** a alg.; dejar a alg. a la cuarta **pregunta**; sacar las **tripa**s a alg.

fleecy clouds cabrillas

flies (have one's ~ undone) tener la **botica** abierta

to be flighty ser ligero/alegre de **cascos**

fling (go on a/have a ~) echar una **cana** al aire

to flip one's lid perder la **chaveta**; pasarse de **rosca**

flip-flop (do a ~) dar un **golpe** de timón

to flit from one man/woman to another ir de **flor** en flor

to flock (birds of a feather ~ together) Dios los cría y ellos se juntan; cada **oveja** con su pareja; no/nunca falta un **roto** para un descosido

to flog a dead horse azotar el **aire**; machacar en hierro frío; arar en el **mar**

floodgates (the ~ of heaven open) a **cántaro**s (example); llover a **chorros/cubos/mar**es/ **torrente**s

floor (wipe the ~ with s.o.) hacer **polvo** a alg.; revolcar a alg.

to floor it hundir el **pedal**

to floor s.o. dejar **clavado** a alg.; partir a alg. por el **eje**; dejar a alg. de una **pieza**

floored (be [completely] ~) quedarse **parado**

floozie la fulana; el pendón; la sota

to flourish fast/greatly/rapidly crecer como la **espuma**

to flourish like the green bay tree crecer como la **espuma**

fluency la labia

fluke (be a ~) sonar la **flauta** [por casualidad]

to flunk s.o. dar **calabaza**s a alg.

flunked (exam) sobresaliente con tres eses

to flush [with anger/excitement/etc.] salírsele/ subírsele a alg. los **color**es

fly (die/drop like flies) caer/morir como **chinche**s

fly (have one's ~ undone) tener la **botica** abierta

fly (s.o. wouldn't harm/hurt a ~) ser incapaz de matar una **mosca**

fly (there are no flies on s.o.) no tener un **pelo** de tonto

to fly (let ~) echar **ajos** [y cebollas]; darse a todos los **demonio**s; pitar

to fly (pigs might ~!) ¡hasta que/cuando meen las **gallina**s!; ¡hasta que/cuando las **rana**s críen pelo!

to fly (when pigs learn to ~) cuando meen las **gallina**s; cuando las **rana**s críen pelo; en la **semana** que no tenga jueves/de tres jueves

to fly a kite lanzar un **globo** de ensayo

to fly a kite (go ~!) ¡anda a **bañar**te!; ¡vete a freír **buñuelos/espárrago**s!

to fly a kite (tell s.o. to go ~) mandar a alg. a freír **buñuelos**/al **cuerno**/a freír **espárrago**s/a hacer **gárgara**s

to fly into a temper (tend to ~) a **flor** de piel

to fly off the handle ponerse como un **basilisco**; exaltársele a alg. la **bilis**; subirse al **campanario**; salirse de sus **casilla**s; ponerse hecho un **demonio**; perder los **estribo**s; hinchársele a alg. las narices (▷ **nariz**); subirse por las **pared**es/a la **parra**

to fly off the handle ([tend to] ~) a **flor** de piel; no poder con el **genio**

fly-by-night (be a ~) no ser alg. **trigo** limpio

flying colors (come off/out with ~) salir a **tambor** batiente

to foam at the mouth echar **espumarajo**s

to foam with rage echar **espumarajo**s

fob watch la patata

focus of attention (be the ~) estar algo/alg. en [el] **candelero**

fogey (old ~) el carroza

foggy (not to have the foggiest [idea]) no distinguir lo **blanco** de lo negro; no saber [ni] la **cartilla**; no tener ni la más remota/ pálida **idea** de algo; no saber ni **jota** de algo

to foist s.th. off on s.o. colar algo a alg.

fold (return to the ~) volver al **redil**

to fold up like a house of cards derrumbarse como un **castillo** de naipes

folk (there's nowt so queer as ~) de todo tiene la/ hay en la **viña** del Señor

to follow s.o.'s example/in s.o.'s footsteps seguir los **pasos** de alg.

to follow the crowd dejarse llevar de/por la
   corriente
fond (be passionately ~ of reading) a más no
   poder
to fondle s.o. hacer **fiesta**s a alg.
food (awful/bad ~) el comistrajo/pisto
food (pick at one's ~) comer como un **gorrión**
food (same old rotten ~) **azote**s y galeras
fool el primo
fool (act/play the ~) hacer el **gracioso/oso**;
   tirarse a muerto
fool (be no ~) tener la **cabeza** en su sitio/bien
   puesta; no **comulgar** con ruedas de
   molino; no chuparse el **dedo**; no tener un
   pelo de tonto; no ser **rana/zurdo**
fool (be no end of a ~) la **mar** de; ser **tonto** del
   bote/de capirote
fool (be nobody's ~) no **comulgar** con ruedas de
   molino; no chuparse el **dedo**; no nació
   alg. ayer (▷ **nacer**); no tener un **pelo** de
   tonto
fool (make a ~ of o.s.) lucirse; hacer el **oso**
fool (make a ~ out of s.o.) dar la **castaña** a alg.
fool (only a ~ never changes his mind) es de
   sabios cambiar de opinión (▷ **el sabio**)
fool (there's no ~ like an old ~) la **cabeza** blanca y
   el seso por venir; a la **vejez**, viruelas
to fool s.o. dar [el] **camelo** a alg.; dársela a alg.
   con **queso**
to fool s.o. (don't [even] try to fool me!) ¡a mí no
   me la cuelas! (▷ **colar**)
fools (children and ~ tell the truth) los **niños** y los
   locos dicen las verdades
fools (not to suffer ~ gladly) no aguantar/sufrir
   pulgas
fool's paradise (live in a ~) tejer la tela de
   Penélope
foot la pata
foot (be dead on one's feet) caerse de cansancio/
   sueño
foot (begin to stand on one's own two feet) alzar/
   levantar el **vuelo**
foot (cheesy/smelly feet) los **queso**s
foot (crow's feet) **pata**s de gallo
foot (cut the ground from under s.o.'s feet) minar
   el **terreno** a alg.
foot (fall/land on one's feet) caer de **pie**s
foot (feet) los **queso**s
foot (get back on one's feet) levantar/alzar
   cabeza; ponerse/salir a **flote**
foot (get cold feet) quedarse **frío**; encogérsele a
   alg. el **ombligo**
foot (get on one's feet again) levantar/alzar
   cabeza; ponerse/salir a **flote**; echar buen
   pelo/buena **pluma**
foot (get under s.o.'s feet) pisar el **terreno** de alg.
foot (get/put s.th./s.o. back on its/his feet) poner/
   sacar algo/a alg. a **flote**

foot (have both/one's feet [firmly] on the ground)
   tener los **pie**s [bien puestos] en/sobre la
   tierra
foot (have one ~ in the grave) estar con un pie en
   el **estribo/hoyo**; tener un pie en la **tumba**
foot (if you keep your mouth shut, you won't put
   your ~ in it) en **boca** cerrada no entran
   moscas
foot (my ~!) ¡ ... mi **abuela**!; ¡ ... ni **hablar**!; ¡y un
   jamón [con chorreras]!
foot (not to get on one's feet again) no levantar/
   alzar **cabeza**
foot (on ~) a **pata**
foot (person who is always putting his ~ in it) el/la
   metepatas
foot (put one's ~ down hard) hundir el **pedal**
foot (put one's ~ in it/in one's mouth) meter la
   pata/pezuña; tirarse una **plancha**; dar un
   resbalón
foot (stamp one's ~) herir el suelo con el pie
to foot the bill ([have to] ~) ser el **paganini/
   pagano**; [tener que] pagar el **pato**
football el cuero
foot-in-mouth disease (person who has ~) el/la
   metepatas
to be footloose and fancy-free ser libre como el
   aire/viento
footsteps (follow in s.o.'s ~) seguir los **paso**s de
   alg.
to force o.s. not to get angry tragar **bilis**
forearmed (forewarned is ~) hombre prevenido
   vale por dos
to forestall s.th. salir al **paso** de algo
forever para los **resto**s
forever (nothing goes on/lasts ~) no hay **bien** ni
   mal que cien años dure
forever (take ~) ser más largo que una
   cuaresma; ser más **largo** que un día sin
   pan
forever (this won't last ~) ya viene/vendrá el tío
   Paco con la rebaja
forewarned is forearmed hombre prevenido vale
   por dos
to forget (clean ~ about s.th.) dejar algo o
   quedársele algo a alg. en el **tintero**
to forget [all] about s.th. pasar la **esponja** sobre
   algo; echar **tierra** sobre/a algo
forget it! ¡ni **pensar**lo!
forget it ([let's] ~) borrón y cuenta nueva
to forget what one was about to do/say írsele a alg.
   el **santo** al cielo
to fork out rascar[se] el **bolsillo**; aflojar/soltar la
   china/mosca; soltar la **pasta**; sacudir/
   soltar la **tela**
forth (and so ~) ... y otras **hierba**s
fortune (be worth a ~) valer algo un **Perú/Potosí**
fortune (cost a ~) costar una **burrada**/un
   dineral/un **huevo**/un **ojo** de la cara/un
   pico/un **riñón**/una **riñonada**; costar la de

San Quintín; costar un **sentido** o los cinco sentidos

fortune (make a ~) **hinchar**se de plata/dinero

fortune smiles on some but not on others unos nacen con **estrella** y otros nacen estrellados

fortune smiles upon s.o. **sonreír**le a alg. la suerte/fortuna

forty winks (have/get ~) echar una **cabezada**/cabezadita; descabezar un sueñecito

foul (smell/taste ~) oler/saber a **demonio**s/**rayo**s

foul (the weather's ~) de **perro**s

foul mood (be in a ~) no estar para **fiesta**s; estar de mala **leche**/de un humor de **perro**s/de mala **uva**

to foul one's own nest manchar el propio **nido**; tirar **piedra**s a su o sobre el propio tejado

fowl (be neither fish nor ~) no ser **carne** ni pescado; no ser ni **chicha** ni limonada/ni **fu** ni fa; ni **pinchar** ni cortar

fox (be an old ~) ser [un] toro **corrido**/[una] liebre corrida; ser [un] **perro**/**zorro** viejo

fox (person) el lagarto

fragile (very ~) de mírame y no me toques (▷ **mirar**)

frail (be old and ~) caerse de viejo; arrastrar los **pies**

to frame s.o. [up] cargar el **mochuelo** a alg.

frankly (speak ~) **cantar**las claras; hablar en **plata**

fraud el petardo

to fray (seam) **nacer**se

free (be [as] ~ as [the] air) ser libre como el **aire**/**viento**

free (let one's imagination run ~) dar **rienda** suelta a algo (example)

free rein (give ~ to s.th.) dar **rienda** suelta a algo

to be free with one's hands ser **largo** de manos; tener las **mano**s largas

freely (act ~) hacer de su **capa** un sayo

freely (speak ~) hablar en **castellano** [puro y llano]

to freeze (be cold enough to ~ the balls off a brass monkey) hacer un frío de cojones (▷ **cojón**)/que pela (▷ **pelar**); de **perro**s

to freeze (s.o.'s blood ~s) helársele a alg. la **sangre**

to freeze (till hell ~s over!) ¡hasta que/cuando meen las **gallina**s!; ¡hasta que/cuando las **rana**s críen pelo!

to freeze [with fear/horror] no quedarle a alg. **gota** de sangre en las venas; quedarse **helado**

freezing (be [absolutely] ~) hacer un frío que pela (▷ **pelar**); de **perro**s

to be freezing cold hacer un frío que pela (▷ **pelar**); de **perro**s

French leave (take ~) despedirse a la francesa (▷ **francés**)

French letter (condom) el calcetín/globo; la goma

fresh (be still very ~) estar algo sangrando (▷ **sangrar**); estar algo chorreando **sangre**

fresh (be very ~: cheeky) ser más fresco que una **lechuga**

fresh (be/feel as ~ as a daisy) estar fresco/fresquito como una **lechuga**

fresh (get ~ [with s.o.]) subirse a las **barba**s de alg.; ponerse **flamenco**

fresh start (let's make a ~) **borrón** y cuenta nueva

friend (a ~ in need is a ~ indeed) en las malas se conoce a los amigos (▷ **malo**)

friendly (like to try to get ~ with men) tomar **vara**s

friends (mobilize all one's influential ~) tocar todos los **resorte**s

friends in high/in the right places (have ~) el enchufe (example)

friends in the right places (have [powerful/influential] ~) tener buenas **aldaba**s/buenos **asidero**s

fright (awful ~) padre (example)

fright (be half-dead with ~) **morir**se de miedo; estar **muerto** de miedo

fright (get the ~ of one's life) no llegarle a uno la **camisa** al cuerpo; **morir**se del susto

fright (give s.o. a [nasty] ~) meter a alg. el **ombligo** para dentro/el **resuello** en el cuerpo

fright (have stage ~) tener **nervio**s

to be frightened out of one's wits no llegarle a uno la **camisa** al cuerpo; estar con los cojones de corbata (▷ **cojón**); **morir**se del susto; quedarse sin **pulso**[s]

frills **perejil**es

fripperies **perejil**es

to be frivolous ser ligero/alegre de **casco**s

frog (it's better to be a big ~ in a small pond than a small ~ in a big pond) más vale ser **cabeza** de ratón que cola de león

front (from right in ~ of me/etc.) en mis/etc. propias o mismísimas **barba**s/narices (▷ **nariz**)

frowning cejijunto

frowsy pad/room la zorrera

fruitcake (be as nutty as a ~) estar mal de la **azotea**; no estar bueno de la **cabeza** o estar ido/mal/tocado de la cabeza o tener pájaros en la cabeza; estar como una **cabra**/**cafetera**; estar [loco] como un **cencerro**; estar **chalado**; estar mal de la **chaveta**; estar **chiflado**

to fry an egg (go ~!) ¡anda a **bañar**te!; ¡vete a freír **buñuelo**s/**espárrago**s!

to fry an egg (tell s.o. to go ~) mandar a alg. a freír **buñuelo**s/al **cuerno**/a freír **espárrago**s/a hacer **gárgara**s

frying pan (jump out of the ~ into the fire) huir de la[s] **ceniza**[s] y caer/dar en la[s] brasa[s]; huir del **fuego** y caer en las brasas; salir de **Guatemala** y entrar en Guatepeor; ir de **Herodes** a Pilatos; salir de las **llama**s y caer en las brasas; salir de **Málaga** y entrar en Malagón; huir del **perejil** y dar en el berenjenal; saltar/caer de la **sartén** y dar en la brasa; huir del **toro** y caer en el arroyo; salir del **trueno** y dar con el relámpago

fuck (not to give a ~ [about s.th.]) **ciscar**se en algo; [no] importar a alg. un **huevo**/una **puñeta**

to fuck [s.o.] (have sex [with s.o.]) pasar a una por las **armas**; **calzar**[se]/**cargar**se a alg.; echar un **casquete**; **cepillar**[se] a una; poner un **clavo** a una; follar/joder [a alg.]; pasar a una mujer por la **piedra**; pisar a alg.; echar un **polvo**; quilar [a alg.]; regar/tapar/**tirar**se/tumbar/**zumbar**se a una mujer

fuck off! ivete al **coño**/a tomar por **culo**!

to fuck off (tell s.o. to ~) mandar a alg. a tomar por **culo**

fuel (add ~ to the fire/flames) echar leña al **fuego**/apagar el fuego con aceite

fuggy pad/room la zorrera

full (enjoy s.th. to the ~) ponerse las **botas**

full (to the ~) hasta la última **gota**

full blast a toda **pastilla**

full of cuajado de

to be full of energy/[youthful] vigor bullirle a alg. la **sangre** en las venas

to be full of holes estar hecho una **criba**

to be full of o.s. no necesitar **abuela**; **pagar**se de sí mismo

full speed/steam/tilt (at ~) a todo **vapor**; a toda **vela**

full-belt a toda **pastilla**

full-blown padre (example)

fully grown hecho y derecho

fully-fledged hecho y derecho

fuming (be [really] ~) estar alg. que arde (▷ **arder**); estar hecho un **basilisco**; estar alg. que brinca (▷ **brincar**); echar

chiribitas/**chispa**s; echar **rayo**s y centellas; estar alg. que trina (▷ **trinar**)

fun (all the ~ of the fair) habido y por **haber**

fun (make ~ of s.o.) dar [el] **camelo** a alg.; pitorrearse de alg.; dar **soga** a alg.

fun (make ~ of/poke ~ at s.th.) poner algo en **solfa**

fun (spoil [all] the ~/s.o.'s ~) amargar el **caldo** a alg.; aguar la **fiesta**

funeral (that's his ~!) arreglárselas (▷ **arreglar**) (example); componérselas (▷ **componer**) (example)

funeral (that's his/etc. ~) con su/etc. pan se/etc. lo coma/etc. (▷ **comer**)

funk (be in a blue ~) **cagar**se/**ciscar**se de miedo (examples); estar **muerto** de miedo

funny ([as] ~ as a barrel of monkeys) descacharrante

funny ([be] hilariously ~) descacharrante; ser para **morir**se de risa

funny farm el loquero

furious (get ~) dar con la **cabeza** en las paredes; subírsele a alg. el **humo**/la **mostaza** a las narices

fuse (blow a ~) fundírsele a alg. los **plomo**s

fuse (have a or be on a [very] short ~) tener mal/mucho **genio**; tener malas **pulga**s

fuss (cause/kick up a tremendous ~) armar la de **Dios** es Cristo; armar la gorda (▷ **gordo**)

fuss (make a great ~ of/over s.o.) hacer **fiesta**s a alg.

fuss (make a [lot of] ~ [about/over s.th.]) hacer [muchas] **alharaca**s

fuss (without any ~) sin **alharaca**s ni bambollas

to fuss about details (not to ~) no andarse con/en chiquitas (▷ la **chiquita**); no andarse con **requilorios**

future (carve out a ~ for o.s.) **labrar**se un porvenir

future (have a bright ~) **sonreír**le a alg. el porvenir

future (past/present and ~) habido y por **haber**

fuzz (police) la bofia/madera/poli/polilla

fuzz (the first ~ is already appearing on s.o.'s upper lip) ya le sombrea el labio superior a alg. (▷ **sombrear**)

G

gab (have the gift of [the] ~) tener buenas **explicaderas**/mucha **labia**/buen **pico**

gaff (blow the ~) levantar la **liebre**; descubrir el **pastel**

gaff (stand the ~) aguantar [la] **mecha**

gaffe el desliz; la plancha

gaffes (person who is always making ~) el/la metepatas

to gain (nothing ventured, nothing ~ed) quien no se arriesga no pasa la **mar**

gains (no pains, no ~) no hay **atajo** sin trabajo; no hay **barranco** sin atranco; la **letra** con sangre entra; no se pescan **trucha**s a bragas enjutas

gainsaying (there's no ~ it) eso o la cosa no tiene vuelta de **hoja**

gallery (shooting ~) el pimpampúm

gallons (drink ~ of) ponerse **morado** de algo

gallows la **ene** de palo

galore a **manta/patada**s**/pote**; a **punta** pala

to gamble away everything [one owns] jugar hasta la **camisa**

game (be on the ~) hacer la **calle**; ser del **oficio**; ser una **peripatética**

game (give the ~ away) tirar de la **manta**; descubrir el **pastel**

game (it's a whole new ball ~ now) se han vuelto las **tornas**; se ha vuelto la **tortilla**

game (know or see [through] s.o.'s little ~) conocerle/verle a alg. el **juego**; descubrir el **pastel**; conocer el **tinglado**

game (play a double ~) jugar con/a dos **baraja**s; jugar/hacer un doble **juego**

game (that's a different ball ~) eso es otro cantar (▷ **el cantar**)

gang [of thieves] la camada

to gape papar **moscas/viento**

to gape (stand around gaping) papar **moscas/viento**

garbage! ¡**naranjas**! ¡**naranjas** chinas! ¡**naranjas** de la China!; ¡**narices**! (▷ **nariz**)

garbage that ends up on paper el **papel** todo lo aguanta

garden (everything in the ~ is lovely) todo marcha a las mil **maravillas**

garters (have s.o.'s guts for ~) **comer**[se] a alg. vivo

to gas darle a la **mui/sinhueso**

gasbag el/la bocazas; la cotorra

to gauge s.th. tomar el **pulso** a algo

gauntlet (take up the ~) recoger el **guante**

gauntlet (throw down the ~ to s.o.) arrojar el **guante** a alg.

to gawk mirar la **luna**; papar **moscas/viento**

to gawp mirar la **luna**; papar **moscas/viento**

gay (arse bandit; fag; faggot; fairy; pansy; poof[ter]; queen; queer) el canco/marica/maricón/mariposa/pluma; la rana; el sarasa

to be gay ser de la otra **acera**

to gaze at s.o. mirar a alg. de **hito** en hito

to be gazing vacantly at the ceiling estar contando las **viga**s

gear (belongings) los bártulos

geezer (old ~) el carroza

gem (he's/she's a real ~!) ¡menuda/buena **alhaja**!

gem[stone] (fake ~) un **culo** de vaso

generous (be [very] ~) no caberle a alg. el **corazón** en el pecho; no dejarse llamar **roñoso**

generous (be far too ~) pecar de + adj. (example)

genitals (male ~) las **alegrías**

genius (be a ~ [at s.th.]) ser un **hacha** [en/para algo]

to get (if you don't ask you don't ~) quien no llora no mama (▷ **llorar**)

to get (what you see is what you ~) no hay más **cera** que la que arde

to get (you ~ what you give) cuál la **pregunta**, tal la respuesta

to get along arreglárselas (▷ **arreglar**); componérselas (▷ **componer**); ir tirando (▷ **tirar**)

to get along (not to ~ with s.o.) **llevar**se mal con alg.; estar de **uña**s con alg.

to get along well/badly with s.o. hacer buenas/malas **miga**s con alg.

to get along with s.o. **llevar**se bien con alg.

to get at (what are you/etc. getting at?) ¿adónde quieres/etc. ir a **parar**?

get away! ¡y un **jamón** [con chorreras]!

to get away (there's no getting away [from that]) impepinable

to get away (you/etc. won't ~ with it/that forever) tanto va el **cántaro** a la fuente, que al fin se rompe

to get by arreglárselas (▷ **arreglar**); componérselas (▷ **componer**); ir tirando (▷ **tirar**)

to get by (do just enough to ~) cubrir el **expediente**

to get everything one can out of s.o. sacar el **jugo** a alg.

to get into (what's got into you/etc.?) ¿qué **mosca** te/etc. ha picado?

to get it (hiding/etc.) ganársela (▷ **ganar**)

to get it (now I ~!) ¡acabáramos! (▷ **acabar**)

to get it across to s.o. (try to ~ every way imaginable/every way one can think of) decírselo a alg. en todos los **tonos**

to get it [at once] (understand) captar la **onda**; cazarlas/cogerlas/pescarlas al **vuelo**

to get off (tell s.o. where to ~) mandar a alg. a hacer **gárgaras**

to get off lightly (have got off lightly [this time]) haber visto las **orejas** del lobo

to get off lightly (I/we/etc. got off lightly!) ¡de buena me he/nos hemos/etc. librado! (▷ **librar**)

to get on (not to ~ with s.o.) **llevar**se mal con alg.; estar de **uñas** con alg.

to get on fine [again] echar buen **pelo**/buena **pluma**

to get on like a house on fire la **mar** de; comer en un/el o del mismo **plato**

to get on well/badly with s.o. hacer buenas/malas **migas** con alg.

to get on with s.o. **llevar**se bien con alg.

to get one's own back (s.o. can't wait to get his own back) tener **sangre** en el ojo

to get onto s.th. descubrir el **pastel**

to get o.s. a husband **pescar**se un marido

get out! irse con la **música** a otra parte (example)

to get out (let's ~ of here!) irse con la **música** a otra parte (example); ¿**pies**, para qué os quiero?

get out of there! ¡quítate de ahí/de en medio! (▷ **quitar**)

to get over that/it (not to ~ easily) llevar/tener qué **rascar**

to get s.o. on the raw llegar a o herir/tocar en lo más **vivo** a alg.

to get s.th. **calzar**se algo

to get s.th. (manage to ~/succeed in getting s.th.) **calzar**se algo

to get s.th. (understand) calzar/diquelar algo

to get s.th. out of it sacar **tajada**

to get s.th. out of s.o. sacar el **buche** a alg.; sonsacar algo a alg.

to get up (be bad about ~ting up) pegársele a alg. las **sábanas**

to get up late pisar el **sapo**

getaway (make a quick ~) poner **tierra** por medio

ghastly time (have a ~) pasar las de **Caín**

ghost (go as white as a ~) ponerse más blanco que la **pared**/que una **sábana**

ghostwriter negro [literario] (▷ **el negro**)

giant strides (with ~) a **pasos** agigantados

gift horse (don't look a ~ in the mouth) a **caballo** regalado no hay que mirarle o no le mires el diente

gift of [the] gab (have the ~) tener buenas **explicaderas**/mucha **labia**/buen **pico**

gifted (be a brilliantly ~ mathematician/etc.) nació alg. para [ser] matemático/etc. (▷ **nacer**)

gigantic bestial; cojonudo; garrafal

gills (be drunk to the ~) estar hecho un **cesto**/una **cuba**/un **cuero**/un **pellejo**/una **uva**

girl (good-looking/handsome ~) una buena **moza**

girl (sweet ~) una boquita de **piñón**

girl ([very] pretty ~) un **monumento** [nacional]; una boquita de **piñón**; la **ricura**

girl (young ~) la polla

git el/la gilipollas

to give (you get what you ~) cuál la **pregunta**, tal la respuesta

to give a damn (I don't ~!) ¡tal día hará un **año**!

to give a damn (I don't ~ what other people say/ think) ande yo **caliente** y ríase la gente

to give a damn/shit about s.th./s.o. (not to ~) **cagar**se en algo/alg.

to give a monkey's/a rap/a [tinker's] damn or cuss/ two hoots (not to ~) no importar a alg. un **ardite**; [no] importar a alg. un **bledo**/ **comino/higo/pepino/pimiento/pito/ rábano**; reírse de los peces de colores

to give in **revenir**se; recoger **velas**; darse por vencido (▷ **vencer**)

to give in (not to ~) no dar su **brazo** a torcer

to give in to s.o. llevar el **genio** a alg.

to give nothing away no soltar **prenda**

to give one's all dejarse la **piel**

to give s.o. a beating/a fine/a kick or a slap in the face propinar algo a alg.

to give s.th. up for lost echar la **bendición** a algo

to give up dar con la **carga** en tierra/en el suelo o echarse con la carga; arrojar/tirar la **esponja**; echarse al o en el **surco**; recoger **velas**; darse por vencido (▷ **vencer**)

to give up (don't ~!) ¡paciencia y barajar!

to give up drinking/smoking **quitar**se del alcohol/tabaco

to give up one's profession/the cloth ahorcar/ colgar los **hábitos**

to give way **revenir**se

glad (be terribly ~) la **mar** de

glad rags (be in one's ~) estar de veinticinco **alfileres**; estar **peripuesto**; estar de **pontifical**; estar/ir de **punta** en blanco

glad rags (one's ~) los **trapos**/trapitos de cristianar

glad rags (put on one's ~) ponerse de veinticinco **alfileres**/de **pontifical**/de **punta** en blanco

glance (at a ~) a **ojo** de buen cubero

glass (a ~ is almost empty) un vaso está temblando (▷ **temblar**)

glass (almost empty a ~) dejar un vaso temblando (▷ **temblar**)

glass (be as smooth as ~) balsa de aceite

glass (fill up the ~es) atizar la **lámpara**

glass eye el **ojo** overo

glass houses (people who live in ~ should not throw stones) eso sería tirar **piedra**s a su o sobre el propio tejado

glasses (pebble [lens] ~) gafas de **culo** de vaso/botella

glasses (see everything/things or the world through rose-colored ~) verlo todo de color de **rosa**

glee (fiendish/malicious ~) el gustazo

glimmer of hope el **rayo** de esperanza

glimmer of hope (there is a ~) hay **luz** al final del túnel

to glitter (all that ~s is not gold) no es **oro** todo lo que reluce

to gloat over s.th. **cebar**se en algo

gloomy view (take a ~ of everything) verlo todo con **cristal** ahumado

to be glorious ser un/de **alucine**

glorious (smell/taste ~) oler/saber a **gloria**

glory (send s.o. to ~) mandar a alg. al otro **barrio/mundo**

glove (be hand in ~) comer en un/el o del mismo **plato**; ser **uña** y carne

glove (be hand in ~: be in cahoots) estar del mismo **palo**

glove (fit [s.o.] like a ~) sentar [a alg.] como **anillo** al dedo/que ni **pintado** o como pintado

gloves (handle/treat s.o. with kid ~) guardar/tener a alg. entre algodones (▷ **algodón**); tratar a alg. con **guante** de seda

glutton el/la tragaldabas; el tragantón/la tragantona; el tragón/la tragona; el/la zampabollos/zampatortas

glutton (be a ~) comer más que un **sabañón**

go (▷ going)

go (be always/constantly on the ~) no criar **moho**; estar siempre con un **pie** en el aire; andar/ir al **retortero**

go (have a real ~ at s.o.) poner a alg. como **chupa** de dómine

go (in one ~) de un **tirón**

go (keep s.o. [constantly] on the ~) no dejar criar **moho** a alg.; no dejar **respirar** a alg.; traer a alg. al **retortero**; traer/llevar a alg. como un **zarandillo**

to go (get s.th./s.o. ~ing [again]) poner/sacar algo/a alg. a **flote**

to go (here he/etc. ~es again!) ¡[siempre] la misma **canción/cantilena**!

to go (here we ~!) ¡ahora van a soltar al **toro**!

to go (keep ~ing) mantenerse a **flote**; ir tirando (▷ **tirar**)

to go (not to ~ to s.th.) **fumar**se algo

to go (not to know any more whether one is coming or ~ing) no saber dónde volver la **cabeza**

to go (tell s.o. where to ~) mandar a alg. a freír **buñuelos**/al **cuerno**/a freír **espárragos**/a hacer **gárgaras**/a **paseo**

to go about it very carefully/cautiously/warily andar con **pies** de plomo; ir con mucho **ten** con ten

to go about s.th. the wrong way asir algo por el **rabo**

to go about things slyly/on the quiet **matar**las callando

to go all out [to + infinitive] batirse el **cobre** por + infinitivo; echar el **resto**; **volcar**se

to go along with s.o. hacer **coro** con alg.

to go along with the crowd dejarse llevar de/por la **corriente**

to go at it hammer and tongs luchar a **brazo** partido; a más no **poder**; a todo **vapor**; a toda **vela**

to go down very badly caer/sentar como una **pedrada**

to go fine or [very] smoothly or swimmingly or extremely/very well balsa de aceite; ir que chuta (▷ **chutar**); estar como un **dado**; de **rechupete**; ir/marchar sobre **ruedas**; ir/marchar como una **seda**

to go flat out quemar el **caucho**; a toda **pastilla** (example); hundir el **pedal**; correr/lanzarse a **tumba** abierta; a todo **vapor** (example); a toda **vela**

to go off at a tangent irse por los **cerros** de Úbeda; salir[se]/escapar[se]/irse por la **tangente**

to go off at the deep end subirse al **campanario**/por las **paredes**

to go off on a different tack sacar los **pies** del plato/de las alforjas

to go off smoothly/without a hitch salir algo **corriente** y moliente

to go off well pitar

to go on (know what's going on) estar al **cabo** de algo/de la calle

to go on (miss nothing of what is going on) no perder **ripio**

to go on (there's s.th. fishy going on [here]) [aquí] hay **gallo** tapado/**gato** encerrado

to go on about s.th. machacar [en/sobre] algo

to go on and on (s.th.) ser más largo que una **cuaresma**

to go on and on (talk) hablar más que una **cotorra**; dar **cuerda** (example); hablar más que un **sacamuelas**

to go on forever (nothing goes on forever) no hay **bien** ni mal que cien años dure

to go out for a merry/good time ir de **juerga**; irse de/a **picos** pardos

to go out like a light dormirse o quedarse dormido como un **ceporro/tronco**

to go out of one's way **volcar**se

to go out on the make/pull salir de **levante**

to go out on the town irse de/a **picos** pardos

to go together correr **parejas**/andar de pareja

to **go together** ([just] not to ~) no pegar ni con **cola**; no **pegar**

to **go with** ([just] not to ~) no pegar ni con **cola**; no **pegar**

to **go with** anybody (a woman who will ~) la ligona

to **go with** s.o. salir con alg.

to **go without** quitarse algo de la **boca**

to **go without** saying caerse de/por su propio peso

go-ahead (give s.th. the ~) dar **luz** verde a algo

goal (come close to one's ~ without reaching it) nadar y nadar, y a la orilla ahogar

goal (not to reach one's ~) hacer las diez de últimas (▷ **último**)

goal (pursue one's ~ ruthlessly) no ponérsele a alg. nada por **delante**

goat (get s.o.'s ~) sacar a alg. de sus **casilla**s; poner **negro** a alg.; hacer a alg. subirse por las **pared**es

goat (randy ~) el garañón

goat (randy old ~) el **viejo** verde

goats (separate the sheep from the ~) apartar las **oveja**s de los cabritos

gob (face) la jeta

gob (spittle) el pollo

to **gobble** comer/mascar a dos **carrillo**s; ponerse como el chico del **esquilador**; comer como una **lima**

go-between la trotaconventos

God (if ~ helps me out this time, . . .) si **Dios** de esta me escapa, nunca me cubrirá de tal capa

God (man proposes and ~ disposes) el **hombre** propone y Dios dispone

God (put your trust in ~ and keep your powder dry) a **Dios** rogando y con el mazo dando

God (swear to ~ [that . . .]) jurar por lo más **sagrado** [que . . .]

God helps those who help themselves a **Dios** rogando y con el mazo dando; a quien madruga, Dios le ayuda (▷ **madrugar**)

goddam[n] puto

goddam[n] (that's none of your ~ business!) ¿qué **coño** te importa?

godforsaken place (live/be at a ~) vivir/estar donde **Cristo** dio las tres voces/etc. o donde el **diablo** perdió el poncho; vivir/estar en el quinto **infierno/pino** o en la quinta **puñeta**

godsend (be a [real] ~) venir como **agua** de mayo/como **anillo** al dedo; venir como llovido/llegar como caído del **cielo**; venir que ni **pintado**/como pintado

goggle box (TV) la **caja** boba/idiota/tonta

to be **goggle-eyed** tener **ojo**s de besugo

going (be tough ~) un **parto** difícil (example); traérselas (▷ **traer**)

going-over (give s.o. a [good] ~: hiding) dar **leña** o cargar de leña a alg.; dar un [buen] **recorrido** a alg.

going-over (give s.o. a [good] ~: wigging) dar un [buen] **recorrido** a alg.

gold (all that glitters is not ~) no es **oro** todo lo que reluce

gold (be as good as ~) ser más bueno que el **pan**

gold (be worth one's/its weight in ~) valer alg./algo su peso en **oro** o valer algo tanto oro como pesa; valer alg. un **Perú/Potosí**

gold (have a voice of ~) tener una **garganta** de oro

gold (treasure s.th. [as if it were ~ or ~ dust]) guardar algo como **oro** en paño

gold mine (source of profit) la mina de **oro**; el Perú

goldbrick (sell s.o. a ~) dar a alg. **gato** por liebre

golden calf (worship the ~) adorar el **becerro** de oro

golden eggs (kill the goose that lays ~) matar la **gallina** de los huevos de oro

good de los **bueno**s

good (be as ~ as gold) ser más bueno que el **pan**

good (be just as/every bit as ~ as s.o.) no ir en **zaga** a alg.

good (be no ~ at anything) no dar **pie** con bola

good (be up to no ~) hacer de las **suya**s

good (be very ~) dar la **hora** [y quitar los cuartos]

good (do ~ to all alike) hacer [el] **bien** sin mirar a quién; haz **bien** y no mires a quién

good (for ~) para los **resto**s

good (it's too ~ to last) ya viene/vendrá el tío **Paco** con la rebaja

good (really ~) señor

good heavens! ¡**caracol**es!

good luck! ¡buena **suerte**!

good luck (chance piece of ~) la breva; el **cabe** de pala

good old snog (have a ~) cambiar **baba**s; morrearse; darse el **pico**

good thing (a change is a ~) entre **col** y col, lechuga; **pan** con pan, comida de tontos

good thing (be [almost] too much of a ~) ser **miel** sobre hojuelas; traérselas (▷ **traer**)

good thing (it's a ~ . . .) menos **mal**

good thing (you can have too much of a ~) bueno está lo bueno [pero no lo demasiado]

good time la juerga

good time (have a/go out for a ~) estar/ir de **juerga**; irse de/a **pico**s pardos

good times (nobody can take away the ~ I've/we've had) ¡que me/nos quiten lo bailado! (▷ **bailar**)

goodby[e] (say ~ to s.th.) echar la **bendición** a algo

goodby[e] (without so much as a word of ~) sin decir **agua** va goodby[e] (you can kiss it/that ~!) ¡échale un **galgo**!

good-for-nothing el/la ablandabrevas; el trasto

good-for-nothing layabout (be a ~) sin **oficio** ni beneficio (example)

good-for-nothings who live from/by or make their living from/by robbing/stealing gente de la **garra**

good-looking girl una buena **moza**

good-natured (be very ~) ser un **pedazo** de pan

goodness (thank ~) menos **mal**

goodness' sake (for ~!) ¡por los **clavos** de Cristo/ de una puerta vieja!

goods (sell s.o. a bill of ~) dar a alg. **gato** por liebre

goods and chattels los bártulos/**trasto**s

goody-goody la beata

goof la pifia/plancha

to goof dar una **pifia**, pifiar

goolies (testicles) las **bolas/canicas**; los cataplines; los cojones (▷ **cojón**); los **conejos/huevos**; las **pelotas**; los pistones (▷ **pistón**)

goose (kill the ~ that lays golden eggs) matar la **gallina** de los huevos de oro

goose (s.o. wouldn't say boo to a ~) ser incapaz de matar una **mosca**

goose (what's sauce for the ~ is sauce for the gander) lo que es **bueno** para uno es bueno para el otro

goose bumps/pimples (give s.o. or get ~) ponerle o ponérsele a alg. [la] **carne** de gallina

gooseberry (play ~) hacer/ir de **carabina**

gooseflesh (give s.o. or get ~) ponerle o ponérsele a alg. [la] **carne** de gallina

Gordian knot (cut the ~) cortar el **nudo** gordiano

to gorge o.s. on s.th. ponerse **morado** de algo

gorgeous cañón; de **rechupete**

to gormandize servir al **vientre**

gospel truth (speak the ~) lo que dice alg. es el **evangelio**

gospel truth (what s.o. says is accepted/taken as ~) lo que dice alg. es el **evangelio**

gossip (be the subject of ~) andar alg. de **boca** en boca; andar en **lenguas**; ser **pasto** de algo

gossip ([old] ~) el/la correve[i]dile

to gossip about s.o. traer en **bocas** a alg.; llevar/ traer a alg. en **lenguas**; cortar un **sayo** a alg.; traer y llevar [a alg.]; cortar un **traje** a alg.

to govern s.o.'s [way of] thinking completely sorber los **sesos** a alg.

government (petticoat ~) el **gobierno** de faldas

to grab s.th. echar la **garra/zarpa** a algo

grace[fulness] la sal

gracefully (move ~) la sal (example)

grain (go [totally] against the ~ with s.o. [to + infinitive]) venirle algo a alg. [muy] a

contrapelo; hacérsele algo a alg. [muy] **cuesta** arriba [+ infinitivo]

grain (not a ~ of) ni **sombra** de

grain (separate the ~ from the chaff) apartar/ separar el **grano** de la paja; apartar las **oveja**s de los cabritos

grain of salt (take s.th. with a ~) tomar algo con un **grano** de sal

grand de muchas **campanilla**s

grand scale (live on a ~) vivir como un/a lo **príncipe**

grand style (live in ~) vivir a todo **tren**

grand time (have a ~) divertirse la **mar**; pasar las **vacas** gordas

grandmother (try to teach one's ~ to suck eggs) querer enseñar el **padrenuestro** al cura

granted (take s.th. for ~) dar algo por **sentado**

grapes ([it's] sour ~!) ¡están **verdes**!

to grapple boldly with s.th. acometer algo de **frente**

to grasp it at once cazarlas/cogerlas/pescarlas al **vuelo**

to grasp s.th. (understand) calzar algo

to grasp the nettle coger el **toro** por los cuernos; hacer de **tripa**s corazón

grass (get high on ~) emporrarse

grass (hear the ~ grow) oír/sentir/ver crecer la **hierba**

grass (informer) el **chivato**/la chivata; el/la correve[i]dile; el **soplón**/la soplona

grass (marijuana) el chocolate/ful; la hierba/ mandanga/mierda; el tate; la yerba

grass (not to let the ~ grow under one's feet) no criar **moho**

to grass on s.o. [to s.o.] chivarse contra/de alg. [con/a alg.]

grass widower (be a ~) estar de **rodríguez**

to grate on s.o.'s nerves alterar/crispar los **nervio**s a alg. o poner los nervios de punta a alg.

grave (be [as] quiet/silent as the ~) balsa de aceite; no se siente/oye [ni] una **mosca**; estar mudo como una **tumba** o ser [como] una tumba

grave (dig one's own ~) cavar su propia **tumba**

grave (have one foot in the ~) estar con un pie en el **estribo/hoyo**; tener un pie en la **tumba**

gray (at night all cats are ~) de noche todos los **gato**s son pardos

gray sky la **panza** de burra

to grease s.o.'s palm untar el **carro**/la **mano**/la **palma** a alg.

greased lightning (like ~) a toda **mecha**

great bestial; de **bigote**; cañón; chachi; cojonudo; dabute[n]/dabuti; que quita el **hipo**; de narices (▷ **nariz**); pistonudo; de **rechupete**

to be great ser un/de **alucine**; ser la **biblia**; dar la **hora** [y quitar los cuartos]; estar algo/ alg. **jamón** great (feel really ~) estar como **abeja** en flor; estar/sentirse como el **pez** en el agua

great (that'd be really ~!) ¡no faltaba/faltaría más! (▷ **faltar**)

great (whopping ~) de los **bueno**s (example); de padre y muy señor mío (▷ **el padre**) (example)

great big de los **bueno**s (example); de padre y muy señor mío (▷ **el padre**) (example)

to be great buddies/pals la **mar** de; comer en un/el o del mismo **plato**

great car (whacking ~) el cochazo

great guns (go ~) a las mil **maravilla**s

great hurry/rush (be in a ~) la **mar** de

great job (do a ~) cañón (example)

great time (have a ~) cañón/chachi (examples); dabute[n]/dabuti (example); correrse una **juerga**; divertirse la **mar**; ponerse como un **Pepe**; pasarlo **pipa**; de **rechupete**; pasar las **vaca**s gordas

greatest (think one is the ~) creerse el no va más (▷ **ir**)

greatest thing (be the ~ since sliced bread) ser el no va más (▷ **ir**)

greedy-guts el/la tragaldabas; el tragantón/la tragantona; el tragón/la tragona; el/la zampabollos/zampatortas

Greek (be all ~ to s.o.) ser **chino** algo para alg.

Greek calends (on the ~) en las **Calendas** griegas

green (be still as ~ as a pea) estar aún con la **leche** en los labios; caerse de un **nido**

green (be still very ~) caerse de un **nido**

green bay tree (flourish like the ~) crecer como la **espuma**

green light (give s.th. the ~) dar **luz** verde a algo

to be green with envy **morir**se de envidia; estar **muerto** de envidia; **perecer**se de envidia

green with envy (make s.o. ~) poner los **diente**s largos a alg.

green years la **edad** burral/ingrata/del pavo

greenhorn (be [still] a [real] ~) caérsele a alg. el **moco**

grey (at night all cats are ~) de noche todos los **gato**s son pardos

to grieve over (what the eye doesn't see, the heart doesn't ~) **ojo**s que no ven, corazón que no siente

to grin and bear it aguantar [la] **mecha**; hacer de **tripa**s corazón

to grin like a Cheshire cat sonreír de oreja a oreja

grindstone (keep one's nose to the ~) trabajar como un **buey**; dar el **callo**; romperse el **culo**; echar/sudar la **hiel**; echar los **hígado**s; darse una **jupa**; trabajar como un **negro**; dejarse la **piel**; **pringar**[las]; sudar el **quilo**; **remar**; **reventar**se; echar los riñones (▷ **riñón**); destripar terrones (▷ **terrón**); sudar **tinta**

grindstone (keep s.o.'s nose to the ~) echar/sudar la **hiel** (example); hacerle sudar **tinta** a alg.

grip (have a good ~ on s.th.) tener algo en la **uña**

grip (have s.o. in one's ~) tener a alg. por el **asa**

to gripe about (have/find s.th. to ~) buscar **pelo**s en la sopa/leche o al huevo

grist (carry ~ to one's own mill) llevar el **agua** a su molino

to grope in the dark oír **campana**s y no saber dónde; dar **palo**s de ciego

grotesque face/mask la carantoña

ground (close to the ~) a **flor** de (example)

ground (cut the ~ from under s.o.'s feet) minar el **terreno** a alg.

ground (gain ~) ganar **terreno**

ground (have both/one's feet [firmly] on the ~) tener los **pie**s [bien puestos] en/sobre la tierra

ground (hold/stand one's ~) no dar su **brazo** a torcer; mantenerse/seguir en sus **trece**

ground (lose ~) perder **terreno**

ground (prepare the ~ for s.th.) preparar el **terreno** a algo

ground (suit s.o. down to the ~) de **perla**s

ground level (at ~) a **flor** de (example)

to grouse about (have/find s.th. to ~) buscar **pelo**s en la sopa/leche o al huevo

to grovel echarse por los **suelo**s

to grow fast/quickly dar un **estirón**

grown ([fully] ~) hecho y derecho

grudge la tirria

grudge (bear a ~) tener **sangre** en el ojo

grudge (have a ~ against s.o.) tener a alg. entre **ceja** y ceja; tener **hincha/tirria** a alg.

grumpy (look ~) tener **cara** de pocos amigos

guard (be on one's ~ [against]) estar/andar sobre los **estribo**s; estar en **guardia** [contra]; estar con/tener la **mosca** detrás de la oreja; estar [con] **ojo** avisor; guardar las **vuelta**s

to guard s.th. with one's life guardar algo como **oro** en paño

guess (at a rough ~) a **ojo** de buen cubero

guess (be a lucky ~) sonar la **flauta** [por casualidad]

guesswork (by ~) a **ojo** de buen cubero

to guffaw reír[se] a **carcajada**s

guitar (strum away at the ~) rascar la guitarra

gullet (s.o. sticks in s.o.'s ~) tener a alg. atravesado/entre **ceja** y ceja/sentado en el **estómago**; tener **hincha** a alg.; no poder ver a alg. ni **pintado**/ni en **pintura**

gullet (s.th. sticks in s.o.'s ~) tener algo atravesado; no poder ver algo ni en **pintura**

to be gullible tener buenas **creedera**s; pecar de + adj. (example); tener buenas **tragadera**s

to gum up the works echarlo todo a **rodar**

273

gumption (have ~: courage) tener cojones (▷ **cojón**); tener **hígado**s/**huevo**s/**redaños**; tener riñones (▷ **riñón**)

gumption (intelligence) la cholla; el coco

gun (as a problem solver) el quitapenas

gun (hold a ~ to s.o.'s head) poner el **puñal** en el pecho a alg.

gun (jump the ~) madrugar

guns (go great ~) a las mil **maravilla**s

guns (spike s.o.'s ~) echar a **rodar** los proyectos de alg.

guns (stick to one's ~) tener **bigote**/tres pares de bigotes; mantenerse/seguir en sus **trece**

to gush (the words come ~ing out) hablar a borbotones/borbollones (▷ **borbotón/ borbollón**)

gut (bust a ~) batir[se] el **cobre**

guts (hate s.o.'s ~) no poder ver a alg. ni en **pintura**

guts (have ~) tener cojones (▷ **cojón**); tener **hígado**s/**huevo**s/**redaños**; tener riñones (▷ **riñón**)

guts (have s.o.'s ~ for garters) **comer**[se] a alg. vivo

guts (slog/sweat one's ~ out) trabajar como un **buey**; dar el **callo**; romperse el **culo**; echar/sudar la **hiel**; echar los **hígado**s; darse una **jupa**; trabajar como un **negro**; dejarse la **piel**; **pringar**[las]; sudar el **quilo**; remar; **reventar**se; echar los riñones (▷ **riñón**); destripar terrones (▷ **terrón**); sudar **tinta**

guts (spew one's ~ out) echar las **entraña**s; arrojar hasta los **hueso**s; echar las **tripa**s

gutter newspaper el **periódico** amarillo

gutter press la **prensa** amarilla o del corazón

guttersnipe el granuja

guy (be a wise ~) más que **siete**

guy (be some ~) ser hombre de pelo en **pecho**

guy (fall ~) un[a] **cabeza** de turco

guy (the ~ with the beard) el barbas

guy (tough ~) el gallito

to guzzle apiparse

guzzler el tragantón/la tragantona; el tragón/ la tragona

H

habit (fall into the [bad] ~ of + gerund) dar en la **flor/tecla** de + infinitivo

habit (man is a creature/slave of ~) la costumbre es otra/segunda **naturaleza**

hack writer el cagatintas/chupatintas

hag (old ~) la tarasca

hag (painted ~) la carantoña

hair (blush to the roots of one's ~) ponerse de mil **color**es

hair (by a ~'s breadth) por un **pelo**/los pelos

hair (escape by a ~'s breadth) salvarse en una **tabla**

hair (hang or be hanging by a ~) colgar/pender o estar colgado/pendiente de un **cabello/ hilo**

hair (have/try a ~ of the dog [that bit you]) la resaca (example)

hair (keep your ~ on!) ¡para el **carro**!; ¡echa el **freno**, Ma[g]daleno!

hair (let one's ~ down) echar una **cana** al aire

hair (make s.o.'s ~ curl) ponerle o ponérsele a alg. los **pelos** de punta

hair (make s.o.'s ~ stand on end/s.o.'s ~ stands on end) ponerle o ponérsele a alg. los **pelos** de punta

hair (not to harm/hurt a ~ on s.o.'s head) no tocar un **pelo** [de la ropa] a alg.

hair (not to see hide nor ~ of s.o.) no ver el **pelo** a alg.

hair (not to turn a ~) quedarse/estar tan **campante/fresco/pancho**

hair (tear one's ~ [out]) dar con la **cabeza** en las paredes; **rasgar**se las vestiduras

hairs (not to split ~) no pararse en **pelillos**

hairs (split ~) discusiones bizantinas (▷ **bizantino**) (example); partir/hender un **cabello** en el aire; hilar delgado/muy fino; pararse en **pelillos**; buscar cinco/tres **pies** al gato

hairy face ([old] ~: person) el barbas

half (be too clever by ~) cortar un **pelo** en el aire

half (do things by halves) aplicar **paños** calientes

half (have got ~ out of the way/over [and done] with) pasar el **ecuador**

half (my better ~) mi [cara] **costilla**; mi media **naranja**

half (not ~: as intensifier) tener mucho **copete** (example); ser más largo que una **cuaresma**; ser más **largo** que un día sin pan; hacer un frío que pela (▷ **pelar**); de **perros**; darse **tono** (example)

half (not to do things by halves) no andarse con **paños** calientes

half (take a bashing and a ~) de padre y muy señor mío (▷ **el padre**) (example)

half an eye (you can see that with ~) lo ve un **ciego**

half measures (do things in ~/take ~) aplicar **paños** calientes

half measures (not to do things in ~/not to go in for ~) no andarse con **paños** calientes

to be half-dead with fear/fright **morir**se de miedo; estar **muerto** de miedo

half-joking[ly], half-serious[ly] entre **bromas** y veras

to be half-seas over estar a medios **pelos**; estar entre dos **velas**

to be halfway through [it] pasar el **ecuador**

halfwit el pasmarote

ham [actor] el maleta

hammer and tongs (go at it ~) luchar a **brazo** partido; a más no **poder**; a todo **vapor**; a toda **vela**

hand (▷ hands)

hand la pata/pezuña

hand (be a dab ~ at s.th.) **pintar**se uno solo/ pintárselas solo para algo

hand ([be able] to do s.th. with one ~ tied behind one's back) [poder/saber] hacer algo con los **ojos** cerrados

hand (be an old ~) ser [un] toro **corrido**/[una] liebre corrida; ser [un] **perro** viejo

hand (be on ~ [to help s.o.]) estar al **quite**

hand (catch s.o. with his ~ in the cookie jar) coger a alg. con las manos en la **masa**

hand (give s.o. a helping ~) echar un **cable** a alg.

hand (know s.th. like the back of one's ~) de **cabo** a cabo/rabo o de punta a cabo; conocer algo al **dedillo**/como la **palma** de la mano; de **pe** a pa

hand (not to do a ~'s turn) no dar **golpe**

hand (s.o. can't see his ~ in front of his face) no ver tres en un **burro**

hand (s.o. who can turn his ~ to anything) servir lo mismo para un **barrido** que para un fregado

hand (steady ~) el **pulso** firme

hand (take a ~ in a matter) tomar **cartas** en un asunto

hand (throw in one's ~) echar la **soga** tras el caldero

hand in glove (be ~) comer en un/el o del mismo **plato**; ser **uña** y carne

hand in glove (be ~: be in cahoots) estar del mismo **palo**

275

hand in hand (go ~) correr **pareja**s/andar de pareja

hand over fist (make money ~) **hinchar**se de plata/dinero

hand to mouth (it's just enough to live from ~) [lo] **comido** por [lo] servido

handful (this child is a real ~) este niño es de **abrigo**

handful of people (only a ~) cuatro **gato**s

handle (drive the sword/etc. up to its ~ into s.th.) meter la espada/etc. hasta la **cruz** en algo

handle (fly off the ~) ponerse como un **basilisco**; exaltársele a alg. la **bilis**; subirse al **campanario**; salirse de sus **casilla**s; ponerse hecho un **demonio**; perder los **estribo**s; hinchársele a alg. las narices (▷ **nariz**); subirse por las **pared**es/a la **parra**

handle ([tend to] fly off the ~) a **flor** de piel; no poder con el **genio**

to handle s.o. (know [very well] how to ~) tener [mucha] **mano** izquierda con alg.; coger las **vuelta**s a alg.

to handle s.o. with kid gloves guardar/tener a alg. entre algodones (▷ **algodón**); tratar a alg. con **guante** de seda

handles to one's name **perejil**es

handrail el quitamiedos

hands (be a puppet in the ~ of s.o.) ser un **juguete** en manos de alg.

hands (be free with one's ~) ser **largo** de manos; tener las **mano**s largas

hands (be putty in s.o.'s ~) ser **juguete** de los caprichos de alg.

hands (change ~) mudar de **mano**s

hands (get one's ~ on s.th.) echar la **zarpa** a algo

hands (have a lot of work on one's ~) haber **tela** que cortar/para rato

hands (have talented/artistic/skillful ~) tener **manita**s de plata/oro

hands (have two left ~) ser un **manaza**s

hands (play into s.o.'s ~) hacer el **caldo** gordo a alg.

hands (put one's ~ on one's hips) ponerse en **jarra**s

hands (rub one's ~) chuparse los **dedo**s [por algo]

hands (sit on one's ~) estar/quedarse con los **brazo**s cruzados; no dar **golpe**

hands (steal anything one can get one's ~ on) ser más ladrón que una **urraca**

hands (s.th./it is in good ~) en buenas manos está el **pandero**

hands (throw one's ~ in the air) llevarse las manos a la **cabeza**

hands (throw up one's ~ [in horror]) llevarse las manos a la **cabeza**; **rasgar**se las vestiduras

hands (wash one's ~ of it) lavarse las **mano**s [en inocencia]; sacudirse las **pulga**s

handsome (be anything but ~) pecar de + adj. (example)

handsome (not to be exactly what you might call ~) pecar de + adj. (example)

handsome girl una buena **moza**

handstand (do a ~) hacer el **pino**

handy (come in very ~) venir de **perilla**[s]; de **perla**s

handyman (be a/the ~) servir lo mismo para un **barrido** que para un fregado

hang (get the ~ of it/s.th.) captar la **onda**; coger el **tranquillo** a algo

hang (have got the ~ of it/s.th.) entender/conocer la **aguja** de marear; tener algo en la **uña**

to hang about (keep s.o. ~ing about) dar **poste** a alg.

to hang on s.o.'s every word/on s.o.'s lips estar **colgado** de las palabras de alg.; estar pendiente de los **labio**s de alg.; beberle a alg. las **palabra**s

to hang or be hanging by a hair/thread colgar/pender o estar colgado/pendiente de un **cabello/hilo**

hangover (after drinking) la goma/resaca

hangover (sleep off a ~) desollar/dormir el **lobo**; dormir la **mona**/el **vino**

haphazardly a tontas y a locas (▷ **tonto**)

to happen (act as if nothing had ~ed) quedarse/ estar tan **campante/fresco/pancho**

to happen (fancy that ~ing at his/etc. age!) a la **vejez**, viruelas

to happen (it had to/was bound to ~!) ¡ciertos son los **toros**!

to happen (things often ~ when you least expect them to) donde/cuando menos se piensa, salta la **liebre**

to happen (whatever ~s) salga el **sol** por Antequera/por donde quiera; a todo **trance**

to happen every day ser el **pan** [nuestro] de cada día

happy (be as ~ as a clam/as a sandboy/as a lark/as Larry) estar [alegre] como unas **castañuela**s; estar [contento] como o más contento que unas pascuas (▷ **Pascua**)

happy (be terribly ~) la **mar** de

to harass s.o. hacer la **pascua** a alg.; poner a alg. en el **potro**

hard (find s.th. [very] ~ [to + infinitive]) hacérsele algo a alg. [muy] **cuesta** arriba [+ infinitivo]

hard (swallow ~) tragar **saliva**

hard (work ~ for s.th.) ganar[se] algo a **pulso**

hard job (have a ~ getting s.o. to understand s.th.) meter algo a alg. con **cuchara**

hard nut to crack (be a ~) ser un **hueso** duro de roer; ser [un huevo] duro de **pelar**

hard nut to crack (find s.th. a ~) pinchar/dar en **hueso**

hard nut to crack (give s.o. a ~) darle a alg. un **hueso** duro de roer

hard time (give s.o. a ~) tratar a alg. a **baquetazo** limpio

hard time (have a ~) pasar un **trago** amargo

hard time (have a [very] ~ [+ gerund]) hacérsele algo a alg. [muy] **cuesta** arriba [+ infinitivo]

to be hard up estar/andar **mal** de algo (example)

hard way (get s.th. the ~) ganar[se] algo a **pulso**

hard way (learn the ~) escarmentar

to be hardened estar curado de **espanto**

hardened (become ~) criar **callos**

hardened boozer (be a ~) ser un borracho **perdido**

hardly a duras **penas**

hard-on el remo

hard-on (get a ~) empalmarse

hard-working (be very ~) ser una **hormiga**

hare (run with the ~ and hunt with the hounds) comer a dos **carrillos**; servir a **Dios** y al diablo

to harm (not to ~ a hair on s.o.'s head) no tocar un **pelo** [de la ropa] a alg.

harness (die in ~) morir con las **botas** puestas/al **pie** del cañón

to harp on [about] s.th. machacar [en/sobre] algo; revolcarse en algo

to harp on the same old theme every time sonar como un disco **rayado**

Harry (every Tom, Dick and ~) todo **bicho** viviente; Cristo y la madre/todo Cristo; todo/cada **quisque**

harshly (treat s.o. ~) tratar a alg. a **baquetazo** limpio

has-been una antigualla

hash (make a ~ of s.th./things) hacer un **pan** como unas hostias

hash (marijuana) el chocolate/ful; la hierba/mandanga/mierda; el tate; la yerba

haste (more ~, less speed!) vísteme despacio, que estoy de prisa/que tengo prisa (▷ **vestir**)

hat (be old ~) ser **periódico** de ayer; ser del tiempo del **rey** que rabió/del rey Wamba

hat (I'll eat my ~ if . . .) soy **Napoleón** si ...

hat (keep s.th. under one's ~) coserse la **boca**

hat (old ~) una antigualla

hat (pull s.th. out of a/the ~) traer algo en/por la **manga**; sacarse algo de la **manga**

hat (s.o. can't keep s.th. under his ~) no caberle algo a alg. en el **pecho**

hat (talk through one's ~) sin **ton** ni son (example)

hatch (batten down the ~es) atrancar las **escotillas**

hatch (down the ~!) ¡hasta verte, **Cristo/Jesús** mío!

to be hatched [out] **cocer**se

hatchet (bury the ~) enterrar el **hacha** de guerra; echar **pelillos** a la mar

hatchet (take up the ~) desenterrar el **hacha** de guerra

to hate s.o.'s guts no poder ver a alg. ni en **pintura**

hatter (be as mad as a ~) estar más loco que una **cabra**; estar/ser **loco** de atar/remate; estar como una **regadera**

hatter (mad ~'s tea party) la **olla** de grillos

to be haughty tener mucho **copete**

haul (make a ~) hacer su **agosto**; ponerse las **botas**; sacar **raja/tajada**

haul (make a big ~) coger una buena **redada**

to haul s.o. over the coals soltar la/una **andanada** a alg.; zurrar la **badana**/dar una **calada** a alg.; poner a alg. como un **trapo**

to have (let s.o. ~ it) zurrar la **badana** o menear/sacudir el **bulto** a alg.; arrimar **candela**/dar **caña**/medir las **costillas**/sentar las **costuras** a alg.; dar **leña** o cargar de leña a alg.; cascarle/machacarle a alg. las **liendres**; sacudir el **polvo** a alg.; poner a alg. como un **pulpo**

to have had it estar algo para el **arrastre**

to have had it up to here with s.th. estar hasta las **cejas**/el **coco**/el **cogote**/[más allá de] la **coronilla** de algo; estar **frito** de algo; estar hasta el **gorro**/el **moño**/las narices (▷ **nariz**)/la **punta** de los pelos o del pelo/los **topes** de algo

to have had just about all one can take colmar la medida

to have had one over the eight estar hecho un **cesto**/una **cuba**/un **cuero**/un **pellejo**/una **uva**

to have had one too many hacérsele a alg. **candelillas** los ojos; estar hecho un **cesto**/una **cuba**/un **cuero**/un **pellejo**/una **uva**

to have it in for s.o. buscar el **bulto** a alg.; tenérsela jurada a alg. (▷ **jurar**); tener/traer a alg. entre **ojos**; tenerla tomado con alg. (▷ **tomar**)

to have it off/away [with s.o.] pasar a una por las **armas**; **calzar**[se]/**cargar**se a alg.; echar un **casquete**; **cepillar**[se] a una; poner un **clavo** a una; follar/joder [a alg.]; pasar a una mujer por la **piedra**; pisar a alg.; echar un **polvo**; quilar [a alg.]; regar/tapar/**tirar**se/tumbar/**zumbar**se a una mujer

to have s.o. on dar [el] **camelo** a alg.; tomarle el **pelo** a alg.; quedarse con alg.

hawk (have eyes like a ~) tener **ojos** de águila/lince

hay (hit the ~) irse a la/echarse en la **petaca**/**piltra**; tender la **raspa**; hacer la **rosca** [de galgo]

hay (make ~ while the sun shines) al **hierro** caliente batir de repente head (you have to make ~ while the sun shines) a la **ocasión** la pintan calva

haystack (look for a needle in a ~) buscar una **aguja** en un pajar

head (▷ bean; bonce; conk; noddle; nut; onion) el casco; la crisma

head (a still tongue makes a wise ~) es de sabios el callar (▷ **el sabio**)

head (bang one's ~ on s.th.) dar de narices contra algo (▷ **nariz**)

head (bash s.o.'s ~ in) romper los **casco**s/la **crisma** a alg.

head ([be able] to do s.th. standing on one's ~) [poder/saber] hacer algo con los **ojos** cerrados

head (be above s.o.'s ~) ser **chino** algo para alg.

head (be like a bear with a sore ~) de **perro**s

head (be off one's ~) estar mal de la **azotea**; no estar bueno de la **cabeza** o estar ido/mal/tocado de la cabeza o tener pájaros en la cabeza; estar como una **cabra/cafetera**; estar [loco] como un **cencerro**; estar **chalado**; estar mal de la **chaveta**; estar **chiflado**

head (be out of one's ~: be drunk) estar hecho un **cesto**; estar hecho una **cuba**/un **cuero**; tener un **globo** [impresionante]; estar/andar **pedo**; estar hecho un **pellejo**/una **uva**

head (be out of one's ~: be on drugs) tener un **globo** [impresionante]; estar/andar **pedo**; estar de **viaje**

head (be soft in the ~) estar mal de la **azotea**; no estar bueno de la **cabeza** o estar ido/mal/tocado de la cabeza o tener pájaros en la cabeza; estar como una **cabra/cafetera**; estar [loco] como un **cencerro**; estar **chalado**; estar mal de la **chaveta**; estar **chiflado**; tener la cabeza llena de **serrín**

head (be taller than s.o. by a ~) llevar a alg. la cabeza

head (bite s.o.'s ~ off) la bronca (example)

head (blow one's/s.o.'s ~ off) levantarse la **tapa** de los sesos; levantarle a alg. la **tapa** de los sesos

head (bury one's ~ in the sand) esconder/meter la **cabeza** bajo el ala

head (crack one's ~ open) romperse la **crisma**

head (drum s.th. into s.o.'s ~) machacar algo a alg.

head (fill s.o.'s ~ [with s.th.]) calentar la **cabeza** a alg.

head (give s.o. ~) hacerle una **mamada** a alg.

head (give s.o. his ~) llevar/seguir la **corriente** a alg.; llevar el **genio** a alg.

head (have eyes in the back of one's ~) tener **ojos** en la nuca

head (have nothing but sawdust in one's ~) tener la cabeza llena de **serrín**

head (have one's ~ buried in one's work) no levantar/alzar **cabeza**

head (have one's ~ in the clouds) estar en **Babia**/en las **Batuecas**/en **Belén**/en la **higuera**; estar/vivir en la **luna**; andar por o estar/vivir en las **nube**s; mirar las **telarañas**

head (have one's ~ screwed on [tight]) tener la **cabeza** en su sitio/bien puesta

head (have rocks in one's ~) faltarle a alg. un **tornillo**/tener flojos los tornillos; tener una **tuerca** floja

head (hold a gun/pistol to s.o.'s ~) poner el **puñal** en el pecho a alg.

head (keep one's ~ above water) mantenerse a **flote**; ir tirando (▷ **tirar**)

head (keep one's ~ down) no levantar/alzar **cabeza**

head (knock s.th. on the ~) echar algo al o por el **suelo**

head (laugh one's ~ off) como un **descosido** (example); reír[se] a **mandíbula** batiente

head (lose one's ~) perder los **estribo**s/la **tramontana**

head (lose one's ~ over s.o.) perder la **chaveta** por alg.

head (make s.o.'s ~ spin) calentar la **cabeza** a alg.

head (not to have [got] eyes in one's ~) tener **telarañas** en los ojos

head (on his [own] ~ be it!) arreglárselas (▷ **arreglar**) (example); componérselas (▷ **componer**) (example)

head (out of one's ~: on drugs) emporrado

head (put a bullet through s.o.'s/one's ~) pasaportear a alg.; levantarle a alg. la **tapa** de los sesos; levantarse la **tapa** de los sesos

head (put ideas into s.o.'s ~) echarle a alg. la **pulga** detrás de la oreja

head (put one's ~ in the lion's mouth) meterse en la **boca** del lobo

head (shake one's ~) negar con la **cabeza**

head (shriek/shout one's ~ off) como un **descosido** (example); desgañifarse; desgañitarse

head (smash s.o.'s ~ in) romper el **bautismo**/los **casco**s a alg.; quitar los **hocico**s a alg.

head (s.o.'s ~ is/starts spinning) calentarse la **cabeza**; cocérsele a alg. los sesos (▷ **cocer**); tener la cabeza como una **olla** de grillos

head (stand on one's ~) hacer el **pino**

head (s.th. goes round and round in s.o.'s ~) bailarle algo a alg. por la **cabeza**

head (s.th. goes to s.o.'s ~) subírsele algo a alg. a la **cabeza**

head (talk one's ~ off) hablar por los **codo**s

head (tremble from ~ to foot) temblarle a alg. las **carne**s head (turn one's ~ the other way) hacer la vista gorda (▷ **gordo**)

head (turn s.o.'s ~) hacer perder el **seso** a alg.

to be head and shoulders above s.o. **comer**se a alg. crudo; dar **quince** y raya/falta a alg.; dar cien **vuelta**s a alg.

to be head over heels in love (a woman/man who is ~) la tórtola; el tórtolo

to be head over heels in love [with s.o.] estar **perdido** por alg.; estar enamorado hasta los **tuétano**s

to be heading for a disaster abocar a

head[s] or tail[s] (make ~ of it) atar/unir **cabo**s

head[s] or tail[s] (s.o. can't make ~ of s.th.) no tener **cabo** ni cuerda/**pie**s ni cabeza

headache (have a throbbing ~) tener la cabeza a las **once**

headlines (hit/make the ~) saltar a las primeras **página**s

headlong (fall ~) caerse/dar de narices [en/contra el suelo] (▷ **nariz**); besar la **tierra**

headstand (do a ~) hacer el **pino**

to be headstrong ser de dura **cerviz**

health (be bursting/brimming with ~) rebosar de salud; vender/prestar **salud**

health (be/look a picture of ~) estar como una **lechuga**; vender/prestar **salud**

health (drink to the ~ of s.o.) beber a la **salud** de alg.

health (here's to ~, wealth and love) ¡salud, amor y pesetas!

health (recover one's ~) levantar/alzar **cabeza**

heap (be struck all of a ~) quedarse de una **pieza**

heap (collapse/fall in a ~) caerse redondo

heap (strike s.o. all of a ~) dejar a alg. de una **pieza**

heap of metal (old ~: car) la antigualla; la **cafetera** [rusa]

to heap abuse on s.o. poner a alg. como un **Cristo**

to heap insults on s.o. poner a alg. de **oro** y azul

to heap praise on s.o. poner a alg. en/por o levantar a alg. a/hasta los **cuerno**s de la luna; levantar a alg. hasta o poner a alg. por las **nube**s

to heap s.th. (honors/etc.) on s.o. colmar a alg. de algo; prodigar algo a alg.

heaps of a **cántaro**s; hasta la **pared** de enfrente; a **pote**; a **punta** pala

heaps of money (have ~) la **mar** de

to hear (be careful what you say, we can be ~d!) ¡hay **ropa** tendida!

to hear (have ~d s.th./noises to that effect) oír **campana**s y no saber dónde

to hear (have never ~d of it) no haberlas visto [nunca] más gordas (▷ **ver**)

to hear (I think I've ~d that one before) me suena a **música** de caballitos

to hear (pretend not to ~) hacerse el **sueco**

to hear (pretend not to have ~d anything [about it]) hacerse de **nueva**s

to hear a pin drop no se siente/oye [ni] una **mosca** (example); poder oír volar una **mosca**

to hear the grass grow oír/sentir/ver crecer la **hierba**

heart (a full stomach makes for a happy ~) barriga llena, corazón contento

heart (break s.o.'s ~) partírsele a alg. el **alma**

heart (cross my ~ and hope to die) jurar por lo más **sagrado** [que ...] (example)

heart (eat and drink to one's ~'s content) a todo **pasto**

heart (have no ~) tener **pelo**s en el corazón

heart (have one's ~ in one's mouth) tener el **alma** en un hilo

heart (lose ~) caérsele a alg. las **ala**s [del corazón]

heart (pour one's ~ out to s.o.) descubrir/abrir el **pecho** a alg.; contar su **película** a alg.

heart (sob one's ~ out) llorar a **lágrima** viva/como una **Magdalena**; llorar a **moco** tendido/a moco y baba

heart (s.o.'s ~ falls/sinks) caérsele a alg. las **ala**s [del corazón]

heart (s.o.'s ~ is in the right place) tener el **corazón** en su sitio o bien puesto

heart (s.o.'s ~ sinks [into his boots]) caérsele a alg. el **alma** a los pies; caérsele a alg. los palos del **sombrajo**

heart (s.o.'s ~'s in his work) poner sus cinco **sentido**s en algo (example)

heart (take ~) sacar **fuerza**s de flaqueza

heart (take s.th. to ~) tomar algo a **pecho**[s]; no echar algo en **saco** roto

heart (to one's ~'s content) a pedir de **boca**; a todo **pasto**

heart (what the eye doesn't see, the ~ doesn't grieve over) **ojos** que no ven, corazón que no siente

heart (when the ~ is full, it's the mouth that overflows) de la **abundancia** del corazón habla la boca

to be heartbroken partírsele a alg. el **alma**

heartily (eat ~) tener buen **saque**

heat (intense ~) la quemazón

heat (police) la bofia/madera/poli/polilla

heat (be an unbearable ~) traérselas (▷ **traer**)

heat (nearly die in the ~/be dying of the ~) abrasarse de calor; **asar**se vivo

heat (what a sweltering/stifling ~!) ¡qué **horno**!

heaven (be in seventh ~) estar en el séptimo/quinto **cielo**; estar en su[s] **gloria**[s]

heaven (be sure to go to ~) irse al cielo vestido y calzado (▷ **vestir**)

heaven (cry out to ~) clamar al cielo

heaven (for ~'s sake!) ¡por los **clavo**s de Cristo/de una puerta vieja!

heaven (good ~s!) ¡caracoles!

heaven (stink to high ~) clamar al cielo

heaven (the floodgates of ~ open) a **cántaros** (example); llover a **chorros/cubos/mares/ torrentes**

heaven and earth (move ~ [to + infintive]) poner toda la **carne** en el asador; [re]mover **cielo** y tierra [para + infinitivo]

heaven only knows! ¡averígüelo **Vargas**!

to be heavenly ser un/de **alucine**; ser **canela** fina

heavenly (smell/taste ~) oler/saber a **gloria**

heavenly wine (be [a] ~) ser un **vino** de dos orejas

heavy (be damn[ed] ~) como el/un **diablo**

heavy drinker (be a ~) beber como una **esponja**; a **pote** (example)

to hedge one's bets [nadar y] guardar la ropa

heebie-jeebies (give s.o. or get the ~) ponerle o ponérsele a alg. [la] **carne** de gallina/los **pelos** de punta

heebie-jeebies (have the ~) tener un **tembleque**

to heed s.th. no echar algo en **saco** roto

heel (hole in the ~: sock/stocking) el tomate

heeled (be well ~) estar **forrado**; tener el **riñón** bien cubierto

heels (be [hot/hard] on s.o.'s ~) pisar los talones a alg. (▷ **talón**)

heels (cool/kick one's ~) estar en/sobre **ascuas**; estar [como] en **brasas**

heels (dog s.o.'s ~) pisar los talones a alg. (▷ **talón**)

heels (show a clean pair of ~) mostrar/levantar los talones (▷ **talón**)

heels (stick [hard] on s.o.'s ~) pegarse a los talones de alg. (▷ **talón**)

heels (take to one's ~) apretar las **calzaderas**; tomar la del **humo**; poner **pies** en polvorosa; salir por **piernas**; mostrar/ levantar los talones (▷ **talón**); tocárselas (▷ **tocar**); tomar/coger las de **Villadiego**; darle al **zancajo**

height of cheek (be the ~) pasar de **castaño** oscuro; pelar la jeta

hell las **caldera**s de Pe[d]ro Botero

to be hell ser un **calvario**

hell (all ~ broke loose) armar la de **San Quintín** (example)

hell (all ~ is let loose) hay **toros** y cañas

hell (be as ugly as ~) ser un **aborto** del diablo; ser el acabóse de feo (▷ **acabar**); ser más feo que **Carracuca**; ser más **feo** que Picio/ que el pecado/etc.; a más no **poder**; dar un **susto** al miedo

hell (be one ~ of a job [to + infinitive]) costar un **huevo** [+ infinitivo]

hell (come ~ or high water) contra **viento** y marea

hell (go through ~) pasar las de **Caín**; pasar las **penas** del purgatorio

hell (go to ~: and you can go to ~!) ¡y tú que te pudras! (▷ **pudrirse**)

hell (go to ~: he/she/etc. can go to ~!) ¡que el **diablo** cargue con él/etc.!; ¡que se pudra! (▷ **pudrirse**); ¡que mal **rayo** le/etc. parta!

hell (go to ~: go to ~!) ¡anda a **bañarte**!; ¡vete a freír **buñuelos**/al **coño**/a freír **espárragos**/ a espulgar un **galgo**!; ¡que te den **morcilla**!; ¡vete a **paseo**/a la **porra**/a la **puñeta**!

hell (go to ~: tell s.o. to go to ~) mandar a alg. a freír **buñuelos**/al **cuerno**/al **demonio**/al **diablo**/a freír **espárragos**/a hacer **gárgaras**/al **infierno**/a la **mierda**/a capar **moscas**/a **paseo**/a hacer la **puñeta**

hell (hurt like ~) como el/un **diablo**

hell (make life ~ for s.o.) llevar/traer a alg. por la **calle** de la amargura; matar a alg. a **fuego** lento

hell (raise ~) armar la de **Dios** es Cristo/la de **San Quintín**

hell (run like ~) ir como **alma** que se lleva el diablo; como el/un **diablo**; a más no **poder**

hell (till ~ freezes over!) ¡hasta que/cuando meen las **gallinas**!; ¡hasta que/cuando las **ranas** críen pelo!

hell (to ~ with everybody else or with work/etc.!) ¡viva la **Pepa**!

hell (to ~ with s.th./s.o.!) **cagar**se en algo/alg. (example); **ciscar**se en algo (example)

hell (what the ~ are you/etc. doing here or up to here?) ¿qué **demonios** estás/etc. haciendo aquí?; ¿qué diablo te pintas tú/etc. por aquí? (▷ **pintar**); ¿qué **puñeta**s estás/etc. haciendo aquí?

hell (why the ~ does it matter to you?) ¿qué **coño** te importa?

hell for leather (run ~) ir como **alma** que se lleva el diablo; a más no **poder**

help (ask s.o. for ~) llamar a la **puerta** de alg.

help (need a lot of ~) necesitar **Dios** y [su] ayuda

help (there's no ~ for it) no hay [más] **remedio**

help (without [any] outside ~) a **cuerpo** gentil

to help (be on hand to ~ s.o.) estar al **quite**

to help (every little ~s) un **grano** no hace granero pero ayuda al compañero

to help (God helps those who ~ themselves) a **Dios** rogando y con el mazo dando; a quien madruga, Dios le ayuda (▷ **madrugar**)

to help (it can't be ~ed) no hay [más] **remedio**

helpful soul (be a ~) ser un **paño** de lágrimas

helping hand (give s.o. a ~) echar un **cable** a alg.

henpecked husband Juan Lanas

Hercules (labor of ~) ser **obra** de romanos

herd (the entire ~: people) el ganado

here (have had it up to ~ with s.th.) estar hasta las **cejas**/el **coco**/el **cogote**/[más allá de] la **coronilla** de algo; estar **frito** de algo; estar

hasta el **gorro**/el **moño**/las narices
(▷ **nariz**)/la **punta** de los pelos o del pelo/
los **tope**s de algo
here (neither ~ nor anywhere) ni aquí/acá ni en
la **China**
here you are! ¡toma! (▷ **tomar**)
hereafter (the ~) la eterna **morada**; la otra **orilla**
here's to health, wealth and love! ¡salud, amor y
pesetas!
here's to you! ¡salud!
hermit (become a ~) **enterrar**se en vida
heroin (snow/stuff) la blanca; el polvo
herring (red ~) la **pista** falsa
hick el rapaterrones
hide (tan s.o.'s ~) zurrar la **badana** o menear/
sacudir el **bulto** a alg.; arrimar **candela**/dar
caña/medir las **costillas**/sentar las
costuras a alg.; dar **leña** o cargar de leña a
alg.; cascarle/machacarle a alg. las
liendres; sacudir el **polvo** a alg.; poner a
alg. como un **pulpo**
hide (not to see ~ nor hair of s.o.) no ver el **pelo** a
alg.
hiding (get a ~) ganársela (▷ **ganar**)
hiding (give s.o. a ~) zurrar la **badana** o menear/
sacudir el **bulto** a alg.; arrimar **candela**/dar
caña/medir las **costillas**/sentar las
costuras a alg.; dar **leña** o cargar de leña a
alg.; cascarle/machacarle a alg. las
liendres; ponerle a alg. la cara nueva
(▷ **nuevo**); sacudir el **polvo** a alg.; poner a
alg. como un **pulpo**; dar [una] **soba** a alg.;
tocar la/dar una **solfa** a alg.; poner a alg.
el culo como un **tomate**; pegar una
tunda/dar una **vuelta**/menear el **zarzo**/dar
una **zurra** a alg.
hiding (good ~) la manta
high (aim ~[er]) hasta los **gatos** quieren
zapatos; picar [más] alto
high (get ~ on grass) emporrarse
high (make s.o. ~) poner a alg. en **órbita**
high (on drugs) emporrado
to be high (on drugs) tener un **globo**; estar en
onda; estar/andar **pedo**; estar de **viaje**
to be high as a kite/as the sky (drunk/on drugs)
tener un **globo** impresionante
high and dry (be left ~) quedarse en la
estacada/a la **luna** de Valencia
high and dry (leave s.o. ~) dejar a alg. en las
astas del toro; dejar a alg. **colgado**/
empantanado; dejar a alg. en la **estaca**da/
a la **luna** de Valencia; plantar o dejar
plantado a alg.
high and low (search ~) buscar con un **candil**
high and mighty (act ~) darse **aire**s de grandeza;
pintar la **cigüeña**
high and mighty (become [very] ~) subírsele a
alg. los **humo**s a la cabeza

high circles (move in ~) codearse con los de
arriba
high horse (be on one's ~) tener muchas **ínfula**s
high horse (get on one's ~) darse **ínfula**s
high jinks (have ~) pasarlo **pipa**
high on the hog (live ~) vivir a todo **tren**
high post (give/get s.o. a ~) poner a alg. en [el]
candelero
high spirits (be in ~) estar [alegre] como unas
castañuelas
to be high up estar alg. en [el] **candelero**
high-class de muchas **campanilla**s
hike (take a ~!) ¡anda a **bañar**te!; ¡vete a freír
buñuelos/**espárrago**s!
to be hilariously funny descacharrante; ser para
morirse de risa
hill (be over the ~) estar alg. para el **arrastre**
hills (be as old as the ~) ser más viejo que
Carracuca/que la **sarna**
hilt (back s.o. up to the ~) **volcar**se (example)
hilt (stab the knife up to the ~ into s.th.) meter el
cuchillo hasta las **cacha**s en algo
hindmost (devil take the ~) ¡el que venga detrás,
que arree! (▷ **arrear**); el último **mono** es el
que se ahoga
hint (drop a ~ to s.o.) tirar a alg. de la **capa**
to be hip [to s.th.] estar en la **onda**
hip (shoot from the ~) no tener **pelo**s en la
lengua
hip flask la petaca
hips (put one's hands on one's ~) ponerse en
jarras
hips (swing/sway one's ~) contonearse
hips (swinging/swaying of the ~) el campaneo/
contoneo
hip-swinging el campaneo/contoneo
to hit (he/etc. won't know what's ~ him/etc.!) ¡se
le/etc. va a caer el **pelo**!
to hit home dar en el **blanco**; dar en la **diana**/
hacer diana
to hit it off with s.o. hacer buenas **miga**s con alg.
to hit it off with s.o. (not to ~) hacer malas **miga**s
con alg.
to hit on s.o. for money dar un **sablazo** a alg.
to hit the bottle darle a la **botella**
to hit the hay/sack irse a la/echarse en la
petaca/**piltra**; tender la **raspa**; hacer la
rosca [de galgo]
to hit the mark dar en el **blanco**/**busilis**; dar en
la **diana**/hacer diana
to hit the nail on the head dar en el **busilis**/
clavo/**quid**; dar en la **tecla**/**yema**
hitch (go off without a ~) salir algo **corriente** y
moliente
to hitch a lift/ride ir[se] a **dedo**/hacer dedo
to hoard [up] anything ser una **urraca**
hoarder (be a ~) ser una **urraca**
hoarse (shout until one is [as] ~ as a crow)
desgargantarse

hoarse (shout/scream o.s. ~) desgargantarse

hoax el camelo; el **cuento** chino

hobby-horse (he's/she's riding or on his/her ~ again) ha vuelto a la misma **canción/ cantilena**

hobby-horse (let s.o. ride his ~) dar **cuerda/soga** a alg.

to hobnob with s.o. **rozar**se con alg.

to hobnob with upper-crust people codearse con los de **arriba**

hodgepodge el **cajón** de sastre

hog (go the whole ~) poner toda la **carne** en el asador; **jugar**se el todo por el todo

hog (live high on the ~) vivir a todo **tren**

to hog the limelight acaparar la atención [de todos]

hoist (be ~ by/with one's own petard) ir por **lana** y volver trasquilado/esquilado; salirle a alg. el **tiro** por la culata

to hoist another one atizar la **lámpara**

to hoist one or a few alzar/empinar el **codo**; mojarse el **garguero**; mojar/refrescar el **gaznate**; atarse/pegarse un **latigazo**; atizarse un **trago**

hold (get/lay ~ of s.th.) echar la **zarpa** a algo

to hold back morder/tascar el **freno**

to hold back one's tears beberse las **lágrimas**

to hold one's ground no dar su **brazo** a torcer; mantenerse/seguir en sus **trece**

to hold one's own **defender**se bien

to hold s.o. back tirar de la **cuerda** a alg.

hold your horses! ¡para el **carro**!; ¡echa el **freno**, Ma[g]daleno!

hole (of a town) de mala **muerte** (example)

hole in the heel (sock/stocking) el tomate

holes (be full of/riddled with ~) estar hecho una **criba**

holes (make a lot of ~ in s.th.) dejar algo como un **colador**

hollow (beat s.o. ~) cascar a alg.; **comer**se a alg. crudo; dar **quince** y raya/falta a alg.; dar cien **vueltas** a alg.

hollow promises jarabe de pico; música celestial

holy (swear by all that is ~ [that . . .]) jurar por lo más **sagrado** [que ...]

holy Joe (be a ~) **comer**se los santos

holy terror (be a ~) ser de la **piel** del diablo

home (at ~) entre sus cuatro **pared**es (example)

home (be nothing to write ~ about) no ser cosa del otro **jueves**; no ser nada/cosa del otro **mundo**

home (feel completely at ~) estar como **abeja** en flor; estar/sentirse como el **pez** en el agua

home (hit/strike ~) dar en el **blanco**; dar en la **diana**/hacer diana

home truths (tell [a lot of] ~) sacar los **trapos** [sucios] a relucir

home truths (tell s.o. a few ~) cantar las cuarenta a alg.; dar a alg. con los **ochos** y los nueves; decirle a alg. cuatro **verdad**es/las verdades del barquero

to be homesick tirar al monte

homosexual (▷ gay)

to be homosexual ser de la otra **acera**

hon el pichón/la pichona

honestly sin **tapujos**

honey (person) el pichón/la pichona

honeymoon la **luna** de miel

hoof (shake a ~) menear/mover el **esqueleto**

to hoof it ir/venir a golpe de **alpargata**/en el **caballo** de San Francisco/a golpe de **calcetín**/en el **coche** de San Francisco o de San Fernando

hook (act on one's own ~) campar por sus respetos

hook (be off the ~) haber salido del **atolladero**

hook (by ~ or by crook) por las buenas o por las malas (▷ **bueno**); por **fas** o por nefas

hook (get s.o. off the ~) sacar a alg. del **atolladero**; echar un **cable** a alg.; sacar el **pie** del lodo a alg.

hook (have s.o. on the ~) tener a alg. en/sobre **ascuas**

hook (sling one's ~) **largar**se

hook, line and sinker (swallow anything ~) **tragar**[se]las como ruedas de molino

to hook o.s. a husband **pescar**se un marido

hooked [on drugs] (get ~) quedar **colgado**

hooker la fulana/sota; el taxi; la zorra

hooker (be a ~) ser del **oficio**

hooker (cheap ~) la pesetera

hooky (play ~) **fumar**se algo; hacer **novillos**; hacer **rabona**

hoot (be a ~) ser para **morir**se de risa

hoot (not to give/care two ~s) no importar a alg. un **ardite**; [no] importar a alg. un **bledo/ comino/higo/pepino/pimiento/pito/ rábano**

hooter (big ~: big nose) la trompa

hooter (nose) el asa; las napias

hooters (breasts) las **aldabas**; los **cántaros/ globos/limones** (▷ **limón**); las marmellas

hop (catch s.o. on the ~) pillar a alg. en **bolas/ bragas**

to hop it **largar**se

hope (bereft of ~) huérfano de

hope (my/etc. ~s are dashed) [todo] mi/etc. o el **gozo** en el/un pozo

hope ([there is a] glimmer of ~) hay **luz** al final del túnel; el **rayo** de esperanza

to hope there's more where that came from saber a más

hopeful (you're ~!) ¡y un **jamón** [con chorreras]!

hopeless por los cuatro **costados**

hopeless case (be a ~) ser un caso **perdido**

to be hopping mad estar hecho un **basilisco**; estar alg. que brinca (▷ **brincar**); echar

chiribitas/chispas; estar alg. que trina
(▷ **trinar**); estar hecho un **vinagre**

hopping mad (get ~) darse a **perro**s

horizon (bright spot on the ~) el **rayo** de
esperanza

horizon (there is a bright spot on the ~) hay **luz** al
final del túnel

horizons (have very narrow ~) no ver más allá de
sus narices (▷ **nariz**)

horn (be on the ~s of a dilemma) estar entre la
espada y la pared/entre dos **fuego**s

horn (blow one's own ~) no necesitar **abuela**;
darse **bombo**; echarse/tirarse **flore**s

horn (draw in one's ~s) apretarse el **cinturón**;
recoger **vela**s

hornet's nest (stir up a ~) meterse en un
avispero

to be horny estar **bruto**

horny (get ~) ponerse **bruto**; empalmarse

to be horrible ser una triste **gracia**

horror (be petrified/paralyzed with ~) no
quedarle a alg. **gota** de sangre en las
venas; quedarse **helado**; quedarse sin
pulso[s]; bajársele a alg. la **sangre** a los
talones; quedarse **yerto**

horror stories (tell ~ about s.th./s.o.) decir
horrores de algo/alg.

hors d'oeuvre (small [but robust] ~) el sello del
estómago

horse (be a ~ of another/a different color) ser
harina de otro costal

horse (be on one's high ~) tener muchas **ínfula**s

horse (be straight from the ~'s mouth) saber algo
de buena **tinta**

horse (bring/take s.o. down off his high ~) quitar
moños a alg.

horse (don't look a gift ~ in the mouth) a **caballo**
regalado no hay que mirarle o no le mires
el diente

horse (eat like a ~) comer más que un **alguacil**;
llenarse la **andorga**; henchir el **baúl**;
comer/mascar a dos **carrillo**s; ponerse
como el chico del **esquilador**; comer como
una **lima**; comer como un **sabañón**

horse (flog a dead ~) azotar el **aire**; machacar en
hierro frío; arar en el **mar**

horse (get on one's high ~) darse **ínfula**s

horse (lock the barn door after the ~ is stolen)
asno muerto, la cebada al rabo; a buenas
horas, mangas verdes

horse (lock/shut the stable door after the ~ has
bolted/gone) asno muerto, la cebada al
rabo; a buenas **hora**s, mangas verdes

horse sense el pesquis

horse trading la componenda

horses (hold your ~!) ¡para el **carro**!; ¡echa el
freno, Ma[g]daleno!

horses (white ~: waves) cabrillas; **paloma**s

horses (wild ~ couldn't drag me/us away from
here) ni a tirones me/nos sacan de aquí
(▷ **tirón**)

horses (wild ~ won't drag it out of him) sacar algo
a alg. con pinzas/sacacorchos/tirabuzón
(example)

horses for courses cada **loco** con su tema; a
cada uno/cual, lo **suyo**

host (reckon without one's ~) no contar con la
huéspeda/echar la cuenta sin la huéspeda

hot (be bloody/damn[ed] ~) hacer un calor de
cojones (▷ **cojón**)

hot (be red ~ on s.th.) pintarse uno solo/
pintárselas solo para algo

hot (be scorching/sizzling ~) de **bigote**

hot (be terribly ~: spicy) picar que rabia
(▷ **rabiar**)

hot (get ~ under the collar) perder los **estribo**s

hot (it's damn[ed]/darn[ed]/terribly/very ~) canta
la **chicharra**; se asan las **mosca**s

hot (things are getting ~) oler a **chamusquina**

hot air jarabe de pico; música celestial

hot and cold (blow ~) dar una de **cal** y otra de
arena

hot cakes (sell like ~) venderse como el **pan**/
como pan caliente; venderse como
rosquillas

hot potato/issue una **patata** caliente

hot stuff (be ~) estar como un **tren**

hot stuff (during the day pious Annie, during the
night ~) de día **beata**, de noche gata

to hot things up **llevar**se todo por delante

hot-air artist el farolero/la farolera

hotchpotch el **cajón** de sastre

hotel (short-time ~) la pensión de **tapujo**

hot-headed caliente de **casco**s

to be hot-tempered tener el **genio** vivo

hounds (run with the hare and hunt with the ~)
comer a dos **carrillo**s; servir a **Dios** y al
diablo

hour of death (be at s.o.'s side/comfort s.o. at the ~)
recoger el postrer **suspiro** de alg.

house (get on like a ~ on fire) la **mar** de; comer
en un/el o del mismo **plato**

house (people who live in glass ~s should not
throw stones) eso sería tirar **piedras** a su o
sobre el propio tejado

house (put one's own ~ in order [first]) barrer en
su propia casa

house (set up ~ together) casarse por detrás de
la iglesia

house of cards (fold up/collapse like a ~)
derrumbarse como un **castillo** de naipes

housebreaker el reventapisos

how (any old ~) a tontas y a locas (▷ **tonto**)
(example)

to howl with the pack dejarse llevar de/por la
corriente

huff (go off in a or get/go into a ~) mosquearse

huge bestial; de **bigote**; cojonudo; garrafal; padre; solemne

huge lies (tell ~) mentir por los **codos**/más que un **sacamuelas**

huge task/work (be a ~) ser **obra** de romanos

human (be only ~) ser de **carne** y hueso.

human (err is ~) quien o el que tiene **boca**, se equivoca

to humble o.s. doblar/bajar la **cerviz**

humble pie (eat ~) pedir **alafia**; doblar el **espinazo**

to humiliate s.o. hacer morder [el] **polvo** a alg.

to humor s.o. llevar/seguir la **corriente** a alg.; llevar el **genio** a alg.; reírle a alg. la[s] **gracia**[s]

hunch (have a ~ that . . .) darle a alg. el **pálpito**/ tener el pálpito de que ...

hundred percent or per cent (one ~) por los cuatro **costados**

hundred years (it will all be the same in a ~) dentro de cien **años** todos calvos

hundred-percenter por los cuatro **costados** (example)

hundreds of (ask s.o. ~ questions) a **granel**

hunger la **salsa** de San Bernardo

hunger (be dying of ~) estar **muerto** de hambre

hunger (ravenous ~) la gazuza; el **hambre** de tres semanas/de lobo

hunger is the best sauce a buen **hambre** no hay pan duro

hunky-dory (everything's ~) a las mil **maravilla**s (example); ir/marchar sobre **rueda**s (example)

hunt (be on the ~ for s.th.) irse a **ojeo** de algo

hurry (be in a great/mortal ~) la **mar** de

hurry (in a great ~) a toda **mecha**

hurry (you won't see the likes of that in a ~) ni buscando con [un] **candil**

to hurt (be very easily ~) a **flor** de piel

to hurt like the devil or like hell/mad/crazy como el/un **diablo**

to hurt s.o. [very] deeply arrancarle a alg. el **alma**; herir a alg. en **carne** viva; llegarle a alg. a las **telas** del corazón; llegar a o herir/tocar en lo más **vivo** a alg.

to hurt the/one's eye[s]/ear[s] herir la vista/el oído

husband (get/hook o.s. a ~) **pescar**se un marido

husband (henpecked ~) Juan Lanas

to hush s.th. up ocultar/tapar la **caca**; echar **tierra** sobre/a algo

hype (give s.th. a lot of ~) dar **bombo** a algo

hype (with a lot of ~) a **bombo** y platillo

to hype s.th. up dar **bombo** a algo

hypocrite un[a] **cabeza** torcida; la **mosca**/ **mosquita** muerta

hypocritically de **dientes** [para] afuera

I

I menda

I (if ~ were you) yo **que** tú/Ud.

I (it's ~[, and nobody else]) el mismo que viste y calza (▷ **vestir**) (example)

ice (cut no ~) ni **pinchar** ni cortar; no **pintar** nada; ni **quitar** ni poner

ice (put s.th. on ~) dar **carpetazo** a algo

iceberg (tip of the ~) la **punta** del iceberg

icing (there's no ~ on the cake) no hay **olla** sin tocino

idea (crazy ~) el golpe de **bombero**

idea (have no ~ what it's [all] about) no saber uno lo que se pesca (▷ **pescar**)

idea (not to have the faintest/foggiest ~ [about s.th.]) no distinguir lo **blanco** de lo negro; no saber [ni] la **cartilla**; no tener ni la más remota/pálida **idea** de algo; no saber ni **jota** de algo

idea (only have a vague ~) oír **campanas** y no saber dónde (example)

idea (you have no ~!) ¡no te digo **nada**!

ideas (a man who has antiquated ~) el carroza

ideas (have peculiar/strange ~) tener sus **lunas**

ideas (put ~ into s.o.'s head) echarle a alg. la **pulga** detrás de la oreja

idiot un [pedazo de] **alcornoque/atún**; el/la **berzas**; un bombero; un[a] **cabeza** de corcho; una calabaza; un alma de **cántaro**; un ceporro/melón/merluzo; un **palomino** atontado; el pasmarote; un pavipollo/percebe

idiot (be a complete/prize ~) a más no **poder**; ser **tonto** del bote/de capirote

to be idle estar de **miranda**; tocarse las narices (▷ **nariz**); no tener ni **oficio** ni beneficio

idle (be bone-~) ser más vago que la **chaqueta** de un guardia; tocarse el **pito**

idle (s.o. was born ~) nació alg. cansado o con la lengua fuera (▷ **nacer**)

idle arguments/discussions (protracted and ~) discusiones bizantinas (▷ **bizantino**)

idle brain (an ~ is the devil's workshop) el **ocio**/la **ociosidad** es la madre de todos los vicios; los **vicios** son los hijos del ocio

idle hands (the devil finds work for ~) el **ocio**/la **ociosidad** es la madre de todos los vicios; los **vicios** son los hijos del ocio

idleness (vices are born of ~) el **ocio**/la **ociosidad** es la madre de todos los vicios; los **vicios** son los hijos del ocio

idleness is the root of all evil el **ocio**/la **ociosidad** es la madre de todos los vicios; los **vicios** son los hijos del ocio

idler el **paseante** en corte

idly (stand ~ by [while others are working]) estar de **miranda**; tocarse las narices (▷ **nariz**)

to idolize s.o. mirarse en alg. como en un **espejo**

if I were you yo **que** tú/Ud.

ignorance of the law is no excuse/defense ignorancia no quita pecado

to ignore s.o. completely hacer **mangas** y capirotes de alg.

to ignore s.o./s.th. dar de **lado** a alg.; echar algo en **saco** roto

ilk (people of that ~) gente de ese **jaez**

ill (be very ~) no levantar/alzar **cabeza**

ill (pretend to be ~) tener calentura de **pollo**

ill (sham ~) tener calentura de **pollo**

ill (speak ~ of s.th./s.o.) arrastrar/poner algo/a alg. por los **suelos**

ill (take it very ~) caer/sentar como una **pedrada**

ill weeds grow apace mala **hierba** nunca muere

ill wind (it's an ~ that blows nobody any good) no hay **mal** que por bien no venga; a **río** revuelto, ganancia de pescadores

illusion (that's an ~) no caerá esa **breva**

image (be the spitting ~/the spit and ~ of s.o.) ser **clavado** a alg./ser alg. clavado; ser escupido el padre/etc. (▷ **escupir**)

imagination (give free rein to one's ~ or let one's ~ run free/wild) dar **rienda** suelta a algo (example)

imaginative (be more than ~) ser más original que el **pecado**

imbecile el/la **berzas**

to be immaculately dressed estar hecho un **brazo** de mar

to immerse o.s. in s.th. **enfrascar**se en algo

immersed (become ~ in s.th.) **cebar**se/**enfrascar**se en algo

to be imminent estar a la **puerta**/en puertas

immoderately como un **descosido**

impact (have a profound ~) hacer **raya**

impatience (be burning/bursting with ~) rabiar de impaciencia; reventar de impaciencia

impatience (be dying of ~) no caérsele a alg. el **pan**

impertinent (be very ~) tener más **cara** que espalda

impertinent (get ~) ponerse **flamenco**

important de muchas **campanilla**s

to be important no ser **grano** de anís

important (think one is ~) subirse a la **parra**; el **postín** (example); darse **pote**

important people gente de alto **copete**

important thing (that's the ~) es lo que hace el **gasto**

importunate (be very ~) meterse por el **ojo** de una aguja

importunate (get ~) ponerse **flamenco**

impossible (ask the ~) pedir **leche** a las cabrillas; pedir la **luna**; pedir **peras** al olmσ

impossible (attempt the ~) tratar de contar las **estrella**s

to be impossible (book/etc.) caerse de las **manos**

impossible (you're ~!) ser de lo que no hay (▷ **haber**)

impoverished (become ~) venir a menos

to impress s.o. strongly dejar **bizco** a alg.

impressed (be very ~) quedarse **bizco**

impression (make a bad ~) tener mala **sombra**

impression (make a good ~) hacer [un] buen **papel**; tener buena **sombra**

impression (make an ~ on s.o.) hacer **mella** en/a alg.; dar el **opio** a alg.

impudent (be very ~) tener más **cara** que espalda

impudent (get ~) ponerse **flamenco**

impulse (sudden ~) el pronto

to be in estar en la **onda**

in (be all ~: exhausted) estar hecho una braga (▷ **bragas**); estar/quedar hecho **cisco**; tener los **huesos** molidos; estar hecho **migas/papilla/pedazo**s; estar hecho un **pingajo**; estar hecho **polvo/puré**; estar reventado (▷ **reventar**); estar hecho unos **zorro**s

in (be well ~ with s.o.) estar muy metido con alg. (▷ **meter**)

to be in for it tocarle a alg. **recibir**

in for it (he's/etc. ~!) ¡se le/etc. va a caer el **pelo**!

to be in on everything (s.o. always wants to be ~) meterse por el **ojo** de una aguja

to be in on it andar/estar en el **ajo**; estar/andar metido en [la] **danza**

to be in on the secret andar/estar en el **ajo**

inappropriate (say s.th. very/singularly ~) hablar de/mentar/nombrar la **soga** en casa del ahorcado

inch (be every ~ a man) hecho y derecho (example)

inch (give s.o. an ~ and he'll take a mile/yard) darle a alg. un **dedo** y se toma hasta el codo; darle a alg. la/una **mano** y se toma el brazo; darle a alg. el **pie** y se toma la mano

inch by inch palmo a palmo

inconsiderately sin pararse en **barra**s

to be incredible ser un/de **alucine**; no tener **nombre**

incredible (this is ~!) ¡esto es la **oca**!

incredible/incredibly bestial; de **bigote**; chachi; cojonudo; dabute[n]/dabuti; escandalosamente (▷ **escandaloso**); que

quita el **hipo**; de **película**; pistonudo; a **rabiar**; solemne

incredibly disgusting/rotten de **bigote**

to be incredibly ugly ser un **aborto** del diablo; ser el acabóse de feo (▷ **acabar**); ser más feo que **Carracuca**; ser más **feo** que Picio/que el pecado/etc.; a más no **poder**; dar un **susto** al miedo

independently (act ~) campar por sus respetos

indignation (s.o.'s eyes blaze/are ablaze with ~) echar **fuego** por los ojos

indiscretion el desliz

individual (annoying ~) el/la chinche

individual (be an extremely annoying ~) tener **sangre** de chinches

individual (worthless ~) el **ñiquiñaque**

to indulge in mental masturbation hacerse una **paja** mental

industrious (be very ~) ser una **hormiga**

ineffective remedies (apply ~) aplicar **paño**s calientes

inevitable impepinable

inevitable (bow to the ~) besar la **cruz**

inexperienced (be still young and ~) estar aún con la **leche** en los labios

infancy (be [still] in its ~) estar en **ciernes**; estar aún/todavía en **pañal**es

to be infatuated with s.o./s.th. caérsele a alg. la **baba** con/por alg./algo

influence (have [a lot of] ~) tener buenas **aldaba**s/buenos **asidero**s

influence (use all one's ~) tocar todos los **resorte**s

influence (use one's ~ to . . .) enchufar a alg. (example)

influential friends (mobilize all one's ~) tocar todos los **resorte**s

influential friends in the right places (have ~) tener buenas **aldaba**s/buenos **asidero**s

to inform s.o. [to s.o.] chivarse contra/de alg. [con/a alg.]

informer el chivato/la chivata; el/la correve[i]dile; el soplón/la soplona

to infuriate s.o. encender/quemar la **sangre** a alg.

to ingratiate o.s. with s.o. hacer la **pelotilla** a alg.

injection of funds/money (the industry needs an ~) la industria necesita una **inyección** financiera

ink-shitter el cagatintas/chupatintas

innocent (be dreadfully ~) caerse de un **nido**

innocent (look ~) mirar con **ojos** de sobrino

innocent air (put on an ~) mirar con **ojos** de sobrino

innocent expression (have an ~ on one's face) mirar con **ojos** de sobrino

ins and outs (have its ~) tener algo muchos **entresijos**

inseparable (be ~) comer en un/el o del mismo **plato**; ser **uña** y carne

to be inside (in prison) estar a la **sombra**/en la **trena**

inside (in prison: put s.o. ~) meter a alg. donde no vea el **sol**; poner a alg. a la **sombra**; zambullir a alg. en la cárcel

inside out (know ~) de **cabo** a cabo/rabo o de punta a cabo; conocer algo al **dedillo**; de **pe** a pa

to be insidious **matar**las callando

insincerely de **dientes** [para] afuera

insincerely (say s.th. ~) decir algo con la **boca** chica

insinuation (make ~s/an ~) echar **varetas**/una vareta

to insist on one's opinion ([stubbornly] ~) casarse con su **opinión**; ponerse de **puntillas**

to insist on s.th. hacer **hincapié** en algo

to be inspired soplar la **musa** a alg.

installments (pay for s.th. in ~) comprar algo a **plazoletas**

instantly (die ~) quedarse en el **sitio**

instincts (have [very] good ~) tener una **nariz** de primera

to be insufficient estar prendido con **alfileres**

insult (to add ~ to injury s.th. else happens) llover sobre mojado

to insult s.o. mojar la **oreja** a alg.

insults (exchange ~) **repiquetears**e

insults (heap/shower ~ on s.o.) poner a alg. como un **estropajo**; poner a alg. de **oro** y azul

intact (nothing remains ~) no dejar/quedar **títere** con cabeza

intellectual (pseudo-~) el **erudito**/la **erudita** a la violeta

intense heat la quemazón

intentions (have bad/evil ~) tener mal **café**; venir con las de **Caín**; tener mala **leche/pipa/uva**

to intercede meter el **bastón**

intercourse (have lesbian ~) hacer una **tortilla**

interest (be of keen current ~) estar algo en [el] **candelero**

interests (put one's own ~ first) arrimar el **ascua** a su sardina

to interfere (in the conversation/etc.) meter **baza** [en]

to interfere (not to ~) no quitar ni poner **rey**

to interfere in other people's affairs meterse en **camisa** de once varas

interlarded with cuajado de; erizado de

to interrupt the conversation cortar el **hilo** de la conversación

to intervene meter el **bastón**

to intervene in a matter tomar **cartas** en un asunto

to intimidate s.o. meter las **cabras** en el corral a alg.; meter a alg. en un **puño**

intrepidly a **pecho** descubierto

intrigue el tinglado

to be introspective estar metido para dentro (▷ **meter**)

to be introverted estar metido para dentro (▷ **meter**)

inured (become ~) criar **callos**

to be invaluable valer algo un **Perú/Potosí**

invention (necessity is the mother of ~) el **hambre** aguza el ingenio; hombre pobre todo es trazas; la **necesidad** hace maestros o aguza el ingenio

inveterate por los cuatro **costados**; hecho y derecho

inveterate drinker (be an ~) ser un borracho **perdido**

to be involved andar/estar en el **ajo**

involved (be deeply ~ with s.o.) estar muy metido con alg. (▷ **meter**)

involved (get/be ~ in it/s.th.) meterse en o estar/andar metido en [la] **danza**; estar [muy] metido en algo (▷ **meter**)

iota (not an ~ of) ni **chispa** de

iron (have more than one or another ~ in the fire) comer a dos **carrillos**; tener una **vela** encendida por si la otra se apaga

iron (have two/several ~s in the fire) tener un **pie** en dos zapatos

iron (strike while the ~ is hot) al **hierro** caliente batir de repente

iron (you have to strike while the ~ is hot) a la **ocasión** la pintan calva

iron constitution (have an ~) tener **carne** de perro

irritable sort el/la cascarrabias

to isolate o.s. hacer **rancho** aparte

issue (dodge/evade the ~) salir[se]/escapar[se]/irse por la **tangente**

issue (talk round the ~) mear fuera del **tiesto**

issue (hot ~) una **patata** caliente

it (be in on ~) andar/estar en el **ajo**; estar/andar metido en [la] **danza**

it (put ~ over on s.o.) dar [el] **camelo** a alg.; pegar un **parche** a alg.; dársela a alg. con **queso**; dar/pegar una **tostada** a alg.

it (this is ~ now!) ¡ahora van a soltar al **toro**!

it (we won't stand for ~!) ¡no somos negros! (▷ **el negro**)

to be itching to + infinitive **perecer**se/rabiar/reventar por + infinitivo

J

jab (give o.s. a ~) **chutar**se; **pinchar**se

jack (every man ~ [of them]) todo **bicho** viviente; Cristo y la madre/todo Cristo; todo/cada **quisque**

to jack off tocar la **campana**; cascársela (▷ **cascar**); machacársela (▷ **machacar**); hacerse una **paja**; pelársela (▷ **pelar**); hacer la **puñeta**; tocársela (▷ **tocar**); zumbársela (▷ **zumbar**)

to jack up (drug) **chutar**se; **pinchar**se

Jack Robinson (before you can say ~) en un decir **amén**/un **credo**/un **dos** por tres; en menos que canta un **gallo**; en un abrir y cerrar de **ojos**; en menos que se reza un **padrenuestro**; en dos **tranco**s

jacket la chupa

jack-of-all-trades (be a ~) servir lo mismo para un **barrido** que para un fregado

jackpot (hit the ~) hacer su **agosto**; ponerse las **bota**s

jail la trena

jail (be in ~) estar a la **sombra**/en la **trena**

jail (clap s.o. in ~) meter a alg. donde no vea el **sol**; poner a alg. a la **sombra**; zambullir a alg. en la cárcel

jail (end up/finish up/land in ~) dar con los/sus **hueso**s en la cárcel

jail (rot in ~) pudrirse en la cárcel

jalop[p]y la **cafetera** [rusa]

jam (be in an awful/a real ~) estar más perdido que **Carracuca**; estar con el **dogal**/la **soga** al cuello

jam (get o.s. into a ~) meterse en un **atolladero**/**berenjenal**; meterse en **camisa** de once varas

jam (get out of a ~) ponerse/salir a **flote**

jam (get s.o. into a [real] ~) poner a alg. en las **astas** del toro

jam (get/help s.o. out of a ~) sacar a alg. del **atolladero**; echar un **cable** a alg.; sacar el **pie** del lodo a alg.; sacar a alg. de un apuro

jam (leave s.o. in a ~) dejar a alg. en las **astas** del toro

to be jam-full no caber ni un **alfiler**; estar de **bote** en bote

to be jammy tener **potra**

to be jam-packed no caber ni un **alfiler**; estar de **bote** en bote

to jar on s.o.'s nerves alterar/crispar los **nervio**s a alg. o poner los nervios de punta a alg.

jaunt (go for/on a ~) zarpar con rumbo desconocido

jaw (s.o.'s ~ drops) quedarse **parado**

jealous (make s.o. ~) poner los **diente**s largos a alg.

jelly (shake like ~) temblar como una hoja/un azogado/un flan

jerk el/la gilipollas

to jerk off tocar la **campana**; cascársela (▷ **cascar**); machacársela (▷ **machacar**); hacerse una **paja**; pelársela (▷ **pelar**); hacer la **puñeta**; tocársela (▷ **tocar**); zumbársela (▷ **zumbar**)

jewel (fake ~) un **culo** de vaso

jiffy (in a ~) en un decir **amén**/un **credo**/un **dos** por tres; en menos que canta un **gallo**

to jilt s.o. dar **calabaza**s a alg.; largar a alg.; dar la **patada** a alg.; plantar o dejar plantado a alg.

jinks (have high ~) pasarlo **pipa**

job (bad/botched ~) el buñuelo

job (be a long ~) haber **tela** que cortar/para rato

job (be a tough ~/the ~ was tough going) un **parto** difícil (example); ser [un huevo] duro de **pelar**; traérselas (▷ **traer**)

job (be one hell of a ~ [to + infinitive]) costar un **huevo** [+ infinitivo]

job (be/face a [very] difficult ~) necesitar **Dios** y [su] ayuda; tocarle a alg. una **papeleta** difícil; traérselas (▷ **traer**)

job (cushy ~) el **bocado** sin hueso; el enchufillo

job (do a blow ~ on s.o.) hacerle una **mamada** a alg.

job (do a great ~) cañón (example)

job (do a thorough ~) emplearse a **fondo**

job (get [s.o.] a cushy ~) enchufar a alg.; enchufarse

job (have a hard ~ getting s.o. to understand s.th.) meter algo a alg. con **cuchara**

job (have a terrible ~ [to + infinitive]) costar **Dios** y ayuda a alg. [+ infinitivo]

job (have more than one [well-paid] ~) comer a dos **carrillo**s

Job (have the patience of ~) tener la paciencia de un **chino**; tener más **paciencia** que Job/que un santo; tener una **paciencia** angelical/de benedictino

job (lousy ~) de mala **muerte** (example)

job (person who has a cushy ~) el enchufado/la enchufada

job (plum ~) la breva

job (put-up ~) el apaño

job (soft ~) el **bocado** sin hueso

job (take on a dangerous/risky ~) poner el **cascabel** al gato job (tough ~) un **parto** difícil/el parto de los montes

job (without a ~) sin **oficio** ni beneficio

to be job-hunting irse a **ojeo** de algo (example)

Joe (be a holy ~) **comers**e los santos

john (have to go to the ~) echar una **carta** al correo (example)

John Q Public Juan Pérez

johnny (condom) el calcetín/globo; la goma

to join in the conversation escupir en **corro**

joint (bar/etc.) el tinglado

joint (bar/etc. where people go to pick s.o. up) el **bar** de ligue/alterne

joint (of marijuana) el petardo/porro

joke el camelo

joke (a ~ can easily turn serious or into s.th. unpleasant) las **caña**s se vuelven lanzas

joke (be beyond a ~) pasar de **castaño** oscuro; pelar la jeta

joke (dirty ~) la verdulería

joke (s.o. can't take a ~) tener malas **cosquillas**/no sufrir cosquillas

joke (take/treat s.th. as a ~) tomarse algo a **chirigota/risa**

jokes (tell dirty ~) decir **verdulería**s

jolly well de narices (▷ **nariz**)

to jot s.th. down escribir/anotar algo a vuela **pluma**

joy (be beside o.s./overwhelmed/wild with ~) no **caber** en sí de alegría; no caberle a alg. el **corazón** en el pecho; no caber en el **pellejo** de alegría

joy (be bubbling over with ~) rebosar de alegría

joy (be bursting with ~) no caberle a alg. el **corazón** en el pecho; no caber en el **pellejo** de alegría

joy (jump for ~) echar las **campana**s al vuelo

joyful expression (put on a ~) vestir el rostro de alegría

to judge a person by the company he keeps (you can ~) dime con quién andas y te diré quién eres (▷ **decir**)

jug (be put in the ~) ponerse el **capuchón**

jug (prison) la trena

to juggle with s.th. hacer **trampa**[s] (example)

juggling (piece of ~: with figures/etc.) el apaño

juice (let s.o. stew in his own ~) dejar a alg. cocer en su propia **salsa**

juice (stew in one's own ~) cocerse en su propia **salsa**

jumble el **cajón** de sastre

to jumble things up mezclar **berza**s con capachos

jump (be always/constantly on the ~) no criar **moho**; estar siempre con un **pie** en el aire; andar/ir al **retortero**

jump (go take a running ~!) ¡anda a **bañar**te!; ¡vete a freír **buñuelos/espárragos**!

jump (keep s.o. [constantly] on the ~) no dejar criar **moho** a alg.; traer a alg. al **retortero**

jump (tell s.o. to go [and] take a running ~) mandar a alg. a freír **buñuelos**/al **cuerno**/a freír **espárragos**/a hacer **gárgaras**

to jump at the chance coger/asir la **ocasión** por los cabellos/pelos

to jump at the chance (you have to ~) a la **ocasión** la pintan calva

to jump down s.o.'s throat saltar a la **cara** a alg.

to jump for joy echar las **campana**s al vuelo

to jump in a lake (go ~!) ¡anda a **bañar**te!; ¡vete a freír **buñuelos/espárragos**!

to jump in a lake (tell s.o. to go [and] ~) mandar a alg. a freír **buñuelos**/al **cuerno**/a freír **espárragos**/a hacer **gárgaras**

to jump out of one's skin no llegarle a uno la **camisa** al cuerpo; **morir**se del susto

to jump out of the frying pan into the fire huir de la[s] **ceniza**[s] y caer/dar en la[s] brasa[s]; huir del **fuego** y caer en las brasas; salir de **Guatemala** y entrar en Guatepeor; ir de **Herodes** a Pilatos; salir de las **llama**s y caer en las brasas; salir de **Málaga** y entrar en Malagón; huir del **perejil** y dar en el berenjenal; saltar/caer de la **sartén** y dar en la brasa; huir del **toro** y caer en el arroyo; salir del **trueno** y dar con el relámpago

to jump the gun madrugar

jungle (law of the ~) la **ley** de la jungla/selva

jungle law la **ley** de la jungla/selva

junk ([piece of] old ~) la antigualla; el vejestorio

junk ([useless] ~) el ñiquiñaque

junkie el/la yonqui

just (only ~) a duras **pena**s; por un **pelo**/los pelos

just (sleep the sleep of the ~) dormir a **pierna** suelta

to be just . . . no **pasar** de ser ...

just after 10/etc. a las diez/etc. y **pico**

to be just an ordinary person ser del **montón**

just deserts (everyone gets his ~ sooner or later) a cada cerdo/puerco le llega su **San Martín**

just fine a pedir de **boca**

just in case por si las **mosca**s

to be just like her (that was ~) hacer de las **suya**s (example)

just like that de buenas a primeras (▷ **bueno**); de **golpe** y porrazo

just like that (come up with s.th. ~) traer algo en/por la **manga**; sacarse algo de la **manga**

just right (come ~) de **perla**s; venir [que ni] **pintiparado**

just to be on the safe side por si las **mosca**s

justice (not to do s.o. ~) no hacer **justicia** a alg.

justice (pervert ~) doblar la **vara** de la justicia

K

to keel over caerse redondo

keen (be as ~ as mustard [on s.th.]) arder de entusiasmo [con/por algo]

keen (be very ~ on s.th.) hipar/rabiar por algo

keen observer (be a ~) tener **ojo** clínico

to keep (make a promise one doesn't intend to ~) de **boquilla** (example); de **dientes** [para] afuera (example)

to keep a secret to o.s. echar **candado** a la boca/a los labios

to keep going mantenerse a **flote**; ir tirando (▷ **tirar**)

to keep it to o.s. (not to ~) írsele a alg. la **burra**

to keep mum coserse la **boca**; echar **candado** a la boca/a los labios; no decir [ni] **chus** ni mus; no decir ni **pío**; sacar algo a alg. con pinzas/sacacorchos/tirabuzón (examples)

to keep mum (s.o. can't ~) no pudrírsele a alg. nada/las cosas en el **pecho**

to keep on about s.th. machacar [en/sobre] algo

to keep one's end up **defender**se bien

to keep one's head down no levantar/alzar **cabeza**

to keep one's mouth shut coserse la **boca**; echar **candado** a la boca/a los labios; no decir [ni] **chus** ni mus; no decir ni **pío**; estar mudo como una **tumba**/ser [como] una tumba

to keep one's mouth shut (if you keep your mouth shut, you won't put your foot in it) en **boca** cerrada no entran moscas

to keep one's mouth shut (s.o. can't keep his mouth shut) no caberle algo a alg. en el **buche**; no pudrírsele a alg. nada/las cosas en el **pecho**

to keep one's troubles/worries to o.s. andarle/irle a alg. la **procesión** por dentro

to keep out of it no **mojar**se

to keep quiet coserse la **boca**; callar[se] como un muerto/una piedra; estar mudo como una **tumba**/ser [como] una tumba

to keep quiet (I would ~ about it if I were you) dar un **cuarto** al pregonero (example)

to keep s.o. waiting dar **perro** a alg.

to keep s.o. waiting [for] an excessively/unduly long time dar **poste** a alg.

to keep s.th. back quedarse con algo entre **pecho** y espalda

to keep s.th. to o.s. coserse la **boca**

to keep s.th. to o.s. (s.o. can't keep s.th. to himself) no caberle algo a alg. en el **buche/pecho**

to keep s.th. under one's hat coserse la **boca**

to keep s.th. under one's hat (s.o. can't keep s.th. under his hat) no caberle algo a alg. en el **pecho**

to keep to o.s. hacer **rancho** aparte

keep your hair/shirt on! ¡para el **carro**!; ¡echa el **freno**, Ma[g]daleno!

keeping (be in or out of ~ with) [no] **rezar** con

keeps (for ~) para los **restos**

kettle (a watched ~ never boils) quien espera, desespera (▷ **esperar**)

kettle of fish (be another/a different ~) ser **harina** de otro costal

kettle of fish (that's [quite] another/a different ~) eso es otro cantar (▷ **el cantar**)

kettle of fish (this is a pretty ~!) meterse en un **berenjenal** (example)

key player (be a ~) jugar/desempeñar un **papel** (example)

key point el quid

keyed up (be all ~) tener los **nervios** de punta

to kick (s.o. could ~ himself or feels like ~ing himself) dar con la **cabeza** en las paredes

to kick against the pricks dar coces contra el aguijón (▷ **coz**)

to kick one's heels estar en/sobre **ascuas**; estar [como] en **brasas**

to kick over the traces salirse de **madre**; sacar los **pies** del plato/de las alforjas

to kick s.o. out echar a alg. a **baquetazo** limpio; echar a alg. a la **calle**/poner a alg. de patitas en la calle; dar **soleta** a alg.

to kick s.o. up the backside dar a alg. una **patada** en el culo

to kick the bucket irse al otro **barrio**; liar los **bártulos**; **cascar**[la]; diñarla; quedarse **frío/frito**; pelar **gallo**; **guiñar**la; hincar el pico; **liar**las o liárselas; palmarla; estirar la **pata**; liar el **petate**; **pringar**la; **reventar**[se]; quedarse **tieso**

to kid s.o. dar [el] **camelo** a alg.

kid gloves (handle/treat s.o. with ~) guardar/tener a alg. entre algodones (▷ **algodón**); tratar a alg. con **guante** de seda

to kill (be dressed to ~) estar de veinticinco **alfiler**es; estar hecho un **brazo** de mar; estar/ir de **punta** en blanco

to kill o.s. (nearly ~) hacerse **rajas**

to kill o.s. (nearly ~ + gerund) rajarse por

to kill o.s. (not to ~) no **herniar**se

to kill o.s. laughing descojonarse; descoyuntarse/desternillarse/rajarse de risa

to kill o.s. with brainwork romperse los **cascos**

to kill s.o. **cargar**se/cascar/**cepillar**[se] a alg.;
freír a alg.; dejar **frito** a alg.; mandar a alg.
al otro **mundo**; pasaportear a alg.; quitar a
alg. de en medio; dejar **tieso** a alg.;
tumbar a alg.

to kill s.o. (shoot and ~) dar el **paseo** a alg.

to kill s.o. (s.th. isn't going to or won't ~) no
caérsele a alg. los **anillos**

to kill s.o. on the spot dejar a alg. en el **sitio**

to kill s.o. stone-dead dejar **seco** a alg.

to kill two birds with one stone matar dos **pájaros**
de un tiro

to kill two birds with one stone (want to ~) querer
ir por **atún** y a ver al duque

killing (make a ~) hacer su **agosto**; ponerse las
botas; sacar **raja**/**tajada**

killjoy (be a ~) aguar la **fiesta**

kilter (be out of ~) estar a las **once**

kind (be two of a ~) se juntaron el **hambre** y las
ganas de comer; ser de la misma **madera**;
cojear del mismo **pie**; ser **tal** para cual

kind (be very/excessively ~) no caberle a alg. el
corazón en el pecho; hacerse de **miel**

kind (it takes all ~s to make a world) de todo
tiene la/hay en la **viña** del Señor

kind (know exactly what ~ of a person s.o. is)
gastarlas

kind (pay s.o. back in ~) pagar a alg. con/en la
misma **moneda**; volver las **torna**s a alg.

kind (people of that ~) gente de ese **jaez**

kindness (be the very soul of ~) no caberle a alg.
el **corazón** en el pecho

king (in the country of the blind the one-eyed man
is ~) en tierra de **ciego**s o en el país/reino
de los ciegos el tuerto es [el] rey

king (live like a ~) vivir a **cuerpo** de rey; vivir
como un/a lo **príncipe**; a lo gran señor
(▷ **el señor**); vivir a todo **tren**

kip (bed) la petaca/piltra

kip (have a ~) planchar/chafar la **oreja**

to kip planchar/chafar la **oreja**; hacer **seda**

to kiss cambiar **baba**s; darse el **pico**

to kiss it/that goodby[e] (you can ~!) iéchale un
galgo!

kiss-off (give s.o. the ~) dar el **bote** a alg.; echar/
despedir a alg. con **caja**s destempladas;
echar a alg. a la **calle**/poner a alg. de
patitas en la calle; plantar a alg. en la
calle; largar a alg.; dar la **licencia**/[el]
pasaporte/la **patada** a alg.

kite (be high as a ~: drunk/on drugs) tener un
globo impresionante

kite (fly a ~) lanzar un **globo** de ensayo

kite (go fly a ~!) ianda a **bañar**te!; ivete a freír
buñuelos/**espárragos**!

kite (tell s.o. to go fly a ~) mandar a alg. a freír
buñuelos/al **cuerno**/a freír **espárragos**/a
hacer **gárgaras**

knack el tranquillo

knack (get the ~ of s.th.) coger el **tranquillo** a
algo

knack (lose the ~) perder los **libros**/la **onda**

to be knackered (exhausted) estar hecho una
braga (▷ **bragas**); estar/quedar hecho
cisco; tener los **huesos** molidos; estar
hecho **migas**/**papilla**/**pedazos**; estar hecho
un **pingajo**; estar hecho **polvo**/**puré**; estar
reventado (▷ **reventar**); estar hecho unos
zorros

knee (have learned/learnt s.th. at one's mother's ~)
haber mamado algo [ya] en/con la **leche**

knees (think one is the bee's ~) creerse el no va
más (▷ **ir**); la **mar** de

knife (as a problem solver) el quitapenas

knife (stab the ~ up to the hilt into s.th.) meter el
cuchillo hasta las **cachas** en algo

knife (turn the ~ in the wound) remover el
cuchillo en la llaga; hurgar en la **herida**

knife-edge (be balanced on a ~) estar en el **filo** de
la navaja

to knight s.o. calzar la[s] **espuela**[s] a alg.

knock (get the ~) mosquearse

to knock a woman off (lay) **tirar**se/tumbar/
zumbarse a una mujer

to knock like crazy echar las **puertas** abajo

to knock off [work] echarse al o en el **surco**

knock on wood! iel **diablo** sea sordo! ilagarto,
lagarto!

to knock s.o. for a loop/for six or sideways partir a
alg. por el **eje**; dejar a alg. de una **pieza**

to knock s.o. into the middle of next week señor

to knock s.o. off (kill) pasaportear a alg.

to knock s.o. up hinchar a alg.; dejar a alg. con el
paquete; hacer una **tripa** a alg.

to knock s.o.'s block off romper el **bautismo**/la
crisma a alg.

to knock spots off s.o. **comer**se a alg. crudo; dar
quince y raya/falta a alg.; dar cien **vueltas**
a alg.

to knock s.th. back echarse algo al **coleto**/entre
pecho y espalda; **soplar**se algo

to knock s.th. for six echar algo al o por el **suelo**

to knock s.th. on the head echar algo al o por el
suelo

to be knocked for a loop/for six or sideways
quedarse de una **pieza**

knockers (breasts) las **aldaba**s; los **cántaro**s/
globos/limones (▷ **limón**); las marmellas

knock-out (be a real ~) estar como un **camión**

knot (cut the Gordian ~) cortar el **nudo** gordiano

know (be in the ~) andar/estar en el **ajo**

to know (and who ~s what else) y qué sé yo
(▷ **saber**)

to know (before you ~ where you are) a las
primeras de cambio

to know (everybody ~s him/etc.) le conocen hasta
los **perros**; ser más conocido que el **tebeo**

to know (heaven only ~s!) iaverígüelo **Vargas**!

to know (he/etc. ~s/etc. what he/etc. can do!) ¡que se/etc. joda/etc.! (▷ **joder**)

to know (he/etc. won't ~ what's hit him/etc.!) ¡se le/etc. va a caer el **pelo**!

to know (how should I ~!) ¡qué sé yo! (▷ **saber**)

to know (not to ~ a single thing) no saber [ni] la **cartilla**

to know (not to ~ any more whether one is coming or going) no saber dónde volver la **cabeza**

to know (not to ~ beans about s.th.) ni **chispa** de; no tener ni la más remota/pálida **idea** de algo; no saber ni **jota/papa/patata** de algo; estar **pez** en algo

to know (not to ~ exactly) oír **campana**s y no saber dónde

to know (not to ~ left from right) no distinguir lo **blanco** de lo negro

to know (not to ~ one end of s.th. from the other) no tener ni la más remota/pálida **idea** de algo; no saber ni **jota** de algo

to know (not to ~ the first thing about s.th.) ni **chispa** de (example); no saber ni **jota** de algo; estar **pez** en algo

to know (not to ~ what to believe/think) no saber a qué **carta** quedarse

to know (not to talk about things one doesn't ~ anything about) no meterse en **teologías**

to know (one can never ~ too much) el **saber** no ocupa lugar

to know (pretend not to have ~n anything [about it]) hacerse de **nuevas**

to know (s.o. doesn't ~ what he wants) hoy le da a alg. por **pito**s y mañana por flautas

to know (stick to what you ~!) ¡zapatero, a tus zapatos!

to know (we don't ~ where all this is going to end) no sabemos en qué va a **parar** todo esto

to know (you ~ what you can do!) ¡vete a la **porra**!

to know a [hell/heck of a] lot about s.th. saber un **huevo**/un **rato** [largo] de algo

to know a lot of tricks ser de muchas **vueltas**

to know a thing or two saber cuántas son **cinco**

to know about [absolutely] everything saber la **biblia** en verso

to know all about (that you/etc. ~) de **marras**

to know all about s.th. estar al **cabo** de algo/de la calle

to know every trick in the book saber más que **Briján**; tener muchas **camándulas/carlancas**; ser más **corrido** que un zorro viejo; **saber**las todas o muy largas

to know everything saber la **biblia** en verso

to know exactly how nasty s.o. can be/get or how s.o. carries on or what kind of a person s.o. is **gastar**las

to know it (don't I ~!) ¡sí lo sabré yo! (▷ **saber**)

to know it (I ~ only too well!) ¡sí lo sabré yo! (▷ **saber**)

to know nothing at all about s.th. estar **pez** en algo

to know one's oats ser del **paño**

to know one's stuff no ser **rana**

to know one's way around entender/conocer la **aguja** de marear

to know s.th. inside out de **cabo** a cabo/rabo o de punta a cabo; conocer algo al **dedillo**; de **pe** a pa

to know s.th. like the back of one's hand de **cabo** a cabo/rabo o de punta a cabo; conocer algo al **dedillo**/como la **palma** de la mano; de **pe** a pa

to know s.th. very well conocer algo a **palmos**; tener algo en la **uña**

to know the lot saber más que **Briján**

to know [very well] how to handle s.o. tener [mucha] **mano** izquierda con alg.; coger las **vuelta**s a alg.

to know [very well] how to manage tener [mucha] **mano** izquierda

to know what one is dealing with conocer el **paño**

to know what one is doing haber sido **cocinero** antes que fraile

to know what s.o. is up to conocerle/verle a alg. el **juego**

to know what the score is estar al **cabo** de algo/de la calle

to know what's going on estar al **cabo** de algo/de la calle

to know what's what saber cuántas son **cinco**; conocer el **paño**

to know what's what [where s.o. is concerned] tener [mucha] **mano** izquierda [con alg.]

to know where the shoe pinches saber dónde aprieta el **zapato**

to know which side one's bread is buttered arrimarse al **sol** que más calienta

to know which way the cat jumps/the cookie crumbles/the wind is blowing saber de qué lado caen las **pera**s/por dónde van los **tiros**

to know who one is dealing with conocer a su **gente**; conocer el **paño**

know-how el pesquis

know-[it-]all (be a ~) más que **siete**

knowledge (be common ~) andar algo de **boca** en boca (example); andar en **coplas**

known (become ~) salir a **luz**

known (become ~ to the public) salir a volar

to be known everywhere ser más conocido que el **tebeo**

to knuckle under doblar el **espinazo**

knuckles (get a rap over the ~) recibir un **rapapolvo**

knuckles (rap s.o. over the ~) cardarle la **lana** a alg.; echar un **rapapolvo** a alg.

kosher (not to be ~) no ser algo **trigo** limpio

L

to label s.o. colgar el **sambenito** a alg.

labor of Hercules ser **obra** de romanos

to labor in vain coger **agua** en cesto; azotar el **aire**; machacar en hierro frío; arar en el **mar**

lack (there's a distinct ~ of s.th.) brillar algo por su **ausencia**

lad (little ~) la media **botella**

lad (young ~) el pollo

ladder (have gone up the social ~) andar/estar en **zancos**

lady (real ~) señor

lady-killer el castigador

lady-killer (be a ~) tener **corazón** de alcachofa

lake (go jump in a ~!) ¡anda a **bañarte**!; ¡vete a freír **buñuelos**/espárragos!

lake (tell s.o. to go [and] jump in a ~) mandar a alg. a freír **buñuelos**/al **cuerno**/a freír **espárragos**/a hacer **gárgaras**

lamb (be a ~) ser una **paloma** sin hiel

lamb (become/be as meek as a ~) quedarse más suave que un **guante**; estar como una **seda**

lamb (mutton dressed up as ~) la carantoña

to lambast[e] s.o. poner a alg. como un **estropajo**/de **oro** y azul

land (be living in never-never ~/in cloud-cuckoo-~) tener la **cabeza** llena de pájaros; vivir en la **luna**; andar por o vivir en las **nubes**

land (see how the ~ lies) tantear/medir el **terreno**

land of milk and honey (people elsewhere in the world don't live in the ~ either) allí tampoco atan los perros con **longaniza**[s]

to land (get ~ed with it) cargar con el **mochuelo**

to land in jail/prison dar con los/sus **huesos** en la cárcel

to land on one's feet caer de **pies**

to land on one's nose caerse/dar de narices [en/contra el suelo] (▷ **nariz**)

to land s.o. one pegar una **leche**/torta a alg.

to land s.o. with s.th. endiñar/endosar algo a alg.; cargar el **mochuelo** a alg.

to land [up] at recalar en

landlubber el **marinero** de agua dulce

landmark (be a ~) marcar un **hito**

landmark decision/discovery/etc. (be a ~) marcar un **hito**

language (use coarse ~) soltar **tacos**

lap (fall/drop into s.o.'s ~) caerle a alg. como llovido del **cielo**; venir a alg. a la[s] **mano**[s]

lapse el desliz

lard (be a tub of ~) estar hecho una **botija**; estar como una **vaca**

lark (be as happy as a ~) estar [alegre] como unas **castañuelas**; estar [contento] como o más contento que unas pascuas (▷ **Pascua**)

lark (blow/stuff s.th. for a ~) estar hasta las **cejas**/el **coco**/[más allá de] la **coronilla** de algo; estar **frito** de algo; estar hasta el **gorro**/el **moño**/las narices (▷ **nariz**)/la **punta** de los pelos o del pelo/los **topes** de algo

lark (have a ~ with s.o.) tomarle el **pelo** a alg.

lark (rise with the ~) levantarse con las **gallinas**

Larry (be as happy as ~) estar [alegre] como unas **castañuelas**; estar [contento] como o más contento que unas pascuas (▷ **Pascua**)

to lash out (be quick to ~) ser **largo** de manos; tener las **manos** largas

to lash out blindly/wildly or like a maniac como un **descosido** (example); a **diestro** y siniestro (example); dar **palos** de ciego; a tontas y a locas (▷ **tonto**) (example)

last (at long ~) al fin y al **cabo**

last (breathe one's ~) estar en las últimas (▷ **último**)

last (stick to your ~!) ¡zapatero, a tus zapatos!

last (to the ~) hasta la última **gota**

last cent/penny (down to the ~) un **real** sobre otro

last place (be the team in ~) ser el **farolillo** rojo

last straw (be the ~) colmar la medida

last straw (this is the ~!) ¡[esto] es el acabóse! (▷ **acabar**)

to last (it's too good to ~) ya viene/vendrá el tío **Paco** con la rebaja

to last forever (nothing ~s forever) no hay **bien** ni mal que cien años dure

to last forever (this won't ~) ya viene/vendrá el tío **Paco** con la rebaja

to last [out] (shoes/etc.) tirar

lasting de **cal** y canto

late (better ~ than never) nunca es tarde si la **dicha** es buena; más vale **tarde** que nunca

late (come too ~) llegar a los **postres**

late (get up ~) pisar el **sapo**

late (terribly/very ~) a las **mil** y quinientas

to laugh (burst out ~ing) soltar la **carcajada**; soltar el **chorro** [de la risa]; reventar de risa; soltar el **trapo**

to laugh (die ~ing) descoyuntarse/desternillarse de risa; ser para **morir**se de risa (example); **perecer**se de risa to laugh (he who ~s last ~s longest/loudest) al **freír** será el reír; quien o el que ríe último, ríe mejor (▷ **reír**)

to laugh (it's enough to make a cat ~) no hay tales **borregos/carneros/cordero**s

to laugh (kill o.s. ~ing) descojonarse; descoyuntarse/desternillarse/rajarse de risa

to laugh (pee/piss/wet o.s. ~ing) descojonarse; **mear**se [de risa]

to laugh (roll around ~ing) revolcarse de la risa

to laugh (split one's sides ~ing) como un **descosido** (example); rajarse/reventar de risa

to laugh one's head off como un **descosido** (example); reír[se] a **mandíbula** batiente

to laugh s.th. off tomarse algo a **risa**

to laugh up one's sleeve **reír**se a solas/para sus adentros

laughing stock [of the city] (be the ~) ser el **hazmerreír** de la ciudad o de la gente; ser la **irrisión** de la cuidad

laughing stock (make a ~ of o.s.) hacer el **oso**

laughter (roar with ~) reír[se] a **carcajadas**; soltar el **chorro** [de la risa]; a más no **poder**

laughter (roll around with ~) revolcarse de la risa

laughter (split one's sides with ~) rajarse/reventar de risa

to launch s.o. poner a alg. en **órbita**

laurels (rest on one's ~) dormirse sobre los/sus **laurel**es

to lavish attentions on s.o. tratar/atender a alg. a **cuerpo** de rey

to lavish s.th. on s.o. colmar a alg. de algo; prodigar algo a alg.

lavishly (entertain s.o. ~) tratar/atender a alg. a **cuerpo** de rey

law (every ~ has its loophole) hecha la **ley**, hecha la trampa

law (ignorance of the ~ is no excuse/defense) ignorancia no quita pecado

law (jungle ~) la **ley** de la jungla/selva

law (necessity knows no ~) la **necesidad** carece de ley

law of the jungle la **ley** de la jungla/selva

lay (easy ~) la ligona

lay (she's an easy ~) está loca por la música (▷ **loco**)

to lay into s.o. poner a alg. de **oro** y azul

to lay it on [too] thick hinchar el perro; forzar la **nota**

to lay on the works for s.o. tratar/atender a alg. a **cuerpo** de rey

to lay s.o. (have sex with s.o.) pasar a una por las **arma**s; calzar[se]/**cargar**se a alg.; **cepillar**[se] a una; poner un **clavo** a una; follar/joder a alg.; pasar a una mujer por la **piedra**; pisar a alg.; quilar a alg.; regar/

tapar/**tirar**se/tumbar/**zumbar**se a una mujer

layabout (be a good-for-nothing ~) sin **oficio** ni beneficio (example)

to laze around ir por o correr la **gandaya**

lazy (be very ~) ser más vago que la **chaqueta** de un guardia

lazy (s.o. was born ~) nació alg. cansado o con la lengua fuera (▷ **nacer**)

lazy bum (be a ~) sin **oficio** ni beneficio (example)

lazy is s.o.'s middle name nació alg. cansado o con la lengua fuera (▷ **nacer**)

lazy time (have a ~ of it) echarse/tenderse/ tumbarse a la **bartola**

lazybones (be a born ~) nació alg. cansado o con la lengua fuera (▷ **nacer**)

lead (swing the ~) hacer la **zanguanga**

to lead s.o. by the nose llevar a alg. del **cabestro**

leader (be a real/true ~) con toda la **barba**

leading light (not to be exactly a ~) no tener dos **dedo**s de frente; nació alg. tarde (▷ **nacer**)

leaf (shake like a ~) temblar como una hoja/un azogado/un flan

leaf (turn over a new ~) doblar/volver la **hoja**; hacer **libro** nuevo

leak (have/take a ~) cambiar el **agua/caldo** a las aceitunas; cambiar el agua al **canario**; echar una **meada**

to lean on the doorbell echar las **puerta**s abajo

to lean over backwards andar/bailar de **coronilla**; **volcar**se

to lean over backwards to make it easy for s.o. tender **puentes** de plata a alg.

lean years las **vaca**s flacas

leaps and bounds (by ~) a **paso**s agigantados

to learn (everyone has to/we all have to ~) nadie nace enseñado (▷ **nacer**); al primer **tapón**, zurrapa[s]

to learn (have learned/learnt s.th. at one's mother's knee/from the cradle) haber mamado algo [ya] en/con la **leche**

to learn (one only ~s from one's own mistakes) nadie escarmienta en cabeza ajena (▷ **escarmentar**)

to learn by s.o. else's mistakes escarmentar en cabeza ajena

to learn from other people's mistakes (you should ~) cuando las **barbas** de tu vecino veas arder, pon las tuyas a remojar

to learn one's lesson escarmentar

to learn the hard way escarmentar

learned (be immensely ~) ser un **pozo** de ciencia

learning (there's no royal road to ~) la **letra** con sangre entra

leash (keep s.o. on a short ~) atar corto a alg.

leather (run hell for ~) ir como **alma** que se lleva el diablo; a más no **poder**

leave (take French ~) despedirse a la francesa (▷ **francés**)

to leave (be about to ~) estar con un pie en el **estribo**

to leave (be on the point of leaving) estar con un pie en el **estribo**

to leave (there's nothing else left for s.o. to try) no quedarle a alg. ninguna **tecla** por tocar

to leave it at that (not to ~) no quedarse ahí **parado**

leave me alone! ¡no me hagas la **puñeta**!

to leave s.o. behind dejar en **zaga** a alg.

to leave s.th. aside dejar algo a un **lado**/de lado

to leave that alone (it's best to ~) peor es meneallo/mejor es no meneallo/más vale no meneallo (▷ **menear**)

leave well enough alone bueno está lo bueno [pero no lo demasiado]

lecher el garañón

lecher (old ~) el **viejo** verde

lecher (old gay ~) el carroza

lecture (endure the ~) aguantar el **chaparrón**

lecture (give s.o. a ~) echar un **sermón** a alg.

leech (cling to s.o. like a ~) pegarse como una **ladilla/lapa** a alg.

left (not to know ~ from right) no distinguir lo **blanco** de lo negro

left and right a **diestro** y siniestro

left, right and centre a **diestro** y siniestro

leftovers las **ruina**s

leg la pata

leg (chair/table/etc.) la pata

leg ([long] ~) la zanca

leg (matchstick ~) la zanca

leg (be on one's last ~s) la **cuerda** no da más; andar/ir con el **culo** a rastras; estar en las últimas/en las diez de últimas (▷ **último**)

leg (break a ~!) ¡buena **suerte**!

leg (get a/one's ~ over) echar un **casquete**; follar/joder; echar un **polvo**; quilar

leg (pull s.o.'s ~) dar [el] **camelo** a alg.; tomarle el **pelo** a alg.; pitorrearse de alg.; quedarse con alg.

leg (shake a ~) menear/mover el **esqueleto**

leg (wooden ~) la **pata** de palo

to leg it salir por **pierna**s

legless (be ~) estar hecho un **cesto**; estar hecho una **cuba**/un **cuero**; estar hecho un **pellejo**/una **sopa**/una **uva**

legless (get ~) **cocer**se; papar una **jumera**; coger una **melopea/merluza**; coger/pillar una **mona**; moñarse; coger una **pea**; agarrar[se] un **pedo**; coger una **pítima**

leg-pulling el camelo

lemon (be a ~: dud/failure) ser una **patata**

length and breadth (throughout the ~ of) a lo **largo** y a lo ancho de

lenient (be too ~) tener **manga** ancha/ser de manga ancha

leopard (a ~ never changes or cannot change its spots) al que nace **barrigón** es al ñudo que lo fajen; quien nace [para] **burro**, muere rebuznando; la **cabra** siempre tira al monte; quien nace **chicharra** muere cantando; genio y figura hasta la sepultura

lesbian la bollera/torti/tortillera

lesbian intercourse (have ~) hacer una **tortilla**

lesson (learn one's ~) escarmentar

lesson (teach s.o. a ~) escarmentar a alg.

to let off [a fart] soltar/tirar[se] un **pedo**; zullarse

to let off a string of farts soltar una **pedorrera**

to let one off silently (fart) **follar**se

to let s.o. down dejar **colgado** a alg.

to let s.o. have it zurrar la **badana** o menear/sacudir el **bulto** a alg.; arrimar **candela**/dar **caña**/medir las **costillas**/sentar las **costuras** a alg.; dar **leña** o cargar de leña a alg.; cascarle/machacarle a alg. las **liendre**s; sacudir el **polvo** a alg.; poner a alg. como un **pulpo**

to let up aflojar las **rienda**s

to let up (s.o.'s bad luck doesn't ~) pasarlas negras (▷ **negro**)

letdown (turn out to be or be a ~) salir/ser algo **rana**

letter (French ~: condom) el calcetín/globo; la goma

letter (to the ~) al **pie** de la letra

level (on a ~ with) a **flor** de

liar (be a chronic/a downright/an out-and-out/a real ~) ser un **costal** de mentiras; de siete **suela**s

liberty (take liberties with s.o.) subirse a las **barba**s de alg.

lick ([at] full ~) a toda **pastilla**

lick (drive/go [at] full ~) quemar el **caucho**; a toda **pastilla** (example); correr/lanzarse a **tumba** abierta

lick and a promise (give s.th. a ~) limpiar algo solamente por donde ve la **suegra** o limpiar solamente lo que ve la suegra

lick and a promise (make do with a ~) lavarse a lo **gato**

to lick s.o.'s boots lavar la **cara** a alg.

lid (flip one's ~) perder la **chaveta**; pasarse de **rosca**

lid (take the ~ off s.th.) tirar de la **manta**; descubrir el **pastel**

lie el camelo; el **cuento** chino

lie (be a downright/a great big/a whopping great/an absolute ~) de los **bueno**s (example); de padre y muy señor mío (▷ **el padre**) (example); solemne

lie (give the ~ to s.o.) coger a alg. en un **renuncio**

lie (tell a barefaced ~) con toda la **barba**; mentir con toda la **boca** to lie (catch s.o. lying) coger a alg. en un **renuncio**

to lie about one's age quitarse/restarse **años**

to lie down (take it lying down) **tragar**lo

to lie down (we won't take that lying down!) ino somos negros! (▷ **el negro**)

to lie down under it **tragar**lo

to lie like nobody's business ... que se las pela (▷ **pelar**)

to lie through one's teeth con toda la **barba**; mentir por los **codos**; mentir más que hablar/que la Gaceta; ... que se las pela (▷ **pelar**); mentir más que un **sacamuelas**

lies (tell huge ~) mentir por los **codos**/más que un **sacamuelas**

lies (tell whopping great ~) decir mentiras como **puños**

lies (your ~ will always catch up with you in the end) antes se coge al **embustero** que al cojo

life (be in the prime of ~) estar en la **flor** de la vida

life (change one's ~) mudar el **pellejo**

life (dog's ~) de **perros**

life (get the fright of one's ~) no llegarle a uno la **camisa** al cuerpo; **morir**se del susto

life (give a sign of ~) resollar

life (guard s.th. with one's ~) guardar algo como **oro** en paño

life (have as many lives as a cat) tener siete **vidas** [como los gatos]

life (have nine lives) tener siete **vidas** [como los gatos]

life (have the time of one's ~) pasar las **vacas** gordas

life (how's your/etc. love ~?) ¿qué tal andas/etc. de **amor**es?

life (live the ~ of Riley) vivir a **cuerpo** de rey/ como **Dios** en Francia; pegarse la **vida** padre

life (live/have an easy ~) vivir como un **canónigo**; pegarse la **vida** padre

life (live/lead a dissolute ~) correr sin **freno**

life (lose one's ~) dar/soltar el **pellejo**

life (make ~ hell for s.o.) llevar/traer a alg. por la **calle** de la amargura; matar a alg. a **fuego** lento

life (make s.o.'s ~ a misery) llevar/traer a alg. por la **calle** de la amargura

life (not for the ~ of one) ni a la de **tres**

life (not on your ~!) ini en **coplas**!; inaranjas!; inaranjas chinas! inaranjas de la China!; ini **pensar**lo!; ini por **soñación**!; ini **soñar**lo!

life (risk one's ~) jugarse el **pellejo**/la **vida**

life (save one's/s.o.'s ~) salvar el **pellejo**; salvar el **pellejo** a alg.

life (s.o.'s ~ is a/is no bed of roses) pasársela en **flores**; [no] estar/dormir sobre un lecho de **rosas**

life (work sweetens ~) el **trabajo** es el encanto de la vida

life (you can bet your ~ on that) apostaría la **cabeza**

life (you can bet your ~ [that] ...) apostar[se] la **cabeza**/el **cuello** a que ...

life (you have only one ~ to live) no se vive más que una vez (▷ **vivir**)

life is full of surprises donde/cuando menos se piensa, salta la **liebre**

life isn't all a bowl of cherries no todo el monte es **orégano**

life isn't [all/always] a bed of roses la vida no es un lecho de **rosas**

lifestyle (live a luxurious ~) vivir a todo **tren**

lift (hitch/thumb a ~) ir[se] a **dedo**/hacer dedo

to lift s.th. (plagiarize) fusilar algo

light (block the/stand in the ~) hacer **sombrajos**

light (bring s.th. to ~) sacar algo a **luz**; tirar de la **manta**

light (come to ~) salir a **luz**

light (give s.th. the green ~) dar **luz** verde a algo

light (go out like a ~) dormirse o quedarse dormido como un **ceporro/tronco**

light (hide one's ~ under a bushel) meter/poner la **luz** bajo el celemín

light (not to be exactly a leading/shining ~) no tener dos **dedos** de frente; nació alg. tarde (▷ **nacer**)

light at the end of the tunnel (there is ~) hay **luz** al final del túnel

to be light-fingered ser **largo** de uñas; tener las **manos** largas

light-fingered person el/la **uñetas**

lightly (have got off ~ [this time]) haber visto las **orejas** del lobo

lightly (I/we/etc. got off ~!) ide buena me he/ nos hemos/etc. librado! (▷ **librar**)

lightly (take s.th. very ~) tomarse algo a **chirigota**

lightning (like greased ~) a toda **mecha**

like (be as ~ as two peas [in a pod]) parecerse como dos **gotas** de agua/como un **huevo** a otro

like (be/look very much ~) ser **primo** hermano de o ser primos hermanos

like (that was just ~ her) hacer de las **suyas** (example)

to like (bet s.o. anything he ~s [that] ...) apostar[se] la **cabeza**/el **cuello** a que ...

to like (do what one ~s with one's own things) hacer de su **capa** un sayo

to like (let s.o. do with one what s.o. ~s) tener a alg. montado en las narices (▷ **nariz**)

to like (say what one bloody/damn well ~s) salirle a alg. de los cojones (▷ **cojón**)

to like (whether one ~s it or not) por las buenas o por las malas (▷ **bueno**)

like it or not por las buenas o por las malas (▷ **bueno**)

to like s.o./s.th. mirar bien a alg.; rezar con; hacer **tilín** a alg.

to like s.o./s.th. (not to ~) caerle **gordo** a alg.; mirar mal a alg.; no ser **plato** de su gusto; no **rezar** con

to be lik[e]able tener buena **sombra**

likes (you won't see the ~ of that again in a hurry) ni buscando con [un] **candil**

limelight (be in the ~) estar algo en [el] **candelero**

limelight (bring s.th./s.o. into the ~) poner algo/a alg. en [el] **candelero**

limelight (hog the ~) acaparar la atención [de todos]

limit (be really the ~) pasar de **castaño** oscuro; pelar la jeta

limit (there's a ~ to everything) tanto va el **cántaro** a la fuente, que al fin se rompe

limit (this is the absolute ~!) ¡[esto] es el acabóse! (▷ **acabar**)

limit (you're the ~!) ser de lo que no hay (▷ **haber**)

to limp ir a la **pata** chula

limpet (cling to s.o. like a ~) pegarse como una **ladilla/lapa** a alg.

line (be really out of ~) pasar de **castaño** oscuro; pelar la jeta

line (drop a few ~s) poner cuatro **letra**s

line (lay it on the ~) no andarse con/en chiquitas (▷ la **chiquita**); andarse por las **rama**s (▷ example); no andarse con **requilorios**

line (shoot a ~) darse **bombo**; echarse/marcarse un **farol**

line (stand in ~) hacer/guardar **cola**

line (step out of ~) meter la **pata/pezuña**; dar una **pitada**

line (swallow anything hook, ~ and sinker) **tragar**[se]las como ruedas de molino

line (take a tougher ~) apretar la **cuerda**; salir por otro **registro**

line (toe the ~) bailar al **son** que le tocan a alg.

to line one's pockets ponerse las **bota**s; chupar del **bote**; **rascar**se para adentro; **redondear**se

to line up hacer/guardar **cola**

linen (not to wash one's dirty ~ in public) lavar los **trapo**s sucios en casa

linen (wash one's dirty ~ in public) lavar los **trapo**s sucios ante el mundo entero

linen (you shouldn't wash your dirty ~ in public) la **ropa** sucia se lava en casa; los **trapo**s sucios se lavan en casa

lion (beard the ~ in his den) entrar en el cubil de la **fiera**

lion (it's better to be the head of a dog than the tail of a ~) más vale ser **cabeza** de ratón que cola de león

lion's den (go/venture into the ~) meterse en la **boca** del lobo

lion's mouth (put one's head in the ~) meterse en la **boca** del lobo

lion's share la **tajada** del león

lion's share (make sure one gets the ~) servirse/despacharse con el **cucharón**

lip (bite one's ~) morderse la **lengua**

lip (button [up] one's ~) no decir ni **mu/pío**

lip (there's many a slip 'twixt cup and ~) del **dicho** al hecho hay mucho trecho; dicho sin hecho no trae provecho; del **plato** a la boca se pierde la sopa

lip service de **boca** [para] afuera; de **boquilla**; de **diente**s [para] afuera

lips (be on everybody's ~) andar algo en **boca** de todos

lips (hang on s.o.'s ~) estar **colgado** de las palabras de alg.; estar pendiente de los **labio**s de alg.; beberle a alg. las **palabra**s

lips (smack one's ~ [over s.th.]) chuparse los **dedo**s [por algo]

lips (s.o.'s ~ are sealed) coserse la **boca**; callar[se] como un muerto/una piedra

list (have a long wish ~) recetar largo

to listen (careful, there are people ~ing!) ¡hay **moro**s en la costa!

to listen (not/refuse to ~ [to s.o.]) escuchar/oír como quien oye **llover**

to listen (there are none so deaf as those who will not ~) no hay peor **sordo** que el que no quiere oír

to listen carefully aplicar el **oído**

to listen to reason (make s.o. ~) meter a alg. en **cintura/costura**

to listen to what s.o. has to say prestar/dar **oído**s a alg.

literally al **pie** de la letra

little (every ~ helps) un **grano** no hace granero pero ayuda al compañero

little by little palmo a palmo

little lad la media **botella**

little squirt el comino/renacuajo

to live (man cannot ~ by bread alone) no sólo de **pan** vive el hombre

to live (you have only one life to ~) no se vive más que una vez (▷ **vivir**)

to live a dissolute life correr sin **freno**

to live a luxurious lifestyle vivir a todo **tren**

to live an easy life vivir como un **canónigo**; pegarse la **vida** padre

to live and let live vivir y dejar vivir

to live at s.o. else's expense andar/vivir de **gorra**; comer la/vivir de la **sopa** boba

to live by sponging vivir de **sablazo**s

to live from/by stealing vivir de la **uña**

to live from/by stealing/robbing (good-for-nothings who ~) gente de la **garra**

to live high on the hog vivir a todo **tren**

to live in a fool's paradise tejer la tela de **Penélope**

to live in cloud-cuckoo-land/in never-never land or in a dream/fantasy world tener la **cabeza** llena de pájaros; vivir en la **luna**; andar por o vivir en las **nubes**

to live in clover vivir como **Dios** en Francia; vivir/estar como **pava** en corral

to live in constant fear of punishment traer/llevar la **soga** arrastrando

to live in grand style vivir como un/a lo **príncipe**; vivir a todo **tren**

to live it up correrse una **juerga**

to live like a cabbage/vegetable vegetar

to live like a king/lord vivir a **cuerpo** de rey; vivir como un/a lo **príncipe**; a lo gran señor (▷ **el señor**); vivir a todo **tren**

to live next door vivir **pared/tabique** por medio

to live on a grand scale vivir como un/a lo **príncipe**

to live on air sustentarse del aire

to live on the fat of the land vivir a **cuerpo** de rey/a todo **tren**

to live on/off other people comer la/vivir de la **sopa** boba

to live the life of Riley vivir a **cuerpo** de rey/como **Dios** en Francia; pegarse la **vida** padre

to live together casarse por detrás de la iglesia

to live without s.o. (s.o. can't ~) no poder **pasar** sin alg.

to live without s.th. (s.o. can ~) poder **pasar** sin algo

live wire el zarandillo

livelong day (all the ~/the whole ~) todo el **santo** día

to liven things up **llevarse** todo por delante

to be livid estar hecho un **basilisco**; estar alg. que brinca (▷ **brincar**); echar **chiribitas/chispas**; estar alg. que trina (▷ **trinar**)

livid (get ~) darse a **perros**

living (earn/make a ~) ganarse los **fríjoles/los garbanzos/el pan/el puchero/la vida**

living (good-for-nothings who make their ~ from/by stealing) gente de la **garra**

living (make a decent ~) tener su/un buen **pasar**

living (make one's ~ from/by stealing) vivir de la **uña**

living (sponge a ~) andar/vivir de **gorra**; comer la/vivir de la **sopa** boba

load (be two bricks shy of a ~) ser de pocas luces/corto de luces o tener pocas luces (▷ **luz**)

load (be/take a [heavy/real] ~ off s.o.'s mind) quitársele a alg. un [gran] **peso** de encima; quitarle a alg. un [gran] **peso** de encima

load of baloney/bull/rubbish el **cuento** chino

load of nonsense/rubbish una **sarta** de (example)

to be loaded tener muchos **cuartos**; estar **forrado**; rebosar en dinero

loads of a **granel**; hasta la **pared** de enfrente; a **punta** pala

loads of things la **mar** de

to loaf around ir por o correr la **gandaya**

loafer paseante en corte; el/la **trotacalles**

to loathe s.o. tener/traer a alg. entre **ojos**

lobster (blush like a ~) ponerse como un **cangrejo** asado o rojo como un cangrejo; subírsele a alg. el **pavo** o ponerse hecho un pavo

to lock (firmly ~ s.th.) cerrar algo a **piedra** y lodo

to be locked up ponerse el **capuchón**

locker (have a shot in the/one's ~) traer algo en/por la **manga**

log (be as easy as falling off a ~) ser **coser** y cantar; ser **pan** comido

log (sleep like a ~) dormir como un **bendito**/un **ceporro**/un **leño**/un **lirón**/una **peña**/un **tronco**

loggerheads (be at ~) tirarse de los **moños**; andar al **pelo**

lolly (money) el barro; el **calé** o calés; la china; [los] **cuartos**; la guita/lana/manteca; [los] monises; la mosca; [los] nipos; el parné; la pasta; el pisto; la tela; el trigo

lone wolf Juan Palomo

lonely (as ~ as a cloud) más solo que un **hongo**

loner Juan Palomo

long (be as ~ as your arm) ser más **largo** que un día sin pan

long (be very ~: s.th.) ser más **largo** que un día sin pan

long (never stay in one place for ~) ser [un] **culo** de mal asiento

long ago año de/tiempo[s] de/días de **Maricastaña**; del año de/en el año de la **nana**; en [los] tiempos de **ñangué**; del año de o en el año de la **pera/polca**; en tiempos del **rey** que rabió/del rey Wamba

long dozen la **docena** del fraile

long in the tooth (be [a bit] ~) estar alg. para el **arrastre**

long job (be a ~) haber **tela** que cortar/para rato

long last (at ~) al fin y al **cabo**

long weekend (take a ~) hacer **puente**

to long for s.th. beber los **aires** por algo; írsele a alg. el **alma** tras algo; hipar por algo; írsele a alg. los **ojos** tras algo; **perecerse**/rabiar por algo; beber los **vientos** por algo

to long to + infinitive **perecerse** por + infinitivo

longjohns los napoleones

loo (have to go to the ~) echar una **carta** al correo (example) look (have a cross/sour ~ on one's face) tener **cara** de pocos amigos

look (not to like the ~ of s.th.) ir tomando algo mal **cariz**; ponerse algo **feo**

look (one can tell just by the ~ on s.o.'s face) se le ve/nota/conoce a alg. en la **cara**; salirle algo a alg. a los **ojos**

to look (one can tell just by ~ing at s.o.) se le ve/nota/conoce a alg. en la **cara**; salirle algo a alg. a los **ojos**

to look after s.o. arreglárselas (▷ **arreglar**) (example); componérselas (▷ **componer**) (example)

to look alike (not to look in the least bit alike) estar tan lejos como lo **blanco** de lo negro/no parecerse ni en el blanco de los ojos; parecerse como un **huevo** a una castaña

to look as if butter wouldn't melt in one's mouth hacerse la/parecer una **mosquita** muerta; no/nunca haber roto un **plato** [en su vida]

to look at s.th./s.o. through different eyes or differently mirar algo/a alg. con otros **ojos**

to look awful on s.o. sentarle algo a alg. como a un santo **cristo** un par de pistolas; pegarle algo a alg. como un **mandil** a una vaca; sentarle algo a alg. como un **tiro**

to look bad ([be] begin[ning] to ~) ir tomando algo mal **cariz**; ponerse algo **feo**

to look black/grumpy/surly tener **cara** de pocos amigos

to look extraordinarily alike/very much like ser **primo** hermano de o ser primos hermanos

to look out estar/andar sobre los **estribos**

look out! ¡oído al parche!

to look ridiculous (make s.o. ~) poner a alg. en **solfa**

to look smashing/terrific estar como un **camión**/**tren**

to look the other way hacer la vista gorda (▷ **gordo**)

to look up to s.o. as a model mirarse en alg. como en un **espejo**

looker (woman) un buen **bocado**; un **monumento** [nacional]

to be looking for a wife andar en pretensiones (▷ **pretensión**)

to be looking [secretly] into s.th. andar a la **husma** de algo

look-out (that's a fine ~!) ¡vaya un **panorama**!

look-out (that's his ~!) arreglárselas (▷ **arreglar**) (example); componérselas (▷ **componer**) (example)

look-out (that's his/etc. ~) con su/etc. pan se/etc. lo coma/etc. (▷ **comer**)

looks (have stunning good ~) estar como un **tren**

looming (see danger ~ ahead) abocar a

loony bin el loquero

loop (be knocked for a ~) quedarse de una **pieza**

loop (knock s.o. for a ~) partir a alg. por el **eje**; dejar a alg. de una **pieza**

loophole (every law has its ~) hecha la **ley**, hecha la trampa

loophole (find a ~) **deslizar**se por [entre] las mallas

loose (cut ~) echar una **cana** al aire

loose ends (tie up ~) atar/unir **cabo**s

loose woman la prójima

to loosen s.o.'s tongue desatar/soltar la **lengua** a alg.; subírsele algo (vino/etc.) a alg. a predicar (▷ **subirse**)

lord (be [as] drunk as a ~) estar hecho un **cesto**/una **cuba**/un **cuero**/un **pellejo**/una **uva**

lord (live like a ~) vivir como un/a lo **príncipe**; a lo gran señor (▷ **el señor**)

lord (play ~ of the manor) darse **aire**s de grandeza; pintar la **cigüeña**

to lose (▷ **lost**)

to lose ([be bound to] ~) llevar las de **perder**/salir perdiendo

to lose (he who has nothing has nothing to ~) quien **poco** tiene, poco teme

to lose ground perder **terreno**

to lose one's cool ponerse como un **basilisco**; exaltársele a alg. la **bilis**; subirse al **campanario**; salirse de sus **casillas**; ponerse hecho un **demonio**; perder los **estribo**s; hinchársele a alg. las narices (▷ **nariz**); subirse por las **pared**es/a la **parra**

to lose one's head perder los **estribo**s/la **tramontana**

to lose one's head over s.o. perder la **chaveta** por alg.

to lose one's life dar/soltar el **pellejo**

to lose one's rag perder los **estribo**s

to lose one's shirt jugar hasta la **camisa**; estar **pelado** (example)

to lose one's temper ([be quick] to ~) perder los **estribo**s; a **flor** de piel

to lose out llevar las de **perder**/salir perdiendo

to lose sleep over s.th. (unnecessarily ~) hacerse una **paja** mental

to lose s.th. trasconejar algo

to lose the knack/one's touch perder los **libro**s/la **onda**

loser (come off a ~) llevar las de **perder**/salir perdiendo

loss (▷ **dead** ~)

loss (be at a [complete] ~ as to what to do [next]) no saber como salir del **atranco**; la **sabiduría** no llega a más; estar como **tonto** en vísperas

loss (not to be at a ~ as to what to do) arreglárselas (▷ **arreglar**); componérselas (▷ **componer**)

lost (get ~!) ¡anda a **bañar**te!; ¡vete a freír **buñuelo**s/**espárrago**s!; ¡vete a **paseo**!; ¡quítate de ahí/de en medio! (▷ **quitar**) lost (give s.th. up for ~) echar la **bendición** a algo

lost (tell s.o. to get ~) mandar a alg. a freír **buñuelo**s/al **cuerno**/a freír **espárragos**/a hacer **gárgaras**/a **paseo**

to be lost for words quedarse **bizco**

lot (a fat ~ I care!) ital día hará un **año**!

lot (bad ~) el tipejo

lot (be a bad ~) ser un **pájaro** de cuenta

lot (clear off with the whole ~) alzarse/salirse con el **santo** y la limosna/cera

lot (know the ~) saber más que **Briján**

lot (the whole ~ [of them]) el ganado

loud fart el cuesco

loudmouth el farolero/la farolera; el voceras

lousy de mala **muerte**

lousy (the weather's ~) de **perro**s

lousy time (have a really ~) puto (example)

lout el morral/patán

love (a woman/man who is head over heels in ~) la tórtola; el tórtolo

love (be burning with ~) abrasarse de amores

love (be head over heels in ~ [with s.o.]) estar **perdido** por alg.; estar enamorado hasta los **tuétano**s

love (be madly in ~ [with s.o.]) abrasarse de amores; beber los **aire**s por alg.; beber/ sorber los **viento**s por alg.

love (make ~ to/with s.o.) hacer el **amor** a/con alg.

love (not for ~ [n]or money) aunque se junten el **cielo** y la tierra; ni para un **remedio**

love (person) el **pedazo** del alma/del corazón/ de las entrañas; la prenda

love (unlucky at cards, lucky in ~) desgraciado en el **juego**, afortunado en amores/de malas en el juego, de buenas en amores

love affair el apaño

to be love at first sight ser un **flechazo**

love life (how's your/etc. ~?) ¿qué tal andas/etc. de **amor**es?

love nest el picadero

to love (play "she ~s me, she ~s me not") deshojar la **margarita**

to love + gerund **perecerse** por + infinitivo

lovebird la tórtola; el tórtolo

lovely couple (make a ~) hacer una buena/bonita **pareja**

to be lovely[-looking] ser una **pintura**

lover la apaña; el apaño

low (be ~ on s.th.) estar/andar **mal** de algo

low (be feeling ~) tener la/estar con la **depre**

low (be having or going through a real ~) estar por los **suelo**s

low man on the totem pole (be the ~) ser el último **mono**

lowest of the low (be the ~) ser el último **mono**

luck la breva

luck (as ~ will have it) salga **pez** o salga rana

luck (basically it all depends on [good] ~) de **hombre** a hombre no va nada

luck (be dogged by bad ~) pasarlas negras (▷ **negro**)

luck (be in ~) campar con su estrella; andar de **ganancia**; tener **potra**; tener el **santo** de cara

luck (be sheer ~) sonar la **flauta** [por casualidad]

luck (chance piece of good ~) la breva; el **cabe** de pala

luck (good ~!) ¡buena **suerte**!

luck (have a streak/run of bad ~) perseguir a alg. la **negra**/tener la negra

luck (have a streak/run of [good] ~) andar de **ganancia**; llevar/tener [todas] las de **ganar**

luck (have bad ~) tocarle a alg. la **china/negra**; tener mala **pata**; tener el **santo** de espaldas

luck (if I get a bit of ~, . . .) sonar la **flauta** [por casualidad] (example)

luck (nobody says no to a bit of ~) a nadie le amarga un **dulce**

luck (s.o.'s bad ~ doesn't let up) pasarlas negras (▷ **negro**)

luck (stroke of ~) la bolichada/breva; el **cabe** de pala

luck (talk about ~!) ¡de buena me he/nos hemos/etc. librado! (▷ **librar**)

luck (there's no such ~) no caerá esa **breva**

luck (trusting to ~) a la buena de Dios (▷ **bueno**); a la **gracia** de Dios

luck (you/etc. shouldn't push your/etc. ~) tanto va el **cántaro** a la fuente, que al fin se rompe

to be lucky campar con su estrella; correr el **dado**; andar de **ganancia**; tener **potra**; tener el **santo** de cara; tener buena **sombra**

lucky (count o.s. ~) darse con un **canto** en los dientes/pechos

lucky (have been ~ [this time]) haber visto las **orejas** del lobo

lucky (he's/etc. always damned ~) hasta la **perra** le/etc. parirá lechones

lucky (it's nice to be ~!) sonar la **flauta** [por casualidad] (example)

lucky (I/we/etc. got ~ there!) ¡de buena me he/ nos hemos/etc. librado! (▷ **librar**)

lucky (s.o. was born ~) nació alg. de pie[s] (▷ **nacer**)

lucky (unlucky at cards, ~ in love) desgraciado en el **juego**, afortunado en amores/de malas en el juego, de buenas en amores

lucky break la bolichada/breva; el **cabe** de pala

lucky coincidence/guess (be a ~) sonar la **flauta** [por casualidad]

lucky person (be a ~) nació alg. de pie[s] (▷ **nacer**)

lucky star (some are born under a ~ and some are born seeing stars) unos nacen con **estrella** y otros nacen estrellados

lucky streak (be on a ~) andar de **ganancia**

to be lucky there salir bien librado (▷ **librar**)

to lumber s.o. with s.th. endiñar/endosar algo a alg.; cargar el **mochuelo** a alg.

to be lumbered with s.o. tener a alg. sobre sus **costillas**

lump (have/get/feel a ~ in one's throat) tener un nudo en la **garganta**/hacérsele a alg. un nudo en la garganta

to lump everything or them all together medirlo todo o medirlos a todos por el mismo **rasero**/con la misma **vara**

to lump everything or them all together (you can't just ~) no se puede medirlo todo o medirlos a todos por el mismo **rasero**/con la misma **vara**

to lump it ([have to] ~) [tener que] tragar **bilis**

lunch (be out to ~) estar en **Babia**/en la **luna**

lunch (blow one's ~) cambiar la **peseta**

lungs (scream/shout at the top of one's ~) como un **descosido** (example); a más no **poder**

lurch (be left in the ~) quedarse en la **estacada**/a la **luna** de Valencia

lurch (leave s.o. in the ~) dejar a alg. en las **asta**s del toro; dejar a alg. **colgado/empantanado**; dejar a alg. en la **estacada**/a la **luna** de Valencia; plantar o dejar plantado a alg.

lush el cuero; la espita/esponja

luxurious lifestyle (live a ~) vivir a todo **tren**

luxury el postín

luxury flash car el cochazo

M

machine (slot ~) el/la tragaperras

mackerel (set/throw a sprat to catch a ~) meter **aguja** para sacar reja; dar un **gallo** para recibir un caballo

mad (be as ~ as a hatter) estar más loco que una **cabra**; estar/ser **loco** de atar/remate; estar como una **regadera**

mad (be as ~ as a March hare) estar más loco que una **cabra**; estar/ser **loco** de atar/remate

mad (be hopping ~: be angry) estar hecho un **basilisco**; estar alg. que brinca (▷ **brincar**); echar **chiribitas/chispas**; estar alg. que trina (▷ **trinar**); estar hecho un **vinagre**

mad (be stark raving/staring ~) estar/ser **loco** de atar/remate

mad (drive s.o. ~) llevar de **cabeza** a alg.; es para volverse **loco**; ser [como] para subirse por las **pared**es

mad (get [hopping] ~: get angry) dar con la **cabeza** en las paredes; subírsele a alg. el **humo**/la **mostaza** a las narices; darse a **perro**s

mad (go ~) perder la **chaveta**

mad (like ~) como un **descosido**; a **rabiar**

mad (run like ~) ir como **alma** que se lleva el diablo; como el/un **diablo**; correr como **gato** por ascuas

to be mad about s.th./s.o. (enthusiastic) ser **forofo** de algo/alg.; estar **perdido** por alg./algo; **perecer**se por algo

mad hatter's tea party la **olla** de grillos

madam[e] (of brothel) la gobernante

madhouse la **olla** de grillos

madman (like a ~) como un **descosido**

madwoman (like a ~) como una descosida (▷ **descosido**)

magic bestial; chachi; cojonudo; dabute[n]/ dabuti; que quita el **hipo**; pistonudo

to be magic ser la **biblia**

magic ([as if] by ~) [como] por arte de **birlibirloque**; [como] por **ensalmo**

magic (have ~) tener **duende**

to magic s.th. away [como] por arte de **birlibirloque** (example)

magnificent bestial; chachi; cojonudo; dabute[n]/dabuti; que quita el **hipo**; pistonudo

magpie (be a ~) ser una **urraca**

maid (be/become an old ~) quedarse para adornar **altar**es; quedar[se] para **tía**

make (go out on the ~) salir de **levante**

to make [it] up darse las **manos**; echar **pelillos** a la mar

to make it [with a woman] comerse una **rosca**

to make off ahuecar el **ala**; salir pitando (▷ **pitar**)

to make off with the money alzarse con el **dinero**

to make off with the whole thing alzarse/salirse con el **santo** y la limosna/cera

to make out that white is black hacer de lo **blanco** negro/volver en blanco lo negro

to make s.th. up [off the top of one's head] sacarse algo de la **manga**

making (be a writer/etc. in the ~) ser un escritor/ etc. en **ciernes**

makings (have the ~ of . . .) tener **madera/vena** de ...

male [gay] prostitute el chapero

malicious delight/glee el gustazo

to malinger hacer la **zanguanga**

mammoth task/work (be a ~) ser **obra** de romanos

man (a ~ who has antiquated ideas) el carroza

man (a ~ who tries to pick/chat up women) el ligón

man (a woman who always has a new ~ in tow) la ligona

man (act/play the elegant/refined ~) meterse a **finolis**

man (be a ~) vestirse por los **pies**

man (be a real ~) con toda la **barba**; tener **braguetas**; hecho y derecho (example); ser muy **hombre**/todo un hombre; ser hombre de pelo en **pecho**

man (be a sanctimonious/an excessively pious ~) **comer**se los santos

man (be every inch/bit a ~) hecho y derecho (example); ser muy **hombre**/todo un hombre

man (be one ~ after another with a woman) la ligona

man (be s.o.'s right-hand ~) ser el **ojo** derecho de alg.; ser **pies** y manos de alg.

man (be the low ~ on the totem pole) ser el último **mono**

man (dirty/randy old ~) el **viejo** verde

man (every ~ for himself!) ¡sálvese quien pueda! (▷ **salvarse**)

man (every ~ for himself [and the devil take the hindmost]) ¡el que venga detrás, que arree! (▷ **arrear**); el último **mono** es el que se ahoga

man (flit from one ~ to another) ir de **flor** en flor

man (like master, like ~) cual el **dueño**, tal el perro

man (like the next ~) como cada/cualquier **hijo** de vecino; como todo/cada **quisque**

man (like to try to get friendly with men) tomar **varas**

man (not to get a/s.o. can't find a ~) sentarse en el **poyetón**; estar al que salte (▷ **saltar**)

man (one ~'s meat is another ~'s poison) nunca llueve a gusto de todos (▷ **llover**)

man (young ~) el pollo

man cannot live by bread alone no sólo de **pan** vive el hombre

the man in the street Juan Pérez

man is a creature/slave of habit la costumbre es otra/segunda **naturaleza**

man jack (every ~ [of them]) todo **bicho** viviente; Cristo y la madre/todo Cristo; todo/cada **quisque**

man of the moment (be the ~) ser el **hombre** del día

the man on the Clapham omnibus Juan Pérez

man proposes and God disposes el **hombre** propone y Dios dispone

to manage arreglárselas (▷ **arreglar**); componérselas (▷ **componer**); ir tirando (▷ **tirar**)

to manage (know [very well] how to ~) tener [mucha] **mano** izquierda

to manage (s.o. can ~ without s.th.) poder **pasar** sin algo

to manage s.th. teclear algo

to manage to + infinitive arreglárselas/ componérselas para + infinitivo (▷ **arreglar/componer**)

to manage to get s.th. **calzar**se algo

manger (be a dog in the ~) ser [como] el **perro** del hortelano[, que ni come la berza ni la deja comer]

maniac (like a ~) como un **descosido**

manna (come like ~ from heaven) venir como llovido/llegar como caído del **cielo**

manner of means (by no ~/not by any ~) ni a la de **tres**

manners (s.o.'s ~ betray/reveal a bad upbringing) saber a la **pega**

mannish woman (tough ~) la sargentona

manor (play lord of the ~) darse **aires** de grandeza; pintar la **cigüeña**

many (have had one too ~) hacérsele a alg. **candelillas** los ojos; estar hecho un **cesto**/ una **cuba**/un **cuero**/un **pellejo**/una **uva**

many (it's better to bring/have/etc. too ~ than too few) pecar por **exceso** (example)

many of that sort (there aren't ~ around) ni buscando con [un] **candil**

marble (be [as] cold as ~) tener **sangre** blanca/de horchata en las venas

marbles (have lost one's ~) estar mal de la **azotea**; no estar bueno de la **cabeza** o estar ido/mal/tocado de la cabeza o tener

pájaros en la cabeza; estar como una **cabra/cafetera**; estar [loco] como un **cencerro**; estar **chalado**; estar mal de la **chaveta**; estar **chiflado**

marbles (pick up one's ~) arrojar/tirar la **esponja/ toalla**

marbles (testicles) las **bolas/canicas**; los cataplines; los cojones (▷ **cojón**); los **conejos/huevos**; las **pelotas**; los pistones (▷ **pistón**)

march (steal a ~ on s.o.) madrugar a alg.

March hare (be as mad as a ~) estar más loco que una **cabra**; estar/ser **loco** de atar/remate

marching orders (give s.o. his ~) dar el **bote** a alg.; echar/despedir a alg. con **cajas** destempladas; echar a alg. a la **calle**/ poner a alg. de patitas en la calle; plantar a alg. en la **calle**; largar a alg.; dar la **licencia**/[el] **pasaporte**/la **patada** a alg.

mare (go/come on Shank's ~) ir/venir a golpe de **alpargata**/en el **caballo** de San Francisco/ a golpe de **calcetín**/en el **coche** de San Francisco o de San Fernando

marijuana (hash; grass; pot; shit; tea; weed) el chocolate/ful; la hierba/mandanga/ mierda; el tate; la yerba

marijuana cigarette el petardo/porro

marines (tell that to the ~!) ¡cuéntaselo a su o cuéntaselo a tu **abuela**!; ¡ésa es **grilla** [y no canta]!; ¡a otro perro con ese **hueso**!; ¡díselo o cuéntaselo al **nuncio**!; ¡cuéntaselo a su o cuéntaselo a tu **suegra**!

marital row (have a blazing/flaming ~) tirarse los **trastos** a la cabeza

mark (hit the ~) dar en el **blanco/busilis**; dar en la **diana**/hacer diana

mark (overshoot/overstep the ~) pasar de la **raya**; tirar más allá del blanco

mark (toe the ~) bailar al **son** que le tocan a alg.

to mark time marcar el **paso**

marker (be the back ~) ser el **farolillo** rojo

marriage (yoke of ~) la coyunda

to marry a rich woman dar un/el **braguetazo**

to marry a woman without a dowry casarse con una mujer en **camisa**

to marry for money dar un/el **braguetazo**

to be marvelous ser **miel** sobre hojuelas

marvelous time (have a ~) divertirse **horror**es

marvelous[ly] bestial; cañón; chachi; cojonudo; dabute[n]/dabuti; que quita el **hipo**; a las mil **maravillas**; pistonudo

marvelously (go ~) de **rechupete**

mask (drop the ~) quitarse la **careta**/el **embozo**/ la **máscara**

mask (grotesque ~) la carantoña

master (like ~, like man) cual el **dueño**, tal el perro

master (no man can serve two ~s) no se puede servir a **Dios** y al diablo

masterpiece (be a [real] ~) ser un **primor**
masterstroke la **baza** maestra
to masturbate (jack off; jerk off; toss off; wank)
tocar la **campana**; cascársela (▷ **cascar**);
machacársela (▷ **machacar**); hacerse una
paja; pelársela (▷ **pelar**); hacer la **puñeta**;
tocársela (▷ **tocar**); zumbársela (▷ **zumbar**)
masturbation (indulge in mental ~) hacerse una
paja mental
match (be a perfect ~) encajar/caer como
pedrada en ojo de boticario
match (be more than a ~ for s.o.) **comer**se a alg.
crudo; dar **quince** y raya/falta a alg.; dar
cien **vuelta**s a alg.
match (find/meet one's ~) encontrar/hallar la
horma de su zapato
match (for fire) el mixto
to be matched by correr **pareja**s/andar de pareja
(example)
matchstick leg la zanca
material (there's plenty of ~) haber **tela** que
cortar/para rato
matter (be no small ~) no ser **grano** de anís
matter (intervene or take a hand in a ~) tomar
cartas en un asunto
matter (it would be quite a different ~ if . . .) otro
gallo cantaría o otro gallo me/etc. cantara
si ...
matter (that's [quite] another/a different ~) eso es
otro cantar (▷ **el cantar**)
to matter (why the hell does it ~ to you?) ¿qué
coño te importa?
matters (make ~ worse) remachar el **clavo**
matters (to make ~ worse s.th. else happens) llover
sobre mojado
meal (accompany or wash down a ~ with wine/have
wine with a ~) regar una comida con vino
meal (be a slap-up ~) haber **arroz** y gallo muerto
meal (slap-up ~) la comilona
meal (things don't/never seem so bad after a good
~) con **pan** y vino se anda el camino
to mean (be meant to be) estar escrito
(▷ **escribir**)
to mean (not to ~ what one says) de **boca** [para]
afuera (example); de **boquilla**; de **dientes**
[para] afuera (example)
to mean (say one thing and ~ another) de **boca**
[para] afuera (example); de **boquilla**; de
dientes [para] afuera (example)
to mean (say s.th. without really ~ing it) decir algo
con la **boca** chica
to mean (this/that doesn't ~ that . . .) esto/eso no
quita que ... (▷ **quitar**)
to mean the world to s.o. para alg. no hay más
Dios [ni Santa María] que ...
mean feat (be no ~) no ser **moco** de pavo
means (by fair ~ or foul) por las buenas o por las
malas (▷ **bueno**)

means (by no/not by any manner of ~) ni a la de
tres
means (work with s.o. else's/other people's ~) tirar
con pólvora del **rey**
measures (do things in half ~/take half ~) aplicar
paños calientes
measures (not to do things in half ~/not to go in
for half ~) no andarse con **paños** calientes
measures (take drastic/extreme ~) sin pararse en
barras (example); cortar por lo **sano**
meat (one man's ~ is another man's poison) nunca
llueve a gusto de todos (▷ **llover**)
to meddle in s.th. mojar en algo
mediocre sin **pena** ni gloria
meek (become/be as ~ as a lamb) quedarse más
suave que un **guante**; estar como una
seda
to meet one's Waterloo llegarle a alg. su S**an
Martín**
melon (unripe ~) el pepino
member (be a ~ of the other party) ser de la otra
acera
memory (have a ~ like a sieve) tener la cabeza
como un **colador**
memory (s.th. engraves/stamps itself [firmly] on
s.o.'s ~) incrustársele algo a alg. en la
memoria (▷ **incrustarse**)
mental masturbation (indulge in ~) hacerse una
paja mental
to mention (don't ~ it!) ¡no faltaba/faltaría más!
(▷ **faltar**)
mercy (be at the ~ of the waves) ser un **juguete**
de las olas
mercy (beg for ~) pedir **alafia**; cantar el **kirie**
mere words jarabe de pico
merry (be very ~) estar [alegre] como unas
castañuelas
merry (eat, drink and be ~, for tomorrow we die)
dentro de cien **años** todos calvos; a beber
y a tragar, que el **mundo** se va a acabar
merry (get ~ after a few glasses of wine) tener el
vino alegre
to be merry (tipsy) estar **piripi**; estar entre dos
velas
merry time la juerga
merry time (have a/go out for a ~) estar/ir de
juerga
mess el **cajón** de sastre; el jaleo
mess (be in a [complete] ~) mezclar **berzas** con
capachos; estar/andar **manga** por hombro
mess (be in a fine/real ~: person) estar más
perdido que **Carracuca**
mess (get o.s. into a [fine/nice] ~) meterse en un
atolladero/berenjenal; meterse en **camisa**
de once varas
mess (get s.o. into a [hell of a or into a real/right
~]) poner a alg. en las **astas** del toro
mess (get things in a complete ~) mezclar **berzas**
con capachos

mess (in a complete ~) **pata**s arriba
mess (make a ~ in one's pants) **cagarse**
mess (make a ~ of it) **hacer**la buena
mess (make a ~ of s.th.) hacer algo con los **pies**
mess (now we're in a right/fine ~!) ¡la hemos fastidiado! (▷ **fastidiar**); ¡estamos **frescos**!
mess (what a ~ you've made of it!) lucirse (example)
to mess it all up echarlo todo a **rodar**
to mess it/s.th./things up cagar algo; **cagar**la; partir algo por el **eje**; escoñar/joder algo; **pringar**la
metal (old heap of ~: car) la antigualla; la **cafetera** [rusa]
Methuselah (be as old as ~) ser más viejo que **Carracuca**/que la **sarna**
to be meticulous hilar delgado o muy fino
mickey (take the ~ out of s.o.) tomarle el **pelo** a alg.; pitorrearse de alg.
middle name (lazy is s.o.'s ~) nació alg. cansado o con la lengua fuera (▷ **nacer**)
middle of next week (knock s.o. into the ~) señor
middle of nowhere (live/be in the ~) vivir/estar donde **Cristo** dio las tres voces/etc. o donde el **diablo** perdió el poncho; vivir/estar en el quinto **infierno/pino** o en la quinta **puñeta**
middle of the night (in the ~) entre **gallo**s y medianoche
middling (be fair to ~) no ser ni **fu** ni fa
midget el gorgojo
mid-morning snack (have a ~) tomar las **once**
midnight oil (burn the ~) quemarse las **ceja**s/**pestaña**s
might is right ([the principle of] ~) la **ley** del más fuerte
mighty (act high and ~) darse **aire**s de grandeza; pintar la **cigüeña**
mighty (become [very] high and ~) subírsele a alg. los **humo**s a la cabeza
milch cow (be the ~) ser la **vaca** de la boda
mile (a miss is as good as a ~) de **casi** no se muere nadie
mile (give s.o. an inch and he'll take a ~) darle a alg. un **dedo** y se toma hasta el codo; darle a alg. la/una **mano** y se toma el brazo; darle a alg. el **pie** y se toma la mano
mile (talk a ~ a minute) hablar como una **chicharra**/a **chorro**s/más que una **cotorra**; como un **descosido** (example); no tener **pepita** en la lengua; hablar más que un **sacamuelas**/que **siete**
to be miles away estar en **Babia**/en las **Batuecas**/en **Belén**/en la **higuera**; estar en la **luna**; andar por o estar en las **nubes**
to be miles better than s.o. dar cien **vuelta**s a alg.
milestone (mark a ~) marcar un **hito**

milk (it's no use crying over spilt ~) lo **hecho**, hecho está/a lo hecho, pecho; agua pasada no mueve molino
milk and honey (people elsewhere in the world don't live in the land of ~ either) allí tampoco atan los perros con **longaniza**[s]
to milk s.o. [dry] dejar a alg. en **calzoncillos**; dejar **pelado** a alg.; dejar a alg. a la cuarta **pregunta**; sacar las **tripa**s a alg.
mill (carry grist to one's own ~) llevar el **agua** a su molino
millpond (as smooth as a ~) balsa de aceite
millstone (be a ~ [a]round s.o.'s neck) ser una **cruz** para alg.
millstone (see through a ~) oír/sentir/ver crecer la **hierba**
to mince (not to ~ one's words) decir lo que se le viene a la **boca** a alg.; **cantar**las claras; no tener **frenillo** en la lengua; no morderse la **lengua**; quitarle al **lucero** del alba; no tener **pelo**s/**pepita** en la lengua
to mince (walk daintily) andar a **trote** corto
mincemeat (make ~ of s.o.) **comer**[se] a alg. vivo; hacer **papilla/picadillo/puré** a alg.
mind (banish s.th. from one's ~) relegar algo al olvido
mind (be in two ~s) estar entre **Pinto** y **Valdemoro**
mind (be smashed out of one's ~) estar cocido (▷ **cocer**) (example)
mind (be/take a [heavy/real] load off s.o.'s ~) quitársele a alg. un [gran] **peso** de encima; quitarle a alg. un [gran] **peso** de encima
mind (change one's ~) doblar/volver la **hoja**
mind (change one's ~ more often than one changes one's underwear) bailar a cualquier **son**; ser un[a] **veleta**
mind (clear one's ~) sacudirse las **telaraña**s
mind (give s.o. a piece of one's ~) soltar la/una **andanada** a alg.; zurrar la **badana**/dar una **calada**/cantar las cuarenta a alg.; decir a alg. cuántas son **cinco**; soltar/decir cuatro **fresca**s a alg.; dar a alg. con los **ocho**s y los nueves; poner a alg. las **pera**s a cuarto; decirle a alg. cuatro **verdad**es/las verdades del barquero; poner a alg. de **vuelta** y media
mind (have an awful lot on one's ~) no saber dónde volver la **cabeza**
mind (have one's ~ on other things) estar en **Babia**/en las **Batuecas**/en **Belén**/en la **higuera**; estar en la **luna**; andar por o estar en las **nubes**
mind (only a fool never changes his ~) es de sabios cambiar de opinión (▷ **el sabio**)
mind (out of sight, out of ~) **ojo**s que no ven, corazón que no siente
mind (s.o. can't make up his ~) estar entre **Pinto** y **Valdemoro**

mind (s.o.'s ~ goes blank/is a blank) quedarse en **blanco**

mind (speak one's ~) decir lo que se le viene a la **boca** a alg.; no tener **frenillo** en la lengua; quitarle al **lucero** del alba

to mind (I wouldn't ~ making a lot of money) no estar nada **mal**

to mind one's own business meterse en sus calzones (▷ **calzón**)

to mind one's own business (it's best to ~) cada uno/cual a lo **suyo**

mind your own business! **meter**se alg. donde no le llaman (example)

minor bureaucrat el chupatintas

mint (make a ~) **hinchar**se de plata/dinero

minute (not to have [got] a ~) no tener tiempo ni para **rascar**se

minute (s.o. can't sit still for a ~) ser [un] **culo** de mal asiento

minute's rest (not to give s.o. a ~) no dejar **respirar** a alg.; traer a alg. al **retortero**; no dejar a alg. [ni] a **sol** ni a sombra

mire (drag s.o.'s name through the ~) arrastrar a alg. por el **fango**

miser el cicatero/la cicatera; el cuentagarbanzos

miserable de mala **muerte**

miserly roñoso

miserly (be very ~) contar los **garbanzos**; ser **largo** como pelo de huevo

misery (be a ~) ser un **calvario**

misery (make s.o.'s life a ~) llevar/traer a alg. por la **calle** de la amargura

misfortune (you can always find a companion in ~) no/nunca falta un **roto** para un descosido

to mislay s.th. trasconejar algo

to misplace s.th. trasconejar algo

miss (a ~ is as good as a mile) de **casi** no se muere nadie

to miss (don't ~ the boat) camarón que se duerme, se lo lleva la corriente

to miss (not to ~ any opportunity/a trick) no dormirse en las **pajas**; no perder **ripio**

to miss it (s.o. can't ~) no tener **pérdida**

to miss nothing of what is going on/is being said no perder **ripio**

mistake (recognize one's ~) apearse de su **burro**

mistake (silly ~) la primada

mistake (there's no ~ about it) no hay que darle **vuelta**s

mistaken (be [totally] ~) el jaleo (example)

mistakes (learn by s.o. else's ~) escarmentar en cabeza ajena

mistakes (one only learns from one's own ~) nadie escarmienta en cabeza ajena (▷ **escarmentar**)

mistakes (the more you talk, the more ~ you'll make) quien mucho habla, mucho yerra (▷ **hablar**)

mistakes (you should learn from other people's ~) cuando las **barbas** de tu vecino veas arder, pon las tuyas a remojar

mistress (during the day pious Annie, during the night ~) de día **beata**, de noche gata

mitt (hand) la pata

to mix up everything tomar/confundir el **culo** por las témporas

mixed up (get/be ~ in it/s.th.) andar/estar en el **ajo**; meterse en o estar/andar metido en [la] **danza**; estar [muy] metido en algo (▷ **meter**)

to mobilize all one's influential friends tocar todos los **resortes**

mockery (hold s.o. up to ~) poner a alg. en **solfa**

model (look up to s.o. as a ~) mirarse en alg. como en un **espejo**

to be modest no necesitar **abuela** (example)

to moil (toil [and ~]) remar

molasses ([as] slow as/slower than ~ [in January]) a paso de **buey/tortuga**

molasses (be [as] slow as/slower than ~ [in January]) ser [más lento que] una **tortuga**

molehill (make a mountain out of a ~) hacer un **castillo** de un grano de arena/un **mar** con un vaso de agua; hacer de una **pulga** un elefante/camello

to mollycoddle s.o. [in his childhood] guardar/tener o criar a alg. entre algodones (▷ **algodón**); criar a alg. en **estufa**

moment (at the ~ of truth) a la **hora** de la verdad

moment (be the man of the ~) ser el **hombre** del día

moment (this is the wrong/isn't the right ~!) ¡no está el **horno** para bollos!

moment's peace (not to give s.o. a ~) no dejar a alg. [ni] a **sol** ni a sombra

mommy's boy/darling (bring s.o. up as ~) guardar/tener o criar a alg. entre algodones (▷ **algodón**)

money la blanca

money (be rolling in ~) nadar en la **abundancia**; tener muchos **cuartos**; apalear **oro**

money (big ~) la **pasta** gansa

money (brass; bread; dosh; dough; lolly; sugar; wampum) el barro; el **calé** o calés; la china; [los] **cuartos**; la guita/lana/manteca; [los] monises; la mosca; [los] nipos; el parné; la pasta; el pisto; la tela; el trigo

money (give s.o. a [good] run for his ~) echar/sudar la **hiel** (example); hacerle sudar **tinta** a alg.

money (have heaps/piles/pots of ~) tener muchos **cuartos**; la **mar** de; rebosar en dinero

money (hit on s.o. or tap/touch s.o. for ~) pegar un **petardo**/dar un **sablazo** a alg.

money (make ~ hand over fist) **hinchar**se de plata/dinero

money (make off with the ~) alzarse con el **dinero**

money (make piles/pots/stacks of ~) a **cántaro**s (example); a más no **poder**; a **pote** (example)

money (marry for ~) dar un/el **braguetazo**

money (not for love [n]or ~) aunque se junten el **cielo** y la tierra; ni para un **remedio**

money (put one's ~ where one's mouth is) predicar con el ejemplo

money (spend [one's] ~ wildly or like it's going out of style or like there was no tomorrow como un **descosido** (example)

money (take the ~ and run) alzarse con el **dinero**

money (the best that ~ can buy) ser la flor de la **canela**

money (throw good ~ after bad) echar la **soga** tras el caldero

money box la ladronera

money for the daily expenses la **taleguilla** de la sal

money makes the world go round poderoso caballero es don Dinero (▷ **el caballero**)

money talks poderoso caballero es don Dinero (▷ **el caballero**)

moneymaker el Perú

money-spinner la mina de **oro**; el Perú

monkey (be a cheeky ~) ser más fresco que una **lechuga**

monkey (be brass ~ weather) hacer un frío que pela (▷ **pelar**); de **perros**

monkey (be cold enough to freeze the balls off a brass ~) hacer un frío de cojones (▷ **cojón**)/que pela (▷ **pelar**); de **perros**

monkey (get one's ~ up) ponerse como un **basilisco**; exaltársele a alg. la **bilis**; subirse al **campanario**; salirse de sus **casillas**; ponerse hecho un **demonio**; hinchársele a alg. las narices (▷ **nariz**); subirse por las **pared**es/a la **parra**

monkey (get s.o.'s ~ up) sacar a alg. de sus **casillas**; poner **negro** a alg.; hacer a alg. subirse por las **pared**es

monkey (have a ~ on one's back) quedar **colgado**

monkey (make a ~ [out] of s.o.) poner a alg. en **solfa**

monkey (not to give/care a ~'s) no importar a alg. un **ardite**; [no] importar a alg. un **bledo**/ **comino/higo/pepino/pimiento/pito/ rábano**

monkey wrench (throw a ~ in[to] the works) meter un **bastón/palo** en la rueda o bastones/ palos en las ruedas [de alg.]

monkeys ([as] funny as a barrel of ~) descacharrante

monotonous fare **azote**s y galeras

monster (be a little ~) ser de la **piel** del diablo

Montezuma's revenge la cagalera; las seguidillas

month (in a ~ of Sundays) en las **Calendas** griegas; cuando meen las **gallinas**; cuando las **rana**s críen pelo; en la **semana** que no tenga jueves/de tres jueves

monumental bestial; cojonudo; garrafal

mood (be in a bad ~ with s.o.) estar de **morro**[s] con alg.

mood (be in a bad/foul/stinking ~) estar de mal **café**; no estar para **fiestas**; estar de mala **leche**/de mala **luna**/de **morro**[s]/de un humor de **perros**/de mala **uva**

mood (be in a good ~) estar de buena **luna/uva**

mood (be in a joking ~) estar de **bromas**

mood (be in no ~ for fun/jokes/laughter) no estar para **bromas/fiestas**

moon (be over the ~) estar en el séptimo/quinto **cielo**

moon (come from the ~) tener **monos** en la cara (example)

moon (once in a blue ~) de **higos** a brevas; cada **muerte** de obispo; de **Pascua**s a Ramos; de **uvas** a peras

moon (promise s.o. the ~) prometerle a alg. montañas de **oro** o el oro y el moro

moon (shoot the ~) mudarse clandestinamente

to be moon-faced tener **cara** de pan

to be mooning [about/around] estar mirando a las **musarañas**

to moonlight comer a dos **carrillos**

moralizer (the devil as a ~) el **diablo** predicador

more (be or there is ~ in/to it/this than meets the eye) tener [su] **miga**; la **procesión** va por dentro

more (hope there's ~ where that came from) saber a más

more (pay the twenty dollars and not a cent ~) a **palo** seco

morning (from ~ to/till evening) de **sol** a sol

moron el/la **berzas**

mortal hurry (be in a ~) la **mar** de

moss (a rolling stone gathers no ~) piedra movediza o el moho no la cobija/piedra movediza no coge musgo

most (at the ~) a todo **tirar**

most (get the ~ out of s.th./s.o.) sacar el **jugo** a algo/alg.

most (make the ~ of s.th.) sacar el **jugo** a algo

mote (see the ~ in one's neighbor's/in s.o. else's eye and not the beam in one's own) ver la **paja** en el ojo ajeno y no la viga en el propio

motel (short-time ~) la pensión de **tapujo**

mother (every ~'s son [of them]) todo **bicho** viviente; Cristo y la madre/todo Cristo; cada/cualquier **hijo** de vecino; todo/cada **quisque**

mother (have learned/learnt s.th. at one's ~'s knee) haber mamado algo [ya] en/con la **leche**

mother (like ~ like daughter) en casa del **gaitero** todos son danzantes; de casta le viene al

galgo ser rabilargo; tal madre tal **hija**; en casa del **tamborilero** todos son danzantes

mother (take the father and ~ of a thrashing) de padre y muy señor mío (▷ **el padre**) (example)

mother of invention (necessity is the ~) el **hambre** aguza el ingenio; hombre pobre todo es trazas; la **necesidad** hace maestros o aguza el ingenio

mother-in-law (a ~ would be bitter even if she were made of sugar) suegra, ni aun de azúcar es buena

motley collection el **cajón** de sastre

motormouth (have a ~) hablar más que una **cotorra**/un **sacamuelas**

mountain (make a ~ out of a molehill) hacer un **castillo** de un grano de arena/un **mar** con un vaso de agua; hacer de una **pulga** un elefante/camello

mouse (be as poor as a church ~) no tener ni para unas **alpargatas**; no tener qué llevarse a la **boca**/donde **caerse** muerto; no tener más que el **pan** y la noche; ser más pobre que una **rata** [de iglesia]

mouse (play a cat-and-~ game with s.o.) jugar al **gato** y al ratón con alg.

mouse (play cat and ~ with s.o.) jugar al **gato** y al ratón con alg.

mouse (when the cat's away, the mice will play) cuando el **gato** duerme, bailan los ratones; cuando el **gato** va a sus devociones, bailan los ratones

mouth (be all ~ [and no trousers]) cacarear y no poner huevos; írsele a alg. la **fuerza** por la boca

mouth (be down in the ~) arrastrar el **ala**; no levantar/alzar **cabeza**

mouth (be straight from the horse's ~) saber algo de buena **tinta**

mouth (button [up] one's ~) no decir ni **mu**/**pío**

mouth (don't look a gift horse in the ~) a **caballo** regalado no hay que mirarle o no le mires el diente

mouth (foam at the ~) echar **espumarajo**s

mouth (have one's heart in one's ~) tener el **alma** en un hilo

mouth (if you keep your ~ shut, you won't put your foot in it) en **boca** cerrada no entran moscas

mouth (it's just enough to live from hand to ~) [lo] **comido** por [lo] servido

mouth (keep one's ~ shut) coserse la **boca**; echar **candado** a la boca/a los labios; no decir [ni] **chus** ni mus; no decir ni **pío**; estar mudo como una **tumba**/ser [como] una tumba

mouth (leave a bad/nasty taste in one's ~) dejar a alg. [con] mal **sabor** de boca

mouth (look as if butter wouldn't melt in one's ~) hacerse la/parecer una **mosquita** muerta; no/nunca haber roto un **plato** [en su vida]

mouth (make s.o.'s ~ water) hacérsele a alg. la boca **agua**; poner los **dientes** largos a alg.

mouth (not to keep one's ~ shut) írsele a alg. la **burra**

mouth (not to open one's ~) no decir esta **boca** es mía; no descoser la **boca**; no decir ni **mu**/**pío**

mouth (open one's ~) abrir el **pico**

mouth (put one's money where one's ~ is) predicar con el ejemplo

mouth (shoot one's ~ off) soltar la **sinhueso**

mouth (shut one's ~) cerrar el **pico**

mouth (s.o. can't keep his ~ shut) no caberle algo a alg. en el **buche**; no pudrírsele a alg. nada/las cosas en el **pecho**

mouth (when the heart is full, it's the ~ that overflows) de la **abundancia** del corazón habla la boca

to move (get moving!) ¡arrea! (▷ **arrear**)

to move (often ~) andar/ir con el **hato** a cuestas

to move gracefully la sal (example)

to move in with each other casarse por detrás de la iglesia

to move with the times ir con el **siglo**

moved (be deeply ~ by s.th.) llegarle algo a alg. al **alma**

to be moved to tears arrancarle a alg. **lágrima**s

mover (be a real ~) la sal (example)

much (▷ too ~)

much (nothing ~) nada entre dos **plato**s

much (without so ~ as a by-your-leave/as an explanation/as a word of goodby[e]) sin decir **agua** va

much-ballyhooed/praised/vaunted cacarear algo (example)

muck (food) el comistrajo/pisto

muck (same old ~) azotes y galeras

to muck it [all] up hacer un **pan** como unas hostias

to muck s.th. up partir algo por el **eje**

mud (drag s.o.'s name through the ~) arrastrar a alg. por el **fango**

mud in your eye! ¡salud!; ¡salud, amor y pesetas!

muddle el jaleo

mug (face) el hocico; la jeta

mug (idiot) el primo

mug (ugly ~: face) la carantoña

to mug up [on] s.th. empollar/machacar algo

muggins menda

mule (be as stubborn as a ~) dar con la **cabeza** en las paredes

mule (person) el/la cabezota

multitude una nube

mum (keep ~) coserse la **boca**; echar **candado** a la boca/a los labios; no decir [ni] **chus** ni mus; no decir ni **pío**; sacar algo a alg. con pinzas/sacacorchos/tirabuzón (examples)

mum (s.o. can't keep ~) no pudrírsele a alg. nada/las cosas en el **pecho**

mum's the word en **boca** cerrada no entran moscas

mummy's boy/darling (bring s.o. up as ~) guardar/ tener o criar a alg. entre algodones (▷ **algodón**)

museum piece (be a ~) ser algo/alg. [una] pieza de **museo**

to mushroom aparecer/brotar/darse como **hongo**s/como las **seta**s

mushrooms (shoot/spring up like ~) aparecer/ brotar/darse como **hongo**s/como las **seta**s

music (canned ~) la **música** enlatada

mustard (be as keen as ~ [on s.th.]) arder de entusiasmo [con/por algo]

muster (pass ~) colar

to muster up [one's] courage revestirse de valor

mutton (be as dead as ~) estar más **muerto** que mi abuela/que una piedra; estar **pata**s arriba

mutton dressed up as lamb la carantoña

N

to nab s.o. coger/pescar el **bulto** a alg.; echar el **guante** a alg.

nail (hit the ~ on the head) dar en el **busilis/clavo/quid**; dar en la **tecla/yema**

nail (pay on the ~) pagar a toca **teja**

nailed down (steal anything that isn't ~) ser más ladrón que una **urraca**

naive (be so/very ~) caerse de un **nido**; pecar de + adj. (example)

naivety (pay for one's ~) pagar la **primada**

naked en traje de **Adán**/como Adán en el paraíso; en **carnes** [vivas]; en **cueros** [vivos]; en traje de **Eva**

naked (as ~ as the day s.o. was born) como Dios lo/etc. trajo al **mundo** o tal como vino/etc. al mundo

naked (be stark ~) estar/ir en **bolas**

naked (stark ~) en traje de **Adán**/como Adán en el paraíso; en **carnes** [vivas]; en **cueros** [vivos]; en traje de **Eva**; como su **madre** le/lo/la echó al mundo; como Dios lo/etc. trajo al **mundo** o tal como vino/etc. al mundo; en **pelota**[s]/**porreta**[s]

name (drag s.o.'s ~ through the mud/mire) arrastrar a alg. por el **fango**

name (handles to one's ~) **perejiles**

name (in ~ only) de **boca** [para] afuera; de **boquilla**; de **dientes** [para] afuera

name (lazy is s.o.'s middle ~) nació/p. ej. cansado o con la lengua fuera (▷ **nacer**)

names (big ~) gente de alto **copete**

names (call s.o. all the ~ under the sun) poner a alg. como un **Cristo**; poner **verde** a alg.

nap (have/take a ~) echar una **cabezada**/cabezadita; descabezar un sueñecito

nark el soplón/la soplona

narrow escape (have a ~) [por] el **canto** de un duro; por un **pelo**/los pelos; salvarse en una **tabla**

narrow shave (be/have a ~) [por] el **canto** de un duro; por un **pelo**/los pelos

to be narrow-minded ver las cosas con **anteojeras**

nasty (be ~) tener mala **uva**

nasty (get ~) ponerse algo **feo**

nasty (get ~ after a few glasses of wine) tener el **vino** agrio

nasty (know exactly how ~ s.o. can be/get) **gastar**las

nasty (there's s.th. ~ coming) oler a **chamusquina**

nasty affair/business (get involved in a ~) meterse en un **fregado**

nasty character (be a ~) ser un mal **bicho**

nasty customer una buena **pieza**

nasty disposition/nature (have a ~) tener mal **café**/mala **leche**/mala **pipa**/malas **pulga**s/mala **uva**

nasty drink el jarope

nasty piece of work el malaleche; el/la malaúva; la tipeja; el tipejo

nasty piece of work (be a ~) ser un mal **bicho**; tener mal **café**/mala **leche**; ser un **pájaro** de cuenta; tener mala **pipa/sombra**; tener mala **uva**

nasty surprise (have a very ~) quedarse **frío**

nasty trick (play a ~ on s.o.) hacer una **faena**/una mala **jugada** a alg.; jugar una mala **partida** a alg.; hacer una **perrada** a alg.; jugar una **pieza** a alg.; dar una **puñalada** trapera a alg.

nasty type (be a ~) ser un **pájaro** de cuenta

natural causes (not to die of ~) morir vestido

natural death (not to die a ~) morir vestido

naturally! ¡no faltaba/faltaría más! (▷ **faltar**)

nature (have a nasty/spiteful ~) tener mal **café**/mala **leche**/mala **pipa**/malas **pulga**s/mala **uva**

nature (have a sweet/peaceful ~) no tener **hiel**; ser una **paloma** sin hiel

nature (reveal one's true ~) descubrir la **oreja**

nature calls echar una **carta** al correo (example)

naughty bits las **alegrías**

nearly ([very] ~) [por] el **canto** de un duro; por un **pelo**/los pelos

necessity (make a virtue of ~) sacar **fuerza**s de flaqueza; hacer de la **necesidad** virtud; hacer de **tripa**s corazón

necessity is the mother of invention el **hambre** aguza el ingenio; hombre pobre todo es trazas; la **necesidad** hace maestros o aguza el ingenio

necessity knows no law la **necesidad** carece de ley

neck (be a millstone [a]round s.o.'s ~) ser una **cruz** para alg.

neck (be a pain in the ~) ser alg. un **plomo**

neck (be up to one's ~ in s.th.) estar con el **agua** al cuello; andar/ir de **cabeza** con algo

neck (break one's neck) romperse la **crisma**

neck (breathe down s.o.'s ~) no dejar a alg. [ni] a **sol** ni a sombra

neck (pain in the ~) el/la chinche

neck (risk one's ~) jugarse el **pellejo/pescuezo/tipo**; jugarse la **vida**

neck (save one's/s.o.'s ~) salvar el **pellejo**; salvar el **pellejo** a alg.

neck (stick one's ~ out [for s.th./s.o.]) poner el **cascabel** al gato; jugársela (▷ **jugar**); romper una **lanza** por algo/alg.

neck (wring s.o.'s ~) retorcer el **pescuezo** a alg.

to neck morrearse

nectar (be pure ~) ser **canela** fina

need (a friend in ~ is a friend indeed) en las malas se conoce a los amigos (▷ **malo**)

to need (be just what s.o. needs/needed) venir como **agua** de mayo/como **anillo** al dedo; venir como llovido/llegar como caído del **cielo**; venir como **pedrada** en ojo de boticario; venirle a alg. al **pelo**; venir de **perilla**[s]; de **perlas**; venir que ni **pintado**/ como pintado; venir [que ni] **pintiparado**; venir **rodado**

needed (. . . and that was all we ~!) ... éramos pocos y parió la **abuela**

need[ed] (that's all I/we ~!) ¡no faltaba/faltaría más! (▷ **faltar**); ¡estamos **frescos**!

needle (be on pins and ~s) tener el **alma** en un hilo; estar en/sobre **ascuas**; estar [como] en **brasas**

needle (keep s.o. on pins and ~s) tener a alg. en el **potro**

needle (look for a ~ in a haystack) buscar una **aguja** en un pajar

to needle s.o. buscar las **pulga**s a alg.; freír la **sangre** a alg.

negligee (in one's ~) en **paño**s menores

to be neither fish nor fowl/one thing nor the other no ser **carne** ni pescado; no ser ni **chicha** ni limonada/ni **fu** ni fa; ni **pinchar** ni cortar

neither here nor anywhere ni aquí/acá ni en la **China**

nerve (cheek) el tupé

nerve (have [got] a lot of/a real/such a ~) tener más **cara** que espalda; ser más fresco que una **lechuga**; tener un **morro** que se lo pisa

nerve (have the ~ to . . .) tener la cara como el **cemento** (example)

nerve (hit a raw ~) poner el **dedo** en la llaga; tocar [a alg.] en la **herida**

nerve (what an incredible ~!) solemne

nerve (you've got a/some ~!) ¡qué **morro** tienes!

nerves (be a bag/bundle of ~) ser un hato/manojo de **nervio**s

nerves (get on s.o.'s ~) hacer la **barba** a alg.; darle por o romper las **bola**s a alg.; romper/calentar los **casco**s a alg.; dar la **coña** a alg.; tener/traer **frito** a alg.; caerle **gordo**/dar la **lata** a alg.; hincharle a alg. las narices; alterar/crispar los **nervio**s a alg. o poner los nervios de punta a alg.; sacar a alg. de **quicio**; dar la **serenata/tabarra** a alg.; tentar la paciencia a alg.

nerves (grate/jar on s.o.'s ~) alterar/crispar los **nervio**s a alg. o poner los nervios de punta a alg.

nerves (have one's ~ on edge) tener los **nervio**s de punta

nerves (put s.o.'s ~ on edge) alterar/crispar los **nervio**s a alg. o poner los nervios de punta a alg.

nerves (s.o.'s ~ are all on edge) a **flor** de piel

nerves of steel (have ~) tener **nervio**s de acero

to be nervous tener **nervio**s

nest (feather one's ~) hacer su **agosto**; ponerse las **botas**; chupar del **bote**; **redondear**se

nest (foul one's own ~) manchar el propio **nido**; tirar **piedra**s a su o sobre el propio tejado

nest (leave the parental ~) alzar/levantar el **vuelo**

nest (stir up a hornet's ~) meterse en un **avispero**

nettle (grasp the ~) coger el **toro** por los cuernos; hacer de **tripas** corazón

network (old-boy ~) el enchufismo

neutral (remain ~) no quitar ni poner **rey**

never en las **Calendas** griegas; cuando meen las **gallinas**; cuando las **rana**s críen pelo; en la **semana** que no tenga jueves/de tres jueves

never (better late than ~) nunca es tarde si la **dicha** es buena; más vale **tarde** que nunca

never (if I ~ see you again it will be too soon!) ¡hasta que/cuando meen las **gallinas**! ¡hasta que/cuando las **rana**s críen pelo!

never again una y no más, Santo Tomás

never say never nunca digas de esta **agua** no beberé

never-never (buy s.th. on the ~) comprar algo a **plazoleta**s

never-never land (be living in ~) tener la **cabeza** llena de pájaros; vivir en la **luna**; andar por o vivir en las **nube**s

new (be very ~ still) estar algo sangrando (▷ **sangrar**); estar algo chorreando **sangre**

new (like spanking ~) como un **oro**

new (there's nothing ~ under the sun) no hay nada **nuevo** bajo el sol/las estrellas

news (be old ~) ser **periódico** de ayer

newspaper (gutter/sensational/yellow ~) el **periódico** amarillo

newt (be as pissed as a ~) estar hecho un **cesto**/una **cuba**/un **cuero**/un **pellejo**/una **uva**

newt (get as pissed as a ~) **cocer**se; papar una **jumera**; coger una **melopea/merluza**; coger/pillar una **mona**; moñarse; coger una **pea**; agarrar[se] un **pedo**; coger una **pítima**

next door (live ~) vivir **pared/tabique** por medio

to be next door to s.th. rozar [con] algo

next man (like the ~) como cada/cualquier **hijo** de vecino; como todo/cada **quisque** nice (be [terribly] ~) ser un **pedazo** de pan; tener buena **sombra**

nick (prison) la trena

to nick s.th. [from s.o.] soplar algo [a alg.]

nickel (be down to one's last ~) andar/estar a la cuarta **pregunta**

nickname el remoquete

night (as sure as ~ follows day) como [que] **tres** y dos son cinco

night (at ~ all cats are gray/grey) de noche todos los **gatos** son pardos

night (have a sleepless ~) pasar la **noche** en blanco

night (in the middle of the ~) entre **gallos** y medianoche

night (in the or at dead of ~) entre **gallos** y medianoche

night (make a ~ of it) andar de **gallo**

night (sleepless ~) la **noche** blanca/toledana/vizcaína

night (spend a ~ on the tiles) irse de/a **picos** pardos

night (study/work far into the ~) quemarse las **cejas/pestañas**

night (work through the ~) defraudar el sueño

night and day (be as different as ~) estar tan lejos como lo **blanco** de lo negro/no parecerse ni en el blanco de los ojos; parecerse como un **huevo** a una castaña

night owl (be a ~) andar de **gallo**

nincompoop un [pedazo de] **alcornoque/atún**; un[a] **cabeza** de corcho; una calabaza; un alma de **cántaro**; un ceporro/melón/merluzo; un **palomino** atontado; un percebe

nine (be on cloud ~) estar en el séptimo/quinto **cielo**; estar en su[s] **gloria**[s]

nine days' wonder una **nube** de verano

nine lives (have ~) tener siete **vidas** [como los gatos]

ninepins (go down like ~) caer/morir como **chinches**

nines (be dressed up to the ~) estar de veinticinco **alfileres**; estar hecho un **brazo** de mar; estar **peripuesto**; estar/ir de **punta** en blanco

nines (get dressed up to the ~) ponerse de veinticinco **alfileres**/de **punta** en blanco

nineteen (talk ~ to the dozen) hablar como una **chicharra/a** chorros/por los **codos**/más que una **cotorra**; como un **descosido** (example); no tener **pepita** en la lengua; hablar más que un **sacamuelas**/que **siete**

to nip s.th. in the bud segar en **flor**; salir al **paso** de algo; cortar algo de **raíz**

nipper la media **botella**

nitty-gritty (get down to the ~) ir al **grano**

nob (be a top ~) tener muchas **campanillas**

nob (top ~[s]) un gran **bonete**; gente de alto **copete**; un **pez** gordo

nobody el ñiquiñaque

nobody (be a [complete] ~) ser un **cero** a la izquierda/el último **mono**/un don **Nadie**/un **piernas**

nobody's business (dance/lie/run like ~) ... que se las pela (▷ **pelar**)

nobody's perfect cada uno/cual tiene lo **suyo**; de todo tiene la/hay en la **viña** del Señor

nod (a ~ is as good as a wink) al buen **entendedor**, pocas palabras [le bastan]

nod (agree with a ~) afirmar con el **gesto**

to nod in agreement afirmar con el **gesto**

to nod [yes] afirmar con la **cabeza**

noddle (head) la calabaza/cebolla/chaveta/cholla/coca; el coco/güiro/güito; la jupa; el melón

no-gooders (bunch of ~) la camada

noise (be a big ~) tener muchas **campanillas**

noise (be a shattering ~) ser un ruido que taladra (▷ **taladrar**)

noise (be an ear-piercing/ear-splitting ~) ser un ruido que taladra los oídos (▷**taladrar**)

noise (big ~) un gran **bonete**; el mandamás; un **pez** gordo

noises (have heard ~ to that effect) oír **campanas** y no saber dónde

none (be second to ~) no ir en **zaga** a alg. (example)

nonentity (be a ~) ser del **montón**

nonsense el golpe de **bombero**

nonsense! ¡naranjas! ¡naranjas chinas! ¡naranjas de la China!; ¡narices! (▷ **nariz**)

nonsense (be utter ~) no pegar ni con **cola**

nonsense (stand no ~) no aguantar/sufrir **pulgas**

nonsense (talk [a lot of] ~) irse por los **cerros** de Úbeda; meter **ripio**

normal (things return to ~) las **aguas** vuelven a su cauce

nose (at 6 [o'clock] on the ~) a las seis clavadas (▷ **clavado**)

nose (be as plain as the ~ on your face) estar más claro que el **agua**; ser más claro que el **sol**

nose (beak; conk; hooter; schnozzle; snout) el asa; las napias

nose (big ~) la narizota; el naso; la trompa

nose (big ~: person) el/la narizotas

nose (blow one's ~) echar una **mocada**; mocar; **mocar**se

nose (cut off one's ~ to spite one's face) escupir al cielo; tirar **piedras** a su o sobre el propio tejado; echarse **tierra** a los ojos

nose (drinker's ~) la nariz de **zanahoria**

nose (from right under my/etc. ~/from under my/etc. very ~) en mis/etc. propias o mismísimas **barbas**/narices (▷ **nariz**)

nose (get up s.o.'s ~) sacar a alg. de sus **casillas**; tocar/hinchar los cojones a alg. (▷ **cojón**);

hincharle a alg. las narices (▷ **nariz**); poner
negro a alg.; hacer a alg. subirse por las
paredes; hinchar las **pelota**s a alg.
nose (have a [very] good ~) tener una **nariz** de
primera
nose (it's/that's no skin off my ~) no me va ni me
viene (▷ **venir**)
nose (keep one's ~ to the grindstone) trabajar
como un **buey**; dar el **callo**; romperse el
culo; echar/sudar la **hiel**; echar los
hígados; darse una **jupa**; trabajar como un
negro; dejarse la **piel**; pringar[las]; sudar
el **quilo**; remar; **reventar**se; echar los
riñones (▷ **riñón**); destripar terrones
(▷ **terrón**); sudar **tinta**
nose (keep s.o.'s ~ to the grindstone) echar/sudar
la **hiel** (example); hacerle sudar **tinta** a
alg.
nose (land on one's ~) caerse/dar de narices [en/
contra el suelo] (▷ **nariz**)
nose (lead s.o. by the ~) llevar a alg. del **cabestro**
nose (pick one's ~) hacer **albondiguillas**; sacar
muebles
nose (poke one's ~ into other people's affairs/
business) meterse en **camisa** de once
varas; **meter**se alg. donde no le llaman
nose (poke one's ~ into s.th.) meter el **hocico** en
algo; meter las narices en algo (▷ **nariz**)
nose (rub s.o.'s ~ in s.th.) refregar algo a alg. [por
las narices]
nose (shove s.th. under s.o.'s ~) meter algo a alg.
por las narices (▷ **nariz**)
nose (snatch s.th. away from under s.o.'s ~) dejar a
alg. con la **miel** en los labios
nose (snub/turned-up ~) la nariz respingona
(▷ **respingón**)
nose (s.o. can't see further than or beyond the end
of his ~) no ver más allá de sus narices
(▷ **nariz**)
nose (thumb one's ~ at s.o.) hacer un **palmo** de
narices a alg.
nose (who asked you to poke your ~ in?) ... vela en
este entierro
nosh-up (great ~) la comilona
to notch up a [plus] point apuntarse un **tanto**
nothing (all or ~) o **césar** o nada; o **todo** o nada
nothing (come to ~) irse al **cuerno**; **escoñar**se;
quedar en **nada**; deshacerse como la **sal**
en el agua
nothing (do ~) echarse/tenderse/tumbarse a la
bartola; estar/quedarse con los **brazos**
cruzados; tocar la **vihuela**
nothing (do ~ about s.th.) dar **carpetazo** a algo
nothing (end up with ~) quedarse **asperges**;
chuparse el **dedo**; quedarse con un **palmo**
de narices
nothing (get ~ right) no dar **palotada**
nothing (give ~ away) no soltar **prenda**

nothing (know ~ at all about s.th.) estar **pez** en
algo
nothing (mere ~) la friolera
nothing (over [absolutely] ~) por un quítame allá
esas **pajas**
nothing (stop at ~) no pararse en **barra**s
nothing (that's absolutely ~ yet!) ¡no te digo
nada!
nothing (work for ~) trabajar para el **obispo**
nothing doing! ¡ni **hablar**!; ¡no hay tu **tía**!
nothing else (there's ~ left for s.o. to try) no
quedarle a alg. ninguna **tecla** por tocar
to be nothing else but . . . no **pasar** de ser ...
to be nothing exceptional/extraordinary no ser
nada/cosa del otro **mundo**
to be nothing exciting no ser cosa del otro **jueves**
nothing goes on/lasts forever no hay **bien** ni mal
que cien años dure
nothing has been decided [yet] la **pelota** está/
sigue en el tejado
nothing much nada entre dos **platos**
nothing of the sort (it's ~) no hay tales **borregos**/
carneros/corderos
to be nothing out of the ordinary no ser cosa del
otro **jueves**
to be nothing special no ser cosa del otro **jueves**;
ser del **montón**; no ser nada/cosa del otro
mundo
nothing to do with (have ~ s.th.) no tocar **pito** en
algo; no tener nada que **ver** con algo
nothing to do with (have nothing whatsoever to do
with a matter/with it) no tener **arte** ni parte
en algo; no pegar ni con **cola**
nothing to do with (I've ~ it/this or the/this
matter) de mis **viñas** vengo
nothing to get upset about (it's ~) no es tan feo el
diablo como le pintan (▷ **pintar**)
nothing to lose (he who has nothing has ~) quien
poco tiene, poco teme
to be nothing to write home about no ser cosa del
otro **jueves**; no ser nada/cosa del otro
mundo
nothing's easy to start off with el primer **paso** es
el que cuesta
notice (come to the ~ of s.o.) llegar a **oído**s de
alg.
notice (don't take ~ of the stupid things people say)
a **palabra**s necias, oídos sordos
notice (take ~ of s.th.) prestar/dar **oído**s a algo
notice (take no ~ [of s.th.]) hacer/prestar **oído**s
sordos [a algo]
to notice (no-one will ~ [in the dark]) de noche
todos los **gatos** son pardos
to notice (pretend not to ~ [s.th.]) hacer la vista
gorda [a algo] (▷ **gordo**); hacerse el **sueco**
notion (sudden ~) el pronto
to be notorious ser de **historia**
nous (intelligence) la **cholla**; el **coco/pesquis**

novice (be no ~) haber sido **cocinero** antes que
fraile

nowhere (get ~) salir con una **mano** atrás y otra
[a]delante; marcar el **paso**; no **pelechar**;
estar tocando el **tambor**

nowhere (get absolutely ~ [with]) no comerse
una **rosca** [con]

nowhere (live/be in the middle of ~) vivir/estar
donde **Cristo** dio las tres voces/etc. o
donde el **diablo** perdió el poncho; vivir/
estar en el quinto **infierno/pino** o en la
quinta **puñeta**

nowt (there's ~ so queer as folk) de todo tiene la/
hay en la **viña** del Señor

nub (essential part) el quid

nude (in the ~) en traje de **Adán**/como Adán en
el paraíso; en traje de **Eva**

nuisance el/la chinche

number (back ~) una antigualla

number (exactly twenty/etc. as a round ~) [el]
veinte/etc. **pelado**

Number One (a person who looks after ~) Juan
Palomo

Number One (look after ~) arrimar el **ascua** a su
sardina; barrer hacia/para dentro; chupar
del **bote**; servirse/despacharse con el
cucharón; **rascar**se para adentro; ir a la
suya/a lo **suyo**

numskull un [pedazo de] **alcornoque/atún**;
un[a] **cabeza** de corcho; una calabaza; un
alma de **cántaro**; un ceporro/melón/
merluzo; un **palomino** atontado; un
percebe

numskull (be a ~) tener la cabeza llena de **serrín**

nut (be a hard ~ to crack) ser un **hueso** duro de
roer; ser [un huevo] duro de **pelar**

nut (be off one's ~) estar mal de la **azotea**; no
estar bueno de la **cabeza** o estar ido/mal/

tocado de la cabeza o tener pájaros en la
cabeza; estar como una **cabra/cafetera**;
estar [loco] como un **cencerro**; estar
chalado; estar mal de la **chaveta**; estar
chiflado; estar a las **once** y cuarto

nut (find s.th. a hard ~ to crack) pinchar/dar en
hueso

nut (give s.o. a hard ~ to crack) darle a alg. un
hueso duro de roer

nut (head) la calabaza/cebolla/chaveta/cholla/
coca; el coco/güiro/güito; la jupa; el
melón

nuthouse el loquero

nuts (drive s.o. ~) traer de **culo** a alg.

nuts (go ~ [about s.o.]) perder la **chaveta** [por
alg.]

nuts (testicles) las **bola**s/**canica**s; los cataplines;
los cojones (▷ **cojón**); los **conejos/huevos**;
las **pelota**s; los pistones (▷ **pistón**)

to be nuts estar mal de la **azotea**; no estar
bueno de la **cabeza** o estar ido/mal/
tocado de la cabeza o tener pájaros en la
cabeza; estar como una/más loco que una
cabra; estar como una **cafetera**; estar
[loco] como un **cencerro**; estar **chalado**;
estar mal de la **chaveta**; estar **chiflado**;
estar/ser **loco** de atar/remate; estar a las
once y cuarto

to be nuts about s.o. estar **chalado/chiflado** por
alg.; beber/sorber los **viento**s por alg.

nutty (be as ~ as a fruitcake) estar mal de la
azotea; no estar bueno de la **cabeza** o
estar ido/mal/tocado de la cabeza o tener
pájaros en la cabeza; estar como una
cabra/cafetera; estar [loco] como un
cencerro; estar **chalado**; estar mal de la
chaveta; estar **chiflado**

o

oaf (be a clumsy ~) ser un **manazas**
oaf (stupid person) un ceporro
oaks (little strokes fell great/big ~) gota a gota se
llena la bota
oar (put/stick/shove one's ~ in) meter **baza** [en];
echar su **cuarto** a espadas; meter su
cuchara
oats (feel one's ~) sentirse en la **cumbre**
oats (know one's ~) ser del **paño**
oats (sow one's wild ~) **correr**la o correr sus
mocedades
obligations (meet one's ~ [on time]) no dolerle
prendas a alg.
oblivion (consign s.th. to ~) relegar algo al olvido
oblivion (fall/sink into ~ for good) caer en el
pozo airón
observer (be a keen ~) tener **ojo** clínico
obstacles (put/place ~ in s.o.'s path/way) poner
chinas a alg.
obstinate (be as ~ as they come) a más no **poder**
obstinate (be extremely/utterly ~) a más no
poder
obtrusive (be very ~) meterse por el **ojo** de una
aguja
to be obvious caerse de/por su propio peso;
estar en la **mano**; estar algo sangrando
(▷ **sangrar**)
occurrence (be an everyday ~) ser el **pan**
[nuestro] de cada día
ocean (be [just] a drop in the ~) ser una **gota** de
agua en el mar
odd character (be an ~) ser un **pájaro** raro
odd fellow (be an ~) ser un **notas**
odd fish (be an ~) ser un **notas**/un **pájaro** raro
odd sort el tipejo
oddball (be an ~) ser un **notas**
odds (against all [the] ~) contra **viento** y marea
odds (all the ~ and sods) todo **bicho** viviente;
Cristo y la madre/todo Cristo; todo/cada
quisque
odds (be at ~ with s.o.) estar de **punta** con alg.
off (it's all ~) [todo] mi/etc. o el **gozo** en el/un
pozo
off with you! ¡quítate de ahí/de en medio!
(▷ **quitar**)
off-chance (on the ~) a la buena de Dios
(▷ **bueno**); a la **gracia** de Dios; salga **pez** o
salga rana
off-the-cuff answer/speech/etc. (give an ~) traer
algo en/por la **manga**
to offend (be very easily ~ed) a **flor** de piel
to offend the/one's eye[s]/ear[s] herir la vista/el
oído

offense (take ~) mosquearse
offer (it's an ~ one can't refuse) a la **ocasión** la
pintan calva
officer (an ~ who has risen from the ranks) un
oficial de **cuchara**
oil (burn the midnight ~) quemarse las **cejas**/
pestañas
oiled wheels (run on ~) ir/marchar sobre **ruedas**
to be old contar muchas **navidades**
old (any ~ how) a tontas y a locas (▷ **tonto**)
(example)
old (be as ~ as the hills/as Methuselah) ser más
viejo que **Carracuca**/que la **sarna**
old (be one/etc. year ~er than s.o.) llevar a alg.
un/etc. año
old (be so ~ s.o. can hardly walk) caerse de viejo
old (be too ~ for that [sort of thing]) ya no estar
para esos **trotes**
old (donkey's years ~) año de/tiempo[s] de/días
de **Maricastaña**; del año de/en el año de
la **nana**; en [los] tiempos de **ñangué**; del
año de o en el año de la **pera/polca**; en
tiempos del **rey** que rabió/del rey Wamba
old (not to be [just] any ~ poet/etc.) ser un poeta/
etc., no así como quiera (▷ **querer**)
old (same ~) de **marras** (example)
old (s.th. is so ~ it is falling to pieces or apart)
caerse [a/en pedazos] de viejo
to be old and frail caerse de viejo; arrastrar los
pies
old bag la tarasca
old banger (car) la antigualla; la **cafetera** [rusa]
old charm (turn on the ~) andar en/andarse con
floreos
old chestnuts una antigualla
to be old chestnuts ser del tiempo del **rey** que
rabió/del rey Wamba
old crock (car) la antigualla; la **cafetera** [rusa];
el vejestorio
old crock (person) una antigualla; el carcamal/
vejestorio
old devil (be a cunning ~) ser [un] toro **corrido**/
[una] liebre corrida; ser [un] **perro/zorro**
viejo
old dodderer el vejestorio
old fog[e]y el carroza
old fool (there's no fool like an ~) la **cabeza**
blanca y el seso por venir; a la **vejez**,
viruelas
old fox (be an ~) ser [un] toro **corrido**/[una]
liebre corrida; ser [un] **perro/zorro** viejo
old gay lecher el carroza
old geezer el carroza

315

old goat (randy ~) el **viejo** verde
old gossip el/la correve[i]dile
old hag la tarasca
old hand (be an ~) ser [un] toro **corrido**/[una] liebre corrida; ser [un] **perro** viejo
old hat una antigualla
to be old hat ser **periódico** de ayer; ser del tiempo del **rey** que rabió/del rey Wamba
old heap of metal (car) la antigualla; la **cafetera** [rusa]
old junk ([piece of] ~) la antigualla; el vejestorio
old lecher el **viejo** verde
old maid (be/become an ~) quedarse para adornar **altar**es; quedar[se] para **tía**
old man (dirty/randy ~) el **viejo** verde
to be old news ser **periódico** de ayer
old queen (old gay) el carroza
old relic (car/thing/person) la/una antigualla; el vejestorio
old salt un viejo **lobo** de mar
old sea dog un viejo **lobo** de mar
old soak el cuero; la espita/esponja
old story (be the same ~ every time) sonar como un disco **rayado**
old story (the same ~ [every time]!) i[siempre] la misma **canción/cantilena**!
old theme (be harping on the same ~ every time) sonar como un disco **rayado**
old thing la antigualla
old tome una antigualla
old wives' tale el **cuento** de viejas
old wreck la antigualla; el carcamal
old-boy network el enchufismo
old-fashioned (very ~) año de/tiempo[s] de/días de **Maricastaña**; del año de/en el año de la **nana**; en [los] tiempos de **ñangué**; del año de o en el año de la **pera/polca**; en tiempos del **rey** que rabió/del rey Wamba
omelet (you can't make an ~ without breaking eggs) no se puede hacer **tortilla**s sin romper huevos
to omit dejar algo a un **lado** o de lado
omnibus (the man on the Clapham ~) Juan Pérez
on (and so ~) ... y otras **hierba**s
once doesn't count una no es ninguna
one (be a deep/quiet ~) tener alg. muchos **entresijo**s; andarle/irle a alg. la **procesión** por dentro
one (be a tough ~: person) tener **pelo**s en la lengua
one (be/face a tough ~) ser un **hueso** duro de roer; tocarle a alg. una **papeleta** difícil; ser [un huevo] duro de **pelar**; tener [mucho] **tomate**; traérselas (▷ **traer**)
one (be the ~ who pays/who has to pay) ser el **paganini/pagano**
one (have ~ for the road) tomar[se] la del **estribo**; tomar la última (▷ **último**)
one (he's/she's a fine ~!) ¡menuda/buena **alhaja**!

one (hoist ~ or a few) alzar/empinar el **codo**; mojarse el **garguero**; mojar/refrescar el **gaznate**; atarse/pegarse un **latigazo**; atizarse un **trago**
one (hoist another ~) atizar la **lámpara**
one (I think I've heard that ~ before) me suena a **música** de caballitos
one (paste/land s.o. ~) pegar una **leche/torta** a alg.
one (pull a fast ~ on s.o.) pegar un **petardo** a alg.; dársela a alg. con **queso**
one (pull the other ~!) ¡cuéntaselo a su o cuéntaselo a tu **abuela**!; ¡a otro perro con ese **hueso**!; ¡cuéntaselo a su o cuéntaselo a tu **suegra**!
one (put ~ over on s.o.) dar [el] **camelo** a alg.; pegar un **parche** a alg.; dársela a alg. con **queso**; dar/pegar una **tostada** a alg.
one (sly ~) el vivo/la viva
one over the eight (have had ~) estar hecho un **cesto**/una **cuba**/un **cuero**/un **pellejo**/una **uva**
one thing (if it isn't ~ it's another) cuando no es por **pitos**, es por flautas
one too many (have had ~) hacérsele a alg. **candelillas** los ojos; estar hecho un **cesto**/una **cuba**/un **cuero**/un **pellejo**/una **uva**
one-armed bandit el/la tragaperras
one-eyed man (in the country of the blind the ~ is king) en tierra de **ciegos** o en el país/reino de los ciegos el tuerto es [el] rey
one's all (give ~) dejarse la **piel**
oneself (by ~) a **cuerpo** gentil
oneself (keep to ~) hacer **rancho** aparte
oneself (think only of ~) ir a la **suya**/a lo **suyo**
onion (head) la calabaza/cebolla/chaveta/cholla/coca; el coco/güiro/güito; la jupa; el melón
only just a duras **pena**s; por un **pelo**/los pelos
open (keep one's eyes ~) avivar el/[los] **ojo**[s]
to open s.o.'s eyes hacer caer la **venda** de los ojos a alg.
opening (good ~) el resquicio
opening (look for an ~) estar a la que salta (▷ **saltar**)
openly sin **tapujo**s
openly (speak ~) hablar en **castellano** [puro y llano]
open-mouthed (leave s.o. ~) dejar **bizco** a alg.
operator (be a very shrewd ~) estudiar con el **demonio**
operator (sharp/smooth ~) el vivo/la viva
opinion (stick firmly to one's ~) estar **caballero** en su opinión; mantenerse/seguir en sus **trece**
opinion (stubbornly defend one's ~ [against s.o.]) tenerlas tiesas [con/a alg.] (▷ **tieso**)
opinion ([stubbornly] insist on one's ~) casarse con su **opinión**; ponerse de **puntillas**

opinion (we know that nobody asked for our ~, but . . .) ... vela en este entierro

opinion (who asked for your ~?) ... vela en este entierro

opportunist (be an ~) arrimarse al **sol** que más calienta

opportunity (at the first best ~) a las **primera**s de cambio

opportunity (clutch at any ~) agarrarse/asirse a un **pelo**

opportunity (good ~) el resquicio

opportunity (not to pass up/miss any ~) no dormirse en las **paja**s; no perder **ripio**

opportunity (seize the ~) coger/asir la **ocasión** por los cabellos/pelos; tender las **vela**s

opportunity (that ~ won't come again) **ojo**s que te vieron ir

opportunity (unexpected ~) el **cabe** de pala

opportunity (wait for the right ~) estar a la que salta (▷ **saltar**)

opportunity (watch out for an ~) estar a la que salta (▷ **saltar**)

opportunity makes the thief la **ocasión** hace al ladrón

optimistic (be ridiculously ~) verlo todo de color de **rosa**

ordeal (be an ~/a terrible ~) ser un **calvario**; ser pasar por las horcas caudinas (▷ **caudino**)

order (put one's own house in ~ [first]) barrer en su propia casa

to order (be just what the doctor ~ed) venir como **agua** de mayo/como **anillo** al dedo; venir como llovido/llegar como caído del **cielo**; venir como **pedrada** en ojo de boticario; venirle a alg. al **pelo**; venir que ni **pintado**/como pintado; venir [que ni] **pintiparado**

orders (give s.o. his marching ~) dar el **bote** a alg.; echar/despedir a alg. con **caja**s destempladas; echar a alg. a la **calle**/poner a alg. de patitas en la calle; plantar a alg. en la **calle**; largar a alg.; dar la **licencia**/[el] **pasaporte**/la **patada** a alg.

ordinary corriente y moliente; sin **pena** ni gloria

ordinary (be nothing out of the ~) no ser cosa del otro **jueves**

ordinary people (even the most ~ aim high/are ambitious) hasta los **gatos** quieren zapatos

ordinary person (be just an ~) ser del **montón**

orgasm (come; shoot off) **correr**se; sacar la **piedra**

origins (betray one's humble/rustic ~) tener el **pelaje/pelo** de la dehesa

ounce (not an ~ of) ni **chispa/sombra** de

out (▷ all ~)

out (be way ~) el jaleo (example)

to be **out** for s.o.'s blood buscar el **bulto** a alg.

out of (be almost ~ s.th.) estar/andar **mal** de algo

out of line (be really ~) pasar de **castaño** oscuro; pelar la jeta

out of sight, out of mind **ojo**s que no ven, corazón que no siente

out of the blue de buenas a primeras (▷ **bueno**)

out of work sin **oficio** ni beneficio

to be out to + infinitive irse a **ojeo** de algo/alg.

to be out to lunch estar en **Babia**/en la **luna**

out with it! ([come on,] ~) sacar a **relucir** algo (example); ¡rompe de una vez! (▷ **romper**); soltar la **sinhueso** (example)

out-and-out por los cuatro **costados**; hecho y derecho; rematado; de siete **suela**s

out-and-out drunkard (be an ~) ser un borracho **perdido**

to outdo s.o. at/in s.th. ganar a alg. en algo

to outlive s.o. enterrar a alg.

out-of-date [and worthless] book una antigualla

outrage (express one's ~) echarse a la **calle**

to be outrageous clamar al cielo; no tener **nombre**

outrageously escandalosamente (▷ **escandaloso**)

outright (tell s.o. ~) a **palo** seco

to outshine s.o. **comer**se a alg. crudo; dar **quince** y raya/falta a alg.; dar cien **vuelta**s a alg.; hacer **sombra** a alg.

outside help (without [any] ~) a **cuerpo** gentil

to be outspoken no tener **pelo**s/**pepita** en la lengua

outstanding bestial; chachi; cojonudo; dabute[n]/dabuti; que quita el **hipo**; pistonudo; sobresaliente

to be outstanding hacer **raya**

outstanding mathematician (be an ~) **pintar**se uno solo/pintárselas solo para algo (example)

outstanding services (have rendered ~) merecer una **estatua**

outstanding student (be an ~) lucir en sus/los estudios

to outstrip s.o. comerle el **terreno** a alg.; dejar en **zaga** a alg.

oven (have a bun in the ~) estar hinchada (▷ **hinchar**)

over (▷ all ~)

over [and done] with (have got half ~) pasar el **ecuador**

over (come after everything is ~) llegar a los **postre**s

over (put one/it ~ on s.o.) dar [el] **camelo** a alg.; pegar un **parche** a alg.; dársela a alg. con **queso**; dar/pegar una **tostada** a alg.

to be overambitious pecar por **exceso** (example)

overboard (throw everything ~) echarlo todo a **rodar**

to overcome o.s. saltar sobre la propia **sombra**

overconfidence (err on the side of ~) pecar por **exceso** (example)

to be overconfident pecar por **exceso** (example)

to overdo it estirar la **cuerda**; pecar por **exceso**; pasarse de **rosca**

to be overflowing with tenderness/affection rebosar de ternura

overhang la **panza** de burro

to be overindulgent tener **manga** ancha/ser de manga ancha

to be overjoyed no caberle a alg. el **corazón** en el pecho

overnight de la **noche** a la mañana

to overshadow s.o. hacer **sombra** a alg.

to overshoot the mark pasar de la **raya**; tirar más allá del blanco

to oversleep pegársele a alg. las **sábanas**

to overstay one's welcome calentar el **asiento**/ pegársele a alg. el asiento

to overstep the mark pasar de la **raya**

to be overwhelmed with joy no **caber** en sí de alegría

owl (be a night ~) andar de **gallo**

owl (be as wise as an ~) ser más **sabio** que Salomón

own (each to his ~) cada uno/cual a lo **suyo**

own (hold one's ~) **defender**se bien

own (s.o. can't wait to get his ~ back) tener **sangre** en el ojo

own (strike out on one's ~) campar por sus respetos

own (the devil looks after his ~) mala **hierba** nunca muere

own (to each his ~) cada **loco** con su tema; a cada uno/cual, lo **suyo**

to own (as if one ~ed the place) como **Pedro** por/ en su casa

ox (work like an ~) trabajar como un **buey**

P

pace (at a snail's ~) a paso de **buey/tortuga**

pace (keep ~) correr **parejas**/andar de pareja

pack (a ~ of lies/nonsense/rubbish) una **sarta** de (examples)

pack (howl/run with the ~) dejarse llevar de/por la **corriente**

pack rat (be a ~) ser una **urraca**

to pack (send s.o. ~ing) dar el **bote** a alg.; echar/ despedir a alg. con **cajas** destempladas; echar a alg. a la **calle**/poner a alg. de patitas en la calle; plantar a alg. en la **calle**; mandar a alg. al **diablo**; largar a alg.; dar la **licencia**/[el] **pasaporte** a alg.; mandar a alg. a **paseo**; dar la **patada** a alg.; mandar a alg. a la **porra**

to pack one's bags/things [and go] liar los **bártulos**; hacer la **maleta**; liar el **petate**; levantar el **tabanque**

to pack up [and go] hacer la **maleta**; liar el **petate**

packed (be absolutely ~) no caber ni un **alfiler**; estar de **bote** en bote

to be packed in like sardines estar como tres en un **zapato**

to be packed out no caber ni un **alfiler**; estar de **bote** en bote

packet (cost a ~) costar una **burrada**/un **dineral**/ un **huevo**/un **ojo** de la cara/un **pico**/un **riñón**/una **riñonada**; costar la de **San Quintín**; costar un **sentido** o los cinco sentidos

packet (make a ~) hacer su **agosto**

pad (bachelor ~) el picadero

pad (frowsy/fuggy/smoky/stuffy ~) la zorrera

paid (put ~ to s.th.) echar algo al o por el **suelo**

pain in the arse/ass/neck el/la chinche

pain in the neck (be a ~) ser alg. un **plomo**

pains (no ~, no gains) no hay **atajo** sin trabajo; no hay **barranco** sin atranco; la **letra** con sangre entra; no se pescan **truchas** a bragas enjutas

pains (withdrawal ~) el mono

paint (be as exciting as watching [the] ~ dry) ser algo un **plomo**; a más no **poder**

painted hag la carantoña

pajamas (think one is the cat's ~) creerse el no va más (▷ **ir**); la **mar** de

pal (be bosom/great ~s) la **mar** de; estar a partir un **piñón** [con alg.]; comer en un/el o del mismo **plato**

palm (carry off the ~) llevarse la **gala/palma**

palm (grease s.o.'s ~) untar el **carro**/la **mano**/la **palma** a alg.

to palm s.th. off on s.o. colar algo a alg.

to pamper s.o. [in his childhood] guardar/tener o criar a alg. entre algodones (▷ **algodón**); criar a alg. en **estufa**

pan (be a flash in the ~) pasar como una **nube** de verano

pan (flash in the ~) una **nube** de verano

pan (jump out of the frying ~ into the fire) huir de la[s] **ceniza**[s] y caer/dar en la[s] brasa[s]; huir del **fuego** y caer en las brasas; salir de **Guatemala** y entrar en Guatepeor; ir de **Herodes** a Pilatos; salir de las **llamas** y caer en las brasas; salir de **Málaga** y entrar en Malagón; huir del **perejil** y dar en el berenjenal; saltar/caer de la **sartén** y dar en la brasa; huir del **toro** y caer en el arroyo; salir del **trueno** y dar con el relámpago

to pan s.th. dar **caña** a algo

pancake (be [as] flat as a ~) ser de **Castellón de la Plana**; ser lisa (▷ **liso**)

pangs of conscience el rescoldo

panic (be in a flat ~) estar con los cojones de corbata (▷ **cojón**)

pansy (gay) el canco/marica/maricón/mariposa/ pluma; la rana; el sarasa

pants (bore the ~ off s.o.) quedarse con alg.

pants (catch s.o. with his ~ down) pillar a alg. en **bolas/bragas**

pants (fill one's ~/make a mess in one's ~) **cagar**se

pants (scare the ~ off s.o.) dar un **susto** de muerte a alg.

pants (wear the ~) cortar el **bacalao**; llevar la **batuta**; llevar/ponerse los calzones (▷ **calzón**); ser el amo del o dirigir el **cotarro**; llevar los pantalones (▷ **pantalón**)/la **voz** cantante

paper (be a scrap/a worthless bit of ~) no ser más que **papel** mojado

paper (garbage/rubbish that ends up on ~) el **papel** todo lo aguanta

paper (not to be worth the ~ [s.th. is written on]) no ser más que **papel** mojado

paper bag (s.o. who couldn't fight his way out of a ~) el/la gallina

par (be on a ~) correr **parejas**/andar de pareja

paradise (live in a fool's ~) tejer la tela de **Penélope**

to be paralyzed with fear/horror no quedarle a alg. **gota** de sangre en las venas; quedarse **helado**; quedarse sin **pulso**[s]; bajársele a alg. la **sangre** a los talones; quedarse **yerto**

to be **parched** abrasarse de sed; estar **muerto** de sed

parental nest (leave the ~) alzar/levantar el **vuelo**

parrot (be as sick as a ~) arrojar hasta los **huesos**

parrot fashion (repeat s.th. ~) hablar con **boca** de ganso

part (play a ~) jugar/desempeñar un **papel**

part (the most difficult ~ is yet/still to come) aún falta/queda la **cola**/el **rabo** por desollar

part (without having [had] any ~ in it) sin **comer**lo ni beberlo

to **participate in s.th.** mojar en algo

to be **particular** hilar delgado/muy fino

party (be a member of the other ~) ser de la otra **acera**

party (keep it with both parties) bailar en la **cuerda** floja

party (mad hatter's tea ~) la **olla** de grillos

party (spoil the ~) aguar la **fiesta**

to **party** (go out/be ~ing) ir/estar de **juerga**

to **pass for** pasar por

to **pass muster** colar

to **pass over s.th.** dejar algo a un **lado** o de lado

passable potable

passenger (pillion ~) el paquete

to be **passionately fond of reading** a más no **poder**

past (be a thing of the ~) ser **agua** pasada

past (be s.o. with a ~) ser de **historia**

past (in the dim and distant ~) en [los] tiempos de **ñangué**

past and future habido y por **haber**

to **paste s.o. one** pegar una **leche/torta** a alg.

pasting (give s.o. a sound ~) poner a alg. como **chupa** de dómine

pat (have/know s.th down/off ~) saber algo al **dedillo**

patch (go through a bad/rough/unlucky ~) pasarlas negras (▷ **negro**); pasar un **trago** amargo

patch (not to be a ~ on s.o.) no **servir** para descalzar a alg.; no llegarle a alg. a la **suela** del zapato/a los **zancajos**

path (tread a ~) tirar por un camino

patience (arm o.s. with ~) revestirse de paciencia

patience (even a saint can lose his ~ with s.o.) poder hacer perder la paciencia a un **santo**

patience (have the ~ of Job/of a saint) tener la paciencia de un **chino**; tener más **paciencia** que Job/que un santo; tener una **paciencia** angelical/de benedictino

patsy (easy victim) el primo

Paul (rob Peter to pay ~) desnudar/desvestir a un **santo** para vestir otro

paunch (start to get a ~) echar **panza/tripa**

pauper el muerto de **hambre**

to **pave the way for s.o./s.th.** preparar el **terreno** a alg./algo

paw (hand) la pata/pezuña

to **pay** (be the one who ~s/who has to ~) ser el **paganini/pagano**

to **pay** (it doesn't ~) [lo] **comido** por [lo] servido

to **pay** (make s.o. ~ for it) pasar la **cuenta** a alg.

to **pay** (you'll ~ for this!) ¡[ya] me las pagarás! (▷ **pagar**)

to **pay** (you'll ~ for this in spades!) ¡[ya] me las pagarás con creces! (▷ **pagar**)

to **pay a visit** (s.o. must just [go and] ~: go to the toilet) echar una **carta** al correo (example); tener que ir a un **sitio**

to **pay attention to s.th.** prestar/dar **oídos** a algo; prestar atención a algo

to **pay cash/on the nail** pagar a toca **teja**

to **pay dearly for s.th.** **salir**le algo a alg. caro

to **pay for one's stupidity/naivety** (have to ~) pagar la **primada**

to **pay for s.th. in installments** comprar algo a **plazoleta**s

to **pay no attention** [to what s.o. says] escuchar/oír como quien oye **llover**

to **pay s.o. back in his own coin/in kind** pagar a alg. con/en la misma **moneda**; volver las **torna**s a alg.

to **pay the twenty dollars and not a cent more** a **palo** seco

to **pay up** (it's time to ~!) ¡tocan a pagar! o ia pagar tocan! (▷ **tocar**)

pea (be as like as two ~s [in a pod]) parecerse como dos **gota**s de agua/como un **huevo** a otro

pea (be still as green as a ~) estar aún con la **leche** en los labios; caerse de un **nido**

peace (not to give s.o. a moment's ~) no dejar a alg. [ni] a **sol** ni a sombra

peaceful nature (have a ~) no tener **hiel**; ser una **paloma** sin hiel

peacefully (die ~) quedarse [muerto] como un **pajarito**

peacock (be as proud as a ~) ser engreído como **gallo** de cortijo

peanuts (not to be ~) no ser **grano** de anís; no ser **moco de pavo**

peanuts (sell/buy s.th. for ~) vender/comprar algo a **huevo**

peanuts (work for ~) cobrar/ganar una **miseria**; trabajar por un **pedazo** de pan

pearls (cast ~ before swine) echar **margarita**s a los puercos

peasouper (thick fog) el puré

pebble [lens] glasses gafas de **culo** de vaso/ botella

pecker el arma/asunto/bolo/calvo/canario/ chorizo/cimbel; la gurrina; el pájaro; la picha/pija; el pijo; la pinga; el pito; la polla/porra; el rabo/troncho

pecker (keep your ~ up!) ¡tente **tieso**!

peculiar ideas (have ~) tener sus **luna**s

to be **pedantic** hilar delgado o muy fino

peddler (ass ~) el chapero

pee (have a ~) cambiar el **agua/caldo** a las aceitunas; cambiar el agua al **canario**

to pee o.s. laughing **mear**se [de risa]

peeled (keep one's eyes ~) avivar el/[los] **ojo**[s]

peep (not to hear a ~ out of or from s.o.) no decir ni **pío**

peg (feel like a square ~ in a round hole) estar/sentirse como **gallina** en corral ajeno

peg (take s.o. down a ~ or two) bajar el **gallo**/los **humo**s a alg.; meter a alg. el **resuello** en el cuerpo

to peg out (die) irse al otro **barrio**; liar los **bártulos**; **cascar**[la]; diñarla; quedarse **frío/frito**; pelar **gallo**; **guiñar**la; hincar el pico; **liar**las o liárselas; palmarla; estirar la **pata**; liar el **petate**; **pringar**la; **reventar**[se]; quedarse **tieso**

the pen is mightier than the sword más fuerte es la **pluma** que la espada

penis (cock; eleventh finger; dick; dong; pecker; prick; weeny; willy) el arma/asunto/bolo/calvo/canario/chorizo/cimbel; el **dedo** veintiuno; la gurrina; el pajarito/pájaro; la picha/pija; el pijo; la pinga; el pito; la polla/porra; el rabo/troncho

penis of children el pajarito

penny (a bad ~ always turns up) mala **hierba** nunca muere

penny (be down to one's last ~) andar/estar a la cuarta **pregunta**

penny (cost a pretty ~) costar una **burrada**/un **dineral**/un **huevo**/un **ojo** de la cara/un **pico**/un **riñón**/una **riñonada**; costar la de **San Quintín**; costar un **sentido** o los cinco sentidos

penny (count every ~) pellizcar los céntimos

penny (down to the last ~) un **real** sobre otro

penny (in for a ~, in for a pound) [una vez] puesto en el **burro**; preso por **mil**, preso por mil quinientos; de **perdido**s, al agua/río

penny (look after the pennies and the pounds will look after themselves or will take care of themselves) a quien cuida la **peseta** nunca le falta un duro; muchos **poco**s hacen un mucho

penny (not to have a ~ to one's name) no tener ni para unas **alpargata**s; estar sin/no tener **blanca**; no tener qué llevarse a la **boca**/donde **caerse** muerto; estar sin un/no tener [ni] un **cuarto**; estar con una **mano** atrás y otra [a]delante; estar sin un/no tener [ni] un **real**

penny ([now] the ~ has dropped) ahora caigo en la **cuenta**/me doy cuenta

penny (spend a ~) cambiar el **agua/caldo** a las aceitunas; cambiar el agua al **canario**

penny (the ~ finally dropped) por fin cayó en la **cuenta**/se dio cuenta

penny-pincher el cicatero/la cicatera; el cuentagarbanzos

pennyworth (put in one's [two] ~) meter **baza** [en]; meter su **cuchara**

penpusher el cagatintas/chupatintas

people (▷ important/ordinary/prominent ~; upper-class/upper-crust ~; well-heeled/well-to-do ~)

people (a whole crowd of ~) ciento y la **madre**

people (all the ~) el ganado

people (live on/off other ~) comer la/vivir de la **sopa** boba

people (only a few ~/a handful of ~) cuatro **gato**s

people (what ~ may/might/will say) el qué dirán (▷ **decir**)

people elsewhere in the world don't live in the land of milk and honey either allí tampoco atan los perros con **longaniza**[s]

people of that ilk/sort/kind gente de ese **jaez**

pebble [lens] glasses gafas de **culo** de vaso/botella

percent or per cent (one hundred ~) por los cuatro **costados**

to be perfect venir/sentar [a alg.] como **anillo** al dedo (example)

perfect (be [absolutely] ~) poder pasar por las **pica**s de Flandes

perfect (nobody's ~) cada uno/cual tiene lo **suyo**; de todo tiene la/hay en la **viña** del Señor

perfectly a pedir de **boca**

perfectly (fit ~) venir/sentar [a alg.] como **anillo** al dedo (example)

perfectly (go/suit ~) de **perlas**

period (have a ~: ▷ she has the **curse** [of Eve]/has the **rag** on/is on the rag)

period (start one's ~) venirle a una mujer el **primo** de América

peroxide blonde la **rubia** de frasco/bote

to persist in one's error no apearse de su **burro**

person (a ~ who has a cushy job) el enchufado/la enchufada

person (a ~ who is all talk and no action) el/la cantamañanas

person (a ~ who is always putting his foot in it/dropping a clanger/making gaffes or who has foot-in-mouth disease) el/la metepatas

person (a ~ who looks after Number One) Juan Palomo

person (amusing ~) el jacarero

person (annoying ~) el/la chinche

person (be a dangerous ~) ser un **pájaro** de cuenta

person (be a fickle ~) bailar a cualquier **son**; ser un[a] **veleta**

person (be a lucky/an unlucky ~) nació alg. de pie[s]/de cabeza (▷ **nacer**)

person (be a sanctimonious/an excessively pious ~)
comerse los santos
person (be an extremely annoying ~) tener **sangre**
de chinches
person (be just an ordinary ~) ser del **montón**
person (cantankerous ~) el/la cascarrabias
person (crafty/sly ~) el zorro
person (know exactly what kind of [a] ~ s.o. is)
gastarlas
person (light-fingered ~) el/la uñetas
person (pig-headed ~) el/la cabezota
person (quick-tempered ~) el/la cascarrabias
person (short, chubby ~) el tapón
person (unlucky ~) el/la malapata
person (unreliable ~) el/la cantamañanas
person ([very] active ~) el zarandillo
personality (be totally different personalities)
estar tan lejos como lo **blanco** de lo
negro/no parecerse ni en el blanco de los
ojos
to pervert justice doblar la **vara** de la justicia
peseta (500-~ bill/note) medio **saco**
peseta (1000-~ bill/note) la lechuga/sábana; el
saco/verde
peseta (coin) la rubia
pest el/la chinche
pest (be a real ~) tener **sangre** de chinches
to pester s.o. dar la **coña/serenata** a alg.
to pester s.o. with questions asar a alg. a
preguntas
pet subject/topic (he's/she's onto his/her ~ again)
ha vuelto a la misma **canción/cantilena**
petard (be hoist by/with one's own ~) ir por **lana** y
volver trasquilado/esquilado; salirle a alg.
el **tiro** por la culata
Peter (rob ~ to pay Paul) desnudar/desvestir a
un **santo** para vestir otro
to be petrified with fear/horror no quedarle a alg.
gota de sangre en las venas; quedarse
helado; quedarse sin **pulso**[s]; bajársele a
alg. la **sangre** a los talones; quedarse
yerto
petticoat government el **gobierno** de faldas
petty clerk el cagatintas/chupatintas
philanderer el castigador
philanderer (be quite a ~) tener **corazón** de
alcachofa
phlegmatic (be very ~) tener la **sangre** gorda
physique (have a good ~) tener buena **percha**
Piccadilly Circus (it's like ~ around here or there)
parece que hay **jubileo** aquí/allí
pick (elite) la **flor** y nata
to pick at one's food comer como un **gorrión**
to pick one's nose hacer **albondiguillas**; sacar
muebles
to pick o.s. up levantar/alzar **cabeza**
to pick s.o. up hacer un **levante** a alg.
to pick s.o. up (a joint where people go to ~) el **bar**
de ligue/alterne

to pick s.o. up (go out trying to ~) salir de **levante**
to pick up (a woman who can be ~ed up easily) la
ligona
to pick up women (a man who tries to ~) el ligón
pickle (get o.s. into a ~) meterse en un
berenjenal/en **camisa** de once varas
pickpocket el cicatero/la cicatera
pick-up (easy/quick ~) el levante
pick-up (go out on the ~) salir de **levante**
picnic (be no ~) no saber a **rosquilla**
picnic (be one sandwich short of a ~) ser de pocas
luces/corto de luces o tener pocas luces
(▷ **luz**)
picture (be in the ~) estar en la **onda**; estar de
viaje
picture of health (be/look a ~) estar como una
lechuga; vender/prestar **salud**
piddle (have a ~) cambiar el **agua/caldo** a las
aceitunas; cambiar el agua al **canario**
pie (be as easy as ~) ser una **breva**; ser **coser** y
cantar; ser **pan** comido
pie (eat humble ~) pedir **alafia**; doblar el
espinazo
piece (nothing remains in one ~) no dejar/quedar
títere con cabeza
piece of cake (be a ~) ser una **breva**; ser **coser** y
cantar; ser **pan** comido
piece of good luck (chance ~) la breva; el **cabe** de
pala
piece of juggling (with figures/etc.) el **apaño**
piece of old junk la antigualla; el vejestorio
piece of one's mind (give s.o. a ~) soltar la/una
andanada a alg.; zurrar la **badana**/dar una
calada/cantar las cuarenta a alg.; decir a
alg. cuántas son **cinco**; soltar/decir cuatro
frescas a alg.; dar a alg. con los **ochos** y
los nueves; poner a alg. las **peras** a cuarto;
decirle a alg. cuatro **verdad**es/las verdades
del barquero; poner a alg. de **vuelta** y
media
piece of stupidity la primada
piece of work (be a nasty ~) ser un mal **bicho**;
tener mal **café**/mala **leche**; ser un **pájaro**
de cuenta; tener mala **pipa/sombra**; tener
mala **uva**
piece of work (nasty ~) el malaleche; el/la
malaúva; la tipeja; el tipejo
pieces (pull s.o. to ~) poner a alg. como un
guiñapo/como **hoja** de perejil; roer los
zancajos a alg.
pieces (smash s.th. to ~) hacer algo **cisco**/[una]
tortilla
pieces (s.th. is so old it is falling to ~) caerse [a/en
pedazos] de viejo
pieces (tear s.o. to ~) poner a alg. como **chupa**
de dómine/como un **guiñapo**/como **hoja**
de perejil; machacar a alg.; hacer **polvo** a
alg.; revolcar a alg.; poner a alg. como un
trapo

to be pie-eyed estar cocido (▷ **cocer**)

piercing wind (a ~ is blowing) corre un **gris** que pela

pig (▷ **pigs**)

pig (be [as] fat as a ~) estar hecho una **botija**; no caber en el **pellejo**

pig (policeman) el bofia/poli/polizonte

pig (make a [real] ~ of o.s.) comer más que un **alguacil**; llenarse la **andorga/barriga**; henchir el **baúl**; ponerse las **botas**; llenarse el **buche**; comer/mascar a dos **carrillo**s; ponerse como el chico del **esquilador**; comer como una **lima**/más que **siete**; llenarse el **vientre**

pig (sweat like a ~) sudar la **gota** gorda

to pig out como un **descosido** (example); más que **siete**

pigeon (stool ~: informer) el chivato/la chivata; el soplón/la soplona

pigeons (set the cat among the ~) meter los **perro**s en danza

to be pigheaded dar con la **cabeza** en las paredes; ser duro de **mollera**; tener la cabeza más dura que un **picador**

pig-headed person el/la cabezota

pigheadedly erre que erre

pigs (police) la bofia/madera/poli/polilla

pigs (when ~ learn to fly) cuando meen las **gallinas**; cuando las **ranas** críen pelo; en la **semana** que no tenga jueves/de tres jueves

pigs might fly! ¡hasta que/cuando meen las **gallinas**!; ¡hasta que/cuando las **ranas** críen pelo!

pikestaff (be as plain as a ~) estar más claro que el **agua**; ser más claro que el **sol**

pile (make a/one's ~) hacer su **agosto**; ponerse las **botas**; **hinchar**se de plata/dinero

piles of a **cántaros**; hasta la **pared** de enfrente; a **punta** pala

piles of money (have ~) la **mar** de

piles of money (make ~) a más no **poder**

pill (be a bitter ~ [to swallow]) ser un **trago** amargo

pill ([have to] swallow the bitter ~) [tener que] tragar **quina**

pill (sweeten/sugar/sugar-coat the ~) dorar la **píldora**

pillar (run/chase from ~ to post) andar de la **Ceca** a la Meca; ir de **Herodes** a Pilatos; dar más vueltas que un **tiovivo**

pillion (ride ~) ir de **paquete**

pillion passenger/rider el paquete

to pillory s.o. poner a alg. en la **picota**

pimp el taxista

pin (as bright/clean as a new ~ or like a new ~) limpio como una **patena**; como una **plata**/una **tacita** de plata

pin (be on ~s and needles) tener el **alma** en un hilo; estar en/sobre **ascuas**; estar [como] en **brasas**

pin (hear a ~ drop) no se siente/oye [ni] una **mosca** (example); poder oír volar una **mosca**

pin (keep s.o. on ~s and needles) tener a alg. en el **potro**

to pin s.th. on s.o. cargar el **mochuelo** a alg.

to pin the blame on s.o. cargar el **baúl/blanco** a alg.; endiñar algo a alg. (example); cargar el **mochuelo/muerto** a alg.; echar el **sambenito** a alg.

pinch of salt (take s.th. with a ~) tomar algo con un **grano** de sal

to pinch (know where the shoe ~es) saber dónde aprieta el **zapato**

to pinch s.th./s.o. (steal) pisar algo/a alg.; **pringar**se algo; soplar algo [a alg.]

to pine for s.th. **perecer**se por algo

pink (be in the ~) vender/prestar **salud**

pink (be tickled ~) alegrarse/estar como [un] **niño** con zapatos nuevos; estar [contento] como o más contento que unas pascuas (▷ **Pascua**)

pink slip (give s.o. the ~) dar el **bote** a alg.; echar/despedir a alg. con **cajas** destempladas; echar a alg. a la **calle**/poner a alg. de patitas en la calle; plantar a alg. en la **calle**; largar a alg.; dar la **licencia**/[el] **pasaporte**/la **patada** a alg.

pious (be an excessively ~ man/woman/person) **comer**se los santos

pious (excessively ~ woman) la beata

pious Annie la beata

pious Annie (be a ~) **comer**se los santos

pious Annie (during the day ~, during the night a bit of all right or hot stuff or mistress) de día **beata**, de noche gata

pipe (put that in your ~ and smoke it!) ¡chúpate ésa! (▷ **chupar**)

to pipe down echar el **cierre**; achantar la **mui**; cerrar el **pico**

to pirate s.th. fusilar algo

piss la meada

piss (have a ~) echar una **meada**; mear

to piss mear

piss off! ¡anda a **bañar**te!; ¡vete al **coño**/a tomar por **culo**!

to piss off (tell s.o. to ~) mandar a alg. a tomar por **culo**/a la **mierda**

to piss on s.th. pasarse algo por el **culo**

to piss o.s. laughing descojonarse; **mear**se [de risa]

to piss s.o. off darle por o romper las **bolas** a alg.; poner a alg. a **parir**; tocar/hinchar los cojones a alg. (▷ **cojón**) pissed (be ~: drunk) estar hecho un **cesto**; estar cocido (▷ **cocer**); estar hecho una **cuba**/un **cuero**/un **pellejo**/una **uva**

pissed (be as ~ as a newt) estar hecho un **cesto**/una **cuba**/un **cuero**/un **pellejo**/una **uva**

pissed (get ~/as ~ as a newt: drunk) cogerse una **castaña**; **cocer**se; papar una **jumera**; coger una **melopea**/**merluza**; coger/pillar una **mona**; moñarse; coger una **pea**; agarrar[se] un **pedo**; coger una **pítima**

to be pissed off estar hasta las **bolas**

pistol la pipa

pistol (as a problem solver) el quitapenas

pistol (hold a ~ to s.o.'s head) poner el **puñal** en el pecho a alg.

pit (be [like] a bottomless ~) ser un **pozo** sin fondo

pitch (queer one's own ~) hacer las diez de últimas (▷ **último**)

pitch (queer s.o.'s ~) echar a **rodar** los proyectos de alg.

to pitch s.o. into the street plantar a alg. en la **calle**

pith el jugo

pittance (earn a ~) cobrar/ganar una **miseria**

pittance (work for a mere ~) trabajar por un **pedazo** de pan

pity (it would be such a ~ not to . . .) sería un **pecado** no ...

place (as if one owned the ~) como **Pedro** por/en su casa

place (be [caught] between a rock and a hard ~) estar entre la **espada** y la pared/entre dos **fuegos**

place (be the team in last ~) ser el **farolillo** rojo

place (be/feel very/wholly out of ~) estar/sentirse como **gallina** en corral ajeno; hacer tanta falta como los **perros** en misa/ser como perro en misa

place (everyone to his ~) cada **mochuelo** a su olivo

place (live/be at a godforsaken ~) vivir/estar donde **Cristo** dio las tres voces/etc. o donde el **diablo** perdió el poncho; vivir/estar en el quinto **infierno**/**pino** o en la quinta **puñeta**

place (miserable ~) de mala **muerte** (example)

place (never stay in one ~ for long) ser [un] **culo** de mal asiento

place (put s.o. in his ~) poner a alg. a **raya**/en su **sitio**

place (there's a time and a ~ for everything) no hay que hablar de/mentar/nombrar la **soga** en casa del ahorcado

place (wreck the ~) no dejar/quedar **títere** con cabeza

place (you can't be in more than one ~ at the same time) no se puede **repicar** y estar en la procesión

places (have [powerful/influential] friends in the right ~) tener buenas **aldaba**s/buenos **asidero**s; el enchufe (example)

places (s.o. wouldn't like to swap ~ with s.o.) no arrendarle la **ganancia** a alg.

to plagiarize s.th. fusilar algo

plague (the ~ is raging) se ceba la peste (▷ **cebar**)

to plague s.o. with questions asar a alg. a preguntas

plain [and simple] mondo y lirondo; sin **tapujos**

plain (be as ~ as a pikestaff/as day/as the nose on your face) estar más claro que el **agua**; ser más claro que el **sol**

plain English/Spanish/German/etc. (in ~) en **cristiano**

plain English/Spanish/German/etc. (say/tell s.th. in ~) hablar en **castellano** [puro y llano]; hablar en **cristiano**

plain sailing (think everything is ~) creer que todo el monte es **orégano**

plan (thwart s.o.'s ~s) echar a **rodar** los proyectos de alg.

planet (come from another ~) tener **monos** en la cara (example)

planks (be as thick as two short ~) ser más tonto que **Abundio**; si le/etc. menean, da **bellota**s; ser más tonto que **Carracuca**; ser más **cerrado** que un cerrojo; ser más **corto** que las mangas de un chaleco; ser más tonto que una **mata** de habas; no saber ni siquiera quitarse los **mocos**; ser más bruto que la **pila** de un pozo

plastered (be ~) estar hecho un **cesto**; estar cocido (▷ **cocer**); estar hecho una **cuba**/un **cuero**; estar/andar **pedo**; estar hecho un **pellejo**/una **sopa**; estar **trompa**; estar hecho una **uva**

plastered (get ~) **cocer**se; papar una **jumera**; coger una **melopea**/**merluza**; coger/pillar una **mona**; moñarse; coger una **pea**; agarrar[se] un **pedo**; coger una **pítima**; coger[se] una **trompa**

plate (have an awful lot on one's ~) no saber dónde volver la **cabeza**

platitude blanco y en botella, leche

play (be child's ~) ser una **breva**; ser **coser** y cantar; ser **pan** comido; ser **tortas** y pan pintado

play (bring s.th. into ~) poner algo en **juego**

to play a dirty/nasty trick on s.o. hacer una **faena**/una mala **jugada** a alg.; jugar una mala **partida** a alg.; hacer una **perrada** a alg.; jugar una **pieza** a alg.; dar una **puñalada** trapera a alg.

to play a role/part jugar/desempeñar un **papel**

to play along with s.o. llevar/seguir la **corriente** a alg.

to play chaperon[e]/gooseberry hacer/ir de **carabina**

to play dead/possum hacerse el **muerto**

to play first fiddle cortar el **bacalao**; llevar la **batuta**; llevar/ponerse los calzones (▷ **calzón**); ser el amo del o dirigir el **cotarro**; llevar la **voz** cantante

to play into s.o.'s hands hacer el **caldo** gordo a alg.

to play it safe [nadar y] guardar la ropa; picar de **vara** larga

to play lord of the manor darse **aires** de grandeza; pintar la **cigüeña**

to play second fiddle ser **plato** de segunda mesa

to play "she loves me, she loves me not" deshojar la **margarita**

to play s.o. for a sucker engañar a alg. como a un **chino**

to play the buffoon/clown/fool hacer el **gracioso/oso**; **tirar**se a muerto

to play the elegant/refined man/woman meterse a **finolis**

to play the field ir de **flor** en flor

to play up to s.o. dar **coba**/hacer **fiestas** a alg.; venir a alg. con **papel**es; hacer la **rosca** a alg.

to play with fire jugar con el **fuego**; atar perros con **longaniza**

player (be a key ~) jugar/desempeñar un **papel** (example)

player (poor ~) el maleta

plaything (be a ~ of the waves) ser un **juguete** de las olas

pleasant (s.th. ~ is always welcome) a nadie le amarga un **dulce**

to please (do [exactly] as one ~s) campar por sus respetos; hacer de su **capa** un sayo; hacer su santa voluntad (▷ **santo**)

to please (try to ~ everybody) nadar entre dos aguas; [nadar y] guardar la ropa

to please (you can't ~ all the people all of the time) nunca llueve a gusto de todos (▷ **llover**)

to please (you can't ~ everybody) nunca llueve a gusto de todos (▷ **llover**)

pleased (be as ~ as Punch) alegrarse/estar como [un] **niño** con zapatos nuevos; estar [contento] como o más contento que unas pascuas (▷ **Pascua**)

pleased (be terribly ~) la **mar** de

pleased (be well ~) darse con un **canto** en los dientes/pechos

plenty (in ~) a **cántaros/pote**

plenty of a **cántaro**s/**manta**; a **punta** pala

pleonasm (use ~) poner dos **albardas** a un burro

to plonk ser un **vino** peleón

plot el tinglado

plot (lay a ~) armar un **tinglado**

to plough (flunk) tirarse una **rosca**

to plough s.o. dar **calabazas** a alg.

pluck (have ~) tener cojones (▷ **cojón**); tener **hígados/huevos/redaños**; tener riñones (▷ **riñón**)

to pluck up [one's] courage sacar **fuerza**s de flaqueza; revestirse de valor; hacer de **tripa**s corazón

plum job la breva

plumes (adorn o.s. with borrowed ~) adornarse con **plumas** ajenas

plunge (take the ~) entrar a por **uvas**

to plunge into s.th. meterse de **cabeza** en algo

plush el postín (example); señor

pocket (carry/have s.o. in one's ~) tener a alg. en el **bote**

pockets (line one's ~) ponerse las **botas**; chupar del **bote**; **rascar**se para adentro; **redondear**se

pockmarked face la cara de **rallo**

point (come/get [straight] to the ~) no andarse con/en chiquitas (▷ la **chiquita**); ir al **grano**; no andarse con **requilorios**

point (fail to see the ~) quedarse en **blanco**

point (get the ~) captar la **onda**

point (key ~) el quid

point (know s.o.'s weak ~[s]) saber de qué **pie** cojea alg.

point (notch up a [plus] ~) apuntarse un **tanto**

point (sore/weak ~) el **punto** flaco

point (that's the ~) es lo que hace el **gasto**

point (touch on a sore ~) poner el **dedo** en la llaga; tocar [a alg.] en la **herida**

point (wander from the ~) irse por los **cerros** de Úbeda; **salir**se del tema

to be pointless no tener **pies** ni cabeza (example)

pointless arguments/discussions (protracted and ~) discusiones bizantinas (▷ **bizantino**)

poison (one man's meat is another man's ~) nunca llueve a gusto de todos (▷ **llover**)

to poke fun at s.th. poner algo en **solfa**

to poke one's nose in (who asked you to poke your nose in?) ... vela en este entierro

to poke one's nose into other people's affairs/business meterse en **camisa** de once varas; **meter**se alg. donde no le llaman

to poke one's nose into s.th. meter el **hocico** en algo; meter las narices en algo (▷ **nariz**)

poker (as stiff as a ~) tieso como un ajo

pole (s.o. wouldn't touch s.th./s.o. with a ten-foot ~) no poder coger algo ni con **papel** de fumar; no poder coger algo/a alg. ni con **tenazas**

to be poles apart estar tan lejos como lo **blanco** de lo negro/no parecerse ni en el blanco de los ojos

police (cops; filth; fuzz; pigs) la bofia/madera/**poli/polilla**

policeman un agente de la **porra**

policeman (cop; copper; pig) el bofia/poli/
polizonte

policy (apply a ~ of the carrot and the stick or a
carrot-and-stick ~) mezclar **bromas** con
veras; dar una de **cal** y otra de arena;
aplicar una política del **palo** y la zanahoria

to polish s.th. off echarse algo al **coleto**/al
estómago/entre **pecho** y espalda

polite (say s.th. just to be ~) decir algo con la
boca chica

politeness and firmness aren't mutually exclusive lo
cortés no quita lo valiente

politeness doesn't have to be a sign of weakness lo
cortés no quita lo valiente

pompous behavior el postín

pompousness el postín

pong ([horrible] ~) el pestazo

to pong oler a **tigre**

pony (for cheating in exam) la chuleta

pony (go/come on Shank's ~) ir/venir a golpe de
alpargata/en el **caballo** de San Francisco/
a golpe de **calcetín**/en el **coche** de San
Francisco o de San Fernando

poof[ter] (gay) el canco/marica/maricón/
mariposa/pluma; la rana; el sarasa

pooh la caca

poop la caca

to be pooped (exhausted) estar hecho una braga
(▷ **bragas**); estar/quedar hecho **cisco**;
tener los **huesos** molidos; estar hecho
migas/papilla/pedazos; estar hecho un
pingajo; estar hecho **polvo/puré**; estar
reventado (▷ **reventar**); estar hecho unos
zorros

poor (be as ~ as a church mouse) no tener ni para
unas **alpargatas**; no tener qué llevarse a la
boca/donde **caerse** muerto; no tener más
que el **pan** y la noche; ser más pobre que
una **rata** [de iglesia]

poor (be very ~) no tener más que el **pan** y la
noche

poor (become desperately ~) quedarse por/a
puertas

poor bullfighter/player el maleta

poorly written letter (a very ~) hacer algo con los
pies (example)

to pop off (die) irse al otro **barrio**; **cascar**[la];
diñarla; quedarse **frío/frito**; pelar **gallo**;
guiñarla; hincar el pico; **liar**las o liárselas;
palmarla; estirar la **pata**; liar el **petate**;
pringarla; **reventar**[se]; quedarse **tieso**

to pop one's clogs/cork (▷ **clogs; cork**)

to pop out (s.o.'s eyes ~ of their sockets/of his head)
saltársele/salírsele a alg. los **ojos** de las
órbitas

poppy (turn as red as a ~) ponerse como una o
más rojo que una **amapola**; ponerse como
un **tomate**

port (any ~ in a storm) a falta de **pan**, buenas
son tortas

porter (of hotel/etc.) la leona

posh pichi; el postín (example); señor; a lo
gran señor (▷ **el señor**)

poshness el postín

position (be in a ~ of authority) estar alg. en [el]
candelero

position (be in a good/high ~) andar/estar en
zancos

position (get a ~) enchufarse

position (hold a good ~) estar bien **sentado**

position (undermine s.o.'s ~) minar el **terreno** a
alg.

possibly (not ~) ni a la de **tres**

possum (play ~) hacerse el **muerto**

post (be as deaf as a ~) ser más sordo que una
tapia

post (get [s.o.] a ~) enchufar a alg.; enchufarse

post (give/get s.o. a high ~) poner a alg. en [el]
candelero

post (run/chase from pillar to ~) andar de la **Ceca**
a la Meca; ir de **Herodes** a Pilatos; dar
más vueltas que un **tiovivo**

posterior (buttocks) donde la **espalda** pierde su
honesto nombre; el mapamundi/pompis;
la popa; el rabel/salvohonor/tafanario/
trasero/traspontín; la trastienda

pot (a watched ~ never boils) quien espera,
desespera (▷ **esperar**)

pot (marijuana) el chocolate/ful; la hierba/
mandanga/mierda; el tate; la yerba

pot (smoke ~) emporrarse

potato (hot ~) una **patata** caliente

pots of a **cántaros/pote**

pots of money (have ~) tener muchos **cuartos**;
rebosar en dinero

pots of money (make ~) a **cántaros** (example); a
más no **poder**; a **pote** (example)

pot-smoker el/la grifota

pounds (look after the pennies and the ~ will look
after themselves or will take care of
themselves) a quien cuida la **peseta** nunca
le falta un duro; muchos **pocos** hacen un
mucho

to pour (it never rains but it ~s) siempre llueve
sobre mojado (▷ **llover**); bien vengas **mal**,
si vienes solo; a **perro** flaco no le faltan
pulgas

to pour one's heart out to s.o. descubrir/abrir el
pecho a alg.; contar su **película** a alg.

to be pouring [down or with rain] a **cántaros**
(example); llover a **chorros/cubos/mares**/
torrentes

to pout hacer **pucheros**

poverty is no sin/is not a crime pobreza no es
vileza

powder (put your trust in God and keep your ~
dry) a **Dios** rogando y con el mazo dando

power (do everything in one's ~) poner toda la **carne** en el asador; emplearse a **fondo**; no dejar **piedra** para mover; tocar todos los **resorte**s

powerful friends in the right places (have ~) tener buenas **aldaba**s/buenos **asidero**s

to practice what one preaches predicar con el ejemplo

praise (give s.o. exaggerated ~) dar **bombo** a alg.

praise (heap ~ on s.o.) poner a alg. en/por o levantar a alg. a/hasta los **cuerno**s de la luna; levantar a alg. hasta o poner a alg. por las **nube**s

praise (sing s.o.'s ~s) poner a alg. en/por o levantar a alg. a/hasta los **cuerno**s de la luna; levantar a alg. hasta o poner a alg. por las **nube**s

to praise s.o. to the skies dar **bombo** a alg.; poner a alg. en/por o levantar a alg. a/hasta los **cuerno**s de la luna; hacerse **lengua**s de alg.; levantar a alg. hasta o poner a alg. por las **nube**s

to praise s.th. to the skies hacerse **lengua**s de algo

praised (much-~) cacarear algo (example)

prat el/la gilipollas

prayer (on a wing and a ~) a la buena de Dios (▷ **bueno**); a la **gracia** de Dios

to preach (practice what one ~es) predicar con el ejemplo

to preach in the wilderness clamar en el desierto; dar **música** a un sordo; predicar en el desierto

precautions (take ~ [against]) ponerse en **guardia** [contra]

pregnant (get ~) salir con [una] **tripita**

pregnant (get/make s.o. ~) hinchar a alg.; dejar a alg. con el **paquete**; hacer una **tripa** a alg.

prehistoric año de/tiempo[s] de/días de **Maricastaña**; del año de/en el año de la **nana**; en [los] tiempos de ñangué; del año de o en el año de la **pera/polca**; en tiempos del **rey** que rabió/del rey Wamba

prematurely (celebrate ~) echar las **campana**s al vuelo

to prepare for the worst ponerse en lo **peor**

to prepare the ground for s.th. preparar el **terreno** a algo

present (all those ~) el ganado

present and future habido y por **haber**

press (gutter/yellow ~) la **prensa** amarilla o del corazón

press (have a bad/good ~) tener buena/mala **prensa**

to press on regardless liarse la **manta** a la cabeza

pressure (put the ~/apply ~ on s.o.) apretar las **clavija**s/los **tornillo**s/las **tuerca**s a alg.

to pretend not to have heard/known anything [about it] hacerse de **nueva**s

to pretend not to hear/notice/see/understand [s.th.] hacer la vista gorda [a algo] (▷ **gordo**); hacerse el **sueco**

to pretend to be dead hacerse el **muerto**

to pretend to be ill/sick tener calentura de **pollo**

to pretend to be surprised hacerse de **nueva**s

pretext (use s.th. as a ~) tomar **pie** de algo

pretty (be anything but ~) pecar de + adj. (example)

pretty (be awfully/very ~) la **mar** de; de narices (▷ **nariz**) (example); ser un **piropo** ambulante

pretty (not to be exactly what you might call ~) pecar de + adj. (example)

pretty ([very] ~ girl/woman) un **monumento** [nacional]; una boquita de **piñón**; la ricura

pretty penny (cost a ~) costar una **burrada**/un **dineral**/un **huevo**/un **ojo** de la cara/un **pico**/un **riñón**/una **riñonada**; costar la de **San Quintín**; costar un **sentido** o los cinco sentidos

to prevaricate andar en/andarse con **floreo**s

prevention (an ounce of ~ is worth a pound of cure) más vale **prevenir** que curar

prevention is better than cure más vale **prevenir** que curar

price (drop the ~) bajar la **mano**

prick el arma/asunto/bolo/calvo/canario/chorizo/cimbel; la gurrina; el pájaro; la picha/pija; el pijo; la pinga; el pito; la polla/porra; el rabo/troncho

to prick up one's ears aguzar el **oído**/las **oreja**s

pricks (kick against the ~) dar coces contra el aguijón (▷ **coz**)

pricks of conscience el rescoldo

prick-teaser la calientapollas

pride (be bursting [at the seams] with ~) no caber en el **pellejo** de orgullo

pride (be the ~ [and joy] of) ser la **gala** de

priesthood (leave the ~) ahorcar/colgar los **hábito**s

prime of life (be in the ~) estar en la **flor** de la vida

Prince Charming el **príncipe** azul; el **príncipe** encantado

print (have it in cold ~) **carta**[s] canta[n]

prison la trena

prison (be in ~) estar en la **trena**

prison (end up/finish up/land in ~) dar con los/sus **hueso**s en la cárcel

private (in ~) de **silla** a silla

private business (tell everyone one's ~) dar un **cuarto** al pregonero

prize idiot (be a ~) ser **tonto** del bote/de capirote

problem (be a case of the solution being worse than the ~) ser peor el **remedio** que la enfermedad problem (know where the ~ lies or the ~s lie) saber dónde aprieta el **zapato**

problem (that's his ~!) arreglárselas (▷ **arreglar**) (example); componérselas (▷ **componer**) (example)

problem (that's his/etc. ~) con su/etc. pan se/etc. lo coma/etc. (▷ **comer**)

problem (that's where the ~ is/lies) ahí está el **busilis**/la madre del **cordero**

problem (the best way to solve a ~ is to attack the root cause of it) muerto el **perro**, se acabó la rabia

problem solver el quitapenas

problems (. . . as if we didn't have enough ~) ... éramos pocos y parió la **abuela**

problems (be up to one's neck in ~) estar con el **agua** al cuello

problems (not to have any ~) pasársela en **flor**es

to proceed very carefully/cautiously/warily andar con **pies** de plomo

to proclaim s.th. from the rooftops echar las **campana**s al vuelo

procuress la trotaconventos

profession (a woman who has the oldest ~ in the world) la horizontal

profession (give up one's ~) ahorcar/colgar los **hábito**s

profession (have no ~) no tener ni **oficio** ni beneficio

profession (without a ~) sin **oficio** ni beneficio

profit (sell at no ~) cambiar el **dinero**

profound impact (have a ~) hacer **raya**

progress (make rapid ~) quemar etapas

to be prohibitive andar/estar por las **nubes**

prominent people gente de alto **copete**

promise (empty/hollow ~s) jarabe de pico; música celestial

promise (give s.th. a lick and a ~) limpiar algo solamente por donde ve la **suegra** o limpiar solamente lo que ve la suegra

promise (make a ~ one doesn't intend to keep) de **boquilla** (example); de **dientes** [para] afuera (example)

promise (make do with a lick and a ~) lavarse a lo **gato**

promise (not to keep one's ~) doblar/volver la **hoja**

to promise s.o. the earth/moon prometerle a alg. montañas de **oro** o el oro y el moro

promising (look very ~) estar como un **dado**

proof (the ~ of the pudding is in the eating) al freír será el reír; al **probar** se ve el mosto

proper (as is ~) como **Dios** manda

proper[ly] como **Dios** manda; con todas las de la **ley**; de padre y muy señor mío (▷ **el padre**)

pros and cons (weigh up the ~) hacer[se] su/una **composición** de lugar

to prosper fast/greatly/rapidly crecer como la **espuma**

prostitute la fulana/horizontal; la **moza** de partido; la paloma/sota; el taxi; la trotacalles/zorra

prostitute (be a ~) ser una **peripatética**; ser de la **vida**

prostitute (cheap ~) la pesetera

prostitute (male [gay] ~) el chapero

prostitution (take to/up ~) echarse al **mundo**/a la **vida**

protection (put o.s. under s.o.'s ~) agarrarse a los faldones de alg. (▷ **faldón**)

protracted and idle/pointless/unresolvable discussions or arguments discusiones bizantinas (▷ **bizantino**)

proud (be as ~ as a peacock) ser engreído como **gallo** de cortijo

providence (tempt ~) tentar a Dios/al diablo

provocative woman (sexually ~) la calientapollas/ **castigadora**

to pry (be/go ~ing [secretly] into s.th.) andar a la **husma** de algo

pseudo-intellectual el **erudito**/la **erudita** a la violeta

pub (do the ~s) andar/ir de **chateo**

pub (go from one ~ to another) andar/ir de **chateo**

pub-crawl (go on a ~) andar/ir de **chateo**

public (become known to the ~) salir a volar

to publish s.th. sacar algo a **luz**

to be published salir a **luz**

pudding (the proof of the ~ is in the eating) al freír será el reír; al **probar** se ve el mosto

to puff o.s. up echar de **bolina**; darse **bombo**; ponerse como una gallina **clueca**; **hinchar**se; ponerse **moño**s

to puke (make s.o. [want to] ~) revolver las **tripa**s a alg.

pull (go out on the ~) salir de **levante**

pull (have [a lot of] ~) tener buenas **aldaba**s/ buenos **asidero**s

to pull a fast one on s.o. pegar un **petardo** a alg.; dársela a alg. con **queso**

to pull it off at the first attempt llegar y besar el **santo**

to pull off s.th. difficult llevar[se] el **gato** al agua

to pull o.s. up by one's [own] bootstraps a **cuerpo** gentil (example)

to pull out rajarse

to pull s.o. to pieces poner a alg. como un **guiñapo**/como **hoja** de perejil; roer los **zancajo**s a alg.

to pull s.o.'s leg dar [el] **camelo** a alg.; tomarle el **pelo** a alg.; pitorrearse de alg.; quedarse con alg.

to pull s.th. out of a/the hat/bag traer algo en/por la **manga**; sacarse algo de la **manga**

pull the other one! ¡cuénteselo a su o cuéntaselo a tu **abuela**!; ¡a otro perro con ese **hueso**!; ¡cuénteselo a su o cuéntaselo a tu **suegra**!

pulp (beat s.o. to a ~) hacer **papilla/picadillo** a alg.

Punch (be as pleased as ~) alegrarse/estar como [un] **niño** con zapatos nuevos; estar [contento] como o más contento que unas pascuas (▷ **Pascua**)

punches (not to pull [one's] ~) no andarse con/en chiquitas (▷ la **chiquita**); no morderse la **lengua**; no andarse con **requilorios**

punches (pull [one's] ~) morderse la **lengua**

punches (roll with the ~) bailar al **son** que le tocan a alg.

to punish s.o. dar a alg. para **castañas**

to punish s.o. severely escarmentar a alg.

punishment (live in constant fear of ~) traer/llevar la **soga** arrastrando

puppet (be a ~ in the hands of s.o.) ser un **juguete** en manos de alg.

purse la chicharra

purse (you can't make a silk ~ out of a sow's ear) aunque la **mona** se vista de seda, mona se queda; no se le puede pedir **peras** al olmo

purse strings (hold the ~) administrar/manejar los **cuarto**s

to pursue one's goal ruthlessly no ponérsele a alg. nada por **delante**

to pursue s.th. very diligently andar/bailar de **coronilla**

push off! irse con la **música** a otra parte (example); ¡quítate de ahí/de en medio! (▷ **quitar**)

to push off (go/leave) darse de **naja**; najarse; salir pitando (▷ **pitar**)

to push s.o. buscar el **bulto** a alg.

to push s.o. (s.o. has to be pushed to do s.th.) hacer algo a **remolque** (example)

to push the boat out echar/tirar la **casa** por la ventana

pushbike la burra

pusher el púcher

pushover (be a ~) ser una **breva**; ser **coser** y cantar; ser **pan** comido

pushy (be very ~) meterse por el **ojo** de una aguja

pushy (get ~) ponerse **flamenco**

pussy la almeja; el bacalao/beo/bollo/chocho/ conejo/coño/higo; la raja/rana/seta

to put everything one has into s.th. rajarse por

to put everything one has into the defense of s.th. defender algo a **capa** y espada

put it there! ¡choca esos **cinco**!

to put up (don't ~ till tomorrow what you can do today) no dejes para **mañana** lo que puedes hacer hoy

to put one/it over on s.o. dar [el] **camelo** a alg.; pegar un **parche** a alg.; dársela a alg. con **queso**; dar/pegar una **tostada** a alg.

to put o.s. first barrer hacia/para dentro

to put paid to s.th. echar algo al o por el **suelo**

to put s.o. on tomarle el **pelo** a alg.; buscar las **pulga**s a alg.

to put s.th. away (food) echarse algo al **coleto**/al **estómago**/entre **pecho** y espalda

to put s.th. behind one echar **tierra** sobre/a algo

to put s.th. up for discussion poner algo sobre el **tapete**

to put up (not to be ~ for discussion) quedar sobre el **tapete**

to put up a good/etc. performance/etc. hacer [un] buen **papel**

to put up with a lot aguantar lo **suyo**; tener buenas **tragaderas**

to put up with anything aguantar **carro**s y carretas; tragárselas (▷ **tragar**)

to put up with it ([have to] ~) [tener que] tragar **bilis/quina**

putty (be ~ in s.o.'s hands) ser **juguete** de los caprichos de alg.

put-up job el apaño

pyjamas (think one is the cat's ~) creerse el no va más (▷ **ir**); la **mar** de

Q

quarrel (pick a ~) **tomar**la con alg.

to quarrel over s.th. andar a la **rebatiña** de algo

queen (gay) el canco/marica/maricón/
  mariposa/pluma; la rana; el sarasa

queen (old ~: gay) el carroza

queer (gay) el canco/marica/maricón/mariposa/
  pluma; la rana; el sarasa

queer (there's nowt so ~ as folk) de todo tiene la/
  hay en la **viña** del Señor

queer fish el tipejo

queer fish (be a ~) ser un **pájaro** raro

to queer one's own pitch hacer las diez de últimas
  (▷ **último**)

to queer s.o.'s pitch echar a **rodar** los proyectos
  de alg.

Queer Street (be in ~) las **trampa**s (example)

question (ask a silly ~, get a silly answer) a
  preguntas necias oídos sordos

question (call s.th. into ~) poner algo en **tela** de
  juicio

question (in ~) de **marras**

question (it's/[that's] out of the ~!) ¡ni **hablar**!; ¡y
  un **jamón** [con chorreras]!; ¡nada de eso!;
  ¡ni hablar del **peluquín**!

to question s.th. poner algo en **tela** de juicio

questions (bombard s.o. with ~ or ask s.o.
  hundreds/a barrage of ~) freír a alg. a
  preguntas; a **granel**

questions (pester/plague s.o. with ~) asar a alg. a
  preguntas

queue (s.o. must have been at the back of the ~
  when they were handing brains out) ser más
  tonto que **Abundio**; si le/etc. menean, da
  bellotas; ser más tonto que **Carracuca**; ser
  más **cerrado** que un cerrojo; ser más
  corto que las mangas de un chaleco; ser
  más tonto que una **mata** de habas; no

saber ni siquiera quitarse los **mocos**; ser
  más bruto que la **pila** de un pozo; tener el
  juicio en los talones (▷ **talón**)

to queue [up] hacer/guardar **cola**

to quibble buscar cinco/tres **pies** al gato

quick (cut s.o. to the ~) herir a alg. en **carne** viva;
  llegar a o herir/tocar en lo más **vivo** a alg.

quick conquest/pick-up el levante

to be quick to lash out ser **largo** de manos; tener
  las **manos** largas

to be quick to lose one's temper a **flor** de piel

to be quick-tempered tener el **genio** vivo; el
  pronto (example)

quick-tempered person el/la cascarrabias

quick-wittedness la sal

quid (cost a few ~) costar unas **perra**s

quiet (be [as] ~ as a Sunday-school party) balsa de
  aceite

quiet (be [as] ~ as the grave) balsa de aceite; no
  se siente/oye [ni] una **mosca**

quiet (I would keep ~ about it if I were you) dar un
  cuarto al pregonero (example)

quiet (it was so ~ you could have heard a pin drop)
  poder oír volar una **mosca**

quiet (keep ~) coserse la **boca**; callar[se] como
  un muerto/una piedra; estar mudo como
  una **tumba**/ser [como] una tumba

quiet (on the ~) a la **chita** callando; a la **sordina**;
  de **tapadillo**

quiet (on the ~: go about things on the ~) **matar**las
  callando

quiet one (be a ~) andarle/irle a alg. la **procesión**
  por dentro

quietly sin **alharaca**s ni bambollas

quietly (very ~) de **puntilla**s

to quit college/one's career/etc. plantar la carrera

330

R

rabbit (poor player) el maleta
to race [along] quemar el **caucho**
to rack one's brains quebrarse/romperse la
  cabeza; darse de **cabezada**s; romperse los
  cascos; comerse el **coco**; estrujarse el
  melón; devanarse/torturarse los **seso**s
racket (noise) la bronca; el jaleo
racketeer el bachiller Trapazas (▷ **trapaza**)
rag (▷ glad rags)
rag (chew the ~) echar un **párrafo**
rag (lose one's ~) perder los **estribo**s
rag (newspaper) el periodicucho
rag (she has the ~ on/is on the ~) está con la
  cuenta
to rag s.o. tomarle el **pelo** a alg.
ragamuffin el granuja
rage (be seething/wild with ~) estar hecho un
  basilisco; estar alg. que brinca (▷ **brincar**);
  echar **chiribitas/chispa**s; echar **rayo**s y
  centellas; estar alg. que trina (▷ **trinar**)
rage (foam/splutter with ~) echar **espumarajo**s
raging (the plague/fire is ~) se ceba la peste/el
  fuego (▷ **cebar**)
raging thirst (have a ~) abrasarse de sed; estar
  muerto de sed
rail (be as thin as a ~) estar como/hecho una
  espátula
to rail [against] despotricar [contra]
to rain (it never ~s but it pours) siempre llueve
  sobre mojado (▷ **llover**); bien vengas **mal**,
  si vienes solo; a **perro** flaco no le faltan
  pulgas
to rain cats and dogs/in torrents a **cántaro**s
  (example); llover a **chorro**s/**cubo**s/**mare**s/
  torrentes
rake (be as thin as a ~) quedarse en el **chasis**;
  salirse por el **corbatín**; estar como/hecho
  una **espátula**; estar más **seco** que una
  pasa
to rake it in ponerse las **bota**s; a **cántaro**s
  (example); **hinchar**se de plata/dinero;
  apalear **oro**
rake-off (get a ~) sacar **raja/tajada**
ramrod (as stiff/straight as a ~) tieso como un
  ajo; derecho como una **vela**
random (at ~) a la buena de Dios (▷ **bueno**); a
  diestro y siniestro; a la **gracia** de Dios
to be randy estar **bruto**
randy (get ~) ponerse **bruto**; empalmarse
randy goat el garañón
randy old goat/man el **viejo** verde
ranker un oficial de **cuchara**
to rant [about] despotricar [contra]

to rant and rave echar **ajo**s [y cebollas]; darse a
  todos los **demonio**s; despotricar; echar
  sapos y culebras
rap (get a ~ over the knuckles) recibir un
  rapapolvo
rap ([have to] take the ~) [tener que] pagar el
  pato/los **plato**s rotos/los **vidrio**s rotos
rap (not to give/care a ~) no importar a alg. un
  ardite; [no] importar a alg. un **bledo**/
  comino/higo/pepino/pimiento/pito/
  rábano
rap on the head la coca; el cocotazo
to rap s.o. over the knuckles cardarle la **lana** a
  alg.; echar un **rapapolvo** a alg.
rarely (very ~) de **higo**s a brevas; cada **muerte**
  de obispo; de **Pascua**s a Ramos; de **uva**s a
  peras
rascal el granuja
rat (be a pack ~) ser una **urraca**
rat (I/we [can] smell a ~ [here]) [aquí] hay **gallo**
  tapado/**gato** encerrado
rat (smell a ~) descubrir el **pastel**; oler el **poste**;
  olerse la **tostada**
to rat on s.o. [to s.o.] chivarse contra/de alg.
  [con/a alg.]
to be rated highly estar algo en [el] **candelero**
to rave (rant and ~) echar **ajo**s [y cebollas]; darse
  a todos los **demonio**s; despotricar; echar
  sapos y culebras
to rave [about] (talk angrily) despotricar [contra]
to rave about s.th./s.o. (talk enthusiastically)
  hacerse **lengua**s de algo/alg.
to rave to s.o. about s.th. cantar algo a alg.
ravenous hunger la gazuza; el **hambre** de tres
  semanas/de lobo
raving mad (stark ~) estar/ser **loco** de atar/
  remate
raw (in the ~) en traje de **Adán**/como Adán en
  el paraíso; en traje de **Eva**; en **porreta**[s]
raw ([really] get/touch s.o. on the ~) llegar a o
  herir/tocar en lo más **vivo** a alg.
raw nerve (hit a ~) poner el **dedo** en la llaga;
  tocar [a alg.] en la **herida**
razor (be [as] sharp as a ~) ser más listo que el
  hambre
razor-sharp (be ~) ser más listo que el **hambre**
razor's edge (be on a ~) estar en el **filo** de la
  navaja
to reach (come close to one's goal without ~ing it)
  nadar y nadar, y a la orilla ahogar
to reach (not to ~ one's goal) hacer las diez de
  últimas (▷ **último**)

to read (be passionately fond of ~ing) a más no **poder**

to read (not to like to ~) estorbarle a alg. lo **negro**

to read (s.o. can't ~) estorbarle a alg. lo **negro**

to read absolutely everything there is to read habido y por **haber**

to read s.th. right through echarse algo al **coleto**

to be ready [to go to s.o.'s aid] estar al **quite**

to be ready for battle estar al **pie** del cañón

to be ready for the breaker's yard or for the scrapheap/scrapyard estar algo para el **arrastre**

to be ready to act estar al **pie** del cañón

to be ready to drop caerse de cansancio/sueño

to be ready to explode a **flor** de piel

real lady señor

real leader (be a ~) con toda la **barba**

real man (be a ~) con toda la **barba**; tener **braguetas**; ser muy **hombre**/todo un hombre; ser hombre de pelo en **pecho**

real[ly] de los **buenos**; hecho y derecho; con todas las de la **ley**; de narices (▷ **nariz**); señor; de siete **suelas**; ni quien tal vio (▷ **ver**)

to reap (as you sow, so you ~) se cosecha lo que se siembra (▷ **cosechar**)

to reap what one has sown cosechar lo que uno ha sembrado

reason (bereft of ~) huérfano de

reason (for no ~ at all) sin **ton** ni son

reason (for no apparent/particular ~) sin **ton** ni son

reason (for one ~ or another) por **hache** o por be

reason (make s.o. listen to or see ~) meter a alg. en **cintura/costura**

reason (there's no rhyme or ~ [to s.th.]) no tener **cabo** ni cuerda/**pies** ni cabeza

reason (without rhyme or ~) sin **ton** ni son; a tontas y a locas (▷ **tonto**)

reasonable potable

reasoning (simple-minded ~) la cuenta de la **lechera**

to rebel dar coces contra el aguijón (▷ **coz**)

to recant cantar la **palinodia**

recantation (make a public ~) cantar la **palinodia**

receiver [of stolen goods] la **capa** [de ladrones]

to reckon without one's host no contar con la **huéspeda**/echar la cuenta sin la huéspeda

reckoning (everyone comes to his day of ~) a cada cerdo/puerco le llega su **San Martín**

to recline ([go and] ~) tomar la **horizontal**

recluse (become a ~) **enterrar**se en vida

recognition (he/she/etc. seeks ~) ¡sí quiere el huevo!

recognition (not to receive due ~) no hacer **justicia** a alg.

record (can't he/etc. change the ~!?) ¡[siempre] la misma **canción/cantilena**!

record (set the ~ straight) poner las cosas en su **sitio**

to recover levantar/alzar **cabeza**

to recover one's health levantar/alzar **cabeza**

red (go ~ [with shame]) salírsele/subírsele a alg. los **colores**

red (go as ~ as a beetroot or turn as ~ as a beet/poppy) ponerse como una o más rojo que una **amapola**; ponerse como un **cangrejo** asado o rojo como un cangrejo; ponerse como un **tomate**

red (go [bright] ~) ponerse como una o más rojo que una **amapola**; ponerse como un **cangrejo** asado o rojo como un cangrejo; ponerse de mil **colores**; subírsele a alg. el **pavo** o ponerse hecho un pavo; ponerse como un **tomate**

red (see ~) subírsele a alg. la **sangre** a la cabeza

red carpet (roll out the ~ [for s.o.]) echar/tirar la **casa** por la ventana

red-carpet treatment (give s.o. the ~) echar/tirar la **casa** por la ventana

red cent (not to be worth a ~) no valer un **ardite/comino/pito**

red cent (not to have a ~ to one's name) no tener ni para unas **alpargatas**; estar sin/no tener **blanca**; no tener qué llevarse a la **boca**/donde **caerse** muerto; estar sin un/no tener [ni] un **cuarto/real**

red-handed (catch s.o. ~) pillar a alg. en **bolas**; coger a alg. en el **garlito**/con las manos en la **masa**

red herring la **pista** falsa

to be red hot on s.th. **pintar**se uno solo/pintárselas solo para algo

red-hot por los cuatro **costados**

to reel (drunk) hacer **caracol**es

refined man/woman (act/play the ~) meterse a **finolis**

refuge (take ~ with s.o.) agarrarse a los faldones de alg. (▷ **faldón**)

to refuse (it's an offer one can't ~) a la **ocasión** la pintan calva

regardless sin pararse en **barras**

regardless (press on ~) liarse la **manta** a la cabeza

regardless of the consequences salga lo que salga/saliere (▷ **salir**)

rein (give free ~ to s.th.) dar **rienda** suelta a algo

rein (keep s.o. on a tight ~) atar corto a alg.; tener a alg. agarrado/cogido por las narices (▷ **nariz**); tener a alg. de la **oreja**

reins (loosen/slacken the ~) aflojar las **riendas**

reins (tighten the ~) sujetar/templar las **riendas**

to rejoice echar las **campanas** al vuelo

to rekindle s.th. avivar el **rescoldo** de algo

relationship (have a ~ with a woman) tener que **ver** con una mujer

to relax darse un **verde**

relic (old ~: car/thing/person) la/una antigualla; el vejestorio

to relieve o.s. echar una **carta** al correo; echar una **firma**; hacer sus **necesidad**es

to relieve s.o. of everything dejar a alg. en **cueros** [vivos]; dejar esquilmado a alg. (▷ **esquilmar**)

reluctantly (do s.th. ~) hacer algo a **remolque**

to remain (nothing ~s intact or in one piece) no dejar/quedar **títere** con cabeza

remarks (make cutting/snide ~ at s.o.) dar **remoquete** a alg.

remedies (apply ineffective ~) aplicar **paños** calientes

to be remote from it all estar en **Babia**/en las **Batuecas**/en **Belén**/en la **higuera**; estar en la **luna**; andar por o estar en las **nubes**

rent boy el chapero

repeat exam la repesca

to repeat o.s. unnecessarily poner dos **albardas** a un burro

to repeat s.th. parrot fashion hablar con **boca** de ganso

repercussions (have [grave] ~) tener/traer **cola**

reputation (have a bad ~) ser de **historia**

to be reserved estar metido para dentro (▷ **meter**)

resistance (put up a firm ~ [to s.o.]) tenerlas tiesas [con/a alg.] (▷ **tieso**)

resort (as a last ~) en última **instancia**

respect (have the greatest ~ for s.o.) tener a alg. en los **altar**es

responsibility ([have to] take the ~) [tener que] pagar los **vidrio**s rotos

rest (not to give s.o. a minute's ~) no dejar **respirar** a alg.; traer a alg. al **retortero**; no dejar a alg. [ni] a **sol** ni a sombra

to rest on one's laurels dormirse sobre los/sus **laurel**es

restless sleeper (be a ~) ser de mala **yacija**

restless soul (be a ~) ser [un] **culo** de mal asiento

to restrain o.s. morder/tascar el **freno**

restraint (abandon/drop all ~) soltarse la **melena**/el **pelo**; sacar los **pies** del plato/ de las alforjas

restroom (go to the ~) hacer lo que otro no puede hacer por uno

to retire into one's shell meterse en su **concha**

to retract volver sobre sus **pasos**

to retreat into one's shell meterse en su **concha**

to reveal one's true feelings/secret thoughts respirar por la **herida**

to reveal one's true nature descubrir la **oreja**

to reveal s.th. desembuchar algo; tirar de la **manta**; descorrer el **velo** sobre algo

to revel in s.th. **cebar**se en algo

revenge (Montezuma's ~) la cagalera; las seguidillas

revenge (want to get/take one's ~) tener **sangre** en el ojo

reward (desert and ~ seldom keep company) de **ingratitud**es/**ingrato**s está el mundo lleno

rhyme or reason (there's no ~ [to s.th.]) no tener **cabo** ni cuerda/**pies** ni cabeza

rhyme or reason (without ~) sin **ton** ni son; a tontas y a locas (▷ **tonto**)

rich (be filthy/stinking ~) tener muchos **cuartos**; estar **podrido** de dinero

rich (get ~) ponerse las **botas**; **redondear**se

rid (get ~ of s.o.: to kill) quitar a alg. de en medio

rid (get ~ of s.th.) quitar algo de en medio

rid (get ~ of s.th./s.o.) **quitar**se algo/a alg. de encima

to riddle s.o. with bullets dejar a alg. como un **colador**; coser/freír a alg. a tiros/balazos

to riddle s.th. with bullets dejar algo como un **colador**

to be riddled with holes estar hecho una **criba**

ride (be [easily] taken for a ~) hacer el **canelo**; comulgar con ruedas de molino; quedarse **fresco**; hacer el **primo**

ride (hitch/thumb a ~) ir[se] a **dedo**/hacer dedo

ride (take s.o. for a ~) dar [el] **camelo** a alg.; engañar a alg. como a un **chino**; dejar **fresco** a alg.; pegársela a alg. (▷ **pegar**); quedarse con alg.

to ride (he's/she's riding his/her hobby-horse again) ha vuelto a la misma **canción/cantilena**

to ride (let s.o. ~ his hobby-horse) dar **cuerda/ soga** a alg.

to ride on the back (of a motorcycle) ir de **paquete**

to ride pillion ir de **paquete**

to ride up (skirt/etc.) respingar

rider (pillion ~) el paquete

ridicule (hold s.o. up to ~) poner a alg. en **solfa**

ridicule (turn s.th. into ~) poner algo en **solfa**

to be ridiculous no tener **cabo** ni cuerda/**pies** ni cabeza

ridiculous (look ~) tener **monos** en la cara

ridiculous (make s.o. look ~) poner a alg. en **solfa**

ridiculous answers (give ~) irse por los **cerros** de Úbeda

to be ridiculously optimistic verlo todo de color de **rosa**

right (come just ~) de **perlas**; venir [que ni] **pintiparado**

right (get nothing ~) no dar **palotada**

right (it serves him/her ~!) ¡que se pudra! (▷ **pudrirse**)

right (serve s.o. ~) calzárselos (▷ **calzar**); sentar bien a alg.

right (s.o. can't do/get a thing ~) no dar **palotada**; no dar **pie** con bola

right ([the principle of] might is ~) la **ley** del más fuerte

right moment (this isn't the ~!) ¡no está el **horno** para bollos!

right off the bat de buenas a primeras (▷ **bueno**)

to be right on dar en el **blanco/clavo**

right time (come at just the ~) venir como **agua** de mayo/como **anillo** al dedo; venir como llovido/llegar como caído del **cielo**; venir que ni **pintado**/como pintado; venir **rodado**

right-hand man (be s.o.'s ~) ser el **ojo** derecho de alg.; ser **pies** y manos de alg.

rightly or wrongly por **fas** o por nefas

to rile s.o. buscar las **cosquillas** a alg.; freír la **sangre** a alg.

Riley (live the life of ~) vivir a **cuerpo** de rey/como **Dios** en Francia; pegarse la **vida** padre

ringer (be a dead ~ for s.o.) ser **clavado** a alg./ser alg. clavado

rings (run ~ around s.o.) dar **quince** y raya/falta a alg.; dar cien **vuelta**s a alg.

to riot echarse a la **calle**

riot act (read the ~ to s.o.) soltar la/una **andanada** a alg.; zurrar la **badana**/dar una **calada** a alg.; cantar/leer la **cartilla** a alg.

to rip (let ~) echar **ajos** [y cebollas]; darse a todos los **demonios**; pitar

ripe (the time is ~) está madura la **breva**

rip-off (be a ~) ser un **robo**

rise (give ~ to) dar **pie** para/a

to rise with the lark levantarse con las **gallina**s

to risk (not to ~ anything) no morir de **cornada** de burro; vivir de **renta**

to risk everything **jugar**se el todo por el todo

to risk everything on one throw jugárselo todo a una [sola] **carta**

to risk one's neck/life jugarse el **pellejo/pescuezo/tipo**; jugarse la **vida**

risk s.th. [for a change]! ¡nadie muere de **cornada** de burro!

risky assignment/job (take on a ~) poner el **cascabel** al gato

river (sell s.o. down the ~) vender a alg.

road (have one for the ~) tomar[se] la del **estribo**; tomar la última (▷ **último**)

road (there's no royal ~ to learning) la **letra** con sangre entra

to roar with laughter reír[se] a **carcajada**s; soltar el **chorro** [de la risa]; a más no **poder**

roaring drunk (get ~) coger una **papalina**

roasting la sofrenada

roasting (give s.o. a ~) soltar la/una **andanada** a alg.; zurrar la **badana** a alg.; dar una **calada**/un **palo** a alg.; echar una **peluca** a alg.; poner a alg. hecho una **salsa**; sofrenar a alg.

to be roasting **asar**se vivo

to rob Peter to pay Paul desnudar/desvestir a un **santo** para vestir otro

to rob s.o. of everything dejar a alg. en **cuero**s [vivos]; dejar esquilmado a alg. (▷ **esquilmar**)

to rob s.o. of s.th. with violence robar algo a alg. a **mano** airada

robbery (be daylight ~) ser un **robo**

robbing (good-for-nothings who live from/by or make their living from/by ~) gente de la **garra**

Robinson (before you can say Jack ~) en un decir **amén**/un **credo**/un **dos** por tres; en menos que canta un **gallo**; en un abrir y cerrar de **ojos**; en menos que se reza un **padrenuestro**; en dos **tranco**s

rock (as solid as a ~) de **cal** y canto

rock (be [caught] between a ~ and a hard place) estar entre la **espada** y la pared/entre dos **fuego**s

rock (be on the ~s: be broke) estar sin/no tener **blanca**; estar sin un/no tener [ni] un **cuarto/real**

rock (be/go on the ~s: marriage) irse al **cuerno**

rock (get one's ~s off) echar un **casquete**; follar/joder; echar un **polvo**; quilar

rock (have ~s in one's head) faltarle a alg. un **tornillo**/tener flojos los tornillos; tener una **tuerca** floja

rock bottom (be at/reach ~) estar por los **suelo**s

rocker (be off one's ~) estar mal de la **azotea**; no estar bueno de la **cabeza** o estar ido/mal/tocado de la cabeza o tener pájaros en la cabeza; estar como una **cabra/cafetera**; estar [loco] como un **cencerro**; estar **chalado**; estar mal de la **chaveta**; estar **chiflado**

rocker (go off one's ~) perder la **chaveta**

rocket (give s.o. a ~) soltar la/una **andanada** a alg.; zurrar la **badana**/dar una **calada**/meter un **paquete** a alg.

rod (pistol) la pipa

rod (pistol: as a problem solver) el quitapenas

rod (spare the ~ and spoil the child) la **letra** con sangre entra

rogue el granuja; una buena **pieza**

role (play a ~) jugar/desempeñar un **papel**

to roll around laughing/with laughter revolcarse de la risa

to roll in the aisles [with laughter] revolcarse de la risa

to roll one's eyes poner los **ojo**s en blanco

to roll up one's sleeves empezar a afilarse las **uña**s

to roll with the punches bailar al **son** que le tocan a alg.

roller skates (be [as] awkward as a cow on ~) a más no **poder**

to be rolling in it estar **forrado**

to be rolling in money nadar en la **abundancia**; tener muchos **cuartos**; apalear **oro**

rolling stone (a ~ gathers no moss) piedra movediza, el moho no la cobija/piedra movediza no coge musgo

roly-poly la foca

Rome (when in ~, do as the Romans [do]) [allí] donde fueres haz como vieres o lo que vieres (▷ **ver**)

Rome was not built in a day no se ganó **Zamora** en una hora

roof (be like a cat on a hot tin ~) estar en/sobre **ascuas**

roof (go through or hit the ~) ponerse como un **basilisco**; exaltársele a alg. la **bilis**; subirse al **campanario**; salirse de sus **casillas**; ponerse hecho un **demonio**; hinchársele a alg. las narices (▷ **nariz**); subirse por las **paredes**/a la **parra**; fundírsele a alg. los **plomos**

rooftops (proclaim/shout s.th. from the ~) echar las **campanas** al vuelo; pregonar/proclamar algo a los cuatro **vientos**

room (frowsy/fuggy/smoky/stuffy ~) la zorrera

roost (cock of the ~) el gallito

roost (rule the ~) cortar el **bacalao**; llevar la **batuta**; llevar/ponerse los calzones (▷ **calzón**); ser el amo del o dirigir el **cotarro**; llevar la **voz** cantante

root (strike at the ~ of the evil/problem) atajar el mal/problema de **raíz**

root (strike right at the ~ of the trouble) cortar por lo **sano**

root and branch ([eradicate s.th.] ~) hasta la **pared** de enfrente; arrancar algo de **raíz**

root cause (the best way to solve a problem is to attack the ~ of it) muerto el **perro**, se acabó la rabia

to root s.th. out completely arrancar algo de **raíz**

rooted to the spot (be/stand ~) quedarse hecho una **estatua**

roots (blush to the ~ of one's hair) ponerse de mil **colores**

roots (put down ~) echar raíces (▷ **raíz**)

rope (be at the end of one's ~) no saber como salir del **atranco**; no saber a qué **santo** encomendarse

rope (safety ~) el quitamiedos

ropes (be on the ~) estar contra/en las **cuerdas**

ropes (don't talk of ~ in the house of a man who was hanged) no hay que hablar de/mentar/nombrar la **soga** en casa del ahorcado

rose (there's no ~ without a thorn) no hay **boda** sin tornaboda/**miel** sin hiel/**rosa**[s] sin espinas

rose-colored glasses (see everything/things or the world through ~) verlo todo de color de **rosa**

roses (be no bed of ~) no saber a **rosquilla**

roses (come up ~) a pedir de **boca**

roses (life isn't [all/always] a bed of ~) la vida no es un lecho de **rosas**

roses (s.o.'s life is a bed of ~) pasársela en **flores**; estar/dormir sobre un lecho de **rosas**

roses (s.o.'s life is no bed of ~) no estar/dormir sobre un lecho de **rosas**

rose-tinted spectacles (see everything/things or the world through ~) verlo todo de color de **rosa**

rot (talk [a lot of] ~) irse por los **cerros** de Úbeda

to rot (let him/her ~!) ¡que se pudra! (▷ **pudrirse**)

to rot in jail pudrirse en la cárcel

rotten (incredibly ~) de **bigote**

the rotten apple spoils the barrel una **manzana** podrida echa un ciento a perder

rotter (be a ~) ser un mal **bicho**

rough (cut up ~) ponerse **negro**

rough (things get a bit ~) batirse el **cobre**

rough ([you've got to] take the ~ with the smooth) tomar las duras con las maduras (▷ **duro**); no todo el monte es **orégano**

rough diamond (be a ~) ser un **diamante** en bruto

rough guess (at a ~) a **ojo** de buen cubero

rough patch (go through a ~) pasarlas negras (▷ **negro**); pasar un **trago** amargo

rough time (have a ~ [of it]) pasarlas moradas (▷ **morado**)/negras (▷ **negro**); pasar un **trago** amargo

roughly a **ojo** de buen cubero

round and round (s.th. goes ~ in s.o.'s head) bailarle algo a alg. por la **cabeza**

round face (have a ~) tener **cara** de pan

round number (exactly twenty/etc. as a ~) [el] veinte/etc. **pelado**

to be round the bend estar mal de la **azotea**; no estar bueno de la **cabeza** o estar ido/mal/tocado de la cabeza o tener pájaros en la cabeza; estar como una **cabra/cafetera**; estar [loco] como un **cencerro**; estar **chalado**; estar mal de la **chaveta**; estar **chiflado**

rounds (be doing/going the ~) andar algo de **boca** en boca

row (cause/kick up a[n almighty] ~) echar a rodar los **bolos**; la camorra (example); armar [un] **cisco**/la de **Dios** es Cristo/la gorda (▷ **gordo**); el jaleo (example); armar la de **San Quintín**; hacer la santísima (▷ **santísimo**)

row (have a blazing/flaming [marital] ~) tirarse los **trastos** a la cabeza row (noise or noisy argument/disturbance) la bronca/camorra; el jaleo; la tremolina

row (there will be a ~) habrá **función**

royal road (there's no ~ to learning) la **letra** con sangre entra

royalty (treat s.o. like ~) tratar/atender a alg. a **cuerpo** de rey

rub (there's/that's the ~) ahí está el **busilis**/la madre del **cordero**

to rub one's hands chuparse los **dedo**s

to rub s.o. up the wrong way sacar a alg. de **quicio**

to rub s.o.'s nose in s.th. refregar algo a alg. [por las narices]

to rub s.th. in refregar algo a alg. [por las narices]

to rub up against s.o.'s legs hacer **fiesta**s a alg.

rubber (condom) el calcetín/globo; la goma

rubbish el **cuento** chino; el ñiquiñaque

rubbish! ¡**naranja**s! ¡**naranja**s chinas! ¡**naranja**s de la China!; ¡narices! (▷ **nariz**)

rubbish (be utter ~) no pegar ni con **cola**

rubbish (talk [a lot of] ~) irse por los **cerro**s de Úbeda

rubbish that ends up on paper el **papel** todo lo aguanta

Rubicon (cross the ~) pasar/atravesar el **Rubicón**

ruckus el jaleo; la tremolina

rude (be [very] ~ to s.o.) soltar la/una **coz** a alg.; tratar a alg. a coces (▷ **coz**)

rudely (treat s.o. very ~) tratar a alg. a coces (▷ **coz**)/a **patada**s/a **zapatazo**s

to ruffle a dog's/cat's fur/neck hacer **fiesta**s a un animal

rug (pull the ~ out from under s.o.) mover la **silla** para que caiga alg.

rug (sweep it under the ~) ocultar los **trapo**s sucios

to ruin one's eyes quebrarse los **ojo**s

to ruin s.th. partir algo por el **eje**; echar algo al o por el **suelo**

to be ruined irse al **cuerno**; **escoñar**se; venirse al **suelo**

ruined (it's all ~) [todo] mi/etc. o el **gozo** en el/un pozo

rule (be under s.o.'s ~) estar bajo la **férula** de alg.

to rule the roost cortar el **bacalao**; llevar la **batuta**; llevar/ponerse los calzones (▷ **calzón**); ser el amo del o dirigir el **cotarro**; llevar la **voz** cantante

rumor (there's a ~ going [a]round that . . .) corre la **voz** [de] que ...

rumor has it that . . . corre la **voz** [de] que ...

rumored (it is ~ that . . .) corre la **voz** [de] que ...

rumpus la tremolina

rumpus (kick up an incredible ~) armar la de **San Quintín**

run (give s.o. a [good] ~ for his money) echar/sudar la **hiel** (example); hacerle sudar **tinta** a alg.

run of bad luck (have a ~) perseguir a alg. la **negra** o tener la negra

run of [good] luck (have a ~) andar de **ganancia**; llevar/tener [todas] las de **ganar**

to **run** (▷ **bat** out of hell; like nobody's **business**; like crazy; like the **devil**; as **fast** as one can; like **hell**; hell for leather; like **mad**; like the **wind**; for all one is **worth**)

to **run** (take the money and ~) alzarse con el **dinero**

to run cold (s.o.'s blood runs cold) helársele a alg. la **sangre**

to run free/wild (let one's imagination ~) dar **rienda** suelta a algo (example)

to run on oiled wheels ir/marchar sobre **rueda**s

to run out the clock vivir de **renta**

to run s.o. down traer en **boca**s a alg.; arrastrar a alg. por el **fango**; poner a alg. como un **guiñapo**/como **hoja** de perejil; poner **mal** a alg.; arrastrar/poner a alg. por los **suelo**s

to run s.th. down arrastrar algo por el **fango**; arrastrar/poner algo por los **suelo**s

to run with the hare and hunt with the hounds comer a dos **carrillo**s; servir a **Dios** y al diablo

to run with the pack dejarse llevar de/por la **corriente**

to be running about/around nonstop andar/ir al **retortero**

running jump (go take a ~!) ¡anda a **bañar**te!; ¡vete a freír **buñuelo**s/**espárrago**s!

running jump (tell s.o. to go [and] take a ~) mandar a alg. a freír **buñuelo**s/al **cuerno**/a freír **espárrago**s/a hacer **gárgara**s

run-of-the-mill corriente y moliente

runs (diarrhea) la cagalera; las seguidillas

runt (person of small stature) el gorgojo/renacuajo

rush (be in a great ~) la **mar** de

to rush s.th./things hacer **manga**s y capirotes de algo

rustic el patán

S

sack (bed) la petaca/piltra

sack (give s.o. the ~) dar el **bote** a alg.; echar/despedir a alg. con **caja**s destempladas; echar a alg. a la **calle**/poner a alg. de patitas en la calle; plantar a alg. en la **calle**; largar a alg.; dar la **licencia**/[el] **pasaporte**/la **patada** a alg.

sack (hit the ~) irse a la/echarse en la **petaca**/**piltra**; tender la **raspa**; hacer la **rosca** [de galgo]

to sack s.o. dar el **bote** a alg.; echar/despedir a alg. con **caja**s destempladas; echar a alg. a la **calle**/poner a alg. de patitas en la calle; plantar a alg. en la **calle**; largar a alg.; dar la **licencia**/[el] **pasaporte**/la **patada** a alg.

saddle (be firmly in the ~) estar bien **sentado**

to saddle s.o. with s.th. endiñar/endosar algo a alg.; cargar el **mochuelo** a alg.

safe (better [to be] ~ than sorry) ¡a **penseque** lo ahorcaron!; más vale un **"por si acaso"** que un **"¿quién pensara?"**; más vale **prevenir** que curar; más vale **prevenir** que lamentar

safe (play it ~) [nadar y] guardar la ropa; picar de **vara** larga

safe side (just to be on the ~) por si las **moscas**

safecracker el reventacajas

safety appliance (handrail/rope/etc.) el quitamiedos

said de **marras**

sailing (think everything is plain ~) creer que todo el monte es **orégano**

sails (trim one's ~ to the wind) cambiar de/la **chaqueta**; bailar al **son** que le tocan a alg.

saint (even a ~ can lose his patience with s.o.) poder hacer perder la paciencia a un **santo**

saint (have the patience of a ~) tener la paciencia de un **chino**; tener más **paciencia** que Job/que un santo; tener una **paciencia** angelical/de benedictino

sake (do s.th. for s.o.'s ~) hacer algo por **amor** de/a alg.

sake (for heaven's/goodness' ~!) ¡por los **clavo**s de Cristo/de una puerta vieja!

salt (old ~) un viejo **lobo** de mar

salt (rub ~ in[to] the wound) remover el **cuchillo** en la llaga; hurgar en la **herida**

salt (take s.th. with a grain/pinch of ~) tomar algo con un **grano** de sal

same (always the ~: food) sota, caballo y rey

same (it will all be the ~ in a hundred years) dentro de cien **año**s todos calvos

same (it's the ~ the whole world over) en todas partes cuecen **habas**; allí tampoco atan los perros con **longaniza**[s]

same (the very ~) el mismo que viste y calza (▷ **vestir**)

same old de **marras** (example)

same old muck or rotten food **azote**s y galeras

sanctimonious woman la beata

sanctimonious man/woman/person (be a ~) **comer**se los santos

sand (build on ~) hacer **castillo**s de arena; sembrar en la arena

sand (bury one's head in the ~) esconder/meter la **cabeza** bajo el ala

sandboy (be as happy as a ~) estar [alegre] como unas **castañuelas**; estar [contento] como o más contento que unas pascuas (▷ **Pascua**)

sandwich (be one ~ short of a picnic) ser de pocas luces/corto de luces o tener pocas luces (▷ **luz**)

sardines (be packed in like ~) estar como tres en un **zapato**

sassy (get ~) ponerse **flamenco**

sauce (hunger is the best ~) a buen **hambre** no hay pan duro

sauce (what's ~ for the goose is ~ for the gander) lo que es **bueno** para uno es bueno para el otro

sausage dog el **perro** salchicha

to save (scrimp and ~) quitarse algo de la **boca**

to save one's/s.o.'s bacon/life/neck/skin) salvar el **pellejo**; salvar el **pellejo** a alg.

to saw away at the violin rascar el violín

to saw off one's own branch matar la **gallina** de los huevos de oro

to saw wood (snore) roncar como un **trompo**

sawdust (have nothing but ~ in one's head) tener la cabeza llena de **serrín**

sawn-off shotgun la chata

say (have a ~) tener **voz** en capítulo

say (have no ~/not to have any ~) ni **pinchar** ni cortar; no **pintar** nada; ni **quitar** ni poner; no tener ni **voz** ni voto

say (they will have no ~/will not be given any ~ in this matter) ... vela en este entierro

to say (be careful what you ~, walls have ears/we can be heard!) ¡hay **ropa** tendida!

to say (forget what one was about to ~) írsele a alg. el **santo** al cielo

to say (I couldn't care less/don't give a damn what other people ~) ande yo **caliente** y ríase la gente to say (just ~ s.th.) de **dientes** [para] afuera (example)

to say (listen to what s.o. has to ~) prestar/dar **oído**s a alg.

to say (make sense with what one ~s) hablar en **cristiano**

to say (miss nothing of what is being said) no perder **ripio**

to say (not to ~ a word) no decir esta **boca** es mía; no descoser la **boca**; coserse la **boca**; echar **candado** a la boca/a los labios; no **chistar**; no decir [ni] **chus** ni mus; no decir ni **mu/pío**; no soltar **prenda**

to say (not to be sincere [in what one ~s]) de **boca** [para] afuera; de **boquilla**; de **dientes** [para] afuera

to say (not to have a good word to ~ about s.o.) poner a alg. como **hoja** de perejil; no dejar **hueso** sano a alg.; roer los **zancajos** a alg.

to say (not to mean what one ~s) de **boca** [para] afuera (example); de **boquilla**; de **dientes** [para] afuera (example)

to say (s.o. can't ~ a word) pegársele a alg. la **lengua** al paladar

to say (suddenly [and unexpectedly] ~ s.th.) descolgarse con algo

to say (what people may/might/will ~) el qué dirán (▷ **decir**)

to say (when all is said and done) al fin y al **cabo**

to say (you could have said that right away!) ¡acabáramos! (▷ **acabar**)

to say absolutely nothing no **respirar**

to say boo to a goose (s.o. wouldn't ~) ser incapaz de matar una **mosca**

to say no (nobody says no to a bit of luck) a nadie le amarga un **dulce**

to say one thing and mean another de **boca** [para] afuera (example); de **boquilla**; de **dientes** [para] afuera (example)

to say s.th. (it's one thing to ~ and another to actually do it) del **dicho** al hecho hay mucho trecho; dicho sin hecho no trae provecho

to say s.th. as cool as you please decir algo tan **fresco**

to say s.th. in plain English/Spanish/German/etc. hablar en **castellano** [puro y llano]; hablar en **cristiano**

to say s.th. insincerely/just to be polite/ without really meaning it decir algo con la **boca** chica

to say s.th. quite boldly/brazenly decir algo tan **fresco**

to say s.th. to o.s. decir algo para su **coleto**

to say s.th. to s.o.'s face decir algo en las **barba**s de alg.

to say too much (harm o.s. by saying too much) perderse por el **pico**

to say uncle darse por vencido (▷ **vencer**)

to say what one bloody/damn well likes salirle a alg. de los cojones (▷ **cojón**)

saying (go without ~) caerse de/por su propio peso

scalawag el granuja

scale (live on a grand ~) vivir como un/a lo **príncipe**

scales (remove the ~ from s.o.'s eyes) hacer caer la **venda** de los ojos a alg.

scales (the ~ fall from s.o.'s eyes) caérsele a alg. la **venda** de los ojos

scandal (be a[n absolute] ~) clamar al cielo; no tener **nombre**

scandal (cause a huge ~) armar la gorda (▷ **gordo**)

scandal (full-blown/huge ~) padre (example)

scandalmonger (be a ~) ser una buena **tijera**

to be scandalous no tener **nombre**

scandalously escandalosamente (▷ **escandaloso**)

scapegoat un[a] **cabeza** de turco

scarce (make o.s. ~) escurrir/escapar/huir el **bulto**; hacerse **humo**/el **perdidizo**; pirarse o pirárselas

scarcely a duras **penas**

to scare s.o. silly dar un **susto** de muerte a alg.

to scare the living daylights out of s.o. dar un **susto** de muerte a alg.

to scare the pants off s.o. dar un **susto** de muerte a alg.

scared (get ~) arrugarse

scared (not to get ~ easily) estar curado de **espanto**

to be scared out of one's wits no llegarle a uno la **camisa** al cuerpo; estar con los cojones de corbata (▷ **cojón**); **morir**se del susto; quedarse sin **pulso**[s]

to be scared shitless **cagar**se/**ciscar**se de miedo (examples)

to be scared stiff tener el **alma** en un hilo; no llegarle a uno la **camisa** al cuerpo; estar con los cojones de corbata (▷ **cojón**); quedarse **helado**; bajársele a alg. la **sangre** a los talones; quedarse **yerto**

to be scared to death tener el **alma** en un hilo; caerse [muerto] de miedo; no llegarle a uno la **camisa** al cuerpo; estar con el alma en un **puño**; bajársele a alg. la **sangre** a los talones

scatterbrain un[a] **cabeza** de chorlito

scatterbrain (be a ~) tener la **cabeza** a pájaros

to be scatterbrained tener la **cabeza** a pájaros

to be scatty tener la **cabeza** a pájaros

scene (cause/make a terrible ~) armar la gorda (▷ **gordo**)

scenes (behind the ~) bajo **cuerda**/por debajo de cuerda

to scent danger oler el **poste**

schemer el bachiller Trapazas (▷ **trapaza**); el urdemalas

scheming bitch la **pájara**

schnozzle (nose) el asa; las napias

scholar (soi-disant ~) el **erudito**/la **erudita** a la violeta

to scoff (eat) menear el **bigote**; comer/mascar a dos **carrillos**; ponerse como el chico del **esquilador**; comer como una **lima**

scolding la bronca

scolding (get a ~ at home) habrá **función** (example)

scoop (bring off a ~) dar el **pisotón**

to be scorching hot de **bigote**

score (by the ~) a **punta** pala

score (know what the ~ is) estar al **cabo** de algo/de la calle

score (settle a ~ with s.o.) ajustar **cuentas** con alg.

scores of a **punta** pala

to scotch a rumor segar en **flor**; cortar algo de **raíz**

scowling cejijunto

to scramble for s.th. andar a la **rebatiña** de algo

scrap la bronca/camorra

scrap (not a ~ of) ni **chispa** de

scrap of paper (be a ~) no ser más que **papel** mojado

to scrape away at the violin rascar el violín

to scrape through the exam (just ~) por un **pelo**/los pelos (example); a duras **penas** (example)

scrapheap (be ready for the ~) estar algo para el **arrastre**

scrapyard (be ready for the ~) estar algo para el **arrastre**

to scratch (you ~ my back and I'll ~ yours) hoy por mí, mañana por tí; una **mano** lava la otra

scratching (eating is like ~: once you start, you don't want to stop or you can't stop) el **comer** es como el rascar, todo es cuestión de empezar

scream ([be] a [real] ~) descacharrante; ser para **morir**se de risa

to scream at the top of one's voice/lungs como un **descosido** (example); a más no **poder**

to scream o.s. hoarse desgargantarse

screw (have a ~: have sex) echar un **casquete**; follar/joder; echar un **polvo**; quilar

screw (have a ~ loose) faltarle a alg. un **tornillo**/tener flojos los tornillos; tener una **tuerca** floja

screw (put the ~s on s.o.) apretar las **clavijas** a alg.; poner a alg. a **parir**; apretar los **tornillos**/las **tuercas** a alg.

to screw o.s. up to do s.th. sacar **fuerzas** de flaqueza; revestirse de valor

to screw [s.o.] (have sex [with s.o.]) pasar a una por las **armas**; **calzar**[se]/**cargar**se a a alg.; echar un **casquete**; **cepillar**[se] a una; poner un **clavo** a una; follar/joder [a alg.]; pasar a una mujer por la **piedra**; pisar a alg.; echar un **polvo**; quilar [a alg.]; regar/tapar/**tirar**se/tumbar/**zumbar**se a una mujer

to screw (tell s.o. to ~ himself) mandar a alg. a la **mierda**

to screw it/s.th./things up **cagar**la; escoñar/joder algo

screw s.th./s.o.! **cagar**se en algo/alg. (example); **ciscar**se en algo (example)

to screw up [one's] courage sacar **fuerzas** de flaqueza; revestirse de valor; hacer de **tripas** corazón

to screw up one's face hacer **pucheros**

screw you! ¡vete a tomar por **culo**!

screwed on [tight] (have one's head ~) tener la **cabeza** en su sitio/bien puesta

to scrimp and save quitarse algo de la **boca**

scrooge el cicatero/la cicatera; el cuentagarbanzos

to scrounge [on s.o.] chupar del **bote**; andar/vivir de **gorra**; dar el **gorrazo** a alg.

to scrounge one's meals comer la/vivir de la **sopa** boba

scrounger la esponja; el/la lameplatos

scrumptious de **rechupete**

scruples el rescoldo

scruples (drop all ~) soltarse la **melena**/el **pelo**

to scrutinize s.th. pasar algo por la **criba**

scuttlebutt has it that . . . corre la **voz** [de] que ...

sea (be [caught] between the devil and the deep blue ~) estar entre la **espada** y la pared/entre dos **fuegos**

sea (worse things happen at ~) más **cornada**s da el hambre; más se perdió en **Cuba**

sea dog (old ~) un viejo **lobo** de mar

sealed (s.o.'s lips are ~) coserse la **boca**; callar[se] como un muerto/una piedra

seams (be bursting at the ~ with pride) no caber en el **pellejo** de orgullo

to search high and low buscar con un **candil**

search me! no sé **nada** de nada; ¡qué sé yo! (▷ **saber**); de mis **viñas** vengo

second fiddle (play ~) ser **plato** de segunda mesa

to be second to none no ir en **zaga** a alg. (example)

to be second-best ser **plato** de segunda mesa

second-rater (be a ~) ser **plato** de segunda mesa

secret (be in on the ~) andar/estar en el **ajo**

secret (have ~s) andar con **tapadillos**

secret (keep a ~ to o.s.) echar **candado** a la boca/a los labios

secretive (be very ~) andar con **tapujos**

secretly de **tapadillo**

securely (shut/close s.th. ~) cerrar algo a **cal** y canto

seductress la **castigadora**
to see (anyone can ~ that) lo ve un **ciego**
to see (be ~ing things) ver visiones (▷ **visión**)
to see (have ~n plenty worse) estar curado de **espanto**
to see (I came, I saw, I conquered) vine, vi y vencí (▷ **vencer**)
to see (I won't ~ you or the money/etc. again) **ojos** que te vieron ir
to see (if I never ~ you again it will be too soon) ¡hasta que/cuando meen las **gallinas**!; ¡hasta que/cuando las **ranas** críen pelo!
to see (not to ~ hide nor hair of s.o.) no ver el **pelo** a alg.
to see (not to want to ~ that one is on the wrong track) meter la cabeza en un **puchero**
to see (oh, I ~!) ¡acabáramos! (▷ **acabar**)
to see (pretend not to ~ [s.th.]) hacer la vista gorda [a algo] (▷ **gordo**); hacerse el **sueco**
to see (s.o. can't ~ a thing) no ver tres en un **burro**
to see (s.o. can't ~ further than or beyond the end of his nose) no ver más allá de sus narices (▷ **nariz**)
to see (s.o. can't ~ his hand in front of his face) no ver tres en un **burro**
to see (what you ~ is what you get) no hay más **cera** que la que arde
to see (you can ~ that with half an eye) lo ve un **ciego**
to see (you can ~ what s.o. is up to/is after/is really thinking) se le ve el **plumero** a alg.
to see (you won't ~ that/him/her again!) ¡échale un **galgo**!
to see (you won't ~ the likes of that in a hurry) ni buscando con [un] **candil**
to see reason (make s.o. ~) meter a alg. en **cintura/costura**
to see red subírsele a alg. la **sangre** a la cabeza
to see s.o. echar la **vista** encima a alg.
to see s.th. coming **ver**las venir
to see through a millstone oír/sentir/ver crecer la **hierba**
to see through it conocer el **tinglado**
to see through s.o.'s little game conocerle/verle a alg. el **juego**; descubrir el **pastel**; conocer el **tinglado**
to see which way the cat jumps/the cookie crumbles/the wind is blowing ver de qué lado caen las **peras**/por dónde van los **tiros**
to seem (things aren't always what they ~) ni están todos los que son, ni son todos los que están (▷ **estar**)
to seem (things don't/never ~ so bad after a good meal) con **pan** y vino se anda el camino
to be seething [with rage] estar alg. que arde (▷ **arder**); estar hecho un **basilisco**; estar alg. que brinca (▷ **brincar**); echar

chiribitas/**chispas**; echar **rayos** y centellas; estar alg. que trina (▷ **trinar**)
to seize s.o./s.th. echar la **garra** a alg./algo
to seize the opportunity coger/asir la **ocasión** por los cabellos/pelos; tender las **velas**
self (be a [mere] shadow of one's former ~) no ser [ni] **sombra** de lo que era/etc.
self-control (lose all ~) salirse de **madre**
to be self-evident caerse de/por su propio peso
selfsame el mismo que viste y calza (▷ **vestir**)
to sell (be sold on o.s.) **pagar**se de sí mismo
to sell at no profit cambiar el **dinero**
sell it elsewhere! irse con la **música** a otra parte (example)
to sell like hot cakes venderse como el **pan**/como pan caliente; venderse como **rosquillas**
to sell one's soul [to the devil] vender el **alma** al diablo
to sell s.o. a bill of goods dar a alg. **gato** por liebre
to sell s.o. a goldbrick dar a alg. **gato** por liebre
to sell s.o. down the river vender a alg.
to sell s.th. for a song vender algo por una **miseria**/por un **pedazo** de pan
to sell s.th. for peanuts vender algo a **huevo**
semen la leche
to send s.o. about his business mandar a alg. a **paseo**
to send s.o. on a trip (make s.o. high) poner a alg. en **órbita**
to send s.o. packing dar el **bote** a alg.; echar/despedir a alg. con **cajas** destempladas; echar a alg. a la **calle**/poner a alg. de patitas en la calle; plantar a alg. en la **calle**; mandar a alg. al **diablo**; largar a alg.; dar la **licencia**/[el] **pasaporte** a alg.; mandar a alg. a **paseo**; dar la **patada** a alg.; mandar a alg. a la **porra**
to send s.o. to glory mandar a alg. al otro **barrio**/**mundo**
sensational newspaper el **periódico** amarillo
sense la mollera; el seso
sense (common/horse ~) el pesquis
sense (make ~ of it) atar/unir **cabos**
sense (make ~ with what one says) hablar en **cristiano**
sense (make no ~ whatsoever) no tener **cabo** ni cuerda/**pies** ni cabeza
sense (not to make ~) no **pegar**
sense (sixth ~) el sexto **sentido**
to sense danger oler el **poste**
to separate the sheep from the goats apartar las **ovejas** de los cabritos
to separate the wheat/grain from the chaff apartar/separar el **grano** de la paja; apartar las **ovejas** de los cabritos
series (a [whole] ~ of) un **rosario** de; una **sarta** de

serious (a joke can easily turn ~) las **cañas** se vuelven lanzas

serious (be getting ~) ir tomando algo mal **cariz**

serious (dead[ly] ~) serio como un **poste**

serious business (this is where we get down to ~) tocan a matar (▷ **tocar**)

serious expression (put on a ~) vestir el rostro de gravedad

seriously (not to take s.th. ~) tomarse algo a **chirigota/risa**; tomar algo a **juego/juerga**

seriously (take s.th. ~) tomar algo a **pecho**[s]

to serve (no man can ~ two masters) no se puede servir a **Dios** y al diablo

to serve s.o. right calzárselos (▷ **calzar**); sentar bien a alg.

to serve s.o. right (it serves him/her right!) ¡que se pudra! (▷ **pudrirse**)

service (at your ~) para **servir**le [a usted]

service (lip ~) de **boca** [para] afuera; de **boquilla**; de **dientes** [para] afuera

services (have rendered outstanding ~) merecer una **estatua**

to be set on s.th. tener algo metido entre **ceja** y ceja

to set s.o. up with a cushy job enchufar a alg. (example)

to set up house together casarse por detrás de la iglesia

to set up in business montar un **tinglado**

to settle a score with s.o. ajustar **cuentas** con alg.

to settle down echar raíces (▷ **raíz**); [a]sentar el **real** o sus reales

to settle down (things are settling down) las **aguas** vuelven a su cauce

settlement ([provisional/temporary] ~) la componenda

set-to la bronca/camorra

seventh heaven (be in ~) estar en el séptimo/quinto **cielo**; estar en su[s] **gloria**[s]

severe de los **buenos**

to sew up (have s.th. all sewn up) tener algo en el **bote**

sex (have ~: ▷ get a/one's **leg** over; get one's **rocks** off; have a **screw/shag**)

sex (have ~ [with s.o.]: ▷ **ball** [s.o.]; bang [s.o.]; bonk [s.o.]; fuck [s.o.]; have it off/away [with s.o.]; knock a woman off; lay s.o.; screw [s.o.]; shag [s.o.])

sexually provocative woman la calientapollas/**castigadora**

to shack up together casarse por detrás de la iglesia

to shackle s.o. poner **trabas** a alg.

shade (put s.o. in the ~) hacer **sombra** a alg.

shadow (be a [mere] ~ of one's former self) no ser [ni] **sombra** de lo que era/etc.

shadow (follow s.o. [around] like a ~) ser la **sombra** de alg.

shadow (not to even trust one's own ~) desconfiar hasta de su **sombra**

shadow (without a ~ of [a] doubt) sin **sombra** de duda

shady business (be involved in some ~) andar con **tapujos**

shady customer (be a ~) no ser alg. **trigo** limpio

shady deal la componenda

shag (have a ~: have sex) echar un **casquete**; follar/joder; echar un **polvo**; quilar

to shag [s.o.] (have sex [with s.o.]) pasar a una por las **armas**; **calzar**[se]/**cargar**se a alg.; echar un **casquete**; **cepillar**[se] a una; poner un **clavo** a una; follar/joder [a alg.]; pasar a una mujer por la **piedra**; pisar a alg.; echar un **polvo**; quilar [a alg.]; regar/tapar/**tirar**se/**tumbar**se/**zumbar**se a una mujer

to be shagged out (exhausted) estar hecho una braga (▷ **bragas**); estar/quedar hecho **cisco**; tener los **huesos** molidos; estar hecho **migas/papilla/pedazos**; estar hecho un **pingajo**; estar hecho **polvo/puré**; estar reventado (▷ **reventar**); estar hecho unos **zorros**

to shake (begin to ~/start shaking) entrarle a alg. **templeques** o un **templeque**

to shake a leg/a hoof/one's stuff menear/mover el **esqueleto**

to shake like a leaf/jelly temblar como una hoja/un azogado/un flan

to shake one's head negar con la **cabeza**

to shake s.o./s.th. off dar [el] **esquinazo**/el **quiebro** a alg.; **quitar**se algo/a alg. de encima

shaken (be deeply ~ by s.th.) llegarle algo a alg. al **alma**

shakes (get the ~) entrarle a alg. **templeques** o un **templeque**

shakes (have the ~) tener un **templeque**

shakes (in two ~) en dos **trancos**

to be shaky estar prendido con **alfileres**

to sham ill tener calentura de **pollo**

shambles (a[n absolute] ~) **patas** arriba

shambles (be a[n absolute] ~) mezclar **berzas** con capachos; cajón de sastre (example)

shame (blush with ~) salírsele/subírsele a alg. los **colores**

shame (feel no ~ [about . . .]) tener la cara como el **cemento**

shame (not to have an ounce/the least bit of ~) ni **sombra** de

shameless (be quite ~ [about . . .]) tener la cara como el **cemento**

Shank's mare/pony (go/come on ~) ir/venir a golpe de **alpargata**/en el **caballo** de San Francisco/a golpe de **calcetín**/en el **coche** de San Francisco o de San Fernando

shape (in pretty bad ~) mal **parado**

to shape up nicely echar buena **pluma**

sharp (at 6 [o'clock] ~) a las seis clavadas
(▷ **clavado**)
sharp (be [as] ~ as a razor) ser más listo que el
hambre
sharp (be [very/pretty] ~) tener muchas
conchas/más conchas que un galápago;
ser más listo que el **hambre**; saber
[mucho] **latín**
sharp operator el **vivo**/la **viva**
sharp's the word! ¡arrea! (▷ **arrear**)
to shatter s.o. hacer **polvo** a alg.
to shatter s.th. hacer algo **cisco**
to shatter s.th. (hopes/etc.) echar algo al o por el
suelo
to be shattered (exhausted) estar hecho una braga
(▷ **bragas**); estar/quedar hecho **cisco**;
tener los **huesos** molidos; estar hecho
migas/**papilla**/**pedazo**s; estar hecho un
pingajo; estar hecho **polvo**/**puré**; estar
reventado (▷ **reventar**); estar hecho unos
zorros
shattering noise (be a ~) ser un ruido que taladra
(▷ **taladrar**)
shave (be/have a close/narrow ~) [por] el **canto**
de un duro; por un **pelo**/los pelos;
salvarse en una **tabla**
sheep (be the black ~ [of the family]) ser el
garbanzo negro [de la familia]
sheep (black ~) la **oveja** negra
sheep (separate the ~ from the goats) apartar las
ovejas de los cabritos
sheep's clothing (wolf in ~) el **diablo** predicador;
un **lobo** con piel de cordero/oveja; el
mátalas callando
sheep's clothing (be a wolf in ~) **matar**las callando
sheep's eyes (make ~ at s.o.) hacer **carantoña**s a
alg.
sheet (go as white as a ~) ponerse más blanco
que la **pared**/que una **sábana**
sheets (be three ~ to/have three ~ in the wind)
estar hecho un **cesto**/una **cuba**/un **cuero**/
un **pellejo**/una **uva**
sheets (come down in ~) a **cántaro**s (example);
llover a **chorros**/**cubos**/**mares**/**torrentes**
shelf (be left on the ~: s.o.) quedarse para
adornar **altares**; sentarse en el **poyetón**;
quedarse para vestir **santos**
shelf (leave s.th. on the ~) dar **carpetazo** a algo
shell (retreat/retire/withdraw into one's ~)
meterse en su **concha**
to shelve s.th. dar **carpetazo** a algo
shindig la **juerga**
to shine at one's studies lucir en sus/los estudios
shiner (have a ~) tener un **ojo** a la funerala
shining light (not to be exactly a ~) no tener dos
dedos de frente; nació alg. tarde (▷ **nacer**)
to shirk hurtar el hombro
shirt (give the ~ off one's back) dar hasta la
camisa; dar la **capa**

shirt (in one's ~) en **paño**s menores
shirt (keep your ~ on!) ¡para el **carro**!; ¡echa el
freno, Ma[g]daleno!
shirt (lose one's ~) jugar hasta la **camisa**; estar
pelado (example)
shit la ñoña/ñorda
shit! ¡me cago en diez/en la mar! (▷ **cagar**)
shit (have/take a ~) cagar; plantar la **estaca**;
hacer de lo **gordo**
shit (marijuana) el chocolate/ful; la hierba/
mandanga/mierda; el tate; la yerba
shit (not to be worth a ~) no valer un **cojón**
shit (not to give a ~ [about s.th./s.o.]) **cagar**se en
algo/alg.; **ciscar**se en algo; pasarse algo
por el **culo**; [no] importar a alg. un **huevo**/
una **puñeta**
to shit cagar; plantar la **estaca**; hacer de lo
gordo
shit creek (be up ~ [without a paddle]) estar
jodido (▷ **joder**)
to shit o.s. **cagar**se; zullarse
to shit o.s. [for fear] **cagar**se/**ciscar**se de miedo
shitless (be scared ~) **cagar**se/**ciscar**se de miedo
(examples)
shits (diarrhea) la cagalera; las seguidillas
shivers (send ~ down s.o.'s spine) ponerle o
ponérsele a alg. [la] **carne** de gallina
shock (be a ~ to s.o.) quitar el **hipo** a alg.
shock (come as a ~) caer/sentar como un **jarro**
de agua fría
to shock s.o. arrancarle a alg. el **alma**
shocked (be completely ~) quedarse **frío**
to be shocked by s.th. llegarle algo a alg. al **alma**
shockingly escandalosamente (▷ **escandaloso**)
to be shockingly expensive costar una **burrada**/un
dineral/un **huevo**/un **ojo** de la cara/un
pico/un **riñón**/una **riñonada**; costar la de
San Quintín; costar un **sentido** o los cinco
sentidos
shoe (I wouldn't like to be in his ~s) no quisiera
estar en su **pellejo**/en sus **zapatos**
shoe (if the ~ fits, wear it) quien o el que se pica,
ajos come; al que le sirva que se lo ponga
(▷ **servir**)
shoe (know where the ~ pinches) saber dónde
aprieta el **zapato**
shoe (now the ~'s on the other foot) se han vuelto
las **tornas**; se ha vuelto la **tortilla**
shoe (s.o. wouldn't like to be in s.o.'s ~s) no
arrendarle la **ganancia** a alg.
shoelaces (not to be fit to tie s.o.'s ~) no llegarle a
alg. a la **suela** del zapato/a los **zancajo**s
shoemaker (the ~'s son always goes barefoot) en
casa de **herrero**, cuchillo de palo
to shoot (be like ~ing fish in a barrel) ser **coser** y
cantar; ser **pan** comido
to shoot a line darse **bombo**; echarse/marcarse
un **farol**
to shoot and kill s.o. dar el **paseo** a alg.

to shoot from the hip no tener **pelos** en la lengua
shoot him/etc.! ¡al **paredón** con él/etc.!
to shoot off (have an orgasm) **correr**se; sacar la **piedra**
to shoot off (leave quickly) desempedrar la **calle**
to shoot one's bolt echar el **resto**
to shoot one's bolt (have shot one's bolt) haber quemado su último **cartucho**
to shoot one's mouth off soltar la **sinhueso**
to shoot s.o. several times propinar algo a alg.
to shoot the breeze/bull cascar; darle a la **sinhueso**
to shoot the moon mudarse clandestinamente
to shoot the works poner toda la **carne** en el asador; **jugar**se el todo por el todo
to shoot up (drug) **chutar**se; **pinchar**se
to shoot up (grow fast) crecer como la **espuma**; dar un **estirón**
to shoot up like mushrooms aparecer/brotar/ darse como **hongo**s/como las **seta**s
shooting gallery el pimpampúm
to be short of s.th. estar/andar **mal** de algo
short, chubby person el tapón
to be short-lived pasar como una **nube** de verano
short-lived (s.th. ~) una **nube** de verano
to be short-tempered tener el **genio** vivo
short-time hotel/motel la pensión de **tapujo**
shorty el renacuajo
shot (be a big ~) tener muchas **campanillas**; ser un **pájaro** gordo
shot (big ~[s]) un gran **bonete**; gente de alto **copete**; gente gorda; el mandamás; un **pez** gordo
shot (call the ~s) cortar el **bacalao**; llevar la **batuta**; llevar/ponerse los calzones (▷ **calzón**); ser el amo del o dirigir el **cotarro**; mover los **hilos**; llevar la **voz** cantante
shot (have a ~ in the/one's locker) traer algo en/ por la **manga**
shot (give ?.s. a ~) **chutar**se; **pinchar**se
shot (of drug) el chute; la picotada; el picotazo
shot (take a ~: photograph) tirar una foto
shot (well, the first ~ was a failure) al primer **tapón**, zurrapa[s]
shot in the arm (the industry needs a ~) la industria necesita una **inyección** financiera
shot in the arm (what they said was a ~ for us) lo que dijeron supuso una **inyección** de optimismo para nosotros
shotgun (sawn-off ~) la chata
shotgun wedding (have a ~) casarse de **penalty**
shoulder (be a ~ for s.o. to cry on) ser el **paño** de lágrimas de alg.
shoulder (give s.o. the cold ~) dar de **lado** a alg.
shoulders (be head and ~ above s.o.) **comer**se a alg. crudo; dar **quince** y raya/falta a alg.; dar cien **vuelta**s a alg.

shoulders (rub ~ with s.o.) **rozar**se con alg.
shoulders (rub ~ with upper-crust people) codearse con los de **arriba**
to shout about s.th. echar las **campanas** al vuelo
to shout at the top of one's voice/lungs como un **descosido** (example); a más no **poder**
to shout one's head off como un **descosido** (example); desgañifarse; desgañitarse
to shout o.s. hoarse desgargantarse
to shout s.th. from the rooftops echar las **campanas** al vuelo; pregonar/proclamar algo a los cuatro **viento**s
to shout until one is [as] hoarse as a crow desgargantarse
to shove s.th. under s.o.'s nose meter algo a alg. por las narices (▷ **nariz**)
show (give the ~ away) tirar de la **manta**; descubrir el **pastel**
show (put on a ~) montar un **número**; hacer el **paripé**
show (run the ~) cortar el **bacalao**; llevar la **batuta**; llevar/ponerse los calzones (▷ **calzón**); ser el amo del o dirigir el **cotarro**; llevar la **voz** cantante
to show (not to ~ one's anger/feelings) andarle/irle a alg. la **procesión** por dentro
to show (we have to ~ who we are) o somos o no somos (▷ **ser**)
to show off darse **charol**; hacer el **paripé**; darse **pisto**; el **postín** (example); darse **pote**; toser fuerte
to show off s.th. **pagar**se de algo
to show [o.s. in] one's true colors quitarse la **careta**; enseñar el **cobre**; quitarse el **embozo**; descubrir la **hilaza**; quitarse la **máscara**; descubrir la **oreja**
to show o.s. up lucirse; meter la **pata/pezuña**
to show s.o. the [way to the] door enseñar/mostrar la **puerta** a alg.
to show up asomar las narices (▷ **nariz**)
to show up (not to ~) **fumar**se algo
to show up at recalar en
to show up at the end llegar a los amenes (▷ **amén**)
to show what one can do hacer [un] buen **papel**
to shower insults on s.o. poner a alg. como un **estropajo**
to shower s.o. with s.th. or s.th. upon s.o. colmar a alg. de algo
showing-off el postín
shreds (tear s.o. to ~) poner a alg. como **chupa** de dómine/como un **guiñapo**/como **hoja** de perejil; machacar a alg.; hacer **polvo** a alg.; revolcar a alg.; poner a alg. como un **trapo**
shrew (woman) una mujer de **armas** tomar; la cascarrabias/tarasca
shrewd (be very ~) tener muchas **camándulas**/**carlancas**

shrewd operator (be a very ~) estudiar con el **demonio**

to shriek one's head off como un **descosido** (example)

shrimp (person of small stature) el renacuajo

to shroud s.th. correr/echar un **velo** sobre algo

to shut one's eyes [to s.th.] hacer la vista gorda [a algo] (▷ **gordo**); cerrar los **ojos** a algo

to shut s.o. up matarle a alg. el **gallo** [en la mano]; tapar la boca a alg.

to shut s.th. all up cerrar algo a **piedra** y lodo

to shut s.th. firmly/tight/securely cerrar algo a **cal** y canto

to shut the door in s.o.'s face dar a alg. con la **puerta** en la cara/en los hocicos/en las narices

to shut up like a clam callar[se] como un muerto/ una piedra; estar mudo como una **tumba**/ ser [como] una tumba

shut-eye (get a bit of or some ~) echar una **cabezada**/cabezadita; descabezar un sueñecito; planchar/chafar la **oreja**; hacer la **rosca** [de galgo]

shy (once bitten twice ~) de los escarmentados nacen los avisados (▷ **escarmentar**); el **gato** escaldado del agua fría huye

shyster el bachiller Trapazas (▷ **trapaza**)

sick (be as ~ as a parrot) arrojar hasta los **huesos**

sick (be very ~) no levantar/alzar **cabeza**

sick (make s.o. ~ to his stomach) revolver el **estómago**/las **tripas** a alg.

sick (pretend to be ~) tener calentura de **pollo**

to be sick and tired of s.o. estar hasta las **cejas**/la **punta** de los pelos o del pelo de alg.

to be sick and tired of s.th. estar hasta las **cejas**/el **coco**/[más allá de] la **coronilla** de algo; estar **frito** de algo; estar hasta el **gorro**/el **moño**/las narices (▷ **nariz**)/la **punta** de los pelos o del pelo/los **topes** de algo

to be sick to the teeth of s.th. estar hasta las **cejas**/el **coco**/[más allá de] la **coronilla** de algo; estar **frito** de algo; estar hasta el **gorro**/el **moño**/las narices (▷ **nariz**)/la **punta** de los pelos o del pelo/los **topes** de algo

side (be at s.o.'s ~ at the hour of death) recoger el postrer **suspiro** de alg.

side (change ~s) cambiar de/la **chaqueta**

side (get out of bed on the wrong ~/get up on the wrong ~ of the bed) levantarse con el **pie** izquierdo o salir con mal pie

side (just to be on the safe ~) por si las **moscas**

side (keep it with both ~s) bailar en la **cuerda** floja

side (on the ~) bajo **cuerda**/por debajo de cuerda

side (put s.th. on one ~) dar **carpetazo** a algo

side (split one's ~s laughing/with laughter) como un **descosido** (example); rajarse/reventar de risa

to side with s.o. ponerse del/al **lado** de alg.

sidelines (watch from the ~) ver los toros desde la **barrera**

sideways (be knocked ~) quedarse de una **pieza**

sideways (knock s.o. ~) partir a alg. por el **eje**; dejar a alg. de una **pieza**

sieve (have a memory like a ~) tener la cabeza como un **colador**

to sift through s.th. pasar algo por la **criba**

sight (be love at first ~) ser un **flechazo**

sight (be out of ~: prices/etc.) andar/estar por las **nubes**

sight (out of ~, out of mind) **ojos** que no ven, corazón que no siente

sight (s.o. can't stand the ~ of s.o.) no poder ver a alg. ni en **pintura**

sight for sore eyes (be a ~) dar **gusto** verlo

sign of life (give a ~) resollar

signal success (achieve a ~) poner una **pica** en Flandes

silence (there's [a] deathly ~) no se siente/oye [ni] una **mosca**

silence gives/implies consent quien calla otorga (▷ **callar**)

silence is golden en **boca** cerrada no entran moscas; por la **boca** muere el pez

to silence s.o. tapar la boca a alg.

silent (be [as] ~ as the grave) estar mudo como una **tumba** o ser [como] una tumba

silent (it's [as] ~ as the grave) no se siente/oye [ni] una **mosca**

silent fart el follón

silently (fart ~) **follar**se

silk purse (you can't make a ~ out of a sow's ear) aunque la **mona** se vista de seda, mona se queda; no se le puede pedir **peras** al olmo

silly gil/gilí

silly (drink o.s. ~) de padre y muy señor mío (▷ **el padre**) (example); coger una **papalina**

silly (scare s.o. ~) dar un **susto** de muerte a alg.

silly answers (give ~) irse por los **cerros** de Úbeda

silly mistake la primada

silly thing [to do] la burrada

silver lining (every cloud has a ~) no hay **mal** que por bien no venga

to be silver-tongued tener un **pico** de oro

similar (be very ~) ser **primo** hermano de o ser primos hermanos

simple-minded reasoning la cuenta de la **lechera**

sin (be as ugly as ~) ser un **aborto** del diablo; ser el acabóse de feo (▷ **acabar**); ser más feo que **Carracuca**; ser más **feo** que Picio/que el pecado/etc.; a más no **poder**; dar un **susto** al miedo

sin (it would be a ~ not to . . .) sería un **pecado** no ...

sin (poverty is no ~) pobreza no es vileza

sincere (not to be ~ [in what one says]) de **boca** [para] afuera; de **boquilla**; de **dientes** [para] afuera

sinecure el **bocado** sin hueso

to sing (inform) cantar; irse de la **mui**

to sing like an angel ... que es un **primor** (example)

to sing s.o.'s praises poner a alg. en/por o levantar a alg. a/hasta los **cuernos** de la luna; levantar a alg. hasta o poner a alg. por las **nubes**

to singe one's wings pillarse los **dedos**

singing voice (have an excellent ~) tener una **garganta** de oro

single-handedly a **cuerpo** gentil

singles bar el **bar** de ligue/alterne

to sink (I'm/etc. sunk) [todo] mi/etc. o el **gozo** en el/un pozo

sinker (swallow anything hook, line and ~) **tragar**[se]las como ruedas de molino

sissy el/la gallina

to sit back and do nothing estar/quedarse con los **brazos** cruzados

to sit on one's backside/butt tocarse los cojones (▷ **cojón**); tocar la **vihuela**

to sit on one's hands estar/quedarse con los **brazos** cruzados; no dar **golpe**

to sit on the fence estar entre dos **aguas**; ver los toros desde la **barrera**; nadar entre dos aguas

to sit on top of a volcano andar/verse en los **cuernos** del toro

to sit still (s.o. can't ~ for a minute) ser [un] **culo** de mal asiento

sitting (at a single/at one ~) de un **tirón**

situation (be in a [very] difficult ~) estar más perdido que **Carracuca**; estar entre la **espada** y la pared/entre dos **fuegos**

situation (change the ~ completely) dar la vuelta a la **tortilla**

situation (the ~ is about to explode/is extremely tense) está para dar un **estallido**

situation (the ~ is [still] unresolved) la **pelota** está/sigue en el tejado

six (be knocked for ~) quedarse de una **pieza**

six (knock s.o./s.th. for ~) partir a alg. por el **eje**; dejar a alg. de una **pieza**; echar algo al o por el **suelo**

six of one and half a dozen of the other (it's ~) lo que no va en **lágrimas**, va en suspiros; lo mismo es ñangá que **ñangué**; olivo y aceituno, todo es uno; tamboril por gaita

sixes (be [all] at ~ and sevens) estar/andar **manga** por hombro

sixth sense el sexto **sentido**

size (cut s.o. down to ~) bajar los **humos** a alg.; poner a alg. en su **sitio**

to be sizzling hot de **bigote**

to skedaddle poner **pies** en polvorosa

skeleton (have a ~ in the closet/cupboard) tener un **cadáver** en el armario

skeletons (bring out the ~ in the closet/cupboard) sacar los **trapos** [sucios] a relucir

skidmark (in the underwear) el palomino

skillful hands (have ~) tener **manitas** de plata/oro

to skim the cream off chuparse [una] buena **breva**

skin (be soaked to the ~) estar calado/mojado hasta los **huesos**; estar hecho un **pato**/una **sopa**; estar mojado hasta los **tuétanos**

skin (by the ~ of one's teeth) [por] el **canto** de un duro; por un **pelo**/los pelos

skin (develop a thick ~) criar **callos**

skin (get soaked to the ~) mojarse hasta el **alma**/los **huesos**

skin (get under s.o.'s ~) alterar/crispar los **nervios** a alg. o poner los nervios de punta a alg.; sacar a alg. de **quicio**

skin (have a thick ~) tener anchas/buenas **espaldas**; tener buen **estómago**

skin (it's/that's no ~ off my nose) no me va ni me viene (▷ **venir**)

skin (jump out of one's ~) no llegarle a uno la **camisa** al cuerpo; **morir**se del susto

skin (save one's/s.o.'s ~) salvar el **pellejo**; salvar el **pellejo** a alg.

skin and bone (be all ~/nothing but ~) ser un/estar hecho un **costal** de huesos; quedarse en el **chasis**; estar en los **huesos**; no tener más que el **pellejo**

to skin (keep one's eyes ~ned) avivar el/[los] **ojo**[s]

to skin a cat (there's more than one way to ~) hay muchas maneras de matar **pulgas**

to skin out (beat it) sacar el **bulto**

to skin s.o. alive **comer**[se] a alg. vivo

skinflint el cicatero/la cicatera; el cuentagarbanzos

to be skinny salirse por el **corbatín**; estar más **seco** que una pasa

skinny-dipping (go ~) estar/ir en **bolas** (example); en **carnes** [vivas] (example); en **cueros** [vivos] (example)

to be skint estar **palmado/pelado**

to skip s.th. **fumar**se algo; dejar algo a un **lado** o de lado

to skive off [s.th.] escurrir/escapar/huir el **bulto**; **fumar**se algo; hurtar el hombro

skunk (be [as] drunk as a ~) estar hecho un **cesto**/una **cuba**/un **cuero**/un **pellejo**/una **uva**

sky (be high as the ~: drunk/on drugs) tener un **globo** impresionante

sky (gray ~) la **panza** de burra
sky (praise s.o. to the skies) dar **bombo** a alg.;
poner a alg. en/por o levantar a alg. a/
hasta los **cuernos** de la luna; hacerse
lenguas de alg.; levantar a alg. hasta o
poner a alg. por las **nube**s
sky (praise s.th. to the skies) hacerse **lengua**s de
algo
to be sky-high andar/estar por las **nube**s
to slack tocarse las narices (▷ **nariz**)
slag (woman) la fulana; el pendón
to slag each other/one another off repiquetearse
to slag s.o. off poner a alg. como **chupa** de
dómine/como **hoja** de perejil; poner a alg.
a **parir**
to slag s.th. off dar **caña** a algo
to slam s.o. poner a alg. como **chupa** de
dómine/como **hoja** de perejil; hacer **polvo**
a alg.
to slam s.th. dar **caña** a algo
to slam the door in s.o.'s face dar a alg. con la
puerta en la cara/en los hocicos/en las
narices
slammer la trena
slammer (be in the ~) estar a la **sombra**/en la
trena
slammer (be put in the ~) ponerse el **capuchón**
slammer (put s.o. in the ~) meter a alg. donde no
vea el **sol**; poner a alg. a la **sombra**;
zambullir a alg. en la cárcel
to slander s.o. arrastrar/poner a alg. por los
suelos
slap in the face la leche
slap [on the mouth] [el]/la tapaboca[s]
slaps in the face (series of ~) la sopapina
slap-up meal la comilona
slap-up meal/do (be a ~) haber **arroz** y gallo
muerto
slash (have a ~) cambiar el **agua/caldo** a las
aceitunas; cambiar el agua al **canario**;
echar una **meada**; mear
slate (wipe the ~ clean) barrer con todo; hacer
borrón y cuenta nueva; hacer **tabla** rasa
to slaughter s.o. cascar a alg.
slave (work like a ~) trabajar como un **negro**
slave of habit (man is a ~) la costumbre es otra/
segunda **naturaleza**
to slave away trabajar como un **buey**; dar el
callo; romperse el **culo**; echar/sudar la
hiel; echar los **hígado**s; darse una **jupa**;
trabajar como un **negro**; dejarse la **piel**;
pringar[las]; sudar el **quilo**; remar;
reventarse; echar los riñones (▷ **riñón**);
destripar terrones (▷ **terrón**); sudar **tinta**
sleep (not to get a wink of ~ all night) defraudar el
sueño; pasar la **noche** en blanco
sleep (unnecessarily lose ~ over s.th.) hacerse una
paja mental

sleep of the dead/just (sleep the ~) dormir a
pierna suelta
to sleep (not to ~ a wink [all night]) pasar la
noche en blanco; no pegar **ojo**
to sleep planchar/chafar la **oreja**; hacer **seda**
to sleep badly ser de mala **yacija**
to to sleep it off desollar/dormir el **lobo**; dormir
la **mona**/el **vino**
to sleep jolly/very well de narices (▷ **nariz**)
(example)
to sleep like a baby dormir como un **bendito**/
lirón
to sleep like a log dormir como un **bendito**/un
ceporro/un **leño**/un **lirón**/una **peña**/un
tronco
to sleep off a hangover desollar/dormir el **lobo**;
dormir la **mona**/el **vino**; hacer **polvo**
to sleep on s.th. consultar algo con la **almohada**
to sleep soundly dormir a **pierna** suelta
to sleep the sleep of the dead/just dormir a **pierna**
suelta
to sleep well (with a clear conscience you ~) la
mejor **almohada** es una conciencia
tranquila
to sleep with s.o. hacer el **amor** con alg.
sleeper (be a restless ~) ser de mala **yacija**
sleeping dogs (let ~ lie) peor es meneallo/mejor
es no meneallo/más vale no meneallo
(▷ **menear**)
sleepless night (have a ~) pasar la **noche** en
blanco
sleepy village balsa de aceite
sleeve (have s.th. up one's ~) traer algo en/por la
manga
sleeve (laugh up one's ~) **reír**se a solas/para sus
adentros
sleeves (roll up one's ~) empezar a afilarse las
uñas
to sling one's hook **largar**se
to slink off with one's tail between one's legs con
las **oreja**s gachas (example); irse con el
rabo entre las piernas/patas
slip (give s.o. the ~) dar [el] **esquinazo** a alg.
slip (give s.o. the pink ~) dar el **bote** a alg.;
echar/despedir a alg. con **cajas**
destempladas; echar a alg. a la **calle**/
poner a alg. de patitas en la calle; plantar
a alg. en la **calle**; largar a alg.; dar la
licencia/[el] **pasaporte**/la **patada** a alg.
slip (mistake) el desliz
slip (there's many a ~ 'twixt cup and lip) del **dicho**
al hecho hay mucho trecho; dicho sin
hecho no trae provecho; del **plato** a la
boca se pierde la sopa
slip of the tongue (be a ~) irse de la **lengua**/írsele
a alg. la lengua
to slip away **deslizar**se; desaparecer por el **foro**;
hacerse el **perdidizo**

to slip out (s.th.) irse de la **lengua**/írsele a alg. la
lengua

to slip s.o. s.th. deslizar algo a alg.

to slip s.th. through colar algo

to slip up dar un **resbalón**

slip-up el desliz

to slog away trabajar como un **buey**; dar el **callo**;
romperse el **culo**; echar/sudar la **hiel**;
echar los **hígado**s; darse una **jupa**; trabajar
como un **negro**; dejarse la **piel**;
pringar[las]; sudar el **quilo**; remar;
reventarse; echar los riñones (▷ **riñón**);
destripar terrones (▷ **terrón**); sudar **tinta**

to slog one's guts out (▷ **guts**)

sloshed (be ~) estar hecho un **cesto**; estar
cocido (▷ **cocer**); estar hecho una **cuba**/un
cuero; estar/andar **pedo**; estar hecho un
pellejo/una **sopa**; estar **trompa**; estar
hecho una **uva**

sloshed (get ~) **cocer**se; papar una **jumera**;
coger una **melopea**/**merluza**; coger/pillar
una **mona**; moñarse; coger una **pea**;
agarrar[se] un **pedo**; coger una **pítima**

slot machine el/la tragaperras

slow ([as] ~ as/~er than molasses [in January]) a
paso de **buey**/**tortuga**

slow (be [as] ~ as/~er than molasses [in January])
ser [más lento que] una **tortuga**

to be slow on the uptake calzar poco; ser corto de
entendederas/tener malas entendederas

slowcoach (be [such] a ~) ser [más lento que]
una **tortuga**

slowly palmo a palmo

slowpoke (be [such] a ~) ser [más lento que] una
tortuga

slut la fulana; el pendón

slut (call a woman a ~) decir a una las cuatro
letras

to be sly tener [mucha] **mano** izquierda; saber
cuántas **púas** tiene un peine

sly (be as ~ as they come) tener muchas
camándulas/**carlanca**s; tener muchas
conchas/más conchas que un galápago;
ser más **corrido** que un zorro viejo; tener
mucha **letra** menuda; ser capaz de contar
los **pelos** al diablo; **saber**las todas o muy
largas; tener mucha **trastienda**

sly (on the ~) a la **chita** callando

sly dog/fellow el lagarto

sly one el vivo/la viva

sly person el zorro

sly sort el **mátalas callando**

sly woman la pájara

slyly (go about things ~) **matar**las callando

smack (walk/run ~ into s.th.) dar de narices
contra algo (▷ **nariz**) (example)

to smack one's lips [over s.th.] chuparse los **dedo**s
[por algo]

small matter (be no ~) no ser **grano** de anís

small thing (not to be just a ~) no ser **moco de
pavo**

small world (it's a ~) el mundo es un **pañuelo**

smart (elegant/etc.) pichi; el **postín** (example);
señor; a lo gran señor (▷ **el señor**)

smart (be as ~ as they come) ser más listo que el
hambre

smart (be pretty/really ~) saber más que **Lepe**

smart (be very ~) saber más que **Briján**; tener
mucha **letra** menuda

smart (think to be very ~) la **mar** de

smart alec[k]/Alec[k] (be a real ~) más que **siete**

to smash (spy ring/etc.) desvertebrar algo

to smash s.o.'s face/head in romper el **bautismo**/
los **casco**s/la **crisma** a alg.; quitar los
hocicos a alg.

to smash s.th. to pieces hacer algo **cisco**/[una]
tortilla

smashed (be ~) estar hecho un **cesto**/una **cuba**/
un **cuero**/un **pellejo**/una **sopa**; estar
trompa; estar hecho una **uva**

smashed (be ~ out of one's mind) estar cocido
(▷ **cocer**) (example)

smashed (get ~) **cocer**se; papar una **jumera**;
coger una **melopea**/**merluza**; coger/pillar
una **mona**; moñarse; coger una **pea**;
agarrar[se] un **pedo**; coger una **pítima**

smasher (girl/woman) un buen **bocado**; un
monumento [nacional]; de **rechupete**

smashing bestial; chachi; cojonudo; dabute[n]/
dabuti; que quita el **hipo**; pistonudo

smashing (look ~) estar como un **camión**

smashing time (have a ~) chachi (example);
dabute[n]/dabuti (example)

smattering (slight knowledge) la tintura

to smell (I/we [can] ~ a rat [here]) [aquí] hay **gallo**
tapado/**gato** encerrado

to smell a rat descubrir el **pastel**; oler el **poste**;
olerse la **tostada**

to smell awful/foul saber a **demonio**s/**rayo**s

to smell divine/heavenly/etc. oler a **gloria**

to smell fishy oler a **camelo**/a **cuerno** quemado

to smell of sweat oler a **tigre**

smelly feet los **queso**s

smile (be all ~s) tener cara de **pascua**s

to smile (fortune ~s on some but not on others)
unos nacen con **estrella** y otros nacen
estrellados

to smile (fortune ~s upon s.o.) **sonreír**le a alg. la
suerte/fortuna

to be smitten with s.o. estar **perdido** por alg.

smoke (go up in ~) deshacerse como la **sal** en el
agua

smoke (there's no ~ without fire/where there's ~,
there's fire) donde **fuego** se hace, humo
sale; cuando el **río** suena, agua lleva o
piedras trae

to smoke (give up smoking) **quitar**se del tabaco

to smoke (put that in your pipe and ~ it!) ¡chúpate ésa! (▷ **chupar**)

to smoke cigarettes only no fumar más que **papel**

to smoke like a chimney fumar como un **carretero**/una **chimenea**; a todo **pasto**

to smoke pot emporrarse

smoky pad/room la zorrera

smooth (as ~ as glass/as a millpond) balsa de aceite

smooth ([you've got to] take the rough with the ~) tomar las duras con las maduras (▷ **duro**); no todo el monte es **orégano**

smooth operator el vivo/la viva

smooth type el mátalas callando

smoothly (go off ~) salir algo **corriente** y moliente

smoothly (go/run [very] ~) balsa de aceite; ir/ marchar sobre **ruedas**/como una **seda**

to be smug **pagar**se de sí mismo

to smuggle s.th. through colar algo; pasar algo de **tapadillo**

smut (talk ~) decir **verdulerías**

snack (have a mid-morning ~) tomar las **once**

snag (there's/that's the ~) ahí está el **busilis**/la madre del **cordero**

snags (have its ~) tener algo muchos **entresijos**

snail's pace (at a ~) a paso de **buey/tortuga**

snake in the grass un judas (▷ **Judas**)

snap (be a ~) ser una **breva**

to snap at s.o. saltar a la **cara** a alg.; soltar la/ una **coz** a alg.

snappy (make it ~!) ¡arrea! (▷ **arrear**)

to snatch s.th. away from under s.o.'s nose dejar a alg. con la **miel** en los labios

sneak el chivato/la chivata; el/la correve[i]dile; el soplón/la soplona

to sneak away escurrir/escapar/huir el **bulto**; **deslizar**se; desaparecer por el **foro**; despedirse a la francesa (▷ **francés**); hacerse el **perdidizo**

to sneak on s.o. [to s.o.] chivarse contra/de alg. [con/a alg.]

to sneeze (not to be ~d at) no ser **moco de pavo**

snide remarks (make ~ at s.o.) dar **remoquete** a alg.

to sniff (not to be ~ed at) no ser **moco de pavo**

to sniffle sorberse los **mocos**

snitch (informer) el chivato/la chivata; el/la correve[i]dile

to snitch on s.o. [to s.o.] chivarse contra/de alg. [con/a alg.]

snog (have a good old ~) cambiar **babas**; morrearse; darse el **pico**

to snoop (be/go ~ing around) andar a la **husma**

snooze (have a ~) echar una **cabezada**/ cabezadita; descabezar un sueñecito

to snore heavily roncar como un **trompo**

snot las **velas**

snout (nose) el asa; las napias

snow (cocaine/heroin) la blanca; el Charly; la coca/nieve

to be snowed under with s.th./work andar/ir de **cabeza** con algo; no **saber** de sí

snowflakes las **moscas** blancas

snub nose la nariz respingona (▷ **respingón**)

to snuff it (die) irse al otro **barrio**; acabársele a alg. la **candela**; cascar[la]; diñarla; quedarse **frío/frito**; pelar **gallo**; **guiñar**la; hincar el pico; **liar**las o liárselas; palmarla; estirar la **pata**; liar el **petate**; **pringar**la; **reventar**[se]; quedarse **tieso**

snug (be as ~ as a bug in a rug) estar en su[s] **gloria**[s]; vivir/estar como **pava** en corral

soak (old ~) el cuero; la espita/esponja

to be soaked to the skin estar calado/mojado hasta los **huesos**; estar hecho un **pato**/ una **sopa**; estar mojado hasta los **tuétanos**

soaked to the skin (get ~) mojarse hasta el **alma**/ los **huesos**

to be soaking wet estar calado/mojado hasta los **huesos**; estar hecho un **pato**/una **sopa**; estar mojado hasta los **tuétanos**

soaking wet (get ~) mojarse hasta el **alma**/los **huesos**

So-and-so (Mr. ~) el señor no sé cuántos (▷ **saber**)

to soap s.o. up dar **coba** a alg.

to be soaring (prices/etc.) andar/estar por las **nubes**

to sob one's heart out llorar a **lágrima** viva/como una **Magdalena**; llorar a **moco** tendido/a moco y baba

to sob uncontrollably llorar a **moco** tendido/a moco y baba

soccer ball el cuero

social ladder (have gone up the ~) andar/estar en **zancos**

sock (put a ~ in it!) ¡echa el **freno**, Ma[g]daleno!

sockets (s.o.'s eyes pop out of their ~) saltársele/ salírsele a alg. los **ojos** de las órbitas

sod (do ~ all) tocarse los cojones (▷ **cojón**)/el **pito**; tocar la **vihuela**

sod (not a ~) ni **quisque**

sod (there isn't/wasn't a ~ here/there) no hay/ había **bicho** viviente; no hay/había ni un **gato**

sods (all the odds and ~) todo **bicho** viviente; Cristo y la madre/todo Cristo; todo/cada **quisque**

soft (be/go ~ on s.o.) caérsele a alg. la **baba** con/ por alg.

to be soft in the head estar mal de la **azotea**; no estar bueno de la **cabeza** o estar ido/mal/ tocado de la cabeza o tener pájaros en la cabeza; estar como una **cabra/cafetera**; estar [loco] como un **cencerro**; estar **chalado**; estar mal de la **chaveta**; estar **chiflado**; tener la cabeza llena de **serrín**

soft job el **bocado** sin hueso
to soft-soap s.o. hacer la **barba**/dorar la **bola**/hacer **carantoñas**/dar **coba**/comer el **coco**/hacer **fiestas**/dar **jabón** a alg.; venir a alg. con **papeles**; hacer la **rosca** a alg.
softy (be a ~) ser un **blandengue**
soi-disant expert/scholar el **erudito**/la **erudita** a la violeta
solid [as a rock] de **cal** y canto
Solomon (be wiser than ~) ser más **sabio** que Salomón
solution (be a case of the ~ being worse than the problem) ser peor el **remedio** que la enfermedad
solution (seek a quick ~) echar/tirar por el **atajo**
some (be pretty and then ~) de narices (▷ **nariz**) (example)
some guy (be ~) ser hombre de pelo en **pecho**
someone else (get ~ to do it!) ¡que lo haga el **nuncio**!
someone else (tell that to ~) ¡díselo o cuéntaselo al **nuncio**!
something (have that certain ~) tener **duende**
something different (it's ~ every time) cuando **pitos** flautas, cuando flautas pitos
somewhere else (go ~) irse con la **música** a otra parte
son (every mother's ~ [of them]) todo **bicho** viviente; Cristo y la madre/todo Cristo; cada/cualquier **hijo** de vecino; todo/cada **quisque**
son (like father like ~) de tal **costilla**, tal astilla; en casa del **gaitero** todos son danzantes; de casta le viene al **galgo** ser rabilargo; tal padre tal **hijo**; de tal **palo**, tal astilla; en casa del **tamborilero** todos son danzantes
son of a bitch el cabrón/cagachín
son of a bitch (be a mean ~) ser un mal **bicho**
song (sell/buy s.th. for a ~) vender algo por una **miseria**/por un **pedazo** de pan; comprar algo por un **pedazo** de pan
song and dance (make a [great] ~ [about s.th.]) hacer [muchas] **alharacas**; a **bombo** y platillo (example)
soon (as ~ as I/etc. turned my/etc. back) a las **primeras** de cambio
soon (don't speak too ~) cantar victoria
soon (if I never see you again it will be too ~) ¡hasta que/cuando meen las **gallinas**!; ¡hasta que/cuando las **ranas** críen pelo!
sooner or later a la corta o a la larga (▷ **largo**)
to be sopping wet estar hecho una **sopa**
sore (open up/reopen an old ~/old ~s) renovar la **herida**/la[s] **llaga**[s]
sore head (be like a bear with a ~) de **perros**
sore point el **punto** flaco
sore point/spot (touch on a ~) poner el **dedo** en la llaga; tocar [a alg.] en la **herida**

sorrow (drain/drink the cup of ~ [down] to the last drop) apurar el **cáliz** de cicuta/de [la] amargura/de dolor hasta las heces
sorry (better [to be] safe than ~) ia **penseque** lo ahorcaron!; más vale un **"por si acaso"** que un **"¿quién pensara?"**; más vale **prevenir** que curar; más vale **prevenir** que lamentar
sort (a woman of that ~) una tal
sort (be a clumsy ~) ser un **manazas**
sort (irritable ~) el/la cascarrabias
sort (it's nothing of the ~) no hay tales **borregos**/**carneros**/**corderos**
sort (odd ~) el tipejo
sort (people of that ~) gente de ese **jaez**
sort (sly ~) el mátalas callando
sort (there aren't many of that ~ around) ni buscando con [un] **candil**
to sort out (he has to sort that out himself!) arreglárselas (▷ **arreglar**) (example); componérselas (▷ **componer**) (example)
sorts (it takes all ~ to make a world) de todo tiene la/hay en la **viña** del Señor
to be so-so no ser ni **fu** ni fa
soul (be a helpful ~) ser un **paño** de lágrimas
soul (be a restless ~) ser [un] **culo** de mal asiento
soul (brevity is the ~ of wit) lo **bueno**, si breve, dos veces bueno
soul (every living ~) todo **bicho** viviente; Cristo y la madre/todo Cristo; todo/cada **quisque**
soul (hardly a ~) cuatro **gatos**
soul (my mother/etc., God rest her/etc. ~) mi madre/etc., que en **gloria** esté/que Dios tenga en la gloria
soul (not a living ~) ni **quisque**
soul (sell one's ~ [to the devil]) vender el **alma** al diablo
soul (there isn't/wasn't a blessed/living ~ here/there) no hay/había **bicho** viviente; no hay/había ni un **gato**
soul of kindness (be the very ~) no caberle a alg. el **corazón** en el pecho
sound de los **buenos**
to sound (it ~s all too familiar) me suena a **música** de caballitos
to sound fishy oler a **camelo**/a **cuerno** quemado
to sound s.o. out meter a alg. los **dedos** en la boca; tirar de la **lengua** a alg.; tomar el **pulso** a alg.
to sound s.th. out tomar el **pulso** a algo
soup (be really in the ~) estar más perdido que **Carracuca**
sour (look ~) torcer el **morro**
sour expression (put on a ~) poner cara de **vinagre**
sour face (make a ~) poner cara de **vinagre**
sour grapes! ¡están **verdes**!

sour look (have a ~ on one's face) tener **cara** de pocos amigos

source (have s.th. from a good/reliable ~) beber en buena **fuente**/en fuente fidedigna

sow (be [as] fat as a ~) estar hecho una **botija**; no caber en el **pellejo**

to sow (as you ~, so you reap) se cosecha lo que se siembra (▷ **cosechar**)

to sow (he who ~s the wind will reap the whirlwind) quien siembra **viento**s recoge tempestades

to sow (reap what one has ~n) cosechar lo que uno ha sembrado

to sow one's wild oats **correr**la o correr sus mocedades

to be sozzled estar a medios **pelos**; estar entre **Pinto y Valdemoro**

space (be staring into ~) estar mirando a las **nubes**; estar contando las **viga**s

to be spaced out estar de **viaje**

spade (call a ~ a ~) llamar las cosas por su **nombre**; llamar al **pan**, pan y al vino, vino

spades (in ~) a **punta** pala

spades (you'll pay for this in ~!) i[ya] me las pagarás con creces! (▷ **pagar**)

Spain (build castles in ~) hacer **castillo**s en el aire

Spaniard (average ~) Juan Español

Spaniard/etc. (be a ~ to the core/through and through) ser español/etc. hasta los **tuétano**s

Spanish (in [plain] ~) en **cristiano**

Spanish (say/tell s.th. in plain ~) hablar en **cristiano**

Spanish (speak ~) hablar en **cristiano**

spanking new (like ~) como un **oro**

spanner (throw a ~ in[to] the works) meter un **bastón/palo** en la rueda o bastones/palos en las ruedas [de alg.]

spare (drive s.o. ~) dar con la **cabeza** en las paredes; sacar a alg. de sus **casillas**; tener/traer **frito** a alg.; hacer a alg. subirse por las **paredes**; ser [como] para subirse por las **paredes**; hacer la santísima a alg. (▷ **santísimo**)

spare (go ~) dar con la **cabeza** en las paredes; subirse al **campanario**/por las **pared**es/a la **parra**

to spare no expense echar/tirar la **casa** por la ventana

to spare nobody no dejar/quedar **títere** con cabeza

to spare s.o. s.th. hacerle a alg. **gracia** de algo

spare the rod and spoil the child la **letra** con sangre entra

spark (not a ~ of) ni **chispa** de

to sparkle with wit tener mucha **chispa**

to speak frankly/bluntly **cantar**las claras; hablar en **plata**

to speak freely/openly/straightforwardly hablar en **castellano** [puro y llano]

to speak ill of s.th./s.o. arrastrar/poner algo o a alg. por los **suelo**s

speak of the devil [and he's sure to appear] hablando del **rey/ruin** de Roma [y él que se asoma o por la puerta asoma]

to speak one's mind decir lo que se le viene a la **boca** a alg.; no tener **frenillo** en la lengua; quitarle al **lucero** del alba

to speak out **cantar**las claras

to speak too soon (don't ~) cantar victoria

special (be nothing ~) no ser cosa del otro **jueves**; ser del **montón**; no ser nada/cosa del otro **mundo**

special (be s.th. ~) salirse del **montón**

special (be very ~) ser **canela** fina

spectacle (make a ~ of o.s.) dar la **nota**

spectacles (see everything/things or the world through rose-tinted ~) verlo todo de color de **rosa**

speechless (be [left] ~) quedarse de una **pieza**

speechless (leave s.o. ~) dejar **clavado** a alg.; quitar el **hipo** a alg.

speed (at full/top ~) a toda **pastilla**; a todo **vapor**; a toda **vela**

speed (go/drive at top ~) hundir el **pedal**

speed (more haste, less ~!) vísteme despacio, que estoy de prisa/que tengo prisa (▷ **vestir**)

to speed [along] quemar el **caucho**

to spend a penny cambiar el **agua/caldo** a las aceitunas; cambiar el agua al **canario**

to spend an awful lot on clothes gastar una barbaridad en **trapos**

to spend [one's] money wildly or like it's going out of style or like there was no tomorrow como un **descosido** (example)

to spend time or a year/etc. doing s.th. **tirar**se tiempo o un año/etc. haciendo algo

to spew one's guts out echar las **entrañas**; arrojar hasta los **huesos**; echar las **tripas**

spice (variety is the ~ of life) entre **col** y col, lechuga; en la variedad está el **gusto**; pan con pan, comida de tontos

spick-and-span como un **oro**; limpio como una **patena**; como una **plata**/una **tacita** de plata

to spike s.o.'s guns echar a **rodar** los proyectos de alg.

to spill the beans cantar; vaciar el **costal**; desembuchar; soltar la **lengua**; irse de la **mui**; no quedarse con nada en el **pecho**; soltar la **sinhueso**

to spin (make s.o.'s head ~) calentar la **cabeza** a alg.

to spin (s.o.'s head is/starts ~ning) calentarse la **cabeza**; cocérsele a alg. los sesos (▷ **cocer**); tener la cabeza como una **olla** de grillos

to be spine-chilling ponerle o ponérsele a alg. los **pelo**s de punta
spirit (fighting ~) tener **garra** (example)
spirits (be in high ~) estar [alegre] como unas **castañuelas**
spit and image (be the ~ of s.o.) ser **clavado** a alg./ser alg. clavado; ser escupido el padre/etc. (▷ **escupir**)
to spit it [all] out no quedarse con nada en el **pecho**; soltar la **sinhueso**
spit it out! ¡rompe de una vez! (▷ **romper**); soltar la **sinhueso** (example)
spiteful disposition/nature (have a ~) tener mal **café**; tener mala **leche/pipa/uva**
spitting image (be the ~ of s.o.) ser **clavado** a alg./ser alg. clavado; ser escupido el padre/etc. (▷ **escupir**)
spittle el pollo
spleen (vent one's ~ on s.o.) descargar la **bilis** en/contra alg.
splendid bestial; chachi; cojonudo; dabute[n]/dabuti; que quita el **hipo**; pistonudo
to be splendid ser un/de **alucine**; ser **canela** fina; estar algo **jamón**
spliff el petardo/porro
to split (beat it) darse el **bote/piro**
to split (seam) **nacer**se
to split one's sides laughing como un **descosido** (example); rajarse/reventar de risa
to splutter (the words come ~ing out) hablar a borbotones/borbollones (▷ **borbotón/borbollón**)
to splutter with rage echar **espumarajo**s
to spoil [all] the fun/s.o.'s fun/the party amargar el **caldo** a alg.; aguar la **fiesta**
to spoil everything echarlo todo a **rodar**
to spoil s.o. guardar/tener a alg. entre algodones (▷ **algodón**)
to spoil s.th./things for s.o. amargar el **caldo** a alg.
to spoil the child (spare the rod and ~) la **letra** con sangre entra
to be spoiled (s.th.) irse al **cuerno**; **escoñar**se
spoilsport (be a ~) aguar la **fiesta**
spoke (put a ~ in s.o.'s wheel) meter un **bastón/palo** en la rueda o bastones/palos en las ruedas de alg.; poner **traba**s a alg.
sponge (throw in the ~) dar con la **carga** en tierra/en el suelo o echarse con la carga; arrojar/tirar la **esponja**; echar la **soga** tras el caldero; arrojar/tirar la **toalla**; recoger **vela**s
to sponge (live by sponging) vivir de **sablazo**s
to sponge [on s.o.] chupar del **bote**; andar/vivir de **gorra**; dar el **gorrazo** a alg.
to sponge a living andar/vivir de **gorra**; comer la o vivir de la **sopa** boba
sponger la esponja; el/la lameplatos
to spoon morrearse

to spoon-feed s.o. with s.th. meter algo a alg. con **cuchara**
spot (▷ spots)
spot (be in a very tight ~) estar con el **dogal**/la **soga** al cuello
spot (be/stand rooted to the ~) quedarse hecho una **estatua**
spot (brown ~ in the underwear) el palomino
spot (die on the ~) quedarse en el **sitio**
spot (get o.s. into a tight ~) meterse en un **berenjenal**/en **camisa** de once varas
spot (get s.o. into a [very] tight ~) poner a alg. en las **asta**s del toro
spot (get/help s.o. out of a tight ~) sacar a alg. del **atolladero**; echar un **cable** a alg.; sacar a alg. de un apuro
spot (kill s.o. on the ~) dejar a alg. en el **sitio**
spot (know s.o.'s weak ~[s]) saber de qué **pie** cojea alg.
spot (leave s.o. in a tight ~) dejar a alg. en las **asta**s del toro
spot (on the ~) de **golpe** y porrazo
spot (put one's finger on the ~) poner el **dedo** en la llaga
spot ([there is a] bright ~ on the horizon) hay **luz** al final del túnel; el **rayo** de esperanza
spot (touch on a sore ~) poner el **dedo** en la llaga; tocar [a alg.] en la **herida**
spot (weak ~) el **punto** flaco
spotless limpio como una **patena**; como una **plata**/una **tacita** de plata
to be spot-on dar en el **blanco/clavo**
spots (knock ~ off s.o.) **comer**se a alg. crudo; dar **quince** y raya/falta a alg.; dar cien **vuelta**s a alg.
spots before one's eyes las **musarañas**
sprat (set/throw a ~ to catch a mackerel/whale) meter **aguja** para sacar reja; dar un **gallo** para recibir un caballo
sprawling (fall in a ~) dar con los/sus **hueso**s en el santo suelo
spread (meal) la comilona
to spread like wildfire extenderse/propagarse/difundirse como una **mancha** de aceite; propagarse como un **reguero** de pólvora
to spread one's wings alzar/levantar el **vuelo**
spree la juerga
spree (be/go on a ~) estar/ir de **juerga**
spree (have a real ~) correrse una **juerga**
to spring up like mushrooms aparecer/brotar/darse como **hongo**s/como las **setas**
to spruce [o.s.] up ponerse de veinticinco **alfilere**s; emperejilar[se]/emperifollar[se]; ponerse de **punta** en blanco
spruced up (be all ~) estar de veinticinco **alfilere**s; estar/ir de **punta** en blanco
spruced up (get all ~) ponerse de veinticinco **alfilere**s/de **punta** en blanco
spunk la leche

to squabble andar en **dares** y tomares/**dimes** y diretes; andar al **pelo**
to squabble (be [always] squabbling) andar a **palos**
to squabble (start squabbling with s.o.) mojar la **oreja** a alg.
squabbling dimes y diretes
squad (put s.o. before a firing ~) mandar a alg. al **paredón**
to squander s.th. **fumar**se algo; tirar algo por la ventana
square (person) el carroza
squeaky clean limpio como una **patena**; como una **plata**/una **tacita** de plata
to squeal (inform) cantar; chivarse; irse de la **mui**
to squeal on s.o. [to s.o.] chivarse contra/de alg. [con/a alg.]
to squeeze (you can't ~ s.o./s.th. into . . .) no caber ni un **alfiler** (examples)
to squeeze a tear llorar con un **ojo**
to squelch s.o. bajar los **humos** a alg.
squirrel (be a ~) ser una **urraca**
squirt (little ~: person) el comino/renacuajo
to stab away at s.o. coser a alg. a **puñaladas**
to stab s.o. in the back dar una **puñalada** trapera a alg.
to stab s.o. repeatedly coser a alg. a **puñaladas**
to stab the knife up to the hilt into s.th. meter el cuchillo hasta las **cachas** en algo
stable door (lock/shut the ~ after the horse has bolted/gone) asno muerto, la cebada al rabo; a buenas **horas**, mangas verdes
stack (blow one's ~) ponerse como un **basilisco**; exaltársele a alg. la **bilis**; subirse al **campanario**; salirse de sus **casillas**; ponerse hecho un **demonio**; hinchársele a alg. las narices (▷ **nariz**); subirse por las **pared**es/a la **parra**
stacks of a **granel**; a **punta** pala
stacks of money (make ~) a más no **poder**
stage fright (have ~) tener **nervio**s
to stagger (drunk) hacer **caracol**es
staggering[ly] cañón
stake (be at ~) estar en **juego**
stake ([pull] up ~s) hacer la **maleta**; liar el **petate**
to stake one's all poner toda la **carne** en el asador
to stake s.th. poner algo en **juego**
stalks (s.o.'s eyes stand out on ~) saltársele/ salírsele a alg. los **ojos** de las órbitas
to stamp (s.th. ~s itself [firmly] on s.o.'s memory) incrustársele algo a alg. en la memoria (▷ **incrustarse**)
to stamp one's foot herir el suelo con el pie
to stand (s.o. can't ~ it any more/longer) no poder con su **alma**
to stand (s.o. can't ~ s.o.) tener a alg. **atravesado**/ entre **ceja** y ceja/sentado en el **estómago**;

caerle **gordo** a alg.; tener **hincha**/no poder **pasar** a alg.; no poder ver a alg. ni **pintado**/ni en **pintura**; no poder **tragar** a alg.
to stand (s.o. can't ~ s.th.) tener algo **atravesado**; no poder ver algo ni en **pintura**
to stand (s.o. can't ~ the sight of s.o.) no poder ver a alg. ni en **pintura**
to stand around gaping papar **moscas**/**viento**
to stand fast/firm no dar su **brazo** a torcer; mantenerse/seguir en sus **trece**
to stand for (we won't ~ it/that!; I'll not ~ that) ¡no somos negros! (▷ **el negro**); a mí no me tose nadie (▷ **toser**)
to stand idly by [while others are working] estar de **miranda**; tocarse las narices (▷ **nariz**)
to stand no nonsense no aguantar/sufrir **pulga**s
to stand on end (make s.o.'s hair ~/s.o.'s hair stands on end) ponerle o ponérsele a alg. los **pelo**s de punta
to stand on one's head hacer el **pino**
to stand on one's head (be able to do s.th. standing on one's head) [poder/saber] hacer algo con los **ojo**s cerrados
to stand on one's own two feet (begin to ~) alzar/ levantar el **vuelo**
to stand one's ground no dar su **brazo** a torcer; mantenerse/seguir en sus **trece**
to stand out from the crowd salirse del **montón**
to stand s.o. up dejar **colgado** a alg.; dar [el] **esquinazo** a alg.; dar **mico** a alg.; plantar o dejar plantado a alg.; dar un **plantón** a alg.; hacer **rabona** a alg.
to stand up for s.o. dar/sacar la **cara** por alg.; ponerse del/al **lado** de alg.
to stand up to s.o. plantar **cara** a alg.
to stand up to the severest criticism poder pasar por las **picas** de Flandes
star (be [written] in the ~s) estar escrito (▷ **escribir**)
star (make s.o. a ~) lanzar a alg. al **estrellato**
star (see ~s) ver las **estrellas**
star (some are born under a lucky ~ and some are born seeing ~s) unos nacen con **estrella** y otros nacen estrellados
stardom (help s.o. to rise to ~) lanzar a alg. al **estrellato**
to stare at s.o. mirar a alg. de **hito** en hito
to be staring into space estar mirando a las **nubes**; estar contando las **vigas**
to be staring vacantly estar mirando a las **musarañas**
stark naked en traje de **Adán**/como Adán en el paraíso; en **carnes** [vivas]; en **cueros** [vivos]; en traje de **Eva**; como su **madre** le/lo/la echó al mundo; como Dios lo/etc. trajo al **mundo** o tal como vino/etc. al mundo; en **pelota**[s]/**porreta**[s]
to be stark naked estar/ir en **bolas**

stark raving/staring mad estar/ser **loco** de atar/ remate

starkers en traje de **Adán**/como Adán en el paraíso; en **carnes** [vivas]; en traje de **Eva**; como Dios lo/etc. trajo al **mundo** o tal como vino/etc. al mundo; en **pelota**[s]/ **porreta**[s]

to be starkers estar/ir en **bola**s

start (from ~ to finish) de **cabo** a cabo/rabo o de punta a cabo; de **pe** a pa

start (let's make a fresh ~) **borrón** y cuenta nueva

to start off (nothing's easy to ~ with) el primer **paso** es el que cuesta

to start out dar los primeros **paso**s

starter (small [but robust] ~) el sello del **estómago**

to be starving estar **muerto** de hambre

starving would be/have been worse más **cornada**s da el hambre

to stay (never ~ in one place for long) ser [un] **culo** de mal asiento

to stay away from s.th. **fumar**se algo

to stay [too] long (on a visit) calentar el **asiento**/ pegársele a alg. el asiento

steady hand el **pulso** firme

to steal a march on s.o. madrugar a alg.

to steal anything one can get one's hands on/that isn't nailed down ser más ladrón que una **urraca**

to steal s.th. [from s.o.] hacer **noche** de algo; soplar algo [a alg.]

to steal s.th./s.o. pisar algo/a alg.

stealing (good-for-nothings who live from/by or make their living from/by ~) gente de la **garra**

stealing (live from/by ~) vivir de la **uña**

stealth (by ~) bajo **cuerda**/por debajo de cuerda; a la **sordina**

stealthily a la **chita** callando; de **tapadillo**

steam (at full ~) a todo **vapor**; a toda **vela**

steam (have still some ~ left) aún quedar **cuerda** a alg./aún tener cuerda

steam (let off ~) dar **rienda** suelta a algo

steel (have nerves of ~) tener **nervio**s de acero

steep (be very ~: rent/etc.) andar/estar por las **nube**s

to steer clear of all work estar haciéndose **viejo**

to steer clear of s.th./s.o. **quitar**se algo/a alg. de encima

stench ([horrible] ~) el pestazo

step by step palmo a palmo

to step in tomar **carta**s en un asunto

to step on it dar/meter **caña**; hundir el **pedal**

steps (take one's first ~) dar los primeros **paso**s

steps (tread in s.o.'s ~) seguir los **paso**s de alg.

to stew (let s.o. ~ in his own juice) dejar a alg. cocer en su propia **salsa**

to stew in one's own juice cocerse en su propia **salsa**

stick (get hold of the wrong end of the ~ oír **campana**s y no saber dónde; tomar el **rábano** por las hojas

stick (get the dirty/short end of the ~) tocarle a alg. bailar con la más fea (▷ **feo**)

to stick firmly to one's opinion estar **caballero** en su opinión; mantenerse/seguir en sus **trece**

to stick it on tener la cara como el **cemento**

to stick it out **sudar**lo

to stick one's neck out [for s.th./s.o.] poner el **cascabel** al gato; jugársela (▷ **jugar**); romper una **lanza** por algo/alg.

to stick to one's decision tener **bigote**/tres pares de bigotes

to stick to one's guns tener **bigote**/tres pares de bigotes; mantenerse/seguir en sus **trece**

stick to what you know! ¡zapatero, a tus zapatos!

stick to your last! ¡zapatero, a tus zapatos!

to stick up for s.o. dar/sacar la **cara** por alg.

sticks (live/be [way] out in the ~) vivir/estar donde **Cristo** dio las tres voces/etc. o donde el **diablo** perdió el poncho; vivir/ estar en el quinto **infierno/pino** o en la quinta **puñeta**

sticks ([pull] up ~) hacer la **maleta**; liar el **petate**

sticky business traérselas (▷ **traer**)

sticky fingers (have ~) ser **largo** de uñas

stiff (as ~ as a poker/ramrod) tieso como un ajo

stiff (be scared ~) tener el **alma** en un hilo; no llegarle a uno la **camisa** al cuerpo; estar con los cojones de corbata (▷ **cojón**); quedarse **helado**; bajársele a alg. la **sangre** a los talones; quedarse **yerto**

to stifle one's anger tragar **bilis**; morder/tascar el **freno**; tragar **quina**

stifling heat (what a ~!) ¡qué **horno**!

still tongue (a ~ makes a wise head) es de sabios el callar (▷ **el sabio**)

still waters run deep del **agua** mansa líbreme Dios que de la brava me libro yo; por fuera no rompe un **plato**, pero tiene la música por dentro; la **procesión** va por dentro

to sting s.o. for s.th. soplar algo [a alg.]

stingy roñoso

stingy (be very ~) contar los **garbanzos**; ser **largo** como pelo de huevo; pellizcar los céntimos

stingy (s.o. doesn't want it to be said that he's ~) no dejarse llamar **roñoso**

stink ([horrible] ~) el pestazo

stink (kick up a ~) armar [un] **cisco**

to stink to high heaven clamar al cielo

stinker (bad/cheap cigar) la tagarnina

stinker (be a real ~) tener [mucho] **tomate**

stinking de **perros**; de siete **suelas**

stinking mood (be in a ~) estar de mala **leche**; de **perros**

to be stinking rich tener muchos **cuarto**s; estar **podrido** de dinero

stir (cause a ~) levantar una **polvareda**

to stir (it's best not to ~ [all] that up) peor es meneallo/mejor es no meneallo/más vale no meneallo (▷ **menear**)

to stir it/s.th. up again revolver el **caldo**

to stir up a hornet's nest meterse en un **avispero**

to stir up the dying embers avivar el **rescoldo**

stitch (not to have a ~ on) en **pelota**[s]

stitch (not to have a dry ~ on one) estar calado/ mojado hasta los **huesos**; estar hecho un **pato**; estar mojado hasta los **tuétanos**

stitches (be in ~) descoyuntarse/desternillarse/ rajarse de risa

stock (take ~) hacer[se] su/una **composición** de lugar

stocky woman la chata

stomach (a full ~ makes for a happy heart) barriga llena, corazón contento

stomach (get an upset ~) cortarse la **digestión**

stomach (have a strong ~) tener buen **estómago**

stomach (have butterflies in the/one's ~) tener los **nervio**s de punta

stomach (make s.o. sick to his ~) revolver el **estómago**/las **tripas** a alg.

stomach (make s.o.'s ~ turn) revolver el **estómago**/las **tripas** a alg.

stomach (s.o.'s eyes are too big for/are bigger than his ~) comer con los **ojos**

stomach (turn s.o.'s ~) revolver el **estómago**/las **tripas** a alg.

stomach (upset s.o.'s ~) sentarle algo a alg. como un **tiro**

to stomach s.o. (s.o. can't ~) tener a alg. **atravesado**/entre **ceja** y ceja/sentado en el **estómago**; tener **hincha** a alg.; no poder ver a alg. ni **pintado**/ni en **pintura**; no poder **tragar** a alg.

to stomach s.th. (s.o. can't ~) tener algo **atravesado**; no poder ver algo ni en **pintura**

stone (a rolling ~ gathers no moss) piedra movediza, el moho no la cobija/piedra movediza no coge musgo

stone (be only a ~'s throw away) estar a [un] **tiro** de piedra

stone (cast the first ~) arrojar/tirar la primera **piedra**

stone (constant dripping wears away a ~) gota a gota se llena la bota

stone (leave no ~ unturned) poner toda la **carne** en el asador; emplearse a **fondo**; no dejar **piedra** para mover; tocar todos los **registro**s/todas las **teclas**

stone (people who live in glass houses should not throw ~s) eso sería tirar **piedra**s a su o sobre el propio tejado

stone (try to get blood out of a ~) sacar **agua** de las piedras/de un palo seco

stone ([want to] kill two birds with one ~) querer ir por **atún** y a ver al duque; matar dos **pájaro**s de un tiro

to stone s.o. to death matar a alg. a **pedrada**s

to be stone-broke estar con una **mano** atrás y otra [a]delante; estar **palmado**; no tener [ni] una **perra**; andar/estar a la cuarta **pregunta**

to be stone cold tener **sangre** blanca/de horchata en las venas

stoned (be ~: be drunk) estar hecho un **cesto**/ una **cuba**/un **cuero**; tener un **globo** [impresionante]; estar/andar **pedo**; estar hecho un **pellejo**/una **uva**

stoned (be ~: from drugs) tener un **globo** [impresionante]; estar/andar **pedo**; estar de **viaje**

stoned (get ~: get drunk) **cocer**se; papar una **jumera**; coger una **melopea**/**merluza**; coger/pillar una **mona**; moñarse; coger una **pea**; agarrar[se] un **pedo**; coger una **pítima**

stoned (from drugs) emporrado

to be stone-dead estar más **muerto** que mi abuela/que una piedra; estar **patas** arriba

stone-dead (kill s.o. ~) dejar **seco** a alg.

to be stone-deaf ser más sordo que una **tapia**

stool pigeon (informer) el **chivato**/la **chivata**; el **soplón**/la soplona

stoolie (informer) el **soplón**/la soplona

to stop at nothing no pararse en **barra**s

stop it! ¡cruz y raya!

to stop talking (s.o. wouldn't ~) hablar como una **chicharra**; hablar a **chorro**s; hablar más que una **cotorra**; dar **cuerda** a alg. (example); hablar más que un **sacamuelas**

stops (pull out all the ~) tocar todos los **registro**s/todas las **teclas**

storm una nube

storm (any port in a ~) a falta de **pan**, buenas son tortas

storm in a teacup una **tormenta** en un vaso de agua

storm in a teacup (cause/start a ~) ahogarse en un vaso de agua

story (be another/a different ~) eso es otro **cantar**; ser **harina** de otro costal

story (be the same old ~ every time) sonar como un disco **rayado**

story (cock-and-bull/tall ~) el **cuento** chino

story (it's a different ~ now) se han vuelto las **tornas**; se ha vuelto la **tortilla**

story (tell horror stories about s.th./s.o.) decir **horrore**s de algo/alg.

story (that's a likely ~!) iésa es **grilla** [y no canta]!

story (that's [quite] another/a different ~) eso es otro cantar (▷ **el cantar**)

story (the same old ~ [every time]!) i[siempre] la misma **canción/cantilena**!

straight (as ~ as a ramrod) derecho como una **vela**

straight (come ~ out with s.th.) no andarse con/en **chiquitas** o con **requilorios**

straight (come/get ~ to the point) no andarse con/en **chiquitas**; ir al **grano**; no andarse con **requilorios**

straight (drink ~ from the bottle/spring/etc.) beber a **morro**

straight (tell s.o. ~ [out]/give it to s.o. ~) **cantar**las claras a alg.; a **palo** seco

straight and narrow (put s.o. [back] on the ~) meter/poner a alg. en **vereda**

straight off/through de un **tirón**

straight whisk[e]y a **palo** seco

straightforwardly (speak ~) hablar en **castellano** [puro y llano]

to strain one's eyes excessively quebrarse los **ojos**

to strain o.s. (not to ~) no **herniarse**

strange customer ni tipejo

strange customer (be a ~) ser un **pájaro** raro

strange ideas (have ~) tener sus **lunas**

to strangle s.th. at birth salir al **paso** de algo

straw (be the last ~) colmar la medida

straw (draw/get the short ~) tocarle a alg. bailar con la más fea (▷ **feo**)

straw (this is the last ~!) i[esto] es el acabóse! (▷ **acabar**)

the straw that/which breaks the camel's back la **gota** que desborda/colma el vaso

straws (clutch at ~) agarrarse a un **clavo** ardiendo; agarrarse/asirse a un **pelo**

streak (be on a lucky ~) andar de **ganancia**

streak of bad luck (have a ~) perseguir a alg. la **negra** o tener la negra

streak of [good] luck (have a ~) andar de **ganancia**; llevar/tener [todas] las de **ganar**

stream (be dealt an endless ~ of blows) a **granel**

stream (hurl/unleash a ~ of abuse/insults at s.o.) soltar una **andanada**/un **chaparrón** de insultos a alg.

streams (sweat ~) sudar a **chorros/mares**

street (be in Queer Street) las **trampas** (example)

street (be right up s.o.'s ~) rezar con; hacer **tilín** a alg.

street (dash along/through the ~) desempedrar la **calle**

street (pitch s.o. into the ~) plantar a alg. en la **calle**

street (the man in the ~) Juan Pérez

streets (take to the ~) echarse a la **calle**

streets (walk/work the ~) hacer la **calle**; ser del **oficio**; ser una **peripatética**

to be streets ahead of s.o. **comer**se a alg. crudo; dar **quince** y raya/falta a alg.; dar cien **vueltas** a alg.

streetwalker la paloma; el taxi; la trotacalles

stress (lay/put [special/particular] ~ on s.th.) hacer **hincapié** en algo

to stress s.th. hacer **hincapié** en algo

stretch (at a ~) de un **tirón**

to be strict hilar delgado o muy fino

strides (with giant ~) a **pasos** agigantados

to strike (hit) írsele a alg. la **mano**

to strike home dar en el **blanco**; dar en la **diana**/hacer diana

to strike it rich ponerse las **botas**

to strike out on one's own campar por sus respetos

to strike s.o. all of a heap dejar a alg. de una **pieza**

to strike s.o. all of a heap (be struck all of a heap) quedarse de una **pieza**

to strike s.o. dumb dejar a alg. de una **pieza**

to strike s.o. dumb (be struck dumb) quedarse de una **pieza**

to strike up a conversation pegar la **hebra**/el **hilo**

strike while the iron is hot al **hierro** caliente batir de repente

to strike while the iron is hot (you have to ~) a la **ocasión** la pintan calva

string (a [whole] ~ of) un **rosario** de; una **sarta** de

string (have more than one or another ~ to one's bow) comer a dos **carrillos**; tener una **vela** encendida por si la otra se apaga

string (have s.o. on a ~) tener a alg. en un **puño**

string (have two/several ~s to one's bow) tener un **pie** en dos zapatos

string of farts la pedorrera

string of farts (let off a ~) soltar una **pedorrera**

string-pulling el enchufismo

strings (be tied to s.o.'s apron ~) estar bajo la **férula** de alg.

strings (hold the purse ~) administrar/manejar los **cuartos**

strings (pull ~) enchufar a alg. (example); enchufe (example)

strings (pull all the ~ [one can]) tocar todos los **resortes**

strings (pull the ~) mover los **hilos**

strip (tear a ~ off s.o.) meter un **paquete** a alg.

stroke of luck la bolichada/breva; el **cabe** de pala

stroke of work (not to do a ~) no rascar **bola**; no dar **palotada**

strokes (little ~ fell great/big oaks) gota a gota se llena la bota

strong (be very ~: wine) arder en un **candil**

strong stuff (be pretty ~: remark/etc.) arder en un **candil**; pasar de **castaño** oscuro; pelar la jeta struggle (be an/[a real] uphill ~ [+ gerund]) hacérsele algo a alg. [muy] **cuesta** arriba [+ infinitivo]; vérselas negras con algo (▷ **negro**)

struggle (have such a ~ to do s.th.) tener que **ver**se y desearse para hacer algo

to struggle [hard] apretar los **puños**; remar

to strum away at the guitar rascar la guitarra

to be stubborn ser de dura **cerviz**; tener la cabeza más dura que un **picador**

stubborn (be as ~ as a mule) dar con la **cabeza** en las paredes

stubborn (remain ~) no apearse de su **burro**

stubbornly erre que erre

to be stuck-up tener mucho **copete**

stuck-up (become [very] ~) subírsele a alg. los **humos** a la cabeza

studded with cuajado de

student (be a brilliant/an outstanding ~) lucir en sus/los estudios

study (shine at one's studies) lucir en sus/los estudios

to study (give up/quit ~ing) ahorcar/colgar los **libros**

to study far into the night quemarse las **cejas**/**pestañas**

to study like mad como un **descosido** (example)

stuff (be hot ~) estar como un **tren**

stuff (be made of the same ~) ser de la misma **madera**

stuff (be pretty strong ~: remark/etc.) arder en un **candil**; pasar de **castaño** oscuro; pelar la jeta

stuff (belongings) los bártulos/**trastos**

stuff (cocaine/heroin) el polvo

stuff (during the day pious Annie, during the night hot ~) de día **beata**, de noche gata

stuff (know one's ~) no ser **rana**

stuff (shake one's ~) menear/mover el **esqueleto**

to stuff one's face comer más que un **alguacil**; llenarse la **andorga**; apiparse; henchir el **baúl**; menear el **bigote**; comer/mascar a dos **carrillos**; como un **descosido** (example); ponerse como el chico del **esquilador**; dar un buen **golpe** a la comida; comer como una **lima**

to stuff o.s. comer más que un **alguacil**; llenarse la **andorga**; apiparse; llenarse la **barriga**; henchir el **baúl**; ponerse las **botas**; llenarse el **buche**; comer/mascar a dos **carrillos**; como un **descosido** (example); ponerse como el chico del **esquilador**; comer como una **lima**; ponerse como un **trompo**; llenarse el **vientre**

to stuff o.s. with s.th. ponerse **morado** de algo

to stuff s.th. for a lark estar hasta las **cejas**/el **coco**/[más allá de] la **coronilla** de algo; estar **frito** de algo; estar hasta el **gorro**/el **moño**/las narices (▷ **nariz**)/la **punta** de los pelos o del pelo/los **topes** de algo

stuffed (get ~!) ivete a tomar por **culo**!; ¡que te jodas! (▷ **joder**); ¡que te den **morcilla**!; ivete a la **puñeta**!

stuffed (tell s.o. to get ~) mandar a alg. a tomar por **culo**/a hacer la **puñeta**

stuffy pad/room la zorrera

to stump s.o. partir a alg. por el **eje**

to stump up rascar[se] el **bolsillo**; aflojar/soltar la **china**/**mosca**; soltar la **pasta**; sacudir/soltar la **tela**

to stun s.o. dejar **bizco** a alg.

stunned como herido por el/un rayo (▷ **herir**)

to be stunned quedarse **bizco**

stunner (woman) un **monumento** [nacional]

stunning good looks (have ~) estar como un **tren**

stunning[ly] cañón

stupid gil/gilí

stupid (be [very] ~) caerse de tonto; gilipollear; no saber uno dónde tiene los **ojos**

stupid (do s.th. ~) gilipollear

stupid (not to be ~) no ser **zurdo**

stupid (you must think I'm ~!) ¡a mí no me la cuelas! (▷ **colar**)

stupid thing [to do] la burrada

stupid things (don't take notice of the ~ people say) a **palabras** necias, oídos sordos

stupidity (pay for one's ~) pagar la **primada**

stupidity (piece of ~) la primada

style (be dressed in the latest ~) ir vestido a la última (▷ **último**)

style (live in grand ~) vivir como un/a lo **príncipe**; vivir a todo **tren**

style (spend money like it's going out of ~) como un **descosido** (example)

subject (change the ~) doblar/volver la **hoja**

subject (digress/wander from the ~) irse por los **cerros** de Úbeda; **salir**se del tema

subject (he's/she's onto his/her favorite/pet ~ again) ha vuelto a la misma **canción**/**cantilena**

subject (talk round the ~) salir[se]/escapar[se]/irse por la **tangente**; mear fuera del **tiesto**

subject (to change the ~) párrafo aparte

subject of gossip (be the ~) andar alg. de **boca** en boca; andar en **lenguas**; ser **pasto** de algo

to submit doblar/bajar la **cerviz**

substance el jugo

substance (get the ~ out of s.th.) sacar el **jugo** a algo

to succeed in getting s.th. **calzar**se algo

success (achieve a signal ~) poner una **pica** en Flandes

success (come close to ~ without attaining it) quedarse con la **miel** en los labios; nadar y nadar, y a la orilla ahogar

success (sweets of ~) las **miel**es del triunfo

success (terrific ~) padre (example)

to be successful campar con su estrella

such luck (there's no ~) no caerá esa **breva**
such thing (there isn't any/there's no ~) no hay tales **borregos/carneros/corderos**
to suck s.o. dry dejar esquilmado a alg. (▷ **esquilmar**); chupar la **sangre** a alg.
to suck s.o. off hacerle una **mamada** a alg.
to suck up to s.o. hacer la **barba**/lavar la **cara**/dar **coba**/hacer la **pelotilla** a alg.
sucker (fool) el primo
sucker (play s.o. for a ~) engañar a alg. como a un **chino**
sudden (all of a ~) de buenas a primeras (▷ **bueno**); de **golpe** y porrazo
sudden feeling/fit/impulse/notion el pronto
suddenly de buenas a primeras (▷ **bueno**); de **golpe** y porrazo; a las **primeras** de cambio
suddenly [and unexpectedly] say/announce s.th. descolgarse con algo
suddenly die quedar **seco**
to suffer (not to ~ fools gladly) no aguantar/sufrir **pulgas**
sugar (go easy on the ~) no estirar los **pies** más de lo que da la frazada
sugar (money) el barro; el **calé** o calés; la china; [los] **cuartos**; la guita/lana/manteca; [los] monises; la mosca; [los] nipos; el parné; la pasta; el pisto; la tela; el trigo
sugar (not to go easy on the ~) estirar la **pierna** más larga que la sábana
to sugar[-coat] the pill dorar la **píldora**
to suit (be well ~ed for s.th.) **pintar**se uno solo/pintárselas solo para algo
to suit (s.th. doesn't ~ s.o. at all) sentarle algo a alg. como a un santo **cristo** un par de pistolas; pegarle algo a alg. como un **mandil** a una vaca; sentarle algo a alg. como un **tiro**
to suit each other/one another (not to ~) no **comulgar** en la misma iglesia
to suit s.o. down to the ground or perfectly de **perlas**
to suit s.o. to a T venir/sentar a alg. como **anillo** al dedo/que ni **pintado** o como pintado
suitcase (live out of a ~) andar/ir con el **hato** a cuestas
sum (cost a tidy ~) costar una **burrada**/un **dineral**/un **huevo**/un **ojo** de la cara/un **pico**/un **riñón**/una **riñonada**; costar la de **San Quintín**; costar un **sentido** o los cinco sentidos
sum (do one's ~s) consultar con el **bolsillo**
sum (get one's ~s wrong) no contar con la **huéspeda**/echar la cuenta sin la huéspeda
summer (one swallow does not make a ~) una **golondrina** no hace verano
to summon up [one's] courage sacar **fuerzas** de flaqueza
sun (block the ~) hacer **sombrajos**

sun (call s.o. all the names under the ~) poner a alg. como un **Cristo**; poner **verde** a alg.
sun (make hay while the ~ shines) al **hierro** caliente batir de repente
sun (talk about everything under the ~) hablar de este **mundo** y del otro
sun (there's nothing new under the ~) no hay nada **nuevo** bajo el sol/las estrellas
sun (you have to make hay while the ~ shines) a la **ocasión** la pintan calva
to sunbathe **tostar**se [al sol]
Sunday best (be in one's ~) estar de veinticinco **alfiler**es; estar **peripuesto**; estar/ir de **punta** en blanco
Sunday best (one's ~) los **trapos**/trapitos de cristianar
Sundays (in a month of ~) en las **Calendas** griegas; cuando meen las **gallinas**; cuando las **ranas** críen pelo; en la **semana** que no tenga jueves/de tres jueves
Sunday-school party ([as] quiet as a ~) balsa de aceite
sundry (tell all and ~ [about it/s.th.]) dar un **cuarto** al pregonero; pregonar/proclamar algo a los cuatro **vientos**
sunk (I'm/etc. ~) [todo] mi/etc. o el **gozo** en el/un pozo
sunrise (from ~ to/till sunset) de **sol** a sol
sunset (from sunrise to/till ~) de **sol** a sol
super bestial; chachi; cojonudo; dabute[n]/dabuti; que quita el **hipo**; pistonudo
to be super ser un/de **alucine**; ser la **biblia**; dar la **hora** [y quitar los cuartos]
superficially (clean [s.th.] [up] ~) limpiar algo solamente por donde ve la **suegra** o limpiar solamente lo que ve la suegra
to suppress one's anger tragar **bilis**; morder/tascar el **freno**; tragar **quina**
supreme effort (make a ~) echar el **resto**; navegar a todo **trapo**
supreme effort (take s.o. a ~ [to + infinitive]) costar **Dios** y ayuda a alg. [+ infinitivo]
sure (as ~ as ~ can be) como [que] **tres** y dos son cinco
sure (as ~ as eggs is/are eggs) como [que] **tres** y dos son cinco
sure (as ~ as night follows day) como [que] **tres** y dos son cinco
sure (as ~ as the day is long) como [que] **tres** y dos son cinco
sure (for ~) impepinable
sure (it ~ is [she]) el mismo que viste y calza (▷ **vestir**) (example)
sure (never be/don't be too ~) nunca digas de esta **agua** no beberé
sure thing (it's a ~) son **habas** contadas
to be sure to go to heaven irse al cielo vestido y calzado (▷ **vestir**)

sure-fire (be a ~ . . .) ser **bueno** como el oro; ser tan seguro como el **evangelio**

surly (look ~) tener **cara** de pocos amigos

to surpass s.o. comerle el **terreno** a alg.

surprise (come as a nasty ~) caer/sentar como un **jarro** de agua fría

surprise (have a very nasty/unpleasant ~) quedarse **frío**

surprise (life is full of ~s) donde/cuando menos se piensa, salta la **liebre**

surprise (take s.o. by ~) coger a alg. de **nuevas**

to surprise (nothing ~s s.o. any more) estar curado de **espanto**

surprised (act ~/pretend to be ~) hacerse de **nuevas**

suspense (be left/kept in ~) estar en **vilo**

suspense (keep s.o. in ~) tener a alg. en/sobre **ascuas**; tener a alg. en el **potro**

suspicious (be [extremely] ~) oler a **cuerno** quemado; estar con/tener la **mosca** detrás de la oreja; estar con cien **ojos**

swallow (one ~ does not make a summer) una **golondrina** no hace verano

to swallow (I'm not going to ~ that!) ¡a mí no me la cuelas! (▷ **colar**)

to swallow (it was as if the earth had ~ed them up) tragarse la **tierra** a alg. (example)

to swallow (s.o. is/feels so ashamed [of himself], he just wants the earth to open and ~ him up) caérsele a alg. la cara de **vergüenza**

to swallow anything comulgar con ruedas de molino; tener buenas **creederas/tragaderas**; **tragar**[se]las como puños

to swallow anything hook, line and sinker **tragar**[se]las como ruedas de molino

to swallow hard tragar **saliva**

to swallow one's anger/feelings tragar **saliva**

to swallow the bitter pill ([have to] ~) [tener que] tragar **quina**

swank el postín

to swank darse **bombo**; darse **charol**; darse **pisto**; el **postín** (example); darse **pote**; toser fuerte

to swap places with s.o. (s.o. wouldn't like to ~) no arrendarle la **ganancia** a alg.

swarm una nube

swarming with cuajado de

to sway one's hips contonearse

swaying of the hips el campaneo/contoneo

to swear (curse and ~) echar **sapos** y culebras

to swear black and blue [that . . .] jurar por lo más **sagrado** [que ...]

to swear by all that is holy [that . . .] jurar por lo más **sagrado** [que ...]

to swear [horribly] echar **ajos** [y cebollas]; blasfemar/jurar como un **carretero**; darse a todos los **demonios**; soltar **tacos**

to swear like a trooper blasfemar/jurar como un **carretero**

to swear to God [that . . .] jurar por lo más **sagrado** [que ...]

sweat (be a real ~) costar un **huevo** [+ infinitivo]

sweat (by the ~ of his/etc. brow) con el sudor de su/etc. **frente**

sweat (drip with ~) sudar a **chorros/mares**

sweat (have such a ~ [to + infinitive]) costar un **huevo** [+ infinitivo]

sweat (have such a ~ to do s.th.) tener que **ver**se y desearse para hacer algo

sweat (smell of ~) oler a **tigre**

to sweat away trabajar como un **buey**; dar el **callo**; romperse el **culo**; echar/sudar la **hiel**; echar los **hígados**; darse una **jupa**; trabajar como un **negro**; dejarse la **piel**; **pringar**[las]; sudar el **quilo**; remar; **reventar**se; echar los riñones (▷ **riñón**); destripar terrones (▷ **terrón**); sudar **tinta**

to sweat blood sudar la **gota** gorda; sudar **sangre**

to sweat buckets/streams sudar a **chorros**/la **gota** gorda/a **mares**

to sweat it out **sudar**lo

to sweat like a bull/pig sudar la **gota** gorda

to sweat one's guts out (▷ guts)

sweep (make a clean ~ of s.th.) barrer con algo; hacer **tabla** rasa [de algo]

to sweep it under the carpet/rug ocultar los **trapos** sucios

sweet (take the bitter with the ~) tomar las duras con las maduras (▷ **duro**)

sweet (the ~s of success/victory) las **miel**es del triunfo

sweet f.a. (do ~) tocarse los cojones (▷ **cojón**)/el **pito**

sweet girl una boquita de **piñón**

sweet nature (have a ~) no tener **hiel**; ser una **paloma** sin hiel

to sweeten (work ~s life) el **trabajo** es el encanto de la vida

to sweeten the pill dorar la **píldora**

sweetheart la prenda

sweetie la pichona (▷ **pichón**)

to sweet-talk s.o. dorar la **bola**/dar **coba**/comer el **coco** a alg.

sweet-tempered (be very ~) no tener **hiel**; ser una **paloma** sin hiel; estar como una **seda**

to be sweltering de **bigote**

sweltering heat (what a ~!) ¡qué **horno**!

swig (have a ~) atizarse un **trago**

swill (food) el comistrajo/pisto

swim (be in the ~) estar en la **onda**

to swim against the tide ir/navegar contra la **corriente**

to swim like a brick nadar como un **plomo**

to swim with the tide dejarse llevar de/por la **corriente**

swimmingly a las mil **maravillas**

swimmingly (go ~) balsa de aceite; ir que chuta (▷ **chutar**); ir/marchar sobre **rueda**s/como una **seda**

swindle el camelo/petardo

to swindle hacer **trampa**[s]

to swindle s.o. dar la **castaña** a alg.; dar a alg. **gato** por liebre; pegar un **parche** a alg.

swindler el bachiller Trapazas (▷ **trapaza**)

swine (cast pearls before ~) echar **margarita**s a los puercos

swine (person) el cabrón/cagachín

to swing one's hips contonearse

to swing the lead hacer la **zanguanga**

swinging of the hips el campaneo/contoneo

to swipe s.th. (steal) **pringar**se algo; soplar algo [a alg.]; echar la **zarpa** a algo

to switch (dishonestly ~ s.th.) dar el **cambiazo** a alg.

sword (be a double-edged ~) ser un arma de dos **filo**s

sword (he who lives by the ~, dies by the ~) el que a **hierro** mata, a hierro muere

sword (the pen is mightier than the ~) más fuerte es la **pluma** que la espada

sword (with fire and ~) a **fuego** y hierro/sangre

swords (cross ~ with s.o.) habérselas con alg. (▷ **haber**)

to swot quemarse las **ceja**s; romperse los **codo**s; empollar; machacar; quemarse las **pestaña**s

to swot up [on] s.th. empollar/machacar algo

sycophant el/la lavacaras

symptoms (withdrawal ~) el mono

T

T (suit/fit [s.o.] to a ~) venir/sentar [a alg.] como **anillo** al dedo/que ni **pintado** o como pintado

table (drink s.o. under the ~) beber hasta **tumbar** a alg.; dar cien **vuelta**s a alg. (example)

tables (turn the ~ on s.o.) devolver la **pelota**/ volver las **torna**s a alg.; cambiar/volver la **tortilla** a alg.

tack (go off on a different ~) sacar los **pie**s del plato/de las alforjas

tacks (get [straight] down to brass ~) no andarse con/en chiquitas (▷ la **chiquita**); ir al **grano**; no andarse con **requilorios**

to tackle s.th. hincar el diente a/en algo

tail (be like a dog with two ~s) alegrarse/estar como [un] **niño** con zapatos nuevos

tail (slink off/go away with one's ~ between one's legs) irse con el **rabo** entre las piernas/ patas

tail (turn ~) poner **pie**s en polvorosa

tail (with one's ~ between one's legs) con las **oreja**s gachas

tail (work one's ~ off) trabajar como un **buey**; dar el **callo**; romperse los **cuerno**s/el **culo**; echar/sudar la **hiel**; echar los **hígado**s; darse una **jupa**; trabajar como un **negro**; dejarse la **piel**; pringar[las]; sudar el **quilo**; remar; **reventar**se; echar los riñones (▷ **riñón**); destripar terrones (▷ **terrón**); sudar **tinta**

tailender (be the ~) ser el **farolillo** rojo

to take (have had just about all one can ~) colmar la medida

to take (I'm not taking anything/that from anybody) a mí no me tose nadie (▷ **toser**)

to take a long time (not to half ~) ser más largo que una **cuaresma**; ser más **largo** que un día sin pan

to take for pasar por

to take forever ser más largo que una **cuaresma**; ser más **largo** que un día sin pan

to take it ([have to] ~) [tener que] tragar **bilis**/ **quina**

to take it (s.o. can't ~ any more/longer) no poder con su **alma**

to take it easy echarse/tenderse/tumbarse a la **bartola**; darse un **verde**

to take it lying down **tragar**lo

to take it or one's anger/fury out on s.o. descargar la **bilis** en/contra alg.; **cebar**se en alg.

to take it out of s.o. batirse el **cobre** (example); hacer **polvo** a alg.

to take it very ill caer/sentar como una **pedrada**

to take over tomar el **remo**

to take s.o. down a peg or two bajar el **gallo**/los **humo**s a alg.; meter a alg. el **resuello** en el cuerpo

to take s.o. down off his high horse quitar **moño**s a alg.

to take s.o. in dar a alg. **gato** por liebre

to take s.o. on echar **raya** a alg.

to take s.o. on (nobody can take him on) a ése no hay quien le tosa (▷ **toser**)

to take s.o. time or a year/etc. to do s.th. **tirar**se tiempo o un año/etc. haciendo algo

to take that lying down (we won't ~!) ¡no somos negros! (▷ **el negro**)

to take things too far (you can ~) bueno está lo bueno [pero no lo demasiado]

to take to s.th. like a duck to water encontrarse en seguida en su **elemento**

to take to/up prostitution echarse al **mundo**/a la **vida**

taken aback (be completely ~) quedarse **frío**; quedarse de una **pieza**

to be taken in hacer el **canelo**; quedarse **fresco**; tragar la **píldora**; hacer el **primo**

tale (old wives' ~) el **cuento** de viejas

tale (tell ~s [out of school]) írsele a alg. la **burra**

talent (go out looking for ~) salir de **levante**

talent (have/show a ~ for . . .) tener **vena** de ...

talented (be a brilliantly ~ mathematician/etc.) nació alg. para [ser] matemático/etc. (▷ **nacer**)

talented hands (have ~) tener **manita**s de plata/ oro

talk (be all ~ [and no action]) cacarear y no poner huevos; írsele a alg. la **fuerza** por la boca

talk (person who is all ~ and no action) el/la cantamañanas

to talk abrir el **pico**

to talk (don't ~ of ropes in the house of a man who was hanged) no hay que hablar de/mentar/ nombrar la **soga** en casa del ahorcado

to talk (encourage s.o. to ~) dar **cuerda/soga** a alg.

to talk (get s.o. to ~/make s.o. ~) sacar el **buche** a alg.; desatar/soltar la **lengua** a alg.

to talk (money ~s) poderoso caballero es don Dinero (▷ **el caballero**)

to talk (reveal) cantar; vaciar el **costal**; irse de la **mui**; no quedarse con nada en el **pecho**; soltar la **sinhueso**

to talk (s.o. wouldn't stop ~ing) hablar como una **chicharra**; hablar a **chorro**s; hablar más

que una **cotorra**; dar **cuerda** a alg.
(example); hablar más que un **sacamuelas**
to talk (the more you ~, the more mistakes you'll
make) quien mucho habla, mucho yerra
(▷ **hablar**)
to talk (try to get s.o. to ~) meter a alg. los **dedos**
en la boca
to talk a lot cascar; darle al **pico**; gastar mucha
prosa
to talk [a lot of] nonsense/rot/rubbish irse por los
cerros de Úbeda; meter **ripio**
to talk a mile a minute hablar como una
chicharra/a **chorros**/más que una **cotorra**;
como un **descosido** (example); no tener
pepita en la lengua; hablar más que un
sacamuelas/que **siete**
to talk about (everybody is talking about s.th.)
andar algo en **boca** de todos
to talk about (not to ~ s.th. any more) dejar la
fiesta en paz
to talk about (not to ~ things one doesn't know
anything about) no meterse en **teologías**
to talk about (there's lots to ~) haber **tela** que
cortar/para rato
to talk about clothes/fashion hablar de **trapos**
to talk about everything under the sun hablar de
este **mundo** y del otro
to talk at deaf ears clamar en el desierto; dar
música a un sordo; predicar en el desierto
to talk behind s.o.'s back cortar un **sayo** a alg.
to talk big echar de **bolina**; escupir por el
colmillo; darse **tono**; no se oye más **voz**
que la suya
to talk in a torrent hablar a borbotones/
borbollones (▷ **borbotón/borbollón**);
hablar a **chorros**
to talk nineteen to the dozen hablar como una
chicharra/a **chorros**/por los **codos**/más
que una **cotorra**; como un **descosido**
(example); no tener **pepita** en la lengua;
hablar más que un **sacamuelas**/que **siete**
talk of angels! hablando del **rey/ruin** de Roma
[y él que se asoma o por la puerta asoma]
talk of the devil [and he's sure to appear]
hablando del **rey/ruin** de Roma [y él que
se asoma o por la puerta asoma]
talk of the town (be the ~) andar algo en **boca** de
todos; ser la **comidilla** de la ciudad/de la
gente/del público; andar en **copla**s/
lenguas
to talk one's head off hablar por los **codos**
to talk round the issue/subject salir[se]/
escapar[se]/irse por la **tangente**; mear
fuera del **tiesto**
to talk smut decir **verdulerías**
to talk the hind legs off a donkey hablar como una
chicharra; hablar más que una **cotorra**/un
sacamuelas
to talk thoughtlessly írsele la **boca** a alg.

to talk through one's hat sin **ton** ni son (example)
to talk to a brick wall ladrar a la **luna**; hablar a la
pared
to talk to the winds clamar en el desierto; dar
música a un sordo; predicar en el desierto
to talk too much hablar por los **codos**; perderse
por el **pico**
to talk too much (talking too much can be
dangerous) por la **boca** muere el pez
to talk turkey [with s.o.] **cantar**las claras [a alg.]
talkativeness la prosa
talking-to (give s.o. a ~) cantar/leer la **cartilla** a
alg.; echar un **rapapolvo/sermón** a alg.
tall story el **cuento** chino
to be taller than s.o. by a head llevar a alg. la
cabeza
tan (get a ~) **tostar**se [al sol]
to tan **tostar**se [al sol]
to tan s.o.'s hide zurrar la **badana** o menear/
sacudir el **bulto** a alg.; arrimar **candela**/dar
caña/medir las **costillas**/sentar las
costuras a alg.; dar **leña** o cargar de leña a
alg.; cascarle/machacarle a alg. las
liendres; sacudir el **polvo** a alg.; poner a
alg. como un **pulpo**
tangent (go off at a ~) irse por los **cerros** de
Úbeda; salir[se]/escapar[se]/irse por la
tangente
tanked up (get ~: get drunk) apiparse; **cocerse**;
papar una **jumera**; coger una **melopea/**
merluza; coger/pillar una **mona**; moñarse;
coger una **pea**; agarrar[se] un **pedo**; coger
una **pítima**
tanning (give s.o. a ~) zurrar la **badana** o
menear/sacudir el **bulto** a alg.; arrimar
candela/dar **caña**/medir las **costillas**/
sentar las **costura**s a alg.; dar **leña** o
cargar de leña a alg.; cascarle/machacarle
a alg. las **liendres**; sacudir el **polvo** a alg.;
poner a alg. como un **pulpo**; tocar la/dar
una **solfa** a alg.; menear el **zarzo**/dar una
zurra a alg.
to tap s.o. for money pegar un **petardo**/dar un
sablazo a alg.
to be tarred with the same brush ser lobos de una
misma **camada**; ser del mismo **jaez**; cojear
del mismo **pie**
tart (cheap ~) la pesetera
tart (prostitute) la fulana/sota; el taxi; la zorra
task (be a huge/mammoth ~) ser **obra** de
romanos
task (face a difficult ~) necesitar **Dios** y [su]
ayuda
task (take s.o. to ~) cantar/leer la **cartilla** a alg.;
dar un **palo** a alg.
taste (leave a bad/nasty ~ in one's mouth) dejar a
alg. [con] mal **sabor** de boca

taste (there's no accounting for ~) sobre **gusto**s no hay nada escrito/para cada gusto se pintó un color

taste (there's no accounting for ~!) hay **gusto**s que merecen palos

to taste awful/foul saber a **demonio**s/**rayo**s

to taste delicious/excellent/etc. saber a **gloria**; saber a más

tasty (person) de **rechupete**

tattletale el/la correve[i]dile; el soplón/la soplona

tax collector el sacamantas

tea (he's/she's not my cup of ~) no es **santo** de mi devoción

tea (marijuana) el chocolate/ful; la hierba/mandanga/mierda; el tate; la yerba

tea (not for all the ~ in China) aunque se junten el **cielo** y la tierra

tea (not to be s.o.'s cup of ~) no ser **plato** de su gusto

tea party (mad hatter's ~) la **olla** de grillos

to teach (try to ~ one's grandmother to suck eggs) querer enseñar el **padrenuestro** al cura

to teach s.o. a lesson escarmentar a alg.

teacup (cause/start a storm in a ~) ahogarse en un vaso de agua

teacup (storm in a ~) una **tormenta** en un vaso de agua

team (be the bottom-of-the-table ~) ser el **farolillo** rojo

team in last place (be the ~) ser el **farolillo** rojo

teapot (cause/start a tempest in a ~) ahogarse en un vaso de agua

teapot (tempest in a ~) una **tormenta** en un vaso de agua

to tear [along] (speed) quemar el **caucho**

to tear (that's/it's torn it) [todo] mi/etc. o el **gozo** en el/un pozo

to tear one's hair [out] dar con la **cabeza** en las paredes; **rasgar**se las vestiduras

to tear s.o. to bits/pieces/shreds poner a alg. como **chupa** de dómine/como un **guiñapo**/como **hoja** de perejil; machacar a alg.; hacer **polvo** a alg.; revolcar a alg.; poner a alg. como un **trapo**

to tear s.th. to bits hacer algo **cisco**

tear (squeeze a ~) llorar con un **ojo**

tears (be bored to ~) aburrirse como una ostra/una almeja/un mono

tears (be moved to ~) arrancarle a alg. **lágrimas**

tears (bring ~ to s.o.'s eyes) arrancarle a alg. **lágrimas**

tears (burst into ~) soltar el **trapo**

tears (hold back or fight back/down one's ~) beberse las **lágrimas**

tears (weep/shed [a few] crocodile ~) llorar/derramar **lágrimas** de cocodrilo; llorar con un **ojo**

to tease s.o. tomarle el **pelo** a alg.; pitorrearse de alg.; buscar las **pulga**s a alg.

teeming with cuajado de

to tell (one can ~ just by looking at s.o./just by the look on s.o.'s face) se le ve/nota/conoce a alg. en la **cara**; salirle algo a alg. a los **ojo**s

to tell (s.th. ~s s.o. that . . .) darle a alg. el **pálpito**/tener el pálpito de que ...

to tell all and sundry [about it/s.th.] dar un **cuarto** al pregonero; pregonar/proclamar algo a los cuatro **viento**s

to tell all one knows cantar de plano

to tell dirty jokes decir **verdulería**s

to tell everyone one's private business dar un **cuarto** al pregonero

to tell s.o. a thing or two decir a alg. cuántas son **cinco**

to tell s.o. off dar un **jabón**/una **jabonadura** a alg.; jabonar a alg.

to tell s.o. or try telling s.o. every way imaginable/every way one can think of decírselo a alg. en todos los **tono**s

to tell s.o. outright/straight [out] **cantar**las claras a alg.; a **palo** seco

to tell s.o. to get lost mandar a alg. a freír **buñuelo**s/al **cuerno**/a freír **espárrago**s/a hacer **gárgaras**/a paseo

to tell s.o. to go [and] jump in a lake/to go [and] take a running jump/to go climb a tree/to go fly a kite/to go fry an egg mandar a alg. a freír **buñuelo**s/al **cuerno**/a freír **espárrago**s/a hacer **gárgaras**

to tell s.o. to go to blazes mandar a alg. al **diablo**/a capar **mosca**s/a paseo

to tell s.o. to go to hell mandar a alg. a freír **buñuelo**s/al **cuerno**/al **demonio**/al **diablo**/a freír **espárrago**s/a hacer **gárgaras**/al **infierno**/a la **mierda**/a capar **mosca**s/a paseo/a hacer la **puñeta**

to tell s.o. what you think of him poner a alg. a **caldo**

to tell s.o. what's what decir a alg. cuántas son **cinco**

to tell s.o. where to get off mandar a alg. a hacer **gárgaras**

to tell s.o. where to go mandar a alg. a freír **buñuelo**s/al **cuerno**/a freír **espárrago**s/a hacer **gárgaras**/a paseo

to tell s.th. in plain English/Spanish/German/etc. hablar en **cristiano**

to tell tales [out of school] írsele a alg. la **burra**

tell that to s.o. else! ídiselo o cuéntaselo al **nuncio**!

tell that to the marines! ¡cuéntaselo a su o cuéntaselo a tu **abuela**!; ¡ésa es **grilla** [y no canta]!; ia otro perro con ese **hueso**!; ídiselo o cuéntaselo al **nuncio**!; ¡cuénteselo a su o cuéntaselo a tu **suegra**!

to tell the world [about it/s.th.] dar un **cuarto** al pregonero

telling-off la bronca

telling-off (give s.o. a ~) soltar la/una **andanada** a alg.; zurrar la **badana** a alg.; dar una **calada**/un **jabón**/una **jabonadura** a alg.; jabonar a alg.; cardarle la **lana** a alg.; dar un **meneo** a alg.; echar un **rapapolvo** a alg.; dar [una] **soba** a alg.; poner a alg. de **vuelta** y media

telling-off (give s.o. a terrific ~) la bronca (example)

telltale el chivato/la chivata; el/la correve[i]dile; el soplón/la soplona

temper ([be quick to] lose one's ~) perder los **estribos**; a **flor** de piel

temper (have a bad/nasty/violent ~) tener mal **café** o mal/mucho **genio** o malas **pulga**s

temper (have a quick ~) el pronto (example)

temper (tend to fly into a ~) a **flor** de piel

tempest in a teapot una **tormenta** en un vaso de agua

tempest in a teapot (cause/start a ~) ahogarse en un vaso de agua

to tempt fate/providence tentar a Dios/al diablo

tempting (look ~) estar algo diciendo cómeme (▷ **comer**)

to tend to flare up very quickly/to fly into a temper/to fly off the handle a **flor** de piel; no poder con el **genio**

tenderness (be overflowing with ~) rebosar de ternura

ten-foot pole (s.o. wouldn't touch s.th./s.o. with a ~) no poder coger algo ni con **papel** de fumar; no poder coger algo/a alg. ni con **tenazas**

tensed up (be all ~) tener los **nervios** de punta

tenterhooks (be on ~) tener el **alma** en un hilo; estar en/sobre **ascuas**; estar [como] en **brasas**

tenterhooks (keep s.o. on ~) tener a alg. en/sobre **ascuas**; tener a alg. en el **potro**

termagant una mujer de **armas** tomar; la cascarrabias/tarasca

terrible blow (be a ~) ser un **trago** amargo

terrible experience (be a ~) ser pasar por las horcas caudinas (▷ **caudino**)

terrible job (have a ~ [to + infinitive]) costar **Dios** y ayuda a alg. [+ infinitivo]

terrible ordeal (be a ~) ser pasar por las horcas caudinas (▷ **caudino**)

terrible things (say ~ about s.th./s.o.) decir **horror**es de algo/alg.

terrible time (have a ~ [of it]) irle a alg. como a los **perros** en misa; puto (example)

terrible/terribly escandalosamente (▷ **escandaloso**); de padre y muy señor mío (▷ **el padre**); de **perros**; a **rabiar**; requete...; solemne

terribly hot (be ~: spicy) picar que rabia (▷ **rabiar**)

terribly hot (it's ~) canta la **chicharra**

to be terribly pleased/glad/happy la **mar** de

terrific bestial; de los **buenos**; chachi; cojonudo; dabute[n]/dabuti; que quita el **hipo**; padre (example); de padre y muy señor mío (▷ **el padre**); pistonudo; señor

to be terrific ser un/de **alucine**

terrific (look ~) estar como un **tren**

to be terrified caerse [muerto] de miedo; no llegarle a uno la **camisa** al cuerpo

terror (be a holy ~) ser de la **piel** del diablo

testicles (balls; bollocks; goolies; marbles; nuts) las **bolas/canicas**; los cataplines; los cojones (▷ **cojón**); los **conejos/huevos**; las **pelotas**; los pistones (▷ **pistón**)

tether (be at the end of one's ~) no saber como salir del **atranco**; no saber a qué **santo** encomendarse

Thames (s.o. won't set the ~ on fire) no haber inventado la **pólvora**

thank goodness menos **mal**

that (come up with s.th. just like ~) traer algo en/por la **manga**; sacarse algo de la **manga**

that (enough of ~!) ¡cruz y raya!

that (first it's this, then it's ~) cuando **pitos** flautas, cuando flautas pitos

that (I'm not taking ~ from anybody) a mí no me tose nadie (▷ **toser**)

that (it's not as bad as all ~) no es tan feo el diablo como le pintan (▷ **pintar**)

that (just like ~) de buenas a primeras (▷ **bueno**); de **golpe** y porrazo

that (not to be as bad as all ~) no llegar la **sangre** al río

that (not to come to ~) no **llegar** a tanto

that (not to leave it at ~) no quedarse ahí **parado**

that (we won't stand for ~!; you/etc. can't do ~ to us! I'll not stand for ~) ¡no somos negros! (▷ **el negro**); a mí no me tose nadie (▷ **toser**)

that (you/etc. know all about de **marras**

that's all there is no hay más **cera** que la que arde

that's that! ([and] ~) sanseacabó

that's the end of that! ¡se acabó! (▷ **acabar**)

theme (be harping on the same old ~ every time) sonar como un disco **rayado**

there (not to be all ~) faltarle a alg. un **tornillo**/tener flojos los tornillos; tener una **tuerca** floja

there you are! ¡toma! (▷ **tomar**)

thick (be a bit ~: unfair/etc.) pasar de **castaño** oscuro; pelar la jeta

thick (be as ~ as a brick/as ~ as they come/as ~ as two short planks) ser más tonto que **Abundio**; si le/etc. menean, da **bellota**s; ser más tonto que **Carracuca**; ser más

cerrado que un cerrojo; ser más **corto** que las mangas de un chaleco; ser más tonto que una **mata** de habas; no saber ni siquiera quitarse los **mocos**; pecar de + adj. (example); ser más bruto que la **pila** de un pozo; ser **tonto** del bote/de capirote

thick (be as ~ as thieves) estar a partir un **piñón** con alg.; ser **uña** y carne

thick (be pretty ~) comulgar con ruedas de molino

thick (be very ~ with s.o.) estar a partir un **piñón** con alg.

thick (lay it on [too] ~) hinchar el perro; forzar la **nota**

thick (through ~ and thin) contra **viento** y marea

thick and fast (the blows came ~) a **granel**

thick ear (give s.o. a ~) ponerle a alg. la cara nueva (▷ **nuevo**); pegar una **torta** a alg.

thick skin (develop a ~) criar **callos**

thick skin (have a ~) tener anchas/buenas **espaldas**; tener buen **estómago**

thick with dirt/etc. cuajado de; estar o ponerse **perdido** de algo

thicko (be a real ~) ser más tonto que **Abundio**; si le/etc. menean, da **bellotas**; ser más tonto que **Carracuca**; ser más **cerrado** que un cerrojo; ser más **corto** que las mangas de un chaleco; ser más tonto que una **mata** de habas; no saber ni siquiera quitarse los **mocos**; ser más bruto que la **pila** de un pozo

thick-skinned (be ~) tener anchas/buenas **espaldas**; tener buen **estómago**

thief el/la **uñetas**

thief (band/gang of thieves) la camada

thief (be a ~) ser **largo** de uñas

thief (be as thick as thieves) estar a partir un **piñón** con alg.; ser **uña** y carne

thief (opportunity makes the ~) la **ocasión** hace al ladrón

thin (be as ~ as a rail/rake) quedarse en el **chasis**; salirse por el **corbatín**; estar como/hecho una **espátula**; estar más **seco** que una pasa

thin (be terribly/very ~) quedarse en el **chasis**; salirse por el **corbatín**

thin (go ~) perder **carnes**

thing (a change is a good ~) entre **col** y col, lechuga; pan con pan, comida de tontos

thing (a fine ~ you've done!) lucirse (example)

thing (be [almost] too much of a good ~) ser **miel** sobre hojuelas; traérselas (▷ **traer**)

thing (be neither one ~ nor the other) no ser **carne** ni pescado; no ser ni **chicha** ni limonada/ni **fu** ni fa; ni **pinchar** ni cortar

thing (be one ~ after another) ser una **gotera**

thing (be the best/greatest ~ since sliced bread) ser el no va más (▷ **ir**)

thing (chuck the whole ~) dar con la **carga** en tierra/en el suelo o echarse con la carga; mandar algo al **cuerno**/a tomar por **culo**/al **diablo** (examples); tirar los **trastos**

thing (find the very ~) encontrar/hallar la **horma** de su zapato

thing (if it isn't one ~ it's another) cuando no es por **pitos**, es por flautas

thing (it boils/comes down to the same ~) llámele usted o llámale **hache**

thing (it's a good ~ . . .) menos **mal**

thing (it's a sure ~) son **habas** contadas

thing (it's one ~ to say s.th. and another to actually do it) del **dicho** al hecho hay mucho trecho; dicho sin hecho no trae provecho

thing (know a ~ or two) saber cuántas son **cinco**

thing (little/minor ~) una **nube** de verano; nada entre dos **platos**; la quisquilla

thing (make off with the whole ~) alzarse/salirse con el **santo** y la limosna/cera

thing (not to be just a small ~) no ser **moco de pavo**

thing ([not] to be s.o.'s ~) [no] **rezar** con; hacer **tilín** a alg.

thing (not to know a single ~) no saber [ni] la **cartilla**

thing (not to know the first ~ about s.th.) ni **chispa** de (example); no saber ni **jota** de algo; estar **pez** en algo

thing (old ~) la antigualla

thing (over some tiny ~) por un quítame allá esas **pajas**

thing (say one ~ and mean another) de **boca** [para] afuera (example); de **boquilla**; de **dientes** [para] afuera (example)

thing (silly/stupid ~ [to do]) la burrada

thing (s.o. can't do/get a ~ right) no dar **palotada**; no dar **pie** con bola

thing (s.o. can't see a ~) no ver tres en un **burro**

thing (tell s.o. a ~ or two) decir a alg. cuántas son **cinco**

thing (that's the important ~) es lo que hace el **gasto**

thing (there isn't any/there's no such ~) no hay tales **borregos/carneros/corderos**

thing (you can have too much of a good ~) bueno está lo bueno [pero no lo demasiado]

thing of the past (be a ~) ser **agua** pasada

things (and many other ~) y qué sé yo (▷ **saber**)

things (be good at explaining ~ [away]) tener buenas **explicaderas**

things (be seeing ~) ver visiones (▷ **visión**)

things (belongings) los bártulos/**trastos**

things (distort/twist ~) hacer de lo **blanco** negro/volver en blanco lo negro

things (do or not to do ~ by halves/in half measures) aplicar **paños** calientes; no andarse con **paños** calientes

things (do useless ~) cazar **moscas**

things (do what one likes with one's own ~) hacer de su **capa** un sayo

things (don't take notice of the stupid ~ people say) a **palabras** necias, oídos sordos

things (get ~ in a complete mess) mezclar **berzas** con capachos

things (go about ~ slyly/on the quiet) **matar**las callando

things (have ~ under control) llevar/tener las **riendas**; tener la **sartén** por el mango

things (have one's mind on other ~) estar en **Babia**/en las **Batuecas**/en **Belén**/en la **higuera**; estar en la **luna**; andar por o estar en las **nubes**

things (jumble ~ up) mezclar **berzas** con capachos

things (let ~ take their course) dejar que ruede la **bola**

things (loads of ~) la **mar** de

things (make ~ difficult for s.o.) poner **chinas** a alg.

things ([not] to waste one's time on little ~) [no] pararse en **pelillos**

things (pack one's ~ [and go]) liar los **bártulos**; hacer la **maleta**; liar el **petate**; levantar el **tabanque**

things (say awful/terrible ~ about s.th./s.o.) decir **horror**es de algo/alg.

things (turn ~ to one's advantage) llevar el **agua** a su molino

things (work ~ to one's own advantage) arrimar el **ascua** a su sardina

things (worse ~ happen at sea) más **cornadas** da el hambre; más se perdió en **Cuba**

things (you can take ~ too far) bueno está lo bueno [pero no lo demasiado]

things are getting hot oler a **chamusquina**

things are settling down/return to normal las **aguas** vuelven a su cauce

things aren't always what they seem ni están todos los que son, ni son todos los que están (▷ **estar**)

things don't/never seem so bad after a good meal con **pan** y vino se anda el camino

things get a bit rough/tough batirse el **cobre**

things often happen when you least expect them to donde/cuando menos se piensa, salta la **liebre**

things would be very different if . . . otro **gallo** cantaría o otro gallo me/etc. cantara si ...

to think (I couldn't care less/don't give a damn what other people ~) ande yo **caliente** y ríase la gente

to think (if you ~ the worst, you won't be far wrong) piensa mal y acertarás (▷ **pensar**)

to think (not to know what to ~) no saber a qué **carta** quedarse

to think (tell s.o. what you ~ of him) poner a alg. a **caldo**

to think (without ~ing) de **golpe** y porrazo; a tontas y a locas (▷ **tonto**)

to think (you can ~ what you like) el pensamiento no tiene/conoce **barreras**

to think (you can see what s.o. is really ~ing) se le ve el **plumero** a alg.

to think a lot of o.s. tener muchas **ínfulas**

to think a lot of s.o. entrar a alg. por el **ojo** derecho

to think better of it apearse de su **burro**

to think everything is plain sailing creer que todo el monte es **orégano**

to think hard comerse el **coco**

to think [it over] long and hard [before doing anything] tentarse la **ropa**

to think no end of o.s. tener muchos **tufos**

to think one has done enough echarse al o en el **surco**

to think one is important subirse a la **parra**; el **postín** (example); darse **pote**

to think one is the cat's pajamas/pyjamas/whiskers or the bee's knees creerse el no va más (▷ **ir**); la **mar** de

to think one is the greatest creerse el no va más (▷ **ir**)

to think only of o.s. ir a la **suya**/a lo **suyo**

to think s.th. over [very] thoroughly requete...

to think to be very clever/smart la **mar** de

thirst (be dying of ~/have a raging ~) abrasarse de sed; estar **muerto** de sed

this (first it's ~, then it's that) cuando **pitos** flautas, cuando flautas pitos

thorough job (do a ~) emplearse a **fondo**

thorough[ly] por los cuatro **costados**; con todas las de la **ley**; requete...

those (all ~ present) el **ganado**

thought (give s.th. a lot of ~) dar muchas **vueltas** a algo

thought (reveal one's secret ~s) respirar por la **herida**

thoughtless error el penseque

thoughtlessly (talk ~) írsele la **boca** a alg.

to thrash s.o. menear/sacudir el **bulto** a alg.; dar un **meneo** a alg.

thrashing (get a ~) ganársela (▷ **ganar**)

thrashing (give s.o. a ~) zurrar la **badana** o menear/sacudir el **bulto** a alg.; arrimar **candela**/dar **caña**/medir las **costillas**/sentar las **costuras** a alg.; dar **leña** o cargar de leña a alg.; cascarle/machacarle a alg. las **liendres**; dar un **meneo** a alg.; dar a alg. para el **pelo**; sacudir el **polvo** a alg.; poner a alg. como un **pulpo**; poner a alg. hecho una **salsa**; tocar la o dar una **solfa** a alg.; poner a alg. el culo como un **tomate**; pegar una **tunda** a alg.

thrashing (take the father and mother of a ~) de padre y muy señor mío (▷ **el padre**) (example) thread (hang or be hanging by a ~) colgar/pender o estar colgado/pendiente de un **cabello/hilo**

thread (lose the ~) perder el **hilo**/cortársele a alg. el hilo

thread (pick up the ~) tomar el **hilo**

to be thrilled to bits with s.th. caérsele a alg. la **baba** con/por algo

throat (jump down s.o.'s ~) saltar a la **cara** a alg.

throats (be at each other's ~) tirarse de los **moños**

throbbing headache (have a ~) tener la cabeza a las **once**

through (fall ~) irse al **cuerno; escoñarse**

through and through por los cuatro **costados**

through and through (be a Spaniard/etc. ~) ser español/etc. hasta los **tuétanos**

throughout [the length and breadth of] a lo **largo** y a lo ancho de

throw (be only a stone's ~ away) estar a [un] **tiro** de piedra

throw (risk everything on one ~) jugárselo todo a una [sola] **carta**

to throw o.s. into s.th. meterse de **cabeza** en algo

to throw s.o. out echar a alg. a **baquetazo** limpio

to throw up [violently] echar las **entrañas**; cambiar la **peseta**; echar las **tripas**

thumb (be under s.o.'s ~) estar bajo la **férula** de alg.

thumb (have/keep s.o. under one's ~) **calzarse** a alg.; tener a alg. en un **puño**

thumb (twiddle one's ~s) estar/quedarse con los **brazos** cruzados; tocarse el **pito**

to thumb a lift/ride ir[se] a **dedo**/hacer dedo

to thumb it ir[se] a **dedo**/hacer dedo

to thumb one's nose at s.o. hacer un **palmo** de narices a alg.

thumbs (be all ~) ser un **manazas**

thunder (look like or as black as ~) tener **cara** de pocos amigos

thunderstorm (be like a dying duck in a ~) quedarse de una **pieza**

thunderstruck como herido por el/un rayo (▷ **herir**)

to thwart s.o.'s plans echar a **rodar** los proyectos de alg.

tick (drink on ~) beber sobre **tarja**

tick (eat until one is [as] full/tight as a ~) a todo **pasto**; a más no **poder**

tick (in a ~) en un decir **amén**/un **credo**/un **dos** por tres; en menos que canta un **gallo**

tick (in two ~s) en dos **trancos**

ticking-off la bronca/sofrenada

ticking-off (give s.o. a ~) soltar la/una **andanada** a alg.; zurrar la **badana**/dar una **calada** a alg.; cantar/leer la **cartilla** a alg.; poner a alg. como **chupa** de dómine; cardarle la **lana** a alg.; echar una **peluca**/un **rapapolvo** a alg.; sofrenar a alg.

ticking-off (give s.o. a terrific ~) la bronca (example)

to tickle s.o.'s curiosity hacer **cosquillas** a alg.

to be tickled pink alegrarse/estar como [un] **niño** con zapatos nuevos; estar [contento] como o más contento que unas pascuas (▷ **Pascua**)

to be tiddly (tipsy) hacérsele a alg. **candelillas** los ojos; estar a medios **pelos**; estar entre **Pinto y Valdemoro**; estar entre dos **velas**

tide (go/swim against the ~) ir/navegar contra la **corriente**

tide (go/swim with the ~) dejarse llevar de/por la **corriente**

tide (now the ~ has turned) se han vuelto las **tornas**; se ha vuelto la **tortilla**

tide (time and ~ wait for no man) camarón que se duerme, se lo lleva la corriente

tidy sum (cost a ~) costar una **burrada**/un **dineral**/un **huevo**/un **ojo** de la cara/un **pico**/un **riñón**/una **riñonada**; costar la de **San Quintín**; costar un **sentido** o los cinco sentidos

tie (end in a ~) salir/quedar **pata**[s]

to tie salir/quedar **pata**[s]

tied ([be able] to do s.th. with one arm ~ behind one's back) [poder/saber] hacer algo con los **ojos** cerrados

tight roñoso

to be tight (drunk) estar hecho un **cesto**; estar cocido (▷ **cocer**); estar hecho una **cuba**/un **cuero**/un **pellejo**/una **sopa**; estar **trompa**; estar hecho una **uva**

tight (be extremely ~ with s.th.) repartir algo como **pan** bendito

tight (get ~: get drunk) **cocerse**; papar una **jumera**; coger una **melopea/merluza**; coger/pillar una **mona**; moñarse; coger una **pea**; agarrar[se] un **pedo**; coger una **pítima**; coger[se] una **trompa**; pillar una **zorra**

tight (shut/close s.th. ~) cerrar algo a **cal** y canto

tight spot (be in a very ~) estar con el **dogal**/la **soga** al cuello

tight spot (get o.s. into a ~) meterse en un **berenjenal**/en **camisa** de once varas

tight spot (get s.o. into a [very] ~) poner a alg. en las **astas** del toro

tight spot (get/help s.o. out of a ~) sacar a alg. del **atolladero**; echar un **cable** a alg.; sacar a alg. de un apuro

to tighten up [on s.o.] apretar las **clavijas** a alg.; apretar la **cuerda**

tight-fisted (be extremely ~ with s.th.) repartir algo como **pan** bendito

tightwad el cicatero/la cicatera; el cuentagarbanzos

tiles (spend a night on the ~) irse de/a **picos** pardos

tilt (at full ~) a todo **vapor**; a toda **vela**

time (be a waste of ~) azotar el **aire**; machacar en hierro frío; arar en el **mar**

time (come at just the right ~/s.th. couldn't have come at a better ~) venir como **agua** de mayo/como **anillo** al dedo; venir como llovido/llegar como caído del **cielo**; venir que ni **pintado**/como pintado; venir **rodado**

time (do ~) estar a la **sombra**/en la **trena**

time (give s.o. a hard/difficult ~) tratar a alg. a **baquetazo** limpio; llevar/traer a alg. por la **calle** de la amargura

time (hardly have ~ to breathe) no tener tiempo ni de **respirar**

time (have a bloody awful/a ghastly/a hard/a lousy/a rough/a terrible/a tough ~ [of it]) pasar las de **Caín**; pasarlas moradas (▷ **morado**)/negras (▷ **negro**); irle a alg. como a los **perro**s en misa; puto (example); pasar un **trago** amargo

time (have a fine/a grand/a great/a fantastic/a marvelous/a smashing/a tremendous/a whale of a/a wonderful ~) cañón/chachi (examples); dabute[n]/dabuti (example); divertirse **horrore**s; correrse una **juerga**; divertirse la **mar**; ponerse como un **Pepe**; pasarlo **pipa**; de **rechupete**; pasar las **vaca**s gordas

time (have a tough ~ doing s.th.) verse **negro** para hacer algo

time (have a [very] hard time [+ gerund]) hacérsele algo a alg. [muy] **cuesta** arriba [+ infinitivo]

time (have an easy/a lazy ~ of it) echarse/tenderse/tumbarse a la **bartola**

time (have the ~ of one's life) pasar las **vaca**s gordas

time (in next to no ~) en un decir **amén**/un **credo**/un **dos** por tres; en menos que canta un **gallo**/se reza un **padrenuestro**

time (it's ~ to pay up!) ¡tocan a pagar! ¡a pagar tocan! (▷ **tocar**)

time (mark ~) marcar el **paso**

time (merry/good ~) la juerga

time (merry/good ~: have a/go out for a) estar/ir de **juerga**; irse de/a **pico**s pardos

time (not to half take a long ~) ser más largo que una **cuaresma**; ser más **largo** que un día sin pan

time (not to have an easy ~ of it) irle a alg. como a los **perro**s en misa

time (not to waste any ~) no andarse con **requilorios**

time ([not] to waste one's ~ on little things) [no] pararse en **pelillo**s

time (play for ~) vivir de **renta**

time (since ~ began) desde que el **mundo** es mundo

time (spend ~ or a year/etc. doing s.th.) **tirar**se tiempo o un año/etc. haciendo algo

time (take s.o. ~ or a year/etc. to do s.th.) **tirar**se tiempo o un año/etc. haciendo algo

time (the ~ is ripe) está madura la **breva**

time (there's a ~ and a place for everything) no hay que hablar de/mentar/nombrar la **soga** en casa del ahorcado

time (this is a bad ~!) ¡no está el **horno** para bollos!

time (waste one's ~) coger **agua** en cesto; azotar el **aire**; matar la **araña**; machacar en hierro frío; arar en el **mar**; estar tocando el **tambor**

time (waste one's ~ and energy) gastar la **pólvora** en salvas

time and tide wait for no man camarón que se duerme, se lo lleva la corriente

time and [time] again requete...

times (be behind the ~) estar fuera de **onda**

times (move with the ~) ir con el **siglo**

times (nobody can take away the good ~ I've/we've had) ¡que me/nos quiten lo bailado! (▷ **bailar**)

tinker's damn/cuss (not to be worth a ~) no valer un **ardite/comino/pito**

tinker's damn/cuss (not to give/care a ~) no importar a alg. un **ardite**; [no] importar a alg. un **bledo/comino/higo/pepino/pimiento/pito/rábano**

tiny thing (over some ~) por un quítame allá esas **paja**s

tip (give a ~) dar el **soplo**

tip of one's tongue (have s.th. on the ~) tener algo en la **punta** de la lengua

tip of the iceberg la **punta** del iceberg

to tip off dar el **soplo**

tip-off el chivatazo

tip-off (give a ~) dar el **chivatazo**; dar el/un **soplo**

to be tipsy hacérsele a alg. **candelilla**s los ojos; estar a medios **pelo**s; estar entre **Pinto y Valdemoro**; estar **piripi**; estar entre dos **velas**

tiptoe (on ~) de **puntillas**

to tiptoe de **puntillas** (example)

tired (be dead ~) estar **muerto** [de cansancio]

tired (be dog-~) estar hecho una braga (▷ **bragas**); caerse de cansancio/sueño; estar/quedar hecho **cisco**; tener los **hueso**s molidos; estar hecho **migas/papilla/pedazo**s; estar hecho un **pingajo**; estar hecho **polvo/puré**; estar reventado (▷ **reventar**); estar hecho unos **zorros**

tired (be sick and ~ of s.o.) estar hasta las **ceja**s de alg.; estar hasta la **punta** de los pelos/del pelo de alg.

tired (be sick and ~ of s.th.) estar hasta las **ceja**s/el **coco**/[más allá de] la **coronilla** de algo; estar **frito** de algo; estar hasta el **gorro**/el **moño**/las narices (▷ **nariz**)/la **punta** de los pelos o del pelo/los **topes** de algo

to be **tired of the endless/long wait** estar cansado del **plantón**

tired out (get ~) calentarse la **cabeza**

tit (▷ **tits**)

tit for tat donde las dan, las toman (▷ **dar**)

tit for tat (give s.o. ~) no quedar a **deber** nada; pagar a alg. con/en la misma **moneda**; volver las **tornas** a alg.

to titivate [o.s.] emperejilar[se]/emperifollar[se]

titles (extra ~) **perejil**es

tits las **aldabas**; los **cántaros**/**globos**/limones (▷ **limón**); las marmellas

tits (big ~) la tetorra

tits (get on s.o.'s ~) darle por o romper las **bolas** a alg.; hinchar las **pelotas** a alg.; sacar a alg. de **quicio**

toady el/la lameplatos/lavacaras; el pelotillero; el/la quitamotas

to toady to s.o. lavar la **cara**/dar **coba**/hacer la **pelotilla** a alg.

tobacco (bad/cheap ~) la tagarnina

tod (all on one's ~) más solo que un **hongo**

today (don't put off till tomorrow what you can do ~) no dejes para **mañana** lo que puedes hacer hoy

to toe the line/mark bailar al **son** que le tocan a alg.

toes (keep s.o. on his ~) no dejar **respirar** a alg.

together (go ~) correr **parejas**/andar de pareja

together ([just] not to go ~) no pegar ni con **cola**; no **pegar**

to toil [and moil] remar

tolerant (be excessively ~) tener buenas **tragaderas**

Tom (every ~, Dick and Harry) todo **bicho** viviente; Cristo y la madre/todo Cristo; todo/cada **quisque**

tome (old ~) una antigualla

tomorrow (don't put off till ~ what you can do today) no dejes para **mañana** lo que puedes hacer hoy

tomorrow (spend money like there was no ~) como un **descosido** (example)

ton (by the ~/tons of) a **punta** pala

ton (weigh a ~) pesar algo lo **suyo**

ton of bricks (come down on s.o. like a ~) soltar la/una **andanada** a alg.; zurrar la **badana** a alg.; la bronca (example); dar una **calada** a alg.; soltar/decir cuatro **frescas** a alg.; hacer **papilla**/echar los **perros** a alg.

tongue la sinhueso

tongue (a still ~ makes a wise head) es de sabios el callar (▷ **el sabio**)

tongue (be a slip of the ~) irse de la **lengua**/írsele a alg. la lengua

tongue (have a vicious/wicked/sharp ~) ser un **alacrán**; tener una **lengua** viperina o de víbora/de serpiente/de escorpión/de hacha

tongue (have s.th. on the tip of one's ~) tener algo en la **punta** de la lengua

tongue (hold one's ~) morderse la **lengua**

tongue (loosen s.o.'s ~) desatar/soltar la **lengua** a alg.; subírsele algo (vino/etc.) a alg. a predicar (▷ **subirse**)

tongue (set [a lot of] ~s wagging) andar algo/alg. de **boca** en boca; ser **pasto** de algo

tongue (sharp/evil ~) la navaja

tongue (with one's ~ hanging out) con la **lengua** fuera

tongue-lashing (give s.o. a ~) soltar la/una **andanada** a alg.; zurrar la **badana**/dar una **calada**/echar una **peluca** a alg.

too (be [far/much] ~ + adj.) pecar de + adj.

too many (it's better to bring/have/etc. ~ than too few) pecar por **exceso** (example)

too much (be really ~) pasar de **castaño** oscuro; pelar la jeta

too much (it's better to bring/have/etc. ~ than too little) pecar por **exceso** (example)

too much (it's better to do ~ rather than too little) pecar por **exceso** (example)

too much (s.th. is ~ for s.o.) venir ancho algo a alg.

too much (talk ~) hablar por los **codos**; perderse por el **pico**

too much of a good thing (be [almost] ~) ser **miel** sobre hojuelas; traérselas (▷ **traer**)

too much of a good thing (you can have ~) bueno está lo bueno [pero no lo demasiado]

tooth (▷ fed up to the back teeth with s.o./s.th.)

tooth (an eye for an eye [and a ~ for a ~]) donde las dan, las toman (▷ **dar**); si haces **mal**, espera otro tal; ojo por ojo, diente por diente

tooth (be [a bit] long in the ~) estar alg. para el **arrastre**

tooth (be sick to the teeth of s.th.) estar hasta las **cejas**/el **coco**/[más allá de] la **coronilla** de algo; estar **frito** de algo; estar hasta el **gorro**/el **moño**/las narices (▷ **nariz**)/la **punta** de los pelos o del pelo/los **topes** de algo

tooth (by the skin of one's teeth) [por] el **canto** de un duro; por un **pelo**/los pelos

tooth (draw the teeth of s.th.) quitar **hierro** a algo

tooth (lie through one's teeth) con toda la **barba**; mentir por los **codos**; mentir más que hablar/que la Gaceta; ... que se las pela (▷ **pelar**); mentir más que un **sacamuelas**

tooth (show one's teeth) enseñar los **colmillos**; enseñar/mostrar las **uñas**

tooth (sink/get one's teeth into s.th.) hincar el diente a/en algo tooth and nail (fight ~ [to defend s.th.]) luchar a **brazo** partido; defender algo a **capa** y espada

tooth-puller el/la sacamuelas

top (blow one's ~) ponerse como un **basilisco**; exaltársele a alg. la **bilis**; subirse al **campanario**; salirse de sus **casillas**; ponerse hecho un **demonio**; hinchársele a alg. las narices (▷ **nariz**); subirse por las **pared**es/a la **parra**; fundírsele a alg. los **plomos**

top (come out on ~) llevarse la mejor **parte**

top (go over the ~) pasarse de **rosca**; tirar más allá del blanco

top (on ~ of all s.th. else happens) llover sobre mojado

top brass gente de alto **copete**

top dog el mandamás

top nob[s] un gran **bonete**; gente de alto **copete**; un **pez** gordo

top of the world (feel on ~) estar como **abeja** en flor; estar/sentirse como el **pez** en el agua

top speed (at ~) a toda **pastilla**; a todo **vapor**; a toda **vela**

top speed (go/drive at ~) hundir el **pedal**

toper el cuero; la espita/esponja

topic (he's/she's onto his/her favorite/pet ~ again) ha vuelto a la misma **canción/cantilena**

tops (be the ~) ser la **biblia**

tops (this is the ~!) ¡esto es la **oca**!

topsy-turvy **patas** arriba

to be topsy-turvy mezclar **berza**s con capachos; estar/andar **manga** por hombro

to torment s.o. poner a alg. en el **potro**

torrent (talk in a ~) hablar a borbotones/borbollones (▷ **borbotón/borbollón**); hablar a **chorros**

torrents (rain in ~) a **cántaro**s (example); llover a **chorros/cubos/mares/torrente**s

to be torture ser un **calvario**; ser pasar por las horcas caudinas (▷ **caudino**)

to toss and turn dar vueltas a la **almohada**

to toss off (masturbate) tocar la **campana**; cascársela (▷ **cascar**); machacársela (▷ **machacar**); hacerse una **paja**; pelársela (▷ **pelar**); hacer la **puñeta**; tocársela (▷ **tocar**); zumbársela (▷ **zumbar**)

to be totally dust-covered estar o ponerse **perdido** de algo

totem pole (be the low man on the ~) ser el último **mono**

touch (add/put the finishing ~[es] to s.th.) dar el último **golpe** a algo; dar el último/[los últimos] **toque**[s] a algo

touch (lose one's ~) perder los **libro**s/la **onda**

to touch on (it's best not to ~ that) peor es meneallo/mejor es no meneallo/más vale no meneallo (▷ **menear**)

to touch s.o. for money dar un **sablazo** a alg.

to touch s.o. on the raw llegar a o herir/tocar en lo más **vivo** a alg.

to touch s.th./s.o. (s.o. wouldn't ~ with a bargepole/ten-foot pole) no poder coger algo ni con **papel** de fumar; no poder coger algo/a alg. ni con **tenazas**

touch wood! ¡el **diablo** sea sordo! ¡lagarto, lagarto!

touched (be deeply ~ by s.th.) llegarle algo a alg. al **alma**

tough (act ~) darse **aire**s de valiente; hacerse el **hombre**

tough (be [really] ~: s.th.) tener [mucho] **tomate**; traérselas (▷ **traer**)

tough (things get a bit ~) batirse el **cobre**

tough assignment (be a ~) pinchar/dar en **hueso**

tough customer (be a/s.o. is a ~) ser de **armas** tomar; no quisiera partir **peras** con alg.

tough going (be ~) un **parto** difícil (example); traérselas (▷ **traer**)

tough guy el gallito

tough job un **parto** difícil/el parto de los montes

tough job (be a ~) un **parto** difícil (example); ser [un huevo] duro de **pelar**; traérselas (▷ **traer**)

tough mannish woman la sargentona

tough one (be a ~: person) tener **pelo**s en la lengua

tough one (be/face a ~) ser un **hueso** duro de roer; tocarle a alg. una **papeleta** difícil; ser [un huevo] duro de **pelar**; tener [mucho] **tomate**; traérselas (▷ **traer**)

tough time (have a ~ doing s.th.) verse **negro** para hacer algo

tough time (have a ~ [of it]) pasarlas moradas (▷ **morado**)/negras (▷ **negro**)

to be tough with s.o. tratar a alg. a **baquetazo** limpio

to toughen o.s. up criar **callo**s

towel (throw in the ~) dar con la **carga** en tierra/en el suelo o echarse con la carga; arrojar/tirar la **esponja**; echar la **soga** tras el caldero; arrojar/tirar la **toalla**; recoger **vela**s

town (go out on the ~) irse de/a **pico**s pardos

toy (be like a child with a new ~) alegrarse/estar como [un] **niño** con zapatos nuevos

trace (disappear/vanish without ~) desaparecer por [el] **escotillón**; hacerse **humo**

traces (kick over the ~) salirse de **madre**; sacar los **pie**s del plato/de las alforjas

track (keep to the beaten ~) seguir la **senda** trillada

track (not to want to accept/see that one is on the wrong ~) meter la cabeza en un **puchero**

tracks (make ~) pelar **gallo**

trade (s.o. was born to the ~) nació alg. mamando el oficio (▷ **nacer**) traitor un judas (▷ **Judas**)

traitor (turn ~) cambiar de/la **chaqueta**

trap (dust ~) el **nido** de polvo

trap (fall/walk into the ~) caer en el **garlito/lazo**; acudir al **paño/reclamo**; caer en la **red**

trap (get caught in one's own ~) ir por **lana** y volver esquilado/trasquilado

trap (mouth) la jeta; el pico

trap (shut one's ~) echar el **cierre**; achantar la **mui**; cerrar el **pico**

trashy weeklies la **prensa** amarilla o del corazón

to tread a path tirar por un camino

to tread in s.o.'s steps seguir los **pasos** de alg.

to tread very carefully/cautiously/warily andar con **pies** de plomo

treasure (person) la prenda

to treasure s.th. [as if it were gold or gold dust] guardar algo como **oro** en paño

treat (be a ~ for the ears) ser un regalo para los **oídos**

treat (be a ~ to see it) dar **gusto** verlo

treat (come on a ~/work a ~) a las mil **maravillas**; ir/marchar sobre **ruedas**

treat (she looks a ~) está para comérsela (▷ **comer**)

to treat s.o. harshly tratar a alg. a **baquetazo** limpio

to treat s.o. like dirt tratar a alg. a coces (▷ **coz**)/ a **patadas**/como a un **perro**/a **zapatazos**

to treat s.o. like royalty tratar/atender a alg. a **cuerpo** de rey

to treat s.o. very badly/rudely tratar a alg. a coces (▷ **coz**)/a **patadas**/a **zapatazos**

to treat s.o. with kid gloves guardar/tener a alg. entre algodones (▷ **algodón**); tratar a alg. con **guante** de seda

tree (bark up the wrong ~) tomar el **rábano** por las hojas

tree (go climb a ~!) ¡anda a **bañarte**!; ¡vete a freír **buñuelos/espárragos**!

tree (tell s.o. to go climb a ~) mandar a alg. a freír **buñuelos**/al **cuerno**/a freír **espárragos**/a hacer **gárgaras**

to tremble (begin to ~/start trembling) entrarle a alg. tembleques o un **tembleque**

to tremble all over/from head to foot temblarle a alg. las **carnes**; temblar como una hoja/un azogado/un flan

tremendous de los **buenos**; padre; de padre y muy señor mío (▷ **el padre**)

tremendous effort (make a ~) batir[se] el **cobre**

tremendous time (have a ~) divertirse **horrores**

tremendously (enjoy o.s. ~) divertirse la **mar**

trencherman (be a good ~) tener buen **saque**

to be trendy estar en la **onda**

trice (in a ~) en un decir **amén**/un **credo**/un **dos** por tres; en menos que canta un **gallo**

trick (know every ~ in the book) saber más que **Briján**; tener muchas **camándulas**/

carlancas; ser más **corrido** que un zorro viejo; **saber**las todas o muy largas

trick (not to miss a ~) no perder **ripio**

trick (play a dirty/nasty ~ on s.o.) hacer una faena/una mala **jugada** a alg.; jugar una mala **partida** a alg.; hacer una **perrada** a alg.; jugar una **pieza** a alg.; dar una **puñalada** trapera a alg.

to trick s.o. pegársela a alg. (▷ **pegar**)

tricks (be/get up to one's old/usual ~) hacer de las **suyas**

tricks (know a lot of ~) ser de muchas **vueltas**

tricky (be [very] ~) tener **bigote**/tres pares de bigotes

tricky (really ~ problem) de narices (▷ **nariz**) (example)

trifle la friolera; una **nube** de verano; nada entre dos **platos**; la quisquilla

trifle (over some ~) por un quítame allá esas **pajas**

trifles ([not] to stick at ~) [no] pararse en **pelillos**

trimmings **perejiles**

trimmings (with all the ~) con toda la **barba**; con todos sus **requisitos**

trip (drug-induced) el pedo

trip (drug-induced: be on a ~) estar/andar **pedo**; estar de **viaje**

trip (drug-induced: send s.o. on a ~) poner a alg. en **órbita**

triteness blanco y en botella, leche

to triumph llevarse la **gala/palma**

triviality blanco y en botella, leche; la quisquilla

trooper (swear like a ~) blasfemar/jurar como un **carretero**

trot (for cheating in exam) la chuleta

trot (keep s.o. on the ~) no dejar criar **moho** a alg.

trots (diarrhea) la cagalera; las seguidillas

trouble (ask for ~) encomendar las **ovejas** al lobo; buscar cinco/tres **pies** al gato

trouble (be in ~ with s.o.) vérselas con alg. (▷ **ver**)

trouble (cause s.o. [a lot of] ~) amargar el **caldo** a alg.; partir a alg. por el **eje**

trouble (cause/give s.o. ~ in spades/no end of ~) a **punta** pala (example)

trouble (get o.s. into ~) meterse en un **avispero**

trouble (go to great ~ to get s.th.) sacar algo de debajo de la **tierra**

trouble (have nothing but ~) no ganar para **sustos**

trouble (keep one's ~s to o.s.) andarle/irle a alg. la **procesión** por dentro

trouble (keep out of ~) quitarse de **ruidos**

trouble (look for ~) la bronca/camorra (examples); buscar cinco/tres **pies** al gato

trouble (make/stir up ~) armar [un] **cisco**; alborotar el **cotarro** trouble (strike right at the root of the ~) cortar por lo **sano**

trouble (take your ~s elsewhere!) irse con la **música** a otra parte (example)

trouble (there's will be ~) habrá **función**

trouble (there's ~ brewing) oler a **chamusquina**

troubled waters (fish in ~) pescar al **candil**; pescar en aguas turbias; pescar en **río** revuelto

troubled waters (there's good fishing in ~) a **río** revuelto, ganancia de pescadores

trouble-free digs el picadero

troublemaker una buena **pieza**

trousers (be all mouth [and no ~]) cacarear y no poner huevos; írsele a alg. la **fuerza** por la boca

trousers (catch s.o. with his ~ down) pillar a alg. en **bolas/bragas**

trousers (wear the ~) cortar el **bacalao**; llevar la **batuta**; llevar/ponerse los calzones (▷ **calzón**); ser el amo del o dirigir el **cotarro**; llevar los pantalones (▷ **pantalón**)/la **voz** cantante

truant (play ~) **fumar**se algo; hacer **novillos/ rabona**

true leader (be a ~) con toda la **barba**

true-blue por los cuatro **costados**

truism blanco y en botella, leche

trump (hold all the ~s) llevar/tener [todas] las de **ganar**; tener todos los **triunfos** [en la mano]

trump card (play one's ~) echar un **triunfo**

trumpet (blow one's own ~) no necesitar **abuela**; darse **bombo**; echarse/tirarse **flores**

trumpeted (much-~) cacarear algo (example)

trust (put your ~ in God and keep your powder dry) a **Dios** rogando y con el mazo dando

trust (win s.o.'s ~) **ganar**se la confianza de alg.

to trust (not to even ~ one's own shadow) desconfiar hasta de su **sombra**

trusting to luck a la buena de Dios (▷ **bueno**); a la **gracia** de Dios

trustworthy (not to be ~) no ser alg. **trigo** limpio

truth (at the moment of ~) a la **hora** de la verdad

truth (children and fools tell the ~) los **niño**s y los locos dicen las verdades

truth (speak the gospel ~) lo que dice alg. es el **evangelio**

truth (there's not a grain of ~ in this) ni **sombra** de

truth (what s.o. says is accepted/taken as gospel ~) lo que dice alg. es el **evangelio**

truths (tell [a lot of] home ~) sacar los **trapo**s [sucios] a relucir

truths (tell s.o. a few home ~) cantar las cuarenta a alg.; dar a alg. con los **ochos** y los nueves; decirle a alg. cuatro **verdad**es/las verdades del barquero

tub of lard (be a ~) estar hecho una **botija**; estar como una **vaca**

tube ([boob] ~: TV) la **caja** boba/idiota/tonta

to tuck in or tuck it away comer/mascar a dos **carrillos**; ponerse como el chico del **esquilador**; comer como una **lima**

tug-of-war el tira y afloja

to tumble (the words come tumbling out) hablar a borbotones/borbollones (▷ **borbotón/ borbollón**)

tune (call the ~) cortar el **bacalao**; llevar la **batuta**; llevar o ponerse los calzones (▷ **calzón**); ser el amo del o dirigir el **cotarro**; llevar la **voz** cantante

tune (dance to s.o.'s ~) llevar/seguir la **corriente** a alg.; bailar al compás de la **música** de alg.

tunnel (there is light at the end of the ~) hay **luz** al final del túnel

tunnel vision (suffer from ~) ver las cosas con **anteojeras**

turd (shit) la **ñoña/ñorda**

turkey (cold ~) el mono

turkey (talk ~ [with s.o.]) **cantar**las claras [a alg.]

turn (be one's ~) estar de **tanda**

to turn (make s.o.'s stomach ~) revolver el **estómago**/las **tripa**s a alg.

to turn (not to know which way to ~) no saber a qué **santo** encomendarse

to turn a deaf ear [to s.th.] escuchar/oír como quien oye **llover**; hacer/prestar **oídos** sordos [a algo]

to turn out [very] differently traspintarse

to turn out well salir algo **corriente** y moliente

to turn over a new leaf doblar/volver la **hoja**; hacer **libro** nuevo

to turn s.o.'s head hacer perder el **seso** a alg.

to turn s.o.'s stomach revolver el **estómago**/las **tripa**s a alg.

to turn things to one's advantage llevar el **agua** a su molino

to turn up (a bad penny always turns up) mala **hierba** nunca muere

to turn up ([suddenly] ~) aparecer por [el] **escotillón**; asomar las narices (▷ **nariz**)

to turn up (whatever turns up) salga lo que salga/ saliere (▷ **salir**)

to turn up at recalar en

turncoat (be a ~) cambiar de/la **chaqueta**

turned-up nose la nariz respingona (▷ **respingón**)

twat (stupid person) el/la gilipollas

twat (vagina) la almeja; el bacalao/beo/bollo/ chocho/conejo/coño/higo; la raja/rana/ seta

twerp el/la gilipollas

to twig it [at once] captar la **onda**; cazarlas/ cogerlas/pescarlas al **vuelo**

to twig s.th. (understand) calzar/diquelar algo

twinkling (in the ~ of an eye) en menos que canta un **gallo**; en un abrir y cerrar de **ojos**

to twist (not to let s.o. ~ one's arm) no dar su **brazo** a torcer

to twist s.o. [a]round one's little finger meterse a alg. en el **bolsillo**; llevar a alg. de un **cabello**

to twist things (truth/facts) hacer de lo **blanco** negro/volver en blanco lo negro

twit un [pedazo de] **alcornoque/atún**; un[a] **cabeza** de corcho; una calabaza; un alma de **cántaro**; un ceporro/melón/merluzo; un **palomino** atontado; un pavipollo/percebe

two (it's just a question of putting ~ and ~ together) por el **hilo** se saca el ovillo

two (put ~ and ~ together) atar/unir **cabos**

to two-time one's husband/etc. echar una **cana** al aire; irse de/a **picos** pardos

type (be a churchy ~) **comerse** los santos

type (be a nasty ~) ser un **pájaro** de cuenta

type (cheerful ~) el jacarero

type (churchy ~) la beata

type (he's/she's not my ~) no es **santo** de mi devoción

type (not to be his/etc. ~) no ser su/etc. **tipo**

type (smooth ~) el mátalas callando

typing error (make a ~) hacer una **mosca**

typo (make a ~) hacer una **mosca**

U

ugly (be as ~ as sin/hell or incredibly ~) ser un **aborto** del diablo; ser el acabóse de feo (▷ **acabar**); ser más feo que **Carracuca**; ser más **feo** que Picio/que el pecado/etc.; a más no **poder**; dar un **susto** al miedo

ugly (get ~) ponerse algo **feo**

ugly face la carantoña

ugly mug (face) la carantoña

ultimate (be the ~) ser el no va más (▷ **ir**)

ultrashort requete...

to be unbearable ser de mala **digestión**

unbearable heat traérselas (▷ **traer**)

to unbosom o.s. to s.o. descubrir/abrir el **pecho** a alg.

uncalled-for (say s.th. that is quite ~) hablar de/mentar/nombrar la **soga** en casa del ahorcado

to be uncertain estar en **tela** de juicio

uncle la **capa** [de ladrones]

uncle (cry/say ~) darse por vencido (▷ **vencer**)

uncommitted (remain ~) ver los toros desde la **barrera**

uncommunicative (be very ~) no soltar **prenda**

to uncover s.th. descorrer el **velo** sobre algo

undauntedly a **pecho** descubierto

to be undecided estar entre dos **aguas**; no saber a qué **carta** quedarse; nadar entre dos aguas; ni ir ni **venir**

undeniable impepinable

to be under discussion estar sobre el **tapete**

underhand way (in an ~) bajo **cuerda**/por debajo de cuerda

to undermine s.o.'s position minar el **terreno** a alg.

to understand captar la **onda**

to understand (have a hard job getting s.o. to ~ s.th.) meter algo a alg. con **cuchara**

to understand (not to ~ a word [of it]) no entender ni **papa/patata**

to understand (now I ~!) ¡acabáramos! (▷ **acabar**)

to understand (pretend not to ~) hacerse el **sueco**

to understand (s.o. [just] doesn't/can't ~) no caberle a alg. en la **cabeza**

to understand s.th. calzar algo

underwear (change one's mind more often than one changes one's ~) bailar a cualquier **son**; ser un[a] **veleta**

undies (in one's ~) en **paños** menores

undistinguished sin **pena** ni gloria

uneasy (feel very ~) estar/sentirse como **gallina** en corral ajeno

unexpected chance/opportunity el **cabe** de pala

unexpectedly a las **primeras** de cambio

unfair world (it's an ~) Dios da pan a quien no tiene dientes

to be unfaithful [to s.o.] echar una **cana** al aire; meter/poner [los] **cuernos** a alg.; jugársela (▷ **jugar**); pegársela a alg. (▷ **pegar**); irse de/a **picos** pardos

uninhibitedly (quite ~) como **Pedro** por/en su casa

universe (center of the ~) el **ombligo** del mundo

to unload s.th. on [to] s.o. endiñar/endosar algo a alg.; cargar el **mochuelo** a alg.

to be unlucky tener mala **pata/sombra**

unlucky (s.o. was born ~) nació alg. de cabeza (▷ **nacer**)

unlucky at cards, lucky in love desgraciado en el **juego**, afortunado en amores/de malas en el juego, de buenas en amores

unlucky patch (go through a ~) pasarlas negras (▷ **negro**)

unlucky person el/la malapata

unlucky person (be an ~) nació alg. de cabeza (▷ **nacer**)

to unmask s.o. quitarle la **careta/máscara** a alg.

unnoticed (come and go almost ~) sin **pena** ni gloria (example)

unperturbed (remain/be totally ~) quedarse/estar tan **fresco**

unpleasant (a joke can easily turn into s.th. ~) las **cañas** se vuelven lanzas

unpleasant (get ~) ponerse algo **feo**

unpleasant character (be an ~) ser un **pájaro** de cuenta; tener mala **sombra**

unpleasant surprise (have a very ~) quedarse **frío**

to be unreliable estar prendido con **alfiler**es

unreliable person el/la cantamañanas

unresolvable arguments/discussions (protracted and ~) discusiones bizantinas (▷ **bizantino**)

unresolved (the situation is [still] ~) la **pelota** está/sigue en el tejado

unripe melon el pepino

unruly (be very ~) ser de la **piel** del diablo

unscathed (get out/emerge ~) caer de **pies**

unscathed (nobody comes through or escapes ~) no dejar/quedar **títere** con cabeza (examples)

unscrupulously sin pararse en **barras**

unshakable de **cal** y canto

to be unspeakable no tener **nombre**

unvarnished sin **tapujos**

to unveil s.th. descorrer el **velo** sobre algo

unwillingly (do s.th. ~) hacer algo a **remolque**

to be utterly obstinate a más no **poder**

up (be well ~) estar en **pinganitos**

to be **up against it** estar contra/en las **cuerdas**
to be **up against s.o.** habérselas con alg. (▷ **haber**)
to be **up for discussion** estar sobre el **tapete**
up in (be well ~ s.th.) ser del **paño**
up to (know/you can see what s.o. is ~) conocerle/
verle a alg. el **juego**; se le ve el **plumero** a
alg.
up to (not to be ~ s.th.) venir ancho algo a alg.
up to (not to be ~ that [sort of thing] any more) ya
no estar para esos **trotes**
to be **up to date** estar en la **onda**
to be **up to no good** hacer de las **suyas**
to be **up to one's old/usual tricks** hacer de las
suyas
to **up stakes/sticks** hacer la **maleta**; liar el **petate**
upbringing (s.o.'s manners betray/reveal a bad ~)
saber a la **pega**
uphill struggle (be an/[a real] ~ [+ gerund])
hacérsele algo a alg. [muy] **cuesta** arriba
[+ infinitivo]; vérselas negras con algo
(▷ **negro**)
upper class[es] (belong to the ~) codearse con los
de **arriba**
upper crust gente gorda
upper crust (belong to the ~) codearse con los de
arriba
upper-class people gente gorda
upper-crust people (rub shoulders or hobnob with
~) codearse con los de **arriba**
upright hecho y derecho
upright (bolt ~) tieso como un ajo; derecho
como una **vela**
upset (get all ~ over nothing) ahogarse en un
vaso de agua
upset (it's nothing to get ~ about) no es tan feo el
diablo como le pintan (▷ **pintar**)

upset stomach (get an ~) cortarse la **digestión**
to **upset s.o.** sentarle algo a alg. como un **tiro**
to **upset s.o.'s stomach** sentarle algo a alg. como
un **tiro**
upside down **patas** arriba
to **upstage s.o.** hacer **sombra** a alg.
uptake (be slow on the ~) calzar poco; ser corto
de **entendederas**/tener malas
entendederas
uptake (be [very] quick on the ~) cazarlas/
cogerlas/pescarlas al **vuelo**
urchin el granuja
urge (I felt a terrible ~ to cry) me entraban unas
ganas locas de llorar
use (for everyday ~) para todo **trote**
use (it's no ~ crying over spilt milk) lo **hecho**,
hecho está/a lo hecho, pecho; agua
pasada no mueve molino
use (the ~ of contacts to obtain advantages/favors)
el enchufismo
to **use s.th. up quickly** no dejar criar **moho** a algo
to be **useless** (s.o.) ser alg. una **calamidad**; ser
[como o lo mismo que] la **carabina** de
Ambrosio; ser un **cero** a la izquierda; no
servir a **Dios** ni al diablo
to be **useless** (s.th.) no ser más que **papel**
mojado
useless things (do ~) cazar **moscas**
utmost (do one's ~) andar/bailar de **coronilla**;
emplearse a **fondo**; echar el **resto**;
volcarse
utter rematado; solemne
to **utter** (not to ~ a word) no **chistar**
to be **utterly obstinate** a más no **poder**

V

vacantly (be gazing ~ at the ceiling) estar contando las **viga**s

vacantly (be staring ~) estar mirando a las **musarañas**

vagina (beaver; cunt; fanny; pussy; twat) la almeja; el bacalao/beo/bollo/chocho/ conejo/coño/higo; la raja/rana/seta

vague idea (only have a ~) oír **campana**s y no saber dónde (example)

vain (labor in ~) coger **agua** en cesto; azotar el **aire**; machacar en hierro frío; arar en el **mar**

vain (wait in ~) esperar sentado

to vamoose **largar**se

to vanish hacerse **noche**

to vanish into thin air desaparecer por [el] **escotillón**; hacerse **humo**

to vanish off the face of the earth tragarse la **tierra** a alg.

to vanish without trace hacerse **humo**

variety is the spice of life entre **col** y col, lechuga; en la variedad está el **gusto**; pan con pan, comida de tontos

vast amount una nube

vaunted (much-~) cacarear algo (example)

VD (have ~) estar picado de la **tarántula**

vegetable (live like a ~) vegetar

to vegetate (person) vegetar

veil (draw a ~ over s.th.) correr/echar un **velo** sobre algo

vengeance (vow ~ against s.o.) jurárselas a alg. (▷ **jurar**)

to vent one's anger/fury/spleen on s.o. descargar la **bilis** en/contra alg.; **cebar**se en alg.

to venture (nothing ~d, nothing gained) quien no se arriesga no pasa la **mar**

verbal exchange dimes y diretes

verbiage la prosa

to verge on s.th. rozar [con] algo

verse (with chapter and ~) con [todos sus] **pelos** y señales

very same el mismo que viste y calza (▷ **vestir**)

very [well] de narices (▷ **nariz**)

vices are born of idleness el **ocio**/la **ociosidad** es la madre de todos los vicios; los **vicio**s son los hijos del ocio

victory (sweets of ~) las **miel**es del triunfo

view (a bird's-eye ~ of) a **vista** de pájaro

view (take a gloomy ~ of everything) verlo todo con **cristal** ahumado

vigor (be full of/bursting with [youthful] ~) bullirle a alg. la **sangre** en las venas

villain una buena **pieza**

violence (rob s.o. of s.th. with ~) robar algo a alg. a **mano** airada

violence (with great ~) a **fuego** y hierro/sangre

violin (scrape/saw away at the ~) rascar el violín

viper (cherish a ~ in one's bosom) criar la **víbora** en el seno

VIPs gente de alto **copete**

virago una mujer de **arma**s tomar; la cascarrabias/tarasca

virtue (make a ~ of necessity) sacar **fuerza**s de flaqueza; hacer de la **necesidad** virtud; hacer de **tripas** corazón

vision (suffer from tunnel ~) ver las cosas con **anteojeras**

visit (s.o. must just [go and] pay a ~: go to the toilet) echar una **carta** al correo (example); tener que ir a un **sitio**

vodka (be as clear as ~) estar más claro que el **agua**

voice (be a ~ crying in the wilderness) clamar en el desierto; dar **música** a un sordo; predicar en el desierto

voice (have an excellent singing ~) tener una **garganta** de oro

voice (scream/shout at the top of one's ~) como un **descosido** (example); a más no **poder**

voice of gold (have a ~) tener una **garganta** de oro

volcano (be sitting on top of a ~) andar/verse en los **cuerno**s del toro

volley (unleash a ~ of insults at s.o.) soltar una **andanada** de insultos a alg.

to vomit cambiar la **peseta**

vote of confidence (propose a ~) plantear la cuestión de **gabinete**

to vow vengeance against s.o. jurárselas a alg. (▷ **jurar**)

W

wag el jacarero

to wag (set [a lot of] tongues ~ging) andar algo/
alg. de **boca** en boca; ser **pasto** de algo

wagon (go on the [water] ~) **quitar**se del alcohol

wait (be in for a long ~/have got a long ~ coming)
esperar sentado (example)

wait (be tired of the endless/long ~) estar cansado
del **plantón**

to wait (be just what s.o. is ~ing for) ser **pasto** de
algo

to wait (just you ~!) ¡[ya] me las pagarás!
(▷ **pagar**)

to wait (keep s.o. ~ing) dar **perro** a alg.

to wait (keep s.o. ~ing [for] an excessively/unduly
long time) dar **poste** a alg.

to wait (s.o. can hardly ~) no caérsele a alg. el
pan

to wait and see (]let's] ~!) ¡paciencia y barajar!

to wait and/to see which way the cat jumps/the
cookie crumbles/the wind is blowing esperar
a ver de qué lado caen las **peras**/por
dónde van los **tiros**

to wait till the cows come home esperar sentado

waiting gets you down quien espera, desespera
(▷ **esperar**)

to be waiting in vain esperar sentado

to walk ir/venir a golpe de **alpargata**/en el
caballo de San Francisco/a golpe de
calcetín/en el **coche** de San Francisco o
de San Fernando

to walk (be so old s.o. can hardly ~) caerse de
viejo

to walk off with s.th. hacer **noche** de algo;
pringarse algo

to walk the streets hacer la **calle**; ser del **oficio**;
ser una **peripatética**

walking antique una antigualla

walking encyclopedia (be a ~) saber más que
Lepe

walking zero (be a ~) ser un **cero** a la izquierda/
un don **Nadie**

walkover (it won't be a ~) no va a ser un **paseo**

wall (▷ walls)

wall (drive s.o. up the ~) dar con la **cabeza** en las
paredes; hacer a alg. subirse por las
paredes; ser [como] para subirse por las
paredes; hacer la santísima a alg.
(▷ **santísimo**)

wall (go up the ~) subirse al **campanario**/por las
paredes/a la **parra**

wall (put him/etc. up against the ~ [and shoot him/
etc.]!) ¡al **paredón** con él/etc.!

wall (put s.o. up against a ~) mandar a alg. al
paredón

wall (talk to a brick ~) ladrar a la **luna**; hablar a
la **pared**

wall (the weakest goes to the ~) la **cuerda** se
rompe siempre por lo más delgado

wallet la chicharra; el cuero

wallflower (be a ~) comer **pavo**

wallop (give s.o. a ~) pegar una **torta** a alg.

walloping (give s.o. a ~) dar [una] **soba** a alg.

walls (within one's own four ~) entre sus cuatro
paredes

walls have ears las **pared**es oyen

walls have ears (be careful what you say, ~!) ¡hay
ropa tendida!

wampum (money) el barro; el **calé** o calés; la
china; [los] **cuartos**; la guita/lana/
manteca; [los] monises; la mosca; [los]
nipos; el parné; la pasta; el pisto; la tela;
el trigo

to wander from the point/subject irse por los
cerros de Úbeda; **salir**se del tema

to wangle o.s. a job/etc. enchufarse

to wangle s.th. teclear algo

wank (have a ~) tocar la **campana**; cascársela
(▷ **cascar**); machacársela (▷ **machacar**);
hacerse una **paja**; pelársela (▷ **pelar**);
hacer la **puñeta**; tocársela (▷ **tocar**);
zumbársela (▷ **zumbar**)

to wank tocar la **campana**; cascársela
(▷ **cascar**); machacársela (▷ **machacar**);
hacerse una **paja**; pelársela (▷ **pelar**);
hacer la **puñeta**; tocársela (▷ **tocar**);
zumbársela (▷ **zumbar**)

wanker el/la gilipollas

to want (find just what one ~ed) encontrar/hallar
la **horma** de su zapato

to want (just the way you ~ it to) a pedir de **boca**

to want (s.o. doesn't know what he ~s) hoy le da a
alg. por **pitos** y mañana por flautas

warily (go about it or proceed/tread very ~) andar
con **pies** de plomo

warning (without [any] ~) sin decir **agua** va; de
buenas a primeras (▷ **bueno**)

wary (be [extremely] ~) estar con/tener la
mosca detrás de la oreja; estar con cien
ojos

to wash (▷ dirty linen)

to wash (excuse/etc.) colar

to wash (s.th. doesn't ~ with s.o.) no tirar algo a
alg.

to wash down a meal with wine regar una comida
con vino

to wash one's hands of it lavarse las **manos** [en inocencia]; sacudirse las **pulga**s

to be washed out (exhausted) estar hecho una braga (▷ **braga**s); estar/quedar hecho **cisco**; tener los **hueso**s molidos; estar hecho **migas/papilla/pedazos**; estar hecho un **pingajo**; estar hecho **polvo/puré**; estar reventado (▷ **reventar**); estar hecho unos **zorros**

washout el/la ablandabrevas/**berza**s

washout (be a [complete] ~) ser alg. una **calamidad**; ser un **cero** a la izquierda/un **pierna**s; ser alg./algo **rana**

washout (turn out to be a ~) salir alg./algo **rana**

waste (lay s.th. ~) a **fuego** y hierro/sangre

waste of time (be a ~) azotar el **aire**; machacar en hierro frío; arar en el **mar**

to waste (not to ~ any time) no andarse con **requilorios**

to waste one's breath ladrar a la **luna**; gastar **saliva**

to waste one's time coger **agua** en cesto; azotar el **aire**; matar la **araña**; machacar en hierro frío; arar en el **mar**; estar tocando el **tambor**

to waste one's [time and] energy gastar la **pólvora** en salvas

to waste one's time on little things ([not] to ~) [no] pararse en **pelillos**

to waste s.o. freír a alg.; dejar **frito** a alg.; tumbar a alg.

wasted effort (be a ~) azotar el **aire**; machacar en hierro frío; arar en el **mar**

watch ([fob] ~) la patata

to watch (be as exciting as ~ing [the] paint dry) ser algo un **plomo**; a más no **poder**

watch out! ¡oído al parche!

to watch out [for] estar/andar sobre los **estribos**; estar en **guardia** [contra]; guardar las **vuelta**s

to watch [out for] (you've got to ~ s.o.) ser de **armas** tomar

to watch [out for] (you've got to ~ that guy) ese tío es de **abrigo**

to watch with one's arms crossed estar/quedarse con los **brazo**s cruzados

watched kettle/pot (a ~ never boils) quien espera, desespera (▷ **esperar**)

water (▷ **water**s)

water (get into deep ~) meterse en **hondura**s

water (keep one's head above ~) mantenerse a **flote**; ir tirando (▷ **tirar**)

water (take to s.th. like a duck to ~) encontrarse en seguida en su **elemento**

water level (at ~) a **flor** de (example)

water off a duck's back (be [like] or run off s.o. like ~) escuchar/oír como quien oye **llover** (example)

to be water under the bridge ser **agua** pasada

water under the bridge (a lot of water has flowed under the bridge [since then]) ha corrido/pasado mucha **agua** bajo el puente; ha llovido mucho desde entonces (▷ **llover**)

water wagon (go on the ~) quitarse del alcohol

to water (make s.o.'s mouth ~) hacérsele a alg. la boca **agua**; poner los **diente**s largos a alg.

to water [down] the wine bautizar/cristianizar el **vino**

Waterloo (meet one's ~) llegarle a alg. su **San Martín**

waters (cast one's bread [up]on the ~) hacer [el] **bien** sin mirar a quién

waters (fish in troubled ~) pescar al **candil**; pescar en aguas turbias; pescar en **río** revuelto

waters (still ~ run deep) del **agua** mansa líbreme Dios que de la brava me libro yo; por fuera no rompe un **plato**, pero tiene la música por dentro; la **procesión** va por dentro

waters (there's good fishing in troubled ~) a **río** revuelto, ganancia de pescadores

waves (be at the mercy of/a plaything of the ~) ser un **juguete** de las olas

wax (be utterly fed up with the whole ball of ~) estar hasta [más allá de] la **coronilla** de algo (example)

wax (buy it, the whole ball of ~) tragar[se]las como puños (example)

way (find a ~) arreglárselas (▷ **arreglar**); componérselas (▷ **componer**)

way (get one's [own] ~) salirse con la **suya**

way (get s.o. in the family ~) dejar a alg. con el **paquete**; hacer una **tripa** a alg.

way (get s.th. out of the ~) quitar algo de en medio

way (get s.th. the hard ~) ganar[se] algo a **pulso**

way (give ~) **revenir**se

way (go about s.th. the wrong ~) asir algo por el **rabo**

way (go one's own ~) sacar los **pie**s del plato/de las alforjas; hacer **rancho** aparte

way (go out of one's ~) **volcar**se

way (have [got] a ~ with s.o.) tener [mucha] **mano** izquierda con alg.

way (have got half out of the ~) pasar el **ecuador**

way (have one's [own] ~ [at all costs]) salirse con la **suya**; hacer su santa voluntad (▷ **santo**)

way (in a bad ~) mal **parado**

way (in an underhand ~) bajo **cuerda**/por debajo de cuerda

way (just the ~ you want it to) a pedir de **boca**

way (know one's ~ around) entender/conocer la **aguja** de marear

way (know which ~ the cat jumps/the cookie crumbles/the wind is blowing) saber de qué lado caen las **pera**s/por dónde van los **tiros** way (learn the hard ~) escarmentar

way (look the other ~/turn one's head the other ~) hacer la vista gorda (▷ **gordo**)

way (no ~!) ¡ni en **coplas**!; ¡no faltaba/faltaría más! (▷ **faltar**); ¡ni **hablar**!; ¡**naranjas**! ¡**naranjas** chinas! ¡**naranjas** de la China!; ¡narices! (▷ **nariz**); ¡ni **pensarlo**!; ¡ni por **soñación**!; ¡ni **soñarlo**!; ¡no hay tu **tía**!

way (not to know which ~ to turn) no saber a qué **santo** encomendarse

way (not to let anything get in one's ~) no ponérsele a alg. nada por **delante**

way (pave the ~ for s.o./s.th.) preparar el **terreno** a alg./algo

way (rub s.o. up the wrong ~) sacar a alg. de **quicio**

way (take the easiest ~ out) echar/tirar por el **atajo**

way (tell s.o./try telling s.o./try to get it across to s.o. every ~ imaginable or every ~ one can think of) decírselo a alg. en todos los **tonos**

way (that's the ~ I am) **gastar**las

way (that's the ~ it is) eso o la cosa no tiene vuelta de **hoja**; impepinable (example); no hay que darle **vueltas**

way (that's the ~ the ball bounces/the cookie crumbles) así es la **vida**

way (there are no two ~s about it) son **habas** contadas; eso o la cosa no tiene vuelta de **hoja**; no hay que darle **vueltas**

way (there's more than one ~ to skin a cat) hay muchas maneras de matar **pulgas**

way (there's no other ~/no ~ around it) no hay más **cáscaras**/[más] **remedio**

way ([wait and/to] see which ~ the cat jumps/the cookie crumbles/the wind is blowing) [esperar a] ver de qué lado caen las **peras**/por dónde van los **tiros**

way (where there's a will, there's a ~) donde hay **gana**, hay maña; querer es poder

to be way out el jaleo (example)

ways (want to have it both ~) querer ir por **atún** y a ver al duque; querer **nadar** y guardar la ropa; encender una **vela** a San Miguel/a Dios y otra al diablo

weak (be very ~) estar hecho una **pavesa**

weak point/spot el **punto** flaco

weak point[s]/spot[s] (know s.o.'s ~) saber de qué **pie** cojea alg.

the weakest goes to the wall la **cuerda** se rompe siempre por lo más delgado

weakling (be a ~) ser un **blandengue**

weakness (politeness doesn't have to be a sign of ~) lo **cortés** no quita lo valiente

weakness[es] (know s.o.'s ~) saber de qué **pie** cojea alg.

wealthy (get ~) **redondear**se

to wear away (constant dripping wears away a stone) gota a gota se llena la bota

to wear out (▷ **worn out**)

to wear s.o. out hacer **polvo** a alg.

weather (be brass monkey ~) hacer un frío que pela (▷ **pelar**); de **perros**

weather (be under the ~) no estar en su **peso**

weather (the ~'s foul/lousy/terrible) de **perros**

weathercock (be a ~) dar una de **cal** y otra de arena; bailar a cualquier **son**; ser un[a] **veleta**

to weave about hacer **caracoles**

wedding (have a shotgun ~) casarse de **penalty**

weed (bad/cheap tobacco) la tagarnina

weed (marijuana) el chocolate/ful; la hierba/mandanga/mierda; el tate; la yerba

weeds (ill ~ grow apace) mala **hierba** nunca muere

week (knock s.o. into the middle of next ~) señor

weekend (take a long ~) hacer **puente**

weeklies (trashy ~) la **prensa** amarilla o del corazón

weeny el pajarito

to weep (be enough to make you ~) ser una triste **gracia**

to weep bitterly llorar como una **Magdalena**

weepy face (make a ~) hacer **pucheros**

to weigh a ton pesar algo lo **suyo**

weight (be worth one's/its ~ in gold) valer alg./algo su peso en **oro** o valer algo tanto oro como pesa; valer alg. un **Perú/Potosí**

weight (lose ~) perder **carnes**

weight (put on ~) echar **panza/tripa**

welcome (overstay one's ~) calentar el **asiento**/pegársele a alg. el asiento

welcome (s.th. pleasant is always ~) a nadie le amarga un **dulce**

welcome (you're ~!) ¡no faltaba/faltaría más! (▷ **faltar**)

to be welcomed with open arms tener todas las **puertas** abiertas

well como **Dios** manda

well (come off/do [very] ~) pescar una buena **breva**

well (come out of s.th. ~) salir bien librado de algo (▷ **librar**)

well (extremely/jolly/very/wonderfully ~) a las mil **maravillas**; de narices (▷ **nariz**); de **perlas**; de **rechupete**; requete...

well (go extremely/very/wonderfully ~) ir que chuta (▷ **chutar**); estar como un **dado**; de **rechupete**

well (go off ~) pitar

well (turn out ~) salir algo **corriente** y moliente

well (work ~) pitar

well enough (leave ~ alone) bueno está lo bueno [pero no lo demasiado]

to be well heeled estar **forrado**; tener el **riñón** bien cubierto well off (be ~) tener su/un buen **pasar**

well stacked (not to be exactly ~) ser de **Castellón de la Plana**; ser lisa (▷ **liso**)

to be well up estar en **pinganitos**

well-heeled people gente de pelo/pelusa

to be well-placed socially estar en **pinganitos**

well-to-do people gente de pelo/pelusa

wet (be dripping/soaking/sopping ~) estar calado/mojado hasta los **huesos**; estar hecho un **pato**/una **sopa**; estar mojado hasta los **tuétanos**

wet (get dripping/soaking ~) mojarse hasta el **alma**/los **huesos**

wet behind the ears (be still ~) llevar todavía el **cascarón** pegado al culo; estar aún con la **leche** en los labios; caerse de un **nido**

wet blanket (be a ~) aguar la **fiesta**

to be wet through estar calado/mojado hasta los **huesos**; estar hecho un **pato**; estar mojado hasta los **tuétanos**

wet through (get ~) mojarse hasta el **alma**/los **huesos**

to wet one's whistle mojarse el **garguero**; mojar/refrescar el **gaznate**

to wet o.s. laughing descojonarse; **mear**se [de risa]

to be whacked (exhausted) estar hecho una braga (▷ **bragas**); estar/quedar hecho **cisco**; tener los **huesos** molidos; estar hecho **migas/papilla/pedazos**; estar hecho un **pingajo**; estar hecho **polvo/puré**; estar reventado (▷ **reventar**); estar hecho unos **zorros**

whacking great car el cochazo

whale (set/throw a sprat to catch a ~) meter **aguja** para sacar reja; dar un **gallo** para recibir un caballo

whale of a time (have a ~) divertirse la **mar**; pasarlo **pipa**

what not (and ~) y qué sé yo (▷ **saber**)

what's what (know ~) saber cuántas son **cinco**; conocer el **paño**

what's what (know ~ [where s.o. is concerned]) tener [mucha] **mano** izquierda [con alg.]

what's what (tell s.o. ~) decir a alg. cuántas son **cinco**

What's-his-name (Mr. ~) el señor no sé cuántos (▷ **saber**)

wheat (separate the ~ from the chaff) apartar/separar el **grano** de la paja; apartar las **oveja**s de los cabritos

wheel (be a big ~) tener muchas **campanillas**; ser un **pájaro** gordo

wheel (be/feel like a fifth ~) sentirse de **carabina**; hacer tanta falta como los **perros** en misa/ser como perro en misa

wheel (big ~[s]) un gran **bonete**; gente gorda; un **pez** gordo

wheel (break a butterfly on the ~) matar **moscas** a cañonazos

wheel (put a spoke in s.o.'s ~) meter un **bastón/palo** en la rueda o bastones/palos en las ruedas de alg.; poner **trabas** a alg.

wheel (run on oiled ~s) ir/marchar sobre **ruedas**

wheeler dealing la componenda

wheeling and dealing la componenda

where to get off (tell s.o. ~) mandar a alg. a hacer **gárgaras**

where to go (tell s.o. ~) mandar a alg. a freír **buñuelos**/al **cuerno**/a freír **espárragos**/a hacer **gárgaras**/a **paseo**

while (it's not worth~) [lo] **comido** por [lo] servido

whipping boy un[a] **cabeza** de turco

whirlwind (he who sows the wind will reap the ~) quien siembra **vientos** recoge tempestades

whisker (come within a ~ of) [por] el **canto** de un duro

whiskers (think one is the cat's ~) creerse el no va más (▷ **ir**); la **mar** de

whisk[e]y (not for all the ~ in Ireland) aunque se junten el **cielo** y la tierra

whisk[e]y (straight ~) a **palo** seco

to whisper s.th. in s.o.'s ear/to s.o. decir algo al **oído** de alg.

whistle (blow the ~ on s.o.) chivarse contra/de alg.

whistle (blow the ~ on s.th.) dar la **puntilla** a algo

whistle (wet one's ~) mojarse el **garguero**; mojar/refrescar el **gaznate**

to whistle for s.th. esperar sentado

white (go as ~ as a ghost/sheet) ponerse más blanco que la **pared**/que una **sábana**

white (make out that ~ is black) hacer de lo **blanco** negro/volver en blanco lo negro

white horses (waves) cabrillas; **palomas**

whiz{z} (be a ~ [at s.th.]) ser un **hacha** [en/para algo]

whole lot/bunch [of them] el ganado

whole-hog por los cuatro **costados**

whole-hogger por los cuatro **costados** (example)

wholly por los cuatro **costados**

to whoop it up echar una **cana** al aire; correrse una **juerga**

whoopee (make ~) correrse una **juerga**

whopping great de los **buenos** (example); de padre y muy señor mío (▷ **el padre**) (example)

whopping great lies (tell ~) decir mentiras como **puños**

whore la fulana/puta/sota/zorra

whore (be a ~) ser del **oficio**

whore (call a woman a ~) decir a una las cuatro **letras**

to whore [around] or go whoring [around] irse de **puta**s

why (that's ~ [it doesn't work/etc.]) ahí está el **busilis**/la madre del **cordero**

wick (get on s.o.'s ~) hacer la **barba** a alg.; darle por o romper las **bola**s a alg.; romper/ calentar los **casco**s a alg.; dar la **coña** a alg.; tener/traer **frito** a alg.; caerle **gordo**/ dar la **lata** a alg.; hincharle a alg. las narices (▷ **nariz**); alterar/crispar los **nervio**s a alg. o poner los nervios de punta a alg.; sacar a alg. de **quicio**; dar la **tabarra** a alg.; tentar la paciencia a alg.

wicked world (this ~) este pícaro **mundo**

widower (be a grass ~) estar de **rodríguez**

wife ([all] the world and his ~) todo **bicho** viviente; Cristo y la madre/todo Cristo; ciento y la **madre**; todo/cada **quisque**

wife (be looking for a ~) andar en pretensiones (▷ **pretensión**)

wife (old wives' tale) el **cuento** de viejas

wigging (endure the ~) aguantar el **chaparrón**

wigging (give s.o. a ~) soltar la/una **andanada** a alg.; zurrar la **badana**/dar una **calada** a alg.; poner a alg. como **chupa** de dómine; dar un **fregado** a alg.; echar una **peluca**/ un **rapapolvo** a alg.; dar un [buen] **recorrido** a alg.; dar [una] **soba** a alg.; echar/soltar el **toro** a alg.; poner **verde** a alg.

wild (let one's imagination run ~) dar **rienda** suelta a algo (example)

to be wild about s.o./s.th. (enthusiastic) caérsele a alg. la **baba** con/por alg./algo; ser **forofo** de algo/alg.; estar **perdido** por alg./algo

wild horses couldn't drag me/us away from here ni a tirones me/nos sacan de aquí (▷ **tirón**)

wild horses won't drag it out of him sacar algo a alg. con pinzas/sacacorchos/tirabuzón (example)

to be wild with joy no **caber** en sí de alegría

to be wild with rage estar hecho un **basilisco**; estar alg. que brinca (▷ **brincar**); echar **chiribitas**/chispas; echar **rayo**s y centellas; estar alg. que trina (▷ **trinar**)

wilderness (be a voice crying in the ~) clamar en el desierto; dar **música** a un sordo; predicar en el desierto

wilderness (preach in the ~) clamar en el desierto; dar **música** a un sordo; predicar en el desierto

wildfire (spread like ~) extenderse/propagarse/ difundirse como una **mancha** de aceite; propagarse como un **reguero** de pólvora

wildly como un **descosido**; a **diestro** y siniestro; a tontas y a locas (▷ **tonto**)

wildly (lash out ~) dar **palos** de ciego

wildly and untiringly (dance ~) ... que se las pela (▷ **pelar**)

will (where there's a ~ there's a way) donde hay **gana**, hay maña; querer es poder

will (work with a ~) batir[se] el **cobre**

willies (give s.o. or get the ~) ponerle o ponérsele a alg. los **pelo**s de punta

willy el pajarito

willy-nilly por las buenas o por las malas (▷ **bueno**)

wily bird (be a ~) ser un **pájaro** de cuenta

wimp Juan Lanas

wimp (be a ~) ser un **blandengue**

to win llevarse la **gala**/**palma**

to win s.o. over ganarse la voluntad de alg.

to win s.o. over to s.th. ganar a alg. para algo

to win s.o.'s favor/trust **ganar**se la confianza/ voluntad de alg.

wind (a piercing ~ is blowing) corre un **gris** que pela

wind (cast s.th. to the ~s) echar algo en **saco** roto

wind (cast/throw caution to the ~[s]) liarse la **manta** a la cabeza

wind (get the ~ up) arrugarse; encogérsele a alg. el **ombligo**

wind (he who sows the ~ will reap the whirlwind) quien siembra **viento**s recoge tempestades

wind (it's an ill ~ that blows nobody any good) no hay **mal** que por bien no venga; a **río** revuelto, ganancia de pescadores

wind (know which way the ~ is blowing) saber de qué lado caen las **peras**/por dónde van los **tiro**s

wind (put the ~ up s.o.) meter a alg. el **ombligo** para dentro/el **resuello** en el cuerpo

wind (run like the ~) beber los **aire**s; ... que se las pela (▷ **pelar**); beber los **viento**s

wind (take the ~ out of s.o.'s sails) dejar a alg. con un **palmo** de narices

wind (talk to the ~s) clamar en el desierto; dar **música** a un sordo; predicar en el desierto

wind (the ~ is [as] cold as a witch's caress) corre un **gris** que pela

wind (there's a cold ~ [blowing]) hace un **gris**

wind (trim one's sails to the ~) cambiar de/la **chaqueta**; bailar al **son** que le tocan a alg.

wind ([wait and/to] see which way the ~ is blowing) [esperar a] ver de qué lado caen las **peras**/por dónde van los **tiros**

to wind s.o. up buscar las **pulga**s a alg.

windbag el/la bocazas; la cotorra

wine (accompany or wash down a meal with ~/have ~ with a meal) regar una comida con vino

wine (be [a] cheap/coarse ~) ser un **vino** peleón

wine (be [an] absolutely wonderful/[a] divine/[a] heavenly ~) ser un **vino** de dos orejas

wine (be [an] excellent ~) ser un **vino** de una oreja

wine (be very strong) arder en un **candil**

wine (get nasty/merry after a few glasses of ~) tener el **vino** agrio/alegre

wine (water [down] the ~) bautizar/cristianizar el **vino**

to wine and dine s.o. tratar/atender a alg. a **cuerpo** de rey

wing (on a ~ and a prayer) a la buena de Dios (▷ **bueno**); a la **gracia** de Dios

wings (clip s.o.'s ~) cortar las **alas**/los **vuelo**s a alg.

wings (spread one's ~) alzar/levantar el **vuelo**

wink (a nod is as good as a ~) al buen **entendedor**, pocas palabras [le bastan]

wink (have/get forty ~s) echar una **cabezada**/cabezadita; descabezar un sueñecito

wink (not to get a ~ of sleep/not to sleep a ~ all night) defraudar el sueño; pasar la **noche** en blanco

wink (not to sleep a ~) no pegar **ojo**

to wink at s.th. hacer la vista gorda a algo (▷ **gordo**)

to winkle everything out of s.o. tirar de la **cuerda**/**lengua** a alg.

to winkle s.th. out of s.o. sacar algo a alg. con pinzas/sacacorchos/tirabuzón; sonsacar algo a alg.

to wipe the floor with s.o. hacer **polvo** a alg.; revolcar a alg.

to wipe the slate clean barrer con todo; hacer **borrón** y cuenta nueva; hacer **tabla** rasa [de algo]

wire (live ~) el zarandillo

wire-pulling el enchufismo

wires (pull ~) el enchufe (example)

wise (a word to the ~ is sufficient/enough) al buen **entendedor**, pocas palabras [le bastan]

wise (be as ~ as an owl) ser más **sabio** que Salomón

wise (get ~ to s.th.) dar en la **cuenta** de algo; descubrir el **pastel**

wise guy (be a ~) más que **siete**

wise head (a still tongue makes a ~) es de sabios el callar (▷ **el sabio**)

to be wise to s.o. conocerle/verle a alg. el **juego**

to be wised up saber [mucho] **latín**

to be wiser than Solomon ser más **sabio** que Salomón

wish (come up with a lot of ~es) recetar largo

to wish (as much as one ~es) a pedir de **boca**

wish list (have a long ~) recetar largo

wit (be at one's ~s' end) no saber como salir del **atranco**; la **sabiduría** no llega a más; no saber a qué **santo** encomendarse

wit (be frightened/scared out of one's ~s) no llegarle a uno la **camisa** al cuerpo; estar con los cojones de corbata (▷ **cojón**); **morir**se del susto; quedarse sin **pulso**[s]

wit (brevity is the soul of ~) lo **bueno**, si breve, dos veces bueno

wit (humor) la sal

wit (sparkle with ~) tener mucha **chispa**

witch's caress (the wind is [as] cold as a ~) corre un **gris** que pela

to be with it estar en la **onda**

to withdraw into one's shell meterse en su **concha**

withdrawal pains/symptoms el mono

without huérfano de

without (do/go ~) quitarse algo de la **boca**

without (s.o. can manage/do/live ~ s.th.) poder **pasar** sin algo

without (s.o. can't live ~ s.o.) no poder **pasar** sin alg.

without a job/profession sin **oficio** ni beneficio

without any fuss sin **alharacas** ni bambollas

without [any] warning sin decir **agua** va; de buenas a primeras (▷ **bueno**)

without much ado sin **alharacas** ni bambollas

without rhyme or reason sin **ton** ni son; a tontas y a locas (▷ **tonto**)

without saying (go ~) caerse de/por su propio peso

without so much as a by-your-leave/as an explanation/as a word of goodby[e] sin decir **agua** va

without thinking de **golpe** y porrazo; a tontas y a locas (▷ **tonto**)

wittiness la sal

wolf (cry ~) gritar ¡al **lobo**!

wolf (keep the ~ from the door) mantenerse a **flote**

wolf (lone ~) Juan Palomo

wolf (throw s.o. to the wolves) arrojar a alg. a los **lobos**

wolf (womanizer) el castigador/ligón

to wolf [down] **soplar**se algo

wolf in sheep's clothing el **diablo** predicador; un **lobo** con piel de cordero/oveja; el mátalas callando

wolf in sheep's clothing (be a ~) **matar**las callando

woman (a ~ of that sort) una tal

woman (a ~ who always has a new man in tow) la ligona

woman (a ~ who can be picked/chatted up easily) la ligona

woman (a ~ who has the oldest profession in the world) la horizontal

woman (a ~ who will go with anybody) la ligona

woman (a man who tries to pick/chat up women) el ligón

woman (act/play the elegant/refined ~) meterse a **finolis**

woman (be a sanctimonious/an excessively pious ~) **comer**se los santos

woman (be one man after another with a ~) la ligona

woman (crafty/sly ~) la pájara

woman (flit from one ~ to another) ir de **flor** en flor

woman (gorgeous/tasty/yummy ~) de **rechupete**

woman (loose ~) la prójima

woman (marry a ~ without a dowry) casarse con una mujer en **camisa**

woman (sanctimonious or excessively pious ~) la beata

woman (sexually provocative ~) la calientapollas/ **castigador**a

woman (stocky ~) la chata

woman (the women) las hijas de **Eva**

woman (tough, mannish ~) la sargentona

woman (very pretty ~) un **monumento** [nacional]

womanizer el castigador/ligón

womanizer (be quite a ~) tener **corazón** de alcachofa

women las hijas de **Eva**

wonder (nine days' ~) una **nube** de verano

wonderful (smell/taste ~) oler/saber a **gloria**

to be wonderful ser un/de **alucine**; ser **canela** fina; ser **miel** sobre hojuelas

wonderful time (have a ~) cañón (example)

wonderful wine (be [an] absolutely ~) ser un **vino** de dos orejas

wonderful[ly] bestial; cañón; chachi, cojonudo; dabute[n]/dabuti; que quita el **hipo**; a las mil **maravilla**s; de **película**; pistonudo; señor

wonderfully well (go ~) de **rechupete**

to woo s.o. arrastrar el **ala** a alg.

wood (knock on/touch ~!) ¡el **diablo** sea sordo! ¡lagarto, lagarto!

wood (saw ~: snore) roncar como un **trompo**

wooden leg la **pata** de palo

wood[s] (be out of the ~) haber salido del **atolladero**

wood[s] (not to be out of the ~ yet) cantar victoria

wool (pull the ~ over s.o.'s eyes) dar a alg. **gato** por liebre

wool (wrap s.o. [up] in cotton ~) guardar/tener o criar a alg. entre algodones (▷ **algodón**)

to be woolgathering estar en **Babia**/en la luna; estar pensando en las **musarañas**

word (a ~ to the wise is sufficient/enough) al buen **entendedor**, pocas palabras [le bastan]

word (be the [very] last ~) ser el no va más (▷ **ir**)

word (hang on s.o.'s every ~) estar **colgado** de las palabras de alg.; estar pendiente de los **labio**s de alg.; beberle a alg. las **palabra**s

word (keep s.o. to his/take s.o. at his ~) coger a alg. la **palabra**

word (mum's the ~) en **boca** cerrada no entran moscas

word (not to breathe/say/utter a ~) no decir esta **boca** es mía; no descoser la **boca**; coserse la **boca**; callar[se] como un muerto/una piedra; echar **candado** a la boca/a los labios; no **chistar**; no decir [ni] **chus** ni mus; no decir ni **mu/pío**; no soltar **prenda**; no **respirar**

word (not to have a good ~ to say about s.o.) poner a alg. como **hoja** de perejil; no dejar **hueso** sano a alg.; roer los **zancajo**s a alg.

word (not to let anybody get a ~ in edgeways/ edgewise) acaparar la palabra; no dejar meter **baza** a nadie

word (not to let s.o. get a ~ in edgeways/edgewise) no dejar meter **baza** a alg.

word (not to understand a ~ [of it]) no entender ni **papa/patata**

word (sharp's the ~!) ¡arrea! (▷ **arrear**)

word (s.o. can't say a ~) pegársele a alg. la **lengua** al paladar

word (without [saying] a ~/so much as a ~) sin decir esta **boca** es mía; sin **chistar** [ni mistar]; sin decir **oste** ni moste; sin **paular** ni maular

word of goodby[e] (without so much as a ~) sin decir **agua** va

word for word al **pie** de la letra

words (actions speak louder than ~) del **dicho** al hecho hay mucho trecho; dicho sin hecho no trae provecho; **obras** son amores, que no buenas razones

words (be lost for ~) quedarse **bizco**

words (mere ~) jarabe de pico

words (not to mince one's ~) decir lo que se le viene a la **boca** a alg.; **cantarlas** claras; no tener **frenillo** en la lengua; no morderse la **lengua**; quitarle al **lucero** del alba; no tener **pelos/pepita** en la lengua

words (the ~ come gushing/spluttering/tumbling out) hablar a borbotones/borbollones (▷ **borbotón/borbollón**)

work (▷ **works**)

work (avoid all ~/steer clear of all ~) estar haciéndose **viejo**

work (be a huge/mammoth ~) ser **obra** de romanos

work (be a nasty piece of ~) ser un mal **bicho**; tener mal **café/mala leche**; ser un **pájaro** de cuenta; tener mala **pipa/sombra**; tener mala **uva**

work (be out of ~) no tener ni **oficio** ni beneficio

work (be totally wrapped up/engrossed in one's ~) no levantar/alzar **cabeza**

work (do s.o.'s dirty ~ for him) sacar las **castañas** del fuego a alg.

work (have a lot of ~ on one's hands) haber **tela** que cortar/para rato

work (have one's head buried in one's ~) no levantar/alzar **cabeza**

work (knock off ~) echarse al o en el **surco**

work (nasty piece of ~) el malaleche; el/la malaúva; la tipeja; el tipejo

work (not to do a stroke of ~) no rascar **bola**; no dar **palotada**

work (out of ~) sin **oficio** ni beneficio
work (set to/start ~) empezar a afilarse las **uña**s
work (some do [all] the ~ and others get [all] the
  credit/one does [all] the ~ and the other [one]
  gets [all] the credit) unos cardan la lana y
  otros tienen/llevan/cobran la **fama**
work (the devil finds ~ for idle hands) el **ocio**/la
  ociosidad es la madre de todos los vicios;
  los **vicio**s son los hijos del ocio
work sweetens life el **trabajo** es el encanto de la
  vida
to work all out to + infinitive batirse el **cobre** por
  + infinitivo
to work far into the night quemarse las **ceja**s/
  pestañas
to work flat out a toda **pastilla** (example); a más
  no **poder**; a todo **vapor** (example); a toda
  vela
to work for nothing trabajar para el **obispo**
to work for peanuts/for a mere pittance cobrar/
  ganar una **miseria**; trabajar por un **pedazo**
  de pan
to work hard for s.th. ganar[se] algo a **pulso**
to work like a bull/an ox/a slave trabajar como un
  buey/negro
to work like a slave trabajar como un **negro**
to work like mad como un **descosido** (example)
to work one's butt/tail off (▷ butt; tail)
to work one's fingers to the bone at s.th. dejarse las
  uñas en algo
to work o.s. to death **reventar**se; echar los
  riñones (▷ **riñón**)
to work the streets hacer la **calle**; ser del **oficio**;
  ser una **peripatética**
to work things to one's own advantage arrimar el
  ascua a su sardina
to work through the night defraudar el sueño
to work very hard trabajar como un **buey**; dar el
  callo; batir[se] el **cobre**; romperse el **culo**;
  echar/sudar la **hiel**; echar los **hígado**s;
  darse una **jupa**; trabajar como un **negro**;
  dejarse la **piel**; pringar[las]; sudar el **quilo**;
  remar; **reventar**se; echar los riñones
  (▷ **riñón**); destripar terrones (▷ **terrón**);
  sudar **tinta**
to work very hard at s.th. dejarse las **uña**s en
  algo
to work [well] pitar
to work with a will batir[se] el **cobre**
to work with s.o. else's/other people's means tirar
  con pólvora del **rey**
worked up (get ~ about nothing [at all]) ahogarse
  en un vaso de agua
worked up (get s.o. ~) romper/calentar los
  cascos a alg.; sacar a alg. de sus **casilla**s;
  poner **negro** a alg.; hacer a alg. subirse por
  las **pared**es; sacar a alg. de **quicio**
works (gum up the ~) echarlo todo a **rodar**

works (lay on the ~ for s.o.) tratar/atender a alg.
  a **cuerpo** de rey
works (shoot the ~) poner toda la **carne** en el
  asador; **jugar**se el todo por el todo
works (throw a spanner/a monkey wrench in[to]
  the ~) meter un **bastón/palo** en la rueda o
  bastones/palos en las ruedas [de alg.]
workshop (an idle brain is the devil's ~) el **ocio**/la
  ociosidad es la madre de todos los vicios;
  los **vicio**s son los hijos del ocio
world (. . . means the ~ to s.o.) para alg. no hay
  más **Dios** [ni Santa María] que ...
world ([all] the ~ and his wife) todo **bicho**
  viviente; Cristo y la madre/todo Cristo;
  ciento y la **madre**; todo/cada **quisque**
world (be living in a dream/fantasy ~) tener la
  cabeza llena de pájaros; vivir en la **luna**;
  andar por o vivir en las **nube**s
world (come down in the ~) venir a menos
world (cut o.s. off from the ~) **enterrar**se en vida
world (feel on top of the ~) estar como **abeja** en
  flor; estar/sentirse como el **pez** en el agua
world (have the best of both ~s) comer a dos
  carrillos
world (it takes all kinds/sorts to make a ~) de todo
  tiene la/hay en la **viña** del Señor
world (it's a small ~) el mundo es un **pañuelo**
world (it's an unfair ~) Dios da pan a quien no
  tiene dientes
world (it's not the end of the ~) más se perdió en
  Cuba
world (it's the same the whole ~ over) en todas
  partes cuecen **haba**s; allí tampoco atan los
  perros con **longaniza**[s]
world (money makes the ~ go round) poderoso
  caballero es don Dinero (▷ **el caballero**)
world (not for anything in the ~) aunque se
  junten el **cielo** y la tierra
world (s.o. won't set the ~ on fire) no haber
  inventado la **pólvora**
world (tell the ~ [about it/s.th.]) dar un **cuarto** al
  pregonero
world (the bottom falls out of s.o.'s ~) caérsele a
  alg. la **casa** encima/a cuestas
world (this wicked ~) este pícaro **mundo**
worldly-wise corrido
to worm s.th. out of s.o. sonsacar algo a alg.
to be worn out (exhausted) estar hecho una braga
  (▷ **braga**s); estar/quedar hecho **cisco**;
  tener los **hueso**s molidos; estar hecho
  migas/**papilla**/**pedazo**s; estar hecho un
  pingajo; estar hecho **polvo/puré**; estar
  reventado (▷ **reventar**); estar hecho unos
  zorros
worry (keep one's worries to o.s.) andarle/irle a
  alg. la **procesión** por dentro
worry (not to have any worries) pasársela en
  flores

to worry (be worried to death) tener el **alma** en un hilo

to worry a lot comerse el **coco**

worse (have seen plenty ~) estar curado de **espanto**

worse (it could be/have been ~) más **cornada**s da el hambre; más se perdió en **Cuba**

worse (starving would be/have been ~) más **cornada**s da el hambre

worse things happen at sea más **cornada**s da el hambre; más se perdió en **Cuba**

to worship the golden calf adorar el **becerro** de oro

worst (come off ~) llevar las de **perder**/salir perdiendo

worst (if [the] ~ comes to [the] ~) en última **instancia**

worst (if you think the ~, you won't be far wrong) piensa mal y acertarás (▷ **pensar**)

worst (prepare for the ~) ponerse en lo **peor**

worst (the ~ [of it] is yet/still to come) aún falta/queda la **cola**/el **rabo** por desollar; quedarle a alg. todavía el **trago** más amargo

worth (not to be ~: ▷ anything; bean; [brass] farthing; [red] cent; shit; [tinker's] damn/cuss)

worth (not to be ~ the paper [s.th. is written on]) no ser más que **papel** mojado

worth (prove one's ~) hacer [un] buen **papel**

worth (run for all one is ~) a más no **poder**

to be worth a fortune valer algo un **Perú/Potosí**

worth it/worthwhile (it's not ~) [lo] **comido** por [lo] servido

to be worth one's/its weight in gold valer alg./algo su peso en **oro** o valer algo tanto oro como pesa; valer alg. un **Perú/Potosí**

worthless bit of paper (be a ~) no ser más que **papel** mojado

worthless individual el **ñiquiñaque**

wound (open up/reopen an old ~/old ~s) renovar la **herida**/la[s] **llaga**[s]

wound (rub salt in[to] the ~) remover el **cuchillo** en la llaga; hurgar en la **herida**

wound (turn the knife in the ~) remover el **cuchillo** en la llaga; hurgar en la **herida**

to wound s.o. arrancarle a alg. el **alma**; herir a alg. en **carne** viva; llegarle a alg. a las **telas** del corazón

to wrap s.o. [up] in cotton wool guardar/tener o criar a alg. entre algodones (▷ **algodón**)

wrapped up (be/become totally ~ in s.th./in one's work) no levantar/alzar **cabeza**; meterse hasta las **cachas** en algo

wrapped up (become ~ in s.th.) **enfrascar**se en algo

wreck (old ~) la antigualla; el carcamal

to wreck s.th. partir algo por el **eje**

to wreck the place no dejar/quedar **títere** con cabeza

wrench (throw a monkey ~ in[to] the works) meter un **bastón/palo** en la rueda o bastones/palos en las ruedas [de alg.]

to wrestle (arm ~) echar un **pulso**

wretched de mis **pecados**

to wring s.o.'s neck retorcer el **pescuezo** a alg.

to write (a very poorly written letter) hacer algo con los **pies** (example)

to write (have s.th. written all over one's face) tener algo escrito en la frente/cara (▷ **escribir**)

to write home (be nothing to ~ about) no ser cosa del otro **jueves**; no ser nada/cosa del otro **mundo**

to write off (you can write that off!) ¡échale un **galgo**!

to write s.o. off (have written s.o. off) contarle a alg. con los **muertos**

to write s.o. up in a big way dar **bombo** a alg.

to write [s.th.] [down] quickly or without much thought escribir/anotar [algo] a vuela **pluma**

to write s.th. off escribir algo en la **ceniza**

writer (hack ~) el cagatintas/chupatintas

wrong (be [totally] ~) el jaleo (example)

wrong (do everything ~) no dar **pie** con bola

wrong (get one's sums ~) no contar con la **huéspeda**/echar la cuenta sin la huéspeda

wrong (go ~) espachurrarse

wrong (if you think the worst, you won't be far ~) piensa mal y acertarás (▷ **pensar**)

wrong (the absentee is always [in the] ~) ausente sin culpa, ni presente sin disculpa

wrong (what's ~ with you/etc.?) ¿qué **mosca** te/etc. ha picado?

wrong end of the stick (get hold of the ~) oír **campana**s y no saber dónde; tomar el **rábano** por las hojas

wrong moment (this is the ~!) ¡no está el **horno** para bollos!

to be wrong nine times out of ten dar una en el **clavo** y ciento en la herradura

wrong side (get out of bed on the ~/get up on the ~ of the bed) levantarse con el **pie** izquierdo o salir con mal pie

wrong way (go about s.th. the ~) asir algo por el **rabo**

wrong way (rub s.o. up the ~) sacar a alg. de **quicio**

Xanthippe una mujer de **arma**s tomar; la
   cascarrabias

Y

to yack darle a la **mui/sinhueso**

to yap darle a la **mui/sinhueso**

yard (give s.o. an inch and he'll take a ~) darle a alg. un **dedo** y se toma hasta el codo; darle a alg. la/una **mano** y se toma el brazo; darle a alg. el **pie** y se toma la mano

year dot ([in/from] the ~) año de/tiempo[s] de/ días de **Maricastaña**; del año de/en el año de la **nana**; en [los] tiempos de ñangué; del año de o en el año de la **pera/polca**; en tiempos del **rey** que rabió/del rey Wamba

to yearn for s.th. beber los **aires** por algo; írsele a alg. el **alma** tras algo; hipar por algo; beber los **vientos** por algo

years (be close to forty/etc. ~ of age) **zumbar**le a alg. los cuarenta/etc. años

years (boom/fat/lean ~) las **vacas** gordas/flacas

years (donkey's ~ ago/old) año de/tiempo[s] de/ días de **Maricastaña**; del año de/en el año de la **nana**; en [los] tiempos de ñangué; del año de o en el año de la **pera/polca**; en tiempos del **rey** que rabió/del rey Wamba

years (green ~) la **edad** burral/ingrata/del pavo

years (it will all be the same in a hundred ~) dentro de cien **años** todos calvos

yellow newspaper el **periódico** amarillo

yellow press la **prensa** amarilla o del corazón

yes-man el pelotillero

yesterday (s.o. wasn't born ~) no **comulgar** con ruedas de molino; no chuparse el **dedo**; no nació alg. ayer (▷ **nacer**)

yob el patán

yoke (throw off the ~) sacudir el **yugo**

yoke of marriage la coyunda

yokel el patán

yokel (country ~) el rapaterrones

you (if I were ~) yo **que** tú/Ud.

you-know-who de **marras**

young and inexperienced (be still ~) estar aún con la **leche** en los labios

young girl la polla

young lad/man el pollo

yours truly menda

youthful vigor (be full of/bursting with ~) bullirle a alg. la **sangre** en las venas

yummy de **rechupete**

Z

zero (be a real/walking ~) ser un **cero** a la izquierda/un don **Nadie**

zilch (be a real ~) ser un **cero** a la izquierda

zip (have ~) tener **garra**

Zs (catch some ~) echar una **cabezada**/ cabezadita; descabezar un sueñecito